LIVING LANGUAGE®

SPANISH
DICTIONARY

SPANISH–ENGLISH
ENGLISH–SPANISH

REVISED & UPDATED

THE LIVING LANGUAGE® SERIES

**Living Language Basic Courses,
  Revised & Updated**

Spanish*	Japanese*
French*	Russian
German*	Italian*

Portuguese (Brazilian)
Portuguese (Continental)
Inglés/English for Spanish Speakers

**Living Language Intermediate
  Courses**

Spanish 2	French 2
German 2	Italian 2

**Living Language Advanced Courses,
  Revised & Updated**

Spanish 3	French 3

Living Language Ultimate™
(formerly All the Way™)

Spanish*	Spanish 2*
French*	French 2*
German*	German 2*
Italian*	Italian 2*
Russian*	Russian 2*
Japanese*	Japanese 2*

Inglés/English for Spanish Speakers*
Inglés/English for Spanish Speakers 2*
Chinese (1999)

**Living Language® Essential Language
  Guides**

Essential Spanish for Healthcare
Essential Spanish for Social Services
Essential Spanish for Law Enforcement
*Essential Language Guide for Hotel &
  Restaurant Employees*

Living Language Children's Courses

Spanish	French

**Living Language Conversational
  English**

for Chinese Speakers
for Japanese Speakers
for Korean Speakers
for Spanish Speakers
for Russian Speakers

Living Language Fast & Easy™

Spanish	Italian	Portuguese
French	Russian	Czech
German	Polish	Hungarian
Japanese	Korean	Mandarin
Arabic	Hebrew	(Chinese)

Inglés/English for Spanish Speakers

Living Language All Audio™

Spanish	French	Italian	German

**Living Language Speak Up!®
  Accent Elimination Courses**

Spanish   American Regional
Asian, Indian and Middle Eastern

Fodor's Languages for Travelers

Spanish	French	Italian	German

**Living Language® Parent/Child
  Activity Kits**

Learn French in the Kitchen
Learn Italian in the Kitchen
Learn Spanish in the Kitchen
Learn French in the Car
Learn Italian in the Car
Learn Spanish in the Car

*Available on Cassette and Compact Disc

SPANISH
DICTIONARY

SPANISH–ENGLISH
ENGLISH–SPANISH

REVISED & UPDATED

REVISED BY IRWIN STERN, PH.D.

Director of Language Programs

Department of Spanish and Portuguese

Columbia University

◆

Based on the original by Ralph Weiman,

O. A. Succar, and Robert E. Hammarstrand

LIVING LANGUAGE®
A Random House Company

This work was previously published under the title *Living Language™ Common Usage Dictionary—Spanish* by Ralph Weiman, O. A. Succar, and Robert E. Hammerstrand.

Published by Living Language, A Random House Company, 201 East 50th Street, New York, New York 10022.

LIVING LANGUAGE is a registered trademark of Crown Publishers, Inc.

Random House, Inc. New York, Toronto, London, Sydney, Auckland

www.livinglanguage.com

Printed in the United States of America

Library of Congress Catalog Card Number: 55-12161

ISBN 0-609-80289-5

10 9 8 7 6 5 4 3 2

CONTENTS

CONTENTS

INTRODUCTION

The *Living Language*® *Spanish Dictionary* lists more than 20,000 of the most frequently used Spanish words, gives their most important meanings, and illustrates their uses. This revised edition contains updated phrases and expressions, as well as many new entries related to business, technology, and the media.

1. More than 1,000 of the most essential words are capitalized to make them easy to find.

2. Numerous definitions are illustrated with phrases, sentences, and idiomatic expressions. Where there is no close English equivalent for a Spanish word or where the English equivalent has several meanings, the context of the illustrative sentences helps to clarify the meanings. Important regionalisms are indicated as such.

3. Because of these useful phrases, the *Living Language*® *Spanish Dictionary* also serves as a phrase book and conversation guide. The dictionary is helpful both to beginners who are building their vocabulary and to advanced students who want to perfect their command of colloquial Spanish.

4. The Spanish expressions (particularly the idiomatic and colloquial ones) have been translated to their English equivalents. However, literal translations have been added to help the beginner. For example, under the entry *mano,* hand, you will find: *Mano a mano.* Even. On equal terms. ("Hand to hand.") This dual feature also makes this dictionary useful for translation work.

EXPLANATORY NOTES

Literal translations are in quotation marks.

Nouns and adjectives are given only in their masculine singular form unless there is a special usage for the feminine singular. Number and agreement follow the rules presented in the conversational Spanish manual.

ABBREVIATIONS

adj.	adjective
adv.	adverb
Amer.	American (Latin America)
Arg.	Argentina
coll.	colloquial
conj.	conjunction
f.	feminine
m.	masculine
math.	mathematics
Mex.	Mexico
mil.	military
n.	noun
pl.	plural
P.R.	Puerto Rico
prep.	preposition
pron.	pronoun
U.S. Span.	United States Spanish

Spanish-English

A

A *to, in, at, on, by, for.*
  Voy a Barcelona. *I'm going to Barcelona.*
  ¿A quién quiere Ud. escribir? *Who(m) do you want to write to?*
  Dígaselo a él. *Tell it to him.*
  A la derecha. *To the right. On the right.*
  A las cinco y cuarto. *At a quarter past five.*
  A veces. *At times.*
  A la vista. *At sight.*
  A tiempo. *In time.*
  A pie. *On foot.*
  Uno a uno. *One by one.*
ABAJO *down, below, under; downstairs.*
  Está abajo. *He's downstairs.*
  De arriba abajo. *From top to bottom. From top to toe. From head to foot.*
  Calle abajo. *Down the street.*
abandonado *adj. abandoned, given up; untidy; careless.*
abandonar *to abandon, to give up, to leave.*
  Después de cinco años lo abandonó. *He gave it up after five years.*
abandono *m. abandonment; slovenliness.*
abanico *m. fan.*
abarcar *to embrace, include, contain; to cover (a subject); to reach, extend to.*
  La tienda abarca toda la cuadra. *The store occupies the whole block.*
abarrotes *m. groceries; grocery (store).*
abastecer *to supply, to provide.*
abastecimiento *m. supply.*
abdomen *m. abdomen.*
abecedario *m. the alphabet; primer (book).*
abeja *f. bee.*
abiertamente *openly, frankly, plainly.*
ABIERTO *adj. open; frank.*
  ¿Hasta qué hora está la tienda abierta? *How late does the store stay open? Till what time does the store stay open?*
  Ha dejado Ud. abierta la ventana. *You've left the window open.*
abogado *m. lawyer, attorney; mediator.*
abonado *adj. reliable, rich; m. subscriber; commuter.*
abonar *to credit to; to pay; to fertilize (the soil).*
abonarse *to subscribe to.*
abono *m. allowance; subscription; commutation ticket; fertilizer.*
aborrecer *to despise, to hate, to dislike.*
aborrecimiento *m. hatred, abhorrence.*
abotonar *to button.*
  Abotónate el chaleco. *Button your vest.*
abrazar *to embrace, to hug.*
abrazo *m. hug, embrace.* Un fuerte abrazo. *A big hug. Best Wishes (farewell in letter, telephone conversation).*
abrelatas *m. can opener.*
abreviar *to abbreviate.*
abreviatura *f. abbreviation.*
abridor *m. opener.*
abrigar *to shelter, to protect; to make or keep warm.*
abrigarse *to take shelter; to cover oneself; to dress warmly.*
ABRIGO *m. shelter; protection; overcoat.*
ABRIL *m. April.*
ABRIR *to open, to unlock.*
  Abra la ventana. *Open the window.*
abrochar *to button; to fasten.*
absceso *m. abscess.*
ABSOLUTAMENTE *absolutely; in no way.*
absoluto *adj. absolute.* En absoluto. *Absolutely not.*
absolver *to absolve, to acquit.*
abstenerse *to abstain, to refrain.*
abstinencia *f. abstinence, temperance.*
absuelto *adj. absolved, acquitted.*
absurdo *adj. absurd.*
abuchear *to boo, hiss.*
abuela *f. grandmother.*
abuelo *m. grandfather.*
abundancia *f. abundance.*
abundante *adj abundant.*
abundar *to abound.*
aburrido *adj. weary, boring, tiresome.*
aburrimiento *m. weariness, boredom.*
aburrir *to bore; to annoy.*
aburrirse *to be (get) bored.*
abusar *to abuse; to take advantage of.*
  Abusa de su bondad. *He's taking advantage of your kindness.*
abuso *m. abuse, misuse.*
  ¡Esto es un abuso! *That's taking advantage!*
ACA *here, this way.*
  ¡Ven acá! *Come here!*
ACABAR *to finish, to complete, to end.*
  ¿Consiguió Ud. acabar su trabajo? *Did you manage to finish your work?*
  Acabar de. *To have just.*
  Acabo de comer. *I've just eaten.*
  El tren acaba de llegar. *The train has just arrived.*
academia *f. academy.*
acampamiento *m. camping, campgrounds.*
acampar *to camp, to encamp.*
acaparamiento *m. monopoly; hoarding.*
acaparar *to monopolize; to control the market; to hoard.*
acariciar *to caress, to pet; to cherish.*
acarrear *to carry, to transport; to cause.*
acarreo *m. carrying, transportation; carriage, cartage.*

ACASO *by chance, perhaps; m. chance, accident.*

Acaso preferiría usted ir en persona. *Perhaps you would prefer to go in person.*

Por si acaso va Ud. allí. *If you happen to go there.*

Llevemos paraguas por si acaso llueve. *Let's take umbrellas in case it rains.*

acatarrarse *to catch cold.*

Estoy acatarrado. *I've caught a cold. I have a cold.*

acceder *to accede, to agree, to consent.*

accesar *to access (files, documents)*

acceso *m. access*

accesorio *adj. accessory, additional.*

accidental *adj. accidental.*

accidentarse *to get into an accident.*

ACCIDENTE *m. accident.*

El accidente ocurrió aquí mismo. *The accident happened right here.*

Fue un accidente. *It was an accident.*

ACCIÓN *f. action, act, deed, feat; share; stock.*

Sus acciones contradicen sus palabras. *His actions contradict his words.*

¿Tiene Ud. acciones de la compañía X? *Have you any shares of the X company?*

accionador *m. switch.*

Accionador de corriente P.ower switch.

accionista *m. and f. stockholder, shareholder.*

aceitar *to oil, to lubricate.*

aceite *m. oil.*

Aceite de oliva. *Olive oil.*

aceitoso *adj. oily.*

aceituna *f. olive.*

acelerador *m. accelerator.*

acelerar *to accelerate, to hasten, to hurry.*

ACENTO *m. accent; accent mark.*

Habla con acento extranjero. *He speaks with a foreign accent.*

acentuar *to accent; to accentuate, to emphasize.*

aceptacíon *f. acceptance; approval.*

ACEPTAR *to accept.*

¿Aceptan ustedes cheques de viajero? *Do you accept travelers' checks?*

acera *f. sidewalk.*

ACERCA *about, concerning, in regard to.*

Le escribimos acerca de su viaje. *We wrote to him concerning your trip.*

acercar *to approach; to bring near.*

Acerque Ud. esa silla. *Pull up that chair. Bring that chair closer.*

acercarse a *to approach, to come near.*

¡Acérquese! *Come nearer!*

El invierno se acerca. *It will soon be winter. ("Winter is approaching.")*

acero *m. steel.*

acertadamente *opportunely, wisely.*

Lo ha dicho Ud. acertadamente. *That's well said (put).*

acertado *adj. fit, apt, proper, to the point.*

Su observación fue muy acertada. *His remark was to the point.*

Eso es lo más acertado. *That's the best thing to do.*

ACERTAR *to hit the mark, to guess right; to succeed.*

Es difícil acertar quien va a ganar. *It's difficult to guess who's going to win.*

Acertó con la casa. *He succeeded in finding the house.*

ácido *m. acid.*

ácido *adj. sour.*

acierto *m. good hit; skill; tact.*

aclaración *f. explanation, clarification.*

aclarar *to explain, to make clear; to clear up; to rinse (clothes).*

¿Aclarará hoy el tiempo? *Will the weather clear up today?*

acoger *to receive, to welcome.*

Le acogieron cordialmente. *They received him cordially.*

acogida *f. reception; welcome.*

Una calurosa acogida. *A warm welcome.*

acomodador *m. usher.*

acomodar *to accommodate, to suit; to arrange, to place.*

Haga Ud. lo que le acomode. *Do as you please.*

acompañante *chaperon, companion.*

acompañar *to accompany, to escort, to attend.*

No puedo persuadirla que nos acompañe. *I can't get (persuade) her to come with us.*

Le acompañaré hasta la esquina. *I'll go with you as far as the corner.*

Si Ud. me permite la acompañaré a su casa. *If you don't mind I'll take you home.*

Acompaño a usted en el sentimiento. *I'm very sorry to hear about your loss.*

acongojarse *to become sad, to grieve.*

aconsejable *adj. advisable.*

aconsejar *to advise.*

¿Qué me aconseja Ud. que haga? *What do you advise me to do?*

acontecer *to happen, to take place.*

acontecimiento *m. event, happening.*

acordar *to agree; to resolve; to remind.*

Tenemos que acordar la hora de salida. *We have to agree on the time of departure.*

ACORDARSE *to come to an agreement; to remember, to keep in mind.*

Se acordó enviarle un telegrama. *It was decided to send him a telegram.*

No me acuerdo de su nombre. *I don't recall his name.*

acordeón *m. accordion*

acortar *to shorten, to cut short.*

ACOSTARSE *to go to bed, to lie down.*

acostumbrar *to accustom, to be accustomed.*

Estoy acostumbrado a acostarme tarde. *I'm used to going to bed late.*

acrecer *to accrue*

acreditar *to credit; to accredit.*

acreedor *m. creditor, mortgagee.*

acrobacia *f. acrobatics.*

acróbata *m. and f. acrobat.*

acta *f. minutes, record of proceedings; certificate.*

Acta de matrimonio. *Marriage certificate.*

actitud *f. attitude.*

actividad *f. activity.*

En plena actividad. *In full swing.*

activista *m. and f. activist*

activo *adj. active; m. assets.*

ACTO *m. act, action, deed; meeting.*

En el acto. *At once.*

Acto seguido. *Then. Immediately afterward.*

Primer acto. *First act.*

Acto dañoso. *Tort.*

actor *m. actor, performer.*

actriz *f. actress.*

actuación *f. way of acting; role; record (of a person); play, work (of a team); pl. proceedings.*

ACTUAL *adj. present, existing. (The equivalent of "actual" is real, verdadero.)*

La moda actual. *The present-day fashion. The fashion now.*

El cinco del actual. *The fifth of this month.*

actualidad *f. present time.*

En la actualidad. *At present.*

actualizarse *to keep up-to-date.*

actualmente *at present, at the present time, nowadays. ("Actually" is realmente.)*

Está actualmente en Madrid. *He's at present in Madrid.*

actuar *to act, to put into action.*

acuatizar *to land on water (a plane.).*

ACUDIR *to rush to, to come to; to turn to; to attend.*

No sé a quién acudir. *I don't know who(m) to turn to.*

Un policía acudió en nuestra ayuda. *A policeman came to our aid.*

Acudir a la vía judicial. *To bring suit.*

acueducto *m. aqueduct.*

ACUERDO *m. agreement, accord, understanding; resolution.*

No estoy de acuerdo con Ud. *I don't agree with you.*

Llegar a un acuerdo. *To come to an understanding. To reach an agreement.*

De común acuerdo. *By mutual consent (agreement).*.

De acuerdo. *All right, okay.*

acumuldor, *m. battery.*

acusación *f. accusation.*

acusado *m. defendant.*

acusar *to accuse, to prosecute; to acknowledge (receipt).*

Acusar recibo. *To acknowledge receipt.*

acústica *f. acoustics.*

adaptable *adj. adaptable.*

adaptar *to adapt, to fit.*

adaptarse *to adapt oneself.*

adecuado *adj. adequate, fit, suited.*

ADELANTADO *adj. anticipated, advance, in advance.*

Pagar adelantado. *To pay in advance.*

Por adelantado. *Beforehand. In advance.*

adelantar *to advance; to pay in advance; to be fast (a watch).*

Mi reloj adelanta. *My watch is fast.*

adelantarse *to take the lead, to come forward.*

ADELANTE *ahead, farther on, forward, onward.*

¡Adelante! 1. *Go on!* 2. *Come in!*

De hoy en adelante. *From today on.*

En adelante. *Henceforth. From now on.*

Más adelante se lo explicaré. *I'll explain to you later on.*

adelanto *m. progress, improvement; advance payment.*

adelgazar *to make thin; to become slender, to lose weight.*

Me parece que usted ha adelgazado un poco. *I think you've gotten a little thinner.*

ademán *m. gesture, motion.*

ADEMAS *moreover, besides, furthermore, too.*

Además de eso. *Moreover. Besides that.*

ADENTRO *inside, within, inwardly.*

Vaya adentro. *Go in.*

Decir a sus adentros. *To say to oneself.*

adeudar *to owe; to pay (duty or freight).*

adeudarse *to get into debt.*

adherente *m. follower, supporter (of a party, society, etc.)*

adherirse *to become a member, to join.*

adhesión *f. adhesion; belonging to.*

adición *f. addition.*

ADICIONAL *adj. additional.*

adiestramiento *m. training.*

adiestrar *to train, to instruct, to teach.*

adinerado *adj. rich, wealthy.*

ADIÓS *m. Good-bye.*

adivinanza *f. riddle, puzzle, guess.*

adivinar *to guess, to foretell.*

adjetivo *m. adjective.*

adjuntar *to enclose, to attach.*

adjunto *adj. enclosed, attached, annexed; m. assistant.*

administración *f. administration, management; office of an administrator.*

administrador *m. administrator, manager.*

administrar *to administer, to manage.*

admirable *adj. admirable.*

admirablemente *admirably.*

admiración *f. admiration, wonder.*

admirador *m. admirer.*

admirar *to admire.*

admirarse *to wonder, to be amazed, to be surprised.*

admisión *f. admission, acceptance.*

ADMITIR *to admit, to accept, to grant.*

ADONDE *where, whither.*
  ¿Adónde? *Where?*
  ¿Adónde va Ud.? *Where are you going?*

adopción *f. adoption, passage (law).*

adoptar *to adopt.*

adorable *adj. adorable.*

adoración *f. adoration.*

adorar *to adore, to worship.*

adormecimiento *m. drowsiness; numbness.*

adornar *to trim, to adorn, to decorate.*

adquirir *to acquire.*

adquisición *f. acquisition.*

aduana *f. customhouse, customs.*

aduanero *m. customs official.*

adulador *m. flatterer.*

adular *to flatter.*

adulón *adj. and m. flatterer.*

adulterio *m. adultery.*

adulto *adj. and n. adult.*

adverbio *m. adverb.*

adversario *m. adversary, enemy.*

adversidad *f. adversity.*

advertencia *f. warning, admonition, notice, advice.*

advertir *to warn, to give notice, to let know; to take notice of.*

aéreo *adj. aerial, by air, air.*
  Por correo aéreo. *By air mail.*

aeróbico *adj. aerobic.*

aeromoza *f. stewardess.*

aeronáutica *f. aeronautics.*

aeronave *f. airship.*

aeroplano *m. airplane.*

aeropuerto *m. airport.*

afán *m. anxiety, eagerness.*

afanarse *to be uneasy, to be anxious; to act eagerly; to work hard or eagerly, to take pains.*
  No se afane tanto. *Don't work so hard. Take it easy.*

afección *f. affection, fondness.*

afectar *to affect, to concern.*

afecto *m. affection, fondness, love.*
  Afecto a. *Fond of.*
  En prueba de mi afecto. *As a token of my affection (esteem).*

afeitadora *f. electric shaver.*

afeitar *to shave.*
  Hojas de afeitar. *Razor blades.*

afeitarse *to shave oneself.*

afianzar *to give security.*

afición *f. fondness; hobby.*

aficionado *adj. fond of; m. fan, amateur.*
  ¿Es Ud. un aficionado a los deportes? *Are you a sports fan? Are you fond of sports?*

afilalápices *m. pencil sharpener*

afilar *to sharpen.*

afiliado *adj. affiliated; m. member (of a society).*

afiliarse *to affiliate oneself, to join, to become a member (of a society).*

afinar *to tune.*

afinidad *f. affinity, analogy, resemblance.*

afirmación *f. affirmation, assertion, statement.*

afirmar *to affirm, to assert; to fasten, to make fast.*

afirmativo *adj. affirmative.*

aflicción *f. affliction, sorrow, grief.*

afligirse *to grieve, to become despondent, to worry.*
  No hay porque afligirse. *There's no reason to worry.*

aflojar *to loosen; to slacken; to become lax.*

afortunadamente *fortunately, luckily.*

afortunado *adj. fortunate, lucky.*
  ¡Qué afortunado es Ud.! *How fortunate (lucky) you are!*

afrenta *f. affront, insult, outrage.*

afrontar *to confront, to face.*

AFUERA *out, outside; f. pl. suburbs, outskirts.*
  Salgamos afuera. *Let's go outside.*
  ¡Afuera! *Get out of the way!*
  La fábrica está en las afueras de la ciudad. *The factory is on the outskirts of the city.*

agacharse *to bend down, to stoop.*

agarrar *to grasp, to seize.*

agarrarse *to clinch; to grapple, to hold on.*

agasajar *to entertain, to receive and treat hospitably.*

agencia *f. agency; branch office.*

agenda f. notebook, memorandum book.

agente m. agent.

ágil adj. agile, light, fast.

agitación f. agitation, excitement.

agitar to agitate, to stir, to shake up.

Agítese antes de usarse. Shake well before using.

agonía f. agony.

agonizar to be dying; to tantalize.

AGOSTO m. August.

agotamiento m. exhaustion.

AGOTAR to drain, to exhaust, to run out of.

Estoy agotado. I'm exhausted.

Se me agotó la gasolina. I ran out of gas.

Esta edición está agotada. This edition is out of print.

Se han agotado las localidades. All the seats are sold out.

AGRADABLE adj. agreeable, pleasant, pleasing.

Pasamos un rato muy agradable. We had a very pleasant time.

AGRADAR to please, to like.

Esto me agrada más. I like this (one) better. This (one) pleases me more.

AGRADECER to give thanks, to be grateful.

Se lo agradezco mucho. I appreciate this very much.

Le estoy muy agradecido. I'm very much obliged to you.

agradecimiento m. gratitude, gratefulness.

agrado m. liking, pleasure.

Ser del agrado de uno. To be to one's taste (liking).

agravarse to grow worse.

agregar to add; to aggregate, to heap together; to assign temporarily.

agresión f. aggression.

agresor m. aggressor.

agriarse to turn sour.

agricultor m. farmer.

agricultura f. farming, agriculture.

AGRIO adj. sour.

agropecuaria, industria f. agriculture and livestock industry.

agroquímico adj. agrochemical.

agrupación f. gathering, crowd; association.

agrupar to bring together; to group, to come together in a group.

AGUA f. water.

Agua corriente. Running water.

Agua fresca. Cold water.

Agua mineral. Mineral water.

Agua potable. Drinking water.

Agua tibia. Lukewarm water.

aguacate m. avocato.

aguacero m. downpour, heavy shower.

aguafiestas m. and f. killjoy, party pooper.

aguantar to bear, to endure; to resist.

Lo siento pero no la puedo aguantar. I'm sorry but I can't stand her.

AGUARDAR to expect; to wait for; to allow time for.

Estoy aguardando a un amigo. I'm expecting (waiting for) a friend.

Podemos aguardar en la sala. We can wait in the living room.

¡Aguarde un momento! Wait a minute!

¡Aguárdeme! Wait for me!

águila f. eagle.

aguinaldo m. Christmas or New Year's gift.

aguja f. needle.

agujero m. hole.

¡ah! ah! oh!

¡Ah, se me olvidaba! Oh, I almost forgot!

ahí there (near the person addressed).

¿Qué tiene Ud. ahí? What have you got there?

Ponlo ahí. Put it there.

¡Ahí viene! There he comes.

Por ahí. Over there. That way.

De ahí que. Hence. Therefore. As a consequence.

ahijado m. godchild; protégé.

ahogado adj. drowned.

ahogar to drown; to choke.

ahogarse to drown; to be suffocated.

AHORA now, at present.

Vámonos ahora. Let's go now.

Ahora me toca a mí. It's my turn now.

Ahora mismo. Right now. This very moment.

Venga Ud. ahora mismo. Come right away (this moment).

ahorcar to hang (to suspend by the neck).

ahorita in a little while, just now, this minute.

Ahorita mismo. Right away.

Ahorita pasará el autobús. The bus will pass by in a little while.

ahorrar to save, to economize; to spare.

Ahorrar algo para el día de mañana. To lay something aside for a rainy day.

ahorro m. savings; thrift.

Libreta de la Caja de Ahorros. Bankbook.

AIRE m. air, wind; aspect, look.

Una corriente de aire. A draft ("current of air").

Voy a salir a tomar un poco de aire. I'm going out for some fresh air.

Tiene un aire muy severo. He has a very severe (stern) look.

Estar en el aire. To be up in the air.

Al aire libre. In the open. Outdoors.

aislacionista m. and f. isolationist.

aislar to isolate.

ajedrez m. chess.

ajeno *another's, of others, other people's, foreign, strange.*

Estoy completamente ajeno a ello. *I'm completely unaware of it. I know absolutely nothing about it.*

Ajeno al asunto. *Foreign to the subject. Having nothing to do with the subject.*

Lo ajeno. *That which belongs to others.*

Bienes ajenos. *Other people's goods (property).*

ají *m. chili.*

ajo *m. garlic.*

ajustar *to adjust; to fit; to settle (an account, matter, etc.).*

AL *(contraction of a + el) to the, at the; on, when. See also* a *and* el.

Aviso al público. *Notice to the public.*

Al contrario. *On the contrary.*

Al amanecer. *At dawn (daybreak).*

Al anochecer. *At dusk (nightfall).*

Al fin y al cabo. *At last. In the end. At length. After all. In the long run.*

Al saberlo. *When I learned that.*

Se rieron mucho al oír eso. *They laughed a lot when they heard that.*

ala *f. wing; brim (of a hat).*

alabar *to praise.*

alabarse *to praise oneself, to boast.*

alacrán *m. scorpion.*

alambrado *m. wire fence, wire net.*

alambre *m. wire.*

alambrista *m. and f. tightrope walker.*

alameda *f. public walk lined with trees.*

alarde *m. ostentation, showing off, boasting.*

Hacer alarde de. *To boast of (about).*

alargar *to lengthen; to stretch; to extend; to prolong, to drag on; to hand over, to pass.*

Alargar el paso. *To walk faster.*

alargarse *to become or grow longer*

Se alargan los días. *The days are growing (getting) longer.*

alarma *f. alarm.*

alarmarse *to become alarmed; to be alarmed.*

alba *f. dawn.*

Al rayar el alba. *At daybreak.*

albacea, *m. and f., executor.*

albañil *m. mason, bricklayer.*

albaricoque *m. apricot.*

albedrío *m. free will.*

albergue *m. lodging, shelter.*

albóndiga *f. meatball.*

alborotarse *to become excited.*

alboroto *m. excitement; disturbance.*

álbum *m. album.*

alcachofa *f. artichoke.*

alcalde *m. mayor.*

alcance *m. reach, range; scope; ability, intelligence.*

De gran alcance. *Far-reaching.*

Estar al alcance de. *To be within the reach of. To be within someone's means.*

Al alcance del tribunal. *In the court's jurisdiction.*

alcanfor *m. camphor.*

alcantarilla *f. sewer, drain.*

alcanzar *to overtake, to catch up with; to catch; to reach; to obtain, to attain, to get; to be enough, to be sufficient; to hand, to pass; to affect.*

Los alcanzaremos con nuestro coche. *We'll overtake them with our car.*

¿Pudieron alcanzar el tren? *Were they able to catch the train?*

No alcanza para todos. *There's not enough for everybody.*

Tenga la bondad de alcanzarme el salero. *Please pass me the saltshaker.*

Alcanzar a comprender. *To understand. To make out.*

Poco se le alcanza. *He doesn't understand it very well. He doesn't care very much about it.*

Alcanzar con la mano. *To reach with one's hand.*

alcoba *f. bedroom.*

alcohol *m. alcohol.*

aldaba *f. door knocker, latch.*

aldea *f. small village.*

alegar *to allege, to plead.*

alegrar *to gladden, to make glad, to enliven.*

ALEGRARSE *to rejoice, to be glad, to be happy.*

Me alegro muchísmo. *I'm very glad. I'm delighted.*

Me alegro de que esté usted mejor. *I'm very glad you're better.*

Me alegro de saberlo. *I'm happy to know it.*

alegre *adj. glad, merry, happy.*

alegría *f. merriment, gaiety, delight, rejoicing, joy.*

Está llena de alegría. *She's very happy.*

alejar *to remove, to take away; to hold off (at a distance).*

alejarse *to go far away; to move away.*

alemán *adj. and n. German.*

alfabetizar *to make literate.*

alfabeto *m. alphabet.*

alfanumérico *adj. alphanumeric.*

alfiler *m. pin.*

alfombra *f. carpet, rug.*

ALGO *some, something, anything, somewhat.*

¿Algo más? *Anything else?*

Algo que comer. *Something to eat.*

En algo. *In some way. Somewhat.*

Por algo. *For some reason.*

¿Hay algo de particular? *Is there anything special?*

¿Necesita Ud. algo más? *Do you need anything else?*

¿Tiene Ud. algo que hacer esta tarde? *Do you have anything to do this afternoon?*

¿Quiere Ud. tomar algo? *Do you want anything to drink?*

Quiero comer algo ligero. *I want something light to eat.*

Tengo algo que decirle. *I have something to tell you.*

Lo encuentro algo caro. *I find it somewhat expensive.*

Comprendo algo. *I understand a little.*

algodón *m. cotton.*

algoritmo *m. algorithm.*

ALGUIEN *somebody, someone.*

Alguien llama a la puerta. *Someone's knocking at the door.*

¿Aguarda Ud. a alguien? *Are you waiting for someone?*

algún *adj. (used only before a masculine noun)* some, any.

¿Tiene Ud. algún libro para prestarme? *Have you a (any) book to lend me?*

Algún día se lo contaré. *I'll tell you some day.*

Durante algún tiempo. *For some time.*

ALGUNO *adj. some, any.*

En modo alguno. *In any way.*

Alguna cosa. *Anything.*

En alguna parte. *Anywhere.*

¿Hay alguna farmacia cerca de aquí? *Is there a drugstore near here?*

Lo habré leído en alguno que otro periódico. *I probably read it in some newspaper or other.*

Déjeme ver algunas camisas. *Let me see some shirts.*

Conozco a algunas personas aquí pero no a todas. *I know some (several) people here but not everyone.*

Alguna que otra vez. *Once in a while. Occasionally.*

alhaja *f. jewel.*

alianza *f. alliance.*

alicates *m. pliers, pincers.*

aliento *m. breath; courage.*

Sin aliento. *Out of breath.*

Dar aliento. *To encourage.*

alimentación *f. feeding, food.*

Alimentación por friccion *Friction-feed.*

alimentar *to feed; to nourish; to cherish.*

alimento *m. food, nourishment; pl. support.*

alistar *to enlist; to get ready.*

aliviar *to lighten; to make things easier; to get better.*

¡Qué se alivie pronto! *I hope you'll get better soon.*

alivio *m. relief, ease.*

¡Qué alivio! *What a relief!*

ALMA *f. soul.*

No hay ningún alma viviente en este lugar. *There's not a living soul in this place.*

Con toda mi alma. *With all my heart.*

Lo siento en el alma. *I deeply regret it. I'm extremely sorry about it.*

almacén *m. warehouse; store, shop.*

Tener en almacén. *To have in stock.*

Almacenes. *Department store.*

almacenamiento *m. storage (computer).*

almacenar *to store; to hoard.*

almanaque *m. almanac, calendar.*

almeja *f. clam.*

almendra *f. almond.*

almendro *m. almond tree.*

almidón *m. starch.*

almidonar *to starch.*

almirante *m. admiral.*

almohada *f. pillow, bolster.*

almohadón *m. large cushion or pillow.*

almorzar *to lunch; to breakfast (Mex.).*

ALMUERZO *m. lunch.*

alojamiento *m. lodging; billeting (soldiers).*

alojar *to lodge; to billet (soldiers).*

alpargata *f. hemp sandal.*

alpinista *m. and f. mountain climber.*

ALQUILAR *to rent, to hire.*

Se alquila. *To let (a room, a house, etc.). For rent.*

Se alquila la casa. *The house is for rent.*

ALQUILER *m. rent, rental, the act of hiring or renting.*

¿Cuánto es el alquiler? *How much is the rent?*

ALREDEDOR *around; pl. outskirts, surroundings.*

Tengo alrededor de veinte dólares. *I have about twenty dollars.*

Un viaje alrededor del mundo. *A trip around the world.*

Vive en los alrededores de Madrid. *He lives in the outskirts of Madrid.*

altavoz *m. loudspeaker.*

alterarse *to become angry, to get annoyed.*

altercado *m. quarrel.*

alternar *to alternate.*

alternativa *f. alternative.*

altibajos *m. pl. ups and downs.*

ALTO *adj. high, tall; loud; halt, stop.*

Es muy alto para su edad. *He's very tall for his age.*

Haga el favor de hablar más alto. *Please speak louder.*

No puedo alcanzarlo, está muy alto. *I can't reach it; it's too high.*

Hacer alto. *To halt.*

Dar alta *To discharge (hospital).*

¡Alto! *Stop!*

¡Alto ahí! *Stop there!*

Se me pasó por alto. *I overlooked it. I didn't notice it.*

A altas horas de la noche. *Late at night.*

altoparlante *m. loudspeaker.*

altura *f. height, altitude.*

aludir *to allude, to refer to.*

alumbrado *m. lighting, illumination.*

alumbrar *to light, to illuminate.*

aluminio *m. aluminum.*

alumno *m. pupil, student.*

alunizar *to land on the moon.*

alza *f. rise, increase (price, stocks, etc.); sight (on a gun, on instruments).*

alzar *to raise, to lift up.*

ALLÁ *there, over there (away from the speaker); in other times, formerly.*

Más allá. *Farther on. Beyond.*

Más allá de. *Beyond.*

Vaya Ud. allá. *Go there.*

¡Allá voy! *I'm coming!*

Allá en España. *Over there in Spain.*

Allá en el sur. *Down South.*

Eso allá él. *It's his own business.*

ALLÍ *there, in that place.*

De allí. *From there. From that place.*

Allí mismo. *Right there. In that very place.*

Lléveme allí. *Take me there.*

Vive allí, en la casa de la esquina. *He lives in the corner house over there.*

Esté Ud. allí a las nueve. *Be there at nine o'clock.*

Por allí. *That way. Over there.*

ama *f. mistress of the house, landlady.*

Ama de casa. *Housewife*

Ama de llaves. *Housekeeper.*

AMABILIDAD *f. amiability, affability, kindness.*

¿Tendría Ud. la amabilidad de decirme la hora? *What time is it, please? Can you please tell me the time?*

Le agradezco mucho su amabilidad. *Thanks for your kindness.*

AMABLE *adj. amiable, kind.*

Ud. es muy amable. *You're very kind. That's very kind of you.*

amador *m. amateur.*

Programa de amadores. *Amateur hour.*

AMANECER *m. daybreak, dawn.*

al amanecer. *At dawn (daybreak).*

amanecer *to dawn; to awaken very early.*

amante *adj. loving; m. and f. lover, sweetheart.*

Ser amante de. *To be fond of.*

AMAR *to love.*

AMARGO *adj. bitter.*

AMARILLO *adj. yellow.*

amarrar *to tie, to fasten; to moor.*

amartillar *to hammer; to cock (a gun).*

amasar *to knead, to mold.*

amatista *f. amethyst.*

ambición *f. ambition.*

ambicioso *adj. ambitious; greedy.*

ambiente *m. environment; atmosphere.*

AMBOS *adj. both.*

Ambos hermanos vinieron a la fiesta. *Both brothers came to the party.*

ambulancia *f. ambulance.*

amenaza *f. menace, threat.*

amenazar *to menace, to threaten.*

ameno *adj. pleasant, agreeable, pleasing; light, entertaining (reading).*

americana *f. man's coat, jacket; an American (woman).*

americanismo, *m. American trait, custom or word.*

americano *m. American.*

ametralladora *f. machine gun.*

amigablemente *amicably, in a friendly manner.*

amígdalas *f. tonsils.*

AMIGO *m. friend.*

Somos amigos íntimos. *We're close friends.*

Vino a vernos con su amiga. *He came to see us with his girl friend.*

Ser amigo de. *To be fond of.*

amistad *f. friendship.*

amistosamente *amicably, in a friendly manner.*

amistoso *adj. friendly.*

amnistía *f. amnesty.*

amo *m. master, lord; proprietor, owner; boss.*

AMOR *m. love.*

Hacer amor. *To make love.*

Amor mío. *Darling.*

amortiguador *m. shock absorber; bumper.*

Amortiguador de ruido. *Muffler.*

amparar *to shelter, to protect, to help.*

Alamparo de. *In reliance on.*

ampliación *f. enlargement.*

ampolla *f. blister; ampule.*

amueblar *to furnish.*

analfabeto *adj. illiterate.*

análisis *m. analysis.*

analista *m. and f. analyst.*

analizar *to analyze.*

anaranjado *adj. orange.*

anatomía *f. anatomy.*

anciano *m. old man.*

Hogar de ancianos *Old age home.*

ancla f. anchor.

ANCHO adj. broad, wide; m. width, breadth.

Estos zapatos me vienen muy anchos. These shoes are too wide for me.

Dos pies de ancho. Two feet wide.

A todo el ancho. Full-width.

Estoy a mis anchas aquí. I'm very comfortable here.

anchura f. width, breadth.

ANDAR to walk; to go; to be.

Andar a pie. To go on foot.

Es demasiado lejos para ir andando. It's too far to walk.

¿Anda bien su reloj? Does your watch keep good time?

Ando mal de dinero. I'm short of money.

Andar triste. To be sad.

Andar en mangas de camisa. To go around in one's shirtsleeves.

¡Andando! Let's get going!

¡Anda! Go on! Come on!

andén m. platform of a railroad station, track.

anécdota f. anecdote.

anemia f. anemia.

anestesia f. anesthesia.

anfitrión m host.

ángel m. angel.

angosto adj. narrow.

anguila f. eel.

ángulo m. angle.

angustia f. anguish, distress, affliction.

anhelar to long for, to yearn.

anhelo m. desire, longing.

anillo m. ring, band.

animal animal; brute.

¡No seas animal! Don't be stupid!

animar to animate, to encourage, to cheer up. to enliven.

animarse to become lively, to feel encouraged, to cheer up.

No me animo a hacerlo. I wouldn't dare to do it.

ANIMO m. courage; mund, feeling.

Los ánimos están excitadísimos. Feeling is running very high.

¡Ánimo! Cheer up!

aniversario m. anniversary.

ANOCHE last night.

¿Se divirtieron Uds. anoche? Did you have a good time last night?

anochecer to grow dark.

Anochecía (se hacía de noche) cuando llegamos a Madrid. It was getting dark when we arrived in Madrid.

Al anochecer. At dusk (nightfall).

anónimo adj. anonymous

Sociedad anónima (S.A.) Incorporated.

anormal adj. abnormal.

anotar to annotate, to make notes; to write down.

ansia f. anxiety, eagerness, longing.

ansiedad f. anxiety.

ansioso adj. anxious, eager.

antácido m. antacid.

ANTE before, in the presence of.

Ante todo. Above all. First of all.

anteanoche adv. the night before last.

ANTEAYER the day before yesterday.

antebrazo m. forearm.

antecedente m. antecedent; pl. data, references, record (of a person).

antecesores m. ancestors.

antemano beforehand.

De antemano. In advance

antena f. antenna, aerial.

anteojos m. pl. glasses, telescope.

Anteojos a larga vista. Binoculars.

antepasado adj. past, last; m. pl. ancestors, forefathers.

anterior adj. anterior, previous, former, preceding.

anteriormente previously.

ANTES before.

Cuanto antes. As soon as possible.

Hágalo cuanto antes. Do it as soon as possible.

Agítese antes de usarse. Shake well before using.

Haga antes un borrador. Make a rough copy first.

Antes de tiempo. Ahead of time.

anticipación f. anticipation.

Si vienes, avísame con anticipación. Let me know in advance if you come.

anticipar to anticipate; to advance (money).

Me anticipó mil pesos. He gave me a thousand pesos in advance.

anticiparse to anticipate; to act or occur before the regular or expected time.

Se anticiparon media hora. They arrived half an hour earlier.

anticipo m. advance payment, advance.

anticuado adj. old-fashioned.

anticuario m. antiques dealer, antiquarian.

anticuerpo m. antibody.

antifaz m. mask.

antiguamente formerly, in ancient times.

antigüedad f. antiquity; antique; seniority.

Tienda de antigüedades. Antique shop.

ANTIGUO adj. antique, ancient, old.

Ese is un dicho muy antiguo. That's a very old saying.

antipatía f. antipathy, dislike, aversion.

antipático adj. displeasing, not congenial.

Me es muy antipático. I don't find him at all congenial, I don't like him.

antiséptico adj. and n. antiseptic.

antojarse *to desire, to long for, to crave.*
Tiene cuanto se la antoja. *She has everything she could wish for.*
Que haga lo que se le antoje. *Let him do as he pleases.*

antojo *m. desire, caprice, whim.*

antología *f. anthology.*

anual *adj. yearly, annual.*

anular *to void, to annul, to make void, to vacate.*

ANUNCIAR *to announce; to advertise.*
Lo acaban de anunciar en la radio. *They just announced that on the radio.*
La tienda anuncia un saldo. *The store is advertising a sale.*

ANUNCIO *m. announcement, notice, sign, advertisment, commercial.*

anzuelo *m. fishhook; bait.*

AÑADIR *to add.*
Añádalo a mi cuenta. *Add it to my bill.*

añejo *adj. aged.*

AÑO *m. year.*
¿En qué año ocurrió? (*In*) *What year did it happen?*
Hace dos años que vivo aquí. *I've been living here for two years.*
Todo el año. *All year. All year round.*
Por año. *Yearly.*
El año pasado. *Last year.*
El año que viene. *Next year.*
¡Feliz año nuevo! *Happy New Year.*
¿Cuántos años tiene Ud.? *How old are you?* ("*How many years do you have?*")
Tengo treinta años. *I am thirty years old.* ("*I have thirty years.*")

apagado automático *automatic shutoff.*

apagar *to quench, to extinguish, to put out.*
Apague la luz. *Turn off the light. Put out the light.*

apagarse *to go out (of a light, fire, etc.).*
Se apagaron las luces. *The lights went out.*

apagón *m. blackout.*

aparador *m. sideboard, cupboard.*

aparato *m. apparatus, appliance, ostentation.*

APARECER *to appear, to show up, to turn up.*
No apareció en todo el día. *He didn't show up all day.*

aparentar *to pretend, to afffect.*
Aparenta ser rico. *He seems to be rich.*

aparentemente *apparently.*
Aparentemente es así. *Apparently it's so.*

apariencia *f. appearance, looks, aspect.*
Las apariencias engañan. *Appearances are deceiving.*
Al juzgar por las apariencias. *To judge by appearances.*

apartado *adj. separated, distant; m. post-office box.*
Apartado de correos. *Post-office box.*

apartamento *m. apartment.* (*also* **apartamiento.**)
Casa de apartamentos. *Apartment house.*
¿Tiene apartamentos por alquilar? *Do you have any vacancies? Are there any apartments for rent?*

apartamiento *m. separation; isolation; apartment.*

apartar *to separate, to lay aside.*

apartarse *to keep away, to get out of the way.*
Apártese del fuego. *Get away from the fire.*
Se apartó de nosotros. *He kept away from us.*

APARTE *aside, separately.*
Ponga este paquete aparte. *Put this package aside.*
Esa es cuestión aparte. *That's another question.*

apatía *f. apathy.*

apearse *to get off.*
Quiero apearme en la próxima parada. *I want to get off at the next stop.*

apelar *to appeal.*

APELLIDO *m. surname, last name, family name.*
Escriba su nombre y apellido. *Write down your first and last names.*

APENAS *scarcely, hardly; no sooner than, as soon as.*
Apenas puedo creerlo. *I can hardly believe it.*
Apenas podía moverse. *He could scarcely move.*
Las dos apenas. *Not quite two o'clock. A little before two.*

apéndice *m. appendix.*

apetecer *to long for, to desire; to appeal to.*

apetito *m. appetite.*

apio *m. celery.*

aplaudir *to applaud.*

aplauso *m. applause, praise; approbation.*
Dar aplausos. *To applaud.*

aplazar *to put off, to postpone, to defer, to convene, to adjourn.*
Han aplazado el viaje hasta el mes que viene. *They've put off the trip until next month.*

aplicación *f. application, investment.*

aplicado *adj. studious, industrious, diligent.*

aplicarse *to apply oneself, to devote oneself to; to study.*

apoderarse *to take possession of.*

apodo *m. nickname.*

aportación *f. contribution.*

apostar to bet; to post (soldiers, etc.).
¿Cuánto apuestas? How much do you bet?

apoyar to favor, to back up, to support, to defend, to aid; to lean.
Apóyalo contra la pared. Lean it against the wall.
Apoyar una moción. To second a motion.

apoyo m. support, aid.
Apoyo para la cabeza. Headrest (car).

apreciación f. estimation, appreciation.

apreciar to estimate, to value, to appreciate, to esteem; to weigh (evidence).

aprecio m. appreciation, esteem, regard.
Le tengo mucho aprecio. I have a high regard for him.

apremiante adj. urgent, pressing.

apremiar to urge, to press.

APRENDER to learn.
Aprendí solamente un poco de español. I learned only a little Spanish.
Apréndaselo de memoria. Learn it by heart.

apresurarse to hurry, to hasten.
Apresúrese si no quiere perder el tren. Hurry up if you don't want to miss the train.

apretado adj. tight.

apretar to tighten, to press, to compress, to squeeze.
Estos zapatos me aprietan un poco. These shoes are a little tight for me.
¡Apriete aquí! Press here!

aprisa fast, swiftly, promptly.
Vaya lo más aprisa posible. Go as quickly as you can.

aprobación f. approval.

aprobar to approve, to approve of; to pass (an examination).
¿Ha sido aprobado el plan? Has the plan been approved?
No me aprobaron en historia. I failed history.

aprovechar to be useful or beneficial; to profit; to make use of.
Hay que aprovechar la ocasión. We must take advantage of the opportunity.
Aprovechar el tiempo. To make good use of one's time.
¡Qué aproveche! I hope you enjoy it (said when entering a room where people are eating).

aprovecharse to take advantage of, to derive profit from, to make use of.
No deje que se aprovechen de Ud. Don't let people take advantage of you.

aprovisionamiento m. supply.

aproximadamente approximately.

aproximarse a to approach, to come near.

aptitud f. aptitude, fitness, ability; pl. qualifications.

apuesta f. bet, wager.
La gané la apuesta. I won the bet from him.

apuntar to aim; to indicate, to point out; to write down.
Apunte la dirección para que no se le olvide. Write down the address so you won't forget it.
Apúntelo en mi cuenta. Charge it to my account.

apuñalar to stab.

apurarse to hurry; to worry, to fret; to exert oneself.
¡Apúrese! Hurry up!
No se apure Ud. que ya saldremos de aprietos. Don't worry, we'll get out of these difficulties.

apuro m. want; affliction; plight; fix, difficulty, scrape.
¿Salió Ud. del apuro? Did you manage to get out of that difficulty?
Estar en apuros. To be in difficulties.

AQUEL that, that one; the former.
Mire aquel avión. Look at that plane.
Aquel negocio le arruinó. That business ruined him.
En aquel mismo momento llegó. He arrived at that very moment.
En aquel entonces. At that time.
No quería éste sino aquél. I didn't want this one but the one over there.

aquella (f. of aquel) that, that one.
Aquella muchacha baila muy bien. That girl (over there) dances very well.
Esta silla es más cómoda que aquélla. This chair is more comfortable than that one.

aquellas (pl. of aquella) those.
Mira aquellas chicas que van allá. Look at those girls walking over there.

aquello (neuter) that (referring to an idea).
Aquello fue horrible. That was horrible.
Ya pasó aquello. That's gone (past) and forgotten. That's water under the bridge.

aquellos (pl. of aquel) those.
¿Te acuerdas de aquellos tiempos? Do you remember the good old days?
¿Cuáles prefieres, éstos o aquéllos? Which do you prefer, these or those?

AQUÍ here, in this place, hereof.
¿Paramos aquí? Do we stop here?
¿Vive Ud. aquí? Do you live here?
¿Se puede telefonear desde aquí? Can we phone from here?

¿Qué demonios hace Ud. aquí? *What on earth are you doing here?*

Venga Ud. por aquí. *Come this way.*

¿Cuánto hay de aquí a Zaragoza? *How far is it from here to Zaragoza?*

Está muy lejos de aquí. *It's quite a distance from here.*

Aquí tiene lo que ha pedido. *Here's what you ordered (asked for).*

De aquí en adelante. *From now on.*

araña f. spider; chandelier.

arañazo m. a long, deep scratch.

árbol m. tree; mast; shaft.

La raíz del árbol. *The root of a tree.*

El tronco del árbol. *The trunk of a tree.*

archipiélago m. archipelago.

archivar to keep in an archive, to file.

archivo m. archives; file, files (computer); records.

Archivo de entrada. *Input file.*

Archivo de salida. *Output file.*

arco m. arch.

arder to burn.

ardilla f. squirrel.

arena f. sand; arena.

arete m. earring.

argumento m. reason; argument; plot (of a novel, play, etc.).

No me convencen sus argumentos. *His arguments don't convince me.*

No me gustó el argumento de la película. *I didn't like the plot of the film.*

aritmética f. arithmetic.

arma f. weapon, arm.

armamento m. armament.

armario m. closet, cabinet.

armisticio m. armistice.

aroma m. aroma.

arquitecto m. architect.

arquitectura f. architecture.

arrabal m. suburb, slum.

arrancar to tear out by the roots, to tear off; to start (car, etc.).

arranque (or **arrancador**) m. starter.

arrastrar to drag, to haul.

arreglar to arrange; to settle; to regulate; to fix.

Todo está arreglado. *Everything has been arranged.*

Arreglar una cuenta. *To settle on account.*

¿Cuánto pide Ud. para arreglar una radio? *How much do you charge to fix a radio?*

arreglarse to make up, to get ready; to manage; to be settled; to come up.

Arréglate un poco y vámonos al cine. *Get yourself ready and we'll go to the movies.*

arrendamiento m. rental, lease, renting.

Contrato de arrendamiento. *Leasing agreement.*

arrendar to rent, to lease, to hire.

arrepentirse to repeat, to regret.

Te arrepentirás de esto. *You'll be sorry for this.*

ARRIBA up, above, over, overhead, upstairs.

Vamos arriba. *Let's go upstairs.*

Patas arriba. *Upside down.*

De arriba abajo. *From top to bottom. From head to foot.*

Calle arriba. *Up the street.*

arriendo m. renting, lease, rental.

arrimar to approach, to draw near; to lay aside.

arrimarse to lean against; to draw near.

arrodillarse to kneel down.

arrojar to throw, to hurl; to show, to leave (a balance).

arte f. art; skill.

Bellas artes. *Fine arts.*

arterial adj. arterial.

Presion arterial. *Blood pressure.*

artículo m. article; clause.

Artículo de fondo. *Editorial.*

Artículos de tocador. *Toilet articles.*

artificial adj. artificial.

artista m. and f. artist.

arzobispo m. archbishop.

as m. ace.

asa f. handle, haft.

asado adj. roasted; m. roast meat.

asador m. spit (for roasting meat).

asaltante m. and f. mugger, assailant.

asalto m. assault; holdup, mugging.

asamblea f. assembly.

asar to roast.

ascender to ascend, to climb; to amount to; to be promoted.

La cuenta asciende a cien pesos. *The bill amounts to one hundred pesos.*

ascenso m. promotion.

ascensor m. elevator.

aseado adj. clean, neat.

asear to clean, to make neat.

asegurar to insure; to secure, to fasten; to assure; to affirm, to assert.

Le aseguro que estaré allí dentro de una hora. *I assure you that I'll be there in an hour.*

El equipaje está asegurado. *The baggage is insured.*

aseo m. cleanliness, neatness.

aserrar to saw.

asesinar to assassinate, to murder.

asesinato m. assassination, murder.

asesino m. assassin, murderer.

asfalto m. asphalt.

ASÍ *so, thus, in this manner, therefore, so that.*
  Así lo espero. *I hope so.*
  Lo debe Ud. hacer así. *You must (have to) do it this way.*
  No es así, se lo aseguro. *I assure you that's not so.*
  Así, así. *So, so.*
  Más vale así. *It's better this way.*
  Así que llegue le avisaré. *As soon as I arrive I'll notify you.*

asiento *m. seat, chair; entry, registry; bottom.*
  ¿Está tomado este asiento? *Is this seat taken?*
  Tome Ud. asiento. *Take a seat. Have a seat.*
  Asiento de atrás. *Backseat.*

asignar *to assign; to appoint; to allot.*

asignatura *f. subject (in school).*

asilamiento *m. commitment (to a hospital).*

asilo *m. asylum, refuge.*

asimismo *likewise, exactly so.*

asir *to grasp, to hold, to grip.*

asirse de *to avail oneself of; to hold to; to take hold of.*

asistente *m. and f. assistant, aide.*
  Asistente de bordo. *Steward, stewardess.*

asistir *to attend; to assist, to help; to be treated by (a doctor).*
  No asistió a clase hoy. *He did not attend class today.*
  ¿Asistió Ud. a la reunión? *Did you attend the meeting?*
  Un médico famoso asiste a mi mujer. *My wife is being treated by a famous doctor.*

asno *m. donkey, ass.*

asociación *f. association.*

asomar *to loom, to become visible, to begin to appear.*

asomarse *to look out of, to lean out (of a window, etc.).*
  Asómese Ud. a la ventana. *Look out (lean out) of the window.*
  ¡Prohibido asomarse! *Don't lean out of the window!*

asombro *m. amazement, astonishment.*
  Figúrese mi asombro. *Imagine my amazement.*
  No salgo de mi asombro. *I can't get over it.*

aspecto *m. aspect, appearance, look.*
  Ud. no tiene mal aspecto. *You don't look ill.*
  Trate de mejorar su aspecto. *Try to improve your appearance.*

aspirante *m. and f. candidate (for a position).*

aspirina *f. aspirin.*

astronauta *m. and f. astronaut.*

astuto *adj. cunning, sly.*

ASUNTO *m. subject, matter, business.*
  Necesito más detalles sobre este asunto. *I need more information on this matter.*
  Conozco a fondo el asunto. *I'm thoroughly acquainted with the matter.*
  ¿Cuál es el asunto de esa comedia? *What's the subject of that play?*

asustar *to frighten.*

asustarse *to be frightened.*
  ¿De qué te asustas? *What are you afraid of?*

atacar *to attack, to challenge.*

ataque *m. attack.*

atar *to bind, to tie, to fasten.*
  Átese los zapatos. *Tie your shoelaces.*

atardecer *to grow late (toward the end of the afternoon).*

ataúd *m. coffin.*

atemorizar *to frighten, to intimidate.*

ATENCIÓN *f. attention.*
  Quisiera llamar la atención de Ud. sobre este punto. *I'd like to bring this point to your attention.*
  Muchas gracias por su atención. *Thanks for your attention.*
  Le estoy muy reconocido por sus atenciones. *I'm grateful for your kindness.*
  En atención a. *Considering. In view of.*

atender *to attend, to pay attention; to look after; to wait on.*

atentado *m. attempt.*

atentar *to try, to attempt.*

atento *adj. attentive, courteous.*
  Su atento y seguro servidor. *Very truly yours.*

aterrizaje *m. landing (of an airplane).*

aterrizar *to land (an airplane).*

atestado *adj. crowded.*

atestiguar *to depose, to testify.*

atinar *to guess right, to hit on.*

Atlántico *m. Atlantic.*

atleta *m. and f. athlete.*

atlético *adj. athletic.*

atletismo *m. track and field.*

atmósfera *f. atmosphere.*

átomo *m. atom.*

atornillar *to screw.*

atracar *to dock, to moor; to hold up.*

atraco *m. assault, holdup.*

atractivo *adj. attractive, appealing.*

atraer *to attract.*

ATRÁS *behind, backwards, past; ago.*
  Quedarse atrás. *To remain behind.*
  Volverse atrás. *To go back on one's word. To retract.*

Hacerse atrás. *To move backward. To back up. To recoil.*

Tres días atrás. *Three days ago.*

atrasar *to retard, to delay; to be in arrears; to be slow (a watch).*

Mi reloj atrasa. *My watch is slow.*

Esto atrasará mucho mi viaje. *This will delay my trip a long time.*

Atrasarse en los pagos. *To fall behind in one's payments.*

atrasarse *to remain behind; to be late; to get behind (in payment).*

Nos estamos atrasando en el trabajo. *We're getting behind in our work.*

atravesar *to cross, to move across; to lay a thing across; to pierce.*

Atravesemos la calle. *Let's cross the street.*

atrayente *adj. attractive.*

atreverse *to dare, to venture.*

atrevido *adj. bold, daring; fresh.*

atribuir *to attribute, to impute.*

atrocidad *f. atrocity.*

¡Qué atrocidad! *What a horrible (awful) thing!*

atropellar *to trample, to run over; to abuse, to insult.*

Fué atropellado por un coche. *He was run over by a car.*

atropello *m. trampling, abuse, outrage.*

atroz *adj. atrocious, outrageous; enormous.*

Tengo un hambre atroz. *I'm famished. ("I have an enormous hunger.")*

atún *m. tuna fish.*

aturdido *adj. bewildered, stunned, dizzy.*

aturdir *to stun.*

audición *f. audition.*

auditorio *m. audience, auditorium.*

aumentar *to augment, to enlarge, to increase.*

aumentarse *to grow larger.*

aumento *m. increase.*

Aumento de precios. *Price increase. Increase in prices.*

Aumento de salario. *Salary increase.*

AUN *yet, still; even (written* **aún** *when it follows a verb).*

Aun no lo sabe. *He doesn't know yet.*

Tengo que escribir aún otra carta. *I've still got another letter to write.*

Aun cuando. *Although. Even though.*

AUNQUE *though, notwithstanding, even if.*

auriculares *m. headphones.*

aurora *f. dawn, daybreak.*

ausencia *f. absence.*

AUSENTARSE *to be absent, to be away.*

AUSENTE *adj. absent.*

austral *m. austral, southern; Argentine currency unit.*

auténtico *adj. authentic, genuine.*

auto *m. automobile, motor car; edict.*

autobús *m. bus.*

¿Dónde para el autobús? *Where does the bus stop?*

¿Dónde queda la parada del autobús? *Where's the bus stop?*

autocar *m. bus (in Spain).*

automático *adj. automatic.*

Contestador automático. *Telephone answering machine.*

automóvil *m. automobile.*

automovilismo *m. car racing*

automovilística *f. automotive industry.*

autor *m. author.*

autoridad *f. authority.*

autoritario *adj., authoritarian*

autorización *f. authorization.*

autorizar *to authorize.*

autorretrato *m. self-portrait.*

autoverificar *to self-test.*

auxiliar *to and, to help; adj. auxiliary*

auxilio *m. help, aid, assistance.*

avaluar *to appraise.*

avance *m. advance, progress.*

avanzar *to advance, to go ahead, to progress.*

ave *f. bird; fowl.*

Aves de corral. *Fowl. Poultry.*

avena *f. oats.*

avenida *f. avenue.*

aventura *f. adventure.*

aventurarse *to venture, to risk, to take a chance.*

No se aventure usted. *Don't take the risk. Don't take a chance.*

avergonzarse *to be ashamed.*

avería *f. damage, loss, breakdown*

averiguar *to inquire, to find out, to investigate.*

Averigüe a qué hora sale el tren. *Find out (at) what time the train leaves.*

aviación *f. aviation.*

aviador *m. aviator.*

ávido *adj. avid, eager.*

avión *m. airplane.*

avisar *to inform, to notify, to let know; to warn.*

Avíseme con tiempo. *Notify me in time.*

Ya le avisaré. *I'll let you know.*

aviso *m. notice; advertisement; warning.*

Aviso al publico. *Public Notice. Notice to the Public.*

avispa *f. wasp.*

axila *f. armpit.*

AYER *yesterday.*

Ayer por la tarde. *Yesterday afternoon.*

ayuda *f. help, assistance, aid.*

ayudante *m. and f. assistant; adjutant (in the army).*

AYUDAR *to aid, to assist, to help.*
    ¿Permítame que le ayude? *May I help you?*
        Allow me to help you.
ayuntamiento *m. city hall.*
azafata *f. stewardess.*
azar *m. chance; hazard.*
    Al azar. *At random.*
azotar *to whip.*
azote *m. whip; whipping, spanking.*
azotea *f. flat roof; roof garden.*
AZÚCAR *m. sugar.*
AZUL *adj. blue.*
    Azul celeste. *Sky blue.*
    Azul marino. *Navy blue.*

bacalao *m. codfish.*
bache *m. pothole.*
bacteria *f. bacteria.*
bagaje *m. baggage.*
bahía *f. bay, harbor.*
bailar *to dance.*
bailarín *m. dancer*
baile *m. dance, ball*
baja *f. fall, depreciation (price); casualty.*
BAJAR *to go (come) down; to get (bring)*
    down; to get off; to lower, let down;
    to drop (fever, temperature, etc.).
    Bajaré dentro de unos minutos. *I'll come*
      (be) down in a few minutes.
    Bajaron del tren. *They got off the train.*
BAJO *low; under, below.*
    El es algo más bajo que yo. *He's a little*
      bit shorter than I am.
    Hable un poco más bajo. *Speak a little*
      lower.
    Tenemos diez grados bajo cero. *It's ten*
      degrees below zero.
bala *f. bullet.*
balance *m. balance.*
balboa *m. Panamanian currency unit.*
balde *m. bucket.*
    De balde. *Free. For nothing.*
baloncesto *m. basketball*
ballena *f. whale.*
ballet *m. ballet.*
banana *f. banana.*
bananal *m. banana grove*
banca *f. banking (industry).*
banco *m. bench; bank.*
banda *f. band; sash, ribbon; gang.*
bandeja *f. tray.*
bandera *f. flag, banner.*
bandido *m. bandit, outlaw.*
banquero *m. banker.*
BAÑO *m. bath; bathroom.*
BARATO *adj. cheap.*

barba *f. chin; beard.*
    En sus barbas. *To his face.*
barbacoa *f. barbecue.*
barbaridad *f. stupidity.*
    ¡Qué barbaridad! *How foolish!*
barbería *f. barbershop.*
barbero *m. barber.*
barca *f. small boat.*
barco *m. boat, vessel, ship.*
barniz *m. varnish.*
barómetro *m. barometer.*
barranco *m. ravine, gully, cliff.*
barrer *to sweep.*
barriada *f. district, slum.*
barriga *f. belly.*
barril *m. barrel.*
barrio *m. district, neighborhood.*
barrio bajo *m. slum.*
barro *m. mud.*
báscula *f. platform scale.*
base *f. base, basis.*
    Base de datos. *Data base.*
básico *adj. basic.*
básquetbol *m. basketball.*
BASTANTE *enough, sufficient.*
    Tiene bastante dinero. *He has enough*
      money.
    Bastante bien. *Pretty well. Rather well.*
BASTAR *to suffice, be enough.*
    Eso basta por ahora. *That's enough for now.*
    ¡Basta, ya! *That's enough!*
bastón *m. cane, walking stick.*
basura *f. refuse, garbage.*
bata *f. robe, housecoat, smock.*
batalla *f. battle, combat, fight.*
batallar *to battle, to fight.*
batallón *m. battalion.*
bate *m. bat (sport).*
batear *to hit, to bat (sport).*
batería *f. battery.*
    Batería de cocina. *Kitchen utensils.*
batido *m. milkshake.*
batir *to beat.*
baudio *m. baud.*
baúl *m. trunk chest.*
bautizar *to baptize, christen.*
bautizo *m. baptism, christening.*
bebé *m. baby.*
BEBER *to drink.*
    ¿Le gustaría beber algo? *Would you like*
      something to drink?
bebida *f. drink, beverage.*
becerro *m. calf; calfskin.*
beís bol *m. baseball.*
belleza *f. beauty*
BELLO *adj. beautiful.*
    Una mujer bella. *A beautiful woman.*
    Las bellas artes. *The fine arts.*
    ¡Qué bello! *How beautiful!*

bendecir *to bless.*
  ¡Dios le bendiga! *God bless you!*
bendición *f. blessing; benediction.*
bendito *adj. blessed; m. simpleton.*
  Es un bendito. *He's a simpleton.*
beneficiar *to benefit, to profit.*
beneficio *m. benefit, profit, privilege.*
berenjena *f. eggplant.*
berro *m. watercress.*
besar *to kiss.*
beso *m. kiss.*
bestia *f. beast.*
betún *m. shoe polish.*
biberón *m. baby bottle.*
bibliografía *f. bibliography.*
biblioteca *f. library; bookcase.*
bicarbonato *m. bicarbonate.*
bicicleta *f. bicycle.*
bicho *m. insect; vermin; a ridiculous person*
  (coll.); homosexual (Puerto Rico.)
  Es un mal bicho. *He's a bad egg.*
  Es un bicho raro. *He's very odd. He's a*
  queer person.
BIEN *well, right.*
  ¿Está Ud. bien? *Are you all right?*
  Muy bien, gracias. *Very well, thank you.*
  No muy bien. *Not so well.*
  ¡Qué lo pase Ud. bien! *Good luck to you!*
  Está bien. *All right. O.K.*
bienes *m. pl. property, estate, possessions.*
  Bienes inmuebles. *Real property.*
  Bienes muebles. *Personal property.*
bienestar *m. well-being, welfare.*
bienvenida *f. welcome.*
  ¡Bienvenido! *Welcome!*
BILLETE *m. ticket; bank note. (See boleto.)*
  ¿Dónde puedo sacar mis billetes? *Where*
  can I buy my tickets?
  ¿Puede usted cambiarme un billete de diez
  dólares? *Can you change a ten-dollar*
  bill for me?
  Billete de ida y vuelta. *Round-trip ticket.*
billetera *f. wallet, pocketbook.*
binario *adj. binary.*
  El dígito binario. *Bit.*
biombo *m. screen.*
biquini *m. bikini.*
bit *m. bit. (computer).*
blanco *adj. white; m. mark, target.*
  Dar en el blanco. *To hit the mark.*
blando *adj. soft, smooth.*
blusa *f. blouse.*
bobo *adj. foolish, silly; m. fool, simpleton.*
boca *f. mouth.*
bocacalle *f. street intersection.*
bocadillo *m. a snack; sandwich.*
bocaditos *m. snacks.*
bocado *m. mouthful, a bite (to eat).*
  No he probado bocado desde ayer. *I*

  haven't had a bite to eat since
  yesterday.
bocina *f. horn (of a car).*
boda *f. wedding.*
bodega *f. wine-cellar; hold (of a ship);*
  storeroom, grocery store.
bofetada *f. a slap in the face.*
  Soltar una bofetada. *To slap in the face.*
boicotear *to boycott.*
boina *f. beret.*
bola *f. ball, globe.*
bolero *m. popular Latin American song.*
BOLETO *m. ticket. (See billete.)*
bolívar *m. Venezuelan currency unit.*
bolsa *f. purse; bag; stock exchange.*
bolsillo *m. pocket.*
bolso *m. change purse; bag.*
bomba *f. pump; fire engine; bomb; Puerto*
  Rican folk dance.
  Bomba de gasolina. *Gasoline pump.*
bombilla *f. light bulb.*
bombón *m. candy, bonbon.*
bombonera *f. candy box.*
bondad *f. goodness, kindness.*
  Tenga Ud. la bondad de sentarse. *Please sit*
  down.
bonito *adj. pretty, good, graceful; m. bonito*
  (a kind of fish).
bordo, a *on board.*
  Todos los pasajeros estaban a bordo. *All*
  the passengers were on board.
borracho *adj. drunk, intoxicated; m.*
  drunkard.
borrador *m. eraser; rough draft.*
borrar *to strike or cross out, to erase.*
borrón *m. blot, stain.*
bosque *m. wood, forest.*
bostezar *to yawn, to gape.*
botar *to launch (a ship); to bounce; to throw*
  out.
bote *m. boat; jar, can, container.*
  Bote salvavidas. *Lifeboat.*
  Un bote de mermelada. *A jar o,*
  marmalade.
  Bote de remos. *Rowboat.*
BOTELLA *f. bottle.*
botica *f. drugstore.*
boticario *m. druggist.*
botiquín *m. medicine cabinet, medicine*
  chest.
botón *m. button; bud.*
botones *m. hotel page, bellboy.*
boxeador *m. boxer.*
boxear *to box.*
boxeo *m. boxing.*
bravo *adj. brave.*
  ¡Bravo! *Bravo!*
braza *f. breaststroke.*
brazalete *m. bracelet.*

BRAZO *m. arm.*

Puede llevar el paquete debajo del brazo. *You can carry the package under your arm.*

Iban del brazo. *They were walking arm in arm.*

BREVE *adj. brief, short.*

En breve. *Shortly. In a little while.*

breveded *f. briefness, brevity.*

brigada *f. brigade.*

brillante *adj. brilliant, sparkling; m. diamond.*

brillar *to shine, to sparkle.*

brindar *to toast; to offer; to invite.*

brindis *m. toast, drinking someone's health.*

brío *m. vigor.*

brisa *f. breeze.*

brocha *f. brush, paintbrush.*

broche *m. clasp; brooch; hook-and-eye.*

broma *f. joke, jest.*

En broma. *As a joke. Jestingly.*

Tomar a broma. *To take as a joke.*

bromear *to joke, to have fun.*

¡Ud. bromea! *You're joking! You're kidding!*

bromista *m. and f. joker.*

bronce *m. bronze, brass.*

bronquio *m. bronchial tube.*

bruma *f. fog, mist.*

brusco *adj. brusque, rude, rough.*

brutal *adj. brutal, brutish.*

bruto *adj. brutal; rude; m. stupid person.*

En bruto. *In the rough. In a rough state. In the raw state.*

Peso bruto. *Gross weight.*

bucear *to skin-dive.*

buceo *m. skindiving.*

budin *m. pudding.*

BUEN (*contraction of* **bueno**; *used only before a masculine noun*)

Pasamos un buen rato en el cine. *We had a good time at the movies.*

¡Buen viaje! *Bon voyage! Have a pleasant trip!*

Tuve un buen día. *I spent a pleasant day.*

Hace muy buen tiempo. *The weather's very nice.*

En buen estado. *In good condition.*

Un buen hombre. *A good man.*

BUENO *adj. good; kind; satisfactory; suited, fit; well.*

¡Buenos días! *Good morning!*

¡Buenas tardes! *Good afternoon! Good evening!*

¡Buenas noches! *Good night!*

Esa es una buena idea. *That's a good idea.*

He pasado muy buena noche. *I've had a very good night's rest.*

¡Qué bueno! *How wonderful!*

¿Tiene Ud. algo de bueno? *Have you anything good (to eat)?*

¡Sé bueno! *Be good!*

Se pasa de bueno. *He's too good.*

¡Tanto bueno por aquí! *Look who's here! I'm glad to see you.*

¡Eso sí que está bueno! *That's a pretty how-do-you-do!*

De buena gana. *Willingly.*

bufete *m. desk; lawyer's office.*

buffer *m. buffer* (*computer*).

buho *m. owl.*

buitre *m. vulture.*

bujía *f. candle; spark plug.*

bulla *f. noise, fuss.*

No metan tanta bulla. *Don't make so much noise.*

bullicio *m. noise, bustle, tumult.*

bulto *m. bundle, parcel, package.*

¿Cabrán estos bultos en su coche? *Will these packages fit in your car?*

buñuelo *m. bun, cruller, fritter, mess.*

buque *m. ship, vessel, steamer.*

buqué *m. bouquet.*

burguesía *f. middle class.*

burla *f. mockery, scoffing, sneering, fun.*

Le hicimos burla de su sombrero. *We made fun of her hat.*

¿Se burla usted de mí? *Are you making fun of me?*

burlón *adj. mocking, bantering; m. mocker, jester, scoffer.*

burro *m. ass, donkey.*

bursátil *adj. stock, stock market.*

BUSCAR *to seek, look for, search; to fetch, get.*

¿Qué busca Ud. *What are you looking for?*

¿A quién busca Ud. *Who(m) do you wish to see? Who(m) are you looking for?*

Está buscando una colocación. *He's looking for a job.*

Voy a buscar mis libros. *I'm going to get my books.*

¿Quién la va a buscar? *Who's going to get her? Who's going after her?*

Enviaron a buscar al médico. *They sent someone for the doctor.*

buscavidas *m and f. busybody; go-getter.*

búsqueda *f. search.*

busto *m. bust, chest.*

butaca *f. easy chair; orchestra seat* (*in a theater*).

Siéntese Ud. en esta butaca. *Sit down in this armchair.*

Sacaré tres butacas. *I'll buy three orchestra seats.*

buzón *m. mailbox.*

Eche Ud. la carta en el buzón. *Put the letter in the mailbox.*

byte *m. byte* (*computer*).

C

cabalgar *to ride on horseback.*
caballa *f. mackerel.*
caballería *f. cavalry; riding horse.*
caballero *m. gentleman; knight; horseman.*
  Es todo un caballero. *He's a perfect gentleman.*
caballo *m. horse; knight (in chess); queen (cards).*
cabaña *f. hut, cabin.*
cabaret *m. cabaret, nightclub.*
cabecera *f. head of a bed or table.*
  Sentarse a la cabecera. *To take one's place (to sit) at the head of the table.*
CABELLO *m. hair.*
CABER *to fit into; to have enough room; to contain.*
  El libro no cabe en el estante. *The book won't fit on the shelf.*
  No cabe más en el baúl. *The trunk won't hold any more. There's no more room in the trunk.*
  No me cabe la menor duda. *I haven't the slightest doubt.*
CABEZA *f. head.*
  Me duele la cabeza. *I've a headache.*
  ¿Le lavo la cabeza? *Do you want a shampoo? ("Shall I wash your hair?")*
  Tiene mala cabeza. *He's reckless.*
  Pagar a tanto por cabeza. *To pay so much per head.*
  De pies a cabeza. *From head to foot.*
  Por cabezas. *Per capita.*
cabina *f. cabin, booth.*
  Cabina telefónica. *Telephone booth.*
cable *m. cable; rope, line.*
cablevisión *f. cable television.*
CABO *m. tip, extremity, end; cape; rope; corporal.*
  Al cabo de día. *At the end of the day.*
  Leyó el libro de cabo a rabo. *She read the book from cover to cover.*
  Al fin y al cabo. *At last. In the end. At length. After all. In the long run.*
  Llevar a cabo. *To accomplish. To carry through.*
cabra *f. goat.*
cacahuete *m. peanut.*
cacao *m. cocoa; cocoa tree.*
cacería *f. hunt, hunting.*
cacerola *f. casserole, pan.*
cacharro *m. coarse earthen pot, piece of junk.*
cachemir *m. cashmere.*
cachete *m. cheek, slap in the face.*
CADA *adj. every, each.*
  Cada hora. *Every hour.*

  Cada cual. *Each one.*
  Cada vez menos. *Less and less.*
  Dar a cada uno lo suyo. *To give everyone his due.*
  Cada día se pone más delgada. *She's growing thinner day by day.*
cadáver *m. corpse, cadaver.*
cadena *f. chain.*
cadera *f. hip.*
cadete *m. cadet.*
CAER *to fall; to tumble down; to drop; to become, fit; to realize.*
  Por poco me caigo. *I almost (nearly) fell down.*
  Cayó enfermo ayer. *He fell ill yesterday. He got sick yesterday.*
  ¿Qué se le ha caído a Ud.? *What have you dropped?*
  Caer bien con. *To match. To match well with.*
  Ese vestido le cae muy bien. *That dress fits her very well.*
  La Pascua cae en marzo este año. *Easter falls (comes) in March this year.*
caerse *to fall down.*
  Me caí. *I fell down.*
café *m. coffee; café.*
  Una taza de café. *A cup of coffee.*
  Café con leche. *Coffee with cream.*
  Café solo. *Black coffee?*
  Tomemos una cerveza en este café. *Let's have some beer in this café.*
cafetera *f. coffeepot.*
caída *f. fall, downfall.*
CAJA *f. box, case; coffin; chest; cash.*
  Quiero una caja de galletas surtidas. *I want a box of assorted cookies.*
  En caja. *Cash. Cash on hand.*
  Pague en la caja. *Pay the cashier.*
  Caja registradora. *Cash register.*
  Caja de ahorros. *Savings bank.*
  Caja fuerte. *A safe. ("Strong box.")*
  Flujo de caja. *Cash flow.*
cajero *m. cashier.*
  Cajero automático. *Bank machine.*
cajón *m. drawer; box, case (made of wood).*
cajuela *f. car trunk.*
calabaza *f. pumpkin, squash.*
  Ella le dió calabazas. *She refused him (a suitor). She gave him the air.*
calabozo *m. dungeon, prison, cell.*
calamar *m. squid.*
calambre *m. cramp.*
calamidad *f. calamity, misfortune.*
calavera *f. skull; m. madcap.*
  Es un calavera. *He leads a wild life.*
calcetín *m. sock.*
calculador *adj. calculating; m. calculator.*
calcular *to calculate, estimate.*

cálculo m. computation; estimate; calculus.

caldo m. broth.

Caldo de gallina. Chicken broth.

calefacción f. heating.

Calefacción central. Central heating.

calendario m. calendar, almanac.

calentador m. heater.

calentar to warm, heat.

calentarse to grow warm, to warm oneself; to become excited, to get angry.

No quiero calentarme la cabeza por eso. I don't want to worry my head about that.

calentura f. fever.

calibre m. caliber; bore; gauge.

calidad f. quality; condition, capacity.

CALIENTE adj. warm, hot.

Prefiero la leche fría a la caliente. I prefer cold milk to warm.

El sol está muy caliente. The sun's very hot.

calificación f. qualification; mark (in an examination).

calificar to qualify; to rate; to describe; to authorize; to attest.

caligrafía f. calligraphy, handwriting.

calma f. calm, calmness, slowness.

Tómelo con calma. Take it easy.

Debemos mirar este asunto con más calma. We must look at this matter more calmly.

calmante m. sedative.

calmar to calm, to quiet.

calmarse to quiet down.

¡Cálmese! Calm yourself!

CALOR m. heat, warmth; thick (of a fight).

Tengo calor. I'm warm. I'm hot.

Hace mucho calor. It's very hot.

calumniar to slander.

caluroso adj. warm, hot.

Es un día caluroso. It's a hot day.

calva f. bald head.

calvicie f. baldness.

calvo adj. bald; barren.

calzada f. highway, road

calzado m. footwear.

calzador m. shoehorn.

calzar to put on shoes; to wedge.

calzoncillos m. undershorts.

callado adj. quiet; silent; discreet, reserved.

callar to keep quiet, to be silent; to conceal.

¡Cállate! Keep quiet!

En este caso vale más callar. In this case it's better to keep quiet (to say nothing).

callarse to be quiet, to shut up.

CALLE f. street; lane.

Atravesemos la calle. Let's cross the street.

¿Qué calle es ésta? What street is this?

¿Cuál es la calle próxima? What's the street after this? What's the next street?

Esta calles es de dirección única. This is a one-way street.

Al otro lado de la calle. Across the street.

Echar a la calle. To throw out. To put out. ("To throw out into the street.")

Quedarse en la calle. To be left penniless.

callejón m. alley.

Callejón sin salida. Blind alley.

callo m. corn, callus.

CAMA f. bed; couch; litter; layer.

Hacer la cama. To make the bed.

Guardar cama. To be confined to bed. To stay in bed.

cámara f. camera

En cámara lenta. In slow motion.

camarada m. and f. comrade.

camerera f. waitress, chambermaid.

camarero m. waiter; steward.

camarón m. shrimp.

camarote m. cabin, stateroom, box (theater).

CAMBIAR to barter, to exchange; to change, to barter.

¿Puede Ud. cambiarme un billete de diez dólares? Can you change a ten-dollar bill for me?

He cambiado mi reloj por uno nuevo. I've exchanged my watch for a new one.

¿En qué estación cambiamos de tren? At what station do we change trains?

¿Ha cambiado Ud. de idea? Have you changed your mind?

Cambiemos de tema. Let's change the subject.

Cambiar la velocidad. To shift gears.

CAMBIO m. barter, exchange; rate of exchange, change.

No tengo cambio. I haven't any change.

¿A cuánto está el cambio? What's the rate of exchange?

Tasa de cambio. Exchange rate.

En cambio. On the other hand. In return.

Cambio de velocidad (de marchas). Gearshift.

Cambio automático. Automatic transmission.

camilla f. small bed; stretcher.

CAMINAR to walk; to march; to move along.

caminata f. hike

CAMINO m. road, way, highway.

¿Adónde va este camino? Where does this road lead to?

¿Voy bien por este camino? Am I on the right road? Am I going the right way?

Indíqueme el camino. Show me the way.

camión m. truck; bus (Mex.).

camioneta *f.* station wagon, small truck, van.

CAMISA *f.* shirt, chemise.
  En mangas de camisa. *In one's shirtsleeves.*

camiseta *f.* undershirt, T-shirt

camisón *m.* nightgown.

campamento *m.* camp, encampment.

campana *f.* bell
  ¿Tocó Ud. la campanilla? *Did you ring the bell?*

campaña *f.* campaign.
  Campaña de ventas. *Sales campaign.*

campeón *m.* champion.

campeonato *m.* championship.

campesino *m.* peasant.

campo *m.* field, country; space.
  Poner en el campo. *To field a team.*

cana *f.* gray hair.

canal *m.* channel, canal.

canario *m.* canary.

canasta *f.* basket, hamper.

canasto *m.* large basket.

cancelar to cancel; to annul.

cáncer *m.* cancer.

CANCIÓN *f.* song.

cancha *f.* sports grounds, playing field.

candado *m.* padlock.

candelero *m.* candlestick.

candidato *m.* candidate.

candidatura *f.* candidacy.

candidez *f.* candor, simplicity.

cándido *adj.* candid, simple.

canela *f.* cinnamon.

cangrejo *m.* crab, crawfish.

canjear to exchange.

canoa *f.* canoe.

CANSADO *adj.* tired; tedious; annoying.

cansancio *m.* fatigue.

cansar to tire; to annoy, to bore.

cansarse to get tired, to get annoyed, to become bored.

cantante *m. and f.* singer.

CANTAR to sing; to reveal a secret.

cantidad *f.* quantity; amount; sum (of money).

cantina *f.* barroom, saloon; canteen.

canto *m.* singing; song; border; edge; front edge of a book; back of a knife; pebble, stone.

caña *f.* cane, reed; leg, upper part of a boot.
  Caña de pescar. *Fishing rod.*
  Caña de azúcar. *Sugar cane.*

cañada *f.* ravine.

cañaveral *m.* reed field, sugar cane plantation.

cañería *f.* conduit, piping; water pipe; main (gas).

caño *m.* pipe, tube, spout.

cañón *m.* cannon, gun; gorge, canyon; tube; funnel (of a chimney).

caoba *f.* mahogany.

caos *m.* chaos.

capa *f.* cape, cloak; layer; coat, coating.

capacidad *f.* capacity.
  Capacidad adquisitiva. *Purchasing power.*

capacitación *f.* training.

capacitar to train.

capataz *m.* foreman, overseer.

CAPAZ *adj.* capable, able; liable, apt; spacious, having plenty of room.
  Es capaz de cualquier cosa. *He's capable of anything.*

capital *adj.* principal, main; *m.* principal (money invested); capital (stock); *f.* capital city (metropolis).

capitán *m.* captain; commander; ringleader.

capítulo *m.* chapter.

capó *m.* hood (car).

capricho *m.* whim.

cápsula *f.* capsule.

CARA *f.* face; front, façade.
  Su cara no me es desconocida. *Your face is familiar.*
  Tiene Ud. muy buena cara. *You look very well.*
  Disco de dos caras. *Two-sided floppy disk.*
  Echar en cara. *To reproach. ("To throw in someone's face.")*
  De cara. *Facing.*
  ¿Cara o cruz? *Heads or tails?*

¡caray! *Good gracious! Goodness! Gosh!*

carácter *m.* character.

carbón *m.* coal; charcoal; carbon.
  Papel carbón. *Carbon paper.*

carburador *m.* carburetor.

carcajada *f.* hearty laughter.
  Reírse a carcajadas. *To laugh uproariously. To split one's sides laughing.*
  Soltar una carcajada. *To burst out laughing.*

cárcel *f.* prison, jail.

cardíaco *adj.* cardiac.

CARECER to lack, to be in want.
  Carecemos del dinero suficiente para eso. *We lack (don't have) enough money for that.*
  carecer de fundamento. *To be unfounded.*

carga *f.* freight; load; cargo; burden.

cargado *adj.* loaded; strong (tea).
  Estaba cargado de razón. *He was absolutely right.*

cargamento *m.* cargo; load.

cargar to load, to boot; to charge; to carry a load.
  Carga en cuenta. *To charge to an account.*
  Cargar un programa. *To load a program (computer).*

caricia *f. caress.*

caridad *f. charity.*

carie *f. decay* (tooth).

cariño *m. fondness, love, affection; pl. regards.*
> Tomar cariño a. *To become attached to.*
> Dar cariños. *To give one's regards.*

cariñoso *adj. affectionate, loving.*

caritativo *adj. charitable.*

carnaval *m. carnival.*

CARNE *f. flesh; meat; pulp* (of fruit).
> Carne asada. *Roast meat.*
> Carne de vaca. *Beef.*
> Ser carne y uña. *To be bosom friends.*

carnero *m. mutton.*

carnet *m. booklet; membership book, membership card.*
> carnet de conducir *driver's license.*

carnicería *f. butcher shop, meat market; slaughter.*

carnicero *m. butcher.*

CARO *adj. dear; expensive.*
> Es muy caro. *It's too expensive* (dear).
> Un amigo caro. *A dear friend.*
> Lo pagará Ud. caro. *You'll pay dearly for it.*
> Cara mitad. *Better half.*

carpintero *m. carpenter.*

carrera *f. career; race.*
> Coche de carreras. *Racing car.*

carreta *f. heavy cart, wagon.*

carrete *m. spool, reel, bobbin, coil; kind of hat* (Mex.).

carretera *f. road, highway, drive.*
> ¿Adónde va esta carretera? *Where does this highway lead?*

carrillo *m. jowl.*

carro *m. cart; car* (Amer.) *carriage* (machine).

carroza *f. float* (parade).

carruaje *m. any kind of vehicle.*

CARTA *f. letter; map, chart; charter; playing card.*
> ¿Cómo tengo que dirigir la carta? *How shall* (do) *I address the letter?*
> Eche Ud. la carta en el buzón. *Put the letter in the mailbox.*
> ¿A qué hora reparten las cartas? *When is the mail delivered?*
> Carta certificada. *Registered letter.*
> Carta urgente. *Special delivery letter.*
> Carta de crédito. *Letter of credit.*
> Vamos a jugar a las cartas. *Let's play cards.*

carta-llave *f. card-key*

cartel *m. placard, poster, cartel.*

cartelera *f. listings* (theater, film).

cartera *f. portfolio; pocketbook, wallet.*
> Le han roboado la cartera. *They've stolen his wallet.*

carterista *m. pickpocket.*

cartero *m. mailman, letter carrier.*

cartón *m. cardboard.*

cartucho *m. cartridge*

CASA *f. house, home; firm, concern*
> Vive en esa casa que hace esquina. *He lives in the corner house.*
> Mándemelo a casa. *Send it to my house.*
> Vamos a mudarnos de casa pronto. *We're going to move soon.*
> ¿Cuándo viene Ud. por mi casa? *When are you coming to my place?*
> Estaré en casa todo el día. *I'll be* (at) *home all day.*
> Está en la casa de Juan. *He's at John's house.*
> Aquí tiene Ud. su casa. *Come again.* ("This is your home.")
> Esta casa goza de buena fama. *This firm has a good reputation.*
> Casa de huéspedes. *Guest house.*
> Casa de apartamentos. *Apartment house.*

casado *adj. married.*

casamiento *m. marriage, wedding.*

casar *to marry; to match.*

casarse *to get married.*

cascanueces *m. nutcracker.*

cáscara *f. peel, husk, shell, bark.*

caserío *m. row of houses, hamlet.*

casero *adj. pertaining to the home, domestic.*
> No hay nada como la comida casera. *There's nothing like home cooking.*
> Remedios caseros. *Home remedies.*
> Computador casero (personal). *Home* (Personal) *computer.*

caseta *f. telephone booth.*

casete *m. cassette tape.*

CASI *almost, nearly.*
> Casi he terminado. *I'm almost finished.*
> La comida está casi lista. *Dinner is about ready.*
> Casi nunca leo los periódicos. *I hardly ever read the newspapers.*

casilla *f. cabin, post-office box* (Amer.).

CASO *m. case, event, accident.*
> ¿Qué caso tan singular! *What a strange case!*
> Bien, vamos al caso. *Well, let's get to the point.*
> Hacer caso. *To pay attention to. To mind.*
> No le haga caso. *Pay no attention to him. Don't mind him.*

caspa *f. dandruff.*

castañuela *f. castanet.*

castellano *adj. Castilian; m. Spanish language.*

castigar *to punish.*

castigo *m. punishment, penalty.*

castizo *adj. pure, genuine*

casual *adj. accidental, casual.*

casualidad *f. chance, coincidence, accident.*

   Me lo encontré de pura casualidad. *I met him by chance.*

   ¿Qué casualidad! *What a coincidence!*

catálogo *m. catalog.*

catarata *f. waterfall, cascade; cataract (of the eye).*

catarro *m. a cold.*

   Tengo un catarro terrible. *I have a bad cold.*

catedral *f. cathedral.*

catedrático *m. professor of a university.*

categoría *f. category, class.*

catolicismo *m. Catholicism.*

católico *adj. Catholic.*

CATORCE *fourteen; fourteenth.*

catre *m. cot.*

caucho *m. rubber.*

caudal *m. estate, property.*

caudillo *m. leader, chieftain.*

CAUSA *f. cause, motive; lawsuit.*

   No vino a causa de la lluvia. *He didn't come on account (because) of the rain.*

   Sin causa. *Without cause. Without a reason.*

causar *to cause.*

   Causa horror. *It's horrible!*

   Causar daño. *To do harm. To cause damage. To injure.*

cautela *f. caution, prudence.*

cauto *adj. cautious, prudent.*

cavar *to dig up, to excavate.*

caverna *f. cave, cavern.*

caza *f. hunting; game.*

cazador *m. hunter.*

cazar *to hunt, to chase.*

cazuela *f. casserole.*

cebada *f. barley.*

cebo *m. bait (fishing).*

cebolla *f. onion.*

ceder *to grant; to give in, yield, to inure to.*

cedro *m. cedar.*

cédula *(f. warrant, certificate.*

   Cédula de identidad. *Identification papers.*

ceguera *f. blindness.*

ceja *f. eyebrow.*

celda *f. cell.*

CELEBRAR *to celebrate; to be glad; to praise; to hold, take place.*

   Lo celebro mucho. *I'm very happy to hear it.*

   ¿Cuándo se celebra la reunión? *When will the meeting take place?*

célebre *adj. famous, renowned.*

celeste *adj. light blue, celestial.*

celos *m. pl. jealousy.*

celoso *adj. jealous.*

célula *f. cell.*

celular *adj. cellular*

   Teléfono celular. *Cellular telephone.*

cementerio *m. cemetery.*

cemento *m. cement.*

CENA *f. supper, dinner.*

cenar *to have supper, to dine.*

cenicero *m. ashtray.*

ceniza *f. ashes.*

censura *f. censorship; reproach.*

censurar *to censure; to reproach; to criticize.*

CENTAVO *m. cent.*

centena *f. a hundred, about a hundred.*

centenar *m. a hundred, about a hundred.*

   A centenares. *By the hundreds.*

centenario *m. centenary.*

centeno *m. rye.*

centésimo *adj. hundredth.*

centígrado *adj. centigrade.*

centímetro *m. centimeter*

CENTRAL *adj. central; f. main office.*

   América Central. *Central America.*

   ¿Dónde está la central telefónica? *Where is the telephone exchange station?*

CENTRO *m. center, middle; core; club, social circle.*

ceño *m. frown.*

cepillar *to brush; to plane, to polish.*

cepillo *m. brush; carpenter's plane.*

   Cepillo de dientes. *Toothbrush.*

cera *f. wax; earwax*

CERCA *near, about, close by; f. fence.*

   ¿Hay alguna farmacia cerca de aquí? *Is there a drugstore near here?*

   Está muy cerca. *It's quite near.*

   Esto me toca de cerca. *This concerns me very much.*

   Por aquí cerca. *Near here. Somewhere around here.*

cercanías *f. vicinity, neighborhood.*

cercano *adj. nearby.*

cercar *to fence, inclose, surround; to besiege.*

cerciorarse *to ascertain, to make sure.*

cerco *m. fence; siege.*

cerdo *m. hog, pig.*

cereal *m. cereal.*

cerebro *m. brain.*

ceremonia *f. ceremony; formality.*

cereza *f. cherry.*

cerezo *m. cherry tree.*

cerilla *f. match stick.*

cero *m. zero; nought.*

   Tenemos diez grados bajo cero. *It's ten degrees below zero.*

cerrado *adj. closed, shut.*
   Cerrado por reformas. *Closed for repairs.*
   Se trató el asunto a puerta cerrada. *The matter was discussed privately.*
cerradura *f. lock.*
CERRAR *to close, lock, shut; to turn off.*
   Cierre la puerta. *Close (shut) the door.*
   Cerrar con llave. *To lock. ("To close with a key.")*
   Haga el favor de cerrar el grifo. *Please turn the water off.*
cerro *m. hill.*
cerrojo *m. bolt, latch.*
certeza *f. certainty, conviction.*
certidumbre *f. certainty.*
certificado *m. certificate.*
   Certificado de depósito. *Certificate of deposit.*
certificar *to certify; to register (a letter, etc.).*
   Quisiera certificar esta carta. *I'd like to register this letter.*
cervecería *f. brewery, beer saloon.*
cerveza *f. beer, ale.*
cesante *adj. unemployed; dismissed, fired.*
CESAR *to cease, stop; to leave (a job).*
   Quédese aquí hasta que cese la lluvia. *Stay here until the rain stops.*
césped *m. grass, lawn.*
cesta *f. basket, hamper.*
cesto *m. hand basket.*
cicatriz *f. scar.*
ciclismo *m. cycling.*
ciclista *m. and f. bicyclist.*
ciclón *m. cyclone.*
ciego *adj. blind; m. a blind person.*
cielo *m. sky; heaven.*
CIEN *(form of* **ciento;** *used before nouns), one hundred.*
   ¿Le bastará a usted con cien pesos? *Will one hundred pesos be enough for you?*
ciencia *f. science.*
científico *adj. scientific.*
cientista *m. and f. scientist.*
CIENTO *adj. and n. one hundred.*
CIERTO *adj. certain.*
   Es cierto. *It's certain. It's true.*
   Eso no es cierto. *That's not certain. That's not true.*
   Lo dimos por cierto. *We assumed that it was true.*
   Hasta cierto punto eso es verdad. *That's true to a certain extent.*
   Esto me lo dijo cierta persona. *A certain person told me that.*
   ¡Sí, por cierto! *Yes, indeed!*
ciervo *m. deer.*
cifra *f. number; cipher, code.*

CIGARRILLO *m. cigarette.*
cigarro *m. cigar; cigarette (Mex.).*
cigüeña *f. stork.*
cilindro *m. cylinder.*
cima *f. summit, top.*
cimiento *m. foundation, base.*
CINCO *adj. and n. five.*
CINCUENTA *adj. and n. fifty.*
CINE *m. movies, motion picture, cinema.*
cineasta *m. and f. filmmaker.*
cinema *m. movies, cinema.*
cinematógrafo *m. movie projector.*
cinta *f. ribbon; tape; film.*
   Cinta magnetofónica. *Tape (for a tape recorder).*
cintura *f. waist.*
cinturón *m. belt.*
   Cinturón de seguridad. *Seat belt.*
cíper *zipper (Mex.).*
ciprés *m. cypress.*
circo *m. circus.*
circulación *f. circulation; traffic.*
circular *adj. circular.*
circular *to circulate.*
círculo *m. circle; circuit; club.*
circunferencia *f. circumference.*
circunstancia *f. circumstance.*
   Lo exigen las circunstancias. *The circumstances demand it. The situation requires it.*
ciruela *f. plum, prune.*
cirujano *m. surgeon.*
   Cirujano plástico. *Plastic surgeon.*
cisne *m. swan.*
CITA *f. appointment, date; summons; quotation.*
   Deseo hacer una cita con Ud. *I'd like to make an appointment with you.*
   Tengo una cita esta noche con mi novia. *I've a date tonight with my girl.*
citación. *f. citation, subpoena.*
citar(se) *to cite; to make an appointment; to summon.*
   Me he citado con él para el lunes. *I've made an appointment with him for next Monday.*
   Citó una porción de casos semejantes. *He cited a number of similar cases.*
cítrico *m. citric fruit.*
CIUDAD *f. city.*
   Ciudad natal. *Hometown. City in which one is born.*
ciudadanía *f. citizenship.*
ciudadano *m. citizen.*
civil *adj. civil; courteous, polite.*
civilización *f. civilization.*
civilizar *to civilize.*
clara *f. white of an egg.*
claraboya *f. skylight.*

claridad *f. clearness; light; distinctness, plainness.*
Escriba Ud. la dirección con claridad. *Write the address clearly.*

clarín *m. bugle; bugler.*

clarinete *m. clarinet; clarinetist.*

CLARO *adj. clear; intelligible; plain, transparent, pure (water, etc.); light (color); bright (room, etc.)*
Poner en claro. *To make (something) clear. To clarify. To clear (something) up. To set-right.*
¡Claro que sí! *Certainly! Of course!*
¡Claro que no! *Of course not!*
Pasé la noche en claro. *I couldn't sleep a wink all night.*

CLASE *f. class; kind; sort; classroom; lesson.*
Clase de español. *Spanish class.*
Es el primero de la clase. *He's at the head of his class.*
¿Qué clase de fruta es esa? *What kind of fruit is that?*
La clase obrera. *The working class.*

clásico *m. classic, typical.*
Este es un caso clásico. *This is a typical case.*

clasificados *m. pl. classified ads.*

clasificar *to classify, to rate.*

clavar *to nail, fasten; to drive in, to pierce; to cheat.*
Clavar la vista en. *To stare at.*

CLAVE *f. key; cipher, code.*

clavel *m. carnation.*

clavo *m. nail; clove.*
Por fin ha dado Ud. en el clavo. *At last you've hit the nail on the head.*

clero *m. clergy.*

cliente *m. and f. client; customer.*

clientela *f. clientele, customers.*

clima *m. climate.*

clínica *f. clinic; dispensary.*

cloaca *f. sewer.*

cloroformo *m. chloroform.*

clóset *m. closet.*

club *m. club.*

coacción *f. duress.*

cobarde *adj. timid, cowardly; m. coward.*

cobija *f. bed cover, blanket.*

cobrador *m. conductor (bus, streetcar, etc.); collector.*

COBRAR *to collect, receive (money); to charge (price).*
Quisiera cobrar este cheque. *I'd like to have this check cashed.*
Cobre Ud. de este dólar. *Take it out of this dollar.*
Llamada por cobrar. *Collect call.*
Cobramos a primero de mes. *We're paid on the first of the month.*

¿Cuánto cobra Ud. por su trabajo? *How much do you charge for your work?*
Cobrar ánimo. *To take courage.*

cobre *m. copper.*

cocer *to cook, boil, bake.*

cocido *m. dish made of boiled meat and vegetables; stew.*

cocina *f. kitchen; cuisine.*

cocinar *to cook.*

cocinero *m. chef, cook.*

coco *m. coconut tree; coconut.*

cóctel *m. cocktail.*

COCHE *m. coach, carriage; car.*
Coche comedor. *Dining car. Diner.*
Coche cama. *Sleeping car. Sleeper.*
Coche de fumar. *Smoking car.*
Cochera *f. garage (Mexico)*

codazo *m. a shove with the elbow.*
Me dió un codazo. *He gave me a shove (with his elbow).*

codiciar *to covet, to desire eagerly.*

codicioso *adj. covetous, greedy; diligent.*

codo *m. elbow.*
Hablar por los codos. *To be a chatterbox.*

codorniz *f. quail.*

COGER *to catch, to take hold of; to gather; to take, to seize; to have room or capacity for. (It's a bad word in Argentina or Uruguay. In those countries use "tomar.")*
Coja Ud. un lápiz y escriba. *Take a pencil and write.*
He cogido un resfriado. *I've caught a cold.*
Esa pregunta me ha cogido de sorpresa. *That question took me by surprise.*
Los niños desbaratan todo lo que cogen. *Children destroy everything they get hold of (lay their hands on).*
Ha cogido mi sombrero en vez del suyo. *He took my hat instead of his own.*
Le cojo la palabra. *I'll take you up on that.*

cohecho *m. bribery.*

cohete *m. rocket.*

coincidencia *f. coincidence.*
Nos encontramos por una simple coincidencia. *We met by pure chance (coincidence).*

coincidir *to coincide.*

cojear *to limp.*
Sé de que pie cojea. *I know his weakness.*

cojera *f. lameness.*

cojo *adj. lame.*

cola *f. tail; rear of a train; glue; line (of people).*
Hacer cola. *To stand in line.*

colaboración *collaboration.*

colaborar *to collaborate.*

colador *m. strainer*

colar *to strain.*

colcha *f. bedspread.*

colchón *m. mattress.*

colección *f. collection.*

coleccionar *to collect.*

colecta *f. collection, collect.*

colectar *to collect; to solicit.*

colectivo *m. bus (Argentina).*

colegio *m. school; association*
> No ha debido aprender gran cosa en el colegio. *I don't think he learned much at school.*
> Colegio de abogados. *Lawyers association. The bar.*
> El colegio de cardinales. *The College of Cardinals.*
> Colegio electoral. *Electoral college.*

cólera *f. anger, fit of temper, rage; m. cholera.*
> Se le pasó la cólera fácilmente. *He got over his fit of temper easily.*

colesterol *m. cholesterol*

COLGAR *to hang, to suspend.*
> Colgaron al criminal. *The criminal was hanged.* (''They hanged the criminal.'')
> Cuelgue su abrigo en la percha. *Hang your coat on the hanger.*
> ¡No cuelgue Ud.! *Don't hang up!*
> Cuelgue el receptor. *Hang up the receiver.*

cólico *m. colic.*

coliflor *f. cauliflower.*

colilla *f. cigar or cigarette stub or butt.*

colina *f. small hill.*

colmena *f. beehive.*

colmillo *m. eyetooth, canine tooth, task.*

colmo *m. heap; climax, limit.*
> ¡Es el colmo! *That's the limit! That's the last straw!*

colocación *f. employment, situation; arrangement.*
> Anda buscando una colocación. *He's looking for a job.*
> Ha obtenido una buena colocación. *He has a good job. He got a good job.*

colocar *to place, to give employment to; to dispose of, to sell; to invest.*
> Colóquelo en su lugar. *Put it back in its place.*
> Se ha colocado en una casa de comerico. *He got a job in a business firm.*

colón *m. Costa Rican and Salvadorean monetary unit; Colón Christopher Columbus.*

colonia *f. colony; residential section in the outskirts of a town; cologne.*

colonial *adj. colonial.*

COLOR *m. color; paint; tendency, policy; aspect; pretext.*
> Es un color muy de moda. *It's a very stylish color.*

A color. *In color.*
> Color firme (sólido). *Fast color. Color that doesn't fade.*
> Color vivo. *Bright color.*
> De color. *Colored.*
> ¿Qué color tiene ese peridódico? *What's that newspaper's policy? How does that newspaper stand politically?*

colorado *adj. red.*
> Ponerse colorado. *To blush.*

colorete *m. rouge.*

colorido *m. colorful.*

columna *f. column, pillar.*

columpiar *to swing.*

columpio *m. swing.*

collar *m. necklace, collar.*

coma *f. comma; m. coma*

comadre *f. term applied both to the godmother and to her relationship with the mother of a child; a midwife.*

comadrear *to gossip.*

comadrona *f. midwife*

comandante *m. commander, commandant.*

comandos *m. commands (computer).*

comarca *f. territory, district.*

combate *m. combat.*
> Poner fuera de combate. *To knock out.*

combatiente *noun and adj. combatant, fighter.*
> No combatiente. *Noncombatant.*

combatir *to combat, fight.*

combinación *f. combination; a slip (for women).*

combinar *to combine.*

combustible *m. combustible, fuel.*

comedia *f. comedy, play; farce.*
> La comedia agradó mucho al auditorio. *The audience liked the play very much.*
> Es una comedia. *It's a farce.*

comediante *m. comedian.*

comedor *m. dining room.*
> Coche comedor. *Diner. Dining car.*

comensal *m. and f. guest (at the table); boarder.*

comentar *to comment.*

comentario *m. comment, commentary.*
> Comentarious del día. *News commentary.*
> Eso se entiende sin comentarios. *That's very clear (obvious, self-evident).*

COMENZAR *to begin, to commence.*
> ¿A qué hora comienza la función? *(At) What time does the play begin?*

COMER *to eat, to dine.*
> ¿Qué quiere Ud. comer? *What do you want (would you like) to eat?*
> Tengo ganas de comer. *I'm hungry.*
> Dar de comer. *To feed.*
> Ser de buen comer. *To have a hearty appetite.*

Se comen el uno al otro. *The fight like cats and dogs.*

Ud. se come las palabras. *You don't enunciate clearly. You swallow half of your words.*

comercializar *to commercialize.*

comerciante *m. and f. businessman, businesswoman.*

comerciar *to deal, to trade.*

comercio *m. commerce, trade.*

comestible *adj. edible; m. pl. food, groceries.*

cometer *to commit; to make (a mistake).*

Todos cometemos errores. *We all make mistakes. Anyone can make a mistake.*

cometido *m. mission, trust, task; duty.*

Yo he cumplido con mi cometido. *I've done my duty.*

Desempeñó su cometido muy bien. *He fulfilled his obligation (commitment) faithfully.*

comezón *f. itching, itch.*

cómico *adj. comic, comical; m. comedian.*

Tiras cómicas. *Comic strips.*

COMIDA *f. food; meal; dinner.*

No debe Ud. tomar nada entre comidas. *You mustn't eat anything between meals.*

No hay nada como la comida casera. *There's nothing like home cooking.*

¿Está la comida? *Is dinner ready?*

La comida está servida. *Dinner's served. Dinner's on the table.*

comienzo *m. beginning, start.*

comillas *f. quotation marks.*

comisaría *f. police station.*

comisario *m. commissioner.*

comisión *f. commission.*

comité *m. committee.*

COMO *how; as, like.*

¿Cómo lo pasa Ud.? *How do you do? How are you getting along?*

¿A cómo estamos? *What's the date?*

¿Cómo se llama Ud.? *What's your name?*

¿A cómo se venden estas medias? *How much are these stockings?*

¡Cómo no! *Yes, of course.*

Como Ud. quiera. *As you wish (like).*

Habla español tan bien como ella. *He speaks Spanish as well as she.*

El pasaje en autobús cuesta tanto como en metro. *It costs as much to ride on a bus as it does on the subway.*

Como si tal cosa. *As if nothing had happened.*

Según y como. *It all depends.*

cómoda *f. chest of drawers, a dresser.*

comodidad *f. comfort; convenience.*

Para su comodidad. *For your convenience.*

Esta casa tiene muchas comodidades. *This house has many (modern) conveniences.*

cómodo *adj. comfortable; convenient, handy.*

Estoy muy cómodo aquí. *I'm very comfortable here.*

computador (a) *m. or f. computer.*

Microcomputador. *Microcomputer.*

Computer science. *Informática.*

Computer language. *Lenguaje de computador.*

compadecer *to pity, to sympathize with.*

Le compadezco. *I pity him. I sympathize with him.*

compadre *m. term applied both to the godfather and to his relationship with the father of a child; friend, pal, buddy (coll.)*

compañero *m. companion; pal; colleague.*

Es mi compañero de cuarto. *He's my roommate.*

compañía *f. company; partnership, society.*

Suárez y Cía. *Suárez and Co.*

comparación *f. comparison.*

En comparación con. *In comparison with.*

COMPARAR *to compare.*

compartir *to share.*

compás *m. compasses, dividers; compass; time (in music).*

compasión *f. pity, sympathy.*

compatible *adj. compatible, consistent with.*

compatriota *m. and f. countryman, countrywoman.*

compensación *f. compensation, reward.*

compensar *to compensate, to reward.*

competencia *f. competition; competence.*

competente *adj. competent, fit; qualified.*

competir *to compete, to contend.*

complacer *to please, to accommodate.*

Uno no puede complacer a todo el mundo. *One can't please everybody.*

complacerse *to be pleased.*

Se complace mucho en lo que hace. *He's very pleased (satisfied) with what he's doing.*

complaciente *adj. accommodating, agreeable, pleasing.*

complemento *m. complement, object (grammar).*

COMPLETAR *to complete.*

Completar un trabajo. *To complete a job (task).*

COMPLETO *adj. full; complete, finished.*

El autobús va completo. *The bus is full.*

Hay un lleno completo esta noche. *There's a full house tonight.*

Por completo. *Completely.*

complicado *adj. complicated.*

complicar *to complicate.*

cómplice *m. and f. accomplice.*

complot *m. conspiracy, plot, intrigue.*

componer *to repair, to mend; to manage; to compose.*

Quiero que me compongan los zapatos. *I'd like to have my shoes repaired.*

Ya sabré componérmelas. *I'll know how to manage. I'll manage all right (one way or another).*

comportamiento *m. behavior.*

comportarse *to behave.*

composición *composition.*

compositor *m. composer; typesetter.*

compostura *f. repair; neatness; modesty; composure.*

compota *f. preserves, stewed fruit.*

COMPRA *f. purchase, shopping.*

Ir de compras. *To go shopping.*

Tengo que hacer unas compras. *I want to make a few purchases. I want to buy a few things.*

comprador *m. buyer, purchaser; customer.*

COMPRAR *to buy, to shop.*

Comprar a crédito. *To buy on credit.*

Comprar al contado. *To buy for cash.*

COMPRENDER *to understand; to comprise, to include.*

¿Me comprende Ud. bien? *Do you understand me ("all right")?*

Le entiendo perfectamente. *I understand you perfectly.*

¡Se comprende! *That's understood. That's clear. That's a matter of course.*

comprendido *adj. understood; including.*

comprensible *comprehensible.*

comprensión *f. comprehension, understanding.*

comprensivo *adj. comprehensive.*

comprimir *to compress; to repress, to restrain.*

comprimirse *to restrain oneself, to control oneself.*

comprobante *m proof, voucher.*

comprobar *to prove, to verify.*

comprometerse *to commit oneself; to become engaged.*

compromiso *m. compromise; obligation; engagement; pledge, commitment.*

Sin compromiso. *Without obligation.*

compuesto *adj. and n. compound.*

compulsorio *adj. compulsory.*

computación *f. computer science.*

COMPUTADOR (A) *m. and f. computer.*

computar *to compute.*

computarizar *to computerize.*

COMÚN *adj. common.*

Sentido común. *Common sense.*

En común. *In common. Jointly.*

Por lo común. *Generally.*

De común acuerdo. *By mutual consent.*

comunicación *f. communication.*

Telefonista, nos ha cortado la comunicación. *Operator, we've been cut off.*

communicar *to announce; to communicate; to be talking on the phone; to inform.*

comunidad *f. community.*

comunión *f. communion, fellowship.*

CON *with, by.*

Viene con nosotros. *She's coming with us.*

Con mucho gusto. *With ("great") pleasure. Gladly.*

Con tal que. *Provided that.*

Con que. *And so. So. Then. Well then.*

¡Con que ésas tenemos! *So that's the story!*

Con todo. *Notwithstanding. Nevertheless. However. Even so.*

Tratar con. *To do business with. To deal with.*

Dar con. *To find. To meet. To come across.*

concebir *to conceive.*

conceder *to grant.*

concentración *f. concentration.*

concentrar *to concentrate.*

concepto *m. concept, idea.*

concernir *to concern.*

Eso no le concierne a Ud. *That doesn't concern you.*

concesión *f. concession.*

conciencia *f. conscience, consciousness.*

concierto *m. concert; agreement.*

conciliación *f. conciliation.*

conciliar *to conciliate, to reconcile.*

conciso *adj. concise.*

concluir *to conclude; to finish; to close (a deal).*

conclusión *f. conclusion, findings.*

concordancia *f. concordance; harmony, agreement.*

concordarse *to agree.*

concretar *to summarize, specify.*

concreto *adj. concrete.*

En concreto. *In short.*

concurrencia *f. audience, crowd.*

concurrir *to concur; to attend.*

concurso *m. competition, contest.*

concha *f. shell.*

conde *m. count (title).*

condecoración *f. decoration, medal.*

condena *f. sentence, penalty.*

condenar *to condemn, to convict; to disapprove.*

Se le condenó a muerte. *He was condemned to death.*

Condeno su proceder. *I disapprove of his behavior.*

condición *f. condition, state; term.*

A condición que. *On (the) condition that. Provided that.*

Convengo en sus condiciones. *I agree to your terms.*

condicional *adj. conditional.*

condimentar *to season (food).*

condimento *m. seasoning, condiment.*

condiscípulo *m. classmate.*

condominio *m. condominium.*

condón *m. condom.*

condonar *to forgive, to pardon.*

cóndor *m. condor.*

CONDUCIR *to drive; to conduct; to carry; to lead.*

¿Sabe Ud. conducir? *Do you know how to drive?*

Este camino nos conducirá al lago. *This road will take us to the lake.*

conducirse *to conduct oneself, to behave.*

conducta *f. conduct, behavior.*

conductor *conductor, driver.*

conejo *m. rabbit.*

conexión *f. connection.*

confeccionar *to make, to manufacture.*

conferencia *f. conference, lecture.*

Asistimos a la conferencia del lunes. *We attended Monday's lecture.*

Ayer hubo una conferencia de prensa. *Yesterday there was a press conference.*

conferenciante *m. and f. lecturer, speaker.*

conferir *to confer, to bestow.*

confesar *to admit, to confess, to acknowledge.*

¿Confiesa Ud. su falta? *Do you admit your guilt?*

confesión *f. confession, acknowledgment.*

confianza *f. confidence; faith; familiarity.*

Digno de confianza. *Reliable. Trustworthy.*

En confianza. *In confidence.*

Tener confianza en. *To trust.*

confiar *to confide; to trust in, to entrust.*

confidencia *f. secret; confidence.*

confidencial *adj. confidential.*

confidente *m. and f. confidant, informant.*

confirmación *f. confirmation.*

confirmar *to confirm, to ratify.*

confitería *f. candy shop; tearoom.*

conflicto *m. conflict, strife; predicament.*

conformar *to conform; to fit, to agree; to comply with.*

Conformarse con. *To agree with. To be satisfied with.*

CONFORME *alike; according to; O.K., correct.*

Conforme a. *According to.*

Estar conforme. *To be in agreement.*

conformidad *f. conformity, agreement.*

De conformidad con. *In accordance with.*

confort *m. comfort.*

confortable *adj. comfortable.*

confortante *adj. comforting.*

confortar *to comfort, to cheer.*

confundir *to confuse; to mistake.*

confundirse *to become confused; to be perplexed.*

confusión *f. confusion, perplexity.*

confuso *adj. confused.*

congelador *m. freezer.*

congelar *to freeze.*

congestión *f. congestion.*

Congestión cerebral. *Stroke.*

congratulación *f. congratulation.*

congratular *to congratulate.*

congregación *f. congregation.*

congregar *to congregate, to assemble.*

conjetura *f. conjecture, guess.*

conjeturar *to conjecture, to guess.*

conjugación *f. conjugation.*

conjugar *to conjugate.*

conjuncion *f. conjunction.*

conjunto *adj. joint, united; m. the whole.*

En conjunto. *On the whole. In all. Altogether.*

conmemoración *f. commemoration.*

conmemorar *to commemorate.*

conmemorativo *adj. commemorative.*

conmigo *with myself, with me.*

¿Quiere Ud. hablar conmigo? *Do you want to speak with (to) me?*

Venga Ud. conmigo. *Come (along) with me.*

conmoción *f. commotion, tumult, disturbance.*

conmutador *m. electric switch.*

CONOCER *to know, to understand, to be acquainted with.*

¿Conoce Ud. a María? *Do you know Mary?*

No la conozco. *I don't know her.*

¿No se conocen Uds.? *Don't you know each other?*

No tengo el gusto de conocerle. *No, I haven't had the pleasure (of meeting him.)*

Dar a conocer. *To make known.*

conocido *adj. well-known; m. acquaintance.*

Es un antiguo conocido nuestro. *He's an old acquaintance of ours.*

conocimiento *m. knowledge, understanding, acquaintance; bill of lading.*

Poner en conocimiento. *To inform. To let know.*

Llegar a conocimiento de. *To come to the knowledge of.*

Tomar conocimiento de. *To take notice of.*

conquista *f. conquest.*

conquistar *to conquer, to win over.*

consciente *adj. conscious.*

consecuencia *f. consequence.*

No es de ninguna consecuencia. *It's of no consequence.*

Como consecuencia. *In consequence. As a consequence.*

En consecuencia. *Therefore. In consequence.*

CONSEGUIR *to obtain, to attain, to get.*

Será difícil conseguirlo. *It'll be difficult to get it.*

No pude conseguir ningún dinero. *I couldn't get (obtain) any money.*

consejero *m. member of a board (council); cunselor, advisor.*

consejo *m. advice; council, advisory board.*

Seguiré sus consejos. *I'll follow your advice.*

Consejo de ministros. *Cabinet (government).*

Consejo de guerra. *Court-martial.*

consentimiento *m. to consent.*

consentir *to consent; to agree, to be willing to; to tolerate; to spoil (a child).*

Nunca consentiré tal cosa. *I'll never tolerate such a thing.*

conserje *m. and f. janitor, concierge.*

conserva *f. preserve, canned food.*

conservación *f. conservation, upkeep, maintenance.*

conservador *adj. and n. preserver; conservative.*

CONSERVAR *to preserve, to keep, to conserve.*

Lo conservé como recuerdo. *I kept it as a souvenir.*

considerable *adj. considerable, large.*

consideración *f. consideration, regard; importance.*

considerar *to consider, to take into account; to treat well.*

consigna *f. watchword; check room.*

Dejaré esta maleta en la consigna. *I'll check this bag. I'll leave this suitcase in the check room.*

consigo *with oneself; with himself; with herself; with yourself, yourselves.*

¿Lo trajo consigo? *Did you bring it with you?*

Lléveselo consigo. *Take it along with you.*

consiguiente *adj. consequent.*

Por consiguiente. *Consequently.*

consistencia *f. consistence, consistency; stability, solidity, firmness.*

consistente *adj. consistent, solid, firm.*

consistir *to consist, to be composed of.*

consolación *f. consolation.*

consolar *to console, to comfort, to cheer.*

conspicuo *adj. famous.*

constante *adj. constant.*

constitución *constitution.*

constituir *to constitute.*

construcción *f. construction, building.*

CONSTRUIR *to construct, to build.*

cónsul *m. consul.*

consulado *m. consulate.*

consulta *f. consultation.*

consultar *to consult, to seek advice.*

Vaya Ud. a consultar al médico. *Go and consult the doctor.*

Consultar algo con la almohada. *To sleep on something. ("To consult with one's pillow.")*

consultor *m. consultant.*

consultorio *m. doctor's office; bureau of information.*

consumidor *m. consumer.*

consumir *to consume, to use.*

consumo *m. consumption; demand (goods).*

Artículo de consumo. *Staple.*

contabilidad *f. bookkeeping, accounting.*

contado *m. cash.*

Se lo pagaré al contado. *I'll pay cash for it.*

contador *m. accountant, purser; meter (gas, electric, etc.).*

contagiar *to infect, to contaminate.*

contagioso *adj. contagious.*

contaminación *f. pollution.*

Contaminación del ambiente. *Environmental pollution.*

contaminar *to contaminate.*

CONTAR *to count; to tell.*

¿Contó Ud. su cambio? *Did you count your change?*

¿Tiene Ud. algo que contarme? *Have you anything to tell me?*

¿Qué cuenta Ud.? *What's new?*

¡Me lo cuenta a mi! *You're telling me!*

¿Puedo contar con Ud.? *Can I count (depend) on you?*

contemplación *f. contemplation.*

contemplar *to contemplate, to consider.*

CONTENER *to hold, to contain.*

Esta botella contiene vino. *This bottle contains wine. There's wine in this bottle.*

contenerse *to refrain, to restrain oneself.*

No puede contenerse. *He can't restrain himelsf.*

contenido *m. contents.*

contentar *to please, to satisfy.*

contentarse *to be pleased, to be contented.*

No se contentará con palabras nada más. *He won't be satisfied with mere words.*

CONTENTO *adj. glad, happy, pleased; m. contentment.*

Parecía contenta. *She looked happy.*

Estamos contentos de su trabajo. *We're pleased with his work.*

contestación *f. answer, reply.*

contestador *adj. answering.*
   Contestador automático. *Telephone answering machine.*
CONTESTAR *to answer, to reply; to attest; to dispute.*
   Le hice una pregunta y no supo contestarme. *I asked him a question and he didn't know the answer.*
   Debe Ud. contestar su carta. *You ought to reply to his letter.*
   No contestan. *They don't answer (phone).*
contigo *with you (familiar, singular).*
contiguo *adj. contiguous; close, near.*
continente *adj. moderate; m. continent.*
continuación *f. continuation.*
CONTINUAR *to continue.*
continuo *adj. continuous.*
   De continuo. *Continually.*
   Sesión continua. *Continuous performances.*
CONTRA *against, contrary to, counter to.*
   Lo hizo contra su voluntad. *She did it against her will.*
   Apóyalo contra la pared. *Lean it against the wall.*
   ¿Sabe Ud. de algún remedio contra el mareo? *Do you know of a remedy for seasickness?*
contrabandista *m. and f..smuggler.*
contrabando *m. contraband, smuggling.*
contradecir *to contradict.*
contradicción *f. contradiction.*
contraer *to contract.*
   Contraer matrimonio. *To get married.*
   Contraer deudas. *To run into debt.*
contrahacer *to counterfeit.*
contrahecho *adj. counterfeit; deformed.*
contraofensiva *f. counteroffensive.*
contrariar *to contradict; to annoy, to vex.*
contrariedad *f. mishap; disappointment; vexation.*
   ¡Qué contrariedad! *What a disappointment!*
contrario *adj. contrary, opposite; m. opponent.*
   A mí me pasa lo contrario. *With me it's the opposite.*
   Dice lo contrario de lo que siente. *He says the opposite of what he thinks.*
   Al contrario. *On the contrary.*
contrarrevolución *f. counterrevolution.*
contraseña *f. watchword; countersign, check.*
contrastar *to contrast.*
contraste *m. contrast; assayer.*
contratar *to engage, to hire; to bargain, to trade; to contract.*
contratiempo *m. mishap, setback, disappointment.*
contrato *m. contract.*
contribución *f. contribution; tax.*
contribuir *to contribute.*

control *m. control.*
   Teclado de control. *Control key (computer).*
   Control remoto. *Remote control.*
controlar *to control.*
contusión *f. bruise, contusion.*
convalecencia *f. convalescence.*
convaleciente *adj. and n. convalescent.*
convencer *to convince.*
conveniencia *f. convenience; fitness, advantage.*
conveniente *adj. convenient, suitable; advantageous.*
convenio *m. pact, agreement, covenant.*
CONVENIR *to agree; to suit, to be advisable.*
   Eso me conviene. *That suits me.*
   No me conviene. *It doesn't suit me. It won't do.*
   No convenimos en el precio. *We didn't agree on the price.*
   Hágalo Ud. como más le convenga. *Do it in the way that's most convenient for you.*
   Al tiempo y en el lugar convenidos. *At the time and place agreed on.*
convento *m. convent.*
conversación *f. conversation, chat, talk.*
   Su conversación es agradable. *It's pleasant to talk with her. ("Her conversation is pleasant.")*
conversar *to converse, to chat.*
convertible *m. convertible.*
convertir *to convert, to change.*
convicción *f. conviction, belief, certainty.*
convicto *adj. guilty, convicted.*
convidado *adj. invited; m. guest.*
convidar *to invite, to treat.*
convoy *m. convoy.*
cónyuge *m. and f. husband or wife.*
coñac *m. cognac, brandy.*
cooperación *f. cooperation.*
cooperar *to cooperate.*
coordinar *to coordinate.*
copa *f. goblet, top of a tree; crown of a hat.*
copia *f. copy, transcript; abundance.*
   Sacar una copia. *To make a copy.*
   Copia dura. *Hard copy (computer).*
   Copia de seguridad. *Backup copy.*
copiar *to copy.*
coqueta *f. flirt, coquette.*
coquetear *to flirt.*
coraje *m. courage; anger.*
CORAZÓN *m. heart; core.*
   Poner el corazón en algo. *To set one's heart on something.*
corbata *f. necktie.*
corcho *m. cork.*
cordel *m. cord, rope.*

cordero m. lamb.

cordial adj. cordial, affectionate.

cordillera f. mountain range.

cordón m. cord, string, lace.

cordura f. prudence, judgment, common sense.

corona f. crown; wreath.

corral m. yard, court; corral.

correa f. leather strap, leash, thong.

corredor m. runner; broker.

    Corredor de inmuebles. Real estate broker.

corregir to correct.

CORREO m. post office; mail.

    ¿Hay una oficina de correos cerca? Is there a post office near by?

    ¿A qué hora sale el correo? (At) What time does the mail leave?

    ¿Ha echado Ud. mi carta al correo? Have you mailed my letter?

    A vuelta de correo. By return mail.

    Por correo aéreo. By airmail.

    Apartado de correos. Post-office box.

CORRER to run; to flow; to elapse; to blow (wind); to draw (curtains, etc.).

    Fuimos allí a todo correr. We rushed there.

    Corre mucho aire. There's a good breeze.

    Corra las cortinas. Draw the curtains.

    No corre prisa. There's no hurry.

    Esto corre de mi cuenta. This is on me. This will be at my own expense.

    Corrió mucho riesgo. He took quite a chance. He ran a great risk.

correrse to slide over, move away.

    Córrase un poco. Move away a little.

correspondencia f. correspondence, mail.

    Estar en correspondencia con. To correspond with.

    Mantener correspondencia con. To correspond with.

    Llevar la correspondencia. To be in charge of the correspondence. To take care of the mail.

correspondiente adj. corresponding.

corresponsal m. correspondent.

corrida f. run, race, course.

    Corrida de toros. Bullfight.

corriente adj. current, present (month or year); ordinary, common; f. current; stream; draft (air).

    Cuenta corriente. Checking account.

    Salgo el quince del corriente. I'm leaving on the fifteenth of this month.

    Hay una corriente de aire. There's a draft.

    Quítese Ud. de la corriente. Get out of the draft.

    Estar al corriente. To be acquainted with. To be familiar with. To be abreast of.

    Poner al corriente. To inform. To acquaint with.

    Tener al corriente. To keep informed.

Corriente alterna. Alternating current (A.C.).

Corriente continua. Direct current (D.C.).

Seguir la corriente. To go with the tide. To follow the crowd.

corroborar to corroborate.

corromper to corrupt.

corrupción f. corruption.

cortaplumas m. penknife.

cortar to cut; to cut off; to shorten.

    Me he cortado. I've cut myself.

    Este cuchillo no corta. This knife doesn't cut well.

    Telefonista, nos ha cortado. Operator, I've been cut off ("you've cut us off").

    Barbero, córteme el pelo. ("Barber, give me a haircut.")

corte cut; edge (of a knife, etc.); court.

    Corte de pelo. Haircut.

    Las Cortes. The Spanish parliament.

    Llamar a Cortes. To convoke the Cortes.

    Hacer la corte. To court.

cortejar to court.

cortés adj. courteous, gentle, polite.

    El es muy cortés. He's very polite.

cortesía f. courtesy, politeness.

corteza f. bark; peel; crust.

    Corteza del árbol. Bark of a tree.

cortina f. curtain, screen.

CORTO adj. short; shy; stupid; backward.

    Las mangas son muy cortas. The sleeves are very short.

    Es muy corto de genio. He's very shy.

    A la corta o larga. Sooner or later.

    Es corto de vista. He's near sighted.

cortocircuito m. short circuit.

cortometraje m. short (film).

COSA f. thing; matter.

    No hay tal cosa. There's no such thing.

    Ninguna cosa. Nothing.

    ¿Desea Ud. alguna otra cosa? Would you like anything else?

    Venga Ud. aquí, tengo que decirle una cosa. Come here, I want to tell you something.

    Como si tal cosa. As if nothing had happened.

    No es cosa de risa. It's no laughing matter.

    Hace cosa de dos meses. It was about two months ago.

    Cosa rara. A strange thing.

    Eso es cosa suya. That's his business.

cosecha f. harvest, crop; harvest time.

cosechar to reap, to gather in the crop.

coser to sew.

    Máquina de coser. Sewing machine.

cosmético adj. cosmetic; pl. m. cosmetics.

cosquillas f. pl. tickling.

cosquillear to tickle.

cosquilloso adj. ticklish, easily offended.

costa f. *coast, shore.*
A lo largo de la costa. *Coastwise. Along the coast.*
costado m. *flank; side.*
COSTAR *to cost.*
¿Cuánto me costará más o menos? *About how much will it cost?*
No me cuesta. *It's no problem for me.*
Me cuesta trabajo creerlo. *It's hard for me to believe it.*
Cueste lo que cueste. *Whatever it costs. At all costs.*
Costar un ojo de la cara. *To cost a fortune.*
costear *to pay the expenses; to sail along the coast.*
costilla f. *rib.*
COSTO m. *cost, expense, price.*
Precio de costo. *Cost price.*
Costo de la vida. *Cost of living.*
costoso adj. *dear, expensive.*
costumbre f. *custom; habit.*
De costumbre. *Usually.*
Como de costumbre. *As usual.*
Tener costumbre de. *To be used to. To be in the habit of.*
costura f. *sewing; needlework; seam.*
Alta costura. *High fashion.*
costurera f. *seamstress.*
cotejar *to confront, to check.*
cotejo m. *comparison; collation.*
cotidiano adj. *daily, everyday.*
cotización f. *quotation (of prices).*
cotizar *to quote (prices).*
coyuntura f. *articulation, joint; opportunity.*
coz f. *kick.*
cráneo m. *skull, cranium.*
crear *to create; to establish, to set up.*
CRECER *to grow; to increase.*
crecimiento m. *increase, growth, increment.*
credencial f. *credential.*
crédito m. *credit; credence; reputation, standing.*
Comprar a crédito. *To buy on credit.*
Vender a crédito. *To sell on credit.*
Dar crédito. *To give credit.*
Tarjeta de crédito. *Credit card.*
Carta de crédito. *Letter of credit.*
creencia f. *belief, credence.*
CREER *to believe; to think.*
Creo que es una buena idea. *I think it's a good idea.*
Creo que sí. *I believe so. I think so.*
Creo que no. *I don't think so.*
Ya lo creo. *I should think (say) so! Of course! Naturally!*
Ver y creer. *Seeing is believing.*
crema f. *cream.*
Crema batida. *Whipped cream.*
Crema (pasta) dentrífica. *Toothpaste.*

criada f. *maid, servant.*
criado m. *a manservant; valet.*
criar *to nurse; to rear, to bring up.*
criatura f.*creature; baby, child.*
crimen m. *crime; guilt.*
criminal m. *and* f. *criminal.*
criollo adj. *and* n. *Creole, native.*
crisantemo m. *chyrsanthemum.*
crisis f. *crisis.*
cristal m. *crystal; glass.*
cristianismo m. *Christianity.*
cristiano adj. *and* n. *Christian.*
criterio m. *criterion, judgment, opinion.*
Lo dejo a su criterio. *I leave it up to you.*
crítica f. *criticism, review.*
criticar *to criticize.*
crítico m. *critic.*
crónica f. *chronicle.*
cronista m. *reporter.*
croqueta f. *croquette.*
cruce m. *crossing; crossroads.*
crucero m. *crossing; cruiser.*
crucigrama m. *crossword puzzle.*
crudo adj. *raw, crude.*
cruel adj. *cruel, hard.*
crueldad f. *cruelty.*
cruz f. *cross.*
cruzar *to cross; to cruise.*
cuaderno m. *notebook; memorandum book.*
cuadra f. *stable; block (of houses).*
cuadrado adj. *square.*
cuadrilla f. *gang, crew.*
cuadro m. *painting, picture; frame; scene (in a play).*
CUAL *which; what; like; as;* el cual *(m.);* la cual *(f.);* los cuales *(m, pl.);* las cuales *(f. pl.) who, which.*
¿Cuál de ellos prefiere Ud.? *Which one do you prefer (like best)?*
¿Cuáles son los últimos modelos? *What are the latest styles?*
Por lo cual. *For that reason.*
Cada cual. *Each one.*
Tal para cual. *Tit for tat. Two of a kind.*
cualquier *any (used immediately before a noun). See also* **cualquiera.**
A cualquier hora. *At any time.*
En cualquier momento. *At any moment.*
cualquiera *any; anyone; anybody.*
(**Cualquiera** *and* **cualquier** *do not change for gender.*)
Cualquiera de los hombres. *Any of the men.*
Tome Ud. cualquiera que le guste. *Take anyone (whichever one) you like.*
Un cualquiera. *A nobody.*
cuan *how, as (used only before adjectives or adverbs).*
¡Cuán lejos! *How far!*
¡Cuán hermoso! *How pretty!*

CUANDO (written **cuándo** *when interrogative*), *when.*
¿Cuándo se marcha Ud.? *When are you leaving?*
Cuando Ud. guste. *Whenever you say. Whenever you wish.*
¿Hasta cuándo? *Until when?*
De vez en cuando. *Once in a while.*
Cuando más (mucho). *At best. At most.*
Cuando menos. *At least.*

CUANTO *as much as, as many as.*
Compre cuantas naranjas encuentre. *Buy as many oranges as you can find.*
Avíseme en cuanto esté libre. *Let me know as soon as it's free.*
Cuanto más le doy tanto más me pide. *The more I give him, the more he asks for.*
Cuanto más gaste tanto menos tendrá. *The more you spend, the less you'll have.*
Cuanto antes. *As soon as possible.*
Por cuanto. *Whereas. Inasmuch as.*
En cuanto a. *In regard to.*

CUÁNTO *how much; how long; how far; how; pl. how many.*
¿Cuánto? *How much?*
¿Cuántos? *How many?*
¿A cuántos estamos? *What's the date?*
¿Cuánto es? *How much is it?*
¿Cuánto hay de aquí a Cali? *How far is it from here to Cali?*
¿Cuánto tiempo se tarda en avión? *How long does it take by airplane?*
¡Cuánto me alegro! *I'm very glad!*

CUARENTA *adj. and n. forty.*

cuartel *m. quarter; barracks; district of a city.*
Cuartel general. *Headquarters.*
Cuartel de bomberos. *Fire station.*

CUARTO *adj. fourth; quarter; m. room.*
Le daré la cuarta parte. *I'll give you a fourth of it.*
A las once menos cuarto. *At a quarter to eleven.*
A las cinco y cuarto. *At a quarter past five.*
¿Tiene Ud. un cuarto para dos personas? *Do you have a double room?*
Es mi compañero de cuarto. *He's my roommate.*

CUATRO *adj. and n. four.*
Son las cuatro. *It's four o'clock.*

cuatrocientos *adj. and n. four hundred.*

Cuba *f. Cuba.*

cubano *adj. and n. Cuban.*

cubeta *f. small barrel; pail, bucket.*

cubierta *f. cover; deck of a ship.*

cubierto *m. cover; place at a table; table d'hôte; shelter.*

cubo *m. bucket; tub; hub of a wheel.*

cubrecama *f. bedspread.*

CUBRIR *to cover; to roof.*

cucaracha *f. cockroach.*

CUCHARA *f. spoon.*
Meter la cuchara. *To meddle.*

cucharada *f. spoonful.*

cucharadita *f. teaspoonful.*

cucharita *f. teaspoon.*

cucharón *m. ladle; large spoon.*

cuchichear *to whisper.*

cuchicheo *m. whispering.*

cuchilla *f. large knife.*

cuchillo *m. knife.*

cuello *m. neck; collar.*

CUENTA *f. count; account; statement; bill; bead.*
Tráigame Ud. la cuenta. *Let me have the bill.*
¿Cuál es el saldo de mi cuenta? *What's the balance of my account?*
Apúntelo en mi cuenta. *Charge it to my account.*
Caer en la cuenta. *To notice.*
Abonar en cuenta. *To credit with.*
Cuenta corriente. *Checking account.*
Cuenta pendiente. *Unpaid balance. Balance due.*
Dar cuenta de. *To report on.*
Darse cuenta de. *To realize.*
Tener en cuenta. *To bear in mind. To take into account (consideration).*
Tomar por su cuenta. *To take upon oneself. To assume responsibility for.*

cuentagotas *m. medicine dropper.*

cuento *m. story, tale; gossip.*
Cuento de hadas. *Fairy tale.*
Traer a cuento. *To bring up. To turn the conversation to a certain point.*
Esto no viene a cuento. *That's beside the point. That's not the case.*
Dejarse de cuentos. *To stop beating around the bush.*

cuerda *f. cord, rope; spring (of a watch).*
¿Le ha dado Ud. cuerda a su reloj? *Have you wound (up) your watch?*
Lo hizo por debajo de cuerda. *He did it in an underhand way.*

cuerdo *adj. in one's senses; wise, prudent.*

cuerno *m. horn.*

cuero *m. leather; hide; skin.*

CUERPO *m. body; element; corps.*

cuervo *m. crow, raven.*

cuesta *f. slope, grade; hill.*
Ir cuesta abajo. *To go downhill.*
Ir cuesta arriba. *To go uphill.*
Cuesta arriba. *With great trouble and difficulty. Painfully.*
A cuestas. *On one's back.*

CUESTIÓN *m. question; dispute, quarrel; problem.*

cueva f. cave; cellar.

CUIDADO m. care, attention; anxiety, worry.

  ¡Cuidado! Be careful!

  Tener cuidado. To be careful.

  ¡Tenga cuidado! Be careful!

  Me tiené sin cuidado. I don't care.

  ¡No tenga Ud. cuidado! Don't worry!

  Estar con cuidado. To be worried.

  Cuidado diurno. Day care.

cuidadoso adj. careful.

cuidar to care, to take care, to mind, to look after.

  ¡Cuídese Ud.! Take good care of yourself.

  Cuidar de. To take care of.

culebra f. snake.

culpa f. fault, guilt; sin.

  ¿Quién tiene la culpa? Whose fault is it?

  Echar la culpa a. To blame.

  Tener la culpa de. To be to blame. To be at fault.

culpable adj. guilty.

culpar to accuse, to blame.

cultivar to cultivate; to till; to improve.

  En Canadá se cultiva mucho el trigo. They grow a lot of wheat in Canada.

cultivo m. farming, cultivation; tillage.

  Cultivo del cuerpo. Cult of the body.

culto adj. well-educated; polished; m. worship; cult, religion.

  Es un hombre culto. He's a well-read (cultured) man.

cultura f. culture; urbanity.

cultural adj. cultural.

cumpleaños m. birthday.

cumplido adj. courteous, polite; full, abundant; m. compliment, attention, courtesy.

cumplimiento m. accomplishment; compliance, fulfillment, enforcement.

  Ofrecer algo por cumplimiento. To offer something out of courtesy.

CUMPLIR to carry out, to fulfill, to keep one's word; to expire.

  Siempre cumple con su deber. He always does his duty. He always fulfills his obligations.

  El plazo se ha cumplido. The time has expired.

  Al cumplir los veinte y un años será mayor de edad. He'll be of age when he's twenty-one.

  Cumplir años. To have a birthday.

cuna f. cradle; family, lineage.

cuña f. wedge.

cuñada f. sister-in-law.

cuñado m. brother-in-law.

cuota f. share; quota; fee.

cura m. priest. f. cure; curing, preserving.

  Los casó el cura. The priest married them.

Este mal tiene cura. This sickness is curable.

curable adj. curable.

curación f. healing, cure.

curar to cure; to heal.

curativo adj. curative.

curiosear to pry into other people's affairs, to be a busybody.

curiosidad f. curiosity; neatness, cleanliness.

curioso adj. curious.

cursar to study.

curso m. course, direction; succession; current.

cursor m. cursor (computer).

curva f. curve.

cúspide f. summit, top.

custodia f. custody, guard; escort.

custodiar to guard, to take into custody.

cutícula f. cuticle.

cutis m. complexion; skin.

cuya (f. of **cuyo**) whose, of which, of whom (pl. **cuyas**).

  La señora a cuya hija le he presentado es amiga de su padre. The lady whose daughter I introduced you to is a friend of your father's.

cuyo whose, of which, of whom (pl. **cuyos**).

  Era un pequeño pueblo, cuyo nombre no recuerdo. It was a small town, the name of which I don't remember.

CH

chabacano adj. coarse, unpolished; m. kind of apricot (Mex.)

chacal m. jackal.

chacota f. noisy merriment; fun.

  Hacer chacota de. To make fun of. To ridicule.

chacra f. farm (Amer.)

chal m. shawl.

chaleco m. vest.

chalet m. chalet; cottage.

chalupa f. sloop; small canoe.

chambón adj. awkward, clumsy.

champaña m. champagne.

champiñón m. mushroom.

champú m. shampoo.

chancear to joke, to fool.

chanclos m. pl. galoshes, rubbers.

chanco adj. dirty, unclean; m. hog, pig.

chantaje m. blackmail.

chantajista m. and f. blackmailer.

chaqueta f. jacket, coat.

charco m. pond, puddle.

charla f. chat, to chatter.

charlatán m. quack, charlatan; babbler, one who is always talking.

chasco m. disappointment; joke.

chasis m. chassis.

chato adj. flat; flat-nosed; ordinary.

chayote m. cheyote.

¡Che! Hey! Listen! (Argentina, Uruguay).

cheque m. check (money).

  Cheque de viajero. Traveler's check.

chequear to get a checkup.

chequeo m. checkup (medical, car, etc.).

chequera f. checkbook.

chicle m. chicle; chewing gum.

chica f. little girl; girl; maid.

  Es una chica encantadora. She's a
    charming girl.

chico adj. small, little; m. boy; pl.
  youngsters.

  Es un chico muy obediente. He's a very
    obedient boy.

chicharrón m. crisp fried bacon or pork fat.

chichón m. lump on the head or in the
  breast.

chiflado adj. silly, crazy.

chillar to scream, to screech; to squeak, to
  creak.

chillido m. scream.

chillón adj. loud, gaudy (color); m.
  screamer.

chimenea f. chimney; fireplace.

chinche f. thumbtack; bedbug, boring person.

chinela f. slipper.

chip m. chip (computer).

chiquero m. pigsty, pigpen.

chiquillo m. little boy; f. little girl.

chiquito adj. small, tiny; m. little boy, f. little
  girl.

chirimoya f. cherimoya.

chisme m. gossip.

chismear to gossip, to tattle.

chismorreo m. gossip.

chismoso adj. talebearing, gossiping; m.
  gossiper.

chispa f. spark.

  Echar chispas. To get raving mad.

  Ser chispa. To be full of life. To sparkle.

chistar to mutter, to mumble.

  Ni siquiera chistó. He didn't say a word.
    He didn't open his mouth.

chiste m. joke.

chistoso adj. witty, humorous.

¡Chito! ¡Chitón! Hush! Silence!

chivo m. kid, goat.

chocante adj. shocking.

chocar to collide; to crash; to shock.

choclo m. cob; ear of corn.

chocolate m. chocolate.

chófer/chofer m. chauffeur.

choque m. collision; clash; shock.

chorizo m. sausage.

chorro m. gush, spurt, jet of water.

choza f. hut, hovel.

chubasco m. squall (rain).

chuchería f. trinket, trifle.

chuleta f. cutlet; chop.

  Chuleta de cordero. Lamb chop.

  Chuleta de puerco. Pork chop.

  Chuleta de ternera. Veal chop.

chupar to suck, to absorb; to sponge on.

churro m. a kind of doughnut, fritter (Spain).

chusma f. riffraff.

D

dactilógrafo m. typist.

dádiva f. gift, present.

dadivoso adj. liberal, generous.

dados m. pl. dice.

dama f. lady, dame; king (in checkers,
  cards).

  Primera dama. Leading lady.

  Jugar a las damas. To play checkers.

daga f. dagger.

dalia f. dahlia.

danzón m. a Cuban dance.

dañado adj. spoiled, damaged.

dañar to damage, to hurt; to spoil.

dañino adj. harmful.

daño m. damage, loss; hurt, harm.

  ¿Te has hecho daño? Did you get hurt?

  ¿Le ha hecho daño la comida? Did the
    food disagree with you?

  Causar daño. To do harm or damage.

DAR to give; to deal (cards); to show (a
  picture); to strike (hours); to hit; to
  take (a walk).

  Denos algo de comer. Give us something to
    eat.

  Deme un poco de pan. Give me some
    bread.

  ¿En cuánto me lo da Ud.? How much will
    you sell ("give") it to me for?

  Le doy dos pesetas por el libro. I'll give
    you two pesetas for the book.

  Ud. da las cartas. You deal (cards).

  La radio dió la noticia. The news came
    over the radio.

  ¿Dónde dan esa película? Where are they
    showing that picture (film)?

  Este reloj da las horas y las medias horas.
    This clock strikes the hours and the
    half-hours.

  Vamos a dar un paseo. Let's take a walk.

  Dar memorias. Dar recuerdos. To give
    one's regards.

  Le doy la razón. I admit you are right.

  Dar aplausos. To clap one's hands.

  Dar a entender. To insinuate. ("To give to
    understand.")

Dar el golpe. *To make a hit. To create a sensation.*

Dar a conocer. *To make known.*

Dar en el clavo. *To hit the nail on the head.*

Dar que decir. *To give cause for criticism.*

Dar de comer. *To feed.*

Dar prestado. *To lend.*

Dar fiado. Dar a crédito. *To give credit.*

Dar con. *To meet. To come across.*

Dar a la calle. *To face the street.*

Dar a luz. *To give birth.*

Dar bien con. *To get along with. To blend with.*

Dar parte. *To report.*

Dar la mano. *To shake hands.*

Dar marcha atrás. *To put in reverse (a car).*

Dar en el blanco. *To hit the mark. To hit the bull's-eye.*

Darse prisa. *To hurry.*

Darse cuenta. *To realize.*

data *f. date.*

datil *m. date (fruit).*

dato *m. datum pl. data.*

DE *of; from; for; by; on; to; with.*

La casa de mi amigo. *My friend's house.*

¿De quién es este libro? *Whose book is this?*

No sé que ha sido de él. *I don't know what's become of him.*

El libro es de ella. *The book is hers.*

¿De dónde es usted? *Where are you from?*

Soy de Madrid. *I'm from Madrid.*

La chica del sombrero verde. *The girl with the green hat.*

Un reloj de oro. *A gold watch.*

Una taza de café. *A cup of coffee.*

Tres pies de largo. *Three feet long.*

Máquina de coser. *Sewing machine.*

Hora de comer. *Time to eat. Dinnertime.*

De pie. *Standing.*

De puntillas. *On tiptoes.*

De prisa. *In a hurry.*

De buena gana. *Willingly.*

De todo un poco. *A little of everything.*

Un día de estos. *One of these days.*

De hoy en adelante. *From now on.*

De día. *In the daytime.*

De noche. *At night.*

De nada. *Don't mention it.*

DEBAJO *under, underneath.*

Debajo de los papeles estaba la carta. *The letter was under the papers.*

debate *m. debate.*

debatir *to debate, to discuss.*

deber *m. obligation, duty.*

DEBER *to owe; to be obliged; must; ought.*

¿Qué se debe hacer? *What can one do? What can be done? What ought (should) one do?*

Debemos irnos. *We must (have to) go.*

Ud. debiera comer más. *You should eat more.*

Debe Ud. aprovechar esta ocasión. *You should take advantage of this opportunity.*

¿Cuánto le debo a Ud.? *How much do I owe you?*

No me debe Ud. nada. *You don't owe me anything.*

Siempre cumple con su deber. *He always does his duty. He always fulfills his obligations.*

debido *adj. due, owing to, an account of; proper.*

Debido a la lluvia no pude venir ayer. *I couldn't come yesterday on account of the rain.*

Redacte Ud. la instancia en debida forma. *Draw up the petition in proper form.*

débil *adj. feeble, weak.*

debilidad *feebleness, weakness.*

debilitar *to weaken, to debilitate.*

débito *m. debt; duty.*

debut *m. debut, first (public) appearance.*

década *f. decade.*

decadencia *f. decay, decadence, decline.*

decaer *to decay, to decline, to die down.*

decano *m. dean.*

decapitar *to decapitate, to behead.*

decena *f. group of ten.*

decente *adj. decent; honest; neat.*

decepción *f. disappointment.*

decididamente *decidedly.*

decidido *adj. decided, firm, determined.*

Es una personal muy decidida. *He's a very determined person.*

DECIDIR *to decide, to resolve, to determine.*

DECIDIRSE *to decide, to make up one's mind.*

No me he decidido todavía. *I haven't decided yet. I haven't made up my mind yet.*

decímetro *m. decimeter.*

décimo *adj. tenth.*

décimoctavo *adj. eighteenth.*

décimocuarto *adj. fourteenth.*

décimonono *adj. nineteenth.*

décimonoveno *adj. nineteenth.*

décimoquinto *adj. fifteenth.*

décimoséptimo *adj. seventeenth.*

décimosexto *sixteenth.*

décimotercero *adj. thirteenth.*

décimotercio *adj. thirteenth.*

decir *m. saying.*
Es sólo un decir. *It's just a saying.*
DECIR *to speak; to say, to tell.*
Dígame, por favor. *Please tell me.*
Dígame dónde está la estación. *Tell me where the station is.*
Dígaselo a él. *Tell it to him.*
Se lo diré. *I'll tell him.*
Dice Ud. bien. *You're right. That's correct. You've said the right thing.*
¡No me diga! *You don't say (so)! ("Don't tell me!")*
¡Diga! ¿Quién habla? *Hello! Who's speaking?*
Decir las cosas claras. *To speak plainly.*
Querer decir. *To mean.*
¿Qué quiere decir esta palabra? *What does this word mean?*
¿Qué me quiere Ud. decir? *What do you want to tell me? What do you mean?*
Por decirlo así. *As it were. So to speak.*
decisión *f. declaration.*
decisivo *adj. decisive.*
declaración *f. declaration.*
Declaración judicial. *Adjudication.*
declarar *to declare; to state; to testify.*
¿Tiene Ud. algo que declarar? *Do you have anything to declare (customs)?*
Declararse en huelga. *To go on strike. To declare a strike.*
Juan se declaró a María. *John proposed to Mary.*
declinar *to decline; to decay.*
decoración *f. decoration; stage scenery.*
decorado *m. decoration; stage scenery; adj. decorated.*
decorar *to decorate.*
decoro *m. decency; decorum; honor.*
decrecer *to decrease.*
decreciente *adj. decreasing.*
decrecimiento *m. decrease.*
decretar *to decree.*
decreto *m. decree.*
dedal *m. thimble.*
dedicar *to dedicate; to devote.*
Se dedica a los negocios. *He's a businessman.*
Se dedicó a la pintura. *He devoted himself to painting.*
dedicatoria *f. dedication.*
dedillo *m. little finger.*
Saber al dedillo. *To have at one's fingertips.*
Me sé la lección al dedillo. *I know the lesson by heart. ("I know it on my fingertips.")*
DEDO *m. finger; toe.*
Dedo meñique. *Little finger, pinky.*
Dedo índice. *Index finger.*

Dedo pulgar. *Thumb.*
Dedo del corazón. *Middle finger.*
Dedo anular. *Ring finger.*
Los zapatos me aprietan los dedos. *The shoes are tight around the toes.*
Está a dos dedos de la tumba. *He's on the brink of death.*
deducción *f. deduction.*
deducir *to deduce; to gather, to understand.*
Deduzco de su carta que no es muy feliz. *I gather from his letter that he's not very happy.*
defecto *m. fault, defect.*
Conozco sus defectos. *I know his faults.*
En defecto de. *In the absence of.*
defectuoso *adj. defective.*
defender *to defend.*
defensa *f. defense.*
defensiva *f. defensive.*
defensor *m. supporter, defender; lawyer, counsel.*
deferencia *f. deference, respect, regard.*
deficiencia *f. deficiency.*
deficiente *adj. deficient.*
déficit *m. shortage, deficit.*
definición *f. definition, explanation.*
definido *adj. definite.*
definir *to define, to determine.*
definitivo *adj. definitive.*
deformación *f. deformation.*
deformar *to deform.*
deforme *adj. deformed; ugly.*
deformidad *f. deformity; ugliness.*
defraudar *to defraud, to swindle.*
defunción *f. death.*
Acta de defunción. *Death certificate.*
degenerado *adj. and n. degenerate.*
degollar *to slash the throat; to decapitate.*
degradante *adj. degrading.*
degradar *to degrade.*
dejado *adj. lazy, negligent, sloppy.*
DEJAR *to leave, to let; to quit, to give up.*
Déjeme verlo. *Let me see it.*
Déjemelo en menos. *Can you let me have it cheaper? ("Give it to me for less.")*
No se nos dejó entrar. *They didn't let us come in.*
¿Puedo dejarle un recado? *May I leave a message for him?*
Déjelo para mañana. *Leave it for tomorrow. Put it off until tomorrow.*
Déjeme en paz. *Let me alone. ("Leave me in peace.")*
Dejar de. *To stop.*
¿Por qué ha dejado Ud. de visitarnos? *Why have you stopped visiting us?*
Dejó su empleo por otro mejor. *He gave up his job for a better one.*

Dejó a su mujer y a sus hijos. *He abandoned his wife and children.*

Le dejaron plantado. *They left him in the lurch.*

No puedo dejar de creerlo. *I can't help believing it.*

Déjese enfriar y sírvase. (*"Let"*) *Cool and serve.*

dejarse *to abandon oneself to; not to take care of oneself, to let oneself go.*

DEL (*contraction of* **de** + **el**) *of the.*

La casa del médico. *The doctor's house.*

Del principio al fin. *From (the) beginning to (the) end.*

No del todo. *Not quite.*

delantal *m. apron.*

DELANTE *before; in front; in the presence of.*

Nos aguarda delante del club. *He's waiting for us in front of the club.*

Firmó el testamento delante de testigos. *He signed his will before witnesses.*

delantera *f. front; start, lead.*

delegación *f. delegation.*

delegado *m. delegate, deputy, proxy.*

deleitar *to please, to delight.*

deleite *m. delight, pleasure; lust.*

deletrear *to spell.*

deletreo *m. spelling.*

delgado *adj. thin, slender.*

deliberación *f. deliberation.*

deliberar *to deliberate.*

delicado *adj. delicate; demanding; fragile; frail.*

delicia *f. delight, pleasure.*

delicioso *adj. delicious, delightful.*

El postre está delicioso. *The dessert is delicious.*

Hemos pasado un rato delicioso. *We had a delightful time.*

delincuente *m. and f. delinquent, offender.*

delinquir *to break the law.*

delirar *to rave; to be delirious.*

Está delirando. *He's talking nonsense. He's raving.*

delirio *m. delirium; raving; wild excitement; nonsense.*

El delirio le duró toda la noche. *The delirium lasted all night.*

La quiere con delirio. *He's madly in love with her. He's head over heels in love with her.*

delito *m. misdemeanor, offense, crime, felony.*

demanda *f. claim, demand, request; inquiry.*

No atendieron su demanda. *They didn't pay any attention to his claim.*

Hay mucha demanda de este artículo. *There's a great demand for this article.*

demandante *m. and f. plaintiff.*

DEMANDAR *to demand, to claim; to take legal action, to enter a claim, to start a suit.*

demarcación *f. demarcation.*

DEMÁS *other; remaining, rest;* **los** (*m.*) **demás; las** (*f.*) **demás** *others; the others.*

Los demás se lo contaré luego. *I'll tell you the rest later.*

Por lo demás me parece bien. *Aside (apart) from that (otherwise), it seems all right to me.*

Esperemos a los demás. *Let's wait for the others.*

DEMASIADO *excessive; too; too much.*

Es demasiado. *It's too much.*

Cuesta demasiado. *It costs too much.*

Este chaleco me aprieta demasiado. *This vest is too tight for me.*

demencia *f. insanity, madness.*

demente *adj. insane, crazy.*

democracia *f. democracy.*

demócrata *m. and f. democrat.*

democrático *adj. democratic.*

demoler *to demolish.*

demolición *f. demolition.*

demonio *m. demon, devil.*

¿Para qué demonio lo querrá (*coll.*)? *What the devil does he need it for?*

¿Qué demonios hace Ud. aquí (*coll.*)? *What on earth are you doing here?*

demostración *f. demonstration.*

demostrar *to demonstrate, to prove, to show.*

Demuéstrelo. Ud. *Prove it.*

Demostró que tenía razón. *He proved he was right.*

No demuestra el menor interés. *He doesn't show the slightest interest.*

demora *f. delay.*

Sin demora. *Without delay.*

demorar *to delay; to remain.*

Se demoraron en el camino. *They were delayed on the road.*

demovilizar *to demobilize.*

denegar *to refuse, to deny.*

denigrante *adj. defamatory, slanderous.*

denigrar *to blacken, to defame.*

denominación *f. denomination.*

denominar *to name.*

denotar *to denote, to indicate, to express.*

densidad *f. density.*

Doble densidad. *Double density.*

denso *adj. dense, thick..*

dentadura *f. set of teeth.*

Dentadura postiza. *False teeth.*

dental *adj. dental.*

dentrífico *toothpaste.*

dentista *m. dentist.*

DENTRO *within, inside.*
　Te espero dentro. *I'll wait for you inside.*
　Hay más gente fuera que dentro. *There are more people outside than inside.*
　El tren sale dentro de cinco minutos. *The train will leave in five minutes.*
　Vuelva dentro de media hora. *Come back in half an hour.*
　Dentro de poco. *Shortly.*
　Hacia dentro. *Toward the inside.*
　Por dentro. *On the inside.*
denuncia *f. complaint; denunciation.*
denunciar *to denounce; to give notice; to inform.*
departamento *m. department; apartment.*
　Tienda de departamentos. *Department store.*
dependencia *f. dependence, dependency; sales staff, personnel of an office, employees; branch office or store.*
DEPENDER *to depend, be dependent on.*
　Depender de. *To depend on. To count on. To rely on.*
dependiente *m. clerk; subordinate; dependent.*
deplorable *adj. deplorable, pitiful.*
deplorar *to deplore, to be sorry, to regret.*
　Deploro mucho lo ocurrido. *I'm sorry about what happened.*
deportar *to deport.*
deporte *m. sport.*
deportista *m. sportsman; f. sportswoman.*
deportivo *adj. having to do with sport(s).*
depositante *m. and f. depositor.*
depositar *to deposit; to place; to put in a safe place; to entrust.*
　Depositaron su dinero en el banco. *They deposited their money in the bank.*
　Deposité en él toda mi confianza. *I placed all my trust in him.*
depositario *m. trustee, custodian; depositary.*
depósito *m. deposit; depot; warehouse; bond, reservoir; tank (of gasoline).*
　Estos edificios son los depósitos de la fábrica. *These buildings are the factory's warehouses.*
　Lléneme el depósito. *Fill the tank up.*
　En depósito. *As a deposit. In bond.*
　Certificado de depósito. *Certificate of deposit.*
depreciación *f. depreciation.*
depresión *f. depression.*
deprimir *to depress.*
DERECHA *f. right side; right hand.*
　A la derecha. *To the right.*
　Es su mano derecha. *He's his right-hand man. ("He's his right hand.")*
DERECHO *m. law, justice; claim, title; right; straight; direct; duties (customs).*

　Es estudiante de derecho. *He's a law student.*
　Ud. no tiene derecho de quejarse. *You have no right to complain. You have no grounds for complaint.*
　Siga derecho. *Keep straight ahead. Go straight ahead.*
　Perdió el brazo derecho en la guerra. *He lost his right arm in the war.*
　Fíjese que esté del derecho. *Make sure it's right side out.*
　Ya es un hombre hecho y derecho. *He's now fully grown-up. He's now a man.*
　Derechos de autor. *Copyright. Royalties.*
　Derechos. *Rights. Fees. Duties.*
　Derechos de aduana. *Customs duties.*
　Libre de derechos. *Duty-free.*
deriva *f. deviation; drift (of a ship or airplane).*
dermatólogo *m. dermatologist.*
derogar *to annul; to repeal.*
derramamiento *m. spilling, shedding.*
derramar *to spill; to shred; to scatter; to spread.*
derrame *m. leakage.*
　Tuvo un derrame cerebral. *He had a cerebral hemorrhage.*
derredor *m. circumference.*
　Al derredor. (En derredor.) *About. Around.*
　Mire en derredor suyo. *Look around you.*
derretir *to melt, to dissolve.*
derribar *to demolish; to knock down; to overthrow.*
　Han derribado muchas casas viejas. *Many old houses have been torn down.*
derrocar *to overthrow.*
derrochador *m. spendthrift, squanderer.*
　Es un derrochador. *He's a spendthrift. Money burns a hole in his pocket.*
derrochar *to squander; to waste away.*
derrota *f. defeat; route, ship's course.*
derrotar *to rout, to defeat.*
derrotero *m. charts; course.*
derrumbamiento *m. collapse; landslide.*
derrumbar *to throw down, to demolish.*
desabotonar *to unbutton.*
desabrido *adj. insipid, tasteless.*
desabrigado *adj. uncovered; without shelter; without enough clothes on.*
desabrigar *to uncover; to leave without shelter.*
　Desabrigarse. *To uncover. To take off one's coat or hat.*
desabrochar *to unbutton, to unclasp, to unfasten.*
desacierto *m. error, blunder.*
desacreditar *to discredit.*
desacuerdo *m. disagreement.*
desafiar *to challenge, to defy.*

desafío *m. challenge; competition.*

desafortunado *adj. unlucky, unfortunate.*

desagradable *adj. disagreeable, unpleasant.*

desagradar *to displease.*

desagradecido *adj. ungrateful.*

desagrado *m. displeasure, discontent.*

desagraviar *to vindicate; to give satisfaction.*

desagravio *m. vindication, justice.*

desaguar *to drain.*

desagüe *m. drainage.*

desahogarse *to find relief (from heat, fatigue, etc.); to free oneself from debt; to open one's heart.*

desahogo *m. ease, relief.*

desahuciar *to evict, to dispossess.*

desairar *to slight, to snub.*

desaire *m. slight, snub.*

desalentar *to discourage.*

desaliento *m. discouragement; dismay.*

desalojar *to dispossess, to evict; to dislodge, to drive out.*

desamparado *adj. abandoned.*

desangrar *to bleed.*

desanimado *adj. discouraged; dull.*
   La fiesta estuvo muy desanimada. *The party was very dull.*

desanimar *to discourage.*

desánimo *m. discouragement.*

desaparecer *to disappear.*

desapercibido *adj. unprepared, not ready; unnoticed.*

desaprobar *to disapprove of.*

desaprovechar *to misuse, not to make good use of.*
   Desaprovechó la oportunidad. *He didn't make (good) use of the opportunity.*

desarmado *adj. unarmed.*

desarmar *to disarm; to dismount, to take apart.*

desarme *m. disarmament.*

desarraigar *to uproot, to extirpate.*

desarreglado *adj. untidy; disarranged, in disorder.*

desarreglar *to disarrange.*

desarreglo *m. disorder, irregularity.*

DESARROLLAR *to develop; to grow; to evolve; to unfold. (See* **revelar** *for "to develop" applied to film, etc.)*

desarrollo *m. development; evolution; growth.*

desaseado *adj. unclean, untidy.*

desaseo *m. slovenliness, untidiness, uncleanliness.*

desasosiego *m. uneasiness, restlessness.*

desastre *m. disaster, calamity.*

desatar *to untie, to loosen.*

desatender *to neglect; to disregard, to pay no attention, to take no notice of; to slight.*

desatento *adj. rude, not attentive.*

desatinar *to talk nonsense; to become confused.*

desatino *m. lack of tact; blunder; nonsense.*

desautorizar *to deprive of authority.*

desavenencia *f. disagreement, discord, misunderstanding.*

desayunarse *to breakfast.*
   ¿Se ha desayunado Ud. ya? *Have you had your breakfast yet?*

desayuno *m. breakfast.*
   Sírvame el desayuno. *Serve my breakfast.*

desbarajuste *m. confusion, disorder.*

desbaratar *to thwart, to upset (a plan); to talk nonsense; to destroy; to disperse, to route (an army); to spoil, to ruin.*

desbocarse *to run away (a horse); to use vile language.*

descabellado *adj. crazy, wild, unrestrained.*
   ¡Qué ideas tan descabelladas tienes! *What crazy ideas you have!*

descalabro *m. calamity, great loss.*

descalificar *to disqualify.*

descalzarse *to take off one's shoes and stockings.*

descalzo *adj. barefoot (ed).*

DESCANSAR *to rest; to sleep.*
   ¿No quiere Ud. descansar un rato? *Don't you want to rest a little?*
   ¡Qué descanse Ud. bien! (¡Qué Ud. descanse!) *Good night, may you sleep well. I hope you sleep well.*

descanso *m. rest; quiet; landing (of a staircase); intermission (in Spain.)*
   Le sentará muy bien un descanso. *A rest will do him good.*

descapotable *m. convertible (car).*

descarado *adj. brazen, impudent.*

descarga *f. discharge; unloading.*

descargar *to unload; to discharge; to acquit.*

descaro *m. boldness; impudence.*

descarrilamiento *m. derailment, running off the rails.*

descarrilar *to derail.*

descartar *to discard; to dismiss.*
   Hay que descartar esa posibilidad. *You must discard that possibility.*
   Me he descartado de un rey. *I discarded the king (at cards).*

descendencia *f. descent, origin.*

descender *to descend, to come down; to drop; to decrease.*

descendiente *adj. and n. descendant.*

descenso *m. descent; decline, fall.*

descifrar *to decipher; to decode.*
   No pude descifrarlo. *I couldn't figure it out. I couldn't make head or tail (out) of it.*

descolgar *to take down; to lift up, to pick up (the receiver).*

descolorido adj. discolored, faded.

descomedido adj. immoderate; excessive; impolite; rude.

Es un muchacho muy descomedido. He's very impolite.

descomponer to spoil, to break; to set at odds; to decompose; to disarrange.

descomponerse to rot;' to be indisposed; to lose one's temper.

decompuesto adj. out of order; spoiled (food); impolite, brazen.

desconcertante adj. confusing, baffling, disconcerting.

desconcertar to disturb, to confuse, to baffle.

desconectar to disconnect.

desconfianza f. distrust.

desconfiar to distrust, to mistrust.

No tiene Ud. razón para desconfiar de él. You have no reason to mistrust him.

El médico desconfiaba de poder salvarlo. The doctor had little hope of saving him.

descongelo m. defrost.

Descongelo automático. Automatic defrost.

desconocer not to recognize; to disavow; to ignore.

desconocido adj. unknown; m. stranger.

Se la acercó un desconocido. A stranger approached her.

La cara de Ud. no me es deconocida. Your face is familiar.

desconocimiento m. ignorance; ingratitude.

desconsiderado adj. thoughtless, inconsiderate.

desconsolador adj. disheartening; sad.

desconsuelo m. affliction, grief.

descontar to discount, to deduct; to take for granted.

descontento adj. not pleased, unhappy; m. discontent, dissatisfaction, disgust.

descorrer to draw (a curtain); to retrace one's steps.

descortés adj. discourteous, impolite.

descortesía f. lack of politeness; rudeness.

descoser to unstitch, to rip out the seams.

descote m. having a low neck (of a dress).

descrédito m. discredit.

descremado adj. skimmed.

descremar to skim (milk).

DESCRIBIR to describe.

descripción f. description.

descubierto adj. discovered, uncovered; bare-headed; m. overdraft; deficit.

Estar en descubierto. To have overdrawn a bank account.

descubrimiento m. discovery.

DESCUBRIR to discover, to find out; to disclose, to bring to light.

Descubrimos que todo era mentira. We

found out (discovered) that it was all a lie.

descuento m. discount.

descuidado adj. negligent, careless, slovenly.

descuidar to neglect, to overlook; to relieve from care.

No descuide Ud. sus asuntos. Don't neglect your business.

Descuide Ud. que no le pasará nada. Don't worry, nothing will happen to her!

descuido m. negligence, carelessness, omission, oversight.

DESDE since, after, from.

Se siente enfermo desde ayer. He's been feeling sick since yesterday.

¿Se puede telefonear desde aquí? Can we phone from here?

Estoy llamando desde hace rato. I have been ringing quite a while.

Desde entonces. Since then. From then (that time) on.

Desde luego. Of course.

Desde que. Ever since.

Desde niño. From childhood.

desdecirse to retract, to go back on one's word.

desdén m. disdain, scorn, contempt.

desdeñar to scorn, to disdain.

desdicha f. misfortune, calamity, unhappiness.

desdichado adj. wretched; unfortunate; unhappy; m. an unfortunate person, a poor fellow.

Es un desdichado. He's a poor devil.

deseable adj. desirable.

DESEAR to wish, to desire.

¿Qué desea Ud.? What do you want (wish)? What would you like?

¿Desea Ud. alguna otra cosa? Do you wish anything else? Would you like anything else?

Desearía hablar dos palabras con Ud. I'd like to have a few words with you.

Le deseo muchas felicidades. Lots of luck!

desechar to discard, to throw away, to scrap; to reject; to dismiss; to depreciate.

Desecharon su propuesta. They rejected his proposal.

desecho m. remainder, residue; refuse; leftovers.

Desechos químicos. Chemical wastes.

desembarazarse to rid oneself of difficulties or hindrances.

desembarcadero m. wharf, pier, landing place.

desembarcar to disembark, to go ashore.

desembarque m. landing, unloading.

desembolsar to pay out, to disburse.

desembolso m. expenditure, disbursement.

desembragar *to release the clutch.*

desempacar *to unpack.*

Tengo que desempacar el equipaje. *I have to unpack the baggage.*

desempaquetar *to unpack.*

desempeñar *to perform, to accomplish; to carry out; to redeem, to take out of pawn; to free from debt.*

Desempeñó muy bien su obligación. *He carried out his mission very well. He fulfilled his obligation (commitment) faithfully.*

desencantar *to disappoint, to disillusion.*

desencanto *m. disappointment, disillusion.*

desenfrenado *adj. unbridled, wild.*

desengañado *adj. disappointed; disillusioned.*

desengañar *to disappoint, to become disillusioned; to disabuse, to rid of a false notion.*

desengaño *m. disappointment, disillusionment.*

desengrasar *to take out (remove) the grease; to scour.*

desenlace *m. outcome, result.*

desenmascarar *to unmask.*

desenredar *to disentangle.*

desenredo *m. disentanglement.*

desenrollar *to unwind, to unroll.*

desentenderse *to shirk; to ignore, to pay no attention.*

desentendido *adj. unaware; unmindful.*

No se haga Ud. el desentendido. *Don't pretend you don't know it.*

desenterrar *to unearth, to dig up.*

desentonado *adj. out of tune.*

desentonar *to be out of tune.*

desenvoltura *f. ease; self-possession; boldness; impudence.*

desenvolver *to unwrap, to unfold; to unravel; to develop.*

DESEO *m. wish, desire.*

No puede refrenar sus deseos. *He has no self-control.*

Tener deseo de. *To desire to.*

Tengo muchos deseos de conocerla. *I'm very eager to meet her.*

deseoso *adj. desirous.*

desequilibrado *adj. unbalanced.*

desequilibrio *m. lack of balance; state of being unbalanced (mind).*

desertar *to desert.*

desertor *m. deserter.*

desesperación *f. despair, desperation; fury.*

desesperado *adj. hopeless, desperate; raving mad.*

desesperarse *to despair, to lose hope; to exasperate.*

Eso me desespera. *That exasperates me.*

desfalcar *to embezzle.*

desfalco *m. embezzlement; diminution.*

desfallecer *to faint; to pine, to languish.*

desfallecimiento *m. fainting; languor.*

desfigurar *to disfigure; to misshape; to distort.*

desfilar *to march in review; to parade.*

desfile *m. review, parade.*

desgarrar *to tear, to rend.*

desgastar *to consume, to-wear out; to waste.*

desgastarse *to lose strength; to wear out.*

desgaste *m. wear and tear; wastage.*

desgracia *f. misfortune; sorrow; accident.*

(**Desgracia** *never means "disgrace." See* **vergüenza, deshonra.**)

¡Qué desgracia! *What a misfortune!*

Por desgracia. *Unfortunately.*

Por desgracia no lo supimos a tiempo. *Unfortunately we didn't find out in time.*

Acaba de ocurrir una desgracia en la calle. *There just was an accident outside ("in the street").*

Caer en desgracia. *To lose favor.*

desgraciadamente *unfortunately.*

desgraciado *adj. unhappy, unfortunate, unlucky; m. wretch, poor fellow.*

Es un desgraciado. *He's a poor devil. He's unlucky (unhappy, unfortunate).*

desgrasar *to remove grease from.*

deshabitado *adj. deserted, uninhabited; vacant.*

deshabitar *to move out.*

deshacer *to undo; to unwrap; to take apart; to melt; to break up (a party); to liquidate (a business); to rout (an army).*

¿Quieres deshacer el paquete? *Would you please unwrap the pacakge?*

Hemos deshecho el negocio. *We've liquidated the business.*

Deshacer el equipaje. *To unpack.*

deshacerse *to do one's best; to get rid of; to get out of order; to grow feeble; to be impatient; to grieve; to vanish.*

¿Se deshizo Ud. de su automóvil? *Did you sell (get rid of) your car?*

Deshacerse en lágrimas. *To burst into tears.*

Deshacerse como el humo. *To vanish into thin air ("To vanish like smoke.")*

deshecho *adj. wasted; in pieces; undone; melted.*

deshelar *to melt; to thaw.*

desheredación *f. disinheritance.*

desheredar *to disinherit.*

deshielo *m. thaw, thawing.*

deshonesto *adj. dishonest; immodest; indecent.*

deshonor *m. dishonor; disgrace.*

deshonra *f. dishonor; disgrace.*

El ser uno pobre no es deshonra. *Poverty is no disgrace.*

deshonrar to dishonor; to disgrace.

deshonroso adj. dishonorable; disgraceful.

deshora f. inconvenient time.

  Viene siempre a deshora. He always comes at the wrong time.

desierto adj. deserted; solitary; m. desert, wilderness.

designar to appoint; to designate.

designio m. intention, design, purpose.

desigual adj. unequal; uneven.

  El terreno era muy desigual. The ground was very uneven.

desilusión f. disillusion.

desilusionar to disillusion.

desinfectante adj. disinfecting; m. disinfectant.

desinfectar to disinfect.

desinflado m. flat tire.

desinflar to deflate.

desinterés m. disinterestedness, unselfishness.

desistir to desist; to waive (one's right).

  Desistió de hacer el viaje. He called off the trip. He didn't make the trip.

desleal adj. disloyal.

deslealtad f. disloyalty.

desligar to untie, to unbind; to free (from an obligation).

desliz m. slip, lapse.

deslizar to slide; to slip; to lapse (in speech or conduct).

  Desliz de la lengua. Slip of the tongue.

deslumbramiento m. glare, overpowering luster or brilliance; bewilderment.

deslumbrar to dazzle; to bewilder.

desmayarse to faint; to become dismayed.

desmayo m. swoon; faint; dismay.

desmedido adj. immoderate; out of proportion.

desmemoriado adj. forgetful.

desmentir to deny; to contradict.

  Lo desmintió rotundamente. He denied it flatly.

desmontar to dismount; to clear (a wood); to take apart (a machine, etc.).

desmoralizado adj. demoralized.

desmoralizar to demoralize.

desnatar to skim (milk products).

desnivel m. unevenness (of ground).

desnudarse to undress, to take one's clothes off.

desnudo adj. naked, nude.

desobedecer to disobey.

desobediencia f. disobedience.

desobediente adj. disobedient.

desocupación f. unemployment; idleness.

desocupado adj. not busy; unemployed.

  Hablaré con Ud. cuando esté desocupado. I'll speak with you when you're not busy.

desocupar to vacate; to empty.

  Tenemos que desocupar la casa antes del mes próximo. We must vacate the house before next month.

desodorante m. deodorant.

desoír to turn a deaf ear; to pretend not to hear; not to heed, to disregard.

desorden m. disorder; excess.

desordenado adj. disorderly; irregular; unruly.

  Lleva una vida desordenada. He lives a very wild (irregular) life.

desorganizar to disorganize.

desorientar to lead astray, to confuse.

despachar to dispatch, to forward; to expedite, to send; to sell; to wait on; to attend to (the mail); to ship; to clear (at the customhouse).

  ¿Quiere Ud. despacharme? Will you wait on me?

  No he despachado todavía la correspondencia de hoy. I still haven't attended to ("sent out") today's correspondence (mail).

despacho m. dispatch; cabinet; office; shipment.

  Estaré en mi despacho entre las ocho y las nueve. I'll be at my office between eight and nine.

  Acaban de recibir un despacho de la embajada. They've just received a dispatch from the embassy.

  Esto lo despacho en un minuto. I'll finish this in a minute.

DESPACIO adj. slowly.

  Hable un poco más despacio. Speak a little slower. Speak more slowly.

  Camine despacio. Walk slowly.

desparramar to scatter, to squander.

despecho m. spite.

despedazar to tear or break into bits.

despedir to fire, to dismiss; to see off; to say good-bye.

despedirse to take leave; to say good-bye; to see off.

despegar to unglue, to detach; to take off.

  El sello se despegó. The stamp came off.

  Acaba de despegar el avión. The plane just took off.

  Se pasó la noche sin despegar los labios. She didn't open her mouth ("lips") all night long.

despegue m. takeoff (aviation).

despeinar to dishevel.

despejado adj. self-possessed; cloudless; smart, bright.

  No creo que llueva, el cielo está despejado. I don't think it will rain. The sky is clear.

  ¡Qué muchacho tan despejado! What a smart boy!

despejarse *to cheer up; to clear up (weather).*
Me parece que el tiempo se está despejando. *I think it's clearing up.*

despensa *f. pantry, provisions.*

desperdiciar *to waste; to squander.*

desperdicio *m. waste.*

despertador *m. alarm clock.*
Ponga el despertador a las siete. *Set the alarm for seven.*

DESPERTAR *to awaken; to wake up.*
¿Se acordará Ud. de despertarme? *Will you remember to wake me?*

despertarse *to wake up.*
Me desperté temprano. *I awoke early.*

despierto *adj. awake; vigilant; lively.*

despilfarrar *to squander, to waste.*

despilfarro *m. slovenliness; waste.*

despistar *to throw off the track; to confuse.*

desplazar *to displace.*

desplegar *to unfold, to unfurl; to hoist (the flag).*

desplomarse *to collapse; to fall flat on the ground.*

despoblado *adj. depopulated; m. deserted, uninhabited place.*

despojar *to deprive, to strip.*
Le han despojado hasta del último centavo. *They took everything he had down to the last penny.*

desposar *to marry.*

déspota *m. despot.*

despreciable *adj. despicable, contemptible.*

despreciar *to despise; to look down on.*

desprecio *m. contempt, scorn.*
Lo trataron con desprecio. *They treated him with contempt.*

desprender *to unfasten, to separate.*

desprenderse *to extricate oneself; to be inferred; to give away; to get rid of.*
Se ha desprendido de toda su fortuna. *He gave away his whole fortune.*

desprendido *adj. generous.*

despreocupado *adj. unconcerned; unconventional, free from prejudice.*

despreocuparse *to become unbiased; not to worry; to ignore, to forget, to pay no attention.*

desproporcionado *adj. disproportionate, out of proportion.*

despropósito *m. absurdity, nonsense.*

desprovisto *adj. unprovided.*

DESPUÉS *after, afterward, later.*
¿Qué pasó después de eso? *What happened after that?*
Llegó media hora después. *He arrived half an hour later.*
Mas bien antes que después. *"Rather before than after."*

desquitarse *to get even.*

desquite *m. revenge; making up for, getting even.*

destacamento *m. detachment (of troops).*

destacar *to detach (troops); to emphasize.*

destajo *m. piecework.*
Trabajamos a destajo. *We do piecework.*

destapar *to uncover; to open, to uncork.*

desteñirse *to fade (color).*

desterrado *adj. exiled; m. exile.*

desterrar *to exile.*

destinar *to appoint; to allot; to assign; to station; to intend for; to address to.*
La carta venía destinada a mí. *The letter was addressed to me.*

destinatario *m. addressee.*

destino *m. destiny; destination; assignment; position.*
Salió con destino a Buenos Aires. *He was bound for Buenos Aires.*
No sé que destino le van a dar a ese edificio. *I don't know what they'll use that building for.*

destornillador *m. screwdriver.*

destornillar *to unscrew.*

destreza *f. skill.*

destróyer *m. destroyer (ship).*

destrozar *to destroy; to smash.*

destrucción *f. destruction.*

destruir *to destroy.*

desvanecerse *to vanish; to faint; to swell, to become puffed up (with pride).*

desvelar *to keep awake.*

desvelo *m. lack of sleep; anxiety.*

desventaja *f. disadvantage.*

desventajoso *adj. disadvantageous.*

desventurado *adj. unfortunate.*

desvergonzado *adj. impudent, unashamed, brazen.*

desvergüenza *f. impudence, brazenness.*

desvestirse *to undress.*

desviación *f. deviation; deflection.*

desviar *to divert; to deviate; to dissuade.*
Desviar la mirada. *To turn one's head away.*

desvío *m. deviation; detour.*

detallar *to detail; to retail.*

detalle *m. detail; retail.*
Comprar al detalle. *To buy at retail.*
Vender al detalle. *To sell at retail.*

detallista *m. retailer.*

detective *m. detective.*

detención *f. detention, arrest; delay.*

detener *to detain; to retain; to withhold; to stop.*

DETENERSE *to stay, stop over; to stop; to pause.*
Nos tendremos que detener en Panamá dos días. *We'll have to stop in Panama for two days.*

Se detuvo un momento para pensarlo. *He paused a moment to think about it.*

detenidamente *slowly, carefully.*

detenido *adj. under arrest.*

detenimiento *m. detention; care.*

detergente *m. detergent.*

deteriorar *to deteriorate.*

deterioro *m. damage, deterioration.*

determinación *f. determination; daring.*

Tomar la determinación. *To resolve. To make the (a) decision.*

determinado *adj. determined, resolute.*

determinar *to determine, to decide.*

determinarse *to resolve, to make up one's mind.*

¿Se determinó a hacer el viaje? *Has he decided to take the trip?*

detestable *adj. detestable.*

detestar *to detest, to abhor.*

DETRÁS *behind; behind one's back.*

Detrás de la puerta. *Behind the door.*

Vienen detrás. *They're following behind.*

Por detrás hablaba mal de él. *He talked about him behind his back.*

deuda *f. debt.*

Pagó todas sus deudas. *He paid all his debts.*

Deuda pendiente. *An unpaid balance.*

Contraer deudas. *To incur debts.*

deudor *m. debtor.*

devastación *f. devastation.*

devastar *to devastate, to ruin.*

devoción *f. devotion.*

devolución *f. return; refund.*

devolver *to restore; to return.*

devorar *to devour, to consume.*

devoto *adj. devout, pious; devoted.*

DÍA *m. day.*

¡Buenos días! *Good morning!*

¿Qué día es hoy? *What's today?*

¿En qué día del mes estamos? *What day of the month is it?*

Dentro de ocho días. *In (within) a week ("eight days").*

Estaré en casa todo el día. *I'll be (at) home all day.*

La veo todos los días. *I see her every day.*

¿Cuál es el plato del día? *What's today's special? ("What's the plate of the day?")*

De día. *In the daytime.*

Un día sí y otro día no. *Every other day.*

Al día siguiente. Al otro día. *On the following day.*

Un día tras otro. *Day after day.*

De día en día. *From day to day.*

Día feriado. *Legal holiday.*

Día de trabajo. (Día laborable). *Weekday. ("Working day.")*

diabetes *f. diabetes.*

diablo *m. devil.*

¡Qué diablos! *What the devil!*

¿En dónde diablos te metiste? *Where on earth did you go? ("Where the devil did you hide yourself?")*

diagnóstico *m. diagnosis.*

diagrama *m. diagram.*

Diagrama de flujo. *Flow chart.*

dialecto *m. dialect.*

diálogo *m. dialogue.*

diamante *m. diamond.*

Diamante en bruto. *Diamond in the rough.*

diámetro *m. diameter.*

diapositiva *f. slide, transparency.*

DIARIO *adj. and n. daily; diary; daily newspaper.*

He leído el diario sólo por encima. *I just glanced at (scanned) the paper.*

Nos vemos a diario. *We see each other every day.*

Los cuartos en este hotel no bajarán de cien pesos diarios. *The rooms in this hotel will cost at least ("won't cost less than") one hundred pesos a day.*

diarrea *f. diarrhea.*

dibujante *m. and f. draftsman, designer.*

dibujar *to draw, to design; to sketch.*

dibujo *m. drawing, design.*

Dibujos animados. *Cartoons.*

diccionario *m. dictionary.*

DICIEMBRE *m. December.*

dictado *m. dictation.*

dictador *m. dictator.*

dictar *to dictate; to issue, to pronounce.*

Escriba Ud. Yo le dictaré. *Take this down, I'll dictate.*

El juez dictó sentencia. *The judge pronounced sentence.*

dicha *f. happiness; good luck.*

¡Qué dicha! *What luck!*

dicho *adj. said; m. saying.*

Niega que lo haya dicho. *He denies that he said it.*

Lo dicho, dicho. *I stick to what I've said. I'll (I'd) say it again.*

Dicho y hecho. *No sooner said than done. ("Said and done.")*

Es un dicho. *It's a saying.*

Tiene unos dichos muy graciosos. *She makes some very witty remarks.*

dichoso *adj. happy; fortunate.*

¡Dichosos los ojos que lo ven a Ud.! *What a pleasure (how nice) to see you!*

DIECINUEVE *adj. and n. nineteen.*

DIECIOCHO *adj. and n. eighteen.*

DIECISÉIS *adj. and n. sixteen.*

DIECISIETE *adj. and n. seventeen.*

DIENTE *m. tooth.*
  Tener buen diente. *To have a hearty appetite ("To have a good tooth.")*
  Cepillo de dientes. *Toothbrush.*
  Diente molar. *Molar.*
  Dientes postizos. *False teeth.*
  Hablar entre dientes. *To mumble. To mutter.*
DIESTRA *f. right hand.*
diestro *adj. and n. skillful, bullfighter.*
dieta *f. diet.*
  Estoy a dieta. *I'm on a diet.*
DIEZ *adj. and n. ten; tenth.*
difamación *f. defamation.*
difamar *to defame.*
DIFERENCIA *f. difference.*
  Partir la diferencia. *To split the difference.*
DIFERENTE *adj. different.*
diferir *to defer, to put off; to differ.*
DIFÍCIL *adj. difficult, hard.*
  No es nada difícil. *It isn't difficult at all.*
  Todo es difícil al principio. *Everything is hard in the beginning.*
  Este escritor es difícil. *This author is difficult to understand.*
dificultad *f. difficulty.*
dificultar *to make difficult, to obstruct.*
dificultoso *adj. difficult; hard to please.*
difteria *f. diphtheria.*
difundir *to diffuse, to divulge; to broadcast.*
difunto *adj. deceased, dead; late; m. corpse.*
difusión *f. diffusion; broadcasting.*
digerir *to digest.*
digestión *f. digestion.*
dignarse *to deign, to condescend.*
dignidad *f. dignity.*
digno *adj. deserving, worthy; dignified.*
  Digno de confianza. *Trustworthy.*
digresión *f. digression.*
dilación *f. delay.*
dilatar *to put off, to delay; to expand.*
dilecto *adj. loved, beloved.*
dilema *m. dilemma.*
  ¡Vaya un dilema! *What a dilemma! What a difficult situation!*
diligencia *f. diligence; haste; business, errand; stagecoach.*
  Estudia con diligencia sus lecciones. *He studies his lessons diligently.*
  Hacer una diligencia. *To attend to some business. To do an errand.*
  Hacer diligencias. *To try, To endeavor.*
  Hay que resolverlo con toda diligencia. *You must solve it quickly.*
diligente *adj. diligent; prompt, swift.*
diluir *to dilute.*
diluviar *to rain heavily.*
  Seguía diluviando cuando partimos. *It was still pouring when we left.*

dimensión *f. dimension.*
diminutivo *adj. diminutive.*
diminuto *adj. diminutive, minute.*
dimisión *f. resignation (from a position, society, etc.)*
dimitir *to resign, to retire.*
dinamita *f. dynamite.*
dínamo *f. dynamo.*
dineral *m. large amount of money.*
DINERO *m. money, currency.*
  Ando mal de dinero. *I'm short of money.*
  Dinero contante. *Ready money. Cash payment.*
  Persona de dinero. *A well-to-do person.*
diodo *m. diode.*
  Diodo electroluminiscente. *Light-emitting diode (LED).*
DIOS *m. God.*
  ¡Dios mío! *My God! Dear me!*
  Dios mediante. *God willing. With the help of God.*
  ¡Por Dios! *For heaven's sake!*
  ¡Válgame Dios! *Goodness! My heavens! Good gracious!*
  ¡No, por Dios! *Good heavens, no!*
  ¡Vaya Ud. con Dios! *Good-bye.*
  ¡Sabe Dios! *God knows!*
  ¡Qué Dios le oiga! *God grant it!*
diploma *m. diploma.*
diplomacia *f. diplomacy.*
diplomático *adj. diplomatic; m. diplomat.*
diptongo *m. diphthong.*
diputado *m. deputy; delegate; representative.*
DIRECCIÓN *f. address; direction, way; control, management, administration; manager's office.*
  ¿En qué dirección va Ud.? *Which way are you going?*
  En esa dirección. *In that direction.*
  Escriba la dirección. *Write (down) the address.*
  Calle de dirección única. *One-way street.*
directamente *directly.*
directivo *adj. managing; f. governing board, board of directors.*
directo *adj. direct; straight; nonstop.*
  ¿Es éste un tren directo o tiene uno que cambiar? *Is that an express or must one change?*
director *adj. and n. directing; manager, director; chief editor; principal (of a school).*
  Director de orquesta. *Orchestra conductor.*
directorio *m. directory; board of directors; executive committee.*
  Presidente del directorio. *Chairman of the Board.*
dirigente *adj. leading, directing; m. leader.*

DIRIGIR *to address; to direct; to conduct, to control; to guide; to drive.*

¿Cómo tengo que dirigir la carta? *How shall I address the letter?*

dirigirse *to apply to; to be bound for; to address.*

¿A quien tengo que dirigirme? *To whom shall I apply?*

¿Se dirige Ud. a nosotros? *Are you speaking to us?*

El lugar hacia el cual se dirigen está aún muy lejos. *The place you're going to is still a good way off.*

discernimiento *m. discernment.*

discernir *to discern; to distinguish.*

disciplina *f. discipline.*

disciplinar *to discipline.*

discípulo *m. disciple; pupil.*

disco *m. disk, record; diskette; dish antenna.*

Disco de dos caras. *Two-sided floppy.*

Disco compacto. *Compact disc (CD).*

Disco duro. *Hard diskette.*

Disco flexible. *Floppy diskette.*

Disco impresor. *Daisy wheel.*

discordante *adj. discordant.*

discordia *f. discord; disagreement; dissension.*

discoteca *f. discotheque.*

discreción *f. discretion; keenness; sagacity.*

A discreción. *At one's discretion. Left to one's discretion. Optional.*

discrepancia *f. discrepancy.*

discrepar *to disagree; to differ from.*

discreto *adj. discreet.*

disculpa *f. excuse, apology.*

disculpar *to excuse.*

discurrir *to wander about; to think over; to flow (a liquid.)*

Discurramos un poco más sobre esto. *Let's consider that a little longer.*

discurso *m. speech.*

Hacer un discurso. *To make a speech. To deliver an address.*

discusión *f. discussion, argument.*

discutible *adj. debatable.*

DISCUTIR *to discuss, to argue.*

diseminar *to disseminate; to scatter.*

disensión *f. dissension, strife.*

disentería *f. dysentery.*

diseñar *to draw, to design, to sketch.*

diseño *m. drawing; sketch, outline.*

Diseño gráfico. *Graphic design.*

disfraz *m. disguise; mask.*

disfrazar *to disguise.*

DISFRUTAR *to enjoy.*

Disfrutaremos más si vamos en grupo. *We'll have more fun if we all go together.*

Disfruta de muy buena salud. *He's enjoying good health.*

disfrute *m. enjoyment.*

disgustar *to displease, to disgust; to offend.*

¿Le disgusta que fume? *Do you mind my smoking?*

disgustarse *to be displeased, to get angry; to quarrel.*

¿No se disgustará Ud? *Won't you be angry?*

disgusto *m. displeasure, disgust, annoyance; quarrel.*

A disgusto. *Against one's will. Not at ease.*

Llevarse un disgusto. *To be disappointed.*

disidente *adj. and n. dissident; dissenter.*

disimulación *f. dissimulation.*

disimulado *adj. dissembling.*

Hacerse el disimulado. *To act dumb.*

disimular *to dissimulate; to overlook.*

disimulo *m. dissimulation; pretense; tolerance.*

diskette *m. See disco.*

dislocación *f. dislocation.*

dislocarse *to sprain; to dislocate.*

disminución *f. lessening, diminishing.*

disminuir *to diminish, to decrease.*

disolver *to melt; to dissolve; to break up (a crowd).*

dispar *adj. different, unlike.*

disparar *to shoot; to fire.*

disparatado *adj. nonsensical, absurd.*

disparatar *to ramble, to talk nonsense; to blunder.*

disparate *m. nonsense; blunder*

disparo *m. discharge, shot.*

DISPENSAR *to excuse; to dispense; to exempt.*

Dispénseme. *Excuse me.*

Dispense Ud. *I beg your pardon.*

Dispénseme, ¿qué hora es? *Excuse me, what time is it?*

Está dispensado. *You're excused.*

dispensario *m. dispensary.*

disperso *adj. dispersed; scattered.*

disponer *to dispose; to arrange; to provide for; to prepare; to determine.*

Disponga Ud. lo que quiera. *Decide whatever you like (wish).*

Me dispongo a salir mañana. *I'm determined to leave tomorrow.*

Dispongo de muy poco tiempo. *I have very little time now ("at my disposal").*

disponible *adj. available.*

disposición *f. service; disposition; state of mind; regulation, order.*

Estoy a su disposición. *I'm at your service.*

Tiene muy buena disposición. *She has a very pleasant disposition.*

Había que sujetarse a la nueva disposición. *We had to submit to the new regulation.*

dispuesto *adj. disposed; ready, arranged; inclined, willing* (*to*).

Bien dispuesto. *Favorably disposed* (*inclined*).

Mal dispuesto. *Unfavorably disposed* (*inclined*).

Estamos dispuestos a todo. *We're prepared for anything.*

disputa *f. dispute; contest; quarrel.*

disputar *to dispute; to quarrel.*

DISTANCIA *f. distance.*

¿Qué distancia hay a Buenos Aires? *How far is it to Buenos Aires?*

Llamada a larga distancia. *Long-distance call.*

DISTANTE *adj. distant, far-off.*

distinción *f. distinction; discrimination; difference.*

Hay que hacer una distinción entre los dos sonidos. *It's necessary to make a distinction between the two sounds.*

Era un hombre de mucha distinción. *He was a very distinguished man.*

A distinción de. *In contrast to.*

distinguido *adj. distinguished, eminent.*

distinguir *to distinguish; to discriminate; to tell (apart); to show regard for.*

¿Cómo puede distinguirlos? *How do (can) you tell them apart?*

distinguirse *to distinguish oneself, to excel.*

distintivo *adj. distinctive; m. badge, insignia.*

DISTINTO *adj. distinct; different.*

distracción *f. oversight; distraction; entertainment; embezzlement.*

La lectura es su distracción favorita. *Reading is his favorite diversion.*

El cine es su distracción favorita. *Going to the movies is his favorite entertainment (diversion).*

distraer *to distract; to entertain.*

Ese ruido me distrae. *That noise distracts me.*

distraerse *to enjoy oneself, to have fun; to be absentminded.*

¿Se ha distraído en la fiesta? *Did you have a good time at the party?*

distraído *adj. inattentive; absentminded.*

distribución *f. distribution.*

distribuidor *adj. distributing; m. distributor.*

Distribuidor automático. *Vending machine.*

distribuir *to distribute; to divide; to allot, to allocate.*

distrito *m. district; region.*

disturbar *to disturb.*

disturbio *m. disturbance.*

disuadir *to dissuade.*

disuasión *f. dissuasion.*

divagación *f. wandering, digression.*

divagar *to wander.*

diván *m. couch.*

divergencia *f. divergence.*

divergente *adj. divergent.*

diversidad *f. diversity; variety.*

diversión *f. amusement, diversion, recreation.*

diverso *adj. diverse; various, several.*

Le he visto en diversas ocasiones. *I've seen him on several occasions.*

divertido *adj. entertaining, amusing; funny.*

Este libro es muy divertido. *This book is very entertaining.*

Todo esto es muy divertido. *All this is very amusing.*

Es una muchacha divertidísima. *She's lots of fun.*

divertimiento *m. diversion, amusement, sport, pastime.*

divertir *to distract; to divert; to amuse.*

Nos contó unos chistes que nos divertieron mucho. *He told us some jokes which amused us very much (a lot).*

DIVERTIRSE *to amuse oneself, to have a good time, to have fun.*

¡Qué se divierta! *Have a good time! Enjoy yourself!*

dividendo *m. dividend.*

DIVIDIR *to divide.*

divinamente *splendidly; divinely, heavenly; very well.*

Canta divinamente. *She sings beautifully* (*"divinely"*). *She has a beautiful voice.*

Este sombrero le sienta divinamente. *This hat is most becoming to you.*

divinidad *f. divinity.*

divino *adj. divine; excellent; heavenly.*

divisa *f. motto; badge; foreign currency.*

divisar *to perceive, to catch sight of.*

división *f. division; partition, compartment.*

divorciarse *to get a divorce, to be divorced.*

divorcio *m. divorce.*

divulgar *to divulge, to publish; to disclose.*

dobladillo *m. hem.*

doblar *to turn; to double; to fold; to bend.*

Doble a la derecha. *Turn to the right.*

Doblar la esquina. *To turn the corner.*

doble *adj. double, twofold; two-faced, deceitful.*

No se fíe Ud. de él, es muy doble. *Don't trust him, he's very deceitful.*

Esto tiene doble sentido. *This has a double meaning.*

doblemente *doubly; deceitfully*

doblez *m. fold; crease; duplicity, double dealing.*

DOCE *adj. and n. twelve; twelfth.*

DOCENA *f. dozen.*

Por docena. *By the dozen.*

dócil *adj. docile; obedient; gentle.*

doctor *m.* doctor.

doctrina *f.* doctrine.

documentación *f.* documentation, documents, papers.

documental *m.* documentary.

documento *m.* document.

    Documentos de identidad. *Identification papers.*

    Documentos mercantiles. *Commercial paper.*

    Documentos públicos. *Public instruments.*

dólar *m.* dollar.

dolencia *f.* ailment; disease.

DOLER *to ache, to cause pain, to hurt.*

    ¿Dónde le duele? *Where does it hurt you?*

    Me duele la cabeza. *I've a headache.*

    El pie me duele muchísimo. *My foot hurts a lot.*

    Me duelen los ojos. *My eyes hurt.*

    Me duele la garganta. *I have a sore throat.*

dolerse (de) *to be sorry (for); to regret; to pity; to complain (of).*

dolo *m.* fraud.

DOLOR *m.* ache, pain; sorrow.

    Tener dolor. *To have a pain.*

    Tener dolor de cabeza. *To have a headache.*

    Dolor de muelas. *Toothache.*

    Dolor de garganta. *A sore throat.*

doloroso *adj.* sorrowful, afflicted; painful.

domar *to tame; to subdue.*

    Sin domar. *Untamed.*

doméstico *adj.* domestic.

domicilio *m.* residence, domicile; home; address.

dominación *f.* domination.

dominante *adj.* dominant.

dominar *to dominate; to master.*

dominarse *to control oneself.*

DOMINGO *m.* Sunday.

dominio *m.* dominion; command, control.

    Tiene un buen dominio del español. *He has an excellent command of Spanish.*

    Tenía un gran dominio sobre sí mismo. *He had great self-control. He had great control over himself.*

don *m.* Don (title of respect used only before Christian names); natural gift.

    Dirija Ud. la carta a Don Antonio. *Address the letter to Antonio.*

    Don de gentes. *Pleasant manners. Social graces. Savoir-faire.*

donación *f.* gift, donation; grant.

donaire *m.* grace; elegance; witty saying.

donar *to donate, to give as a gift.*

donativo *m.* gift, donation.

DONDE *where.*

    ¿Dónde vive? *Where do you live?*

    ¿Dónde está el teléfono? *Where is the telephone?*

    Iremos donde a Ud. le plazca. *We'll go wherever you like.*

    ¿De dónde? *From where?*

    ¿Hacia dónde? *In what direction?*

    ¿Por dónde? *Which way?*

dondequiera *anywhere; wherever.*

    Iré dondequiera que me mande. *I'll go wherever you send me.*

doña *(f. of* **don**) *lady; madam.*

    Doña Angela está enferma. *Doña Angela is ill.*

dorado *adj.* gilt, gilded.

dormilón *adj.* fond of sleeping; *m.* sleepyhead.

DORMIR *to sleep.*

    ¿Ha dormido Ud. bien? *Did you sleep well?*

    No he podido dormir. *I couldn't sleep.*

DORMIRSE *to fall asleep.*

    Debo haberme dormido. *I must have been asleep.*

    Se ha quedado dormido. *He's fallen asleep.*

dormitar *to doze, to be half asleep.*

dormitorio *m.* dormitory; bedroom.

DOS *adj. and n.* two; second (day of the month).

    Dos a dos. *Two by two.*

    De dos en dos. *Two abreast.*

    En un dos por tres. *In the twinkling of an eye.*

    Para entre los dos. *Between you and me.*

    Son las dos. *It's two o'clock.*

    Las dos hermanas se parecen. *Both sisters look alike.*

    ¿Tiene Ud. un cuarto para dos personas? *Do you have a double room?*

    Está a dos pasos de aqui. *It's only a few steps from here.*

DOSCIENTOS *m. pl.* two hundred.

dosis *f.* dose.

dotación *f.* crew; equipment; allocation.

dotar *to provide (with); to allocate; to give a dowry; to endow with.*

dote *m. and f.* dowry; *pl.* gifts, talents.

drama *m.* drama.

dramático *adj.* dramatic.

dramatizar *to dramatize.*

drástico *adj.* drastic.

dril *m.* denim.

droga *f.* drug.

drogadicto *m.* drug addict; junkie.

droguería *f.* drugstore.

ducha *f.* shower (bath).

DUDA *f.* doubt.

    No me cabe la menor duda. *I haven't the slightest doubt.*

    Sin duda. *Without a doubt. Undoubtedly.*

DUDAR *to doubt.*
   Lo dudo. *I doubt it.*
   Dudo que venga. *I doubt if he'll come.*
   Nadie lo duda. *Nobody doubts it.*
dudoso *adj. doubtful, borderline; uncertain.*
duelo *m. duel; mourning; grief; affliction.*
duende *m. ghost.*
dueña *f. owner; landlady; mistress.*
dueño *m. owner; landlord; master.*
   Hacerse dueño. *To take possession.*
   Dueño de sí mismo. *Self-controlled.*
     ("Master of oneself.")
DULCE *adj. sweet; agreeable; m. candy.*
dulzura *f. sweetness; gentleness.*
dúo *m. duo, duet.*
duodécimo *adj. twelfth.*
duplicado *m. duplicate; copy.*
duplicar *to duplicate, to repeat.*
duque *m. duke.*
duquesa *f. duchess.*
durable *adj. durable; lasting.*
   ¿Es durable esta tela? *Will this cloth wear well?*
duración *f. duration.*
duradero *adj. durable; lasting.*
DURANTE *during, for.*
   Durante el día. *During the day.*
   Durante la noche. *During the night.*
   Durante algún tiempo. *For some time.*
DURAR *to last; to continue; to wear well.*
   ¿Cuánto dura la película? *How long does the picture last?*
   Este abrigo me ha durado mucho tiempo. *This overcoat has lasted me a long time.*
   El viaje en barco durará cinco días. *The voyage will take five days.*
durazno *m. peach (Amer.).*
dureza *f. hardness; harshness.*
durmiente *adj. sleeping; m. sleeper.*
DURO *adj. hard; unbearable; obstinate; stingy; harsh; m. five pesetas (Spain); a small amount (Spain).*
   No sea duro con él. *Don't be hard on him.*
   A duras penas. *Scarcely. Hardly. With difficulty.*
   Five pesetas (mh;.5q Spain); a small amount *(Spain).*
   No te doy ni un duro. *I won't give you a red cent.*

E

e *and (used before words beginning with i or hi).*
   Padre e hijo. *Father and son.*
ebanista *m. cabinetmaker.*
ebrio *adj. intoxicated, drunk.*

   Ebrios habituales. *Habitual drunkards.*
economía *f. economy, economics, saving.*
   Economía política. *Political economy.*
económico *adj. economic; economical, not too expensive.*
economizar *to economize; to save.*
ecosistema *m. ecosystem.*
ECHAR *to throw; to throw out; to fire; to sprout; to shoot; to lay down; to start to.*
   Eche esto a la basura. *Throw this in the garbage.*
   Lo echaron de su empleo por holgazán. *They fired him because he was too lazy.*
   Eche un poco de agua caliente en la tetera. *Pour some hot water in the teapot.*
   Eche Ud. la carta al buzón. *Put this letter in the mailbox.*
   Lo echaron a patadas. *They kicked him out.*
   Echar mano a. *To grab. To get hold of. To arrest.*
   Echar a correr. *To start to run.*
   Echar a perder. *To spoil.*
   Echar la culpa a alguno. *To blame someone.*
   Echar de menos. *To miss.*
   Echar raíces. *To take root.*
   Echar el ancla. *To drop anchor.*
ECHARSE *to lie down; to throw oneself, to plunge; to rush, to dash.*
   Se echó en la cama. *He lay down on the bed.*
   Se echó a reír. *He burst out laughing.*
EDAD *f. age; era, epoch, time.*
   ¿Qué edad tiene Ud? *How old are you? What's your age?*
   Somos de la misma edad. *We're (of) the same age.*
   Ser menor de edad. *To be a minor.*
   Mayor de edad. *Of age.*
   Es un hombre de edad. *He's well along in years.*
   Edad media. *Middle Ages.*
edición *f. edition, issue; publication.*
   Edición en pantalla. *Screen editing.*
   Edición de texto. *Text editing.*
edificar *to construct, to build.*
   Van a edificar una nueva escuela. *They are going to build a new school.*
edificio *m. building.*
   Este edificio es bonito por fuera. *This building looks (is) nice from the outside.*
editor *adj. and n. publishing; m. publisher.*
   Casa editora. *Publishing house.*
   Fuí a ver a un editor. *I went to see a publisher.*
editorial *adj. editorial; f. publishing house..*
educación *f. education; bringing up, breeding.*
   Es un hombre sin educación. *He's ill-bred. He has no breeding.*

educar *to educate; to bring up; to train.*
Es muy mal educado. *He has no breeding.*
Es una chica muy bien educada. *She's a very well-bred girl.*
educativo *adj. educational, instructive.*
efectivo *adj. effective, certain, real, actual; m. cash.*
Pagar en efectivo. *To pay in cash.*
Efectivo en caja. *Cash on hand.*
Valor efectivo. *Real value.*
Hacer efectivo. *To make effective. To put into effect. To cash (a check, etc.).*
EFECTO *m. effect, result, consequence; impression; pl. effects, assets, goods, belongings.*
Sus palabras causaron mal efecto. *His words made a bad impression.*
En efecto, no sabe nada. *In fact, he doesn't know anything.*
A tal efecto. *For this purpose.*
A cuyo efecto. *For the purpose of which. To which end.*
Por efecto de. *As a result of.*
Llevar a efecto. *To carry out. To put into practice (effect).*
Dejar sin efecto. *To cancel. To annul. To make (declare) void.*
Efectos personales. *Personal belongings.*
eficaz *adj. effective, efficient.*
eficiente *adj. effective, efficient.*
eje *m. axle, axis.*
ejecución *f. execution, carrying out, performance.*
ejecutar *to execute, to carry out, to perform, to run.*
ejecutivo *adj. executive; m. executive.*
ejemplar *adj. exemplary, serving as an example; m. copy; sample.*
No pude conseguir otro ejemplar del libro. *I couldn't get another copy of the book.*
EJEMPLO *m. example; pattern.*
Por ejemplo. *For example.*
ejercer *to exercise, to perform, to practice.*
Ejercer la medicina. *To practice medicine.*
ejercicio *m. exercise; drill.*
Ejercicio de tiro. *Target practice.*
ejército *m. army.*
EL *(article m.) the.*
El libro. *The book.*
¿No le gusta el frío? *Don't you like the cold?*
¿Cuál es el mejor hotel? *Which is the best hotel?*
EL *(pronoun m.) he, him.*
¿Qué dijo él? *What did he say?*
Dígaselo a él. *Tell it to him.*
elaboración *f. elaboration, working out.*

elaborado *adj. elaborate; manufactured.*
elaborar *to elaborate; to work out; to manufacture.*
elasticidad *f. elasticity.*
elástico *adj. and n. elastic.*
ele *f. name of the letter l.*
elección *f. election; choice, selection.*
Hoy se celebran las elecciones. *Elections will be held today.*
Hizo una buena elección. *He made a good choice.*
electricidad *f. electricity.*
eléctrico *adj. electric.*
Luz eléctrica. *Electric light.*
electrodoméstico *m. appliance.*
electrónico *adj. electronic.*
elefante *m. elephant.*
elegancia *f. elegance; refinement.*
Viste con elegancia. *She dresses neatly.*
elegante *adj. elegant, refined, well dressed.*
elegir *to elect; to choose.*
elemental *adj. elementary; elemental.*
elemento *m. element; pl. elements, rudiments, first principles.*
elenco *m. cast (play, etc.), list.*
elevación *f. elevation.*
elevador *m. elevator; hoist.*
elevar *to elevate; to lift up.*
eliminación *f. elimination.*
eliminar *to eliminate.*
elocuencia *f. eloquence.*
elocuente *adj. eloquent.*
elogiar *to praise.*
elogio *m. praise, eulogy.*
eludir *to elude, to evade.*
Deje de eludir la cuestión: vamos al grano. *Stop evading the issue; let's get to the point.*
ELLA *(f. of él) she, her.*
¿Cómo es ella? *What does she look like?*
Vamos con ella. *We are going with her.*
ELLAS *(pl. of ella) they, them.*
¿Quiénes son ellas? *Who are they?*
Lo prepara para ellas. *He is preparing it for them.*
ELLO *(neuter of él and ella) it.*
Hablemos de ello. *Let's talk about that.*
Para ello. *For the purpose.*
Ello es que. *The fact is (that).*
ELLOS *(pl. of él) they, them.*
Ellos se van, pero yo me quedo. *They're leaving but I'll stay.*
Ninguno de ellos tiene dinero. *None of them has money.*
embajada *f. embassy.*
embajador *m. ambassador.*
embalaje *m. packing; putting in bales; packing-box.*
embalar *to pack in bales; to pack.*

embarazada *adj. pregnant.*
   Estú embarazada de cinco meses. *She's five months pregnant.*

embarcación *f. vessel, ship, boat; embarkation.*

embarcadero *m. wharf, place of embarkation.*

embarcar *to embark.*

embarcarse *to go on board a ship, to embark.*

embargo *m. embargo.*
   Sin embargo. *Nevertheless.*

embarque *m. embarkation, shipment, shipping.*
   Puerta de embarque. *Gate (at an airport).*
   Pase de embarque. *Boarding pass.*

embestida *f. assault, attack.*

emborrachar *to intoxicate.*

emborracharse *to get drunk.*

emboscar *to ambush.*

emboscarse *to lie in ambush.*

embotellar *to bottle*

embrague *m. clutch (car).*

embrollo *m. jumble, tangle; fix, jam.*
   No sé como salir de este embrollo. *I don't know how to get out of this fix (tight spot, jam).*

embustero *m. liar, fibber.*

embutido *m. inlaid work; sausage.*

emergencia *f. emergency.*

emigración *f. emigration.*

emigrante *m. emigrant.*

emigrar *to emigrate.*

eminente *adj. eminent.*

emisora *f. broadcasting station.*

emitir *to emit, to send forth; to issue (bonds, etc.); to utter, to express; to broadcast (news, etc.).*

emoción *f. emotion.*

emocional *adj. emotional.*

emocionante *adj. touching, thrilling.*

emocionarse *to be moved.*
   Se emociona fácilmente. *He's very emotional.*

empacar *to pack.*

empalmar *to join; to splice.*

empanada *f. meat pie.*

empañar *to diaper; to blur; to sully.*

empapar *to soak.*

empaparse *to be soaked, to be drenched.*

empapelar *to paper.*

empaquetar *to pack.*

emparedado *m. sandwich.*

emparentado *adj. related.*

emparentar *to become related.*

empastar *to paste; to bind (books); to fill (a tooth).*

empaste *m. filling (tooth).*

empatar *to equal, to tie.*
   Los dos equipos empataron. *The game ended in a tie. ("The two teams tied.")*

empate *m. tie, draw.*

empeñar *to pawn; to pledge; to engage.*
   Empeñé mi palabra. *I gave (pledged) my word.*
   Está empeñado hasta los ojos. *He's up to his neck in debt.*

empeñarse *to get into debt.*

empeño *m. pledge, obligation; determination; earnest desire; persistence.*
   Estudia con empeño. *He's studying diligently.*
   Tener empeño en. *To be bent on.*

EMPEZAR *to begin.*

emplazamiento *m. summons.*

empleado *m. employee, clerk; servant.*
   Empleado puertas adentro. *Live-in help.*

EMPLEAR *to employ; to hire; to use; to spend.*
   ¿En qué empleó Ud. la tarde? *How did you spend the afternoon?*
   Empleamos dos días en hacerlo. *It took us two days to do it.*
   Estoy empleado en su casa. *I work in his firm.*
   Se acaba de emplear. *He just got a job.*
   Emplearon un centenar do obreros esta mañana. *They hired a hundred workers this morning.*

EMPLEO *m. employment, job, occupation; use.*
   Tiene un buen empleo. *He has a good job.*
   El empleo de esa palabra no es correcto. *That word is not used correctly.*

emprender *to undertake, to take up, to set off.*

empresa *f. company; undertaking; enterprise.*

empresario *m. impresario, contractor, manager.*

empréstito *m. loan.*

empujar *to push.*
   ¡No me empuje! *Don't push me!*

empuje *m. push; impulse.*
   Es un hombre de empuje. *He's an energetic man.*

empujón *m. push; shove.*
   A empujones. *By fits and starts.*

EN *in, into, on, at, by.*
   Lo tengo en la mano. *I have it in my hand.*
   En buen estado. *In good condition.*
   Entremos en esta tienda. *Let's go into this store.*
   Métase en la cama. *Get into bed.*
   He venido en avión. *I came by plane.*

¿En qué fecha? *On what date?*

En casa. *At home.*

En vano. *In vain.*

En general. *In general.*

En adelante. *From now on.*

En cambio. *On the other hand.*

En vez (lugar) de. *Instead of.*

En todas partes. *Everywhere.*

En medio de. *In the middle (midst) of.*

En seguida. *Right away.*

enamorado *adj. in love.*

enamorarse *to fall in love.*

enano *m. dwarf; midget.*

encabezar *to write a heading; to register, to enroll; to head.*

encadenar *to chain, to link together.*

encajar *to fit in; to gear; to inlay; to palm, to pass off.*

encaje *m. lace.*

encaminar *to guide; to direct.*

encaminarse *to be on the way; to take the road to.*

encanecer *to turn gray, to grow old.*

encantador *adj. charming.*

Es una chica encantadora. *She's charming. She's a charming girl.*

encantar *to enchant; to delight; to fascinate.*

Me encantan las flores. *I love (am fond of) flowers.*

Quedaré encantado. *I shall be delighted.*

encanto *m. charm; delight; fascination.*

Es un encanto de criatura. *She's a charming girl.*

encapricharse *to become stubborn; to be infatuated; to indulge in whims.*

encarcelar *to imprison.*

encarecer *to raise the price; to urge.*

Ha encarecido el precio de la carne. *The price of meat has gone up.*

encargado *m. person in charge; agent.*

encargar *to ask, to have someone go on an errand; to entrust; to undertake; to instruct.*

Le encargué que me lo comprara. *I asked her to buy it for me.*

encargarse *to take charge, to take care.*

¿Quién se encargará de los niños? *Who'll take care of the children?*

encargo *m. request; errand; order, charge.*

encarnado *adj. red; m. flesh color.*

Se puso encarnada. *She blushed.*

encendedor *m. cigarette lighter.*

encender *to kindle; to light; to incite.*

Haga el favor de encender la luz. *Please put on the light.*

encendido *m. ignition.*

encerar *to wax.*

encerrar *to close in, to shut up, to confine; to contain.*

encerrarse *to lock oneself in; to live in seclusion.*

encía *f. gum (of the teeth).*

ENCIMA *above, over, at the top.*

Encima de la mesa. *On the table.*

Encima de los árboles. *Above the trees.*

Por encima. *Superficially.*

Por encima de todo. *Above all.*

Estar muy por encima de. *To be far and away above.*

¿Cuánto dinero lleva Ud. encima? *How much money do you have with you?*

encinta *adj. pregnant.*

encoger *to shrink.*

encolar *to glue.*

encomendar *to commend; to entrust; to praise, to extol.*

encomendarse *to commit oneself, to place oneself into the hands of.*

encomienda *f. parcel; parcel post (Amer.).*

ENCONTRAR *to find; to meet.*

¿Encontraste lo que buscabas? *Did you find what you were looking for?*

¿Cómo encuentra Ud. el trabajo? *How do you find the work?*

ENCONTRARSE *to meet, to come across; to clash; to differ with; to be, to feel.*

¿Cómo se encuentra Ud.? *How do you feel?*

Hoy me encuentro mejor. *I feel better today.*

Me encontré con Juan en la calle. *I met John in the street.*

encorvado *adj. bent; curved.*

encrespar *to curl; to frizzle.*

encresparse *to become rough (sea); to be involved (in an affair).*

encubrir *to hide, to conceal.*

ENCUENTRO *m. meeting; encounter.*

encharcar *to form puddles; to inundate.*

enchilada *f. a Mexican corn-flour pancake with chili alone, beef and bean, or chili mixed with meat, fowl, or seafood.*

enchufar *to plug in; to fit one tube into another; to telescope.*

enchufe *m. plug, socket; coupling, joint (for pipes).*

enderezar *to straighten; to set right.*

endeudarse *to get into debt.*

endosar *to endorse.*

endurecer *to harden, to make hard.*

ene *f. name of the letter* **n**.

enemigo *adj. unfriendly, hostile; m. enemy, foe.*

Es enemigo del tabaco. *He's against the use of tobacco.*

enemistad *f. enmity; hatred.*

energía *f. energy, power.*

Crisis de energía. *Energy crisis.*

Energía nuclear. *Nuclear energy.*

Energía solar. *Solar energy.*

enérgico *adj. energetic.*

ENERO *m. January.*

enfadar *to annoy, to make someone angry.*

enfadarse *to get angry, to become angry.*

enfado *m. anger.*

enfermar *to get ill; to fall sick.*

Ud. va a acabar por enfermarse. *You'll end up by getting sick.*

enfermizo *adj. infirm, not healthy, sickly.*

enfermo *adj. ill, sick; m. patient.*

Me siento enfermo. *I feel ill. I don't feel well.*

Está gravemente enfermo. *He's very ill.*

¿Cómo sigue el enfermo? *How is the patient getting along?*

enfocar *to focus.*

enfrentar *to face, to confront.*

ENFRENTE *in front of, opposite.*

El automóvil está parado enfrente de aquel edificio. *The car's parked in front of that building.*

Viven en la casa de enfrente. *They live in the house across the street.*

enfriamiento *m. cooling; refrigeration; cold.*

Enfriamiento por aire. *Air cooling.*

enfriar *to cool.*

enfriarse *to cool off, to get cool.*

enfurecer *to infuriate, to enrage.*

enfurecerse *to become furious.*

enganchar *to hook; to get caught; to hitch; to couple; to recruit.*

engañar *to deceive, to fool.*

engañarse *to deceive oneself.*

Ud. se engaña. *You're deceiving (fooling) yourself.*

engañoso *adj. deceitful; tricky.*

engendrar *to bring into existence; to produce, to create.*

engordar *to fatten; to grow fat.*

engranaje *m. gear.*

engrasar *to grease, to lubricate.*

engrase *m. lubrication.*

enhorabuena *f. congratulation.*

¡La enhorabuena! *Congratulations!*

enjabonar *to soap; to wash with soap.*

enjaular *to cage; to imprison.*

enjuagar *to rinse.*

enjuague *m. rinse.*

Enjuague dental. *Mouthwash.*

enjugar *to dry; to wipe off.*

enlace *m. connection; marriage; liaison, wedding, joining.*

El enlace de trenes es excelente en esta estación. *The train connections are excellent at this station.*

Un feliz enlace. *A happy marriage.*

enlazar *to join, to bind, to connect; to catch with a lasso.*

enmendar *to correct, to amend, to reform.*

enmudecer *to silence.*

enmudecerse *to become dumb; to be silent.*

enojado *adj. angry, cross.*

Estar enojado. *To be angry.*

enojar *to irritate, to make angry.*

enojarse *to get angry.*

enredar *to entangle; to make trouble; to upset.*

enredarse *to become entangled.*

enredo *m. entanglement.*

enriquecer *to enrich; to improve.*

enriquecerse *to get rich.*

ENROLLAR *to roll, to entangle, to get involved.*

enronquecerse *to become hoarse.*

ensalada *f. salad.*

Ensalada mixta. *Tossed salad.*

ENSAYAR *to try, to rehearse, to test.*

ensayarse *to train, to practice.*

ensayo *m. trial; rehearsal.*

enseñanza *f. teaching, instruction.*

ENSEÑAR *to teach; to point out, to show.*

¿Quiere Ud. enseñarme a hablar español? *Would you like to teach me to speak Spanish?*

Enseñe Ud. el camino al señor. *Show this gentleman the way.*

No se lo enseñe a ella. *Don't show it to her.*

enseñarse *to accustom oneself.*

ensordecer *to deafen.*

ensordecerse *to become deaf.*

ensordecimiento *m. deafness.*

ensuciar *to dirty, to soil.*

ensuciarse *to get dirty; to lower oneself.*

entablar *to begin, to start.*

Entablar demanda. *To bring a lawsuit.*

entender *m. understanding; opinion.*

A mi entender. *In my opinion.*

ENTENDER *to understand.*

¿Entiende Ud. español? *Do you understand Spanish?*

No pude entender lo que decían. *I couldn't understand what they were saying.*

Entendido. *It's understood.*

Es un obrero muy entendido en su oficio. *He's very skilled in his trade.*

Según tenemos entendido. *As far as we know.*

Entender de. *To be an expert in. To be familiar with.*

entenderse *to understand one another; to come to an understanding, to agree, to arrange; to be understood; to be meant.*

Entenderse con. *To have to do with. To*

deal with. To come to an
understanding with. To arrange with.

entendimiento m. understanding.

enteramente entirely, completely, quite,
fully.

enterar to inform, to acquaint.
Estamos enterados de sus planes. We know
what his plans are.

enterarse to learn, to find out.
Entérate de cuando sale el tren. Find out
when the train leaves.
Acabo de enterarme de la noticia. I've just
heard the news.

enternecer to soften; to move, to touch.

enternecerse to pity; to be affected with
emotion, to be moved.

ENTERO adj. entire, whole, complete.
Por entero. Entirely. Completely.
Color entero. Solid color.

enterrar to bury.

entidad f. entity.

entierro m. interment, burial, funeral.

entonación f. intonation; tone.

entonar to tune, to intone.

ENTONCES then, at that time.
Era entonces un niño. He was a child then.
Por entonces. At the time.
Desde entonces. Since then. From then on.

ENTRADA f. entrance; entry; admission;
ticket; entree; input (computer).
¿Cuánto cuesta la entrada? How much is
the admission?
Debemos comprar las entradas ahora
mismo. We have to buy the tickets
right away.
¿Qué desea Ud. como entrada? What would
you like as an entree?
"Se prohibe la entrada." "No
admittance."
Entrada libre. Admission free.

entrante adj. entering; coming; next (day,
week, month, etc.); m. next month.

ENTRAR to enter, to go in; to fit in.
¿Se puede entrar? May I come in?
Que no entre nadie. Don't let anyone
come in.

ENTRE between; in; among.
Lo hicieron entre los dos. They did it
between the two of them.
Mire entre los papeles. Look among the
papers.
Parta Ud. 300 entre 3. Divide 300 by 3.
Reírse entre sí. To laugh to oneself.
Entre manos. In hand.
Por entre. Through.

entreacto m. intermission.

entrega f. delivery; surrender.
Entrega a domicilio. Home delivery.
Entrega inmediata. Special delivery.

entregar to deliver; to surrender.
¿A quién ha entregado Ud. la carta?
Who(m) did you give the letter to?
No han entregado la mercancía todavía.
They haven't delivered the goods yet.

entregarse to take to, to abandon oneself to;
to give oneself up.
El criminal se entregó a la policía. The
criminal gave himself up to the
police.
Se ha entregado a la embriaguez. He's
taken to drink.

entremés m. hors d'oeuvre, appetizer; short
play.

entremeter to place between, to insert.

entremeterse to meddle, to intrude, to
interfere.

entremetido m. meddler, busybody, intruder.

entrenador m. coach, trainer.

entrenamiento m. training.

entrenar to train, to coach.

entresuelo m. mezzanine.

ENTRETANTO meanwhile.

ENTRETENER to entertain, to amuse; to
put off, to delay.

entretenido adj. pleasant, amusing.

entretenimiento m. amusement,
entertainment.

entrevista f. interview, conference.

entristecer to grieve, to be unhappy.

entristecerse to be sad, to become sad.

entrometer. See **entremeter.**

enturbiar to make muddy; to muddle.

entusiasmar to fill with enthusiasm; to elate.

entusiasmarse to become enthusiastic.

entusiasmo m. enthusiasm.

entusiasta adj. enthusiastic; m. and f.
enthusiast

envasar to can; to package; to bottle.

envase m. container, packaging.

envejecer to make old; to grow old.

envenenar to poison.

ENVIAR to send; to dispatch.
¿Puede Ud. enviar mi equipaje al hotel?
Can you send my luggage to the
hotel?
Enviaron a buscar al médico. They sent
someone for the doctor.

envidia f. envy.

envidiable adj. enviable.

envidiar to envy.

envidioso adj. envious, jealous.

envío m. sending, remittance, shipment.

enviudar to become a widow or a widower.

envoltorio m. bundle.

envolver to wrap up, to make into a
package; to surround, to envelop; to
disguise.

época f. epoch, age, era, period.

equipaje m. baggage; equipment; crew (of a ship).
    Coche de equipaje. Baggage car.
    Equipaje de mano. Hand luggage.
equipar to equip, to furnish.
equipo m. equipment; team (sports).
equis f. name of the letter **x.**
equivocación f. mistake.
EQUIVOCADO adj. mistaken, wrong.
    Ud. está muy equivocado. You're entirely mistaken.
    Número equivocado. Wrong number.
equivocar to mistake.
EQUIVOCARSE to be wrong, to make a mistake.
    Se equivoca Ud. You're wrong. You're making a mistake.
era f. era; age, time.
ere f. name of the letter **r.**
erario m. public funds.
erección f. erection.
erguir to erect, to raise.
erigir to erect, to build; to establish.
ERRAR to err, to go wrong, to make a mistake, to miss; to wander.
    Todos somos susceptibles de errar. We are all liable to make mistakes.
    Errar el tiro. To miss the target.
errata f. erratum, error in writing or printing.
erre f. name of the letter **rr.**
ERROR m. error, fault, mistake.
erudición f. erudition, learning.
erudito adj. erudite, learned; m. scholar, erudite person.
ESA (f. of **ese**) that; pl. **esas** those.
    Esa mujer. That woman.
    Vamos por esa calle. Let's go down that street.
    No se ocupe Ud. de esas cosas. Don't pay any attention to such things.
ÉSA (f. of **ése**) that, that one, that person, that thing; pl. **ésas** those.
    Ésa es su mujer. That (woman) is his wife.
    Deme ésa. Give me that one.
    Ni por ésas. Not even so. Not even for those.
esbelto adj. slim, slender; elegant.
escabeche m. pickle; pickled fish.
escabroso adj. rugged, harsh; smutty.
escala f. stepladder; scale; port of call.
    Hacer escala en. To stop. To call at a port.
escalera f. staircase; ladder.
escalofrío m. chill.
    Tengo escalofríos. I have the chills.
escamoteo m. juggling; swindling.
escapar to escape, to flee.
escaparate m. show window, glass case; cupboard; cabinet.

escape m. escape.
escarabajo m. beetle; scribbling.
escarbar to scratch (as fowls); to dig; to poke (fire); to probe.
escarcha f. frost.
escaso adj. scarce, scanty; short of.
    Estoy escaso de dinero. I'm short of money.
escena f. stage; scene; view; episode.
    Poner en escena. To stage (produce) a play.
escenario m. stage (theater).
escenográfico adj. scenic.
escéptico adj. skeptical; m. a skeptic.
esclavitud f. slavery.
esclavo m. slave.
escoba f. broom.
ESCOGER to choose, to pick out.
escogido adj. selected, choice.
escolta f. escort.
escoltar to escort.
escombro m. debris, rubbish.
esconder to hide, to conceal.
esconderse to hide, to remain hidden.
escondido adj. hidden.
escopeta f. shotgun.
escorpión m. scorpion.
escribano m. notary.
ESCRIBIR to write.
    Escriba claro. Write clearly.
    ¿Cómo se escribe esa palabra? How is that word written (spelled)? How do you write that word?
    Escriba Ud. a estas señas. Address it this way. Write this address.
    Escribir a máquina. To type.
escrito adj. written; m. writing; manuscript; communication.
    Por escrito. In writing.
escritor m. writer, author.
escritorio m. writing desk.
escritura f. writing; deed.
    Escritura social. Deed of a partnership.
    Escritura de préstamo. Loan agreement.
escrutinio m. scrutiny; election returns.
escuadra f. fleet; squad; square (instrument).
ESCUCHAR to listen; to heed.
    Escúcheme Ud. Listen to me.
    No quiere escuchar razones. He won't listen to reason.
escudo m. shield; Chilean monetary unit.
ESCUELA f. school; schoolhouse.
escupir to spit.
escurrir to drain; to wring; to slip; to glide.
ese f. name of the letter **s.**
ESE (demonstrative adjective m.) that; pl. **esos** those.
    Ese hombre. That man.
    Esos hombres. Those men.

ÉSE (*demonstrative pronoun m.*) *that, that one, that person, that thing; pl.* **ésos** *those.*
  Dígale a ése que no venga. *Tell that man not to come.*
  Ésos no saben lo que dicen. *Those men don't know what they're talking about.*

esencia *f. essence.*

esencial *adj. essential.*

esfera *f. sphere.*

esforzar *to strengthen; to force, to strain.*

esforzarse *to try hard, to endeavor, to strive, to make an effort.*

esfuerzo *m. effort; endeavor.*
  Es inútil hacer mayores esfuerzos. *It's useless to continue trying ("to make further efforts").*

esgrima *f. fencing.*

eslabón *m. link (of a chain).*

esmalte *m. enamel, nail polish.*

esmaltar *to enamel, to polish one's nails.*

esmeradamente *with the greatest care; nicely.*

esmerado *adj. done with care, carefully done.*

esmeralda *f. emerald.*

esmerar *to polish.*

esmerarse *to do one's best.*
  Se esmera en todo. *She tries her hardest in everything (she does).*

ESO (*neuter of* esea *and* ésa) *it; that, that thing.*
  Eso es. *That's it.*
  Eso de. *That matter of.*
  A eso de. *At about. Toward.*
  Por eso. *Therefore. For that reason.*
  ¿Cómo es eso? *How's that?*
  Eso no me gusta. *I don't like that.*
  Eso no me importa. *That makes no difference to me. That doesn't matter to me.*

espaciado *m. spacing.*

espaciador *m. space bar.*

ESPACIO *m. space, room; distance.*
  Un pequeño espacio de terreno. *A small piece of land.*
  Anduvimos por espacio de dos horas. *We walked for two hours.*

espada *f. sword; spade (cards).*
  De capa e espada. *Cloak and dagger.*

ESPALDA *f. back.*
  ¿ Siente Ud. dolor en la espalda? *Does your back ache?*
  A espaldas. *Behind one's back.*
  Dar la espalda. *To turn one's back.*

espantar *to frighten; to chase out.*

espantarse *to be frightened.*

espanto *m. fright.*

espantosamente *frightfully.*

espantoso *adj. frightful.*

España *f. Spain.*

español *adj. and n. Spanish; Spaniard; m. Spanish language.*
  Yo soy español *I'm a Spaniard.*
  Aquí se habla español. *Spanish spoken here.*

esparadrapo *m. adhesive tape.*

esparcir *to scatter; to divulge, to make public.*

especial *adj. special, particular.*
  En especial. *Especially. Specially. In particular.*

especialidad *f. specialty.*

especie *f. species; motive; kind, sort.*

espectáculo *m. spectacle, show.*

espectador *m. spectator.*

especulación *f. speculation.*

especular *to speculate.*

espejo *m. looking glass, mirror.*
  Mírese Ud. al espejo. *Look at yourself in the mirror.*

espera *f. waiting; pause; adjournment.*
  ¿Dónde está la sala de espera? *Where's the waiting room?*

esperanza *f. hope.*

ESPERAR *to hope; to expect, to wait for.*
  Así lo espero. *I hope so.*
  Espero que no. *I hope not.*
  Espéreme. *Wait for me.*
  ¿Espera Ud. visitas? *Do you expect company?*
  Espero volver a verle. *I hope I'll see you again.*

espeso *adj. thick, dense.*

espía *m. and f. spy.*

espiga *f. ear (of corn, wheat, etc.); peg.*

espina *f. thorn; splinter; fishbone; spine.*

espinaca *f. spinach.*

espíritu *m. spirit, soul.*

espiritual *adj. spiritual.*

espléndido *adj. splendid, magnificent; brilliant.*

esplendor *m. splendor, magnificence.*

ESPOSA *f. wife.*

esposas *f. pl. handcuffs.*

ESPOSO *m. husband.*

espuela *f. spur; incentive.*

espuma *f. foam, froth.*

esquela *f. note, slip of paper; death notice.*

esquí *m. ski.*
  Esquí acuático. *Water skiing.*

esquiar *to ski.*

ESQUINA *f. corner.*
  Doblar la esquina. *To turn the corner.*
  A la vuelta de la esquina. *Around the corner.*

ESTA (*f. of* este) *this; pl.* **estas** *these.*
  Esta mujer y aquel hombre son hermanos.

This woman and that man are brother and sister.

Hágalo de esta manera. *Do it this way. Do it in this manner.*

Esta mañana. *This morning.*

Esta noche. *Tonight.*

A estas horas. *At the present time. By now.*

ÉSTA (*f. of* **éste**) *this, this one, the latter; pl.* **éstas** *these.*

En ésta no hay novedad. *There's nothing new here.*

Ésta y aquélla. *This one and that one.*

establecer *to establish.*

establecerse *to establish oneself, to set up in business.*

Un nuevo médico acaba de establecerse en esta calle. *A new doctor has just opened his office on this street.*

Esto es lo que establece la ley. *This is what the law provides.*

establo *m. stable.*

ESTACIÓN *f. station; railroad station; season of the year.*

¿Dónde está la estación? *Where is the station?*

El invierno es la estación más fría del año. *Winter is the coldest season of the year.*

estacionamiento *m. parking lot.*

estacionar *to stop; to park.*

ESTADO *m. state; condition.*

¿Cómo sigue el estado del enfermo? *How is the patient's condition?*

En buen estado. *In good condition.*

Estado de cuenta. *Statement (of an account).*

Hombre de estado. *Statesman.*

Ministerio de Estado. *State Department.*

Estado Mayor. *General Staff.*

Estado de guerra. *State of war.*

Estados Unidos de América *m. pl. United States of America.*

Ella está en estado. *She's pregnant.*

estadounidense *m. and f. North American (from U.S.A.).*

estafa *f. fraud, trick, swindle.*

estampa *f. picture; print; stamp.*

estampilla *f. postage stamp (Amer.).*

estancia *f. stay; ranch (in Latin America).*

estanco *m. cigar store (Spain).*

estanque *m. pond; reservoir.*

estante *m. shelf.*

Estante para libros. *Bookcase.*

estaño *m. tin (metal).*

ESTAR *to be.*

¿Cómo está Ud? *How are you?*

Estoy bien, gracias. *I'm well, thank you.*

Estoy cansado. *I'm tired.*

Estamos listos. *We're ready.*

¿Qué está haciendo? *What are you doing?*

Estoy afeitándome. *I'm shaving.*

¿Dónde está Juan? *Where's John?*

Está en la oficina. *He's at the office.*

He estado en Washington. *I've been in Washington.*

¿Dónde está el correo? *Where's the post office?*

Está cerca. *It's near.*

Está en la calle de Alcalá. *It's on Alcala Street.*

Boston está en los Estados Unidos. *Boston is in the United States.*

Hay que estar allí a las nueve. *We must be there at nine.*

Estaré de vuelta a las cinco. *I'll be back at five o'clock.*

¿A cuánto estamos? *What's the date?*

Hoy estamos a diez. *Today's the tenth.*

La ventana está abierta. *The window's open.*

Está muy nublado. *It's very cloudy.*

Estar de viaje. *To be on a journey.*

Estar de prisa. *To be in a hurry.*

Estar de pie. *To stand. To be on one's feet.*

estático *adj. and m. static.*

estatua *f. statue.*

estatura *f. stature, height of a person.*

estatuto *m. statute, law, by-law.*

ESTE *m. east.*

Esa calle está al este de la ciudad. *This street is on the east side of the city.*

ESTE (*demonstrative adj. m.*) *this; pl.* **estos** *these.*

Éste hombre. *This man.*

Estos libros. *These books.*

ÉSTE (*demonstrative pron. m.*) *this, this one; pl.* **éstos** *these.*

Éste es el mío y aquél es el tuyo. *This one is mine and that one is yours.*

Éstos y aquéllos. *These and those.*

Éstos no saben lo que dicen. *These men don't know what they're talking about.*

estenógrafa *f. stenographer.*

estibador *m. stevedore, longshoreman.*

estilar *to be customary, to be in the habit of.*

ESTILO *m. style, manner; method, way.*

Por el estilo. *Of the kind. Like that. In that manner.*

Y así por el estilo. *And so forth.*

estima *f. esteem, respect; dead reckoning (navigation).*

estimación *f. estimation, valuation.*

estimar *to esteem; to estimate, to deem.*

Era muy estimado de cuantos le conocían. *He was held in esteem by all who knew him.*

Se estima que este trabajo costará mil dólares. *It's estimated that this work will cost a thousand dollars.*

estimular *to stimulate.*

estímulo *m. stimulus.*

estirar *to stretch; to pull.*

estirarse *to stretch, to put on airs.*

estirpe *f. race, stock, origin.*

ESTO *(neuter) this; this thing.*
  ¿Qué es esto? *What's this?*
  ¿Para qué sirve esto? *What's this for?*
  Esto es mío. *This belongs to me.*
  Todo esto es muy divertido. *All this is very amusing.*
  Esto es todo cuanto tengo que decir. *This is all I have to say.*
  Por esto. *For this. Hereby. Therefore. For this reason. On account of this.*
  En esto. *At this time. At this juncture.*
  Con esto. *Herewith.*
  Esto es. *That is. Namely.*

estocado *f. stab, thrust.*

estofado *m. stew; stewed meat.*

estómago *m. stomach.*

estoque *m. stock.*

estorbar *to hinder, to be in the way.*
  ¿Le estorba a Ud. esta maleta? *Is this suitcase in your way?*

estorbo *m. nuisance.*

estornudar *to sneeze.*

estornudo *m. sneeze.*

estrategia *f. strategy.*

estratégico *adj. strategic.*

estrechar *to tighten; to narrow; to squeeze.*
  Estrechar la mano. *To shake hands.*

estrechez *f. tightness, narrowness.*

estrecho *adj. tight, narrow.*

estrella *f. star.*
  Estrella de cine. *Movie star.*

estrellar *to dash, to hurl, to shatter; to fry (eggs).*
  Por poco nos estrellamos. *We had a narrow escape.*
  ¿Quiere los huevos estrellados? *Do you want your eggs fried?*

estremecer *to shake, to tremble.*

estremecerse *to shudder, to tremble, to shake.*

estremecimiento *m. tremor; shudder; trembling, shaking; thrill.*

estrenar *to wear or put on something for the first time; to show for the first time.*
  Estrené este traje ayer. *I wore this suit for the first time yesterday.*

estrenarse *to appear for the first time, to make one's debut.*
  La película se estrena el viernes. *The film opens on Friday.*

estreno *m. première, first public performance.*

estreñimiento *m. constipation.*

estrés *m. stress*

estricto *adj. strict.*

estropear *to ruin, to damage, to spoil.*

estructura *f. structure.*

estruendo *m. loud noise, din, clatter; turmoil; ostentation.*

estuche *m. case, small box, kit.*

estudiante *m. and f. student.*

ESTUDIAR *to study.*

ESTUDIO *m. study; examination; consideration; survey; office; studio.*
  Están haciendo un estudio de la situación. *They're making a survey of the situation.*
  Estar en estudio. *To be under consideration (study).*
  El estudio del pintor. *The painter's studio.*
  Estudio cinematográfico. *Film studio.*

estudioso *adj. studious.*

estufa *f. stove; heater.*
  Arrímese a la estufa. *Draw up (come closer) to the heater.*

estupendo *adj. stupendous, wonderful, terrific, great.*

estupidez *f. stupidity.*

estúpido *adj. stupid.*

etapa *f. stage, phase.*

etcétera *f. et cetera.*

éter *m. ether.*

eternidad *f. eternity.*

eterno *adj. eternal, everlasting, endless.*

ética *f. ethics.*

ético *adj. ethical, moral.*

etiqueta *f. etiquette; label.*
  Vestido de etiqueta. *Evening dress.*
  ¿Qué dice la etiqueta de la botella? *What does the label on the bottle say?*

evacuación *f. evacuation.*

evacuar *to evacuate; to quit; to vacate; to move the bowels.*

evadir *to evade; to avoid.*

evaluación *f. evaluation.*

evaluar *to appraise, to value.*

evalúo *m. appraisal.*

evangelio *m. gospel.*

evaporar *to evaporate.*

evasión *f. evasion, escape.*

evasiva *f. pretext, excuse; subterfuge.*

evasivo *adj. evasive.*

evento *m. event.*

eventual *adj. eventual.*

evidencia *f. evidence.*
  Poner en evidencia. *To make evident (clear, obvious). To make conspicuous.*

evidente *adj. evident.*

evitable *adj. avoidable.*

EVITAR *to avoid; to spare.*
  Evitar un disgusto. *To avoid an unpleasant situation.*

evocar *to evoke.*
evolución *f. evolution.*
exactamente *exactly.*
exactitud *f. accuracy.*
EXACTO *adj. exact, just, accurate, correct.*
exageración *f. exaggeration.*
exagerar *to exaggerate.*
exaltación *f. exaltation.*
exaltar *to exalt, to praise.*
exaltarse *to become excited.*
examen *m. examination; test.*
EXAMINAR *to examine, to investigate, to look into, to study.*
exasperación *f. exasperation.*
exasperar *to exasperate.*
excedente *adj. excessive.*
exceder *to exceed.*
excederse *to overstep, to go too far.*
excelencia *f. excellence.*
EXCELENTE *adj. excellent.*
excepción *f. exception.*
excepcional *adj. exceptional, unusual.*
excepto *except that, excepting.*
exceptuar *to except, to exempt.*
excesivo *adj. excessive, too much.*
exceso *m. excess, surplus.*
  En exceso. *In excess.*
  Exceso de equipaje. *Excess luggage.*
excitable *adj. excitable.*
excitación *f. excitement.*
excitante *adj. exciting.*
excitar *to excite, to stir up.*
exclamación *f. exclamation.*
exclamar *to exclaim.*
excluir *to exclude, to keep out; to rule out.*
exclusión *f. exclusion*
exclusiva *f. exclusive (right); refusal, rejection.*
exclusivamente *exclusively.*
exclusivo *exclusive.*
excursión *f. excursion, trip.*
excusa *f. excuse, apology.*
excusable *adj. excusable.*
excusado *adj. excused, exempted; m. toilet.*
excusar *to excuse; to apologize; to exempt.*
  Excusamos decir. *It's needless to say.*
  Excusarse de. *To refuse to.*
exención *f. exemption.*
exento *adj. exempt, free; duty free.*
  Estar exento de. *To be exempt from. To be free from.*
exhalar *to exhale.*
exhibición *f. exhibition.*
exhibir *to exhibit.*
exhortar *to exhort, to admonish.*
exigencia *f. urgent need; demand for immediate action or attention, exigency.*
exigente *adj. demanding, hard to please.*

  Es muy exigente. *He's a very hard person to please.*
  No seas tan exigente. *Don't be so difficult (demanding, hard to please, particular).*
exigir *to demand; to require; to exact.*
  Lo exigen las circunstancias.
  The situation requires it.
eximir *to exempt, to excuse.*
existencia *f. existence; stock, supply.*
  En existencia. *In stock.*
  Agotarse las existencias. *To be out of stock.*
existente *adj. existing, existent.*
EXISTIR *to exist, to be.*
  En mi opinión existen pruebas bastante claras de ello. *There are, it seems to me, pretty strong proofs of it.*
ÉXITO *m. success.*
  Le felicito por el éxito obtenido. *I congratulate you on your success.*
exoneración *f. exoneration, release.*
expedición *f. expedition; shipment.*
  Gastos de expedición. *Shipping expenses.*
expedidor *m. dispatcher, sender.*
expediente *m. expedient; document, dossier; proceedings*
  Incoar expediente. *To start proceedings.*
EXPEDIR *to expedite; to dispatch, to send, to forward; to issue, to make out (a check, etc.).*
expeler *to expel.*
expensas *f. pl. expenses, charges, costs.*
  A expensas de. *At the expense of.*
experiencia *f. experience; trial.*
experimentar *to try on/out; to experience.*
experimento *m. experiment.*
experto *adj. experienced; able; m. expert.*
explicable. *adj. explainable.*
explicación *f. explanation.*
EXPLICAR *to explain.*
  Déjeme Ud. que se lo explique. *Let me explain it to you.*
explicarse *to explain oneself; to account for.*
  No podemos explicárnoslo. *We can't make it out (account for it.).*
explicativo *adj. explanatory.*
explícito *adj. explicit.*
exploración *f. exploration.*
explorador *m. explorer, scout.*
explorar *to explore.*
explosión *f. explosion, outbursts.*
  Hacer explosión. *To explode.*
explotar *to exploit; to operate; to profiteer.*
exponente *m. and f. exponent; exhibitor.*
exponer *to expound, to explain; to make clear; to expose*
exponerse *to expose oneself; to run a risk.*
exportación *f. export.*

exportador *adj. exporting; m. exporter.*
   Casa exportadora. *Export house (firm).*
exportar *to export.*
exposición *f. exposition, show, exhibition; explanation; peril, risk, exposure; statement.*
expositor *m. exhibitor; exponent.*
expresar *to express; to set forth, to state.*
expresarse *to express oneself.*
expresión *f. expression.*
expresivo *adj. expressive.*
expreso *adj. express; clear; m. express (train); special delivery.*
exprimidor *m. squeezer; wringer.*
exprimir *to squeeze.*
   Exprimir un limón. *To squeeze a lemon.*
expuesto *adj. explained, stated; exposed (to); liable (to).*
   Lo expuesto. *What has been stated.*
   Todos estamos expuestos a equivocarnos. *Anyone is liable (apt) to make a mistake.*
expulsar *to expel, to eject, to throw out.*
expulsión *f. expulsion.*
exquisito *adj. exquisite, excellent, choice.*
extender *to extend, to stretch out; to make out (a check, a document).*
extensión *f. extension, extent.*
   En toda su extensión. *To the full extent. In every sense.*
extensivo *adj. extensive, ample, far-reaching.*
extenso *adj. extensive, vast.*
extenuación *f. extenuation.*
extenuar *to extenuate.*
exterior *adj. exterior; foreign.*
   Comercio exterior. *Foreign trade.*
   Política exterior. *Foreign policy.*
externo *adj. external, on the outside.*
extinguir *to extinguish; to put out.*
extra *extra.*
extractar *to extract, to abridge, to summarize.*
extracto *m. extract, abridgment, summary.*
extraer *to extract, to pull out.*
EXTRANJERO *adj. foreign; m. foreigner, alien.*
   Estar en el extranjero. *To be abroad.*
   Ir al extranjero. *To go abroad.*
extrañar *to wonder at, to find strange.*
   No es de extrañar que. *It's not surprising that.*
extrañarse *to be surprised.*
   Me extraña su conducta. *I'm surprised at his behavior.*
extrañeza *f. wonder, surprise.*
extraño *strange, rare, odd, queer.*
   Es un hombre extraño. *He's a queer fellow.*
extraoficial *adj. unofficial, off the record.*
extraordinario *adj. extraordinary.*

Tiene una memoria extraordinaria. *He has an extraordinary memory.*
extravagancia *f. folly; extravagance.*
extravagante *adj. odd, extravagant.*
extraviado *adj. astray; missing; mislaid.*
extraviar *to mislead; to mislay.*
extraviarse *to go astray; to get lost.*
extravío *m. straying; deviation, misplacement; misguidance.*
extremadamente *extremely, exceedingly.*
extremar *to go to extremes.*
extremarse *to exert oneself to the utmost.*
extremidad *f. extremity; very end.*
extremo *adj. and n. extreme, last, very end.*
   En caso extremo. *As a last resort.*
   Al extremo de que. *To such an extent that.*
   De extremo a extremo. *From end to end.*
   En extremo (Por extremo). *Extremely.*

F

fa *m. fa, F (fourth note in the musical scale).*
fabada *f. dish of pork and beans.*
fábrica *f. factory, mill, plant; fabrication; structure, building.*
fabricación *f. manufacturing.*
fabricante *m. manufacturer.*
fabricar *to manufacture, to make; to build.*
fábula *f. fable, story, tale.*
fabuloso *adj. fabulous; incredible.*
FÁCIL *adj. easy.*
   Parece fácil pero es difícil. *It looks easy but it's difficult.*
facilidad *f. ease, facility.*
   Con facilidad. *Easily. With ease.*
   Facilidad de pagos. *Easy terms. Easy payments.*
facilitar *to facilitate, to make easy; to supply, to provide.*
   Facilitar dinero. *To supply (provide) money.*
fácilmente *easily.*
   A mí no se me engaña tan fácilmente. *You can't fool me that easily.*
   No puedo expresarme fácilmente. *I can't express myself easily.*
factor *m. factor, element; agent.*
factoría *f. factory (U.S. Spanish).*
factura *f. invoice, bill.*
   ¿A cuánto monta la factura? *What does the bill amount to?*
   La factura sube a mil pesetas. *The invoice amounts to one thousand pesetas.*
facturación *f. billing, invoicing.*
facturar *to bill, to invoice; to check (baggage).*
   Tendrá que facturar el baúl. *You'll have to check the trunk.*

facultad *f. faculty; school.*

facultar *to authorize, to empower.*

facultativo *adj. optional; m. physician.*

facha *f. appearance, look.*

fachada *f. façade; bearing (of a person).*

faena *f. work, task, labor.*

faja *f. band; girdle.*

fajar *to band; to girdle.*

fajo *m. bundle; roll (bills).*

falda *f. skirt; the lap.*

falsear *to falsify; to forge, to distort, to adulterate.*

falsedad *f. falsehood, untruth.*

falsificación *f. falsification; forgery.*

falsificar *to falsify; to forge.*

falso *adj. false; incorrect; deceitful; counterfeit.*

    Esta noticia es falsa. *This news is false.*

    Me han dado una moneda falsa. *They've given me a counterfeit coin.*

FALTA *f. fault; defect; need; lack; absence, mistake.*

    Tenemos que disculpar sus faltas. *We must excuse his faults.*

    Hacer falta. *To be needed. To be necessary.*

    ¿Qué le hace falta? *What do you need?*

    No hace falta. *It's not necessary. It's not needed.*

    Sin falta. *Without fail.*

    Tener falta de. *To be in need of.*

    Por falta de. *For lack of. Owing to the shortage of.*

    Falta de pago. *Non-payment.*

FALTAR *to be lacking; to be absent; to miss (classes); to fail; not to fulfill one's promise; to offend, to be rude.*

    Aquí faltan tres libros. *Three books are missing here.*

    Me falta tiempo ahora. *I don't have time now.*

    Ud. faltó a su palabra. *You didn't keep your word.*

    Faltó a la oficina esta mañana. *He wasn't (present) at the office this morning.*

    Faltó a su padre. *He was rude to his father.*

    No faltes a clase. *Don't miss school.*

    Faltar a la verdad. *To lie.*

    No faltaba más. *That's the last straw.*

falto *adj. wanting, lacking, short of.*

    Estar falto de. *To be short of.*

    Falto de peso. *Underweight. Lacking the proper weight.*

falla *f. failure; fault.*

fallar *to deliver a verdict, pronounce a sentence; to fail.*

fallecer *to die.*

    Falleció repentinamente. *He died suddenly.*

fallo *m. sentence, verdict, judgment, finding, decision.*

    El juez dio el fallo. *The judge gave the verdict.*

fama *f. fame; reputation; rumor.*

FAMILIA *f. family; household.*

familiar *adj. familiar; m. close friend, relative.*

famoso *adj. famous; excellent.*

fanático *adj. fanatic. fan.*

fanfarrón *adj. boasting; m. bully, boaster, braggart.*

fanfarronada *f. boast, bragging, bluff.*

fanfarronear *to boast, to brag.*

fango *m. mire, mud.*

fangoso *adj. muddy.*

fantasía *f. fantasy, fancy.*

fantasma *m. phantom; scarecrow; ghost.*

fantástico *adj. fantastic.*

fantoche *m. puppet; ridiculous fellow.*

fardo *m. bale of goods, parcel, bundle.*

faringe *f. pharynx.*

farmacéutico *m. pharmacist, druggist.*

farmacia *f. pharmacy, drugstore.*

faro *m. lighthouse; beacon; headlight.*

farol *m. lantern; street lamp; light.*

    Farol delantero. *Headlight.*

    Farol trasero (de cola). *Taillight.*

farolero *adj. conceited, showing-off; m. a braggart; a lamplighter.*

farsa *f. farce.*

farsante *adj. and n. impostor.*

fascinar *to fascinate, to charm; to allure.*

fascista *adj. and m. and f. fascist.*

fase *f. phase; aspect.*

fastidiar *to annoy, to disgust.*

fastidio *m. disgust, annoyance; boredom.*

fastidioso *adj. squeamish; annoying, disgusting; tiresome.*

fatal *adj. fatal, unfortunate.*

fatiga *f. tiredness, fatigue, weariness, toil.*

fatigado *adj. tired, fatigued.*

fatigar *to tire; to annoy.*

fatigoso *adj. tiring; tiresome.*

fatuo *adj. fatuous, stupid, silly.*

fauna *f. fauna, animal life.*

fausto *adj. happy, fortunate; m. splendor.*

FAVOR *m. favor, good turn, service; good graces.*

    Me hace Ud. un gran favor. *You're doing me a great favor (service).*

    Por favor. *Please.*

    Me hace Ud. el favor. *Please. If you please.*

    Hágame Ud. el favor de. *Please ("Do me the favor of").*

    Haga el favor de pasarme la sal. *Please pass me the salt.*

    Por favor, póngame en comunicación con

el número ... *Please connect me with number ...*

A favor de. *In favor of.*

favorable *adj. favorable.*

favorecer *to favor; to help.*

favorito *adj. favorite.*

FAX *m. fax, facsimile machine.*

faz *f. face, front.*

FE *f. faith; credit.*

Lo hizo de buena fe. *He did it in good faith.*

Lo dijo de mala fe. *He said it deceitfully.*

La fe católica. *The Catholic religion.*

Dar fe. *To attest. To certify. To give credit.*

FEBRERO *m. February.*

fecundo *adj. fruitful, productive, fecund, fertile, prolific.*

FECHA *f. date.*

¿Qué fecha es hoy? *What's the date today? What's today's date?*

¿En qué fecha estamos? *What day of the month is it?*

Hasta la fecha. *To date. Up to today.*

Para estas fechas. *By this time.*

A dos meses de la fecha. *Two months from today.*

fechar *to date (a letter).*

La carta está fechada el seis del corriente. *The letter is dated the sixth of this month.*

fechoría *f. misdeed, a wicked action.*

federación *f. federation.*

felicidad *f. happiness.*

¡Muchas felicidades! *Congratulations!*

felicitación *f. congratulation.*

Felicitaciones! *Congratulations!*

felicitar *to congratulate, to felicitate.*

Le felicito a Ud. *Congratulations! ("I congratulate you.")*

FELIZ *adj. happy, fortunate.*

¡Feliz año nuevo! *Happy New Year!*

¡Feliz cumpleaños! *Happy birthday. Many happy returns of the day.*

¡Que las tenga Ud. muy felices! *Many happy returns of the day.*

femenino *adj. feminine.*

fémur *m. femur, thigh bone.*

fenómeno *m. phenomenon.*

feo *adj. ugly, unpleasant.*

feria *f. fair, show, market.*

feriado *adj. relating to a holiday; m. holiday.*

Día feriado. *Holiday.*

fermentación *f. fermentation.*

fermentar *to ferment.*

fermento *m. ferment; leavening.*

feroz *adj. ferocious, fierce, cruel.*

férreo *adj. iron, ferrous.*

ferretería *f. hardware; hardware store.*

ferrocarril *m. railway, railroad.*

Por ferrocarril. *By railway.*

Estación de ferrocarril. *Train station.*

fértil *adj. fertile, fruitful.*

fervor *m. fervor, zeal.*

festejar *to celebrate.*

Festejar su cumpleaños. *To celebrate one's birthday.*

festividad *f. festivity; holiday.*

festivo *adj. festive, merry.*

Día festivo. *Holiday.*

fiado (en) *on credit.*

Comprar al fiado. *To buy on credit.*

Dar fiado. *To give credit. To sell on credit.*

fiador *m. guarantor; stop, catch.*

fiambre *m. cold meat, cold cuts, cold lunch.*

fianza *f. guarantee, security, bail, bond.*

fiar *to trust, to confide; to sell on credit.*

Se lo puedo fiar. *I can sell it to you on credit.*

No me fío de él. *I don't trust him.*

Puede Ud. fiarse de su palabra. *You may rely (depend) on his word.*

fibra *f. fiber.*

ficha *f. chip (used in games); card, token.*

fideo *m. noodle.*

fiebre *f. fever; rush, exitement.*

fiel *adj. faithful, loyal; true, right; m. pointer, needle (of a balance, scale).*

fiera *f. wild beast.*

fiero *adj. fierce, cruel.*

fierro *m. iron (Amer.).*

FIESTA *f. feast, party; holiday.*

¡Qué fiesta más agradable! *What a lovely party!*

Mañana es día de fiesta. *Tomorrow is a holiday.*

figura *f. figure, form, appearance, image.*

Tiene muy linda figura. *She has a nice figure.*

figurar *to figure; to appear.*

No figura en la lista de invitados. *His name was not on the guest list.*

figurarse *to imagine, to fancy.*

¡Figúrese! *Just imagine!*

fijar *to fix, set (a date); to post (a notice).*

"Prohibido fijar carteles." "*Post no bills.*"

fijarse *to look at, to take notice, to pay attention to.*

Fíjese en la hora. *Look at the time. Look what time it is! Watch the time!*

¿Por qué no se fija Ud. mejor en lo que hace? *Why don't you pay more attention to what you're doing?*

fijo *adj. fixed, firm, fast; permanent.*

Precio fijo. *Fixed price.*

fila *f. row, line, rank.*

En fila. *In line. In a row.*

Una fila de sillas. *A row of chairs.*

filatelia *f. stamp collecting, philately.*

filete *m. fillet, hem; tenderloin, filet mignon.*

filiación *f. relationship; file, record, description (of a person).*

filial *adj. filial; f. branch.*

film/filme *m. film, movie.*

filmadora *m. movie camera.*

filmar *to film, to make a moving picture.*

filmoteca *f. film library.*

filosofía *f. philosophy.*

filósofo *m. philosopher.*

filtrar *to filter, to strain.*

filtrarse *to leak out, to leak through.*

filtro *m. filter.*

FIN *m. end; object, aim, purpose.*
   A fin de mes. *At the end of the month.*
   A fines de año. *In the latter part of the year. Toward the end of the year.*
   Dar fin a. *To finish.*
   Por fin. *Finally.*
   Al fin. *At last.*
   Sin fin. *Endless.*
   Al fin y al cabo. *At last. In the end. At length. After all. In the long run.*
   Con el fin de. *For the purpose of. With the object of.*
   A fin de. *In order that.*
   Con este fin. *To this end. With this end (purpose) in view.*

finado *m. deceased, late.*

FINAL *adj. final, last; m. end; pl. finals (in a contest).*
   La letra final de una palabra. *The last letter of a word.*
   Punto final. *Period. Full stop.*
   Al final. *At the end. At the foot (of a page).*
   Al final de la calle. *At the end of the street.*
   El final de la línea. *The end of the line (train, bus, etc.).*
   Final de trayecto. *Last stop.*

finalizar *to finish; to conclude, to expire.*
   Al finalizar el contrato. *When the contract expires.*

FINALMENTE *finally, at last.*

financiación *f. financing.*

financiamiento *m. financing.*

financiar *to finance.*

financiero *adj. financial; m. fiancier.*

finca *f. farm; real estate, property.*

fineza *f. fineness; delicacy; courtesy.*

fingir *to feign, to pretend.*

fino *adj. fine, delicate; cunning, keen; polite.*
   Esta es una tela muy fina. *This is a very fine material.*
   Es un niño muy fino. *He's a very polite boy.*

FIRMA *f. signature; firm; business concern.*
   Trabaja con una firma norteamericana. *He works for a North American firm.*

firmar *to sign.*

firme *adj. firm, fast, stable, secure, resolute.*
   Mantenerse firme. *To stand one's ground.*
   Color firme. *Fast color.*

fiscal *adj. fiscal; m. public prosecutor.*

física *f. physics.*

físico *adj. physical, m. physicist; physique.*
   Tiene un defecto físico. *He has a physical defect.*

fisiología *f. physiology.*

fisonomía *f. features, physiognomy.*

flaco *adj. lean, thin, weak; m. weak point.*

flagrante *adj. flagrant.*
   En flagrante. *In the very act. Red-handed.*

flamenco *m. Andalusian song and dance/gypsy folk music and dance.*

flan *m. custard.*

flaqueza *f. weakness, feebleness.*

flauta *f. flute.*

fleco *m. fringe, purl; bang (hair) (Mex.).*

flecha *f. arrow, dart.*

fletar *to charter (a ship, etc.).*

flete *m. freight, cargo.*

flexible *adj. flexible, pliable; docile.*

flexión *f. push-up.*

flirtear *to flirt.*

flojo *adj. lax, slack, lazy; loose; not tight; light.*
   Es un hombre flojo. *He's not too bright.*
   La cuerda está floja. *The string's loose.*
   Vino flojo. *Light wine.*

flor *f. flower.*
   ¿Cómo se llama esta flor? *What's the name of this flower?*
   Estar en flor. *To be in blossom.*

florecer *to blossom; to bloom.*

florero *m. flower vase, flower stand.*

florista *m. and f. florist.*

flota *f. fleet.*

flote *m. floating.*
   A flote. *Afloat.*
   Sostenerse a flote. *To keep afloat.*

flúido *adj. fluid, fluent; m. fluid.*

flujo *m. flow.*
   Flujo de caja. *Cash flow.*

fluoruro *m. fluoride.*

fobia *f. phobia.*

foca *f. seal.*

foco *m. focus.*

fogón *m. fireplace; cooking stove.*

fogonazo *m. flash (of a gun).*

fogoso *adj. fiery, impetuous.*

folio *m. leaf of a book, folio.*

folklore *m. folklore.*

folletín *m. feuilleton, a novel in installments, serial story in a newspaper.*

folleto *m. pamphlet.*

fomentar *to foment, to encourage.*

fonda *f. inn, hotel, boardinghouse.*

FONDO *m. bottom; background; fund.*
  Artículo de fondo. *Editorial.*
  En el fondo del pozo. *At the bottom of the well.*
  Conocer a fondo. *To know well. To be thoroughly acquainted with.*
  En el fondo. *At heart. At bottom. Basically. As a matter of fact.*
  Irse a fondo. *To sink. To go to the bottom.*
  Fondos de reserva. *Reserve funds.*
fonética *f. phonetics.*
fonógrafo *m. phonograph.*
forastero *adj.. foreign, strange; m. stranger, foreigner.*
forjar *to forge; to frame.*
FORMA *f. form, shape; mold; manner, way.*
  Ponerse en forma. *To get into shape.*
  No hay forma de hacerlo. *There's no way of doing it.*
  En forma de. *In the shape of.*
  En forma. *In due form.*
  De forma que. *In order that. In such a manner that.*
formación *f. formation.*
formal *adj. formal, proper, serious.*
formalidad *f. formality.*
formar *to form; to shape.*
  La parada se formará a las doce. *The parade will form at twelve o'clock.*
  Formaron una sociedad. *They formed a company.*
formarse *to take form, to develop, to grow.*
  Formarse una idea. *To get an idea.*
formatear *to format.*
formateo *m. formatting (computer).*
formato *m. format.*
formidable *adj. formidable.*
fórmula *f. formula; recipe.*
formular *to formulate.*
formulario *m. form, blank, application, questionnaire.*
  Llene este formulario. *Fill out this application blank.*
forrar *to line (clothes, etc.); to cover (books).*
  El abrigo está forrado por dentro. *The coat is lined inside.*
fortalecer *to fortify, to strengthen.*
fortaleza *f. fortress, stronghold; strength, fortitude.*
fortificación *f. fortification.*
fortificar *to fortify, to strengthen.*
fortitud *f. strength, fortitude.*
fortuito *adj. fortuitous, accidental.*
  Un caso fortuito. *An accident; a fortuitous event.*
fortuna *f. fortune.*
  Por fortuna. *Fortunately.*
forzar *to force, to compel, to oblige.*

forzosamente *necessarily, of necessity.*
forzoso *adj. compulsory, compelling.*
forzudo *adj. strong, robust.*
fosa *f. pit, hole; grave*
fósforo *m. phosphorus; match (to light with).*
  ¿Tiene Ud. fósforos? *Do you have some matches?*
fósil *m. fossil; adj. old, outdated.*
foso *m. pit, ditch.*
foto *f. (abbreviation of* **fotografía**) *photo, picture.*
  Las fotos salieron bien. *The pictures came out all right.*
fotografía *f. photography; photograph, photo, picture.*
fotografiar *to photograph.*
fotógrafo *m. photographer.*
frac *m. dress coat, tails.*
fracasar *to fail, to come out badly.*
fracaso *m. failure.*
  La función fue un fracaso. *The play was a failure.*
fracción *f. fraction.*
fragancia *f. fragrance, pleasing odor.*
fragante *adj. fragant.*
frágil *adj. fragile, brittle; weak, frail (morally).*
fragmento *m. fragment.*
fragua *f. forge.*
fraguar *to forge; to scheme, to plot.*
fraile *m. friar.*
frambuesa *f. raspberry.*
francamente *frankly, openly.*
francés *adj. French; m. Frenchman; French language, f. Frenchwoman.*
FRANCO *adj. frank, free, open, plain; m. French franc.*
  Puerto franco. *Free port.*
  Franco de porte. *Freight prepaid.*
franela *f. flannel.*
franquear *to put a stamp on a letter, to prepay postage; to clear from obstacle; to free (a slave).*
  ¿Ha franqueado las cartas? *Did you put stamps on the letters?*
  Franquear el paso. *To clear the way.*
franqueo *m. postage.*
franqueza *f. frankness, sincerity.*
  Hable con franqueza. *Speak frankly.*
frasco *m. flask, bottle.*
frase *f. sentence.*
  Esta frase no está bien escrita. *This sentence isn't well written.*
fraternidad *f. fraternity, brotherhood.*
frazada *f. blanket.*
frecuencia *f. frequency.*
  Se veían con frecuencia. *They saw one another frequently.*
frecuentar *to frequent, to visit often.*

Este bar es muy frecuentado por mis amigos. *My friends go to this bar a lot.*

frecuente *adj. frequent.*

frecuentemente *often, frequently.*

fregar *to scrub; to wash dishes; to annoy.*

freír *to fry.*

FRENAR *to put on the brakes, to slow up or stop by using a brake; to bridle; to curb.*

¡Frene! *Put on the brakes!*

frenético *adj. mad frantic.*

freno *m. brake; bridle, bit, curb.*

Quite el freno. *Release the brake.*

FRENTE *f. forehead; face; m. front; façade.*

En frente. *In front. Opposite. Across the way.*

Estar al frente de. *To be in charge of.*

Hacer frente a. *To face. To cope with.*

Frente a frente. *Face to face.*

fresa *f. strawberry.*

fresco *adj. cool; fresh; recent; bold; forward; m. fresco (painting); fresh air, breeze; a fresh person.*

El agua está fresca. *The water is cool.*

Ese es un fresco. *He's very fresh. He's a very impudent person.*

Tomar el fresco. *To go out for some fresh air.*

Aire fresco. *Fresh air.*

frescura *f. freshness.*

fricción *f. friction, rubbing.*

frijol *m. kidney bean.*

FRÍO *adj. and n. cold.*

Tengo mucho frío. *I'm very cold.*

Hace frío. *It's cold (of the weather).*

Está frío. *It's cold (of an object).*

Sangre fría. *1. Cold blood. 2. Sang-froid. Presence of mind.*

Le mataron a sangre fría. *They killed him in cold blood.*

friolento *adj. sensitive to cold.*

friolera *f. trifle.*

fritada *f. dish of fried fish or meat.*

frito *adj. fried.*

frontera *f. frontier, border.*

frontón *m. handball court; the wall of a handball court.*

frotar *to rub.*

fructífero *adj. fruitful.*

fructificar *to bear fruit; to yield profit.*

frugal *adj. frugal, thrifty.*

fruncir *to frown; to knit (the brows).*

Fruncir las cejas. *To knit one's brows. To frown. To scowl.*

frustrar *to frustrate.*

fruta *f. fruit.*

frutería *f. fruit store.*

FUEGO *m. fire.*

No deje apagarse el fuego. *Don't let the fire go out.*

Prender fuego a. *To set fire to.*

Armas de fuego. *Firearms.*

Fuegos artificiales. *Fireworks.*

FUENTE *f. spring, fountain, source; platter, large shallow dish.*

Fuente de alimentación. *Power supply.*

Lo sé de buena fuente. *I have it on good authority.*

FUERA *out, outside.*

Hay más gente fuera que dentro. *There are more people outside than inside.*

¡Fuera! *Get out!*

Estar fuera. *To be absent. To be out.*

Por fuera. *On the outside.*

Hacia fuera. *Outwards. Toward the outside.*

Fuera de eso. *Besides. Moreover. In addition (to that).*

Fuera de sí. *Frantic. Beside oneself.*

fueros *m. pl. local laws.*

FUERTE *adj. strong; powerful; excessive; heavy (meal); loud (voice); deep (breath); hard; violent (quarrel); firm, fast; m. forte, strong point; fort, fortress.*

No hable tan fuerte. *Don't speak so loud.*

Este boxeador es más fuerte que el otro. *This boxer is stronger than the other one.*

Es una tela muy fuerte. *This material is very strong.*

Le pegó muy fuerte. *He hit him very hard.*

Respire Ud. fuerte. *Breathe deeply.*

Hubo un fuerte altercado. *There was a violent quarrel.*

Comer fuerte. *To eat too much. To have a heavy meal.*

La música es su fuerte. *Music is his forte.*

FUERZA *f. force, strength, power.*

De por fuerza. *Forcibly. Necessarily. By force.*

Por fuerza. *By force.*

A fuerza de. *By dint of.*

A viva fuerza. *By main force.*

A la fuerza. *By sheer force.*

Por fuerza mayor. *Owing to circumstances beyond one's control. Act of God.*

Fuerzas armadas. *Armed forces.*

fuga *f. escape; flight.*

Poner en fuga. *To put to flight. To rout.*

fugarse *to escape, to run away, to flee.*

fugaz *adj. short-lived, passing soon, not lasting, transient.*

fugitivo *adj. and n. fugitive.*

FULANO *m. So-and-so, What's-his-name.*

El señor fulano de tal. *Mr. So-and-So. Mr. What's-his-name.*

fumador *m. smoker.*

fumar *to smoke* (*cigarettes, etc.*).

Se prohibe fumar. *No smoking.*

función *f. function, performance, play.*

funcionar *to function; to work, to run* (*a machine*).

Esta máquina no funciona. *This machine doesn't work.*

funcionario *m. official, officer, person who holds a public position.*

funda *f. pillowcase; case* (*of a pistol*).

fundación *f. foundation.*

fundador *m. founder.*

fundamental *adj. fundamental.*

fundamento *m. foundation, base, ground, cause.*

Sin fundamento. *Groundless.*

Carecer de fundamento. *To be without foundation, logic or reason.*

fundar *to found, to base.*

Han fundado una nueva sociedad. *They've founded a new society.*

fundarse *to base something on.*

¿En qué se funda Ud. sus esperanzas? *On what do you base your hopes?*

fundición *f. foundry, casting, melting.*

fundir *to melt, fuse; to burn out* (*a bulb*).

fúnebre *adj. mournful, sad.*

funeral *adj. funeral, funereal; m. pl. funeral.*

furgón *m. baggage car; freight car.*

furgoneta *f. station wagon, van.*

furia *f. fury, rage, fit of madness.*

furioso *adj. furious, mad, frantic.*

furor *m. fury.*

fusible *m. fuse* (*electricity*).

fusil *m. rifle.*

fusilar *to shoot.*

fútbol *m. football* (*soccer*).

Fútbol norteamericano. *U.S. football.*

futbolista *m. and f. soccer player.*

FUTURO *adj. future; m. future; fiancé, husband.*

En un futuro próximo. *In the near future.*

En lo futuro. *In the future.*

gabán *m. overcoat.*

gabardina *f. raincoat.*

gabinete *m. cabinet; study, studio, laboratory.*

Gabinete de lectura. *Reading room.*

gaceta *f. gazette, official government journal; newspaper.*

gacetilla *f. a short news article; a gossip column.*

gafa *f. grapple hook; pl. eyeglasses.*

gaita *f. bagpipe.*

gaitero *m. bagpiper.*

gajo *m. branch of a tree.*

gala *f. gala occasion, gala affair; full dress.*

De gala. *Full dress.*

Hacer gala de. *To boast of.*

galán *m. leading man* (*theater*); *gallant, lover.*

Primer galán. *Leading man.*

galante *adj. gallant; generous.*

galantear *to court, to make love.*

galantería *f. gallantry, politeness and attention to women; elegance; generosity.*

galería *f. gallery, balcony.*

gales *m. Welsh; Gales, Wales*

galgo *m. greyhound.*

galón *m. gallon, stripe* (*on uniform*).

galopar *to gallop.*

galope *m. gallop.*

galvanizar *to galvanize.*

gallardo *adj. gallant, brave, daring; handsome.*

galleta *f. cookie, biscuit.*

gallina *f. hen; coward.*

Es un gallina. *He's a coward. He's yellow.*

gallinero *m. chicken coop; top balcony* (*in a theater*).

gallo *m. cock, rooster.*

gamo *m. buck, male deer.*

gamuza *f. suede, chamois.*

GANA *f. appetite, hunger; desire, inclination, will.*

No tengo ganas de comer ahora. *I'm not hungry now. I don't feel like eating now.*

De buena gana. *Willingly. With pleasure.*

De mala gana. *Unwillingly. Reluctantly.*

Trabajó de mala gana. *He worked unwillingly* (*against his will, reluctantly*).

Comer con gana. *To eat with an appetite.*

No me da la gana. *I don't want to. I don't feel like. I won't.*

Hace siempre lo que le da la gana. *She always does what she pleases.*

Tener ganas de. *To desire. To want to. To feel like. To have a mind to.*

Dan ganas de. *One feels inclined to. One feels like.*

ganadería *f. cattle raising, cattle ranch; livestock.*

ganadero *m. cattleman, cattle dealer; rancher.*

ganado *m. cattle, livestock.*

ganador *m. winner.*

ganancia *f. gain, profit.*

Ganancias y pérdidas. *Profit and loss.*

Sacar ganancia. *To make a profit.*

GANAR *to gain; to earn; to win; to reach.*

¿Cuánto quiere Ud. ganar? *What salary do*

you want? ("*How much do you want to earn?*")

Le gané la apuesta. *I won the bet from him.*

No es capaz de ganarse la vida (ganarse el pan). *He's not capable of earning a living.*

gancho *m.* hook; hairpin; clip.

gandul *m.* tramp, loafer, vagabond; bean (*P. R.*).

ganga *f.* bargain; bargain sale.

A precio de ganga. *At a bargain price.*

ganso *m.* gander, goose; a slow (*clumsy*) person; a simpleton.

garaje *m.* garage.

¿Me puede decir dónde hay un garaje cerca? *Can you please tell me where there's a garage near here?*

garantía *f.* guarantee; guaranty, bond.

garantizar *to vouch, to guarantee.*

gardenia *f.* gardenia.

garganta *f.* throat; neck; gorge; instep.

Tengo dolor de garganta. *I have a sore throat.*

gárgara *f.* gargle; gargling.

Hacer gárgaras. *To gargle.*

garra *f.* claw, talon; clutch.

garrafa *f.* carafe, decanter.

garrapata *f.* tick (*insect*).

garrocha *f.* good; stock; pole (*for jumping*).

Salto a la garrocha. *Pole vaulting.*

garrote *m.* cudgel, club; garrote.

gas *m.* gas.

Estufa de gas. *Gas stove.*

gasa *f.* gauze.

gaseosa *f.* carbonated water.

gasolina *f.* gasoline.

Me he quedado sin gasolina. *I've run out of gas.*

Estación de gasolina. (Puesto de gasolina.) *Gas station.*

gasolinera *f.* gasoline pump or station

GASTAR *to spend, to wear out; to waste; to wear, to use.*

Gastó más de mil pesos. *He spent more than a thousand pesos.*

Gastar bromas. *To make jokes. To joke.*

Gastar palabras en vano. *To waste words.*

GASTO *m.* expense, cost; expenditure; consumption.

Gastos menudos. *Petty cash.* ("*Small expenses.*")

Gastos generales. *General expenses, overhead.*

Gasto adicional. *Additional expense.*

gastronomía *f.* gastronomy.

gata *f.* cat.

A gatas. *On all fours.*

gatillo *m.* trigger.

gato *m.* cat, tomcat; jack (*car*).

El gato me ha arañado la mano. *The cat scratched my hand.*

Nos hace falta un gato para levantar el coche. *We need a jack to raise the car.*

gaucho *m.* gaucho, cowboy (*Arg.*).

gaveta *f.* drawer (*of a desk*); locker.

gavilán *m.* sparrow-hawk.

gavilla *f.* sheaf (*of wheat, etc.*); a gang of thugs.

gaviota *f.* seagull.

ge *f.* name of the letter g.

gelatina *f.* gelatine, jelly.

gema *f.* gem; bud.

gemelo *m.* twin; pl. binoculars; cufflinks.

gemido *m.* groan, moan.

gemir *to groan, to moan, to howl.*

generación *f.* generation.

GENERAL *adj.* general, usual; *m.* general.

Por lo general. *As a rule. Usually.*

En general. *In general. On the whole.*

Es general. *He's a general.*

generalmente *generally.*

GÉNERO *m.* cloth, material, stuff; class, kind, sort; gender, sex; pl. goods.

Género para vestidos. *Dress material.*

Género humano. *Mankind.*

generosidad *f.* generosity.

generoso *adj.* generous, liberal.

genial *adj.* outstanding, brilliant, gifted; genial, pleasant.

Tiene un carácter genial. *He's a pleasant person.*

Es una idea genial. *It's a brilliant idea.*

genio *m.* genius; nature, disposition, temper.

Es un verdadero genio. *He's a real genius.*

Tiene muy mal genio. *He has a bad temper.*

GENTE *f.* people, crowd.

Aquí hay mucha gente. *There are many people here.*

Don de gentes. *Pleasant manners. Social graces. Savoir-faire.*

gentil *adj.* courteous; graceful; *m.* gentile, heathen.

gentileza *f.* politeness, courtesy, kindness.

gentío *m.* crowd.

genuíno *adj.* genuine, real.

geografía *f.* geography.

geometría *f.* geometry.

geranio *m.* geranium.

gerencia *f.* management.

gerente *m.* manager.

gerigonza *f.* gibberish.

germen *m.* germ.

germinar *to germinate, to sprout, to start growing or developing.*

gerundio *m.* gerund, present participle.

gesticular *to gesticulate, to make gestures.*

gestión *f. management; negotiation; attempt to obtain or accomplish.*

Encárguese Ud. de esa gestión. *You attend to that matter.*

Está haciendo gestiones para conseguir un puesto. *He's trying to get a job.*

¿Cuáles fueron los resultados de la gestión? *What were the results of the negotiations?*

gestionar *to manage; to negotiate; to try, to take the necessary steps to obtain or accomplish something; to attend to.*

Están gestionando la solución de la huelga. *They're trying to find a way to settle the strike.*

gesto *m. gesture; grimace; facial expression.*

gigante *adj. gigantic; m. giant.*

gimnasia *f. gymnastics, exercise.*

Hacer gimnasia. *To exercise.*

Aparatos de gimnasia. *Exercise equipment.*

gimnasio *m. gymnasium.*

ginebra *f. gin (liquor); Geneva (Switzerland).*

ginecólogo *m. gynecologist.*

GIRAR *to rotate, turn; to draw (a draft, etc.); to operate.*

La tierra gira alrededor del sol. *The earth rotates around the sun.*

Esta casa gira bajo la razón social de X. *This firm does business (operates) under the name of X.*

Girar contra. *To draw on.*

girasol *m. sunflower.*

GIRO *m. turn; rotation; course (of events); draft, money order.*

Giro postal. *Money order.*

Giro bancario. *Bank draft.*

gitano *m. gypsy.*

glacial *adj. glacial, icy.*

Corre un viento glacial. *There's an icy wind.*

global *global, total.*

globo *m. globe; balloon.*

gloria *f. glory; pleasure, delight.*

Esta comida sabe a gloria. *This food's delicious (wonderful).*

glorioso *adj. glorious*

glosa *f. gloss, comment.*

glotón *adj. and n. gluttonous; glutton.*

gobernación *f. administration, government. See gobierno.*

Ministerio de la gobernación. *Department of the Interior.*

gobernador *m. governor.*

gobernante *m. ruler.*

gobernar *to govern, to rule; to control, to steer; to regulate; to direct.*

Gobernar un barco. *To steer a ship.*

gobierno *m. government; control.*

Para su gobierno. *For your guidance.*

Hombre de gobierno. *Statesman.*

goce *m. enjoyment; possession.*

gol *goal (sports).*

golf *m. golf.*

golfo *m. gulf; idler, tramp.*

Golfo de México. *Gulf of Mexico.*

Golfo Pérsico. *Persian Gulf.*

golondrina *f. swallow (bird).*

Empresa golondrina. *A fly-by-night business.*

golosina *f. dainty, delicacy, tidbit; candy.*

goloso *adj. fond of sweets, having a sweet tooth.*

GOLPE *m. blow, stroke, hot; knock; shock.*

Eso fué un golpe muy fuerte. *That was a heavy blow.*

De golpe. *Suddenly. All at once.*

Golpe de estado. *Coup d'état.*

Golpe de gracia. *Coup de grâce. Finishing stroke.*

Golpe de fortuna. *Stroke of fortune.*

De un golpe. *With one blow.*

Golpe de mar. *Surf. Heavy sea.*

golpear *to stroke, to hit, to beat; to knock; to pound.*

Deje de golpear la mesa. *Stop pounding the table.*

goma *f. gum, glue; rubber; eraser; condom.*

Tacones de goma. *Rubber heels.*

Goma de mascar. *Chewing gum.*

gordo *adj. fat, stout; big; m. lard, suet; first prize in a lottery.*

Es un hombre muy gordo. *He's a fat man. He's very fat.*

Dedo gordo. *Thumb.*

gordura *f. stoutness, obesity.*

gorila *m. gorilla.*

gorra *f. cap (for the head).*

De gorra. *Sponging. At someone else's expense.*

gorrión *n. sparrow; sponger (Spain).*

gorre *m. cap, hood.*

gota *f. drop (of liquid); gout.*

Gota a gota. *Drop by drop.*

gotear *to drip, to dribble; to leak.*

goteo *m. dripping, leaking.*

gotera *f. drip, leak; gutter.*

GOZAR *to enjoy; to have, to possess.*

Goza de buena salud. *He enjoys good health.*

Goza de muy buena reputación. *He has a very good reputation.*

gozarse *to rejoice; to find pleasure (in).*

Se goza en . . . He finds pleasure in . . . He takes pleasure in . . .

gozo *m. joy, pleasure.*

No cabe en sí de gozo. *He's very happy. ("He can't contain himself for joy.")*

gozoso adj. cheerful, glad, merry.

grabado m. picture, illustration; engraving; adj. recorded, taped.

grabadora f. tape recorder.

grabar to engrave; to record, to tape; to impress upon the mind.

GRACIA f. grace; favor; pardon; wit, humor; name (of a person); pl. thanks.

Muchas gracias. Thank you very much.

Gracias a Dios. Thank God.

Un millón de gracias. Thanks a lot. (''A million thanks.'')

Dar gracias. To thank.

¿Cuál es su gracia? What's your name?

Eso tiene gracia. That's funny.

Caer en gracia. To take one's fancy.

Hacer gracia. To amuse.

gracioso adj. graceful; witty, funny.

Un dicho gracioso. A witty remark.

grada f. step (of a staircase).

Gradas. Bleachers (stadium).

GRADO m. degree, rank; grade; will; pleasure.

Tenemos diez grados bajo cero. It's ten degrees below zero.

Acaba de recibir el grado de doctor. She has just received her doctor's degree.

Tenía un grado superior en el ejército. He held a high rank in the army.

Está en el cuarto grado. He's in the fourth grade.

De buen grado. Willingly. With pleasure.

gradual adj. gradual, by degrees.

graduar to graduate; to give military rank to; to adjust.

graduarse to graduate, to receive a degree.

gráfico adj. graphic; vivid; m. graph, diagram.

gramática f. grammar.

GRAN (contraction of **grande**) big, great.

Me hace Ud. un gran favor. You're doing me a great favor.

Es un hombre de gran talento. He's a man of great talent.

Es un gran embustero. He's a big liar.

granada f./m. grenade, shell; pomegranate.

GRANDE adj. great, large, huge.

Separe Ud. los grandes de los pequeños. Separate the large ones from the small.

Vive en una casa muy grande. She lives in a very large house.

Estos zapatos me quedan muy grandes. These shoes are too big for me.

En grande. On a large scale.

grandeza f. greatness.

grandioso adj. grand, magnificent.

granero m. granary, barn.

granizar to hail.

Graniza. (Está granizando.) It's hailing.

granizo m. hail.

granja f. grange, farm; country house.

granjear to gain, to win (somebody's affection or goodwill).

grano m. grain; cereal bean (of coffee); pimple.

Vamos al grano. Let's get to the point. Let's get down to brass tacks.

grasa f. grease, fat.

grasiento adj. greasy.

grasoso adj. greasy.

gratamente gratefully.

gratificación f. gratuity, tip, reward; allowance.

gratificar to reward, to gratify, to tip.

gratis adj. gratis, free.

La entrada será gratis. Admission will be free.

gratitud f. gratitude, thankfulness, gratefulness.

GRATO adj. pleasing, gratifying, pleasant.

Me es grato. I'm pleased to.

Me será grato hacerlo. I'll be glad to do it.

gratuito adj. gratis, free.

gravamen m. encumbrance; burden, obligation.

grave adj. grave; serious.

gravedad f. gravity, seriousness.

grávida adj. pregnant.

gremio m. trade union, guild.

grieta f. crevice, crack, fissure; chap (skin).

grifo m. faucet; griffin.

Haga Ud. el favor de cerrar el grifo. Please turn the water off.

grillo m. cricket (insect).

grillos pl. fetters, shackles.

gringo m. name given to North Americans and Englishmen in Latin America.

gripe f. grippe, influenza.

gris adj. gray.

gritar to shout, to scream.

No grites tanto. Don't shout so. Don't scream like that.

grito m. cry, scream, shout.

Llamó a gritos. He yelled (screamed). He called out loud.

Poner el grito en el cielo. To complain bitterly. To make a big fuss.

grosella f. currant (fruit).

grosería f. coarseness, rudeness.

grosero adj. coarse, rude, impolite.

grúa f. crane, derrick, hoist.

gruesa f. gross (144).

GRUESO adj. thick, coarse, bulky.

Una tajada gruesa. A thick slice.

El tronco de ese árbol es muy grueso. This tree has a very thick trunk.

grulla f. crane (bird).

gruñido m. grunt.

gruñir to grumble, to grunt.

grupo m. group.

gruta f. grotto, cavern.

guagua f. bus (P. R.).

guanábana f. breadfruit.

guano m. guano, manure of sea birds, fertilizer.

guante m. glove.

Echar el guante. To catch. To arrest.

guantera f. glove compartment.

guapo adj. good-looking, pretty, handsome; courageous, bold, brave (Amer.).

¿Es guapa la hija? Is the daughter pretty? Es guapísima. She's very pretty.

guarache m. leather sandal (Mex.).

guaraní m. Guarani Indian; Paraguayan currency unit.

guarapo m. fermented sugar cane juice.

guarda f. and m. guard, watchman, keeper; custody, guardianship.

GUARDAR to keep, to guard, to take care of.

Guarde su dinero en la caja fuerte. Keep your money in the safe.

No le guardo ningún rencor. I don't bear him any grudge.

Ha tenido que guardar cama. He had to stay in bed. He was confined to bed.

guardarse to be on guard; to guard against; to abstain from.

guardarropa f. wardrobe; m. cloakroom, the cloakroom attendant.

guardia f. guard (a body of soldiers); watch (on a ship); m. guard (a person), policeman.

Cualquier guardia puede indicarle el camino. Any policeman can direct you (show you the way).

Está de guardia. He's on duty.

guarecer to shelter, to protect.

guarnecer to trim, to garnish; to garrison.

guarnición f. trimming, garniture; setting (in gold, silver, etc.); garrison; pl. harness.

guaso m. (Amer.) nonsense; dullness; joke, fun.

guayaba f. guava (fruit).

GUERRA f. war; trouble.

Estar en guerra. To be at war.

Hacer guerra. To wage war.

Estos chicos dan mucha guerra. These children are a lot of trouble.

guerrero adj. warlike; m. warrior.

guerrillero m. guerrilla fighter.

GUÍA m. guide; cicerone; f. guidebook; directory

¿Dónde puedo encontrar un guía que me acompañe? Where can I get a guide to accompany me?

Guía telefónica. Telephone directory.

Servir de guía. To serve as a guide.

guiar to guide, to direct; to drive.

¿Sabe Ud. guiar? Do you know how to drive?

guijarro m. pebble.

guillotina f. guillotine.

guinda f. kind of cherry.

guineo m. sweet banana.

guiñar to wink; to deviate (a ship).

guión m. hyphen; script (play, film).

guisado m. ragout stew

guisante m. pea.

guisar to cook.

guiso m. stew.

guitarra f. guitar.

gusano m. worm.

GUSTAR to taste; to like.

¿Le gusta a Ud. la fruta? Do you like fruit?

A mí no me gusta el café. I don't like coffee.

¿Le gusta a Ud. eso? Do you like that?

No me gusta. I don't like it.

Nos gustó la comida. We enjoyed the food.

Me gusta más el vino. I like wine better.

Como Ud. guste. As you please.

Me gustaría mucho ir a España. I'd like very much to go to Spain.

GUSTO m. taste; pleasure; liking.

Esto tiene un gusto extraño. This has a strange (funny) taste.

Con (mucho) gusto. With (much) pleasure.

Tengo mucho gusto en conocerle. I'm glad to have met you. Glad to know you.

A mi gusto. To my liking.

Estar (encontrarse, sentirse) a gusto. To feel at home. To be comfortable.

Dar gusto. To please.

Tener gusto en. To take pleasure in.

gustoso adj. tasty; glad, willing, with pleasure.

H

¡ha! ah! alas!

haba f. broad bean.

haber m. credit (bookkeeping); assets.

HABER to have (as an auxiliary verb); to be, to exist.

Hay. There is. There are.

Había. There was. There were.

Hubo. There was. There were.

Habrá. There will be.

Habría. There would be.

Haya. There may be.

Que haya. Let there be.

Hubiera (hubiese). *There might be.*

Si hubiera (hubiese). *If there were. If there should be.*

Ha habido. *There has (have) been.*

Había (hubo) habido. *There had been.*

Habría habido. *There should (would) have been.*

Hay que. *It's necessary.*

Habrá que. *It will be necessary.*

Hubo que. *It was necessary.*

Ha de ser. *It must be.*

He de hacer un largo viaje. *I have (I've got) to make a long trip.*

He aquí. *Here is.*

¿Ha escrito la carta? *Has she written the letter?*

No la ha escrito todavía. *She hasn't written it yet.*

Pudo haber sucedido. *It might have happened.*

Debían haber llegado anoche. *They were supposed to have come last night.*

Debe haber cartas para mí. *There must be some letters for me.*

¿Habrá alguien en la estación esperándome? *Will there be someone at the station to meet me?*

Hemos de ir el martes a su casa. *We must go (we have to go) to his (her) house on Tuesday.*

No habíamos comido desde hacía muchas horas. *We hadn't eaten for many hours.*

Me alegro de haberle visto. *I'm glad to have seen you.*

Hace una semana que la vi. *I saw her a week ago.*

Habérsela con. *To have to deal with. To cope with. To contend with.*

haberes *m. pl.* possessions, property.

habichuela *f.* bean; kidney bean.

Habichuelas verdes. *String beans.*

HÁBIL *adj.* able; clever; skillful; capable.

Es muy hábil. *He's very clever.*

Día hábil. *Working day.*

Testigos hábiles. *Competent witnesses.*

habilidad *f.* ability, skill.

habilitar *to qualify; to enable, to provide; to supply with.*

habitación *f.* room; dwelling; place to live in.

¿Cuántas habitaciones tiene el apartamento? *How many rooms does the apartment have?*

habitante *m. and f.* inhabitant; tenant.

habitar *to inhabit, to live in, to reside.*

¿Qué tal es el piso que habitan? *What kind of an apartment do you live in?*

hábito *m.* habit, custom; cowl, habit (*worn by members of a religous order*).

Tenía el hábito de levantarse temprano. *He was in the habit of getting up early.*

habituar *to accustom.*

habituarse *to become accustomed.*

habla *f.* speech, talk.

Perdió el habla. *He was speechless.*

hablador *adj.* talkative; *m.* gossip, chatterbox, talker.

HABLAR *to speak, to talk.*

¿Habla Ud. español? *Do you speak Spanish?*

Yo no hablo español. *I don't speak Spanish.*

Aquí se habla español. *Spanish is spoken here.*

¡Hable! *Speak!*

¿Quién habla? *Who's speaking (telephone)?*

¡Diga! (¡Holá!) ¿Quién habla? *Hello! Who's this (telephone)?*

Hable más despacio. *Speak slower.*

Nunca habla mal de nadie. *He never says anything bad about anyone.*

Hablando en serio, eso no está bien. *Seriously, that's not right.*

Hablar con. *To speak with.*

Hablar por demás. *To talk too much. Not to talk to the point.*

Hablar por hablar. *To talk for the sake of talking.*

Hablar hasta por los codos. *To chatter. To talk constantly. To be a chatterbox.*

hacendado *m.* rancher, landowner (*Amer.*).

HACER *to make; to do; to cause; to be (cold, warm, etc.).*

Hágame Ud. el favor de. *Please.*

¡Haga el favor de pasarme la sal! *Please pass me the salt.*

¿Me permite que le haga una pregunta? *May I ask you a question?*

Hacen muy buenos pasteles aquí. *They make very good pies here.*

He mandado hacer un traje a la medida. *I'm having a suit made to order.*

Hicimos los planes de común acuerdo. *We made (laid) the plans for mutual agreement.*

Tengo mucho que hacer hoy. *I've a lot to do today.*

¿Qué hago? *What shall I do?*

Haga Ud. lo que quiera. *Do as you please (like).*

¿Qué hemos de hacer? *What are we to do?*

Hace lo que puede. *He does his best.*

Queda mucho por hacer. *Much still remains to be done.*

Me ha dado mucho que hacer. *He's given me a lot of trouble.*

Ya está hecho. *It's already done (finished).*

Dicho y hecho. *No sooner said than done.*

Ropa hecha. *Ready-made clothes.*

Haga Ud. por venir. *Try to come.*

Salió hace un rato. *He left a while ago.*

No hace mucho. *Not long ago.*

Hace cosa de dos meses. *It was about two months ago.*

Se va haciendo tarde. *It's getting late.*

Hace frío. *It's cold.*

Hace calor. *It's warm.*

Hace sol. *It's sunny.*

Hace viento. *It's windy.*

Hace mal tiempo. *The weather's bad. It's nasty out.*

Hacer falta. *To need. To be lacking.*

No hace falta. *It's not necessary.*

Hacer caso. *To pay attention.*

Hacer burla. *To make fun.*

Hacer alto. *To halt.*

Hacer un paréntesis. *To pause.*

Hacer de las suyas. *To be up to one's old tricks again.*

Hacer de cuenta. *To pretend.*

Hacer gimnasia. *To exercise.*

Hacer una convocatoria. *To call a meeting.*

Hacer cola. *To stand in line.*

Hacer frente a. *To face. To resist.*

Hacer ver. *To show.*

Hacer volver. *To send back.*

Hacer esperar. *To keep waiting.*

Hacer saber. *To make known. To inform.*

Hacer juego. *To match.*

Hacer mal. *To do harm.*

Hacerlo bien (mal). *To do it well (badly).*

Hacer fuego. *To fire (gun). To shoot.*

Hacer cuentas. *To figure. To reckon.*

Hacer la corte. *To court. To woo.*

HACERSE *to become; to accustom oneself; to pretend; to be able to.*

¿Puede Ud. hacerse entender en inglés? *Can you make yourself understood in English?*

Juan está en camino de hacerse rico. *John's getting rich. ("John's on the way to becoming rich.")*

Se hacía más loco de lo que era. *He pretended to be crazier than he really was.*

Me hice un lío. *I was all mixed up.*

Hacerse rogar. *To like to be coaxed.*

Hacerse cargo de. *To take charge of. To take into consideration.*

Hacerse atrás. *To fall back.*

Hacerse una sopa. *To become drenched. To get soaked to the skin.*

Hacerse de. *To obtain. To get.*

Hacerse con alguna cosa. *To get hold of something. To obtain something.*

Hacerse el tonto. *To play the fool.*

¡Hazte allá! *Move on! Make way! Get out of the way!*

HACIA *toward, in the direction of.*

Iba hacia su casa. *He was going toward his house.*

Se dirigieron hacia la puerta. *They went toward the door.*

Hacia abajo. *Downwards.*

Hacia arriba. *Upwards.*

Hacia acá. *Over here. Toward this place.*

Hacia allá. *Over there. Toward that place.*

Hacia adelante. *Forward. Onward. Toward the front.*

hacienda *f. property, lands, ranch, plantation, large estate, restaurant (Amer.); fortune, wealth; treasury; finance.*

Ministerio de Hacienda. *The Treasury.*

hacha *f. ax, hatchet.*

hache *f. name of the letter* **h.**

hada *f. fairy.*

Cuentos de hadas. *Fairy tales.*

hado *m. destiny, fate.*

halagüeño *adj. pleasing, nice; flattering, attractive.*

halar *to pull (Amer.).*

Hale la cuerda. *Pull the rope.*

hálito *m. breath.*

HALLAR *to find, to meet with.*

Hallé muchas faltas en esta carta. *I found many mistakes in this letter.*

No lo hallo en ninguna parte. *I can't find it anywhere.*

hallarse *to find oneself, to be.*

Se halla muy bien. *He's very well. He's fine.*

Me hallo sin dinero. *I find myself without any money.*

hallazgo *m. finding; thing found.*

hamaca *f. hammock.*

HAMBRE *m. hunger.*

Tengo hambre. *I'm hungry.*

No tengo hambre. *I'm not hungry.*

Me estoy muriendo de hambre. *I'm starving.*

hambriento *adj. hungry; starved; greedy.*

hamburguesa *f. hamburger.*

hangar *m. airplane, hangar.*

haragán *adj. and n. lazy; indolent; loafer.*

harapo *m. tatter; rag.*

hardware *m. hardware (computer).*

harina *f. flour.*

hartarse *to stuff oneself, to gorge.*

Tomó helado hasta hartarse. *He stuffed himself with ice cream.*

harto *adj. satiated, full; fed up; enough.*

Estoy harto de todo esto. *I'm fed up with all this.*

HASTA *until; as far as; up to; also, even.*

Hasta luego. *So long. See you later.*

Hasta después. *I'll see you later.*

¡Hasta la vista! *Till we meet again! I'll be seeing you soon! See you soon!*

Hasta muy pronto. *I'll see you soon. See you later.*

Hasta mañana. *Until tomorrow. See you tomorrow.*

Hasta el lunes. *Until Monday.*

Fuimos andando hasta el parque. *We walked as far as the park.*

Hay ascensor hasta el quinto piso. *There is an elevator to the fifth floor.*

¿Hasta dónde va el camino? *How far does the road go?*

Hasta cierto punto. *To a certain extent.*

Hasta ahora. *Up to now. Up to this time.*

HAY (*see* **haber**) *there is, there are.*

¿Hay vino? *Is there any wine?*

¿Hay algo para mí? *Is there anything for me?*

¿Qué hay de bueno? *What's new?*

No hay novedad. *Nothing new. The same old thing. The same as usual.*

¿Qué hay? *What's the matter? What's up?*

¡No hay de qué! *Don't mention it! You're welcome!*

Hay un hombre esperándole. *There's a man waiting for you.*

Hay que ver lo que se puede hacer por ella. *We must see what can be done for her.*

haz *m. bundle; fagot; f. face; right side (of a cloth).*

hazaña *f. prowess, feat, exploit.*

he *look here, take notice (used with* **aquí, ahí, allí,** *and* **me, te, la, le, lo, las,** *and* **los**).

He aquí las razones. *These are the reasons (indicating what follows).*

Héme aquí. *Here I am.*

hebilla *f. buckle.*

hebra *f. thread; fiber.*

Pasar la hebra por el ojo de la aguja. *To thread a needle.*

hectárea *f. hectare (10,000 square meters).*

hechicero *adj. fascinating, charming; m. wizard.*

Tiene un semblante hechicero. *She has a fascinating face.*

hechizar *to fascinate, to charm, to bewitch.*

HECHO *adj. made, done; m. fact; deed; action; event.*

Mal hecho. *That's wrong. Poorly made.*

Bien hecho. *Well done.*

Ropa hecha. *Ready-made clothes.*

El hecho es . . . *The fact is . . .*

Dicho y hecho. *Said and done.*

Hecho y derecho. *Perfect in every respect.*

De hecho. *In fact. Actually.*

De hecho y de derecho. *"By act and right."*

hechura *f. workmanship, making, cut, shape, form.*

heder *to stink.*

helada *f. frost.*

helado *adj. frozen; icy; astonished, amazed, astounded; m. ice cream.*

Traiga dos helados de chocolate. *Bring two orders of chocolate ice cream.*

La noticia me dejó helado. *The news astounded me.*

helar *to freeze; to astonish.*

hélice *f. propeller.*

helicóptero *m. helicopter.*

hembra *f. female; woman; eye of a hook.*

hemisferio *m. hemisphere.*

hemorragia *f. hemorrhage.*

hendidura *f. fissure, crevice.*

hemorroide *m. hemorrhoid.*

heno *m. hay.*

hepatitis *f. hepatitis.*

heredad *f. property, land, farm.*

heredar *to inherit.*

heredera *f. heiress.*

heredero *m. heir.*

hereditario *adj. hereditary.*

herencia *f. inheritance, heritage, legacy.*

herida *f. wound, injury.*

herido *adj. wounded, injured; m. wounded man.*

Fue herido en el brazo. *He was wounded in the arm.*

El herido sigue mejor. *The wounded man is improving.*

herir *to wound, to hurt.*

HERMANA *f sister.*

hermanastro *m. stepbrother.*

HERMANO *m. brother.*

HERMOSO *adj. beautiful; lovely, fine.*

¡Qué paisaje tan hermoso! *What beautiful scenery! What a lovely landscape!*

¡Qué día más hermoso! *What a beautiful day!*

hermosura *f. beauty.*

héroe *m. hero.*

heroico *adj. heroic.*

heroína *f. heroine; heroin (drug).*

hervir *to boil.*

Hierva el agua antes de beberla. *Boil the water before you drink it.*

Agua hirviendo. *Boiling water.*

herradura *f. horseshoe.*

herramienta *f. tool; set of tools.*

herrero *m. blacksmith.*

hidalgo *m. nobleman.*

hidrofobia *f. hydrophobia; rabies.*

hidroplano *m. seaplane.*

hiedra *f. ivy.*

hiel *f. gall, bile.*

hielo *m. ice; frost; indifference.*

hiena *f. hyena.*

hierba *f. herb; weed; grass.*
    Hierba maté. *Maté (tea).*

hierro *m. iron; poker.*

hígado *m. liver.*

higiene *f. hygiene.*

higiénico *adj. hygienic, sanitary.*

higienista *m. and f. hygienist.*

higo *m. fig.*

higuera *f. fig tree.*

HIJA *f. daughter.*

hijastro *m. stepchild.*

HIJO *m. son; pl. children.*
    ¿Tiene Ud. hijos? *Do you have any children?*
    Tal padre, tal hijo. *Like father, like son.*

hilar *to spin.*

hilarante *adj. hilarious.*

hilera *f. row, file.*

HILO *m. thread; string; linen; wire.*
    Pañuelo de hilo. *Linen handkerchief.*
    No puedo seguir el hilo de la conversación. *I can't follow the conversation.*
    Perder el hilo. *To lose the thread (of what one is saying, etc.).*

hilván *m. tacking, basting.*

hilvanar *to tack, to baste; to do a thing hurriedly.*

himno *m. hymn.*

hincapié *m. foot stamping.*
    Hacer hincapié. *To insist on. To emphasize. To dwell on. To stand firm.*

hincha *m. and f. rooter, fan (sports).*

hinchado *adj. swollen.*

hinchar *to swell, to inflate; to root for.*

hincharse *to swell; to become arrogant.*

hinchazón *m. swelling; vanity.*

hipertensión *f. hypertension.*

hipnotismo *m. hypnotism.*

hipo *m. hiccough.*

hipocresía *f. hypocrisy.*

hipócrita *adj. and n. hypocritical, not sincere; hypocrite.*

hipódromo *m. racetrack; hippodrome.*

hipoteca *f. mortgage.*

hipotecar *to mortgage.*

hipótesis *f. hypothesis.*

hispánico *adj. Hispanic.*

hispano *adj. Hispanic; Spanish; m. Spanish speaker of the U.S.A.*

hispanoamericano *adj. Spanish American.*

histérico *adj. hysterical.*

historia *f. history; story.*
    Me vino con una larga historia. *He came to me with a long story.*

historiador *m. historian.*

histórico *adj. historic.*

historieta *f. short story; anecdote.*

hocico *m. snout; muzzle.*
    Meter el hocico en todo. *To be nosy. To poke one's nose into everything.*

hockey *m. hockey.*

hogar *m. fireplace; home.*
    Hogar de ancianos. *Old-age home.*

hoguera *f. bonfire; blaze.*

HOJA *f. leaf; blade; sheet.*
    En otoño caen las hojas. *The leaves fall in autumn.*
    Doblemos la hoja. *Let's change the subject.*
    Hoja en blanco. *Blank sheet.*
    Hoja de servicio. *Service record.*
    Hoja de afeitar. *Razor blade.*

hojalata *f. tin plate.*

hojear *to turn the leaves or glance at a book; to look over hastily.*

holgarse *to be pleased with, to take pleasure in, to amuse oneself.*

holgazán *adj. lazy, idle; m. a lazy person. idler.*

¡hola! *Hello!*

hombre *m. man.*
    Es hombre de mundo. *He's a man of the world.*
    Hombre de bien. *An honest man.*
    Hombre de Estado. *Statesman.*

HOMBRO *m. shoulder.*
    Se lastimó el hombro. *He hurt his shoulder.*
    Encogerse de hombros. *To shrug one's shoulders.*

homenaje *m. homage, honor, respect.*
    Rendir homenaje. *To pay homage to.*

homosexual *adj./n. homosexual.*

hondo *adj. profound; deep.*

honesto *adj. decent, honest.*

honor *m. honor.*
    Dio su palabra de honor. *He gave his word of honor.*

honra *f. honor, respect.*
    Tener a honra. *To regard as an honor. To consider it an honor. To be proud of.*
    A mucha honra. *I (we) consider it an honor. I (we) are honored. I'm (or we're) proud of it.*

honradez *f. honesty, integrity.*

honrado *adj. honest, honorable.*
    Era un hombre honrado. *He was an honest man.*

honrar *to honor.*

honrarse *to deem something an honor, to be honored.*

HORA *f. hour; time.*
    ¿Qué hora es? *What time is it?*
    ¿Qué hora será? *I wonder what time it is.*

¿A qué hora empieza la función. (*At*) *What time does the show begin?*

¿A qué hora sale el correo? (*At*) *What time does the mail leave?*

Ya es hora de levantarse. *It's ("already") time to get up.*

Este reloj da las horas y las medias horas. *This clock strikes the hours and the half hours.*

Llegó media hora después. *He arrived half an hour later.*

A la hora. *On time.*

A la hora en punto. *On the dot.*

A la misma hora. *At the same time.*

A estas horas. *By this time. By now.*

Hora de punta. *Rush hour.*

horario *adj. hourly; m. hour-hand; timetable.*

Horario estelar. *Prime-time (television).*

horca *f. gallows; pitchfork.*

horizontal *adj. horizontal.*

horizonte *m. horizon.*

horma *f. form, mold; dry wall.*

hormiga *f. ant.*

hormigón *m. concrete (for building).*

hornada *f. batch (of bread).*

hornillo *m. portable stove; burner; blast hole.*

horno *m. oven; furnace.*

(Horno) microondas. *m. Microwave (oven).*

horóscopo *m. horoscope.*

hortaliza *f. vegetables (for cooking), garden greens.*

horrible *adj. horrible.*

horror *m. horror.*

horroroso *adj. horrible, frightful, dreadful.*

hosco *adj. sullen, gloomy; dark-colored.*

hospedaje *m. lodging; board.*

hospedar *to lodge; to entertain (guests).*

hospicio *m. orphanage; poorhouse, hospice.*

hospital *m. hospital.*

hospitalizar *to hospitalize.*

hostelero *m. innkeeper, tavern keeper.*

hostia *f. host (in the Catholic Church).*

¡Hostia! *Damn it! (Spain, expletive).*

hostil *adj. hostile.*

hostilizar *to harass, to antagonize.*

HOTEL *m. hotel; villa; cottage.*

¿Dónte queda el hotel más próximo? *Where's the nearest hotel?*

HOY *today.*

¿Qué día es hoy? *What day is today? What's today?*

De hoy en adelante. *From now on. Henceforth.*

Hoy en día. Hoy día. *Nowadays.*

hoyo *m. hole, pockmark.*

hoz *f. sickle.*

hueco *m. hole, hollow, empty space.*

huelga *f. strike (of workers).*

huelguista *m. striker, a workman on strike.*

huella *f. track, footprint, trail.*

Huellas digitales. *Fingerprints.*

huérfano *m. orphan.*

Quedarse huérfano. *To be left an orphan.*

huerta *f. orchard; irrigated land.*

huerto *m. small orchard; vegetable garden.*

hueso *m. bone; stone (of fruit); drudgery.*

A otro perro con ese hueso. *Tell it to the marines. You expect me to believe that?*

huésped *m. and f. guest; lodger; innkeeper, host.*

Casa de huéspedes. *Guest house.*

HUEVO *m. egg.*

¿Cómo quiere Ud. los huevos? *How do you like your eggs?*

Huevos y tocino. *Bacon and eggs.*

Huevos fritos. *Fried eggs.*

Huevos pasados por agua. *Soft-boiled eggs.*

Huevos revueltos. *Scrambled eggs.*

huída *f. flight, escape.*

huir *to flee, to escape; to run away.*

hule *m. oilcloth; linoleum.*

humanidad *f. mankind, humanity.*

humanitario *adj. humanitarian, philanthropic.*

HUMANO *adj. human; humane; m. man, human being.*

Eso fue un acto humano. *That was a humane act.*

Un ser humano. *A human being.*

humear *to smoke (chimneys, etc.).*

humedad *f. humidity, dampness, moisture.*

humedecer *to moisten, to dampen.*

húmedo *adj. humid, moist, damp.*

humildad *f. humility, humbleness.*

humilde *adj. poor; humble; unaffected.*

humillación *f. humiliation; affront.*

humillante *adj. humiliating.*

humillar *to humiliate, to lower.*

humo *m. smoke; fume; pl. airs, conceit.*

HUMOR *m. humor; disposition; temper.*

Estar de buen humor. *To be in a good mood.*

Estar de mal humor. *To be in a bad mood. To have the blues.*

humorista *m. and f. humorist.*

hundimiento *m. sinking; collapse, downfall.*

hundir *to sink; to submerge.*

hundirse *to sink; to cave in; to collapse.*

huraño *unsociable.*

hurtadillas (a) *by stealth, on the sly.*

Me miró a hurtadillas. *He looked at me out of the corner of his eye.*

Lo hizo a hurtadillas. *He did it on the sly.*

hurtar *to steal, to rob.*

Hurtar el cuerpo. *To shy away.*

hurto *m. stealing; theft.*

husmear *to smell, to scent; to pry into; to begin to smell (meat).*

I

ida *f. going; one-way trip, trip to a place.*
Billete de ida. *One-way ticket.*
Billete de ida y vuelta. *Round-trip ticket.*

IDEA *f. idea; mind.*
No tengo la menor idea. *I haven't the least idea.*
Creo que es una buena idea. *I think it's a good idea.*
No es mala idea. *That's not a bad idea.*
¿Ha cambiado Ud. de idea? *Have you changed your mind?*

ideal *adj. and n. ideal.*

idealizar *to idealize.*

idear *to think of, to conceive; to devise; to plan.*
Ideó un juego divertidísimo. *He thought up a very amusing game.*
Idear nuevos métodos. *To devise new methods.*

idéntico *adj. identical, the same.*

identidad *f. identity.*
¿Tiene Ud. sus documentos de identidad? *Do you have your identification papers?*

identificación *f. identification.*

identificar *to identify.*

idioma *m. language.*

idiota *adj. idiotic; m. and f. idiot.*

ídolo *m. idol.*

Iglesia *f. church.*

ignominia *f. infamy; disgrace.*

ignorancia *f. ignorance.*

IGNORANTE *adj. ignorant; unaware; m. ignoramus, ignorant person.*
Estaba ignorante de lo que ocurría. *He was unaware of what was happening.*
Es un ignorante. *He's an ignorant man. He's an ignoramus.*

IGNORAR *to be ignorant of, not to know; to be unknown.*
Ignoro su nombre. *I don't know his name.*
Se ignora su paradero. *His whereabouts are unknown.*

IGUAL *adj. equal; similar, like; even.*
Mi corbata es igual que la suya. *My tie is like yours.*
Me es igual. *It's all the same to me. It makes no difference (to me).*
Al igual que los demás. *The same as the others.*
Igual a la muestra. *Like the sample.*
Por igual. *Equally. In a like manner.*

No tener igual. *To be matchless. To have no equal.*

igualar *to equalize; to compare, to liken; to make even.*

igualarse *to put oneself on the same level with someone else.*

igualdad *f. equality.*
En igualdad de condiciones. *On equal terms.*

igualmente *equally.*
Igualmente. *The same to you.*

ilegal *adj. illegal, unlawful.*

ilegible *adj. illegible.*

ilegítimo *adj. illegitimate, spurious.*

ileso *adj. unhurt, unscathed, not harmed.*

ilimltado *adj. unlimited.*

iluminación *f. illumination.*

iluminar *to illuminate.*

ilusión *f. illusion.*

ilustración *f. illustration.*

ilustrado *adj. illustrated; m. well-educated person.*

ilustrar *to illustrate; to explain.*

ilustrarse *to acquire knowledge.*

ilustre *adj. illustrious, celebrated.*

imagen *f. image, figure.*

imaginación *f. imagination.*

IMAGINAR *to imagine, to think, to suspect.*

IMAGINARSE *to imagine.*
¡Imagínese Ud.! *You can imagine!*
Me imagino lo que pensaría de mí. *I can imagine what he thought of me.*

imán *m. magnet.*

imbécil *adj. and n. imbecile.*

imbecilidad *f. imbecility, stupidity.*

imitación *f. imitation.*

imitar *to imitate; to mimic.*

impaciencia *f. impatience.*

impacientar *to vex, to irritate, to make someone impatient.*

impacientarse *to become impatient.*

impaciente *adj. impatient, restless.*

impar *adj. odd, uneven.*
Números impares. *Odd numbers.*

imparcial *adj. impartial, unbiased.*

impedimento *m. impediment, hindrance, obstacle; inability to act.*

IMPEDIR *to hinder, to prevent, to keep from.*
El ruido me impidió dormir. *The noise kept me from sleeping. The noise kept me awake.*

impenetrable *adj. impenetrable; inscrutable, mysterious.*

imperativo *adj. and n. imperative.*

imperdible *m. safety pin.*

imperfecto *adj. imperfect, faulty; m. imperfect (tense).*

imperio *m. empire; dominion.*

impermeabilizar *to make waterproof.*

impermeable *adj. impermeable, waterproof;*
m. raincoat.

impersonal *adj. impersonal.*

impertinente *adj. impertinent, out of place;*
importunate.

ímpetu *m. impulse, impetus.*

impetuoso *adj. impulsive, impetuous.*

impío *adj. wicked; impious, ungodly.*

implicar *to implicate; to imply.*

implícito *adj. implicit.*

implorar *to implore; to beg.*

imponer *to impose; to acquaint with; to have*
personal knowledge of; to command
(respect).

imponerse *to assert oneself, to command*
respect.

importación *f. import; importation.*

IMPORTANCIA *f. importance.*

IMPORTANTE *adj. important.*

IMPORTAR *to import; to matter; to cost.*

   Esta casa importa café del Brasil. *This firm*
     imports coffee from Brazil.

   Este libro importa un dólar. *This book*
     costs a dollar.

   ¿Que importa? *What difference does it*
     make?

   No importa. *Never mind. It doesn't matter.*

   Importa mucho. *It matters a lot. It's very*
     important.

   No se meta en lo que no le importa. *Mind*
     your own business.

importe *m. amount; value, cost.*

importunar *to importune, to annoy.*

imposibilidad *f. impossibility.*

imposibilitar *to make impossible.*

IMPOSIBLE *adj. impossible.*

imposición *f. imposition.*

impostor *m. impostor, deceiver.*

impotencia *f. inability, impotence.*

impotente *adj. powerless, helpless, impotent.*

impracticable *adj. impracticable, not*
practical.

imprenta *f. printing; printing plant.*

impresión *f. impression; print, printing.*

impresionante *adj. impressive.*

impresionar *to impress; to move; to affect.*

impresionista *adj. and m. and f.*
impressionist.

impreso *adj. printed; stamped; m. printed*
matter.

impresora *f. printer.*

   Impresora laser. *Laser printer.*

   Impresora de margarita. *Daisy-wheel*
     printer.

   Impresora de matriz de puntos. *Dot-matrix*
     printer.

imprevisto *adj. unforeseen, unexpected;*
sudden.

   Llegó de imprevisto. *He arrived*
     unexpectedly.

imprimir *to print; to imprint.*

improbable *adj. unlikely, improbable.*

impropio *adj. improper, not correct, unfit;*
unbecoming.

improvisar *to improvise, to extemporize; to*
make or do something offhand.

improviso *adj. unexpected.*

   De improviso. *Unexpectedly.*

imprudencia *f. lack of prudence,*
imprudence.

imprudente *adj. imprudent; indiscreet.*

impuesto *adj. imposed; informed; m. tax,*
duty.

   Impuesto a la renta. *Income tax.*

   Impuesto a las ventas. *Sales tax.*

impulsar *to impel; to drive; to urge.*

impulso *m. impulse; spur; urge.*

   Dar impulsos a. *To get something going*
     (started).

impunidad *f. impunity.*

impureza *f. impurity; contamination.*

impuro *adj. impure, not pure, adulterated.*

imputar *to impute, to blame, to attribute.*

inaceptable *adj. not acceptable.*

inactivo *adj. inactive, idle.*

inadaptable *adj. not adaptable.*

inadecuado *adj. inadequate, not adequate.*

inadmisible *adj. inadmissible, objectionable.*

inadvertido *adj. unnoticed.*

inalterable *adj. unalterable, changeless.*

inauguración *f. inauguration.*

inaugurar *to inaugurate; to begin.*

incansable *adj. untiring.*

incapacidad *f. incapacity, inability;*
incompetence, disability.

incapaz *adj. incapable, inefficient,*
incompetent.

   Es incapaz de hacerlo. *He's incapable of*
     doing it.

incautación *f. seizure, taking over.*

incautarse *to take over, to seize.*

incendiar *to set on fire.*

incendio *m. fire.*

incertidumbre *f. uncertainty.*

incesante *adj. incessant, continual.*

   Un ruido incesante. *A continual noise.*

incidente *adj. incidental; m. incident.*

incierto *adj. uncertain.*

incisión *f. incision.*

inciso *m. parenthetic clause, article*
(contract).

incitar *to incite, to stimulate.*

inclemencia *f. inclemency; severity.*

   La inclemencia del tiempo no nos permitió
     salir. *The bad weather kept us at*
     home.

inclinación *f. inclination; leaning, tendency.*

inclinar *to incline, to bend.*

inclinarse *to incline, to tend to, to lean toward.*

INCLUIR *to include; to enclose.*
> ¿Está incluído el vino? *Is wine included?*
> Incluya su nombre en la lista. *Include his name on the list.*
> Incluí el recibo en la carta. *I enclosed the receipt in the letter.*

inclusive *adj. inclusive, including.*

incluso *adj. enclosed; including.*

incógnito *adj. unknown; incognito.*
> Viajó de incógnito. *He traveled incognito.*

incoherente *adj. incoherent; disconnected.*

incombustible *adj. incombustible.*

incomodar *to disturb, to inconvenience, to bother.*
> Si eso no le incomoda. *If it doesn't inconvenience you.*

incómodo *adj. uncomfortable; inconvenient.*

incomparable *adj. matchless, without equal.*

incompatible *adj. incompatible.*

incompetencia *f. incompetency.*

incompleto *adj. incomplete, unfinished.*

incomprensible *adj. incomprehensible, impossible to understand.*

incomunicado *adj. incommunicado.*

incomunicar *to isolate, to hold someone incommunicado.*

inconcebible *adj. inconceivable, unthinkable, incredible.*

incondicional *adj. unconditional.*

incongruencia *f. incongruity, being out of place, being inconsistent.*

inconsciencia *f. unconsciousness.*

inconsciente *adj. unconscious.*

inconstancia *f. inconstancy, unsteadiness, fickleness.*

inconveniente *adj. inconvenient.*
> Tener inconveniente en. *To object to.*
> No tener inconveniente en. *Not to mind. Not to object to.*

incorporar *to incorporate; to join.*

incorporarse *to sit up or rise from a lying position.*

incorrección *f. incorrectness; inaccuracy.*

incorrecto *adj. incorrect, inaccurate, wrong, improper.*

incorregible *adj. incorrigible.*

incredulidad *f. incredulity, lack of belief.*

incrédulo *adj. incredulous.*

increíble *adj. incredible.*

incremento *m. increment, increase.*
> Tomar incremento. *To increase.*

increpar *to reproach, to rebuke.*

incubadora *f. incubator.*

inculcar *to inculcate, to impress by repetition.*

inculto *adj. uncultivated; uncultured, uneducated, boorish.*

incumbencia *f. duty, concern.*

incumbir *to concern, to pertain.*

incumplimiento *m. nonfulfillment, breach.*

incurable *adj. incurable; hopeless.*

incurrir *to incur; to make (a mistake).*
> Incurrir en deudas. *To get into debt.*

indagar *to inquire, to investigate.*

indebidamente *improperly, unduly, wrongly.*

indebido *adj. improper; wrong; undue; illegal.*

indecente *adj. indecent; unbecoming.*

indecisión *f. indecision, hesitation.*

indeciso *adj. undecided, hesitant.*

indefenso *adj. defenseless.*

indefinido *adj. indefinite.*

indeleble *adj. indelible.*

indemnización *f. indemnity, indemnification, compensation.*

indemnizar *to indemnify, to make good, to compensate.*

independencia *f. independence.*

independiente *adj. independent.*

indeseable *adj. undesirable.*

indeterminado *adj. indeterminate; doubtful; undecided.*

indicación *f. indication, hint, sign; suggestion; pl. instructions.*
> Eso era una buena indicación. *That was a good sign.*
> Lo hizo por indicación de su amigo. *He did it at his friend's suggestion.*
> Una indicación de Ud. es bastante. *A hint from you is enough.*
> Siguió las indicaciones del médico. *He followed the doctor's instructions.*
> Para usarlo, siga las indicaciones siguientes. *To use it, follow these instructions.*

indicador *m. indicator, pointer, gauge.*

INDICAR *to indicate; to point out.*
> Haga el favor de indicarme el camino. *Please show me the way.*

índice *m. index; hand (of a clock, etc.).*
> Dedo índice. *Index finger.*

indicio *m. indication, mark, clue.*

indiferencia *f. indifference.*

indiferente *adj. indifferent.*
> Me es indiferente. *It makes no difference to me.*

indígena *adj. native.*

indigencia *f. poverty, indigence.*

indigente *adj. poor, indigent.*

indigestión *f. indigestion.*

indigesto *adj. hard to digest.*

indignación *f. indignation, anger.*

indignar *to irritate, to annoy, to anger.*

indignidad *f. indignity.*

indigno *adj. unworthy, undeserving; unbecoming; disgraceful.*

indio *m. Indian; Hindu.*

indirecta *f. hint.*

indirecto *adj. indirect.*

indiscreción *f. indiscretion.*

indiscreto *adj. indiscreet, imprudent.*

indiscutible *adj. unquestionable, indisputable.*

indispensable *adj. indispensable, essential.*

indisponer *to indispose; to become ill; to cause enmity or quarrels.*

   ¿Está Ud. indispuesto? *Are you ill (indisposed)?*

indisposición *f. indisposition.*

individual *adj. individual.*

individualmente *individually.*

individuo *m. individual, person.*

índole *f. disposition, character; kind, class.*

inducir *to induce; to persuade.*

indudable *adj. indubitable, certain.*

indulgencia *f. indulgence.*

indulgente *adj. indulgent, lenient.*

indultar *to pardon (a prisoner, etc.).*

indulto *m. pardon.*

indumentaria *f. clothing, clothes, outfit.*

industria *f. industry; diligence.*

industrial *adj. industrial, manufacturing; m. industrialist.*

   Relaciones industriales. *Industrial relations.*

ineficacia *f. inefficiency.*

ineficaz *adj. inefficient.*

ineludible *adj. unavoidable.*

ineptitud *f. ineptitude, inability, unfitness.*

inepto *adj. inept, incompetent; unfit.*

inequívoco *adj. unmistakable.*

inerte *adj. inert; slothful, sluggish.*

inesperadamente *unexpectedly.*

inesperado *adj. unexpected, unforeseen.*

inevitable *adj. inevitable, unavoidable.*

inexactitud *f. inaccuracy.*

inexacto *adj. inexact, inaccurate.*

inexperto *adj. inexperienced; inexpert.*

inexplicable *adj. inexplicable, impossible to explain.*

infalible *adj. infallible.*

infamar *to disgrace, to dishonor, to defame.*

infame *adj. infamous, shameful.*

infamia *f. infamy, disgrace.*

infancia *f. childhood.*

infantería *f. infantry.*

infantil *adj. infantile; childish.*

   Parálisis infantil. *Infantile paralysis.*

infarto *m. heart attack.*

infatigable *adj. tireless, untiring.*

infección *f. infection.*

infectar *to infect, to spread disease.*

infectarse *to become infected.*

infeliz *adj. unhappy; unfortunate; m. a naïve (good-hearted, gullible) person.*

INFERIOR *adj. inferior; lower; subordinate; m. an inferior, a subordinate.*

   Es una tela de calidad inferior. *This material is of inferior quality.*

   Trata muy bien a sus inferiores. *He treats his subordinates well.*

   Labio inferior. *Lower lip.*

inferioridad *f. inferiority.*

inferir *to infer; to imply; to inflict (wounds, injuries, etc.).*

infiel *adj. unfaithful.*

   Si no me es infiel la memoria. *If my memory doesn't fail me. If I remember correctly.*

infierno *m. hell, inferno.*

ínfimo *adj. lowest; least.*

   No lo quiero vender a precio tan ínfimo. *I don't want to sell it at such a low price. I don't want to sell it for so little.*

infinidad *f. infinity; too many, a vast number.*

   Hay infinidad de gente que no piensa así. *There are many (a lot of) people who don't think so.*

infinitamente *infinitely, immensely.*

infinitivo *m. infinitive (grammar).*

infinito *adj. infinite.*

inflación *f. inflation.*

inflamable *adj. inflammable.*

inflamación *f. inflammation.*

inflamar *to catch fire; to inflame.*

   Tenga Ud. cuidado porque se inflama fácilmente. *Be careful, it's inflammable.*

   Tiene los ojos inflamados. *His eyes are inflamed.*

inflar *to inflate.*

influencia *f. influence.*

influenza *f. influenza, grippe, flu.*

INFLUIR *to influence.*

   La propaganda influye mucho en el público. *Advertising has a great influence on the public.*

   Influya usted para que ... *Use your influence to ...*

INFORMACIÓN *f. information; inquiry; investigation.*

informador *m. spokesman.*

informal *adj. unreliable, not to be depended on; not serious; unbusinesslike.*

informalidad *f. informality; lack of reliability, not being dependable.*

informar *to report, to inform, to let know; to plead (law).*

informarse *to find out, to learn.*

   Acabo de informarme del asunto. *I've just learned about the matter.*

informática *f. computer science.*

informe *adj. shapeless; m. information; report; plea, allegation; pl. references.*

Dar un informe. *To give information. To make a report.*

informes *m. information.*

infortunado *adj. unlucky, unfortunate.*

infracción *f. infraction, violation, infringement.*

infrecuente *adj. infrequent, unusual.*

infringir *to infringe, to violate.*

infructuoso *adj. unsuccessful, vain, fruitless.*

infundado *adj. unfounded, groundless, without cause or reason.*

infundir *to give (courage), to command (respect), to make (some suspicious).*

Infundir ánimo. *To give courage.*

Infunde respeto. *It commands respect.*

Me infunde sospechas. *His actions make me suspect him.*

ingeniería *f. engineering.*

ingeniero *m. engineer.*

ingenio *m. ingenuity; talent; mill.*

Fue un escritor de mucho ingenio. *He was a very talented writer.*

Mi hermano trabaja en un ingenio de azúcar. *My brother works at a sugar mill.*

ingenioso *adj. ingenious, clever.*

ingenuidad *f. naïveté, simplicity.*

ingenuo *adj. naïve, simple.*

ingerir *to ingest, to take food.*

INGLÉS *adj. and n. English; Englishman; English language.*

Se habla inglés. *English spoken here.*

Habla muy mal el inglés. *He speaks English very badly.*

El señor es inglés. *The gentleman is an Englishman (is English).*

ingratitud *f. ingratitude, lack of gratitude.*

ingrato *adj. ungrateful.*

ingresar *to enter.*

ingreso *m. entry (bookkeeping); money received; pl. f. income, revenue, returns.*

Ingresó en el ejército como soldado. *He joined the army as a private.*

Hubo más gastos que ingresos. *There were more expenses than profits.*

inhábil *adj. incapable; unfit, unqualified.*

inhalar *to inhale.*

inhibición *f. inhibition*

Inhibición de teclas. *Key lockout (computer).*

inhospitalario *adj. inhospitable.*

inhumano *adj. inhuman, cruel, hard-hearted.*

inicial *adj. initial; f. initial.*

iniciar *to initiate; to begin.*

iniciativa *f. initiative.*

Tomar la iniciativa. *To take the initiative.*

inicuo *adj. wicked.*

iniquidad *f. wickedness, iniquity.*

injerto *m. graft (of trees).*

injuria *f. insult, injury, offense.*

injustamente *adv. unjustly.*

injusticia *f. injustice.*

injusto *adj. unjust, unfair.*

Eso es injusto. *That's not fair. That's unjust.*

inmediación *f. contiguity, nearness; vicinity.*

INMEDIATAMENTE *immediately.*

inmediato *adj. immediate; contiguous.*

inmejorable *adj. the very best, unsurpassable.*

inmensamente *immensely.*

inmenso *adj. immense, huge, vast.*

inmerecido *adj. undeserved.*

inmesurable *adj. boundless, immeasurable.*

inmiscuir *to mix.*

inmiscuirse *to meddle, to interfere.*

inmoderado *adj. immoderate, not moderate.*

inmoral *adj. immoral.*

inmortal *adj. immortal.*

inmóvil *adj. immovable, firmly fixed; deathlike.*

inmovilizar *to immobilize.*

inmueble *m. property; real estate.*

inmundicie *f. filth, dirt.*

inmundo *adj. filthy, dirty, unclean.*

inmutable *adj. unchangeable, immutable, neverchanging.*

innecesario *adj. unnecessary, not necessary.*

innegable *adj. undeniable, unquestionable.*

inocencia *f. innocence.*

inocente *adj. innocent.*

inodoro *adj. odorless; m. toilet.*

¿Dónde está el inodoro? *Where's the toilet?*

inofensivo *adj. inoffensive, harmless.*

inoportuno *adj. inopportune, untimely; said or done at the wrong time.*

No sea Ud. inoportuno. *Don't come at the wrong time (do things at the wrong time, say the wrong things).*

inquebrantable *adj. tenacious, unyielding.*

inquietar *to disturb, to cause anxiety.*

inquietarse *to become anxious or worried; to be uneasy or restless.*

inquieto *adj. restless, uneasy, worried.*

Pasó toda la noche inquieto. *He was restless all night.*

inquietud *f. uneasiness, anxiety, restlessness.*

inquilino *m. tenant.*

inquirir *to inquire.*

insalubre *adj. unhealthful.*

insano *adj. insane, mad.*

inscribir *to inscribe; to register, to record.*

inscribirse *to register (at a school, etc.).*

inscripción f. inscription.
insecticida adj. insecticide.
insecto m. insect.
inseguro adj. uncertain.
insensatez f. foolishness, stupidity.
insensato adj. stupid, foolish.
insensible adj. not sensitive, unfeeling, heartless.
inseparable adj. inseparable.
insertar to insert, to introduce.
inservible adj. useless, good-for-nothing.
insidioso adj. insidious, sly.
insigne adj. famous, noted.
insignia f. badge; pl. insignia.
insignificante adj. insignificant.
insinuar to insinuate, to hint.
insipidez f. insipidity; lack of flavor (taste).
insípido adj. insipid, tasteless.
insistencia f. insistence, persistence.
insistir to insist.
insolación f. sunstroke.
insolencia f. insolence, rudeness.
insolente adj. insolent, rude.
insolvente adj. insolvent, not able to pay, broke.
insomnio m. insomnia, sleeplessness.
inspección f. inspection.
inspeccionar to inspect, to examine.
inspector m. inspector; superintendent.
inspiración f. inspiration.
inspirar to inspire; to inhale.
    Le inspiró mucha simpatía. He found her to be very pleasant.
instalación f. installation; fixtures.
    Instalación eléctrica. Electrical fixtures.
instalar to install; to set up.
instancia f. instance; request.
    A instancia de. At the request of.
instantáneamente instantly, at once.
    Contestó instantáneamente. He answered at once (right away).
INSTANTE m. instant.
    Aguárdame un instante. Wait for me a moment.
    Me contestó al instante. He answered me right away.
instar to urge, to press.
instaurar to establish, to restore.
instintivamente instinctively.
instinto m. instinct.
institución f. institution, establishment.
instituir to institute, to establish.
instituto m. institute; high school.
instrucción f. instruction; education; pl. directions.
    Instrucción pública. Public education.
    ¿Tiene Ud. las instrucciones para el manejo de esta máquina? Do you have

    the directions for the use of this machine?
instructivo adj. instructive.
instructor m. instructor, teacher.
instruir to instruct, to teach.
instrumento m. instrument.
    ¿Qué instrumento toca Ud.? What instrument do you play?
insubordinado adj. insubordinate.
insubordinarse to rebel; to mutiny.
insuficiencia f. insufficiency.
insuficiente adj. not enough, insufficient.
insufrible adj. unbearable.
insultar to insult.
insulto m. insult, offense.
insuperable adj. insuperable, insurmountable.
intacto adj. intact, untouched, whole.
intachable adj. irreproachable, faultless.
integral adj. integral; whole.
    Pan integral. Whole-wheat bread.
integrar to integrate.
integridad f. integrity.
ÍNTEGRO adj. entire, whole, in full; upright, honest.
    Es un hombre íntegro. He's an honest man. He's very upright.
    La suma íntegra. The amount in full.
intelectual adj. and n. intellectual.
inteligencia f. intelligence; understanding.
    En la inteligencia de que. With the understanding that.
    Inteligencia artificial Artificial intelligence.
INTELIGENTE adj. intelligent.
inteligible adj. intelligible.
intemperie f. rough or bad weather.
    A la intemperie. Outdoors. In the open.
INTENCIÓN f. intention, mind, meaning.
    ¿Cuál es su intención? What does he intend to do?
    Lo dijo con segunda intención. What he said had a double meaning.
    Tener buena intención. To mean well.
    Tener mala intención. Not to mean well.
    Tener la intención de. To intend to.
intendencia f. administration, management; quartermaster (corps).
intendente m. quartermaster (officer); superintendent.
intensidad f. intensity.
intenso adj. intense.
intentar to try, to attempt, to intend, to endeavor.
    Es inútil que intente. It's useless to try.
intento m. intent, purpose.
    No lo hice de intento. I didn't do it on purpose.
intercalar to intercalate, to put in between.
intercambio m. interchange; exchange.

interceder *to intercede, to plead in another's behalf.*

interceptar *to intercept; to block.*

INTERÉS *m. interest.*

No demuestra el menor interés. *He doesn't show the slightest interest.*

Pone interés en hacerlo bien. *He tries hard to do it well.*

Devengar intereses. *To pay interest.*

Tasa de interés. *Interest rate.*

interesado *adj. interested, concerned.*

INTERESANTE *adj. interesting.*

Es una novela poco interesante. *It's not a very interesting novel.*

INTERESAR *to interest, to concern.*

No me interesa. 1. *It doesn't interest me.* 2. *I don't care for him (her, it, etc.).*

INTERESARSE *to be concerned; to become interested.*

Se interesó mucho en el negocio. *He became very interested in the business.*

interino *adj. provisional, temporary, acting.*

INTERIOR *adj. interior, internal; m. interior; inside.*

Un cuarto interior. *An inside room.*

Lo dijo para su interior. *He said it to himself.*

El comercio interior. *Domestic trade.*

El Ministerio de Interior. *Department of the Interior.*

Ropa interior. *Underwear.*

Navegación interior. *Inland navigation.*

intermediar *to mediate.*

intermediario *adj. and n. intermediary.*

intermedio *adj. intermediate; m. interval, recess.*

internacional *adj. international.*

internar *to intern, to confine, to hospitalize.*

internista *m. and f. internist.*

interno *adj. internal; interior; m. boarding student; intern.*

Para uso interno. *For internal use.*

interponer *to interpose.*

interpretación *f. interpretation, meaning, acting,*

interpretar *to interpret; to understand.*

Interpretar bien. *To understand correctly.*

No interpretar bien. *To misunderstand.*

intérprete *m. and f. interpreter.*

intervalo *m. interval.*

intervenir *to intervene; to mediate.*

interrogación *f. interrogation, questioning; question, inquiry; question mark.*

Signo de interrogación. *Question mark.*

interrogar *to interrogate, to question.*

interrogatorio *f. cross examination.*

INTERRUMPIR *to interrupt.*

Dispense Ud. que le interrumpa. *Pardon me for interrupting you.*

interrupción *f. interruption; stop.*

Sin interrupción. *Without stopping.*

interruptor *m. switch (electricity); circuit breaker.*

intestino *adj. intestinal; domestic, internal; m. pl. intestines.*

intimar *to intimate, to hint; to order; to become intimate.*

intimidad *f. intimacy, close friendship.*

intimidar *to intimidate, to frighten.*

íntimo *adj. intimate, close.*

Eran amigos íntimos. *They were very close friends.*

Tuvimos una conversación íntima. *We had an intimate conversation. We had a tête-à-tête.*

intolerable *adj. intolerable, unbearable.*

intolerancia *f. intolerance.*

intolerante *adj. intolerant.*

intoxicación *f. intoxication, poisoning.*

intranquilo *adj. restless.*

intransigencia *f. intransigence.*

intransigente *adj. uncompromising, unyielding, die-hard, intransigent.*

intransitable *adj. impassable.*

intratable *adj. hard to deal with, unsociable.*

intrepidez *f. intrepidity, courage.*

intrépido *adj. intrepid, fearless.*

intriga *f. intrigue, plot.*

intrigante *adj. intriguing; m. intriguer.*

intrincado *adj. intricate, entangled, complicated.*

introducción *f. introduction. See* **presentación** *and* **recomendación.**

introducir *to introduce, to put in; to input. See* **presentar.**

Introduje la carta en el buzón. *I put the letter in the mailbox.*

intromisión *f. interference.*

intruso *adj. intruding; m. and f. intruder.*

intuición *f. intuition.*

inundar *to inundate, to flood.*

INÚTIL *useless; fruitless; unnecessary.*

Es inútil que se lo pida. *There's no use (in) asking him.*

Es un hombre inútil. *He's good-for-nothing. He can't do anything.*

inutilidad *f. uselessness.*

inutilizar *to spoil, to ruin, to disable.*

INÚTILMENTE *uselessly, in vain.*

Hicimos el viaje inútilmente. *We made the trip in vain.*

invadir *to invade.*

invalidar *to invalidate, to nullify, to render void.*

inválido *adj. invalid, null; crippled; m. an invalid; a cripple.*

invariable *adj. unchangeable, invariable.*

invasión *f. invasion.*

invención *f. invention.*

inventar *to invent.*

inventario *m. inventory.*

invento *m. invention.*

invernar *to winter, to spend the winter.*

Fueron a invernar a California. *They went to spend the winter in California.*

inverosímil *adj. improbable, unlikely; incredible.*

Me pareció inverosímil el relato. *The story seemed improbable to me.*

invertir *to invert, to turn upside down; to spend, to take (time); to invest (money).*

investigación *f. investigation.*

investigar *to investigate.*

INVIERNO *m. winter.*

invisible *adj. invisible.*

invitación *f. invitation.*

INVITADO *adj. invited; m. guest.*

Estamos invitados a una reunión mañana. *We are invited to go to a meeting tomorrow.*

Hoy tendremos invitados. *We're having guests today.*

INVITAR *to invite.*

inyección *f. injection.*

inyectar *to inject.*

inyectarse *to inject oneself with a substance; to "shoot up" drugs.*

iodo *m. iodine. See* **yodo.**

IR *to go; to be; to concern, to have to do with.*

¡Vámonos! *Let's go!*

¡Voy! *I'm coming!*

Me voy. *I'm going away. I'm leaving.*

Voy a mi casa. *I'm going home.*

Debemos irnos. *We must go.*

¡Váyase! *Go away!*

¡Qué se vaya! *Let him go!*

No se vaya Ud. *Don't go away.*

No puedo ir. *I can't go.*

¿Cómo le va? (¿Cómo vamos?) *How are you? How are you getting along?*

¿Cómo van los negocios? *How's business?*

El paciente va mucho mejor. *The patient is much better.*

Van a dar las doce. *It will soon be twelve.*

Vamos a ver. *Let's ee.*

Vamos a dar un paseo. *Let's take a walk.*

Vamos, Juan, dígamelo Ud. *Go on, John, tell it to me.*

Vamos, déjame ya. *Come on, let me alone (don't bother me).*

¡Qué se le ha de hacer! *It can't be helped!*

Vamos al grano. *Let's get to the point.*

¿Quién va? *Who's there?*

¡Vaya! *Go on! I don't believe it!*

¡Vaya una ocurrencia! *What an idea!*

¡Vaya Ud. con Dios! *Good-bye! Good luck to you! ("Go with God.")*

¡Vaya por Dios! *Good gracious!*

¡Qué va! *Nonsense!*

Ahora va de veras. *Now it's really serious.*

¡Ahí va eso! *Here it comes! Catch!*

La situación va de mal en peor. *The situation is getting worse and worse.*

Eso no me va ni me viene *It (that) doesn't concern me in the least.*

Eso no va conmigo. *That doesn't concern me.*

El buque se fué a pique. *The ship sank.*

Ir a pie. *To walk. To go on foot.*

Ir a caballo. *To ride. To go on horseback.*

Ir de bares (fam.). *To go bar-hopping.*

Ir en coche. *To drive.*

Ir de brazo. *To walk arm-in-arm.*

Ir a medias. *To go half-and-half. To share equally.*

ira *f. anger, fury, rage.*

Tuvo un repente de ira. *He had a fit of temper.*

iracundo *adj. irate, angry; enraged.*

Estaba iracunda por lo que dije. *She was furious at what I said.*

ironía *f. irony.*

irónico *adj. ironical.*

irradiar *to irradiate.*

irreal *adj. unreal.*

irreflexivo *adj. thoughtless, rash.*

irregular *adj irregular.*

irrespetuoso *adj. disrespectful, showing no respect.*

irresponsabilidad *f. irresponsibility, lack of responsibility.*

irresponsable *adj. irresponsible.*

irrigar *to irrigate.*

irritado *adj. irritated, angry.*

irritar *to irritate, to exasperate.*

Ella la irrita. *She exasperates him.*

irrompible *adj. unbreakable.*

isla *f. isle, island.*

italiano *adj. and n. Italian.*

itinerario *n. itinerary; route.*

¿Qué itinerario seguirán? *Which route will you take?*

IZQUIERDO *adj. left; left-handed; f. left hand.*

A ia izquerda. *To the left.*

Estaba sentado a mi izquierda. *He was sitting on my left.*

Es un cero a la izquierda. *He doesn't count. He's a nonentity.*

J

jabalí *m. wild boar.*

jabón *m. soap.*

jabonar *to soap.*

jabonera *f. soapdish.*

jaca *f. nag, pony.*

jacinto *m. hyacinth.*

jactancia *f. boasting.*

jactarse *to boast, to brag.*

Se jacta de haber viajado mucho por el mundo. *He boasts of having traveled all over the world.*

jalea *f. jelly.*

jalear *to encourage, to urge on.*

jaleo *m. clapping of hands to encourage a dancer; Andalusian dance; noisy party, revelry, racket.*

Armar un jaleo. *To start a fuss.*

JAMÁS *never.*

Jamás he visto una corrida de toros. *I've never seen a bullfight.*

Jamás lo hubiera hecho yo. *I'd never have done it.*

Nunca jamás. *Never. Never again.*

Para siempre jamás. *For ever and ever.*

Jamás de los jamases. *Never again.*

jamón *m. ham (smoked or cured).*

jaque *m. check (in chess); braggart*

Jaque mate. *Checkmate.*

jaqueca *f. migraine, headache.*

Tengo jaqueca. *I have a very bad headache.*

jarabe *m. syrup.*

Jarabe para la tos. *Cough syrup.*

jardín *m. garden.*

jardinero *m. gardener; outfielder (baseball).*

jarra *f. jug, pitcher.*

En jarras. *With arms akimbo.*

jarro *m. pitcher, pot, jug; babbler.*

jarrón *m. vase, large jar.*

jaula *f. cage.*

jazmín *m. jasmine.*

jazz *m. jazz.*

jefa *f. chief; mother (Mex.).*

jefatura *f. headquarters.*

Jefatura de Policía. *Police headquarters.*

JEFE *m. chief; head, principal; leader; boss, employer.*

Jefe de taller. *Foreman.*

El jefe del gobierno. *The head of the government.*

El jefe de la oficina. *The office manager.*

Jefe de estación. *Stationmaster.*

jerarquía *f. hierarchy.*

jerez *m. sherry wine.*

jerga *f. jargon.*

jeringa *f. syringe.*

Jesucristo *m. Jesus Christ.*

jesuíta *m. Jesuit; hypocrite.*

Jesús *Jesus.*

¡Jesús! *Good heavens! God bless you (said when someone sneezes)!*

jinete *m. horseman, rider.*

JIRA *f. outing, excursion, picnic; tour.*

Jira de inspección. *Tour of inspection.*

jirafa *f. giraffe.*

jornada *f. journey, trip; day's travel; one day's work.*

Una jornada de cinco días. *A five days' journey (trip).*

Los obreros trabajan jornadas de ocho horas. *The laborers work eight hours a day.*

jornal *m. day's pay; wages.*

Trabaja a jornal. *He works by the day.*

Jornal mínimo. *Minimum wage.*

jornalero *m. day laborer.*

joroba *f. hump.*

jorobado *m. hunchback.*

jorobar *to importune, to annoy.*

jota *f. name of the letter j; a typical Spanish dance; iota.*

No entender ni jota. *Not to understand anything.*

JOVEN *adj. young; m. young man; f. young lady.*

Todavía es muy joven. *She's still very young.*

¿Quién es esa joven? *Who's that young lady?*

Es un joven muy simpático. *He's a very nice young man.*

jovial *adj. jovial, merry.*

joya *f. jewel, gem; precious, wonderful.*

Llevaba muy lindas joyas. *She wore very beautiful jewels.*

Esa muchacha es una joya. *She's a wonderful girl.*

joyas *f. jewelry.*

jubilar *to pension off, to retire from service.*

judía *f. bean; string bean; Jewess.*

Estas judías verdes son excelentes. *These string beans are excellent.*

judío *adj. Jewish; m. Jew.*

JUEGO *m. play, game; gambling; set; play, movement.*

¿Qué juego prefiere? *Which game do you like best?*

Este sombrero no hace juego con mi vestido. *This hat doesn't match my dress.*

Ya te veo el juego. *I see what your intentions are. I see what you're driving (getting) at.*

Compró un juego de loza. *She bought a set of dishes.*

Juegos olímpicos. *Olympics.*

Juego de azar. *Game of chance.*

Juego de naipes (cartas). *Card game.*

Hacer juego. *To match.*

Estar en juego. *To be at stake.*

Poner en juego. *To bring to bear upon. To put into play.*

JUEVES m. Thursday.

juez m. judge.

Juez de paz. Justice of the peace.

jugada f. play; move (chess); turn (cards); mean trick.

Jugada de bolsa. Stock market speculation.

jugador m. gambler; player.

JUGAR to play; to gamble; to stake; to take part.

Juega bien al tenis. He plays tennis well.

Ha jugado todo su dinero. He's gambled all his money.

Juega su última carta. He's playing his last card. That's his last card.

jugarreta f. dirty trick.

jugo m. juice.

jugoso adj. juicy.

juguete m. toy, plaything; laughingstock.

Le regalaron un juguete. They gave him a toy as a present.

Está sirviendo de juguete. He's being made a laughingstock.

juicio m. judgment; mind; opinion; wisdom, good judgment; lawsuit, trial.

¿Ha perdido Ud. el juicio? Have you lost your mind?

Es un hombre de juicio. He's a man of good judgment. He has good judgment.

A mi juicio. In my opinion.

Someter a juicio. To bring to trial.

Pedir en juicio. To sue (at law).

juicioso adj. prudent, sensible, wise, well-behaved.

JULIO m. July.

JUNIO m. June.

junta f. board, council, junta, committee; meeting; joint, coupling, union, junction.

¿A qué hora fue la junta? What time did the meeting take place?

Junta directiva. Board of directors. Executive committee.

Junta de comercio. Board of trade.

Junta de acreedores. Creditors' meeting.

Junta de sanidad. Board of health.

Junta remachada. Riveted joint.

JUNTAR to join, to unite; to assemble, to gather; to pile up (money); to leave ajar (door).

Junte toda la ropa y póngala en la maleta. Get all the clothes together and put them in the suitcase.

Junte la puerta. Leave the door ajar (open).

Juntar dinero. To pile up money.

JUNTARSE to get together, to meet; to join, to associate with, to keep company.

Se junta con mala gente. He keeps bad company.

Se juntó mucha gente para oír al orador. Quite a crowd gathered to hear the speaker.

No me gusta con quien se junta. I don't like the people you associate with.

JUNTO near, close to; together.

Déjalo junto a la puerta. Leave it near the door.

Pasa por junto de. To pass near. To pass by.

Emprenderemos el negocio juntos. We're going into this business together.

Si Ud. quiere, vamos juntos. If you wish, we'll go together.

jura f. oath of allegiance; swearing in.

jurado m. jury, juryman, juror.

jurar to swear, to take oath.

No se lo creo aunque me lo jure. I won't believe you even if you swear that it's true.

justicia f. justice; fairness; law.

Hacer justicia. To do justice. To be just.

Hacerse justicia por sí mismo. To take the law into one's hands.

La justicia. The police.

justificación f. justification.

justificar to justify.

JUSTO adj. just; fair; exact, to the point; scarce; tight; m. a just and pious man.

Eso no es justo. That's not fair.

Al año justo de. Just a year after.

El peso justo. The exact weight.

El sombrero me está muy justo. My hat is very tight.

Vivimos muy justos. We live from hand to mouth.

juvenil adj. juvenile, youthful.

juventud f. youth, youthfulness.

juzgado m. tribunal, court (of justice).

JUZGAR to judge; to think.

Lo ha juzgado Ud. mal. You have judged it wrongly.

¿Lo juzga Ud. conveniente? Do you think it's advisable?

K

ka f. name of the letter **k.**

kilo m. kilo, kilogram (2.2046 pounds).

Deme un kilo de azúcar. Give me a kilogram of sugar.

kilo-byte (KB) m. kilobyte.

kilogramo m. kilogram.

kilometraje m. mileage.

kilométrico kilometric; mileage (ticket).

kilómetro m. kilometer.

kimono m. kimono, dressing gown.

kiosco m. kiosk, newsstand.

L

LA (*f. article*) *the; pl.* **las** *the. See* **los.**
   La muchacha. *The girl.*
   Las muchachas. *The girls.*
   Las dos hermanas se parecen. *Both sisters look alike.*
   Los padres. *The parents.*

LA (*f. direct object pronoun*) *you, her, it; pl.* **las** *them, you. See* **los** *and* **les.**
   ¿La vió Ud. en la fiesta? *Did you see her at the party?*
   No la ví. *I didn't see her.*
   Me alegro de verla. *I'm glad to see you (a woman).*
   Dámela. *Give it (f.) to me.*
   Traduzca estas palabras al español y léalas en voz alta. *Translate these words into Spanish and read them aloud.*

la *m. la, A* (sixth note of the musical scale).

labia *f. gift of gab, sweet talk.*
   Tiene mucha labia para vender. *He has a good sales pitch.*

LABIO *m. lip.*
   Lápiz de labios. *Lipstick.*

labor *f. labor, task; needlework, embroidery.*

laborable *adj. workable; working.*
   Día laborable. *Working day.*

laborar *to labor; to work; to till.*

laboratorio *m. laboratory.*

laborioso *adj. laborious; hardworking.*

labrador *m. farmer, peasant.*

labranza *f. farming; farm.*

labrar *to till, to cultivate (land); to carve (wood, etc.).*

labriego *m. farmhand.*

laca *f. hair spray.*

lacerar *to lacerate; to mangle.*

lacio *adj. withered; languid; straight (hair).*

lacónico *adj. laconic, brief.*

lacrar *to seal (with wax).*

lacre *m. sealing wax.*

ladear *to tilt, to incline; to skirt.*

ladera *f. slope.*

ladino *adj. shrewd; crafty, cunning.*

LADO *m. side; party, faction.*
   Siéntese a mi lado. *Sit next to me. Sit beside me.*
   Al otro lado de la calle. *Across the street. On the other side of the street.*
   Vive en la casa de al lado. *She lives next door. She lives in the next house.*
   Ese edificio queda al otro lado del parque. *That building's on the other side of the park.*
   Nos quedamos a este lado del lago. *We'll stay on this side of the lake.*

Por un lado. *On the one hand. On one side.*
Por un lado me gusta, pero por el otro no. *On the one hand I like it, on the other I don't.*
¡Mire Ud. al otro lado! *Look on the other side!*
¿Quiere hacerse a un lado? *Please move aside.*
No cabe de lado. *It won't fit sideways.*
Trabajaron lado a lado. *They worked side by side.*
Mirar de lado. *To look askance. To look out of the corner of one's eye. To look down on.*
Dejemos esto a un lado. *Let's put this aside.*
Conozco muy bien su lado flaco. *I know his weakness (weak side) very well.*

ladrar *to bark.*

ladrido *m. barking; criticism; calumny.*

ladrillo *m. brick, tile*

ladrón *m. thief, robber.*

lagartija *f. small lizard.*

lagarto *m. lizard, alligator (Amer.).*

lago *m. lake.*

lágrima *f. tear; drop.*

laguna *f. pond; gap, blank*

lamentable *adj. regrettable, deplorable.*
   Es lamentable. *It's regrettable.*

lamentar *to regret, to deplore; to mourn.*
   Lo lamento mucho. *I'm very sorry.*
   Lamento mucho lo ocurrido. *I regret what happened.*

lamer *to lick.*

lámina *f. plate, sheet of metal; engraving, print, picture.*

lámpara *f. lamp*

lana *f. wool.*

lance *m. event, occurrence.*

lancha *f. launch, boat.*

langosta *f. lobster, locust.*

lánguido *adj. languid, faint, weak.*

lanzacohetes *m. rocket launcher.*

lanzamiento *m. launching (of a ship); throwing.*

lanzar *to throw; to launch.*

lapicero *m. pencil holder.*

lápida *f. a flat stone with an inscription; gravestone.*

LÁPIZ *m. pencil; crayon.*
   Lápiz de labios. *Lipstick.*

lapso *m. lapse (of time).*

larga *f. delay, adjournment.*

largar *to loosen; to let go.*
   Largarse. *To leave. To go away.*
   ¡Lárguese de aquí! *Get out of here (not polite)!*

LARGO *adj. long; lengthy; m. length.*

Tiene los brazos muy largos. *He has very long arms.*

Tiene cinco pies de largo. *It's five feet long.*

No ponga Ud. esa cara tan larga. *Don't pull such a long face.*

Tres horas largas. *Three whole hours.*

A lo largo. 1. *In the distance.* 2. *Lengthwise.*

A lo largo de. *Along.*

A la corta o a la larga. *Sooner or later.*

A lo más largo. *At most.*

¡Largo de aquí! *Get out of here!*

Largo de mano. *Light-fingered.*

largometraje *m. full-length film.*

laringe *f. larynx.*

laringitis *f. laryngitis.*

larva *f. larva.*

las *f. pl. See* la *the.*

láser *m. laser ray.*

LÁSTIMA *f. pity; compassion.*

Es lástima. *It's a pity.*

¡Qué lástima! *What a pity! It's too bad! What a shame!*

Me da mucha lástima. *I feel very sorry for him.*

lastimar *to hurt; to injure.*

¿Se ha lastimado Ud.? *Have (did) you hurt yourself?*

Me lastimé una pierna al caer. *I hurt my leg when I fell (down).*

lastre *m. ballast.*

lata *f. tin; tin can; nuisance; bore.*

lateral *adj. lateral.*

latido *m. beat; throbbing.*

latigazo *m. lash; crack (of a whip).*

látigo *m. whip.*

latín *m. Latin.*

latino *adj. Latin.*

latir *to palpitate, to beat.*

latoso *adj. tiresome; boring.*

lava *f. lava.*

lavable *adj. washable.*

lavabo *m. washstand; washroom.*

lavadero *m. laundry, washing-place.*

lavado *m. washing.*

Lavado y planchado. *Laundry.*

lavandera *f. laundress, washwoman.*

lavandería *f. laundry.*

lavaplatos *m. dishwasher.*

lavar *to wash; to launder.*

Láveme estos calcetines. *Wash these socks for me.*

¿Le lavo la cabeza? *Do you want a shampoo?*

Lavar a seco. *To dry-clean.*

lavarse *to wash oneself.*

Lavarse las manos. *To wash one's hands.*

¿Quiere lavarse antes de comer? *Do you want to wash up before eating?*

lavativa *f. enema.*

laxante *adj. and n. laxative.*

lazo *m. bow; lasso, loop.*

Corbata de lazo. *Bow tie.*

LE *him, her, it (Spain); to him, to her, to it. See* les.

¿Qué la pasa? *What's the matter with him (her)?*

Le di el libro (a ella). *I gave her the book.*

Le expliqué el caso a mi esposa. *I explained the matter to my wife.*

leal *adj. loyal.*

lealtad *f. loyalty.*

lección *f. lesson.*

lector *adj. reader.*

lectura *f. reading.*

LECHE *f. milk.*

lechería *f. dairy.*

lechero *m. milkman.*

lecho *m. bed; bed of a river; stratum.*

lechón *m. little pig, suckling pig.*

lechuga *f. lettuce.*

lechuza *f. owl.*

LEER *to read.*

Puedo leer español pero no lo puedo hablar. *I can read Spanish but I can't speak it.*

legajo *m. file.*

legal *adj. legal, lawful; standard.*

Peso legal. *Standard weight.*

legalizar *to legalize.*

legar *to bequeath; to delegate.*

legendario *adj. legendary.*

legible *adj. legible.*

legión *f. legion.*

legislación *f. legislation.*

legislar *to legislate.*

legislatura *f. legislature.*

legitimar *to make legitimate, to legalize.*

legítimo *adj. legitimate; authentic.*

legua *f. league (measure of distance—about three miles).*

legumbre *f. vegetable.*

leído *adj. well-read, well-educated.*

Es un hombre muy leído. *He's a well-read man.*

lejano *adj. distant, remote, far.*

Un país lejano. *A distant country.*

LEJOS *far, far away, distant.*

¿Es muy lejos de aquí? *Is it very far from here?*

Algo lejos. *Rather far.*

A lo lejos. *In the distance.*

Desde (de) lejos. *From afar. From a distance.*

lema *m. motto.*

lempira *m. Honduran currency unit.*

lencería *f. linen goods, linen shop; linen trade.*

LENGUA *f. tongue; language.*
Lengua española. *Spanish language.*
Lengua madre. *Mother tongue.*
Tirar de la lengua. *To draw one out.*
No morderse la lengua. *Not to be afraid to talk.*
Morderse la lengua. *To hold one's tongue.* (*"To bite one's tongue."*)
Irsele a uno la lengua. *To speak out of turn.*
Pegarse la lengua al paladar. *To be speechless with excitement or fear.*
lenguaje *m. language; style.*
Lenguaje de máquina. *Machine language.*
LENTAMENTE *slowly.*
lente *m. lens; pl. eyeglasses.*
Lente de contacto. *Contact lens.*
lenteja *f. lentil.*
lentitud *f. slowness.*
LENTO *adj. slow; sluggish.*
leña *f. firewood.*
A falta de carbón quemaremos leña. *If there's no coal, we'll burn wood.*
Echar leña al fuego. *To add fuel to the fire.*
leñador *m. woodcutter.*
leño *m. log, block.*
Dormir como un leño. *To sleep like a log.*
león *m. lion.*
leona *f. lioness; brave woman.*
leopardo *m. leopard.*
lepra *f. leprosy.*
LES *to them; to you (pl.); them, you (pl. Spain)* See **le.**
Les escribiré. *I'll write to them.*
Les estimo mucho. *I have a high regard for them (you, pl.).*
Les encantará (a Uds.). *You (pl.) will love it.*
lesbia *f. lesbian.*
lesión *f. lesion, injury, wound.*
lesionar *to hurt; to wound; to injure.*
LETRA *f. letter; handwriting; printing type; words of a song; draft, bill (of exchange).*
Tiene buena letra. *She has a good handwriting.*
A la letra. *To the letter. Literally. Verbatim.*
Letra de cambio. *Bill of exchange.*
letrado *adj. learned, erudite; m. lawyer.*
letrero *m. inscription; sign; label.*
No me había fijado en el letrero. *I didn't notice the sign.*
letrina *f. latrine.*
levadura *f. leaven, yeast.*
levantamiento *m. raising, uprising, revolt.*
LEVANTAR *to raise, to lift, to pick up; to remove, to clear (the table).*
¿Puede Ud. levantar ese peso? *Can you lift*

that weight?
Levante la mesa. *Clear the table.*
Levanta ese papel del suelo. *Pick up that paper from the floor.*
Levantar cabeza. *To raise one's head again. To get on one's feet again.*
Empezó a levantar la voz. *He began to raise his voice.*
Llegamos en el momento de levantar el telón. *We arrived just as the curtain was going up.*
Levantar la vista. *To life one's eyes. To look up.*
LEVANTARSE *to raise, to get up.*
¿A qué hora se levanta Ud.? *What time do you get up?*
Me levanto temprano. *I get up early.*
Es hora de levantarse. *It's time to get up.*
leve *adj. light (weight); slight.*
léxico *m. lexicon.*
LEY *f. law, act; legal standard of quality, weight or measure.*
Proyecto de ley. *Bill (of Congress).*
La ley fue aprobada en el senado. *The law was passed in (by) the Senate.*
leyenda *f. legend; inscription (on coins, metals, etc.).*
liar *to tie, to bind; to enroil.*
liberación *f. liberation.*
Liberación condicional. *Parole.*
liberal *adj. and n. liberal.*
liberar *See* **libertar.**
libertad *f. liberty, freedom.*
libertador *adj. liberating; m. liberator.*
libertar *to liberate, to free.*
libertino *adj. and n. dissolute, licentious; libertine.*
libra *f. pound.*
Déme media libra de café. *Give me half a pound of coffee.*
Libra esterlina. *Pound sterling.*
libranza *f. draft; money order.*
LIBRE *adj. free.*
Libre cambio. *Free trade.*
Libre a bordo. *Free on board (F.O.B.).*
Entrada libre. *Admission free.*
librería *f. bookstore; library; bookcase.*
librero *m. bookseller.*
libreta *f. memorandum book.*
Libreta de apuntes. *Notebook.*
Libreta de depósitos. *Bankbook.*
LIBRO *m. book.*
Libro en rústica. *Paper-bound book.*
Firme en el libro de registro. *Sign the register.*
licencia *f. license; leave, furlough; permit; certificate; degree.*
Tomar una licencia. *To take a leave.*
licenciado *m. university graduate; lawyer.*

licenciar *to license; to allow; to discharge (a soldier).*

licitador *m. bidder.*

licitar *to bid on, to auction.*

lícito *adj. licit, lawful, just, fair.*

licor *m. liquor.*

licorería *f. liquor store.*

líder *m. leader.*

lidiar *to combat, to fight; to contend.*

liebre *f. hare.*
> Donde menos se piensa salta la liebre. *Things happen unexpectedly.*

lienzo *m. linen cloth; canvas (painting).*

liga *f. garter; league; alloy.*

ligar *to bind, to tie; to alloy.*

ligereza *f. lightness; fickleness; hastiness.*

LIGERO *adj. quick, swift, light (weight); hasty.*
> Hágalo ligero. *Do it quickly.*

lija *f. sandpaper; dogfish.*

lila *f. lilac; lilac color.*

lima *f. lime (fruit); file (tool).*

limar *to file (with a tool); to polish.*

limitado *adj. limited.*

limitar *to limit; to restrain.*
> Limitarse a decir. *To confine oneself to say.*

límite *f. limit, boundary, border.*
> Todo tiene sus límites. *There's a limit to everything. One must draw the line somewhere.*

limón *m. lemon.*

limonada *f. lemonade; slum.*

limosna *f. alms, charity.*
> Pedir limosna. *To beg.*

limpiabotas *m. shoe shiner.*

limpiador *m. cleaner; cleanser.*

limpiaparabrisas *m. windshield wiper.*

limpiar *to clean, to cleanse; to mop up.*
> Quiero que me limpie en seco este traje. *I'd like this suit dry-cleaned.*
> Quiero que me limpien los zapatos. *I want my shoes shined. I want a shoeshine.*

limpieza *f. cleaning; cleanliness; honesty.*

LIMPIO *adj. clean; neat; pure.*
> Tiene su casa muy limpia. *She keeps her house very clean.*
> Poner en limpio. *To make a good (final, "clean") copy.*
> Sacar en limpio. *To make out. To conclude. To infer.*
> Jugar limpio. *To play fair. To deal fairly.*

linaza *f. linseed; flaxseed.*

lince *adj. keen, sharp-sighted; m. lynx.*

linchar *to lynch.*

lindar *to adjoin, to border.*

linde *m. limit, boundary; landmark.*

lindero *adj. adjoining, bordering; m. boundary.*

LINDO *adj. pretty; neat.*

¡Qué muchacha tan linda! *What a pretty girl!*
> Nos divertimos de lo lindo. *We had a wonderful time.*

LÍNEA *f. line.*
> Tire Ud. una línea recta. *Draw a straight line.*
> La línea está ocupada. *The line is busy.*
> Escribir cuatro líneas. *To write a few lines. To drop someone a note.*
> Línea telefónica. *Telephone line.*
> Línea aérea. *Airline.*
> En toda la línea. *All along the line.*

lingote *m. ingot.*

lingüista *m. and f. linguist.*

linimento *m. liniment.*

lino *m. flax; linen.*

linóleo *m. linoleum.*

linterna *f. lantern; flashlight.*

lío *m. bundle, parcel; row, fix, mess.*
> En buen lío nos hemos metido. *We got ourselves in quite a fix.*
> Armar un lío. *To start a row.*

liquidación *f. liquidation; clearance sale.*

liquidar *to liquidate.*

LÍQUIDO *adj. liquid; clear, net; m. liquid, fluid.*
> Producto líquido. *Net proceeds.*

lírico *adj. lyric, lyrical.*

lirio *m. lily.*

lisiado *adj. maimed, crippled.*

liso *adj. smooth, even; plain.*
> Tela lisa. *Plain cloth.*

lisonja *f. flattery.*

lisonjear *to flatter; to please.*

lisonjero *adj. flattering, pleasing; n. flatterer.*
> Él habla de Ud. de una manera muy lisonjera. *He speaks well of you.*

LISTA *f. list; roll; menu; stripe.*
> Aquí está la lista de platos. *Here is the menu.*
> Pasar lista. *To call the roll.*
> Tela a listas. *Striped cloth.*

listado *adj. striped; m. listing (computer).*
> Listado en papel. *Hard copy.*

LISTO *adj. ready; quick; bright, clever, smart, cunning.*
> ¿Está Ud. listo? *Are you ready?*
> No crea, es más listo de lo que parece. *Don't get the wrong idea; he's smarter than he looks.*

litera *berth (train); bunk.*

literario *adj. literary.*

literato *m. learned man; writer.*

literatura *f. literature.*

litigio *m. litigation, lawsuit.*

litografía *f. lithography.*

litoral *adj. littoral; m. coast; seacoast.*

litro *m. liter.*

liviano *adj. light (weight); fickle; lewd.*

lívido *adj. livid; pale.*

> Se puso lívido. *He became pale.*

LO *(neuter article) the . . . thing; the . . . part.*

> Lo mejor de . . . *The best thing about. . . .*

> Lo dicho. *What's said.*

> Lo mío y lo tuyo. *What's mine and what's yours.*

> Lo demás importa poco. *The rest doesn't matter a great deal. The rest is not very important.*

> Eso es lo que quiero. *That's what I want.*

> A lo lejos. *At a distance. In the distance.*

> A lo sumo. *At the most.*

LO *(m. and neuter direct object pronoun) it, him, you.*

> ¿Me lo das? *Will you give it to me?*

> Démelo. *Give it to me.*

> ¿Están Uds. listos? —Lo estamos. *Are you ready? —We are.*

> No lo conozco. *I don't know him.*

> Se lo llevaron a casa. *They took (carried) him home.*

> No lo puedo remediar. *I can't help it.*

lobo *m. wolf.*

lóbulo *m. lobe, lobule.*

lóbrego *adj. murky, dark; sad.*

local *adj. local; m. place; quarters.*

> Costumbre local. *Local custom.*

> Este local es muy pequeño. *This place (hall, etc.) is very small.*

localidad *f. locality, place; seat (theater).*

localizar *to localize, to locate.*

loción *f. lotion, wash.*

> Loción humectante. *Moisturizer.*

> Loción bronceadora. *Tanning lotion.*

loco *adj. mad, insane, crazy; m. madman.*

> Volverse loco. *To lose one's mind. To become insane.*

> Estar loco. *To be crazy.*

> Está loco por ella. *He's head over heels in love with her. He's crazy about her.*

> Hablar a tontas y a locas. *To tell idle stories (tales).*

locuaz *adj. loquacious, talkative.*

locura *f. insanity, madness, folly.*

> Eso es una locura. *That's a crazy thing to do. That's absurd.*

locutor *m. announcer, emcee.*

lodo *m. mud, mire.*

lógica *f. logic.*

> Carece de lógica y de sentido común. *It lacks logic and common sense.*

lógico *adj. logical, reasonable.*

LOGRAR *to obtain, to get; to attain; to manage, to succeed.*

> Por fin logró lo que quería. *He finally got what he wanted.*

> Debe haber algún medio de lograrlo. *There must be some way of getting it (of obtaining it).*

> Lograron hacerlo. *They managed to do it.*

logro *m. gain; attainment; achievement.*

loma *f. hillock, little hill.*

lombriz *f. earthworm.*

lomo *m. loin; back (of a book); ridge (agriculture).*

> Llevar a lomo. *To carry on one's back.*

lona *f. canvas.*

> Zapatos de lona. *Sneakers.*

longaniza *f. a kind of sausage.*

longitud *f. longitude.*

lonja *f. exchange market; warehouse.*

loro *m. parrot.*

LOS *(pl. of el) the. See* **la, lo.**

> Los hombres. *The men.*

> Los dos. *Both. The two of them.*

> Los míos. *My people, My family. My folks.*

> Límpiate los dientes. *Brush your teeth.*

LOS *(pl. direct object pronoun) they, them; you (pl.). See* **le** *and* **les.**

> ¿Cómo los quiere Ud.? *How do you want them?*

> Los aguardábamos (a Uds.). *We were waiting for you (pl.).*

> Se los daré mañana. *I'll give them to you (them) tomorrow.*

losa *f. tombstone.*

lote *m. lot; portion, share.*

loza *f. chinaware; crockery.*

lozanía *f. vigor; exuberance, liveliness.*

lozano *adj. healthy; sprightly, lively.*

lubricación *f. lubrication.*

lubricante *adj. lubricating; m. lubricant.*

lubricar *to lubricate.*

lucidez *f. lucidity, clearness.*

lúcido *adj. lucid, brilliant.*

luciérnaga *f. glowworm, firefly.*

lucir *to shine, to show off.*

lucirse *to outshine; to show off.*

lucrativo *adj. lucrative, profitable.*

lucro *m. gain, profit.*

lucha *f. fight, struggle, strife.*

> La lucha por la vida. *The struggle for existence.*

luchador *wrestler, fighter.*

luchar *to fight, to wrestle, to struggle.*

LUEGO *immediately, soon, afterward, then, later.*

> ¡Hasta luego! *See you later. So long.*

> Cenaremos y luego iremos al teatro. *We'll have dinner and then we'll go to the theater.*

> Desde luego. *Of course.*

> Avíseme luego que lo reciba. *As soon as you receive it, let me know.*

LUGAR *m. place; time; occasion; motive, cause.*

Ponga las cosas en su lugar. *Put the things in their place. Put everything in its place.*

Yo en su lugar, no iría. *If I were you (in your place) I wouldn't go.*

¿A qué hora tendrá lugar la boda? *What time will the wedding take place?*

En lugar de. *Instead of.*

Dar lugar a. *To give cause for. To give occasion for. To lead up to.*

lugarteniente *m. deputy, substitute, lieutenant.*

lujo *m. luxury.*

Edición de lujo. *Deluxe edition.*

lujoso *adj. luxurious.*

lujuria *f. lust; excess.*

lumbre *f. fire, light.*

luminoso *adj. shining, luminous.*

LUNA *f. moon; glass plate for mirrors.*

Hay luna esta noche. *The moon is out tonight.*

Luna de miel. *Honeymoon.*

lunático *adj. lunatic, mad, eccentric.*

LUNES *m. Monday*

lustrar *to polish, to shine.*

lustre *m. luster, gloss; splendor.*

luto *m. mourning; grief, sorrow.*

De luto. *In mourning.*

LUZ *f. light, daylight.*

Encienda la luz. *Put the light on.*

Apague la luz. *Turn the light off. Put the light out.*

Se apagaron las luces. *The lights went out.*

Luz alta. *Beam (car lights).*

Dar a luz. 1. *To give birth.* 2. *To publish.*

Salir a luz. *To be published. To appear (a book).*

lycra *f. lycra.*

LL

llaga *f. ulcer, wound.*

llama *f. flame; llama (animal).*

llamada *f. telephone call; knock (at the door).*

Hacer una llamada. *To make a telephone call.*

llamamiento *m. calling; call; appeal.*

LLAMAR *to call; to appeal; to name; to send for; to knock (at the door).*

¿Ha llamado Ud.? *Did you call?*

Llamar por teléfono. *To phone.*

Llame Ud. un taxi, por favor. *Please call a taxi.*

Llaman a la puerta. *Somebody's knocking at the door. Someone's at the door.*

Mande a llamar al doctor. *Send for the doctor.*

Llamar la atención. *To call attention to.*

LLAMARSE *to be called or named.*

¿Cómo se llama Ud.? *What's your name?*

Me llamo . . . *My name is . . .*

¿Cómo se llama esta calle? *What's the name of this street?*

llamarada *f. blaze; flushing (of the face).*

llamativo *adj. conspicuous, striking, attractive, showy.*

llanamente *simple, plainly, clearly; sincerely.*

llaneza *f. simplicity, plainness.*

llano *adj. even, smooth, flat; frank; m. plain, flatland.*

Un campo llano. *A smooth terrain.*

llanta *f. rim; tire.*

llanto *m. weeping, crying.*

llanura *f. plain, flatlands.*

LLAVE *f. key; wrench; faucet, spigot.*

¿Dónde está la llave de mi cuarto? *Where's the key to my room?*

Cerrar con llave. *To lock.*

llavero *m. key-ring.*

llegada *f. arrival, coming.*

Avíseme de su llegada. *Let me know when you'll (he'll) arrive.*

LLEGAR *to arrive; to come; to reach, to succeed; to amount.*

¿A qué hora llega el tren? *(At) What time does the train arrive?*

El tren llega con dos horas de retraso. *The train is two hours late.*

¿Llegó Ud. a tiempo? *Were you in time?*

Llegó a hacerlo. *He managed to do it.*

Tenía prisa por llegar a la hora. *He was in a hurry to get there on time.*

Ha llegado a mis oídos que . . . *I've heard that . . .*

Llegar a ser. *To become.*

Llegar a las manos. *To come to blows.*

LLENAR *to fill, to fill out/up; to occupy; to satisfy; to fulfill.*

Llene la botella de vino. *Fill the bottle with wine.*

Llene el formulario de impuestos. *Fill out the tax form.*

Llenar una receta. *To fill a prescription.*

Llenar completamente. *To fill up (completely).*

LLENO *adj. full; complete; m. fullness, abundance.*

Estoy lleno. *I'm full. I've had enough.*

El vaso está lleno. *The glass is full.*

LLEVAR *to carry, to take; to take away; to set (a price); to wear (clothes); to be (older, late, etc.).*

Taxi, lléveme a la estación. *Taxi, take me to the station.*

Lleve estas cartas al correo. *Take these letters to the post office.*

¿Llevamos paraguas? *Shall we take umbrellas?*

No llevo bastante dinero. *I don't have enough money on me.*

Ayúdeme a llevar este hombre en la camilla. *Help me carry this man on the stretcher.*

Lléveselo. *Take it.*

Me lo llevo si me lo deja en tres dólares. *I'll take it if you'll let me have it for three dollars.*

Hace una semana que llevo este traje. *I've worn this suit for a week.*

Llevar al revés. *To wear on the wrong side.*

¿Cuánto tiempo lleva Ud. esperándome? *How long have you been waiting for me?*

El tren lleva una hora de retraso. *The train is an hour late.*

Le llevo cinco años. *I'm five years older than he.*

Llevar a cuestas. *To carry on one's shoulders.*

Llevar a cabo. *To carry out. To bring about. To put through.*

Llevar consigo. *To carry along with one. To carry with it. To imply.*

Llevar la delantera. *To lead. To be ahead.*

Llevar lo mejor. *To get the best. To get the best part of.*

llevarse *to take or carry away; to get along.*

Llévese Ud. estos libros. *Take these books away.*

Se llevó la palma. *He carried the day.*

Llevarse bien. *To get along well (together).*

Llevarse mal. *To be on bad terms.*

Llevarse un chasco. *To suffer a bitter disappointment.*

llorar *to weep, to cry; to lament.*

lloro *m weeping, crying.*

LLOVER *to rain, to shower.*

Está lloviendo. *It's raining.*

Parece que va a llover. *It looks as if it's going to rain.*

Llueve a cántaros. *It's pouring. It's raining cats and dogs.*

Eso ya es llover sobre mojado. *That's adding insult to injury.*

llovizna *f. drizzle.*

lloviznar *to drizzle.*

LLUEVE *It's raining*

LLUVIA *f. rain, shower.*

M

macanudo *adj. (Amer.) fine, excellent, first-rate.*

macarrones *m. pl. macaroni.*

maceta *f. flowerpot; mallet.*

macizo *adj. solid; massive; firm.*

machacar *to pound; to crush; to harp; to dwell (on a subject).*

machete *m. machete.*

macho *adj. male; masculine; virile; m. male animal; mule.*

machucar *to pound, to bruise.*

madame *f. madam.*

madeja *f. hank, skein; lock of hair.*

MADERA *f. wood; lumber; timber.*

Esto es de madera. *This is made of wood.*

maderero *m. dealer in lumber.*

madero *m. beam; timber; piece of lumber.*

madrastra *f. stepmother.*

madre *f. mother; bed (of a river).*

madreselva *f. honeysuckle.*

madriguera *f. burrow; den.*

madrina *f. godmother; bridesmaid; sponsor, patroness.*

madrugada *f. dawn; early morning.*

De madrugada. *At dawn.*

En la madrugada. *In the early morning.*

madrugador *adj. early riser.*

¡Ud. es muy madrugador! *You're an early bird!*

madrugar *to get up early; to get ahead of.*

Tú sí que has madrugado. *But you're up early!*

A quien madruga Dios le ayuda. *The early bird catches the worm.*

madurar *to ripen; to mature.*

madurez *f. maturity; ripeness.*

maduro *adj. ripe; mature.*

La fruta todavía no está madura. *The fruit isn't ripe yet.*

maestro *adj. masterly, master; m. teacher; skilled craftsman; master.*

Una obra maestra. *A masterpiece.*

Es un maestro. *He's a teacher.*

Maestro de obras. *Builder.*

magia *f. magic.*

mágico *adj. magic; marvelous.*

magisterio *m. teaching profession; teachers (as a group).*

magistrado *m. magistrate.*

magnánimo *adj. magnanimous.*

magnesia *f. magnesia.*

magnético *adj. magnetic.*

magnífico *adj. magnificent, splendid, wonderful.*

Habrá que felicitarle por su magnífica labor. *We ought to (must) congratulate him on his wonderful achievement.*

magnitud *f. magnitude; importance, greatness.*

magno *adj. great.*

Alejandro Magno. *Alexander the Great.*

Es una obra magna. *It's an excellent piece of work.*

magnolia *f. magnolia.*

mago *m. magician, wizard.*

maguey *m. maguey (fruit), American aloe.*

mahometano *adj. and n. Mohammedan.*

maicena *f. corn flour.*

maíz *m. maize, Indian corn.*

Rosetas de maíz. *Popcorn.*

maizal *m. corn field.*

majadero *adj. and n. silly; bore, pest.*

majestad *f. majesty.*

majestuoso *adj. majestic, imposing.*

MAL *adj. (shortening of* **malo** *used before masc. nouns) bad; adv. badly, poorly; m. evil; harm; disease; illness.*

Hace mal tiempo. *The weather's bad.*

Está de muy mal humor. *He's in a very bad mood.*

No está mal. *Not bad. It's not bad.*

Este libro está mal escrito. *This book is badly written.*

Ando mal de dinero. *I'm short of money.*

De mal en peor. *Worse and worse. From bad to worse.*

Hacer mal. *To do harm. To do wrong. To act wrongly.*

Este abrigo me está mal. *This coat doesn't fit me.*

Mal hecho. *Badly done.*

Mal que le pese. *In spite of him.*

Mal de su grado. *Unwillingly.*

El bíen y el mal. *Right and wrong. Good and evil.*

Tomemos del mal el menos. *Let's choose the lesser of the two evils.*

Mal de garganta. *Sore throat.*

Este mal tiene cura. *This sickness (disease) is curable.*

malagradecido *adj. ungrateful.*

malaria *f. malaria; paludism.*

malbaratar *to undersell; to squander.*

malcriado *adj. ill-bred; naughty.*

maldad *f. wickedness.*

maldecir *to damn, to curse.*

maldición *f. curse.*

maldito *adj. wicked; damned; cursed.*

malecón *m. sea wall, jetty*

maleducado *adj. bad-mannered.*

maleficio *m. witchcraft, enchantment.*

malestar *m. indisposition, discomfort.*

Sentir un malestar. *To be indisposed.*

maleta *f. valise, suitcase.*

maletera *f. trunk (car).*

maleza *f. underbrush, thicket.*

malgastar *to squander, to waste.*

malhablado *adj. foul-mouthed.*

malhechor *m. malefactor, criminal.*

malhumorado *adj. ill-humored, peevish.*

malicia *f. malice; suspicion.*

malicioso *adj. malicious, suspicious.*

maligno *adj. malignant.*

malintencionado *adj. evil-minded, ill-disposed.*

MALO *adj. bad; wicked; ill; difficult; poorly.*

No es mala idea. *That's not a bad idea.*

¿Qué hay de malo en eso? *What harm is there in that? What's wrong with it?*

¿Te sientes malo? *Do you feel ill?*

¿Tiene Ud. los ojos malos? *Are your eyes sore?*

Ese niño es muy malo. *This child is very bad.*

Estos huevos están malos. *These eggs are bad.*

Lo dijo de mala fe. *He said it deceitfully.*

Lo malo es que no tengo tiempo. *The trouble is that I've no time.*

Tiene mala cabeza. *He's reckless.*

Trabajó de mala gana. *He worked unwillingly.*

Tener malas pulgas. *To be hot-tempered. To be hotheaded (hot-blooded).*

Por malas o por buenas. *Willingly or unwillingly. Willy-nilly.*

malsano *adj. unhealthy, unhealthful.*

Es un clima muy malsano. *It's a very unhealthful climate.*

maltratar *to treat roughly, to mistreat, to abuse; to harm.*

maltrato *m. ill-treatment.*

malvado *adj. wicked.*

mamá *f. mama, mommy.*

mamar *to suck.*

mamarracho *m. ridiculous thing; rubbish; idiot.*

mamey *m. mamee (tree and its fruit).*

mamífero *adj. mammalian; m. pl. mammals.*

manantial *m. spring, source.*

manar *to flow; to ooze.*

manco *adj. one-handed; one-armed; crippled.*

mancomún (de) *adj. jointly, in common; by mutual consent.*

mancomunar *to associate; to subject to joint liability.*

mancha *f. stain, spot; blemish.*

manchado *adj. stained, spotted.*

manchar *to stain, to spot, to soil.*

mandadero *m. messenger; errand boy.*

mandado *m. errand.*

¿Puede Ud. hacerme un mandado? *Will (can) you do (run) an errand for me?*

mandamiento *m. mandate; commandment.*

MANDAR *to send; to will, bequeath; to order; to command; to govern.*

Mande el paquete a estas señas. *Send the package to this address.*

¿Me ha mandado Ud. llamar? *Did you send for me? Have you sent for me?*

Le mandé venir inmediatamente. *I had him come immediately.*

Mande por una ambulancia. *Send for an ambulance.*

He mandado hacer un traje a la medida. *I'm having a suit made to order.*

Mandar decir. *To send word.*

mandarina *f. mandarin, tangerine.*

mandatario *m. attorney; agent; proxy.*

mandato *m. mandate, order.*

mandíbula *f. jaw, jawbone.*

mando *m. command, authority, control.*

Mando medio. *Middle management.*

Mando para juegos. *Joystick.*

mandolina *f. mandolin.*

mandón *adj. domineering, bossy.*

manecilla *f. small hand; hand of a clock or watch.*

manejar *to handle; to drive; to govern; to manage.*

¿Sabe Ud. manejar? *Do you know how to drive?*

manejo *m. management; handling.*

Manejo de personal. *Personnel management.*

MANERA *f. manner, way, method.*

Hágalo de cualquier manera. *Do it any way you can. Do it any old way.*

No hay manera de traducirlo. *There's no way to translate it.*

No tiene buenas maneras. *He has no manners.*

¿De manera que no viene Ud.? *So you're not coming?*

Le alabó en gran manera. *He praised him very highly.*

En cierta manera. *To a certain extent.*

De ninguna manera. *By no means.*

De todas maneras iremos. *We'll go in any case.*

De manera que. *So then. So as to. In such a manner as to.*

Escríbalo de manera que se pueda leer. *Write it so that it can be read (that one can read it).*

manga *f. sleeve; hose (for water); strainer.*

Tener manga ancha. *To be broad-minded.*

En mangas de camisa. *In shirtsleeves.*

mango *m. handle, haft; mango (tree and its fruit).*

mangonear *to sponge; to loaf; to meddle, to pry.*

mangoneo *m. meddling; pettifogging; sponging.*

manguera *f. hose.*

manía *f. mania, frenzy, whim.*

maniático *adj. and n. maniac.*

manicomio *m. insane asylum.*

manicura *f. manicure.*

manifestación *f. manifestation, demonstration.*

manifestante *m. and f. protestor.*

manifestar *to manifest; to state; to reveal.*

manifiesto *adj. manifest; clear, obvious.*

maniobra *f. maneuver; handiwork.*

manipulación *f. handling, manipulation.*

manipular *to handle, to manipulate; to manage.*

maniquí *m. mannequin.*

manivela *f. crank (handle).*

manjar *m. dish, food; victuals.*

MANO *f. hand; forefoot; coat (of paint, etc.); first hand (cards).*

Lo tengo en la mano. *I have it in my hand.*

Le dió la mano al verle. *He shook hands with him when he saw him.*

Mano izquierda. *Left hand.*

Mano derecha. *Right hand.*

El es mi mano derecha. *He's my right-hand man.*

Pidió la mano de mi hermana. *He asked for my sister's hand (in marriage).*

Dejo el asunto en sus manos. *I leave the matter in your hands. I leave it up to you.*

¡Manos a la obra! *Get it started! Get to work! Let's start (it)!*

¡Manos arriba! *Hands up!*

Suelte Ud. las manos. *Let go!*

Vinieron a las manos. *They came to blows.*

Bajo mano. (Debajo de mano.) *Underhandedly. In an underhand manner.*

De buena mano. *On good authority. From a reliable source.*

Mano a mano. *Even. On equal terms (Hand to hand.)*

A mano. 1. *At hand. Nearby.* 2. *By hand.*

Hecho a mano. *Made by hand. Hand-made.*

De primera mano. *First-hand.*

manojo *m. handful, bunch.*

manosear *to handle; to feel; to rumple.*

mansión *f. mansion; residence.*

manso *adj. tame; gentle.*

manta *f. blanket.*

manteca *f. lard; fat; butter.*

mantecado *m. vanilla ice cream; milk shake.*

mantel *m. tablecloth.*

mantener *to feed, to support, to maintain; to keep up; to uphold (an opinion).*

Tiene que mantener dos familias. *He has to support two families.*

Mantener correspondencia. *To keep up a correspondence.*

Mantener una opinión. *To hold to (maintain) an opinion.*

mantenerse *to support oneself, to earn one's living; to stick to; to hold one's own; to remain; to stay.*

En este termos el agua se mantiene fresca. *The water stays cold in this thermos bottle.*

Me mantengo en lo dicho. *I maintain (stick to) what I've said.*

Se mantuvieron firmes hasta el fin. *They held their ground till the very end.*

mantenimiento *m. maintenance, support.*

MANTEQUILLA *f. butter.*

manto *m. mantle, cloak.*

mantón *m. large shawl.*

manual *adj. manual; m. handbook; manual.*

manufacturar *to manufacture.*

manuscrito *adj. written by hand; m. manuscript.*

manutención *f. support, maintenance.*

manzana *f. apple; block (street).*

manzanilla *f. camomile (plant); manzanilla (a strong white wine).*

manzano *m. apple tree.*

maña *f. dexterity, skill, cunning; knack, trick, habit.*

mañana *f. morning; tomorrow.*

Esta mañana. *This morning.*

Hasta mañana. *See you tomorrow.*

Mañana por la mañana. *Tomorrow morning.*

Pasado mañana. *The day after tomorrow.*

mañoso *adj. handy, skillful; cunning.*

mapa *m. map, chart.*

mapamundi *m. map of the world.*

maquilladora *f. Mexican border assembly plant (in-bond industry).*

maquillaje *m. makeup, cosmetics.*

maquillista *m. and f. makeup artist.*

máquina *f. machine; engine.*

Máquina de escribir. *Typewriter.*

A máquina. *By machine.*

maquinaria *f. machinery.*

maquinilla *f. small machine.*

Maquinilla de afeitar. *Electric shaver.*

maquinista *m. machinist; engineer, engine driver.*

MAR *m. and f. sea.*

Iremos por mar. *We'll go by sea.*

Viaje por mar. *Sea voyage.*

En el mar. *At sea.*

maraca *m. maraca (musical instrument).*

maraña *f. entanglement, perplexity, puzzle.*

maravilla *f. marvel, wonder.*

A maravilla. *Marvelously.*

maravillarse *to marvel, to admire.*

maravilloso *adj. marvelous, wonderful.*

marca *f. mark; brand; make*

Es una marca renombrada. *It's a well-known brand.*

marcar *to mark; to brand; to register.*

El termómetro marca treinta grados a la sombra. *The thermometer registers thirty degrees in the shade. It's thirty degrees in the shade.*

Marcar un número. *To dial (a number).*

Marca registrada. *Trademark.*

marcial *adj. martial, military.*

Artes marciales. *Martial arts.*

marco *m. frame.*

marcha *f. march.*

marchante *m. customer; client.*

MARCHAR *to go; to go off; to leave; to march.*

¿Se marcha Ud. ya? *Are you leaving already?*

Tengo que marcharme en seguida. *I have to go immediately.*

Se marcha al extranjero. *He's going abroad.*

El sargento marchaba delante de la compañía. *The sergeant was marching in front of the company.*

marchitar *to wither, to fade.*

marchito *adj. faded, withered.*

marea *f. tide.*

mareado *adj. seasick*

marearse *to get seasick.*

mareo *m. seasickness; dizziness.*

marfil *m. ivory.*

margarina *f. margarine.*

margen *m. and f. margin, border; bank (of a river).*

mariachi *m. and f. musician (Mexico).*

marica *m. (pejorative) gay, homosexual.*

maricón *(pejorative) m. gay, homosexual.*

marido *m. husband.*

Marido y mujer. *Husband and wife.*

marina *f. navy.*

marinero *adj. seaworthy; m. sailor.*

marino *m. seaman; navy blue.*

mariposa *f. butterfly.*

marítimo *adj. maritime.*

marmita *f. kettle, saucepan.*

mármol *m. marble.*

marqués *m. marquis.*

marquesa *f. marchioness.*

MARTES *m. Tuesday.*

martillar *to hammer.*

martillazo *m. a hammer blow.*

martillo *m. hammer.*

mártir *m. martyr.*

MARZO *m. March.*

marrano *m. hog, pig; dirty person.*

marrón *adj. brown.*

mas *conj. but, yet, however.*

Parecen distintos mas no lo son. *They seem different but they're not.*

MÁS *adv. more; most; over; besides; plus.*

Más o menos. *More or less.*

¿Cuánto me costará, más o menos? *About how much will it cost?*

¿Nada más? *Is that all? Nothing else?*

No se me ocurre nada más. *I can't think of anything else.*

No hay más. *There are (there is) no more.*

¿A quién quiere Ud. más? *Who(m) do you like (love) the best (more)?*

Cinco más dos son siete. *Five plus two are seven.*

Es la cosa más fácil del mundo. *It's the easiest thing in the world.*

Más adelante se lo explicaré. *Later on, I'll explain it to you.*

Son más de las diez. *It's after ten o'clock.*

¡Qué papel más malo! *What bad (poor, awful) paper!*

¡Más vale así! *So much the better!*

Eso es lo más acertado. *That's the best thing to do.*

No faltaba más que eso. *That's all we needed. That's the limit.*

Acérquese un poco más al micrófono. *Come a little closer to the microphone.*

Las más de las veces. *Most of the time.*

Lo más pronto. *As soon as possible.*

A lo más. *At most.*

Más tarde o más temprano. *Sooner or later.*

A más tardar. *At the latest.*

Más de. *More than. Over.*

De más. *Too much. Too many.*

Sin más mi más. *Without much ado.*

Más bien. *Rather.*

masa *f. dough; mass; crowd.*

En masa. *In bulk.*

masaje *m. massage.*

Dar un masaje. *To massage. To give a massage.*

masajista *m. and f. masseur, masseuse.*

mascar *to chew.*

máscara *f. mask; disguise.*

mascota *f. mascot.*

masculino *adj. masculine.*

Género masculino. *Masculine gender.*

masón *m. Freemason.*

masonería *f. Freemasonry.*

masticar *to chew, to masticate.*

Mastique bien la comida. *Chew your food well.*

mástil *m. mast, post.*

mata *f. plant, shrub.*

matadero *m. slaughterhouse.*

matanza *f. slaughter, massacre.*

matar *to kill, to murder.*

No matarás. *Thou shalt not kill!*

Matar el tiempo. *To kill time.*

mate *adj. dull (finish); m. checkmate; maté, Paraguay tea; dull color.*

matemáticas *m. mathematics.*

matemático *m. mathematician.*

materia *f. matter; material; subject.*

Materia prima. *Raw material.*

material *adj. material; m. material; equipment.*

Ese material no sirve. *This material is no good.*

Material rodante. *Rolling stock.*

materializar *to materialize; to realize.*

maternal *adj. maternal.*

maternidad *f. maternity.*

materno *adj. maternal, motherly.*

matiz *m. shade of color.*

matón *m. bully.*

matorral *m. thicket, bushes.*

matrícula *f. register; list; matriculation.*

matricular *to matriculate, to register.*

¿En qué escuela te has matriculado? *At what school did you register?*

matrimonio *m. marriage, matrimony; married couple.*

Matrimonio natural. *Common-law marriage.*

mausoleo *m. mausoleum.*

máxima *f. maxim, rule; proverb.*

máximo *adj. maximum, highest, largest, chief, principal.*

Máxima altura. *Highest point. Peak.*

El precio máximo es de diez dólares. *The maximum price is ten dollars.*

MAYO *m. May.*

mayonesa *f. mayonnaise.*

MAYOR *adj. greater, greatest; larger, largest; elder, eldest; m. major.*

Fue mayor en el ejército. *He was a major in the army.*

¿Cuál es la ciudad mayor del mundo? *What is the largest city in the world?*

¿Es su hermana mayor o menor que Ud.? *Is your sister older or younger than you?*

Ser mayor de edad. *To be of age.*

Este asunto es del mayor interés. *This matter is of the greatest interest.*

La mayor parte de la gente lo cree. *Most (of the) people believe it.*

Viven en la calle Mayor. *They live on Main Street.*

Sólo vendemos al por mayor. *We sell wholesale only.*

mayordomo *m. majordomo, steward, butler; administrator.*

mayoría *f. majority; plurality.*

Así piensan la mayoría de los hombres. *Most men think that way.*

mayúscula *f. capital letter.*

mazapán *m. marzipan.*

mazorca *f. ear, cob (of corn).*

Deme unas mazorcas de maíz. *Give me some corn on the cob.*

ME *pron. me; to me; myself.*

Me lo dió. *He gave it to me.*

Dámelo. *Give it to me.*

Me es indiferente. *It makes no difference to me.*

Me duele la cabeza. *I have a headache.*

Me he cortado. *I've cut myself.*

Me dije para mis adentros. *I said to myself.*

mecánica *f. mechanics.*

mecánico *adj. mechanical; m. mechanic.*

mecanismo *m. mechanism.*

mecanógrafa *f. typist.*

Se necesita una mecanógrafa. *Typist wanted.*

mecanógrafo *m. typist.*

mecedora *f. rocking chair.*

mecha *f. wick; fuse; lock of hair.*

mechar *to lard.*

mechón *m. lock of hair.*

medalla *f. metal.*

media *f. stocking; mean (mathematics), media (communications industry).*

¿Quiere Ud. medias de seda o de nilón? *Do you want silk or nylon stockings?*

Media diferencial. *Arithmetical mean.*

mediación *f. mediation, intervention.*

mediador *mediator, go-between.*

mediados *about the middle.*

A mediados de marzo. *About the middle of March.*

mediano *adj. medium, middling, not so good, mediocre.*

medianoche *f. midnight.*

A medianoche. *At midnight.*

mediante *by means of, by virtue of.*

Lo obtuve mediante su ayuda. *I got it through his help.*

Dios mediante. *God willing.*

mediar *to mediate, to intercede.*

medicina *m. medicine; remedy.*

médico *adj. medical; m. physician, doctor.*

MEDIDA *f. measure; measurement.*

Medida patrón. *Standard measure.*

Se tomaron las medidas necesarias en contra de la epidemia. *They took the necessary measures against the epidemic.*

A la medida. *Made to order (suit, dress, etc.).*

A medida que reciba la mercadería, envíemela. *Send me the goods as you receive them.*

Escriba estos números a medida que se los vaya diciendo. *Write these numbers down as I give them to you.*

MEDIO *adj. and adv. half; halfway; midway; means; average; m. middle, center; way, method; pl. means.*

Déme media libra de café. *Give me half a pound of coffee.*

A las dos y media. *At half past two.*

Una hora y media. *An hour and a half.*

La clase media. *The middle class.*

En un término medio. *On an average.*

Los medias de comunicación. *Media.*

Estoy medio muerto de cansancio. *I'm exhausted. I'm half dead.*

Hicimos el trabajo a medias. *We did the work between (the two of) us.*

Lo puso de vuelta y media. *He gave him a dressing down.*

¡Quítese de en medio! *Get out of the way!*

No había medio de saberlo. *There was no way of finding out.*

Vive según sus medios. *He lives according to his means.*

Media vuelta. *About face. Right about-face.*

En medio. *In the middle.*

Medio en broma, medio en serio. *Half in fun, half in earnest.*

Medio muerto de hambre. *Half-starved.*

A medio vestir. *To be half dressed.*

Medio asado. *Medium (of roasted meat). ("Half roasted.")*

mediocre *adj. mediocre.*

mediocridad *f. mediocrity.*

mediodía *m. midday, noon.*

Al mediodía. *At noon.*

medir *to measure.*

meditación *f. meditation.*

meditar *to meditate.*

médula *f. medulla, marrow; pitch.*

Médula ósea. *Bone marrow.*

mega-octeto *m. megabyte.*

mejilla *f. cheek.*

Mejillas rosadas. *Rosy cheeks.*

MEJOR *adj. and adv. better; rather.*

Me siento mejor. *I feel better.*

Esta es la mejor señal de mejoría. *That's the best sign of improvement.*

Escribe el español mejor que yo. *He writes Spanish better than I do.*

Tal vez eso sea mejor. *Perhaps that would be better.*

Hice lo mejor que pude. *I did the best I could.*

Tanto mejor. *All the better. So much the better.*

Tanto mejor si no viene. *So much the better if he doesn't come.*

Cuanto antes mejor. *The sooner the better.*

A lo mejor mañana no llueve. *Perhaps it won't rain tomorrow.*

Mejor que mejor si Ud. puede venir. *So*

    much the better (all the better) if you can come.

mejora f. improvement.
    Eso es una gran mejora. That's a great improvement.

mejorar to improve; to outbid.
    Sigue mejorando. He's improving.
    El tiempo ha mejorado. The weather has improved.

mejoría f. improvement; recovery.

melaza f. molasses.

melocotón m. peach.

melodía f. melody.

melón m. melon.

mella f. notch; dent; gap; impression.

mellizo adj. twin.

membrete m. letterhead; memorandum, note.

membrillo m. quince (tree and its fruit).

memorable adj. memorable.

MEMORIA f. memory; memoir; report; pl. regards, compliments.
    Tiene una memoria extraordinaria. He has an extraordinary memory.
    Si la memoria no me es infiel. If my memory doesn't fail me. If I remember correctly.
    Memoria residente. Internal memory.
    El computador ofrece memoria ampliable. The computer offers an expandable memory.
    Apréndaselo de memoria. Learn it by heart.

menaje m. household goods, furnishings, furniture.

mencionar to mention.

mendigar to beg, to ask charity.

mendigo m. beggar

mendrugo m. crust, crumb.

menear to move, to stir; to wag.

menester m. need; occupation.
    Es menester que lo hagamos. We must do it. It's necessary that we do it.

menesteroso adj. needy.

mengua f. decrease; decline; poverty; disgrace.

menguar to decay; to diminish, to wane.

MENOR adj. less; smaller; younger; m. minor, a person under age.
    No me cabe la menor duda. I haven't the slightest doubt.
    No le hicieron el menor caso. They didn't pay the slightest attention to him.
    El es menor que ella. He's younger than she is.
    Es menor de edad. She's a minor (underage).

MENOS adj. and adv. less; least; minus; except.

    Es poco más o menos la misma cosa. It's more or less the same thing.
    Tengo cinco pesetas de menos. I'm five pesetas short.
    Eso es lo de menos. That's the least of it.
    Todos fueron menos yo. Everyone went but me.
    A las once menos cuarto. At a quarter to eleven.
    Echar de menos a. To miss someone or something.
    ¿Echa Ud. de menos algo? Is anything missing?
    No puedo menos que hacerlo. I can't help doing it.
    Menos mal que no le vió. It's a good thing that he didn't see you.
    Tiene a menos hablarles. He considered it beneath him to speak to them.
    ¡Si yo tuviera veinte años menos! If only I were twenty years younger!
    Tiene poco más o menos treinta años. He's about thirty.
    No iré a menos que Ud. me acompañe. I won't go unless you go with me (accompany me).
    Su familia ha ido muy a menos. His family has become poor.
    Es lo menos que puede Ud. hacer. It's the least you can do.

menoscabo m. damage, loss; detriment.
    Con menoscabo de. To the detriment of.

menospreciar to underrate; to despise, to slight.

menosprecio m. underrating; scorn, contempt.

mensaje m. message.
    Quisiera enviarle un mensaje. I'd like to send him a message.

mensajero m. messenger.

mensual adj. monthly.

mensualidad f. monthly salary; monthly payment.

menta f. mint, peppermint.

mental adj. mental.

mentalidad f. mentality.

MENTE f. mind, understanding.
    Téngalo siempre en mente. Always bear it in mind.

mentecato adj. silly, stupid; m. fool.

mentir to lie, to tell lies.

mentira f. lie, falsehood.

mentiroso adj. lying, false, deceitful; m. liar.

menú m. menu (restaurant, computer).

menudeo m. retail trade.

menudillos m. pl. giblet (of fowl).

MENUDO adj. small; minute; m. change (money); entrails (of animals).

¿Tiene Ud. menudo? *Do you have any change?*

Déjese Ud. ver más a menudo. *Come around more often.*

Sucede a menudo. *It happens very often.*

Gente menuda. *Children.*

meñique *m. little finger.*

El dedo meñique. *The little finger.*

mercadeo *m. marketing.*

mercader *m. merchant, dealer.*

mercadería *f. commodity, merchandise, goods.*

mercado *m. market; marketplace.*

La sirvienta fue de compras al mercado. *The maid went to the market to do the shopping.*

mercadotecnia *f. marketing.*

mercancía *f. merchandise, goods.*

mercante *adj. merchant, mercantile.*

Marina mercante. *Merchant Marine.*

mercantil *adj. commercial, mercantile.*

Derecho mercantil. *Commercial law.*

merced *f. gift, favor; mercy.*

Tener merced. *To show mercy. To be merciful.*

Merced a. *Thanks to.*

Estar a merced de. *To be at someone's mercy.*

mercenario *adj. mercenary.*

mercería *f. drygoods store.*

merecer *to deserve, to merit.*

Se lo merece. *He deserves it.*

merecido *m. "just desserts."*

merendar *to eat a light meal.*

merengue *m. meringue (pastry); dance.*

meridiano *adj. and n. meridian.*

merienda *f. light meal.*

mérito *m. merit, worth; value.*

mermar *to decrease, to dwindle, to diminish.*

mermelada *f. marmalade.*

mero *adj. mere, only, pure, simple.*

Es una mera broma. *It's only a joke.*

Por mera casualidad. *By a mere coincidence.*

MES *m. month; monthly wages.*

¿Qué día del mes tenemos? (¿En qué día del mes estamos?) *What day of the month is it?*

Hace cosa de dos meses. *It was about two months ago.*

El mes que viene. *Next month.*

El mes pasado. *Last month.*

A últimos de mes. *Toward the end of the month.*

A principios del mes que viene. *In the early part of next month.*

MESA *f. table; chair, chairman and other officers of an assembly.*

¿Quién va a servir a la mesa? *Who's going to wait on the table?*

Levante la mesa. *Clear the table.*

Ponga la mesa. *Set the table.*

Mesa redonda. *Round table (discussion).*

mesero *m. waiter.*

meseta *f. plateau; landing (of staircase).*

mestizo *adj. and n. mestizo; of white and Indian parents.*

mesura *f. moderation; politeness.*

meta *f. object, end, goal.*

Alcanzó la meta. *He reached his goal.*

metal *m. metal.*

metálico *adj. metallic.*

metalúrgica *f. metals industry.*

METER *to put in; to smuggle; to insert.*

Meter la mano en el bolsillo. *To put one's hand in one's pocket.*

Meta Ud. el dinero en el bolsillo. *Put the money in your pocket.*

Meter bulla. *To make a lot of noise.*

Meter la pata. *To put one's foot in it.*

METERSE *to meddle, to interfere; to become; to choose a profession or trade; to pick (a quarrel); to give oneself to; to get oneself in.*

No quiero meterme en líos. *I don't want to get myself involved in difficulties.*

En buen lío nos hemos metido. *We got ourselves in quite a fix.*

No se meta en lo que no le importa. *Mind your own business. Don't meddle in other people's affairs.*

Mete las narices en todo. *He's a busybody.*

No se meta Ud. de por medio. *Don't interfere in this.*

Meterse en vidas ajenas. *To meddle in other people's affairs.*

Se metió a cura. *He became a priest.*

Jamás se me metió en la cabeza idea semejante. *Such an idea never entered my head.*

¿Por qué se mete Ud. conmigo? *Why do you pick on me?*

Meterse en la cama. *To get into bed.*

¿En dónde diablos se ha estado metido Ud.? *Where on earth have you been?*

metódico *adj. methodical.*

método *m. method.*

metro *m. meter (39.37 inches); subway.*

metrópoli *f. metropolis.*

mezcla *f. mixture, blending; mortar (for holding bricks or stones together).*

Sin mezcla. *Unmixed. Pure.*

mezclar *to mix, to blend, to mingle.*

No mezcle estas cosas. *Don't mix these things.*

mezquino *adj. stingy; mean; petty.*

MI *(possessive adj.) my; pl.* **mis.**

Mi libro. *My book.*

Mis libros. *My books.*

Siéntese a mi lado. *Sit next to me. ("Sit at my side.")*

MÍ *(pron. used after a preposition)* me.

Para mí. *For me.*

Me llaman a mí. *They're calling me.*

¡Me lo cuenta a mí! *You're telling me!*

MÍA *(f. of* **mío***)* mine; *pl.* **mías.**

Esta corbata es mía. *This tie is mine. This is my tie.*

Es una amiga mía. *She's a friend of mine.*

Son amigas mías. *They're friends of mine.*

¡Querida mía! *My darling!*

Muy señora mía (salutation in a letter). *Dear Madam.*

microbio *m.* microbe.

microcomputador *m.* microcomputer.

micrófono *m.* microphone.

microondas *m.* microwave.

microprocesador *m.* microprocessor.

microscópico *adj.* microscopic.

microscopio *m.* microscope.

miedo *m.* fear, dread.

Tener miedo. *To be afraid.*

No tengas miedo. *Don't be afraid.*

miedoso *adj.* fearful, easily frightened.

miel. *f.* honey.

Luna de miel. *Honeymoon.*

miembro *m.* member, limb.

MIENTRAS in the meantime, while.

Entró mientras leía. *He came in while I was reading.*

Mientras tanto. *Meantime. In the meantime. In the meanwhile.*

MIÉRCOLES *m.* Wednesday.

Miércoles de ceniza. *Ash Wednesday.*

miga *f.* crumb, fragment, bit.

Hacer buenas migas. *To be in perfect harmony.*

MIL *m.* thousand.

Su carta está fechada el veintitrés de mayo de mil novecientos noventay dos. *Your letter is dated May the twenty-third, nineteen hundred and ninety-two.*

Lo hizo a las mil maravillas. *He did it wonderfully.*

Mil gracias. *Many thanks.*

milagro *m.* miracle, wonder.

milagroso *adj.* miraculous, marvelous.

milésimo *adj. and n.* thousandth.

miligramo *m.* milligram.

milímetro *m.* millimeter.

militante *adj.* militant; *m. and f.* militant.

militar *adj.* military; *m.* military man, soldier.

milla *f.* mile.

¿Cuántas millas hay de aquí a Quito? *How many miles is it from here to Quito?*

millar *m.* thousand (group); *pl.* a great number.

millón *m.* million.

millonario *adj. and n.* millionaire.

mimado *adj.* spoiled.

Es un niño mimado. *He's a spoiled child.*

mimar to spoil (a child).

mímico *m.* mime, mimic.

mina *f.* mine.

mineral *adj. and n.* mineral.

minería *f.* mining, working of a mine.

minero *m.* miner.

miniatura *f.* miniature.

minifalda *f.* miniskirt.

minidepartamento *m.* studio apartment.

mínimo *adj.* minimum; least, smallest.

La cosa más mínima. *The smallest thing.*

Este es el precio mínimo. *This is the lowest price.*

ministerio *m.* cabinet, ministry; secretary's office.

ministro *m.* Secretary (Cabinet); minister.

minorista *m.* retailer.

minusválido *m.* handicapped.

minuta *f.* minutes (record); memorandum.

minutero *m.* minute hand.

minuto *m.* minute (of an hour).

¡Espere un minuto! *Wait a minute!*

Estará listo dentro de unos minutos. *It will be ready in a few minutes.*

MÍO *mine,* pl. **míos.**

Son amigos míos. *They're friends of mine.*

Esto es mío. *This is mine. This belongs to me.*

Lo que es mío es suyo. *What's mine is yours.*

El gusto es mío, señor. *The pleasure is mine, sir.*

Hijo mío. *My son.*

Muy señor mío (salutation in a letter). *Dear Sir.*

miope *adj. and n.* nearsighted.

mirada *f.* glance, look.

mirado *adj.* looked at.

Es una persona bien mirada. *He's very respected (well-considered).*

MIRAR to look, to behold; to observe; to watch; to consider.

¡Mire Ud.! *Look!*

¡Mírelo, ahí está! *Look at it, there it is!*

Déjeme mirarlo bien. *Let me take a good look at you.*

Mire Ud. bien lo que hace. *Consider carefully ("well") what you're doing.*

¿No tienen a nadie que mire por ellos? *Don't they have anyone to look after them?*

Miraba lo que estábamos haciendo. *He watched what we were doing.*

Mirar de reojo. *To look askance. To look out of the corner of one's eye.*

Bien mirado. 1. *Carefully considered.* 2. *Well-considered. Respected.*

mirarse *to look at oneself; to look at each other.*

Mírese Ud. al espejo. *Look at yourself in the mirror.*

misa *f. mass.*

miserable *adj. miserable, wretched; miserly, avaricious.*

Vive una vida miserable. *He leads a miserable life.*

miseria *f. misery, destitution; stinginess; trifle.*

misericordia *f. mercy.*

misión *f. mission, errand.*

misionero *m. missionary.*

MISMA (*f. of* **mismo**) *same; similar, equal; self.*

Ella misma lo dice. *She says it herself.*

No es ya la misma persona. *He's no longer the same person. He's changed a great deal.*

MISMO *adj. same; similar; equal; self.*

El mismo día. *The same day.*

No es ya lo mismo. *It's no longer the same (thing).*

Yo mismo lo vi. *I myself saw it.*

Yo mismo lo haré. *I'll do it myself.*

Soy del mismo parecer. *I'm of the same opinion.*

No piensa sino en sí mismo. *He only thinks of himself.*

Ahora mismo. *Right now.*

Allí mismo. *In that very place.*

Te espero aquí mismo. *I'll wait for you right here.*

Ayer mismo. *Only yesterday.*

Mañana mismo voy. *I'll come tomorrow without fail.*

Te estás engañando a ti mismo. *You're fooling yourself.*

Me da lo mismo. *It's all the same to me. It makes no difference to me.*

Lo mismo que si. *Just as if.*

Pienso precisamente lo mismo. *I think exactly the same thing (the same way).*

misterio *m. mystery.*

misterioso *adj. mysterious.*

MITAD *f. half; middle, center.*

Déme la mitad. *Give me half.*

Mi cara mitad. *My better half.*

Fui la mitad del camino a pie y la otra mitad a caballo. *I went one half of the way on foot and the other half on horseback.*

mitigar *to mitigate; to quench.*

mitin *m. meeting.*

mito *m. myth.*

mitología *f. mythology.*

mixto *adj. mixed, mingled.*

Una escuela mixta. *A mixed school (for both boys and girls). Co-educational school.*

Ensalada mixta. *Tossed salad.*

mobiliario *m. furniture, furnishings.*

mocedad *f. youth.*

moción *f. motion.*

Ambas mociones fueron rechazadas. *Both motions were rejected.*

mochila *f. knapsack.*

moda *f. fashion, style.*

Es un color muy de moda. *It's a fashionable color.*

Estar de moda. *To be in style; to be chic.*

La última moda. *The latest style.*

modales *m. pl. manners, breeding.*

Este niño tiene muy buenos modales. *This child has very good manners.*

Sus modales le hacen odioso. *His manners make people dislike (hate) him.*

modalidad *f. modality; form.*

modelo *m. model, pattern; style.*

¿Cuáles son los últimos modelos? *What are the latest styles?*

modem *m. modem.*

moderación *f. moderation.*

moderado *adj. moderate; mild.*

moderar *to moderate, to restrain; to slow up.*

Modere la velocidad. *Slow up. Slow down.*

modernista *adj. and m. and f. modernist.*

MODERNO *adj. modern.*

modestia *f. modesty.*

modesto *adj. modest.*

módico *adj. moderate; m. reasonable price.*

Es un precio módico. *It's a reasonable price.*

modificar *to modify, to alter.*

modismo *m. idiom; expression.*

modista *f. modiste, dressmaker.*

MODO *m. mode; method, manner; mood.*

Es el mejor modo de hacerlo. *It's the best way to do it.*

De este modo. *In this way.*

No me parece bien su modo de hablar. *I don't approve of (like) his manner of speaking.*

De modo que. *So that.*

Hable de modo que se le pueda oír. *Speak so that they can hear you (you can be heard).*

Hágalo de cualquier modo. *Do it any way.*

De todos modos. *Anyway.*

De todos modos iré a su casa. *I'll go to his house anyway (anyhow).*

De ningún modo. *By no means. In no way. Not at all.*

mofa *f. mockery; scoff, sneer.*

mofarse *to mock, to scoff, to jeer.*

mojar *to wet; to moisten; to dampen.*

Las calles están mojadas. *The streets are wet.*

Eso ya es llover sobre mojado. *That's adding insult to injury.*

molde *m. mold; pattern, model.*

En letras de molde. *In print (letters).*

moldura *f. molding.*

moler *to grind; to mill; to bore; to pound.*

molestar *to disturb, to trouble, to bother, to annoy; to tease.*

Siento mucho molestarle. *I'm sorry to bother you.*

¿Le molesta a Ud. el humo? *Does the smoke bother you?*

No se moleste Ud., lo haré yo mismo. *Don't bother, I'll do it myself.*

Deje Ud. de molestarme. *Stop bothering me.*

molestia *f. trouble, bother, annoyance.*

No es ninguna molestia. *Why, it's no bother. It's no trouble at all.*

Siento darle a Ud. tanta molestia. *I'm sorry to trouble you so much.*

Tomarse la molestia de. *To take the trouble to.*

molesto *adj. bothersome; uncomfortable; annoying, boring.*

¡Qué molesto es! *How annoying he is!*

No tenía porque sentirse molesto. *He had no reason to be annoyed.*

molino *m. mill.*

momentáneo *adj. momentary.*

MOMENTO *m. moment.*

No tengo ni un momento libre. *I don't have a free moment.*

Un momento, que suena el teléfono. *Just a moment, the phone is ringing.*

Momentito. *Just a moment.*

Le espero de un momento a otro. *I expect him any minute now.*

Por el momento. *For the moment. For the present.*

En cualquier momento. *At any moment.*

Al momento. *In a moment. Immediately.*

monarca *m. monarch.*

monarquía *f. monarchy.*

mondadientes *m. toothpick.*

mondar *to clean; to husk, to remove the bark; to peel.*

moneda *f. coin; money.*

monitor *m. monitor.*

monja *f. nun.*

monje *m. monk.*

mono *adj. pretty, cute, nice; m. monkey, ape.*

¡Qué mono! ¿Verdad? *Isn't it cute! It's cute, isn't it?*

Tiene dos hijas muy monas. *He has two very pretty daughters.*

He conseguido un apartamento monísimo. *I found the coziest apartment.*

monólogo *m. monologue, soliloquy.*

monopolio *m. monopoly.*

monopolizar *to monopolize.*

monorriel *m. monorail.*

monotonía *f. monotony.*

monótono *adj. monotonous.*

monousuario *m. single user.*

monstruo *m. monster.*

monstruosidad *f. monstrosity.*

monstruoso *adj. monstrous; huge.*

monta *f. amount, total sum.*

De poca monta. *Of little importance.*

montacargas *m. hoist.*

montaña *f. mountain.*

montar *to mount; to ride; to amount to; to set (a diamond); to put together, to fit together, to assemble.*

¿Monta Ud. a caballo? *Can you ride (a horse)?*

¿Monta Ud. en bicicleta? *Can you ride a bicycle?*

¿A cuánto monta la cuenta? *How much does the bill come to?*

Monte esta máquina. *Put this machine together.*

monte *m. mountain; wood, forest; monte (card game).*

montepío *m. pawnshop.*

montón *m. heap, mass.*

montura *f. mount, saddle horse; saddle and trappings.*

monumental *adj. monumental.*

monumento *m. monument.*

mora *f. delay; mulberry; blackberry.*

morada *f. dwelling, abode.*

morado *adj. purple.*

morador *m. resident, inhabitant.*

moral *adj. moral; f. ethics; morale; m. mulberry tree; blackberry bush.*

morar *to inhabit, to reside.*

mordedura *f. bite.*

morder *to bite.*

mordisco *m. bite; biting; a piece bitten off.*

morena *f. brunette.*

moreno *adj. brown; dark, swarthy.*

morera *f. white mulberry tree.*

moribundo *adj. dying.*

MORIR *to die.*

Murió de pena. *She died of a broken heart.*

Morir de risa. *To die laughing.*

Morirse de hambre. *To starve.*

Morirse de frío. *To freeze to death.*

mortadela *f. (bologna) sausage.*

mortaja f. shroud.

mortal adj. mortal, fatal.

mortalidad f. mortality; death rate.

mortero m. mortar.

mortificación f. mortification, humiliation.

mortificar to humiliate, to vex.

mosca f. fly; dough, money (coll.).

moscatel m. muscatel (grape or wine).

mosquito m. mosquito.

mostaza f. mustard; mustard seed.

mosto m. must, grape juice; new wine.

mostrador m. counter.

MOSTRAR to show; to exhibit; to prove.

¿Me lo puede mostrar? Can you show it to me?

motín m. riot, insurrection.

motivo m. motive, reason; motif.

No tiene motivo para quejarse. You have no reason to complain. You have no grounds for complaint.

Sus afirmaciones dieron motivo a una seria disputa. His statements led to a serious quarrel.

motocicleta f. motorcycle.

motociclista m. and f. motorcyclist.

motor m. motor; engine.

El motor no funciona. The motor doesn't work.

MOVER to move; to stir up; to shake.

No mueva la mesa. Don't shake the table.

No dejó piedra que no moviese. He left no stone unturned. He searched high and low.

Apenas podía hablar. He could scarcely talk.

móvil adj. movable; mobile; m. motive.

movilización f. mobilization.

movilizar to mobilize.

movimiento m. movement, motion; traffic.

moza f. girl; maid, servant.

mozo adj. young; m. young man; waiter; porter.

¡Vaya un buen mozo! What a good-looking man!

Mozo, tráigame una cerveza. Waiter, bring me a (glass of) beer.

El mozo le subirá la maleta al tren. The porter will put your suitcase on the train.

MUCHA adj. (f. of mucho) much, very much, a great deal, a lot; very; pl. many, a great many, too many.

Mucha agua. A lot of water.

Había mucha gente. There was a big crowd.

Muchas veces. Many times.

Muchas cosas. Many things.

Esto y muchas otras cosas más. This and many other things.

Muchísimas gracias. Thank you very much.

MUCHACHA m. girl; servant, maid.

¡Qué muchacha tan encantadora! What a lovely girl! What a charming girl!

MUCHACHO m. boy; lad.

Es un muchacho muy inteligente. He's a very intelligent boy.

muchedumbre f. multitude; crowd.

MUCHO adj. much, very much, a great deal of, a lot; very; long (time); pl. many, a great many, too many; very.

Mucho dinero. A lot of money.

Escribe mucho. He writes a great deal.

Mucho más grande. Much larger.

Tiene muchos amigos. He has a lot of friends.

Esto es mucho mejor. This is much better.

Tengo mucho que hacer hoy. I've a lot to do today.

Con mucho gusto. Gladly. With (much) pleasure.

Hace mucho tiempo. It's been a long time. A long time ago.

Hace mucho frío. It's very cold.

Se lo agradezco muchísimo. Thank you very much.

Tengo muchísimo trabajo. I have a great deal of work to do.

Lo cuidaré mucho. I'll take good care of it.

muda f. change of clothes, change of linen.

mudanza f. change; moving out.

MUDAR to change; to alter; to remove; to molt.

He mudado de parecer. I've changed my mind.

MUDARSE to change (clothes); to move (household).

Tengo que mudarme de ropa. I have to change my clothes.

Mi amigo se ha mudado de casa. My friend has moved.

Vamos a mudarnos de casa pronto. We're going to move soon.

mudo adj. dumb, mute, silent.

MUEBLE m. piece of furniture.

Con muebles. Furnished.

Una habitación sin muebles. An unfurnished room.

mueca f. grimace, wry face.

muela f. millstone; molar tooth. tooth.

Muela de juicio. Wisdom tooth.

muelle adj. tender, soft; easy (life); m. pier, quay, dock, wharf; spring (metal).

MUERTE f. death

Se le condenó a muerte. He was condemned to death.

Muerte repentina. Sudden death.

muerto adj. dead; languid; m. corpse.

Muerto de hambre. Starved.

Muerto de cansancio. *Dead tired.*

Medio muerto. *Half dead.*

Estar muerto por alguna persona. *To be madly in love with someone.*

muestra *f. sample; specimen.*

muestrario *m. collection of samples.*

MUJER *f. woman; wife.*

¡Qué mujer más hermosa! *What a beautiful woman!*

Su mujer es joven. *His wife is young.*

mula *f. she-mule.*

muleta *f. crutch.*

mulo *m. mule.*

multa *f. fine, penalty.*

multar *to fine.*

múltiple *adj. multiple.*

multiplicar *to multiply.*

multitud *f. multitude; crowd.*

multiusuario *m. multi-user.*

MUNDO *m. world; multitude; great quantity.*

Quiere ver el mundo. *He (she) wants to see the world.*

Todo el mundo quiere ir. *Everyone wants to go.*

Este hombre se ríe de todo el mundo. *He ("this man") laughs at (ridicules) everybody.*

Tener mundo. *To know one's way around.*

Tercer mundo. *Third World.*

munición *f. ammunition.*

municipal *adj. municipal.*

municipalidad *f. municipality; town hall.*

municipio *m. municipality.*

muñeca *f. wrist; doll; figure (in dressmaking).*

muñeco *m. puppet; doll.*

Nunca se cansa de leer los muñecos. *She never gets tired of reading the comics (funnies).*

muralla *f. wall; rampart.*

murmuro *m. murmur, whisper.*

murmurar *to murmur, to whisper.*

muro *m. wall; rampart.*

músculo *m. muscle.*

museo *m. museum.*

¿Qué días está abierto el museo? *What days is the museum open?*

música *f. music.*

Tiene talento para la música. *She has a gift for music.*

Váyase con la música a otra parte. *Go away, don't bother me.*

musical *adj. musical.*

músico *m. musician.*

muslo *m. thigh.*

mutilar *to mutilate.*

mutuo *adj. mutual.*

Se detestan mutuamente. *They detest each other.*

MUY *very; greatly.*

Muy bien, gracias. *Very well, thank you.*

No muy bien. *Not so well. Not very well.*

Muy mal. *Very bad.*

Ese vestido le cae muy bien. *That dress fits her very well.*

Vino muy de mañana. *He came very early in the morning.*

Estoy muy molesto. *I'm very much annoyed.*

N

nabo *m. turnip.*

NACER *to be born; to sprout; to rise (sun); to originate.*

Nació en Madrid. *He was born in Madrid.*

nacimiento *m. birth; origin; source.*

Partida de nacimiento. *Birth certificate.*

nación *f. nation.*

nacional *adj. national.*

nacionalidad *f. nationality.*

NADA *nothing; by no means.*

No quiero nada. *I don't want anything.*

Nada de particular. *Nothing special. Nothing in particular.*

De nada. *Don't mention it.*

No es nada. *It's nothing at all.*

No importa nada. *It doesn't matter at all.*

No vale nada. *It's worthless.*

¿Nada más? *Is that all?*

Nada de eso. *Nothing of the sort.*

Por nada. *For nothing. Under no circumstances.*

¿No se puede hacer nada? *Can't something be done?*

No quiero nada con él. *I don't want to have anything to do with him.*

No me acuerdo de nada. *I don't remember it at all. I don't remember anything.*

Antes que nada. *First of all. Before anything else.*

nadador *m. swimmer.*

nadar *to swim, to float.*

Sabe nadar muy bien. *She swims very well.*

NADIE *nobody, anybody, no one, anyone, none.*

Nadie lo duda. *Nobody doubts it.*

Eso no lo cree nadie. *Nobody believes it.*

Nunca hable mal de nadie. *He never says anything bad about anyone.*

No teme a nadie. *He's not afraid of anyone.*

naipe *m. playing card.*

naranja *f. orange.*

naranjada *f. orangeade.*

naranjo *m. orange tree.*

narcomanía *f. drug addiction.*

narcómano *m. drug addict.*

narcótico *adj. and n. narcotic.*

narcotraficante *m. and f. drug dealer; drug pusher.*

narcotráfico *m. drug traffic.*

NARIZ *f. nose; nostril.*

Nariz aguileña. *An aquiline nose.*

Nariz chata. *A flat nose.*

Mete las narices en todo. *He's a busybody.*

Estamos hasta las narices. *We are fed up.*

Le dieron con la puerta en las narices. *They slammed the door in his face ("nose").*

Tener de (por) las narices. *To have someone under your control.*

narración *f. account, narration; story.*

narrar *to narrate; to relate.*

nata *f. cream; best part.*

Es de la flor y nata. *He's crème de la crème.*

natación *f. swimming.*

natal *adj. natal, native.*

natalidad *f. birth rate.*

natillas *f. pl. custard.*

nativo *adj. native.*

natural *adj. and n. natural; native.*

Eso es muy natural. *That's quite natural.*

Dibujar del natural. *To draw from life.*

Son naturales de esta isla. *They're natives of this island.*

naturaleza *f. nature.*

NATURALMENTE *of course, naturally.*

Naturalmente que lo haré. *Of course I'll do it.*

¿Estará Ud. allí?—Naturalmente. *Will you be there?—Naturally.*

naturismo *m. naturalism.*

naturista *m. and f. nature-lover; naturalist.*

naufragar *to be shipwrecked; to fail.*

naufragio *m. shipwreck; failure.*

náusea *f. nausea.*

náutica *f. navigation.*

naval *adj. naval.*

nave *f. ship, vessel.*

navegable *adj. navigable.*

navegación *f. navigation; shipping.*

navegante *m. navigator.*

navegar *to navigate; to sail.*

Navidad *f. Nativity; Christmas.*

Por Navidad. *For Christmas.*

¡Feliz Navidad! ¡Felices Pascuas! *Merry Christmas!*

naviero *adj; shipping; m. shipowner.*

navío *m. warship, ship.*

neblina *f. mist, light fog.*

necesariamente *necessarily.*

NECESARIO *adj. necessary.*

Es necesario hacer esto inmediatamente. *It's necessary to do this right away.*

¿Cree Ud. que tendrá los medios necesarios? *Do you think you'll have the necessary means?*

NECESIDAD *f. necessity; need, want.*

Tengo necesidad de ir al banco. *I have (need) to go to the bank.*

Verse en la necesidad de. *To be in the need of. To be compelled to.*

necesitado *adj. very poor; needy; m. person in need.*

Está necesitado. *He's in want. He's down and out.*

NECESITAR *to need; to be in need; to want.*

¿Necesita Ud. algo más? *Do you need anything else?*

Necesito un nuevo par de zapatos. *I need a new pair of shoes.*

Necesita tomar un taxi para ir al aeropuerto. *He has to take a taxi to get to the airport.*

Se necesita una mecanógrafa. *Typist wanted.*

necio *adj. ignorant, stupid; fool.*

necrología *f. necrology, obituary.*

nefasto *adj. ill-fated; unlucky.*

Día nefasto. *Unlucky day.*

NEGAR *to deny; to refuse; to disown.*

No lo niego. *I don't deny it.*

Lo negó de plano. *He denied it flatly.*

Ella se negó a aceptarlo. *She refused to accept it.*

negativa. *f. refusal.*

negativo *adj. negative.*

Una respuesta negativa. *A negative answer.*

negligencia *f. negligence, neglect.*

negligente *adj. negligent, careless.*

negociado *m. bureau, department.*

negociante *m. businessman, merchant, trader.*

Es un negociante muy hábil. *He's a clever (good) businessman.*

negociar *to negotiate.*

NEGOCIO *m. business; affair; transaction.*

¿A qué negocio se dedica Ud.? *What business are you in?*

Hacer negocios. *To do (conduct) business.*

Retirarse de los negocios. *To retire from business.*

Proyecciones de negocios. *Business forecasts.*

Pequeño negocio. *Small business.*

NEGRO *adj. black; gloomy; m. Negro.*

Vestirse de negro. *To dress in black.*

nervio *m. nerve.*

Tengo los nervios de punta. *My nerves are on edge.*

nervioso *adj. nervous.*

¡No se ponga nervioso! *Don't get nervous!*

neto *adj. neat, pure; net.*

Peso neto. *Net weight.*

neumático *m. tire.*

Se me ha pinchado un neumático. *I have a flat (tire). One of my tires blew out.*

neurótico *adj. neurotic.*

neutral *adj. neutral*

nevar *to snow.*

Está nevando. *It's snowing.*

nevera *f. refrigerator, icebox.*

NI *neither, either, nor.*

Ni come ni bebe. *He doesn't eat or drink.*

Ni mi hermano ni yo le podíamos ayudar. *Neither my brother nor I could (were able to) help him.*

Ni siquiera eso. *Not even that.*

nicho *m. niche.*

nicotina *f. nicotine.*

nido *m. nest.*

niebla *f. fog, haze.*

Hay niebla. *It's foggy.*

nieta *f. granddaughter.*

nieto *m. grandson.*

NIEVA. *It's snowing.*

nieve *f. snow.*

nilón *m. nylon.*

NINGÚN *adj. (shortening of* **ninguno** *used only before a masculine noun) no, none, any.*

Ningún hombre. *No man.*

De ningún modo. *By no means. In no way.*

A ningún precio. *Not at any price.*

NINGUNA *adj. (f. of* **ninguno***) no, none, any, no one, anybody.*

No he visto a ninguna de las chicas. *I haven't seen any of the girls.*

Al presente no tenemos ninguna noticia. *At present we have no news (haven't any news).*

No quiero ir a ninguna parte esta noche. *I don't want to go anywhere tonight.*

De ninguna manera. *By no means. In no way.*

NINGUNO *adj. no, none, not one, any; indefinite pronoun none, no one, nobody.*

No tengo ninguno. *I haven't any.*

Ninguno ha venido. *Nobody has come.*

Ninguno de nosotros. *None of us.*

NIÑA *f. girl; pupil (of the eye).*

niñera *f. baby-sitter.*

niñez *f. childhood, infancy.*

NIÑO *m. child; pl. children.*

Niño explorador. *Boy scout.*

Desde niño. *From childhood.*

níquel *m. nickel (metal).*

NO *no, not.*

Le tuve que decir que no. *I had to say no to him.*

Ciertamente que no. *Certainly not.*

¡Por supuesto que no! *No, indeed!*

Todavía no. *Not yet.*

¿Cómo dice? No oigo nada. *What are you saying? I can't hear anything.*

¿No quiere Ud. sentarse? *Won't you sit down?*

No hay nadie aquí. *There's no one here.*

No está mal. *It's not bad.*

No corre prisa. *There's no hurry.*

Ya no. *No longer.*

No del todo. *Not quite. Not altogether.*

No tengo mucho tiempo. *I haven't much time.*

No hay de que. *Don't mention it.*

¡No importa! *It doesn't matter!*

¡No me diga! *You don't say (so)! Don't tell me!*

noble *adj. noble; m. nobleman.*

nobleza *f. nobleness, nobility.*

noción *f. notion, idea.*

No tenía noción de que fuera posible. *I had no idea that it would be possible.*

nocivo *adj. harmful.*

nocturno *adj. nocturnal, night, in the night.*

Trabajo nocturno. *Night work.*

NOCHE *f. night.*

¡Buenas noches! *Good night!*

Esta noche. *Tonight.*

Mañana por la noche. *Tomorrow night.*

¿Sale Ud. todas las noches? *Do you go out every night?*

Ya es de noche. *It's dark.*

Por la noche. *At night.*

Durante la noche. *During the night.*

A medianoche. *At midnight.*

A altas horas de la noche. *Late at night.*

Que pase Ud. buena noche. *I hope you have a good night's sleep.*

Pasar la noche. *To spend the night.*

nochebuena *f. Christmas Eve.*

Esta noche es nochebuena. *Tonight's Christmas Eve.*

nombramiento *m. nomination; appointment.*

nombrar *to appoint, to nominate; to name.*

Fue nombrado gobernador de la isla. *He was appointed governor of the island.*

Al niño le nombraron José. *They named the child Joseph.*

NOMBRE *m. name; noun.*

¿Su nombre y profesión, por favor? *Your name and occupation?*

No conozco a nadie con ese nombre. *I don't know anyone by that name.*

Salúdele en mi nombre. *Remember me to him.*

Va a poner a su hijo el nombre de Antonio. *He's going to name his son Anthony.*

nómina *f. payroll.*

nopal *m. small cactus.*

norma *f. rule, standard, model.*

normal *adj. normal; f. normal school.*

normalidad *f. normality.*

NORTE *m. north.*

norteamericano *adj. and n. North America; American (restricted to persons or things from the United States).*

NOS *we; us; to us.*

  Nos hace falta dinero. *We need money.*

  Dénoslo. *Give it to us.*

  No nos dejaron entrar. *They didn't let us in.*

NOSOTRAS *(f. of nosotros) we; us; ourselves.*

  (Nosotras) Somos sus hermanas. *We're his sisters.*

  Nosotras las mujeres. *We women.*

NOSOTROS *we; us; ourselves.*

  (Nosotros) Somos vecinos. *We're neighbors.*

  Lo haremos nosotros mismos. *We'll do it ourselves.*

  Quiere venir con nosotros. *She wants to come with us.*

nostalgia *f. nostalgia, homesickness.*

NOTA *f. note.*

  Tomar nota. *To take note.*

  Cuaderno de notas. *Notebook.*

  Nota marginal. *Marginal note.*

  Nota musical. *Musical note.*

notable *adj. notable; worthy of notice.*

  Es un hecho notable. *It's an outstanding fact.*

  Es un hombre notable. *He's an outstanding man.*

notar *to note; to notice.*

  ¿Notó Ud. algo raro? *Did you notice anything strange?*

notario *m. notary.*

NOTICIA *f. piece of news; information; notice; pl. news.*

  La radio dio la noticia. *The news came over the radio.*

  Las noticias del día. *The news of the day.*

  Hay buenas noticias. *There's good news. Good news!*

noticiario *or* **noticiero** *m. newscast.*

notificación *f. notification.*

notificar *to notify; to inform.*

notorio *adj. well-known, evident.*

novato *adj. novice, beginner.*

novecientos *adj. and n. nine hundred.*

NOVEDAD *f. novelty; latest news or fashion.*

  ¿Qué hay de novedad? *What's new?*

  Sin novedad. *As usual. Nothing new.*

  Llegamos a Toluca sin novedad. *We arrived in Toluca safely.*

  Ultima novedad. *Latest style.*

novela *f. novel; television soap opera.*

novelista *m. and f. novelist.*

noventa *f. adj. and n. ninety.*

novia *f. sweetheart, girl friend; fiancée; bride.*

noviazgo *m. engagement, betrothal.*

novicio *adj. novice; apprentice.*

novio *m. sweetheart, boyfriend; fiancé; bridegroom.*

  Los novios. *The engaged couple. The newlyweds.*

nube *f. cloud; film (on the eyeball).*

  Hay muchas nubes. *There are many clouds. It's cloudy.*

nublado *adj. cloudy.*

  Está nublado. *It's cloudy.*

nuca *f. nape, back of the neck.*

nuclear *adj. nuclear.*

  Bomba nuclear. *Nuclear bomb.*

  Industria nuclear. *Nuclear industry.*

  Energía nuclear. *Nuclear energy.*

  Central nuclear. *Nuclear plants.*

nudo *m. knot.*

nuera *f. daughter-in-law.*

NUESTRA *(f. of nuestro) our, ours; pl. nuestras.*

  Nuestra hermana. *Our sister.*

  Nuestras hermanas. *Our sisters.*

  Ella es vecina nuestra. *She's a neighbor of ours.*

  La nuestra. *Ours.*

NUESTRO *our; ours; pl. nuestros.*

  Nuestro amigo. *Our friend.*

  Nuestros derechos. *Our rights.*

  Es un antiguo conocido nuestro. *He's an old acquaintance of ours.*

  El nuestro. *Ours.*

  Los nuestros. *Our folks (people).*

nuevamente *adv. once again.*

NUEVE *adj. and n. nine.*

NUEVO *adj. new.*

  ¿Es nuevo ese sombrero? *Is that hat new? Is that a new hat?*

  ¿Qué hay de nuevo? *What's new?*

  Hágalo Ud. de nuevo. *Do it again.*

  ¡Feliz Año Nuevo! *Happy New Year!*

nuez *f. walnut; nut; Adam's apple.*

nulidad *f. nullity; nonentity; incompetent person.*

nulo *adj. null, void; not binding.*

numerar *to number.*

número *m. number; figure; issue (of a magazine).*

  ¿Cuál es su número de teléfono? *What is your telephone number?*

  Escriba el número. *Write the number.*

  Por favor, póngame en comunicación con el número . . . *Kindly connect me with number . . .*

Número equivocado. *Wrong number.*

En números redondos. *In round numbers (figures).*

No me gustó ese número. *I didn't like that act, issue.*

NUNCA *never, ever.*

¡Nunca! *Never!*

Nunca tomo café. *I never take coffee.*

Nunca lo consentiré. *I'll never consent (agree to it).*

Más vale tarde que nunca. *Better late than never.*

nupcial *adj. nuptial.*

nupcias *f. pl. nuptials, wedding.*

nutrición *f. nutrition, nourishment.*

nutrir *to nourish, to feed.*

nutritivo *adj. nutritious, nourishing.*

ñame *m. yam (plant).*

ñapa (also **yapa**) *f. bonus.*

ñato *adj. flat-nosed.*

O *or, either.*

Más o menos. *More or less.*

Más tarde o más temprano. *Sooner or later.*

Lo he visto o en Roma o en París. *I saw him either in Rome or in Paris.*

obcecado *adj. stubborn, obdurate.*

obedecer *to obey.*

Quiero que me obedezcan. *I expect to be obeyed.*

Eso obedece a otras razones. *This is due to other reasons.*

obediencia *f. obedience.*

obediente *adj. obedient.*

obesidad *f. obesity.*

obeso *adj. obese, extremely fat.*

obispo *m. bishop.*

objetar *to object, to oppose.*

objetivo *m. objective, aim.*

OBJETO *m. object, thing, article; purpose, aim.*

No tengo objetos de valor que declarar. *I have nothing of value to declare.*

Por fin logró su objeto. *Finally he reached his goal.*

Ser objeto de burla. *To be the laughingstock.*

Llenar su objeto. *To suit one's purpose.*

oblicuo *adj. oblique.*

obligación *f. obligation; duty; pl. liabilities.*

obligar *to oblige; to compel; to obligate.*

Me veré obligado a dar parte a la policía. *I'll have (be compelled) to report it to the police.*

obligatorio *adj. obligatory, compulsory.*

OBRA *f. work; labor; book; play (theater); building; repairs (in a house); means; deed, action.*

¿Dan ya esa obra? *Are they already performing that play?*

Es una obra de tres tomos. *The work is in three volumes.*

Obra maestra. *Masterpiece.*

Obras públicas. *Public works.*

Poner en obra. *To put into practice. To set into operation.*

Obra de arte. *Work of art.*

obrar *to work; to act; to do things.*

No me gusta su modo de obrar. *I don't like the way he does things.*

obrero *m. worker, workman.*

obscurecer *to darken; to grow dark.*

obscurecerse *to get dark.*

Está obscureciendo. *It's getting dark.*

obscuridad *f. obscurity; darkness.*

obscuro *adj. obscure; dark.*

Una noche obscura. *A dark night.*

obsequiar *to entertain, to treat; to make a present, to give a gift.*

Me han obsequiado un libro. *They gave me a book (as a gift).*

obsequio *m. entertainment; gift, present.*

Le agradezco mucho su obsequio. *Thank you very much for your present.*

observación *f. observation; remark.*

observar *to observe, to notice; to keep, to follow (the law, etc.); to make a remark; to look.*

observatorio *m. observatory.*

obsesión *f. obsession.*

obstáculo *m. obstacle.*

obstante (*preceded by* no) *notwithstanding, in spite of.*

No obstante. *Notwithstanding. Regardless.*

obstinación *f. obstinacy, stubbornness.*

obstinado *adj. obstinate.*

obstinarse *to be obstinate; to persist.*

obstruir *to obstruct, to block.*

Obstruir el tráfico. *To block traffic.*

obstención *f. attainment; accomplishment.*

OBTENER *to obtain, to get; to attain.*

Ha obtenido una buena colocación. *He got a good job.*

obturación *filling (tooth).*

obturador *m. shutter (of a camera); plug, stopper.*

obtuso *adj. obtuse, blunt.*

obús *m. howitzer, shell (of a gun).*

obvio *adj. obvious, evident.*

OCASIÓN *f. occasion; opportunity.*
   He perdido una buena ocasión. *I missed a good opportunity.*
   Iré a Bolivia en la primera ocasión. *I'll go to Bolivia at the first opportunity.*
   Aprovechar la ocasión. *To take advantage of the opportunity.*
   Con (en) ocasión de. *On the occasion of.*
ocasionar *to cause; to bring about.*
occidental *adj. western, occidental.*
occidente *m. west, occident.*
océano *m. ocean.*
   Océano Atlántico. *Atlantic Ocean.*
   Océano Pacífico. *Pacific Ocean.*
ocio *m. idleness, leisure; pastime.*
ociosidad *f. idleness, leisure.*
ocioso *adj. idle, useless.*
octavo *adj. eighth.*
OCTUBRE *m. October.*
oculista *m. and f. oculist, optometrist.*
ocultar *to conceal; to hide.*
oculto *adj. concealed, hidden.*
ocupación *f. occupation, business, trade.*
   ¿Cuál es su nombre y ocupación? *What is your name and occupation?*
OCUPADO *adj. occupied; busy; engaged.*
   Últimamente he estado muy ocupado. *I've been very busy lately.*
   La línea está ocupada. *The line is busy.*
OCUPAR *to occupy; to take possession of; to give work to; to hold a position.*
   ¿Está este asiento ocupado? *Is this seat taken (occupied)?*
   Ocupa un puesto muy importante. *He holds a very important position.*
   Nuestras tropas han ocupado la ciudad. *Our troops have occupied the city.*
   El edificio ocupa toda una manzana. *The building occupies an entire block.*
OCUPARSE *to pay attention to; to be concerned about; to attend to; to be encouraged in; to have as one's business.*
   No se ocupe Ud. de esas cosas. *Don't pay attention to such things.*
   Ocuparse de. *To look into. To take care of.*
   El asunto que nos ocupa. *The matter in question.*
ocurrencia *f. occurrence, incident; wisecrack, joke.*
   Fue una ocurrencia desgraciada. *It was an unfortunate accident.*
   ¡Qué ocurrencia! 1. *What an idea!* 2. *What a joke!*
   Siempre dice muchas ocurrencias. *He's always telling jokes.*
OCURRIR *to occur, to happen.*
   ¿Qué ocurre? *What's the matter? What's happening? What's up?*

No ha ocurrido nada de nuevo. *Nothing new has happened.*
   ¿Cuándo ocurrió eso? *When did that happen?*
   El accidente occurió aquí mismo. *The accident happened right here (in this very place).*
ocurrirse *to occur to one, to strike one (an idea).*
   Se me ocurre una idea. *An idea occurred to me. I have an idea.*
OCHENTA *adj. and n. eighty.*
OCHO *adj. and n. eight.*
   Dentro de ocho días. *A week from today.*
odiar *to hate.*
odio *m. hatred.*
odioso *adj. hateful.*
odontología *f. dentistry.*
OESTE *m. west.*
ofender *to offend.*
ofenderse *to take offense, to be offended.*
   Se ofende por nada. *He (she) gets offended over the least little thing.*
ofensa *f. offense.*
ofensiva *f. offensive.*
   Tomar la ofensiva. *To take the offensive.*
oferta *f. offer, bid; offering, gift.*
   Es su última oferta. *That's his last (final) offer.*
   Oferta y demanda. *Supply and demand.*
oficial *adj. official; m. officer, official; trained worker.*
oficialmente *officially.*
oficina *f. office; workshop.*
   ¿Cuál es la dirección de su oficina? *What's your office address?*
oficinista *m. and f. office worker.*
oficio *m. occupation, work, trade, business; written communication.*
   ¿Qué oficio tiene? *What's your profession? What do you do for a living?*
OFRECER *to offer; to present.*
   Nos ofreció su ayuda. *He offered us his help. He offered to help us.*
   ¿Qué se le ofrece? *What can I do for you?*
   Me ofreció dos dólares por el libro. *He offered me two dollars for the book.*
ofrecimiento *m. offer, offering.*
oftalmólogo *m. ophthalmologist.*
¡oh! *Oh!*
OÍDO *m. hearing; ear (inner).*
   Tengo dolor de oído. *I have an earache.*
   Tiene oído para la música. *He has a good ear for music.*
   Le dijo algo al oído y se marchó. *He whispered something in his ear and left.*
   Ha llegado a mis oídos que . . . *I've heard that . . .*

OÍR *to hear; to listen.*

¡Oye! (¡Oiga! ¡Oígame!) *Say! Say there! Listen! Look here!*

¿Cómo dice? No oigo nada. *What are you saying? I can't hear a thing.*

No oí el despertador. *I didn't hear the alarm clock.*

¿Ha oído Ud. la última noticia? *Have you heard the latest news?*

¡Qué Dios le oiga! *Let's hope so! ("God grant it!")*

ojal *m. buttonhole.*

¡Ojalá! *God grant (it)! Would that . . .*

¡Ojalá que venga! *I wish she would come.*

¡Ojalá fuera así! *I wish it were so! Would that it were so!*

OJO *m. eye; attention, care; keyhole.*

Tengo los ojos cansados de tanto leer. *My eyes are tired from reading so much.*

No pude pegar los ojos en toda la noche. *I couldn't sleep a wink all night.*

Hay que tener mucho ojo. *One should be very careful.*

Le costó un ojo de la cara. *It cost him a mint of money. It cost him a small fortune.*

ola *f. wave (of water).*

OLER *to smell.*

Huelo algo. *I smell something.*

Me huele a quemado. *I smell something burning.*

Esto no me huele bien. *There's something fishy about it.*

olfatear *to smell.*

olfato *m. sense of smell.*

oliva *f. olive.*

Aceite de oliva. *Olive oil.*

olivo *m. olive tree.*

olor *m. scent, odor.*

oloroso *adj. fragrant.*

OLVIDAR *to forget.*

Olvidé los guantes. *I forgot my gloves.*

Se me olvidó el paraguas. *I forgot my umbrella.*

Siempre se me olvida su nombre. *I always forget his name.*

¡Ah, se me olvidaba! *Oh, I almost forgot!*

Olvidemos lo pasado. *Let bygones be bygones.*

olvido *m. forgetfulness; oversight.*

Nos ha echado al olvido. *He's forgotten us.*

Fue un olvido. *It was an oversight.*

olla *f. pot; kettle.*

Olla a presión. *Pressure cooker.*

ombligo *m. navel.*

omisión *f. omission.*

omitir *to omit, to leave out.*

Ud. ha omitido varias frases. *You've omitted several sentences.*

ómnibus *m. bus.*

¿Dónde queda la parada del ómnibus? *Where is the bus stop?*

ONCE *adj. and n. eleven.*

onda *f. wave; ripple.*

Onda corta. *Short wave.*

onza *f. ounce.*

opaco *adj. opaque; dull; not transparent.*

opción *f. option, choice.*

ópera *f. opera.*

operación *f. operation.*

operador *m. operator.*

operar *to operate; to act, to take effect; to operate on.*

Hay que operar al enfermo. *It's necessary to operate on the patient.*

Me operan del corazón. *I am having heart surgery.*

operario *m. factory worker; operator.*

opinar *to give an opinion.*

Opino que debes hacerlo. *I think you should do it.*

¿Qué opina Ud. de esto? *What do you think of that? What's your opinion about that?*

opinión *f. opinion.*

Esta es la opinión de todos. *Everyone is of that opinion.*

He cambiado de opinión. *I've changed my mind.*

oponer *to oppose, to go against.*

No opuso la menor dificultad. *He didn't raise any difficulties.*

oponerse *to be against, to object to.*

Me opongo a eso. *I'm against that.*

oportunamente *opportunely, in good time.*

oportunidad *f. opportunity, good chance.*

oportuno *adj. opportune.*

oposición *f. opposition; competition for a position.*

opositor *m. opponent; competitor.*

opresión *f. oppression.*

opresivo *adj. oppressive.*

opresor *m. oppressor.*

oprimir *to press, to squeeze; to oppress.*

optar *to choose, to pick up.*

Optar por. *To choose.*

óptico *adj. optic, optical; m. optician.*

optimismo *m. optimism.*

optimista *m. and f. optimist.*

opuesto *adj. opposed, opposite, contrary.*

oración *f. prayer; sentence (grammar).*

orador *m. orator, speaker.*

oral *adj. oral.*

orar *to pray.*

ORDEN *m. order, arrangement; f. order, command; brotherhood, society, order.*

A sus órdenes. *At your service.*

Por orden de. *By order of.*

Llamar al orden. *Call to order.*
En orden. *In order.*
Dar orden. *To instruct.*
La orden del día. *The order of the day.*
El orden del día. *Agenda.*
Mantener el orden público. *To preserve the
("public") peace.*
ORDENADOR *m. computer (Spain).*
ordenanza *f. order; statute, ordinance; m.
orderly.*
ordenar *to arrange; to order; to command;
to ordain.*
ordeñar *to milk.*
ordinariamente *ordinarily.*
ORDINARIO *adj. ordinary; vulgar,
unrefined.*
Es una mujer ordinaria. *She's vulgar.*
De ordinario. *Usually. Ordinarily.*
oreja *f. ear (external); flange, lug.*
orfandad *f. orphanhood.*
orgánico *adj. organic.*
organismo *m. organism.*
organización *f. organization.*
organizar *to organize; to form; to arrange.*
órgano *m. organ; means, agency.*
orgasmo *m. orgasm.*
orgullo *m. pride; haughtiness.*
orgulloso *adj. proud; haughty.*
oriental *adj. oriental, eastern; m. oriental.*
orientar *to orient.*
orientarse *to find one's bearings, to find
one's way around.*
Es difícil orientarse en una ciudad
desconocida. *It's difficult to find one's
way around in a strange city.*
ORIENTE *m. Orient, East.*
origen *m. origin, source.*
original *adj. and n. original.*
originalidad *f. originality.*
originar *to cause, to originate.*
Los gastos originados. *The cost.*
orilla *f. border, edge; shore; bank (of a
river).*
ornamento *m. ornament, decoration.*
ornar *to adorn.*
ORO *m. gold; pl. diamonds (at cards).*
Perdí mi reloj de oro. *I lost my gold watch.*
orquesta *f. orchestra.*
ortografía *f. orthography, spelling.*
oruga *f. caterpillar.*
os *(dative and accusative of* **vos** *and*
vosotros *used in Spain) you, to you.*
Os invito a cenar. *I'm inviting you to
dinner.*
oscuro *m. dark.*
oso *m. bear.*
ostentar *to display; to show off, to boast.*
OTOÑO *m. autumn, fall.*
otorgar *to consent, to agree to; to grant.*

Quien calla otorga. *Silence gives consent.*
OTRA *(f. of* **otro***) other, another; pl.* **otras.**
Mi otra hija. *My other daughter.*
¿Desea alguna otra cosa? *Would you like
anything else?*
Parece otra. *She looks quite different. She
looks changed.*
Otra vez. *Again. Once more.*
Otras veces. *Other times.*
OTRO *adj. other, another; pl.* **otros.**
¡Otro vaso de cerveza! *Another glass of
beer!*
Busco otro. *I'm looking for another
(one).*
Busco el otro. *I'm looking for the other
(one).*
Queremos otros. *We want some others.*
Otro tanto. *As much more.*
Otros tantos. *As many more.*
Debe haber otros dos. *There must be two
more.*
Al otro lado de la calle. *Across the street.*
Algún otro. *Someone else.*
Otro día. *Another day.*
El otro día. *The other day.*
De otro modo. *Otherwise.*
ovación *f. ovation.*
oval *adj. oval.*
oveja *f. sheep.*
oyente *m. and f. hearer; listener; pl.
audience, listeners.*

pabellón *m. pavilion; flag, colors.*
paciencia *f. patience.*
Tenga paciencia. *Be patient. Have
patience.*
Estoy perdiendo la paciencia. *I'm losing
my patience.*
paciente *adj. patient; m. patient.*
pacífico *adj. peaceful; mild.*
pacotilla *f. venture; stock of goods.*
Ser de pacotilla. *To be flimsy, trashy,
worthless.*
pactar *to reach an agreement, to sign a pact,
to agree upon.*
pacto *m. pact, agreement.*
padecer *to suffer; to be liable to.*
Ha padecido mucho. *He's suffered a lot.*
Padezco mucho de dolores de cabeza. *I
suffer from headaches a lot.*
padecimiento *m. suffering.*
padrastro *m. stepfather.*
PADRE *m. father; pl. parents.*
De tal padre, tal hijo. *Like father, like
son.*

padrino *m. godfather; best man (at a wedding); second (in a duel); sponsor.*

paella *f. a popular Valencian rice dish.*

paga *f. payment; pay, wages, fee.*

pagadero *adj. payable.*

pagador *m. payer; paymaster; paying teller.*

pagaduría *f. paymaster's office.*

pagano *m. pagan, heathen.*

PAGAR *to pay, to pay for; to return (a visit, a favor).*

  ¿Nos pagarán hoy? *Will they pay us today?*

  Pagar al contado. *To pay cash.*

  Pagar a crédito (plazos). *To pay on credit (in installments).*

  Pagar en la misma moneda. *To give a taste of the same medicine.*

  Pagar una visita. *To return a visit.*

  Me las pagará. *I'll make him pay for it.*

  Pagar el pato. *To be blamed for something. To take the blame for something.*

  Está muy pagado de sí. *He has a high opinion of himself.*

pagaré *m. promissory note, I.O.U.*

PÁGINA *f. page (of a book, etc.).*

  La página siguiente. *The following page.*

pago *m. payment; reward.*

  En pago de. *In payment of.*

  Suspender los pagos. *To stop payment.*

país *m. country (nation).*

paisaje *m. landscape, view.*

paisano *adj. coming from the same country; m. fellow countryman; civilian.*

  Somos paisanos. *We are fellow countrymen.*

  Iba vestido de paisano. *He was dressed in civilian clothes.*

paja *f. straw*

  Sombrero de paja. *Straw hat.*

pájaro *m. bird; darling (term of affection).*

PALABRA *f. word; promise.*

  ¿Qué quiere decir esta palabra? *What does this word mean?*

  No entiendo palabra. *I don't understand a word.*

  Desearía hablar dos palabras con Ud. *I should like to have a few words with you.*

  Me quitó la palabra de la boca. *He took the words right out of my mouth.*

  No falte a su palabra. *Don't break your promise.*

  Pido la palabra. *May I have the floor?*

  Dió su palabra de honor. *He gave his word of honor.*

  Libertad de palabra. *Freedom of speech.*

  De palabra. *By word of mouth.*

  Dirigir la palabra. *To address.*

  Palabra de matrimonio *Promise of marraige.*

  Empeñar la palabra. *To give one's word.*

palacio *m. palace.*

paladar *m. palate; taste.*

palanca *f. lever; crowbar.*

palangana *f. washbowl; basin.*

palco *m. grandstand; box (in a theater).*

palidecer *to turn pale.*

pálido *adj. pale.*

palillo *m. toothpick; pl. chopsticks; castanets; drumsticks.*

paliza *f. spanking; beating.*

palma *f. palm tree; palm leaf; palm (of the hand).*

  Llevarse la palma. *To carry the day.*

  Batir palmas. *To applaud.*

palmada *f. pat, clap; clapping.*

  Dar palmadas. *To clap one's hands.*

palmo *m. span, measure of length.*

  Palmo a palmo. *Inch by inch.*

palo *m. stick; cudgel; timber; blow.*

  Palo de escoba. *Broomstick.*

  De tal palo tal astilla. *A chip off the old block. Like father, like son.*

paloma *f. pigeon; dove.*

  Paloma mensajera. *Homing pigeon. Carrier pigeon.*

palomar *m. pigeon house, dovecot.*

palpable *adj. palpable, evident.*

palpar *to feel, to touch.*

palpitar *to beat, to throb, to palpitate.*

paludismo *m. paludism; malaria.*

pampa *f. pampas, vast treeless plain of Argentina and Uruguay.*

PAN *m. bread; loaf.*

  Pan con mantequilla. *Bread and butter.*

  Ganarse el pan. *To earn a living.*

  Pan de maíz. *Corn bread.*

  Pan integral. *Whole-wheat bread.*

  Ser pan comido. *To be easy.*

pana *f. corduroy.*

panadería *f. bakery.*

panadero *m. baker.*

panal *m. honeycomb; hornet's nest.*

pandereta *f. tambourine.*

pandilla *f. gang.*

panecillo *m. roll (bread).*

panera *f. breadbasket; granary.*

pánico *adj. panic; m. panic.*

panorama *m. landscape, view.*

panorámico *adj. panoramic.*

pantalones *m. pants, trousers.*

  Pantalones vaqueros. *Jeans.*

pantalla *f. lamp shade; screen (computer, television, film).*

pantano *m. marsh, swamp.*

pantera *f. panther.*

pantimedias *f. panty hose.*

pantomima f. pantomine.

pantorrilla f. calf (of the leg).

panza f. paunch, belly.

pañal m. diaper.

Pañales desechables. Disposable diapers.

paño m. woolen material, cloth, fabric; (by
  extension) any woven material.

¿Le queda a Ud. bastante paño para hacer
  otro traje? Have you enough material
  left to make another suit?

Paños menores. Underwear.

pañuelo m. handkerchief.

Pañuelos de papel. Tissues.

papa f. potato; m. Pope.

papá m. papa, daddy.

papagayo m. parrot.

papel m. paper; role; part (in a play).

¿Quiere darme un pliego de papel? Will
  you please give me a sheet of paper?

Escríbalo en este papel. Write it on this
  paper.

Hay papel de escribir en el cajón. There's
  some writing paper in the drawer.

Hizo el papel de tonto. He played the fool.

Hacer un papel. To play a part. To play a
  role.

Papel moneda. Paper money (currency).

Papel de estraza. Brown wrapping paper.

Papel de seda. Tissue paper.

Papel de fumar. Cigarette paper.

papelera f. writing desk; (paper) folder.

papelería f. stationery store.

papeleta f. slip (deposit, etc.).

PAQUETE m. package; parcel.

Mande el paquete a estas señas. Send the
  package to this address.

PAR adj. equal; par (value); even (number);
  m. pair, couple; team; peer.

Es una mujer sin par. There's nobody like
  her.

La peseta estaba a la par. The peseta was
  at par value.

La puerta estaba abierta de par en par. The
  door was wide open.

Un par de zapatos. A pair of shoes.

Llegará dentro de un par de días. He'll
  arrive in a couple of days.

¿Toma Ud. pares o nones? Do you take
  odds or evens?

PARA for, to, until, about, in order to,
  toward.

¿Para qué? What for? For what purpose?

¿Para quién es esto? For whom is this?

Esta carta es para Ud. This letter is for
  you.

¿Para qué sirve esto? What's this for?
  What's this good for?

Tengo una cita para las cuatro. I have an
  appointment for four o'clock.

Déjelo para mañana. Leave it until
  tomorrow.

Tiene talento para la música. She has a gift
  for music.

Me abrigo para no tener frío. I dress
  warmly so as not to be cold.

Bueno para comer. Good to eat.

Estoy para salir. I'm about to leave.

El tren está para partir. The train is about
  to leave.

Trabajar para comer. To work for a living.

Estudia para médico. He's studying to be a
  doctor.

Para siempre. Forever.

Para entre los dos. Between ourselves.

parabién m. congratulations.

parábola f. parable; parabola.

parabrisas m. windshield.

paracaídas m. parachute.

paracaidista m. parachutist.

parada f. stop; pause; halt; parade; wager.

¿Dónde está la parada más cerca del
  autobús? Where is the nearest bus
  stop?

Cinco minutos de parada. Five minutes'
  stop.

La parada se formará a las doce. The
  parade will form at twelve o'clock.

paradero m. whereabouts; terminus; end.

parado adj. stopped, at a standstill; closed
  (a factory); unemployed; standing up
  (Amer.).

paradoja f. paradox.

PARAGUAS m. umbrella.

¿Llevamos paraguas? Shall we take (our)
  umbrellas?

paraíso m. paradise.

paralelo adj. and n. parallel.

parálisis f. paralysis.

paralítico adj. paralytic.

paralizar to paralyze; to bring to a
  standstill; to impede, to hinder.

PARAR to stop, to halt, to stay; to stand
  (Amer.).

¿Paramos aquí? Do we stop here?

Pare Ud. en frente de la estación. Stop in
  front of the station.

Mi reloj se paró. My watch stopped.

No para de llover desde ayer. It hasn't
  stopped raining since yesterday.

¿En qué hotel pararán sus amigos? At what
  hotel will your friends stay?

Paró la oreja para oír lo que decíamos. He
  pricked up his ears to hear what we
  were saying.

No paró bien aquel negocio. That business
  didn't end very well.

¿Dónde irá a parar todo esto? How's all
  this going to end?

pararse to stop; to stand up (*Amer.*).

Se pararon (*Amer.*) al verla llegar. *They stood up when they saw her coming.*

Párese (*Amer.*) en esta esquina que ahorita pasará el autobús. *Stand on this corner; the bus will pass by in a little while.*

pararrayos m. lightning rod.

parásito m. parasite.

parcela f. parcel; piece of land.

parcial adj. partial.

parcialidad f. partiality, bias.

parcialmente partially, partly.

parchar to patch.

pardo adj. brown; dark.

PARECER to appear, to show up, to turn up; to seem, to look, to look like, to resemble; m. opinion; appearance.

¿Qué le parece? *What do you think of it? How do you like it? How does it seem to you?*

Léalo Ud. despacio y dígame lo que le parece. *Read it carefully and let me know what you think of it.*

¿Le parece que vayamos al cine? *What do you say to our going to the movies?*

Me parece barato a ese precio. *I think it's cheap at that price.*

Está enfermo, pero no lo parece. *He's sick but he doesn't look it.*

Al parecer vendrá la semana próxima. *Apparently he's coming next week.*

También soy yo del mismo parecer. *I'm also of the same opinion.*

No me gusta su parecer. *I don't like his appearance.*

parecerse to look alike, to resemble.

Este niño se parece a su padre. *This child looks like his father.*

Se parecen como dos gotas de agua. *They are as alike as two peas in a pod.*

PARECIDO adj. like, similar, resembling; (good or bad) looking; m. likeness.

Yo tengo un traje muy parecido al suyo. *I have a suit very much like yours.*

Los dos trabajos son muy parecidos. *The two jobs are very similar.*

Su hijo es muy bien parecido. *Your son is very good-looking.*

PARED f. wall.

Apóyalo contra la pared. *Lean it against the wall.*

Entre la espada y la pared. *Between the devil and the deep blue sea.*

pareja f. pair; couple; team (of horses); dancing partner.

paréntesis m. parenthesis.

PARIENTE m. relative, relation.

¿Tiene Ud. parientes en esta ciudad? *Do you have any relatives in this town?*

parir to give birth.

parlamento m. parliament; parley.

paro m. unemployment; stoppage of work.

Paro forzoso. *Lockout.*

párpado m. eyelid.

parque m. park.

parqueadero m. parking lot.

parra f. grapevine.

párrafo m. paragraph.

Echar un párrafo. *To have a chat.*

parrilla f. grill; steak house.

A la parrilla. *Grilled.*

parrillada f. grilled fish or meats.

parroquia f. parish.

parroquiano m. parishoner.

PARTE f. part; portion; share; side; role; party; m. report, communication, dispatch.

¿En qué parte de la ciudad vive Ud.? *In what part of the city do you live?*

Hagamos el trabajo por partes iguales. *Let's divide the work equally.*

Cada uno pagó su parte. *Each one paid his share.*

Traigo esto de parte del señor Sucre. *This is from Mr. Sucre.*

Salude a Juan de mi parte. *Give John my regards.*

Recibimos felicitaciones de ambas partes. *We received congratulations from both sides.*

He leído la mayor parte del libro, pero no todo. *I've read most of the book, but not all.*

No tengo arte ni parte en el asunto. *I've nothing to do with the matter.*

¿Le ha visto en alguna parte? *Have you seen him anywhere?*

No lo hallo en ninguna parte. *I can't find it anywhere.*

En todas partes. *Everywhere.*

En parte. *In part.*

En gran parte. *Largely.*

De cinco días a esta parte. *Within the(se) last few days.*

Parte de la oración. *Part of the speech.*

Dar parte. *To inform. To notify.*

Le he dado parte de mi llegada. *I've sent him word of my arrival.*

Por mi parte. *As far as I'm concerned. For my part.*

Por una parte. *On one hand.*

Por otra parte. *On the other hand. Besides.*

La parte interesada. *The interested party.*

¿De parte de quién? *Who's calling?*

participación f. participation, share.

participar *to participate, to take part, to share; to inform, to notify.*

No se crea que yo participo de sus ideas. *Don't think that I share his views.*

Le participo mi decisión. *I'm informing you of my decision.*

¿Participaron Uds. en el juego? *Did you take part in the game?*

particular *adj. particular, unusual, peculiar; m. private citizen; individual.*

Eso no tiene nada de particular. *There's nothing unusual about it.*

¿Hay algo de nuevo?—Nada de particular. *Anything new?—Nothing in particular.*

En particular. *In particular.*

particularidad *f. particularity, peculiarity.*

particularmente *particularly, especially.*

partida *f. departure; entry, item (in an account); lot; one game; certificate (birth, etc.).*

Punto de partida. *Point of departure. Starting point.*

Partida de nacimiento. *Birth certificate.*

Echemos una partida de ajedrez. *Let's play a game of chess.*

Partida doble. *Double entry.*

partidario *adj. and n. partisan, follower, supporter.*

Soy partidario de los paseos al aire libre. *I like to take walks in the fresh air.*

Es partidario de la política nacionalista. *He's in favor of nationalistic policies.*

partido *adj. divided, split; broken; m. party; advantage; game.*

Ese vaso está partido. *That glass is broken.*

La tabla esta partida. *The board is split.*

No sabía qué partido tomar. *I didn't know what to do.*

Pertenecen al mismo partido. *They belong to the same party.*

¿Quiere Ud. ver el partido de fútbol? *Would you like to see the football (soccer) game?*

¿Cuál fue el resultado del partido? *What was the final score of the game?*

PARTIR *to divide, to split; to leave; to cut; to break.*

El tren está para partir. *The train is about to leave.*

Partiremos el primero del mes. *We'll leave on the first of the month.*

Seguía diluviando cuando partimos. *It was still pouring when we left.*

Necesito un cuchillo para partir este pan. *I need a knife to cut this bread.*

La tabla se ha partido en dos. *The board broke in two.*

Partió la manzana en dos. *He divided (split) the apple in two.*

Parta Ud. 300 entre 3. *Divide 3 into 300.*

Partieron el terreno en varios lotes. *They divided the land into several lots.*

Al partirse el hielo cayeron al agua. *When the ice broke, they fell into the water.*

Partir la diferencia. *To split the difference.*

parto *m. childbirth.*

parvo *adj. small, little.*

párvulo *m. small child.*

pasa *f. raisin.*

PASADO *m. past; past tense.*

Pasados dos días. *After two days.*

Lo pasado. *The past.*

El martes pasado, tres de marzo. *Last Tuesday, March the third.*

Pasado mañana. *The day after tomorrow.*

pasaje *m. passage; fare, ticket; strait.*

¿Cuánto cuesta el pasaje? *What's the fare?*

pasajero *adj. passing transitory; m. passenger.*

pasaporte *m. passport.*

PASAR *to pass, to go by, to go across; to come over, to come in, to call (visit); to spend (the time); to get along; to be taken for; to put on, to pretend; to overlook; to surpass; to happen.*

Pásame la sal, por favor. *Pass the salt, please.*

Pase Ud. y siéntese. *Come in and sit down.*

Pase Ud. por aquí. *Come this way.*

Pase por aquí otro día. *Drop in again some time.*

¿Puede Ud. pasar por mi oficina mañana? *Can you call at my office tomorrow?*

Pasamos el río a nado. *We swam across the river.*

Ya pasó el tren. *The train has already passed.*

Pasaron por aquí hace poco. *They went by this place a moment ago.*

Pasamos por la calle de Arenal. *We passed through Arenal Street.*

Pasa por norteamericano, pero no lo es. *He passes for an American but he isn't really.*

Los años se pasan rapidamente. *The years pass quickly.*

¿Cómo se llama este pueblo que acabamos de pasar? *What's the name of the village we just passed?*

Se pasó todo el día leyendo. *She spent the whole day reading.*

¿Qué pasa? *What's the matter?*

¿Cómo lo pasa Ud.? *How are you getting along?*

¿Qué le pasa a Ud.? *What's the matter with you?*

Que pase Ud. buena noche. *I hope you*

have a good night's sleep (rest), *Sleep well.*

Lo pasa uno bien allí. *Life is pleasant there.*

Yo no sé lo que le pasa. *I don't know what's the matter with him.*

Ud. no sabe lo que ha pasado. *You don't know what has happened.*

Sólo Dios sabe qué pasará. *(Only) God knows what will happen.*

Esta lluvia pasará pronto. *The (this) rain will stop soon.*

Ya se le pasará. *He'll get over it.*

Ya pasó aquello. *That's gone (past) and forgotten.*

Eso ha pasado de moda. *That's gone out of style.*

Se pasa de buena. *She's too good.*

Se me pasó por alto. *I overlooked it. I didn't (take) notice.*

Voy a pasar lista a la clase. *I'm going to call the class roll.*

Estamos pasando el rato. *We're killing time. We're having fun.*

pasarela *f.* gangway, catwalk.

pasatiempo *m.* pastime, amusement.

Pascua *f.* Christmas; Easter; Passover.

¡Felices Pascuas! *Merry Christmas!*

Está como unas pascuas. *He's as happy as a lark.*

pase *m.* pass, permit; thrust.

paseante *m.* stroller.

PASEAR to walk; to ride; to take a walk.

Vamos a pasear. *Let's go for a walk.*

Saca los niños a pasear. *Take the children out for a walk.*

pasearse to go for a walk.

PASEO *m.* walk, stroll; ride; drive; avenue or road bordered by trees.

Demos un paseo. *Let's take a walk.*

Vamos a dar un paseo en coche. *Let's go for a drive.*

Hay muchos árboles en el paseo de Recoletos. *There are a lot of trees on Recoletos.*

pasillo *m.* corridor; aisle; hall; basting stitch.

Iré al pasillo para llamar por teléfono. *I'll go out into the hall to phone.*

Asiento al pasillo. *Aisle seat.*

pasión *f.* passion.

pasivo *adj.* passive; *m.* liabilities.

PASO *m.* step; pass; passage; place; gait.

Está a dos pasos de aquí. *It's only a few steps from here.*

Los pasos que sentí no parecían de mujer. *The steps I heard didn't sound like a woman's.*

Tuvimos que abrirnos paso por entre la multitud. *We had to make our way through the crowd.*

Este caballo tiene un paso excelente. *This horse has a fine gait.*

Apretemos el paso para llegar a tiempo. *Let's hurry so that we'll get there on time.*

De paso. *By the way. Incidentally.*

Salir de paso. *To get out of a difficulty.*

Dar los pasos necesarios. *To take the necessary steps.*

Paso a paso. *Step by step.*

Llevar el paso. *To keep in step.*

Marcar el paso. *To mark time.*

"Prohibido el paso." "Keep out." "No trespassing."

pasta *f.* paste; dough; binding (of a book).

Pasta de dientes. *Toothpaste.*

pastel *m.* pie, cake; chopped meat cooked in a banana leaf (P. R.).

pastelería *f.* pastry shop; pastry.

pastelero *m.* pastry cook.

pastilla *f.* drop, lozenge; cake (of soap).

Pastillas de menta. *Mint drops.*

Pastillas para la tos. *Cough drops.*

pastor *m.* shepherd; pastor.

pata *f.* foot and leg of an animal; leg (of a table, chair, etc.); duck.

Ha roto la pata de la mesa. *He broke the leg of the table.*

A pata (coll.). *On foot.*

Patas arriba. *Upside down.*

Meter la pata. *To make a blunder. To put one's foot in it.*

patalear to stamp (the foot).

patata *f.* potato.

Patatas fritas. *French fries.*

patente *adj.* patent, obvious; *f.* patent; grant, privilege.

Hacer patente. *To make clear.*

patillas *f. pl.* sideburns.

patín *m.* skate.

Patín de ruedas. *Roller skates.*

patinaje *m.* skating.

Patinaje sobre ruedas. *Roller skating.*

Patinaje sobre hielo. *Ice skating.*

patinar to skate; to skid.

patio *m.* patio; yard; pit (theater).

pato *m.* drake, duck.

Pagar el pato. *To be made the scapegoat.*

patraña *f.* falsehood, hoax.

patria *f.* native country, fatherland.

patriota *m.* patriot.

patriótico *adj.* patriotic.

patriotismo *m.* patriotism.

patrocinar to patronize.

patrón *m.* master, skipper (of a ship); employer, boss; pattern; standard (gold).

patrono *m.* employer; patron saint.

patrulla f. patrol.

paulatinamente slowly, by degrees.

paulatino adj. slow, gradual.

pausa f. pause.

pauta f. paper ruler; guidelines; example, model.

pava f. turkey hen.

　　Pelar la pava. To flirt.

PAVIMENTO m. pavement.

pavo m. turkey.

　　Pavo real. Peacock.

pavor m. fear, terror.

payaso m. clown.

PAZ f. peace.

　　¿Por qué no hacen las paces? Why don't they bury the hatchet? Why don't they make up?

　　En paz. Even. Quits. On even terms.

　　Déjeme en paz. Let me alone.

pe f. name of the letter **p**.

　　De pe a pa. Entirely. Thoroughly. From top to bottom. From beginning to end.

peaje m. toll.

peatón m. pedestrian.

pecado m. sin.

pecar to sin.

peculiar adj. peculiar.

peculiaridad f. peculiarity.

PECHO m. chest; breast; bosom.

　　Me duele el pecho. My chest hurts me.

　　Es un hombre de pelo en pecho. He's a daring (bold, brave, aggressive) fellow.

　　No lo tome Ud. a pecho. Don't take it to heart.

　　Dar el pecho. To breastfeed.

pechuga f. breast (of a fowl).

pedagogo m. pedagogue, teacher.

pedal m. pedal, treadle.

PEDAZO m. bit, piece, morsel.

　　Sírvame otro pedazo de carne. May I have another piece of meat?

　　Hacer pedazos. To break into pieces.

　　¡Pedazo de bruto! Blockhead!

pedestal m. pedestal; support.

pedido m. order (for goods); request.

　　No podemos servir el pedido. We can't fill the order.

　　Hacer un pedido. To order (goods). To place an order.

　　A pedido de. At the request of.

PEDIR to ask for; to beg; to demand; to wish; to order (goods).

　　Me ha pedido que le haga un favor. He asked me to do him a favor.

　　¿Ya pidió Ud. el desayuno? Have you ordered breakfast?

　　Tengo que pedirle permiso. I have to ask his permission.

　　Pido la palabra. May I have the floor?

　　Pidió socorro a voces. She cried out for help.

　　El público entusiasmado pidió la repetición. The enthusiastic audience called for an encore.

　　Pedir informes. To ask for information. To inquire.

pegajoso adj. sticky, viscous; contagious.

pegar to paste, to glue; to sew on; to hit, to beat; to stop.

　　Pegue las etiquetas. Paste the labels on.

　　Pegar a una persona. To hit (beat up) a person.

　　Pegar fuego a. To set fire to.

　　No pude pegar los ojos en toda la noche. I couldn't sleep a wink all night.

peinado m. hairstyle, coiffure, hairdo.

　　¿Qué peinado prefiere? What hairstyle do you prefer?

peinar to comb.

　　Péineme el pelo hacia atrás. Comb my hair back.

peinarse to do or to comb one's hair.

　　Ella se peina muy bien. She does her hair very nicely.

　　Sólo me falta peinarme. I just (only) have to comb my hair.

PEINE m. comb.

pelado adj. plucked, bare, bald, nude; penniless, broke (Amer.).

pelar to peel; to cut somebody's hair; to pluck, to rob, to cheat.

　　Péleme esa manzana. Peel that apple for me.

　　Es duro de pelar. He's (it's) a hard nut to crack.

peldaño m. step (of staircase).

pelea f. fight, struggle.

pelear to fight.

peletería f. furrier's, fur shop.

película f. film.

　　La película resultó muy aburrida. The picture was dull.

　　¿Qué película dan esta noche? What's showing tonight?

peligro m. peril, danger.

　　No hay peligro. There's no danger.

peligroso adj. dangerous.

PELO m. hair.

　　Quiero que me corten el pelo. I want a haircut.

　　¡No me tome Ud. el pelo! Don't make fun of me! Don't kid me! Don't tease me!

pelota f. ball.

　　Pelota vasca. Jai-alai.

peluca f. wig.

peluquería f. barber shop.

　　Peluquería de señoras. Beauty parlor.

peluquero *m. barber; wigmaker.*

pellejo *m. hide; skin.*

pellizcar *to pinch.*

pena *f. penalty, punishment; grief, sorrow, hardship, toil.*

Murió de pena. *She died of a broken heart.*

Ha sufrido muchas penas. *He has been through many hardships.*

Lo hizo a duras penas. *He did it with great difficulty.*

No vale la pena hacerlo. *It's not worthwhile doing.*

Bajo pena de. *Under penalty of.*

Pena capital. *Capital punishment. Death penalty.*

penal *adj. penal; m. prison.*

penalidad *f. hardship; penalty.*

penar *to suffer; to be in agony.*

pender *to hang; to be pending.*

pendiente *adj. pendent; pending; m. earrings. f. slope.*

Cuestión pendiente. *An open question. A question still pending.*

Eso queda pendiente. *That's still pending.*

Deuda pendiente. *Balance due.*

Lleva unos pendientes muy bonitos. *She's wearing very pretty earrings.*

Bajar una pendiente. *To descend (go down) a hill.*

penetrante *adj. penetrating, piercing.*

penetrar *to penetrate; to fathom, to comprehend.*

península *f. peninsula.*

penitente *adj. and n. penitent.*

penoso *adj. painful; difficult, arduous; distressing.*

pensado *adj. deliberate; thought out.*

Está muy bien pensado. *It's (very) well thought out.*

Tengo pensado comprarlo. *I intend to buy (buying) it.*

pensador *m. thinker; thinking.*

Libre pensador. *Free thinker.*

pensamiento *m. thought; idea; pansy.*

PENSAR *to think; to consider, to intend.*

Piense antes de hablar. *Think before you speak.*

Lo hice sin pensar. *I did it without thinking.*

¿En qué piensa Ud.? *What are you thinking about?*

Esto me da en que pensar. *This gives me something to think about.*

¿Qué piensa Ud. de eso? *What do you think about that?*

Pienso igual que Ud.. *I think the same as you. I agree with you.*

Pensaban estar aquí para el lunes. *They planned to be here about Monday.*

¿Cuándo piensa Ud. marcharse? *When do you intend to leave?*

¿En qué hotel piensa Ud. parar? *At what hotel do you expect to stop?*

pensativo *adj. pensive, thoughtful.*

pensión *f. pension; board; boardinghouse.*

pensionista *m. and f. pensioner; boarder.*

penúltimo *adj. penultimate, last but one.*

peña *f. rock, large stone; circle (of friends).*

peñón *m. large rock; cliff; rocky mountain.*

El peñón de Gibraltar. *The rock of Gibraltar.*

peón *m. peon; pawn (in chess); pedestrian; (spinning) top.*

PEOR *adj. and adv. worse; worst.*

Sigue peor. *He's getting worse.*

Eso es lo peor. *That's the worst of it.*

Tanto peor. *All the worse. So much the worse.*

Llevar la peor parte. *To get the worst of it.*

El mes pasado fue el peor de todos. *Last month was the worst of all.*

La situación va (sigue) de mal en peor. *The situation is going from bad to worse.*

pepinillos *m. pl. pickles.*

pepino *m. cucumber.*

pequeñez *f. a trifle; pettiness.*

Discutieron sobre una pequeñez. *They argued over a trifle.*

PEQUEÑO *adj. little, small, tiny; young; m. child.*

Su hijo es muy pequeño. *His child is very young.*

Tiene los dientes blancos y pequeños. *She has small white teeth.*

¿Cómo están los pequeños? *How are the children?*

PERA *f. pear.*

Partir peras con alguno. *To treat a person familiarly.*

peral *m. pear tree.*

percance *m. misfortune, mishap, accident.*

percepción *f. perception.*

perceptible *adj. perceptible, perceivable.*

percibir *to perceive, to get.*

No percibo bien lo que dice. *I don't quite get what he's saying.*

Percibe un sueldo de mil pesos. *He has (receives) a salary of a thousand pesos a month.*

percha *f. pole, coat hanger.*

PERDER *to lose.*

He perdido mi cartera. *I've lost my wallet.*

No tengo tiempo que perder. *I haven't any time to lose.*

Estuvo a punto de perder la vida. *He nearly lost his life.*

Echar a perder. *To spoil.*

Está echado a perder. *He's spoiled.*

No lo pierdas de vista. *Don't lose sight of him.*

He perdido una buena ocasión. *I missed a good opportunity.*

Lo hice a ratos perdidos. *I did it in my spare moments (time).*

Está borracho perdido. *He's dead drunk.*

¿Este color no pierde? *Does this color fade?*

Ha perdido la razón. *He's lost his reason (mind).*

Perdió la vista. *He lost his eyesight.*

Perder la vergüenza. *To lose all sense of shame.*

Perder el respeto. *To lose respect for.*

Perder el habla. *To become speechless.*

perderse *to get lost; to spoil, to get spoiled; to go astray.*

La comida se va a perder si no se come hoy. *The food will spoil if it's not eaten today.*

Perderse en el bosque. *To get lost in the woods.*

perdición *f. perdition; ruin.*

pérdida *f. loss; damage; leakage.*

Reparar una pérdida. *To recover a loss.*

perdidamente *desperately.*

Está perdidamente enamorado. *He's head over heels in love.*

perdiz *f. partridge.*

perdón *m. pardon.*

¡Perdón! *Pardon me!*

PERDONAR *to excuse, to pardon, to forgive.*

Perdóneme Ud. *Excuse me.*

Le suplico a Ud. que me perdone. *Please excuse me.*

Perdone mi tardanza. *Pardon my lateness.*

Esta vez te lo perdono. *This time I forgive you.*

No perdonar ni un detalle. *To leave nothing untold.*

perecer *to perish, to die.*

peregrino *adj. migratory; m. pilgrim.*

perejil *m. parsley.*

pereza *f. laziness, idleness.*

perezoso *adj. lazy, indolent.*

perfección *f. perfection, improvement, perfecting.*

perfeccionar *to make perfect, to improve.*

perfeccionarse *to improve oneself, to increase one's knowledge.*

PERFECTO *adj. perfect.*

Es un trabajo perfecto. *It's a perfect piece of work.*

perfidia *f. perfidy, treachery, foul play.*

perfil *m. profile; outline.*

perfume *m. perfume; scent, fragrance.*

perfumería *f. perfume store.*

pericia *f. skill; knowledge.*

periférico *adj. peripheral; n. peripheral (computer).*

perilla *f. knob, doorknob.*

Déle vuelta a la perilla. *Turn the knob.*

periódico *adj. periodic(al); m. newspaper, magazine, periodical.*

periodismo *m. journalism.*

periodista *m. and f. journalist, newspaperman, newspaperwoman.*

período *m. period, time.*

perito *adj. experienced, skillful; m. expert; appraiser.*

perjudicar *to damage, to injure, to hurt.*

perjudicial *adj. prejudicial, harmful.*

perjuicio *m. damage, injury, loss.*

perjuro *adj. perjured; m. perjurer.*

perla *f. pearl.*

permanecer *to remain, to stay.*

¿Cuánto tiempo permanecerá Ud. fuera de la ciudad? *How long will you be (remain) out of town?*

permanencia *f. permanence; stay.*

PERMANENTE *adj. and n. permanent.*

Un lugar permanente. *A permanent place.*

La peluquera le hizo una permanente. *The hairdresser gave her a permanent.*

permeable *adj. permeable.*

PERMISO *m. permission; permit, authorization, consent; pardon me.*

Tener permiso de. *To have permission to.*

Con su permiso. *If I may. With your permission.*

No lo haga Ud. sin mi permiso. *Don't do it without my permission.*

Permiso de llevar armas de fuego. *A permit to carry firearms.*

Permiso para guiar. *A driver's license.*

permitir *to permit, to let, to allow.*

¿Me permite Ud. que fume? *May I smoke? Do you mind if I smoke?*

¿Me permite que le haga una pregunta. *May I ask you a question?*

No permitiré tal cosa. *I won't allow such a thing.*

Permítame Ud. que le presente a mi amigo. *Allow me to introduce you to my friend.*

permuta *f. exchange; barter.*

permutar *to barter, to exchange.*

pernicioso *adj. pernicious, injurious, harmful.*

PERO *but, yet, except; m. defect, fault.*

Ud. no querrá ir, pero yo sí. *You may not want to go, but I do.*

Pero no es así. *But that's not the case.*

Pero él dice otra cosa. *But he tells a different story.*

No hay pero que valga. *No ands, ifs, or buts.*

Poner peros. *To find fault.*

perpendicular *adj. and n. perpendicular.*

perpetuar *to perpetuate.*

perpetuidad *f. perpetuity.*

perpetuo *adj. perpetual, everlasting.*

perplejo *adj. perplexed, bewildered, puzzled.*

Me siento perplejo. *I'm perplexed (puzzled).*

perra *f. bitch.*

PERRO *m. dog.*

persecución *f. persecution.*

perseguir *to persecute; to pursue; to harass.*

perseverancia *f. perseverance.*

perseverar *to persevere, to persist.*

persiana *f. window blind; pl. Venetian blind.*

persistencia *f. persistence, obstinacy.*

persistente *adj. persistent, firm.*

persistir *to persist.*

PERSONA *f. person.*

Es muy buena persona. *He's a very nice person.*

Esto me lo dijo cierta persona. *A certain person told me that.*

En este salón caben más de cien personas. *This hall can accommodate over a hundred people.*

personaje *m. character (in a play); celebrity.*

personal *adj. personal; m. personnel, staff.*

Estos artículos son de mi uso personal. *These articles are for my personal use.*

Manejo de personal. *Personnel management.*

personalidad *f. personality.*

perspectiva *f. perspective.*

perspicacia *f. perspicacity.*

perspicaz *adj. perspicacious, acute, sagacious, quick-sighted.*

persuadir *to persuade; to convince.*

persuasión *f. persuasion.*

pertenecer *to belong.*

Esto pertenece a ... *This belongs to ...*

Esa pluma me pertenece. *That pen belongs to me.*

pertinente *adj. pertinent.*

perturba *to perturb, agitate.*

perversidad *f. perversity, wickedness.*

perversión *f. perversion.*

perverso *adj. perverse.*

pervertir *to pervert.*

pesa *f. weight.*

Levantar pesas. *Weightlifting.*

Pesas y medidas. *Weights and measures.*

pesadilla *f. nightmare.*

pesado *adj. heavy; tedious; tiresome; m. bore.*

El hierro es pesado. *Iron is heavy.*

Es un pesado. *He's a bore.*

pésame *m. condolence; message of condolence.*

PESAR *to weigh, to be of weight; to cause regret; m. grief, sorrow; regret.*

¿Cuánto pesa Ud.? *How much do you weigh?*

Vale lo que pesa. *It's worth its weight in gold.*

Me pesa mucho haberle ofendido. *I'm sorry I offended him.*

Aunque me pese no puedo menos que hacerlo. *Although I regret it, I can't help doing it.*

Lo haremos a pesar de todo. *We'll do it in spite of everything.*

pesca *f. fishing; fishery.*

PESCADO *m. fish (after it is caught; see pez).*

pescar *to fish; to catch.*

pescuezo *m. neck (animal).*

pesebre *m. crib, manger.*

peseta *f. peseta (Spanish coin).*

pesimismo *m. pessimism.*

pesimista *adj. pessimistic; m. and f. pessimist.*

pésimo *adj. very bad.*

peso *m. weight; weighing; scales; importance; burden; peso (standard monetary unit in some Spanish American countries).*

Le presté cinco pesos. *I lent him five pesos.*

Ponga Ud. esto en el peso. *Put that on the scales.*

Me han quitado un peso de encima. *That took a load off my mind.*

Sobre nosotros cayó todo el peso de la lucha. *We bore the brunt of the struggle.*

Eso cae de su peso. *That goes without saying.*

Peso neto. *Net weight.*

Peso bruto. *Gross weight.*

De peso. *Of weight. Of importance.*

pestaña *f. eyelash; fringe, edging.*

peste *f. plague; pestilence.*

pestillo *m. door latch, bolt.*

petición *f. petition; claim; demand; plea.*

petróleo *m. petroleum; mineral oil.*

petrolero *m. oil-tanker.*

pez *m. fish (in the water; see pescado); f. pitch, tar.*

pezuña *f. hoof.*

piadoso *adj. pious; merciful.*

pianista *m. and f. pianist.*

piano *m. piano.*

picadillo *m. hash; minced meat.*

picadura *f. prick; puncture; bite (of an insect or snake).*

picante *adj. hot, highly seasoned; cutting, sarcastic, pungent (wit).*

picaporte *m. latch.*

picar *to bite, to sting; to prick; to itch; to chop; to nibble; to spur; to be hot (pepper, etc.).*

Me ha picado una abeja. *I was stung by a bee.*

Me pica la espalda. *My back itches.*

Picar la carne. *To chop (up) meat.*

Esta pimienta pica mucho. *This pepper is very hot (strong).*

El sol pica. *The sun is scorching.*

Picar el caballo. *To spur a horse.*

Picar alto. *To aim too high.*

picarse *to begin to rot (fruit); to decay; to be piqued; to be moth-eaten; to become choppy (sea).*

El vino empieza a picarse. *The wine is turning sour (fermenting).*

Tengo un diente picado. *I have a cavity in one of my teeth.*

picardía *f. knavery; deceit, malice.*

pícaro *adj. roguish; mischievous; m. and f. rogue, rascal, scoundrel.*

Tiene trazas de ser un pícaro. *He looks like a rascal.*

picazón *f. itch, itching.*

pico *adj. odd, leftover; m. beak, bill; pick; spout; peak.*

Subieron al pico más alto de la sierra. *They climbed to the highest peak of the mountain ridge.*

Tiene mucho pico. *She's a chatterbox.*

Son las once y pico. *It's a little after eleven.*

Veinte dólares y pico. *Twenty dollars and some odd cents.*

picor *m. itching.*

pichincha *f. bargain.*

PIE *m. foot, leg; footing, basis.*

Me duele mucho el pie. *My foot hurts a lot.*

Esta mesa tiene seis pies de largo. *This table is six feet long.*

A pie. *On foot.*

Nos fuimos a pie al hotel. *We walked to the hotel.*

Al pie del cerro. *At the foot of the hill.*

De (en) pie. *Standing (up).*

Al pie de la letra. *Literally. To the letter.*

Ponerse en pie. *To stand up.*

Quedar en pie. *To hold good. To be (still) pending.*

No tiene pies ni cabeza. *It doesn't make any sense.*

Tiene buenos pies. *She's a good walker.*

Ha nacido de pie. *He was born with a silver spoon in his mouth.*

piedad *f. mercy; pity.*

piedra *f. stone; gravel; hail.*

Piedras preciosas. *Precious stones.*

Este pan es duro como una piedra. *The bread's hard as a rock.*

No dejar piedra por mover. *To leave no stone unturned. To move heaven and earth.*

PIEL *f. skin; hide; fur.*

Tiene la piel como seda. *She has very soft skin.*

Abrigo de pieles. *Fur coat.*

Quiero este libro encuadernado en piel. *I want this volume bound in leather.*

PIERNA *f. leg.*

Dormir a pierna tendida. *To sleep soundly.*

PIEZA *f. piece; part; room; a play.*

Esta pieza tiene dos ventanas. *This room has two windows.*

Géneros de pieza. *Piece goods. Yard goods.*

Piezas de repuesto. *Spare parts.*

pijamas *m. pl. pajamas.*

pila *f. stone trough or basin; fountain; holy-water basin, font; sink (kitchen, etc.); pile, heap; battery.*

Pila de cocina. *Kitchen sink.*

Una pila de leña. *A pile of wood.*

Pila seca. *Dry cell (battery).*

Nombre de pila. *Christian name. ("Baptismal name.")*

pilar *m. pillar, column, post.*

píldora *f. pill.*

piloto *m. pilot; first mate.*

pillo *m. rogue, rascal.*

pimentón *m. ground red pepper; paprika.*

pimienta *f. pepper.*

pimiento *m. pepper, pimento.*

pincel *m. artist's brush.*

pinchar *to prick, to puncture.*

Se pinchó el dedo. *He pricked his finger.*

Se me ha pinchado un neumático. *I have a flat tire. One of my tires blew out.*

pinchazo *m. puncture; flat tire; prick.*

pinchos *m. pl. snacks.*

pino *m. pine.*

pinta *f. appearance (quality).*

Tiene mala pinta. *It looks awful.*

pintado *adj. painted; spotted; just right, exact.*

Ese traje le queda como pintado. *That dress fits her just right.*

Pintado de rojo. *Painted red.*

No puedo verle ni pintado. *I can't stand the sight of him.*

pintar *to paint; to describe; to begin to ripen.*

¿Qué pinta Ud.? *What are you painting?*

Pinte de azul la pared. *Paint the wall blue.*

Empiezan a pintar las uvas. *The grapes are becoming (getting) ripe.*

pintor *m. painter.*

pintura *f. painting.*

La pintura no está seca. *The paint is still wet.*

Pintura al óleo. *Oil painting.*

Esa es una pintura histórica. *That's an historical painting.*

pinza *f. claw.*

Pinzas. *Tweezers, tongs.*

piña *f. pineapple.*

piojo *m. louse.*

pipa *f. tobacco pipe; cask, barrel (wine).*

pique *(a) sink (used with the verb* **echar** *and* **ir**).

El buque se fue a pique. *The ship sank.*

Echar a pique. *To sink. To send to the bottom.*

pirámide *f. pyramid.*

pirata *m. pirate.*

piropear *to flatter (a girl or a woman).*

pisada *f. footstep; footprint.*

pisar *to tread, to step on; to press; to cover.*

Mire Ud. donde pisa. *Watch your step. Watch where you're going.*

Pise el acelerador. *Step on the gas.*

piscina *f. swimming pool.*

Piscina calentada. *Heated pool.*

PISO *m. floor; pavement; story, apartment.*

¿Se alquila este piso? *Is this apartment for rent?*

¿Cuántos roperos tiene este piso? *How many closets are there in this apartment?*

Ella vive en el segundo piso. *She lives on the second floor.*

Suban Uds. un piso más. *Walk up another flight.*

pisotear *to tread, to trample; to step on someone's foot.*

pisotón *m. tread; stepping on someone's foot.*

Me dió un pisotón. *He stepped on my foot.*

pista *f. trail, track, footprint; trace, clue; racetrack.*

Seguir la pista. *To follow the trail.*

Le estamos siguiendo la pista. *We're on his trail (track).*

pistola *f. pistol.*

pitillo *m. cigarette.*

No tengo ni pitillos ni cerillas. *I have neither cigarettes nor matches.*

pito *m. whistle; penis (slang).*

Eso no vale un pito. *It isn't worth a thing.*

pivote *m. pivot.*

pizarra *f. slate; chalkboard.*

pizca *f. mite, bit; pinch.*

Tiene su pizca de gracia. *It has its funny side.*

placa *f. plate; plaque; license plate.*

Tiene un serio problema de placa en los dientes. *He has a serious plaque problem with his teeth.*

Una placa metálica. *A metal plate.*

PLACER *to please; m. pleasure, enjoyment.*

Es un placer conversar con ella. *It's a pleasure to talk to (with) her.*

Tener placer en. *To take pleasure in.*

Tendré mucho placer en hacerlo. *I'll be very pleased (happy) to do it.*

Me será un gran placer conocerle. *I'd be very happy to meet him (you).*

plaga *f. plague; epidemic.*

plan *m. plan; scheme; drawing.*

Ser plan. *To be one's intention.*

No era plan quedarnos aquí. *It was not our intention to stay here.*

plana *f. page.*

Lo leí en primera plana. *I read it on the first page of the newspaper.*

plancha *f. plate (metal); iron (for clothes); blunder; gangplank.*

La plancha está muy caliente. *The iron is very hot.*

Plancha de acero. *Steel plate.*

Hizo una plancha. *He made a blunder. He put his foot in it.*

planchado *m. ironing; linen to be ironed.*

Lavado y planchado. *Washed and ironed laundry.*

planchar *to iron, to press (clothes).*

Quiero que me planchen el traje. *I'd like to have my suit pressed.*

Ella misma lava y plancha la ropa. *She washes and irons the clothes herself.*

planeta *m. planet.*

planicie *f. plain (land).*

planificación *f. planning.*

Planificación y desarrollo. *Planning and development.*

plano *adj. level, flat; m. plane, map; plan.*

Lo negó de plano. *He denied it flatly.*

Quisiera un plano de la ciudad. *I'd like a map of the city.*

Levantar un plano. *To draw a map (of a place).*

planta *f. plant; sole (of the foot).*

La planta ha echado raíces. *The plant has taken root.*

He alquilado un cuarto en la planta baja. *I've rented a room on the ground floor.*

plantación *f. plantation; planting.*

plantar *to plant; to drive in (the ground); to hit, to punch; to throw out.*

Van a plantar unos árboles en el jardín. *They're going to plant some trees in the garden.*

Lo dejaron plantado. *They left him in the lurch.*

Plantar una bofetada. *To slap in the face.*

Lo plantaron en la calle. *They threw him out. They put him out on the street.*

plantilla *f. insole; payroll; pattern.*

plástico *adj. plastic.*

PLATA *f. silver*

¿Tienes plata? *Do you have any money?*

Plata fina. *Sterling silver.*

plátano *m. banana, plantain.*

platillo *m. saucer; cymbal.*

platino *m. platinum.*

PLATO *m. dish, plate, course.*

Este plato está a pedir de boca. *This dish is delicious.*

¿Cuál es el plato del día? *What's today's special?*

Hay que secar los platos. *We have to dry the dishes.*

¿Puedo repetir de este plato? *May I have a second helping?*

Pagar los platos rotos. *To be made the scapegoat. To be blamed for everything.*

Plato hondo (sopero). *Soup plate.*

Plato llano (de mesa). *Dinner plate.*

Ser plato de segunda mesa. *To play second fiddle.*

playa *f. shore, beach.*

Playa de estacionamiento. *Parking lot.*

PLAZA *f. plaza, square; market; fortified place.*

Vamos a dar una vuelta por la plaza. *Let's take a stroll around the square.*

Hoy no habían naranjas en la plaza. *There weren't any oranges in the market today.*

Plaza de toros. *Bullring.*

Plaza fuerte. *Stronghold. Fortress.*

plazo *m. term, time; credit.*

¿En cuántos plazos debo pagar este automóvil? *How many payments do I have to make on this car?*

A plazos. *On credit. On the installment plan.*

A corto plazo. *Short-term.*

A largo plazo. *Long-term.*

Comprar a plazos. *To be on the installment plan.*

El plazo se ha cumplido. *The time has expired.*

plegable. *adj. folding; pliable.*

plegar *to fold; to plait.*

pleito *m. litigation; lawsuit; dispute, quarrel.*

Entabló un pleito contra ellos. *He brought a lawsuit against them.*

plena *f. Puerto Rican folk dance.*

plenamente *fully, completely.*

plenitud *f. plenitude, fullness.*

PLENO *adj. full, complete.*

Plenos poderes. *Full powers.*

Sesión plena. *Joint session.*

En pleno. *In full. As a whole.*

pliego *m. sheet of paper; sealed document.*

¿Quiere darme un pliego de papel? *Will you please give me a sheet of paper?*

pliegue *m. pleat; crease; fold.*

plomero *m. plumber.*

plomo *m. lead; a bore, a dull person.*

El plomo se funde fácilmente. *Lead melts easily.*

Ande con pies de plomo. *Proceed cautiously.*

pluma *f. pen; feather.*

plural *adj. and n. plural.*

población *f. population; town.*

poblado *m. town, village, inhabited place.*

poblar *to populate, to inhabit, to colonize; to bud, to put forth leaves.*

POBRE *adj. poor; m. poor person; a beggar.*

Es un hombre muy pobre. *He's a very poor man.*

El pobre no da pie en bola. *The poor fellow can't do anything right.*

¡Pobrecito! *Poor little thing!*

¡Qué de pobres hay en esta ciudad! *What a lot of beggars there are in this city!*

pobreza *f. poverty.*

POCO *adj. and adv. little; small; scanty; m. a little, a small part; pl. a few.*

¿Le sirvo un poco de vino? *May I serve (offer) you some wine?*

Deme un poco de leche. *Give me a little milk.*

Acérquese un poco más al micrófono. *Come a little closer to the microphone.*

Me gusta un poco. *I like it a little.*

Sabe un poco de todo. *He knows a little about everything.*

Hágame un poco de sitio. *Make a little room for me.*

Es hombre de poco talento. *He doesn't have much ability.*

Me queda muy poco dinero. *I have very little money left.*

Llegará dentro de poco. *He'll arrive soon.*

Poco importa. *It's not very important. It doesn't matter.*

Por poco se muere. *He almost died.*

Lo demás importa poco. *The rest doesn't matter very much.*

Lo tiene en poco. *He attaches very little value to it.*

Era poco tolerante. *He wasn't very tolerant.*

Poco a poco. *Little by little.*

Hace poco. *A little while ago.*

Pocas veces. *A few times.*

A pocos pasos de aquí. *A few steps from here. Very near.*

podar *to prune (trees).*

PODER *to be able; can; may; m. power, authority; capacity.*

¿En qué puedo servirle? *What can I do for you?*

¿Puedo ir? *May I go?*

¿Podrá Ud. venir? *Will you be able to come?*

¿Puedo entrar? *May I come in?*

¡No puede ser! *That can't be! That's impossible!*

¿Qué puedo ofrecerle a Ud.? *What can I offer you?*

¿Puedo contar con Ud.? *Can I count (depend) on you?*

Hice lo mejor que pude. *I did the best I could.*

A ese tipo no lo puedo ni ver. *I can't bear the sight of that fellow.*

No puedo con él. *I can't stand him.*

Puede que vaya a Australia el próximo año. *I may go to Australia next year.*

Querer es poder. *Where there's a will there's a way.*

Ha dado poder general a su padre. *He has given his father power of attorney.*

El dictador se arrogó el poder. *The dictator usurped power.*

Estudia a más no poder. *He studies as much as he possibly can.*

poderoso *adj. mighty, powerful; wealthy.*

podrir. *(See pudrir.)*

poema *m. poem.*

poesía *f. poetry.*

poeta *m. poet.*

polémica *f. polemics; controversy (literary or political).*

polémico *adj. polemical.*

policía *f. police; public order; m. policeman.*

Un policía acudió en nuestra ayuda. *A policeman came to our aid.*

La policía registró su casa. *The police searched his house.*

polígamo *adj. polygamist.*

polilla *f. moth.*

política *f. politics; policy.*

Tener influencia política. *To have good political connections.*

político *adj. politic, political; in-law; m. politician.*

póliza *f. policy (insurance, etc.).*

Póliza de seguro. *Insurance policy.*

polo *m. pole; polo (game).*

POLVO *m. dust; powder.*

Hay mucho polvo. *It's very dusty.*

Quitar el polvo. *To dust.*

pólvora *f. gunpowder.*

polla *f. pullet, chicken.*

POLLO *m. chicken; nestling.*

Pollo frito. *Fried chicken.*

Pollo asado. *Roast chicken.*

Arroz con pollo. *Chicken and rice.*

pomada *f. pomade, salve.*

pómulo *m. cheekbone.*

ponche *m. punch (drink).*

poncho *m. poncho (a kind of cloak worn in Latin America).*

ponderar *to ponder, to weigh; to praise highly.*

Lo ponderan mucho. *It's highly recommended.*

PONER *to put; to set (a table); to suppose; to lay (eggs); to send (a telegram); to write.*

Ponga el libro en su lugar. *Put the book in its place.*

Mandó poner otra cama en su cuarto. *He had another bed put in his room.*

Hay que poner punto final a esto. *We must put a stop to this.*

Ponga la mesa. *Set the table.*

Le pondré unas líneas. *I'll drop him a few lines.*

Póngalo por escrito. *Put it in writing.*

El médico me ha puesto a régimen. *The doctor has put me on a diet.*

¿Dónde habré puesto mi sombrero? *Where can I have put my hat?*

Acaba de poner una tienda. *He's just opened a store.*

Hay que poner en claro este lío. *We must clear up this mess. We must get to the bottom of this.*

Poner huevos. *To lay eggs.*

Aquí se necesita alguien que ponga orden. *We need someone here who'll keep order.*

Pone en tela de juicio todo lo que le dicen. *He questions everything they tell him.*

Poner un telegrama. *To send a telegram.*

Poner precio. *To set a price.*

Poner al corriente. *To inform.*

Poner al sol. *To put in the sun.*

PONERSE *to set (the sun); to put on (clothes); to become; to make one become; to reach, to come to; to start to.*

El sol se pone más temprano en invierno. *The sun sets earlier in winter.*

Se puso el sombrero y salió. *He put on his hat and left.*

¿Qué me pondré? *What shall I wear (put on)?*

Se puso encarnada. *She blushed.*

Al oír aquello se puso pálida. *When she heard that, she turned pale.*

Se ha puesto muy gordo. *He's become (gotten) very fat.*

Se puso a reír. *She began to laugh.*

Se pone mal con todos. *He gets in bad with everybody.*

Ponerse a trabajar. *To start working.*

Ponerse en marcha. *To start. To put out (a train).*

Ponerse de acuerdo. *To agree. To come to an agreement.*

Ponerse nervioso. *To become (get) nervous.*

Ponerse en pie. *To stand up.*

Ponerse al día. *To be up-to-date.*

poniente *m. west; west wind.*

popular *adj. popular.*

Es una canción popular. *It's a popular song.*

popularidad *f. popularity.*

POR *for; by; through; about.*

Por correo aéreo. *By airmail.*

Ganó por pocos puntos. *He won by a few points.*

"Don Quijote" fue escrito por Cervantes. *"Don Quixote" was written by Cervantes.*

La casa está por alquilar. *The house is for rent.*

¿Quiere Ud. ir por el correo? *Will you go for (go get) the mail?*

Queda una cosa por hacer. *Something still remains to be done.*

No votaré ni por el uno ni por el otro. *I won't vote for either one.*

El pasaporte es válido por un año. *The passport is valid just for a year.*

Entrar por la puerta. *To enter through the door.*

Pasar por la casa. *To pass by the house.*

Lo hace por miedo. *He does it out of fear.*

Por grande que sea. *However large it may be.*

Haga Ud. por venir. *Try to come. Do your best to come.*

Ella se interesa mucho por él. *She's very much interested in him.*

Por el buen parecer. *For the sake of appearances.*

Por poco me caigo. *I almost (nearly) fell down.*

Viven por aquí cerca. *They live near here.*

Eso está por ver. *That remains to be seen.*

Quedan diez páginas por copiar. *Ten pages remain to be copied.*

Por la calle no pasaba un alma. *Not a soul was passing in the street.*

Por adelantado. *In advance.*

Por docena. *By the dozen.*

Por mes. *By the month.*

Por mucho tiempo. *For a long time.*

Por la mañana. *In the morning.*

Por la tarde. *In the afternoon.*

Por la noche. *At night.*

Por ahora. *For the present.*

Por dentro. *On the inside.*

Por fuera. *On the outside.*

Por entonces. *At that time.*

Por consiguiente. *Consequently.*

Por fin. *Finally.*

¿Por qué? *Why?*

Por todas partes. *Everywhere.*

¡Por Dios! *For heaven's sake!*

Por más que. *No matter how. However much.*

Por lo visto. *Apparently.*

Por lo demás. *Furthermore. Aside from this. As to the rest.*

Por esto. *For this reason.*

Por cuanto. *For that reason. Since. Considering that. Whereas.*

Por tanto. *So. For that reason. Therefore.*

Por otra parte. *On the other hand.*

Por ejemplo. *For example.*

Por supuesto. *Of course.*

porcelana *f. porcelain; chinaware.*

La vajilla es de porcelana. *The dinner set is of porcelain.*

porción *f. portion, part; a great many.*

Ya se lo había dicho una porción de veces. *I'd already told him so several times.*

pordiosero *m. beggar.*

porfía *f. insistence; obstinacy.*

porfiado *adj. stubborn, obstinate.*

porfiar *to persist.*

pormenor *m. detail; pl. particulars.*

Eso es simplemente un pormenor. *It's just a detail.*

Para más pomenores averigüe en ... *For further details inquire at ...*

PORQUE *because, on account of, for, as.*

No vino porque estaba ocupado. *He didn't come because he was busy.*

Corrían porque tenían prisa. *They ran because they were in a hurry.*

porqué *m. cause, reason.*

No acierto a explicarme el porqué de su actitud. *I can't understand the reason for his behavior.*

¿POR QUÉ? *why?*

¿Por qué no vino Ud. ayer? *Why didn't you come yesterday?*

No sé por qué. *I don't know why.*

porquería *f. filth; nastiness; worthless thing.*

porrazo *m. blow (with a stick).*

portaaviones *m. aircraft carrier.*

portada *f. cover (of a book, etc.).*

portador *m. bearer; holder, carrier.*

portaequipajes *m. luggage-rack.*

portal *m. vestibule; hall, entrance, doorway; portico.*

portamonedas *m. coin purse.*

portarse *to behave, to act.*

  ¿Cómo se porta? *How does he behave?*

  Se portó muy mal conmigo. *He didn't behave very well toward me.*

portátil *adj. portable.*

  Radio portátil. *Portable radio.*

portavoz *m. and f. spokesman, spokeswoman.*

porte *m. carriage, postage, freight (cost); behavior.*

  ¿Ha pagado Ud. el porte? *Did you pay the postage?*

  Franco de porte. *Free delivery.*

portento *m. wonder, portent, prodigy.*

portería *f. superintendent's office (of a building), concierge's; goalpost.*

portero *m. doorman, janitor.*

porvenir *m. future, time to come.*

pos (en) *after; in pursuit (of).*

  Ir en pos de. *To go after.*

posada *f. inn, lodging house, boardinghouse.*

posadero *m. innkeeper.*

posar *to pose (for an artist); to lodge; to perch (birds).*

POSEER *to possess, to have.*

  Posee una casa en el campo. *He has a house in the country.*

posesión *f. possession.*

posesionar *to give possession.*

posesionarse *to take possession.*

posibilidad *f. possibility.*

POSIBLE *adj. possible; m. pl. means, wealth.*

  No me será posible hacerlo. *It won't be possible for me to do it.*

  Haré por Ud. cuanto me sea posible. *I'll do as much as I can for you.*

  Todo cabe en lo posible. *Everything's possible.*

posición *f. position; status, situation.*

  Goza de una posición holgada. *He's well-to-do.*

  Una posición estratégica. *A strategic position.*

positivamente *positively.*

  Estoy positivamente seguro. *I'm positively certain.*

positivo *adj. positive, sure, certain.*

postal *adj. postal.*

  Giro postal. *Money order.*

  Paquete postal. *Parcel post.*

postergar *to defer, to put off, to delay.*

posteridad *f. posterity.*

posterior *adj. rear, back; later, subsequent.*

  La parte posterior de la cabeza. *The back of the head.*

  Esta ley ha quedado anulada por otra posterior. *This law was superseded by a later one.*

posteriormente *subsequently.*

posguerra *f. postwar period.*

postizo *adj. artificial, false.*

  Dientes postizos. *False teeth.*

postor *m. bidder.*

  Al mejor postor. *To the highest bidder.*

postración *f. depression, exhaustion, state of being depressed.*

postrado *adj. depressed, exhausted.*

postre *adj. last in order; m. dessert.*

  Llegamos a los postres. *We came when they were having dessert.*

  A la postre. *In the long run. At last.*

postrer *(a shortening of* **postrero** *used before a noun) last.*

  Un postrer deseo. *A last wish.*

postrero *adj. last.*

postulado *m. candidate.*

postularse *to present oneself as a candidate.*

póstumo *adj. posthumous.*

postura *f. posture, position; bid; wager.*

potable *adj. drinkable.*

  ¿Hay agua potable aquí? *Is there any drinking water here?*

potaje *m. stew.*

potencia *f. power; strength, force; faculty.*

  Las grandes potencias. *The great powers.*

potentado *m. potentate, monarch; rich man.*

potente *adj. potent, powerful, mighty.*

potro *m. colt.*

pozo *m. well; pit.*

práctica *f. practice, exercise.*

practicante *adj. practicing; m. practitioner; hospital intern.*

práctico *adj. practical; skillful; m. (harbor) pilot.*

  Es un hombre muy práctico. *He's very practical.*

pradera *f. meadow, prairie.*

prado *m. lawn, meadow, pasture ground.*

preámbulo *m. preamble, introduction.*

  Es un preámbulo interesante. *It's an interesting preface.*

  Déjese Ud. de preámbulos, y diga lo que quiere. *Stop beating around the bush (stop evading the issue) and tell me what you want.*

precario *adj. precarious.*

precaución *f. precaution, prudence.*

precaver *to prevent.*

precaverse *to take precautions; to be on one's guard.*

precedencia *f. precedence.*

precedente *adj. preceding; m. precedent.*

preceder *to precede.*

precepto *m. precept, order.*

preciar *to value, to appraise.*

preciarse *to take pride in, to boast.*

Se precia de saber español. *He boasts (is very proud) about his knowledge of Spanish.*

PRECIO *m. price; value.*

¿Qué precio tiene? *What's the price?*

Es precio fijo. *It's a fixed price.*

Precio de fábrica. *Cost price.*

Precio corriente. *Regular price.*

Ultimo precio. *Lowest price.*

A ningún precio. *Not at any price.*

A precio de ganga. *At a bargain price.*

Fijación de precio. *Price fixing.*

preciosidad *f. preciousness; precious or beautiful object; a beauty.*

Es una preciosidad de criatura. *She's a beautiful child.*

precioso *adj. precious; beautiful, delightful.*

Piedras preciosas. *Precious stones.*

Es un sitio precioso para pasar el verano. *It's a delightful spot to spend the summer.*

precipicio *m. precipice; ruin, destruction.*

precipitación *f. rash, haste.*

precipitadamente *hastily, in a rush.*

precipitar *to precipitate; to hasten, to rush; to hurl.*

precipitarse *to rush headlong into; to rush, to hurry.*

precisamente *precisely.*

precisar *to fix, to set; to compel.*

Hay que precisar la hora de la cita. *We have to set the time for the appointment.*

Me vi precisado a hacerlo. *I was compelled to do it.*

precisión *f. precision, accuracy; necessity; compulsion.*

Instrumento de precisión. *Precision instrument.*

Tengo precisión de hacer eso. *I'm obliged to do that.*

Habla con precisión. *He's very precise in his speech. He speaks to the point.*

PRECISO *adj. necessary; precise; clear.*

Es preciso que Ud. reúna el dinero hoy mismo. *You must get the money today.*

Es preciso practicar un idioma para dominarlo. *It's necessary to practice a language in order to master it.*

precoz *adj. precocious.*

predecir *to predict, to foretell.*

predicar *to preach.*

predicción *f. prediction.*

Salieron mal mis predicciones. *My*

predictions didn't come true.

predilección *f. predilection, preference.*

Tener predilección por. *To have a fondness for. To have a predilection for.*

predilecto *adj. favorite.*

Es mi primo predilecto. *He's my favorite cousin.*

predispuesto *adj. predisposed.*

predominar *to prevail, to predominate.*

prefacio *m. preface.*

prefecto *m. prefect, chief administrative official of a county or province.*

prefectura *f. office, jurisdiction, territory and official residence of a prefect; prefecture.*

preferencia *f. preference, choice.*

La tratan con preferencia. *She's given preferential treatment.*

preferente *adj. preferable, preferring.*

preferible *adj. preferable.*

Es preferible ir personalmente. *It's preferable to go in person.*

PREFERIR *to prefer, to like best.*

¿Prefiere vino o cerveza? *Do you prefer wine or beer.*

Prefiero el vino a la cerveza. *I prefer wine to beer.*

prefijo *m. prefix.*

pregonar *to proclaim in public, to make known.*

PREGUNTA *f. question.*

Hacer una pregunta. *To ask a question.*

¿Me permite que le haga una pregunta? *May I ask you a question?*

PREGUNTAR *to ask, to inquire.*

¿Por qué me lo preguntas? *Why do you ask me?*

¿Le preguntó a Ud. algo? *Did he ask you anything?*

Alguien pregunta por Ud. *Someone's asking for you.*

preguntarse *to wonder.*

preguntón *m. inquisitive person.*

prehistórico *adj. prehistoric.*

prejuicio *m. prejudice, bias.*

preliminar *adj. and n. preliminary.*

preludio *m. prelude, introduction.*

Ser el preludio de. *To lead to.*

prematuro *adj. premature.*

premeditación *f. premeditation.*

premeditar *to premeditate, to think out.*

premiar *to reward, to remunerate.*

premio *m. prize; reward*

premura *f. haste, hurry, urgency.*

prenda *f. pledge, security, pawn; piece of jewelry; garment; forfeit; a very dear person; token; pl. qualities, talents.*

Prendas de vestir. *Articles of clothing.*

En prenda. *As security.*

Es un hombre de buenas prendas. *He's a man of fine qualities.*

prendar *to pledge, to give or take something as security; to ingratiate oneself.*

prendarse *to take a fancy to, to be taken with (the beauty of something, etc.), to become fond of, to fall in love.*

prendedor *m. clasp; breastpin, brooch.*

PRENDER *to clasp, to grasp; to catch; to arrest; to take root (a plant); to burn.*

Prender con alfileres. *To fasten with pins.*

¿Quién prendió al ladrón? *Who arrested (caught) the thief?*

La leña no prende. *The wood won't burn.*

La planta ha prendido. *The plant has taken root.*

PRENSA *f. press (newspaper).*

preñada *adj. pregnant.*

preocupación *f. preoccupation, concern, worry.*

preocupar *to preoccupy; to cause concern.*

Está algo preocupado. *He has something on his mind.*

preocuparse *to be worried, to care about, to be concerned.*

No se preocupe tanto. *Don't worry so much.*

Se preocupa por la suerte de su hija. *He's concerned (worried) about his daughter.*

preparación *f. preparation.*

preparador *m. trainer, coach.*

PREPARAR *to prepare, to get ready.*

Nos preparamos a partir. *We're getting ready to start.*

Prepare Ud. su billete. *Get your ticket ready.*

prepararse *to prepare oneself, to be prepared.*

Prepárese. *Get ready.*

Prepararse para un viaje. *To get ready (prepare) for a trip.*

preparativo *m. preparation.*

Estamos haciendo los preparativos para el viaje. *We're making preparations for the trip.*

preparatorio *adj. preparatory.*

preponderancia *f. preponderance.*

preponderar *to prevail.*

preposición *f. preposition.*

presa *f. capture; prey; dam.*

presagiar *to predict, to give warning.*

presagio *m. omen, prediction.*

prescindir *to do without, to dispense with, to do away with.*

prescribir *to prescribe.*

prescripción *f. prescription.*

presencia *f. presence.*

Se exige su presencia. *His presence is required.*

Lo dije en su presencia. *I said it in his presence.*

Hacer acto de presencia. *To put in an appearance.*

Presencia de ánimo. *Presence of mind.*

presenciar *to be present, to witness, to see.*

Acabamos de presenciar ... *We've just witnessed ...*

presentador *m. anchorman (television).*

PRESENTAR *to present; to introduce; to show.*

No la conozco, preséntemela. *I don't know her. Will you introduce me? (Introduce her to me.)*

Le presento a mi prometido. *I'd like you to meet my fiancé.*

Presente este talón al reclamar su equipaje. *Present this check when you claim your baggage.*

Presentaron una queja a la dirección. *They complained to the management.*

presentarse *to put in an appearance, to show up.*

Se presentó inesperadamente. *He showed up unexpectedly.*

PRESENTE *adj. present; m. gift; present.*

¡Presente! *Present (in a roll call)!*

Al presente no tenemos ninguna noticia. *At present we have no news.*

Tengo presente lo que me dijo. *I'm bearing in mind what he told me.*

Tendré siempre presente su bondad. *I shall always remember your kindness.*

Lo dije en voz alta a fin de que lo oyesen todos los presentes. *I said it out loud, so that everyone present could hear it.*

Un presente de valor. *An expensive (valuable) gift.*

presentimiento *m. premonition.*

presentir *to have a premonition.*

preservación *f. preservation.*

preservar *to preserve; to maintain; to keep.*

presidencia *f. presidency; (presidential) chair; chairmanship.*

Ocupar la presidencia. *To preside.*

presidente *m. president; chairman.*

presidiario *m. convict.*

presidio *m. penitentiary, prison.*

presidir *to preside over; to direct, to lead.*

presión *f. pressure.*

presionar *to type; to press; to hit; to pressure.*

preso *adj. and n. imprisoned, prisoner.*

prestado *adj. lent, loaned.*

Vino a pedirme prestado un libro. *He came to borrow a book from me.*

Dar prestado. *To lend.*

Tomar (pedir) prestado. *To borrow.*

prestamista *m. and f. money lender; pawnbroker.*

préstamo *m. loan.*

PRESTAR *to lend, to aid; to pay (attention).*

Me prestó un libro muy interesante. *He lent me a very interesting book.*

Le presté cinco pesos. *I lent him five dollars.*

¿Quiere Ud. prestarnos su ayuda? *Will you give (lend) us a hand?*

Prestar atención. *To pay attention.*

Me ha prestado Ud. un gran servicio. *You've done (rendered) me a great service.*

prestarse *to offer to; to be apt to, to lend itself to.*

Se prestó a ayudarnos. *He offered to help us.*

Eso se prestará a malas interpretaciones. *That is apt to be misinterpreted.*

presteza *f. quickness, speed, haste.*

Con presteza. *Quickly.*

prestigio *m. prestige; good name.*

prestigioso *adj. famous.*

PRESTO *adj. quick, prompt; ready; adv. quickly; soon.*

Estamos prestos para salir. *We're ready to go out.*

Vístete presto. *Get dressed quickly.*

De presto. *Promptly. Swiftly.*

presumido *adj. and n. vain, conceited; conceited person.*

Es muy presumida. *She's very conceited.*

presumir *to presume; to assume; to be conceited.*

Presume ser listo. *He thinks he's smart.*

Era de presumir que . . . *It was to be expected that . . . It was to be presumed . . .*

presunción *f. presumption; presumptuousness, conceit.*

presunto *adj. presumed; apparent.*

Presunto heredero. *Heir apparent.*

presuntuoso *adj. presumptuous, vain.*

presuponer *to presuppose, to take for granted in advance, to assume beforehand.*

presupuestar *to estimate, to budget.*

presupuesto *m. budget; estimate.*

pretencioso *adj. presumptuous, conceited.*

pretender *to pretend; to apply for; to try, to endeavor.*

Pretender un empleo. *To apply for a job.*

Pretende su mano. *He's asking for her hand in marriage.*

Pretendió convencerme. *He tried to convince me.*

pretendiente *adj. and n. pretender; suitor; candidate.*

pretensión *f. pretension; contention.*

pretexto *m. pretext.*

prevalecer *to prevail.*

prevención *f. prevention; foresight; prejudice.*

prevenir *to prepare; to prevent; to foresee; to forewarn, to warn.*

Estámos prevenidos. *We're prepared (on guard).*

Le prevengo a Ud. que no lo haga. *I warned you not to do it.*

prever *to foresee, to see ahead, to anticipate, to provide for.*

Prevemos el éxito. *We anticipate success.*

Es de prever. *It's to be expected.*

previamente *previously.*

previo *adj. previous; prior to.*

Una cuestión previa. *Previous question (parliamentary procedure).*

Previo pago de. *Upon payment of.*

previsto *adj. foreseen.*

En las condiciones previstas en el acuerdo . . . *Under (In) the conditions which have been provided for in the agreement . . .*

prima *f. premium; female cousin.*

Prima de seguro. *Insurance premium.*

María es mi prima. *Mary is my cousin.*

primario *adj. primary.*

Escuela primaria. *Elementary school. Primary school.*

PRIMAVERA *f. spring (the season).*

PRIMER *(a shortening of primero used before a noun) first.*

Primer galán. *Leading man.*

En primer lugar. *In the first place.*

El primer año. *The first year.*

primeramente *first, firstly, in the first place.*

PRIMERO *adj. and n. first; former.*

Tráiganos primero un poco de sopa. *Bring us some soup first.*

Es el primero de la clase. *He ranks highest in his class.*

Veamos primero la hora que es. *Let's first see what time it is.*

Sírvase Ud. darme dos billetes de primera para Madrid. *Two first-class tickets to Madrid, please.*

Es un nadador de primera. *He's an excellent swimmer.*

Primera velocidad. *First gear.*

Primera dama. *Leading lady.*

La primera vez. *The first time.*

Primera enseñanza. *Primary education.*

De primera. *Of superior quality. Highest grade.*

Al primero del mes que viene. *On the first of next month.*

A primeros del mes que viene. *In the early part of next month.*

Primeros auxilios. *First aid.*

De buenas a primeras. *All of a sudden.*

primitivo *adj. primitive.*

primo *m. cousin.*

Primo hermano. *First cousin.*

primor *m. beauty, exquisiteness; dexterity, skill.*

Ese borado es un primor. *That embroidery is very lovely.*

princesa *f. princess.*

PRINCIPAL *adj. principal, main, chief, most important; m. capital; head (of a concern).*

Este es uno de los argumentos principales de su tesis. *This is one of the main arguments of his thesis.*

príncipe *m. prince; ruler.*

principiante *adj. and n. beginner, apprentice.*

principiar *to begin, to commence.*

Van a principiar la construcción. *They're beginning to build.*

PRINCIPIO *m. beginning; origin; principle.*

Al principio me parecía fácil. *It seemed easy to me at first.*

Le pagarán a principios del mes que viene. *They'll pay you the early part of next month.*

Al principios de la semana entrante. *Early next week.*

Dar principio. *To begin.*

¿En qué principio basa Ud. su teoría? *On what principle do you base your theory?*

En principio no me parece mal la idea. *That idea doesn't seem bad in principle.*

prioridad *f. priority.*

PRISA *f. haste, hurry; urgency.*

Tengo mucha prisa. *I'm in a great hurry.*

No corre prisa. *There's no hurry.*

Siempre anda de prisa. *He's always in a hurry.*

¡Démonos prisa, que es tarde! *Let's hurry, it's late.*

¿Por qué tanta prisa? *Why such a hurry?*

Dele Ud. prisa. *Make him (get him to) hurry up.*

prisión *f. imprisonment; prison.*

prisionero *m. prisoner.*

privación. *f. privation, want.*

privado *adj. private, intimate; personal.*

Vida privada. *Private life.*

En privado. *Confidentially.*

Carta privada. *Personal letter.*

privar *to deprive; to forbid*

Privarse de. *To do without.*

No se priva de nada. *He doesn't deprive himself of anything.*

Privado del conocimiento. *Unconscious.*

privilegiado *adj. privileged.*

privilegio *m. privilege.*

pro *m. and f. profit, advantage; pro.*

En pro de. *In favor of.*

El pro y el contra. *The pros and the cons.*

proa *f. prow, bow (of a ship).*

probabilidad *f. probability, likelihood.*

PROBABLE *adj. probable, likely.*

Es poco probable. *It's not likely.*

Es más que probable. *It's more than probable.*

PROBABLEMENTE *probably, likely.*

probabo, *adj. proved, tried.*

Eso está probado. *That's been proved.*

PROBAR *to try; to taste; to prove; to try on.*

Pruebe Ud. este vino, a ver si le gusta. *Taste this wine and see if you like it.*

Me probaré estos zapatos. *I'll try these shoes on.*

Pruebe otra vez. *Try again. Try once more.*

PROBLEMA *m. problem.*

procaz *adj. insolent, impudent, bold.*

procedencia *f. origin; place of sailing.*

procedente *adj. coming or proceeding from; according to law, rules, or practices.*

PROCEDER *to proceed, to act, to behave; m. behavior, conduct.*

Procedió correctamente. *He acted properly.*

Lo que procede hacer. *The correct and proper thing (to do).*

Proceder a. *To proceed with.*

Proceder de. *To come from.*

Proceder contra. *To proceed against. To take action against.*

No me gusta su proceder. *I don't like his behavior.*

procedimiento *m. procedure; method.*

procesado *adj. indicted; m. and f. defendant.*

procesador *m. processor.*

Procesador de palabras. *Word processor.*

procesamiento *m., processing.*

Procesamiento de datos. *Data processing.*

procesar *to sue; to indict; to process.*

procesión *f. procession, parade.*

proceso *m. legal proceedings, (legal) process, lawsuit.*

proclamación *f. proclamation.*

proclamar *to proclaim; to promulgate.*

Se ha proclamado la ley marcial. *Martial law has been proclaimed.*

procrear *to procreate.*

PROCURAR *to endeavor, to try.*

Procuraré estar a tiempo. *I'll try to be on time.*

Procuró levantarse pero no pudo. *He tried to get up but he couldn't.*

Procure no faltar. *Don't fail to come (do it, etc.).* Try your best to come *(do it, etc.).*

prodigio *m. wonder, marvel.*

prodigioso *adj. prodigious, marvelous.*

prodigo *adj. prodigal, wasteful, lavish.*

producción *f. production; output.*

PRODUCIR *to produce; to yield; to bear; to bring as evidence (law).*

Producen 200 aviones al día. *They turn out (produce) 200 planes per day.*

Todo aquello le producía risa. *That made him laugh.*

Producir sus efectos. *To take effect.*

producirse *to be produced.*

productivo *adj. productive.*

producto *m. product; amount.*

Productos alimenticios. *Foodstuffs. Food products. Food.*

productor *m. producer.*

profanación *f. profanation.*

profanar *to profane.*

profano *adj. profane; secular; irreverent.*

profecía *f. prophecy.*

proferir *to utter, to say.*

profesar *to profess; to declare openly.*

profesión *f. profession.*

¿Su nombre y profesión, por favor? *Your name and profession?*

profesional *adj. professional.*

profesor *m. professor, teacher.*

profeta *m. prophet.*

profético *prophetic.*

prófugo *adj. fugitive; m. draft dodger, slacker.*

profundamente *deeply; soundly (sleep).*

Lo siento profundamente. *I regret it deeply.*

Anoche, dormí profundamente. *I slept soundly last night.*

profundidad *f. profundity, depth.*

¿Qué profundidad tiene este lago? *What's the depth of this lake?*

200 pies de profundidad. *200 feet deep.*

profundizar *to deepen; to delve into, to fathom.*

PROFUNDO *adj. profound, deep, intense.*

Dolor profundo. *Intense pain.*

Es un pozo muy profundo. *It's a very deep well.*

Nos perdimos en lo más profundo del bosque. *We were lost in the depths of the woods.*

programa *m. program, plan; curriculum.*

¿Cuál es el programa de hoy? *What is today's program?*

¿Hasta qué punto del programa han estudiado? *How far did they get in the curriculum?*

programable *adj. programmable.*

programación *f. programming.*

programador *m. programmer.*

programar *to program.*

progresar *to progress, to make progress.*

progreso *m. progress.*

Hacer progresos. *To progress. To make progress.*

prohibición *f. prohibition.*

prohibido *adj. forbidden.*

"Prohibido fumar." *"No smoking."*

"Prohibido por la ley." *"Prohibited by law."*

"Prohibido pasar." *"No thoroughfare." "Do not pass beyond here." "No trespassing."*

"Prohibido el tráfico." *"Closed to traffic."*

"Prohibida la entrada." *"No admittance."*

PROHIBIR *to prohibit, to forbid.*

Le prohibo hacer eso. *I forbid you to do that.*

Está prohibido llevar perros en los autobuses. *Dogs are not allowed on the busses.*

"Se prohibe la entrada." *"No admittance."*

"Se prohibe fumar." *"No smoking."*

prójimo *m. fellow man, neighbor.*

proletariado *m. proletariat, working class.*

proletario *adj. proletarian; of the working class.*

La clase proletaria. *The working class.*

prolijo *adj. tedious, wordy, too long.*

prólogo *m. prologue, preface, introduction.*

prolongación *f. prolongation, lengthening.*

prolongar *to prolong, to extend.*

promedio *m. average, mean.*

promesa *f. promise, assurance.*

PROMETER *to promise.*

¿Por qué no me ha escrito Ud. como me prometió? *Why haven't you written to me as you promised?*

Nunca cumple lo que promete. *He never does what he promises.*

Este negocio no promete mucho. *This business is not very promising.*

prometido *adj. promised; m. fiancé; f. fiancée.*

Cumplir lo prometido. *To keep a promise.*

Mi prometido. *My fiancé.*

prominencia *f. prominence; protuberance.*

prominente *adj. prominent; conspicuous.*

Ocupa un puesto prominente en el gobierno. *He occupies a prominent position in the government.*

promoción *f. promotion, special sale.*

promover *to promote; to advance.*

promulgar *to promulgate, to publish.*

pronombre *m. pronoun.*

pronosticar *to forecast.*

pronóstico *m. forecast, prediction; prognosis.*
Pronóstico del tiempo. *Weather forecast.*
prontitud *f. promptness, swiftness.*
PRONTO *adj. prompt, quick; ready; adv. promptly, quickly; soon.*
Hasta muy pronto. *So long. I'll see you soon.*
¡Venga pronto! *Come quickly! Come right away!*
Mientras más pronto mejor. *The sooner the better.*
Hizo muy pronto el trabajo. *He did the work very quickly.*
Me dijo que estaría de vuelta pronto. *She told me she would be back soon.*
Su respuesta fue muy pronta. *He replied (very) promptly.*
Estoy pronto para empezar. *I'm ready to begin.*
De pronto. *Suddenly. All of a sudden.*
De pronto ocurrió algo. *All of a sudden something happened.*
Por de pronto. *For the time being.*
pronunciación *f. pronunciation.*
pronunciar *to pronounce; to utter; to deliver (a speech).*
Ud. pronuncia muy bien el español. *You pronounce Spanish very well.*
Pronunciará un discurso sobre historia contemporánea. *He's going to give a lecture on modern history.*
Pronunciar sentencia. *To pronounce sentence.*
propagación *f. propagation, dissemination.*
propaganda *f. propaganda, advertising.*
propagandista *m. and f. propagandist.*
propagar *to propagate; to spread (news, knowledge, etc.).*
propasarse *to take undue liberties; to exceed one's authority.*
propender *to tend, to incline to.*
propensión *f. propensity, inclination.*
propenso *adj. inclined to, disposed to.*
Está propenso a hacerlo. *He's inclined to do it.*
propiamente *properly.*
propicio *adj. propitious, favorable.*
Una ocasión propicia. *A favorable opportunity.*
propiedad *f. ownership; property.*
Esas casas son de su propiedad. *Those houses belong to him (are his property).*
El jabón tiene la propiedad de quitar la mugre. *Soap has the property of removing dirt.*
Acabo de comprar esa propiedad. *I've just bought that property.*
propietario *m. proprietor, owner, landlord.*

propina *f. tip, gratuity.*
PROPIO *adj. own, self; proper, fit, suitable.*
Sus propias palabras. *His own words.*
Le deseo lo propio. *I wish you the same. The same to you.*
Eso es un juego propio de niños. *It's a game suitable for children.*
Eso sería lo propio. *That would fit the case.*
Estimación propia. *Self-respect.*
Amor proprio. *Self-conceit.*
proponer *to propose; to suggest; to move.*
Me propongo ir a verle. *I intend to go to see him.*
Propongo que vayamos todos a casa. *I suggest we all go home.*
Señor presidente, propongo que se levante la sesión. *Mr. Chairman, I move that the meeting be adjourned.*
Le será difícil llevar a cabo lo que se propone. *It will be hard to carry out what you have in mind (intend).*
proporción *f. proportion.*
proporcional *adj. proportional.*
proporcionar *to provide, to furnish, to supply; to proportion, to fit.*
proposición *f. proposition; proposal, motion.*
PROPÓSITO *m. purpose, intention.*
Lo hizo de propósito. *He did it on purpose.*
A propósito. *By the way.*
Fuera de propósito. *Not to the point. Irrelevant. Foreign to the subject.*
A propósito de. *With regards to. Regarding.*
propuesta *f. proposal, offer; nomination.*
Aceptaron nuestra propuesta. *They accepted our proposal.*
prórroga *f. extension of time, renewal.*
Dar prórroga. *To extend the time of payment. To grant an extension.*
prorrogar *to extend (time), to prolong.*
prosa *f. prose.*
prosaico *adj. prosaic.*
proseguir *to pursue, to carry on, to go on, to continue, to proceed.*
prosista *m. prose writer.*
prospecto *m. prospectus, catalogue.*
prosperar *to prosper, to thrive, to be successful, to get rich.*
próspero *adj. prosperous.*
protagonista *m. and f. protagonist.*
protección *f. protection, support.*
protector *m. protector.*
proteger *to protect; to support.*
protesta *f. protest.*
protestante *adj. and n. protesting; Protestant.*
protestar *to protest.*
PROVECHO *m. profit; benefit, advantage.*
Ser de provecho. *To be useful.*

Sacar provecho. *To derive profit from. To turn to advantage.*

En su provecho. *In your favor. To your advantage.*

¡Buen provecho (said at meals)! *I hope you enjoy your food. Hearty appetite!*

provechoso *adj. profitable, beneficial.*

proveer *to provide; to furnish, to supply; to dispose.*

Proveer de fondos. *To provide with funds.*

Proveerse de. *To supply oneself with.*

provenir *to be due to; to derive from, to come from.*

Eso puede provenir de un resfriado. *That can come from (be caused by) a cold.*

proverbio *m. proverb.*

providencia *f. providence; pl. dispositions, measures.*

Tomar providencias. *To take measures.*

provincia *f. province.*

provisión *f. provision; stock, supply.*

Provisiones alimenticias. *Foodstuffs. Food.*

provisional *adj. provisional, temporary.*

provisionalmente *provisionally, temporarily.*

provisto *adj. provided for, supplied.*

La tienda está muy bien provista de mercaderías. *The store is well stocked with merchandise.*

provocación *f. provocation.*

provocador *m. troublemaker.*

provocar *to provoke, to vex, to make angry.*

PRÓXIMO *adj. near, next, neighboring.*

La próxima estación. *The next station.*

La semana próxima. *Next week.*

¿Cuál es la calle próxima? *What's the street after this?*

proyección *f. projection; screening.*

Proyecciones de negocios. *Business forecasts.*

proyecto *m. project; plan, scheme; design.*

prudencia *f. prudence; moderation.*

prudente *adj. prudent, cautious.*

PRUEBA *f. proof; test; fitting (of garments).*

Existen pruebas bastante claras de ello. *There are pretty strong proofs of it.*

Las pruebas de las fotos son excelentes. *The photo proofs are excellent.*

Sala da pruebas. *Fitting room.*

A prueba de fuego. *Fireproof.*

psicología *f. psychology.*

psicológico *adj. psychological.*

psicólogo *m. psychologist.*

psiquiatra *m. psychiatrist.*

psiquiatría *f. psychiatry.*

púa *f. sharp point, prong.*

Alambre de púas. *Barbed wire.*

publicación *f. publication.*

publicar(se) *to publish; to announce.*

Acaba de publicarse este libro. *This book has just been published.*

Va a publicar un artículo en el periódico de mañana. *He's going to publish an article in tomorrow's paper.*

Publíquese y ejecútese. *Let it be made public and put into effect.*

publicidad *f. publicity, advertising.*

PÚBLICO *adj. public, not private; m. public, crowd, audience.*

Salud pública. *Public health.*

Sacarán la casa a pública subasta. *They'll sell the house at public auction.*

En público. *Publicly. In public.*

"Aviso al público." *"Notice to the public."*

puchero *m. earthen pot; dish of stewed vegetables and meats.*

pudiente *adj. powerful; wealthy, rich.*

pudín *m. pudding.*

pudor *m. modesty, shyness.*

pudrir *to rot.*

Las manzanas se están pudriendo. *The apples are spoiling (rotting).*

PUEBLO *m. village, town; population; people.*

¿Qué pueblo es éste? *What town is this?*

Pueblo natal. *Native town.*

El pueblo español. *The Spanish people.*

puente *m. bridge.*

puerco *adj. nasty, filthy, dirty; m. hog.*

PUERTA *f. door; doorway; gate.*

Abra la puerta. *Open the door.*

Cierre la puerta con llave cuando salga. *Lock the door when you leave.*

La puerta trasera da al jardín. *The back door opens out into the garden.*

Puerta de seguridad. *Security gate.*

puerto *m. port, harbor; haven; pass through the mountains.*

Puerto franco. *Free port.*

Puerto de destino. *Port of destination.*

Puerto paralelo *Parallel port (computer).*

Puerto serial *Serial port (computer).*

PUES *as, since; so; well; then; why; now; indeed.*

Pues vamos. *Then let's go.*

¿Pues qué quiere? *What do you want?*

¡Pues sí! *Yes, indeed!*

¡Pues hombre! *Why, man!*

¡Pues mira, chico! *Now look here, pal!*

Pues vámonos ya. *Let's run along.*

¡Pues no faltaba más! *Well, that's the last straw!*

Pues, como no fumo, no compro tabaco. *Since I don't smoke, I don't buy tobacco.*

Pues bien. *Well, then.*

¿Y pues? *What of it? So what?*

¿Pues qué? *Why not?*

¿Pues y qué? *So what?*

Pues no. *Not at all.*

¡Pues bien, iré! *All right then, I'll go!*

Pues no puede ser. *But it can't be. But it's impossible.*

puesta *f. set, setting; laying (eggs).*

La puesta del sol. *The sunset.*

PUESTO *adj. put, placed; on; set (table); m. place; stand; post; position, employment.*

La mesa está puesta. *The table is set.*

Esto está mal puesto. *This is in the wrong place.*

Llevaba puesto su traje nuevo. *He had his new suit on.*

Puesto que. *Since. Inasmuch as.*

Le compré en un puesto del mercado. *I bought it at a stand in the market.*

¿Dónde habrá un puesto de gasolina? *Where do you suppose there's a filling station?*

Tiene un buen puesto. *He has a good position.*

Puesto militar. *Military post.*

Puesto a bordo. *Free on board.*

Puesto en Nueva York. *Delivered free in New York.*

púgil, pugilista *m. prizefighter.*

pugna *f. struggle.*

pulcro *adj. neat, tidy.*

pulga *f. flea.*

Tiene malas pulgas. *He's bad-tempered.*

pulgada *f. inch.*

pulgar *m. thumb.*

pulir *to polish.*

pulmón *m. lung.*

pulmonía *f. pneumonia.*

pulpa *f. pulp.*

pulsera *f. bracelet.*

pulso *m. pulse; steadiness of the hand; tact.*

Déjeme tomarle el pulso. *Let me feel your pulse.*

Obra con gran pulso. *He acts with great circumspection.*

punta *f. point; tip; edge; cape; headland.*

La punta del lápiz. *Pencil point.*

Sáquele punta al lápiz. *Sharpen the pencil.*

Tengo los nervios de punta. *My nerves are on edge.*

Va de punta en blanco. *She's all dressed up.*

Hora de punta. *Rush hour.*

puntada *f. stitch.*

puntapié *m. kick.*

puntería *f. aim, aiming, marksmanship.*

puntiagudo *adj. sharp-pointed.*

puntilla *adj. narrow lace edging.*

De puntillas. *On tiptoe.*

PUNTO *m. point; dot; period; place; stitch; loop (in knitting); net (cloth material); hole (in a stocking).*

Punto de partida. *Starting point. Point of departure.*

Punto y coma. *Semicolon.*

Dos puntos. *Colon.*

Ganó por pocos puntos. *He won by a few points.*

Nos veremos en el mismo punto. *We'll meet at the same place.*

Punto por punto. *Point by point.*

Ha dado Ud. en el punto. *You've put your finger on it.*

Llevaba un traje de puntos blancos. *She wore a dress with white polka dots.*

Un vestido de punto. *A knitted dress.*

Hay que poner punto final a esto. *We must put a stop to this.*

Estábamos a punto de salir cuando llegaron. *We were just about to leave (on the point of leaving) when they arrived.*

A la hora en punto. *On the dot.*

Hasta cierto punto es verdad. *To a certain extent it's true.*

Estuvo a punto de perder la vida. *He nearly lost his life.*

Su cólera subía de punto. *He became angrier by the minute.*

No sé a punto fijo. *I don't know for certain.*

La comida está en su punto. *The food is just right.*

Punto cardinal. *Cardinal point.*

puntuación *f. punctuation.*

Signos de puntuación. *Punctuation marks.*

puntual *adj. punctual, prompt, on time; exact.*

Sea Ud. puntual. *Be on time. Be punctual.*

puntualizar *to give a detailed account of: to emphasize.*

puntualmente *punctually, on time.*

punzada *f. puncture, prick; acute pain.*

punzante *sharp.*

punzar *to prick, to puncture, to stick.*

puñado *m. handful; a few.*

Un puñado de soldados defendieron la posición. *A few soldiers defended the position.*

puñal *m. dagger.*

puñetazo *m. a punch.*

puño *m. fist; handle (of an umbrella); head (of a cane).*

Firmado de mi puño y letra. *Signed by me.*

pupila *f. pupil (of the eye).*

pupilo *m. ward (under someone's guardianship); boarder; a student.*

pupitre *m. writing desk.*

puré m. puree, thick soup.

Puré de guisantes. *Pea soup.*

Puré de patatas (papas). *Mashed potatoes.*

pureza f. purity.

purga f. purge; drain valve.

purgante m. laxative; purgative.

purgatorio m. purgatory.

Está pasando las penas del purgatorio. *He's suffering many hardships.*

purificar to purify.

PURO adj. pure; clean; plain; m. cigar.

Aire puro. *Pure air.*

Le digo a Ud. la pura verdad. *I'm telling you the plain truth.*

Me lo encontré de pura casualidad. *I met him by ("pure") chance.*

Pruebe estos puros. *Try these cigars.*

pútrido adj. putrid, rotten.

Q

QUE (*rel. pron.*) that, which, who, whom; conj. that, than, whether.

El que. *He who, the one which.*

La que. *She who, the one which.*

Los que (m. pl.). *They who, those who, the ones who.*

Las que (f. pl.). *They who, those who, the ones who.*

Lo que. *That which, which, that, what.*

Yo fui la que lo dijo. *It's I who said it. I was the one who said it.*

El que está hablando. *The one who's speaking. The one speaking.*

Yo no sé lo que le pasa. *I don't know what's the matter with him.*

Alguno que otro. *Someone or another.*

Dice que lo hará. *He said he'd (he'll) do it.*

Vale mucho más de lo que se figuran. *It's worth much more than they imagine.*

Que le guste o no. *Whether he likes it or not.*

Que no entre nadie. *Don't let anyone come in.*

QUÉ (*interrogative pron.*) what; how.

¿Qué es esto? *What's this?*

¿Qué hora es? *What time is it?*

¿Qué busca Ud.? *What are you looking for?*

¿Qué pasa? *What's going on?*

¿Qué van a tomar Uds.? *What are you going to have?*

¿Qué hora será? *I wonder what time it is.*

¿Pues y qué? *So what?*

No sé qué hacer. *I don't know what to do.*

¿De qué está hablando? *What's he talking about?*

¿En qué quedamos? *How do we stand?*

¡Qué va! *Nonsense!*

¡Qué barbaridad! *How awful!*

¿Qué sé yo? *How do I know?*

¡Qué gracia! *How amusing!*

¡Ay qué risa! *How funny! What a joke!*

¡Qué hombre! *What a man!*

No hay de qué. *Don't mention it. You're welcome.*

quebrada f. ravine, gorge.

quebradizo adj. brittle, fragile.

quebrado adj. broken; bankrupt; ruptured; m. fraction (math.).

quebradura f. fissure; fracture; rupture, hernia.

quebrantado adj. tottering, broken-down; failing (health).

Salud quebrantada. *Failing health.*

quebrantamiento m. breaking, breach (of law, promise, etc.).

quebrantar to break, to crush; to trespass; to violate (the law).

quebranto m. weakness; failure; great loss, severe damage; grief.

QUEBRAR(SE) to break; to rupture (hernia); to become bankrupt.

Al caer se quebró un brazo. *He broke his arm when he fell.*

El negocio quebró. *The business failed.*

QUEDAR(SE) to remain; to stop; to be; to fit; to be left; to agree.

¿Cuántos dólares le quedan? *How many dollars do you have left?*

¿Queda lejos el hotel? *Is the hotel far from here?*

Este traje le queda como mandado a hacer. *This suit fits you as if it were made to order.*

Me quedan un poco estrechos. *They're a little tight for me.*

Todo quedó muy mal. *Everything came off (turned out) badly.*

No le queda a Ud. mucho tiempo. *You haven't much time left.*

Quedaron en hacer el trabajo. *They agreed to do the work.*

Quédese sentado. *Remain seated. Keep your seats.*

Nuestro amigo se quedó en Europa. *Our friend stayed in Europe.*

Me quedaré aquí un ratito. *I'll stay here (for) awhile.*

¿En qué quedamos? *How do we stand? What's the final agreement?*

Esto queda entre los dos. *This is just between the two of us.*

Quedarse con. *To keep. To take.*

Se quedó con el libro. *He kept the book. He didn't return the book.*

Me quedo con esta camisa. *I'll take (buy) this shirt.*

Quedarse sin dinero. *To be left penniless.*

quehacer *m. occupation, work.*

Quehaceres domésticos. *Housework.*

queja *f. complaint; resentment; groan.*

quejarse *to complain.*

Ella se queja de Ud. *She complains (is complaining) about you.*

Se queja de dolor de cabeza. *She complains of a headache.*

Eso le dará motivo para quejarse. *That will give him grounds for complaint.*

quejoso *adj. complaining; plaintive.*

quemado *adj. burnt.*

Huele a quemado. *I smell something burning.*

quemadura *f. burn; scald.*

QUEMAR(SE) *to burn; to scald; to parch; to be very hot.*

Cuidado con quemarse. *Be careful, don't burn yourself.*

Por poco me quemo la lengua. *I nearly (almost) burned my tongue.*

Este teatro se ha quemado dos veces. *This theater has burned down twice.*

El sol quema hoy. *The sun's scorching today.*

querella *f. complaint; quarrel.*

querellarse *to complain.*

querencia *f. affection, fondness.*

QUERER *to wish, to want, to desire; to like; to love.*

¿Qué quiere Ud.? *What do you want? What would you like?*

¿Quiere Ud. ver el piso? *Do you want (would you like) to see the apartment?*

¿Quiere Ud. callarse? *Will you keep quiet?*

¿Lo quiere? *Do you want it?*

Yo no lo quiero. *I don't want it.*

Si Ud. quiere. *If you like.*

Haz lo que quieras. *Do as you please.*

Como quieras. *As you like.*

¿A quién quieres más? *Who do you love most? Who do you love the best?*

La quiere mucho. *He loves her very much.*

Yo quisiera un vaso de vino tinto. *I would like a glass of red wine.*

Quiero comprar un reloj. *I want to buy a watch.*

Hubiera querido ver aquella película. *I should like to have seen that film.*

No quiero nada más. *I don't care for anything more.*

¿Qué quiere decir esta palabra? *What does this word mean?*

Sin querer. *Without wanting (wishing) to.*

Querer es poder. *Where there's a will there's a way.*

Como Ud. quiera. *As you wish (like).*

Si Ud. quiere. *If you like.*

querido *adj. beloved, dear; m. lover; f. mistress.*

Querido amigo. *Dear friend.*

queso *m. cheese.*

quetzal *m. quetzal (bird); Guatemalan currency unit.*

¡quiá! *Come now! Not at all! No, indeed!*

quicio *m. hinge.*

Estar fuera de quicio. *To be out of one's mind.*

Sacar de quicio. *To drive one crazy. To exasperate.*

QUIEN *who, which; pl.* **quienes.**

¿Quién es Ud.? *Who are you?*

¿Quiénes son los otros invitados? *Who are the other guests?*

¿Quién habla? *Who's speaking?*

¿Quién lo quiere? *Who wants it?*

¿De quién es este sombrero? *Whose hat is this?*

¿Para quién es? *For whom is it?*

¿Quién va? *Who's there?*

¿A quién busca Ud.? *Who are you looking for?*

Quien así piensa se equivoca. *Whoever thinks so is wrong.*

¡Quién sabe! *Who knows! Heaven knows!*

¿A quién de ellos conoce Ud.? *Which one of them do you know?*

quienquiera *whoever.*

QUIETO *adj. quiet, still.*

¡Estése quieto! *Be quiet!*

quietud *f. quietness, quiet, tranquility.*

quijada *f. jaw.*

quilla *f. keel.*

química *f. chemistry.*

químico *adj. chemical, m. chemist.*

quimono *m. kimono.*

QUINCE *adj. and n. fifteen.*

Hace quince días estaba aquí. *He was here two weeks ago.*

quinceañera *f. girl's fifteenth birthday party.*

quincena *f. fortnight, period of two weeks.*

Nos pagan por quincena. *They pay us every two weeks.*

quincenal *biweekly.*

quinientos *adj. and n. five hundred.*

quinina *f. quinine.*

quinta *f. country house; draft (military).*

quintal *m. quintal, hundredweight.*

quinto *adj. and n. fifth.*

quíntuplo *adj. quintuple, fivefold.*

quiosco *m. kiosk, stand.*

Quiosco de periódicos. *Newspaper stand.*

quirúrgico *adj. surgical.*

quisquilloso *adj. touchy, too sensitive, difficult.*

quitaesmalte *m. nail polish remover.*

QUITAR *to remove; to take away; to rob.*

Quita los pies de la silla. *Take your feet off the chair.*

Me han quitado el reloj. *They have taken my watch.*

Esta crema quita las pecas. *This cream removes freckles.*

Quite el freno. *Release the brake.*

quitarse *to get rid of; to take off.*

Al entrar en la iglesia se quitó el sombrero. *He took his hat off when he entered the church.*

Ya se me quitó el resfriado. *I've gotten rid of my cold.*

Quitarse a uno de encima. *To get rid of someone.*

QUIZÁ, QUIZÁS *perhaps, maybe.*

Quizá sea verdad lo que dice. *Perhaps what he says is true.*

Quizá lo haga. *I might do it. Maybe I'll do it.*

R

rábano *m. radish.*

rabia *f. rabies, hydrophobia; rage, anger.*

Me da rabia. *It makes me angry (mad).*

rabiar *to be furious, to rage, to be angry.*

Rabiar por algo. *To be extremely eager (anxious) for something.*

rabioso *adj. furious, mad.*

Perro rabioso. *Mad dog.*

rabo *m. tail.*

racimo *m. bunch (grapes), cluster.*

ración *f. ration.*

racional *adj. rational, reasonable.*

racionar *to ration.*

racismo *m. racism.*

radiador *m. radiator.*

radiar *to radiate; to broadcast.*

radical *adj. and n. radical.*

RADIO *m. radius; radium; f. radio.*

Radio portátil. *Portable radio.*

radiodifusión *f. broadcasting.*

radioemisora *broadcasting station.*

radioescucha *m. and f. radio listener.*

radiografía *f. radiography, X-ray photography.*

radiooyente *m. and f. radio listener.*

raíz *f. root; foundation.*

El árbol fue arrancado de raíz. *The tree was uprooted.*

Echar raíces. *To take root.*

rajar *to split, to cleave.*

rallador *m. grater.*

rallar *to grate.*

Queso rallado. *Grated cheese.*

rama *f. branch.*

Tabaco en rama. *Leaf tobacco.*

Algodón en rama. *Cotton wool. Raw cotton.*

Andarse por las ramas. *To beat around the bush.*

ramal *m. strand (of a rope); halter; branch, line (railway); ramification.*

ramificación *f. ramification.*

ramillete *m. bouquet.*

ramo *m. branch, line; bunch; bouquet.*

Esa clase de mercancía no es de nuestro ramo. *That type of merchandise is not in our line.*

Le obsequió un ramo de flores. *He gave her a bouquet of flowers.*

rampa *f. ramp, slope.*

rana *f. frog.*

rancio *adj. rancid, stale.*

ranchero *m. rancher.*

rancho *m. mess; hut; slum; ranch.*

Sirvieron el rancho a las doce. *Mess was served at twelve.*

Tiene un rancho muy grande. *He has a big ranch.*

rango *m. rank; position.*

ranura *f. slot, groove.*

RAPIDAMENTE *rapidly.*

rapidez *f. rapidity, swiftness.*

RÁPIDO *adj. rapid; fast; swift; quick; m. express train; m. pl. rapids (water).*

Fue una operación rápida. *It was a swift move.*

¿Es este un rápido? *Is this an express train?*

rapiña *f. robbery, plundering.*

Ave de rapiña. *Bird of prey.*

raptar *to abduct, to kidnap.*

rapto *m. kidnapping, abduction.*

raqueta *f. racket (tennis).*

raramente *seldom.*

Raramente vamos a su casa. *We rarely go to his house.*

rareza *f. rarity; queer habit, queer way.*

Ese chico tiene muchas rarezas. *That boy has many queer habits.*

RARO *adj. rare; unusual; odd, queer, strange.*

Es un hombre muy raro. *He's a very queer person.*

Era raro el día que no recibía cartas. *Hardly a day would go by without her getting a letter.*

Se equivoca raras veces. *He seldom makes a mistake.*

rascacielos *m. skyscraper.*

rascar *to scratch.*

rasgadura *f. tear.*

rasgar *to tear, to rend, to rip.*

rasgo *m. dash, stroke (in writing); feature, characteristic; deed, feat.*
  Rasgo de pluma. *A stroke of the pen.*
  Rasgo característico. *Outstanding feature.*
  Un rasgo heroico. *A heroic action.*
  A grandes rasgos. *In bold strokes. Broadly. In outline.*

rasguño *m. scratch.*

raso *adj. clear; flat; plain; m. satin.*
  Cielo raso. *Ceiling.*
  Un soldado raso. *Private. Buck private.*
  Pasamos la noche al raso. *We spent the night in the open air.*

raspador *m. scraper; eraser.*

raspar *to scrape; to rasp; to erase.*

rastrillo *m. rake; hackle; iron grating.*

rastro *m. track; trail; trace, sign.*
  Ni encontrar rastro de. *Not to find any trace of.*

rata *f. rat.*

ratero *m. petty thief; pickpocket.*

ratificación *f. ratification.*

ratificar *to ratify, to sanction.*

RATO *m. little while, short time.*
  ¿No quiere Ud. descansar un rato? *Won't you take a little rest? Don't you want to rest awhile?*
  Salió hace un rato. *He left a little while ago.*
  Nos vemos en un rato. *We'll see each other shortly.*
  Lo haré a ratos perdidos. *I'll do it in my spare time.*

ratón *m. mouse.*

ratonera *f. mousetrap.*

raya *f. dash; stripe, line; part, color streak (hair).*
  Prefiero esa camisa de rayas. *I'd rather have that striped shirt.*
  Tener (poner) a raya. *To hold at bay (at a distance). To keep within limits.*
  Pon la raya del lado derecho. *Part my hair on the right side.*

rayado *adj. striped.*
  Tela rayada. *Striped material (cloth).*

rayar *to draw lines; to rule (paper); to dawn.*
  Al rayar el alba. *At daybreak.*

rayo *m. ray, beam; spoke (of wheel); thunderbolt; flash of lightning.*
  Rayo de sol. *Sunbeam.*
  Rayos equis (X). *X rays.*

raza *f. race (of people, animals, etc.).*

RAZÓN *f. reason; cause; rate; right.*
  Tiene Ud. razón. *You're right.*
  No tiene razón. *He's wrong.*
  No tener razón de ser. *To be without foundation. To have no raison d'être.*
  Atender a razones. *To listen to reason.*
  Por razones. *For reasons.*
  A razón de. *At the rate of.*
  Ponerse en razón. *To be reasonable.*
  Dar razón de. *To give an account of. To account for. To give information about.*
  Dar la razón. *To agree with.*
  En razón a. *Concerning. As regards. In regard to.*
  Perder la razón. *To lose one's reason.*
  Razón social. *Firm. Name of a concern. Firm name.*
  Aquí no hay quien dé razón. *There's no one here to give any information.*
  ¡Con razón! *I can see it now!*

razonable *adj. reasonable, fair.*

razonamiento *m. reasoning.*

razonar *to reason; to argue.*

re *m., re (musical note).*

reacción *f. reaction.*

reaccionar *to react.*
  Reaccionó violentamente al oír esas palabras. *He reacted violently when he heard that.*

reaccionario *adj. reactionary.*

reacio *adj. obstinate, stubborn.*

REAL *adj. real, actual; royal.*

realidad *f. reality; truth.*
  En realidad. *In reality. Really. Actually.*

realismo *m. realism.*

realizar *to realize, to sell out; to accomplish, to fulfill; to materialize.*

realmente *in reality, really, actually.*

reanudar *to renew; to resume.*
  Reanudar un negocio. *To resume a business.*

reaparecer *to reappear.*

rebaja *f. reduction; deduction; abatement, diminution.*
  ¿Puede Ud. hacerme una rebaja en el precio? *Can you let me have it cheaper?*

rebajar *to reduce; to lower; to diminish.*
  Han rebajado un poco los precios. *They've reduced the prices a little.*

rebajarse *to lower oneself.*

rebanada *f. a slice.*

rebanar *to slice.*

rebaño *m. flock, herd of cattle.*

rebatir *to repel; to refute.*

rebelarse *to rebel, to revolt.*

rebelde *adj. hard to manage, rebellious; stubborn; m. rebel.*

rebelión *f. rebellion.*

rebobinar *to rewind (tape).*

rebosar *to muffle up; to dip into batter; to overflow.*

rebotar *to bounce, to rebound.*

rebozo *m. shawl.*

rebuscar *to search; to glean.*

recado *m. message; errand.*
>Lo mandaron a un recado. *They sent him on an errand.*
>¿Tiene Ud. algún recado para mí? *Have you a message for me?*

recaer *to fall back; to relapse.*
>Recayó a los pocos días de haberse levantado. *He had a relapse a few days after he got up (got out of bed.).*

recaída *f. relapse.*

recalcar *to emphasize, to stress.*

recalentar *to heat again; to overheat.*

recámara *f. dressing room.*

recapacitar *to think over, to recollect, to recall.*

recargado *adj. overloaded; strong; heavy.*

recargar *to overcharge; recharge; to overload; to make an additional charge; to increase (a sentence).*

recargo *m. overload; surcharge; overcharge; additional tax; new charge or accusation; increase (of sentence).*

recatado *adj. circumspect, prudent, cautious.*

recatarse *to act carefully, to be cautious.*

recaudación *f. collection (of rent, taxes, etc.); collector's office.*

recaudar *to collect (rent or taxes).*

recelar *to suspect, to distrust.*

recelo *m. misgiving, suspicion, mistrust.*

receloso *adj. suspicious, apprehensive.*

recepción *f. reception.*

receptor *m. receiver.*
>Descuelgue el receptor. *Pick up the receiver.*
>Cuelgue el receptor. *Hang up the receiver.*

recesión *f. recession.*

receta *f. prescription; recipe.*
>¿Puede Ud. prepararme esta receta? *Can you fill this prescription for me?*
>Receta de cocina. *Recipe.*

recetar *to prescribe a medicine.*

RECIBIR *to receive; to accept.*
>Recibí hoy una carta de mi hermano. *I received a letter from my brother today.*

recibirse *to graduate (as a doctor, lawyer, etc.).*

recibo *m. receipt.*
>Acusar recibo. *To acknowledge receipt.*

recién *(used immediately before past participles) recently; lately.*
>Recién casado. *Newly wed.*
>Recién nocido. *Newborn.*
>El recién llegado. *The newcomer.*

RECIENTE *adj. recent, new, fresh; modern.*
>Un acontecimiento reciente. *A recent event.*

RECIENTEMENTE *recently.*
>Falleció recientemente. *He died recently.*

recinto *m. precinct; inclosure; place.*

recio *adj. strong, vigorous; loud (voice); coarse, thick; severe (weather).*
>Hombre de recia constitución. *A man of strong constitution.*
>Hablar recio. *To talk in a loud voice.*
>De recio. *Strongly. Violently.*

recipiente *adj. receiving; m. container.*

reciprocar *to reciprocate.*

recíproco *adj. reciprocal, mutual.*
>A la recíproca. *Reciprocally.*
>Deben Uds. ayudarse recíprocamente. *You should help each other.*

reclamación *f. demand; complaint.*

reclamante *m. and f. claimant.*

reclamar *to demand, to claim.*

reclamo *m. advertisement; decoy bird (Amer.); claim.*

recluir *to shut up, to confine.*

recluso *adj. imprisoned; m. recluse; convict.*

recluta *f. recruiting; m. recruit.*

reclutar *to recruit.*

recobrar *to recover; to regain.*
>Recobrar la salud. *To regain one's health.*

RECOGER *to pick up; to call for someone; to gather; to collect; to shelter.*
>Recoja Ud. eso que se le ha caído. *Pick up what you dropped.*
>Puedes venir a recogerme a las seis. *You can come to pick me up at six o'clock.*

recogerse *to retire, to go home, to take a rest.*
>Se recoge temprano. *He goes to bed early.*

recolección *f. gathering; compilation; harvest; summary.*

recolectar *to gather, to harvest.*

recomendable *adj. recommendable.*

recomendación *f. recommendation; praise.*
>Carta de recomendación. *Letter of introduction. Letter of recommendation.*

RECOMENDAR *to recommend; to commend; to advise.*
>La persona a quien me recomendó Ud. me ha prometido un empleo. *The person you recommended me to has promised me a job.*
>Le recomiendo a Ud. que lo haga de prisa. *I advise you to do it quickly.*

recompensa *f. reward, compensation.*
>En recompensa. *In return.*

recompensar *to recompense, to reward, to make up for.*

reconciliación *f. reconciliation, bringing together again.*

reconciliar *to reconcile, to make friends again.*

RECONOCER *to recognize; to admit; to inspect, to reconnoiter; to consider; to appreciate.*

¿Reconoce Ud. esta letra? *Do you recognize this handwriting?*

Fue necesario reconocer todo el equipaje. *All the baggage had to be inspected.*

Le estoy muy reconocido por sus atenciones. *I'm grateful to you for your attention.*

reconocimiento *m. recognition, acknowledgment; appreciation, gratitude; reconnaissance.*

reconstituyente *m. tonic (medicine).*

reconstrucción *f. reconstruction.*

reconstruir *to reconstruct, to rebuild.*

recopilar *to compile, to collect.*

record *m. record (sports, etc.).*

Batir el record. *To break the record.*

Tiempo record. *Record time.*

recordar *to remind.*

No puedo recordar su apellido. *I don't recall his name.*

Se lo recordaré. *I'll remind you of it.*

recordatorio *m. reminder.*

recorrer *to travel over; to go over; to look over.*

Ayer recorrimos diez millas. *Yesterday we covered ten miles.*

Esta mañana recorrimos casi todas las tiendas. *This morning we went to nearly all the stores.*

recorrido *m. distance traveled; run, way, line.*

¿Es éste el final del recorrido? *Is this the end of the line (train, bus, etc.)?*

recortar *to cut, to trim, to clip; to shorten.*

recorte *m. clipping; outline; pl. cuttings; trimmings.*

Le envié un recorte del periódico. *I sent him a newspaper clipping.*

recostar *to lean against.*

recostarse *to lean back, to recline.*

recreación *f. recreation, diversion, amusement.*

recrear *to entertain, to amuse, to delight.*

recrearse *to have a little distraction, to have a good time.*

recreo *m. recreation, diversion, amusement.*

rectángulo *m. rectangle.*

rectificar *to rectify; to correct.*

rectitud *f. rectitude, straightforwardness, honesty.*

RECTO *adj. straight; just, upright; erect.*

Trace una línea recta. *Draw a straight line.*

Era un hombre recto. *He was a very upright man.*

rector *m. rector, the head of a college or university.*

recuento *m. checking, recount, inventory.*

recuerdo *m. recollection; memory; souvenir.*

Este pañuelo es un recuerdo. *This handkerchief is a souvenir.*

Dele recuerdos de mi parte. *Remember me to him. Give him my regards.*

recuperar *to recuperate, to recover.*

recurrir *to recur, to appeal; to resort to, to turn to.*

Tuvimos que recurrir a su ayuda. *We had to turn to him for help.*

recurso *m. recourse; appeal; resource; pl. means.*

Sin recursos. *Without means.*

rechazar *to repulse, to reject, to refuse.*

red *f. net; network; trap, snare.*

Los pescadores tendieron la red. *The fisherman spread out the net.*

Cayó en las redes que le tendieron. *He fell into the trap they set for him.*

Red ferroviaria. *Railroad system.*

redacción *f. wording; editing; newspaper office, newspaper staff.*

redactar *to edit; to word, to write.*

Redactar una carta. *To draft a letter.*

El manuscrito estaba bien redactado. *The manuscript was well written.*

redactor *m. editor.*

rededor *m. surroundings.*

Al rededor de. *Around. About. More or less. Nearly.*

redención *f. redemption; recovery.*

redimir *to redeem, to recover, to buy back.*

rédito *m. interest; revenue, yield of invested capital.*

redoblar *to intensify, to redouble; to roll (a drum); to toll (bells).*

REDONDO *adj. round.*

La mesa es redonda. *The table is round.*

En números redondos. *In round numbers.*

Boleto de viaje redondo (Mex). *Round-trip ticket.*

reducción *f. reduction, decrease.*

REDUCIR *to reduce; to cut down; to make smaller; to subdue.*

De hoy en adelante reduciré mis gastos. *From now on I'll cut down on my expenses.*

Todo se redujo a nada. *It didn't amount to anything.*

Reducir la marcha. *To slow down.*

Reducir a polvo. *To pulverize.*

redundancia *f. redundance.*

redundante *adj. redundant.*

redundar *to redound, to turn to, to result.*

Redundará todo en nuestro beneficio. *Everything will turn out to be to our advantage.*

reelección *f. re-election.*

reelegir to re-elect.

reembolsar to get one's money back, to get a refund.

reembolso m. refund.

Enviar contra reembolso. To send C.O.D.

reemplazar to replace; to restore.

reemplazo m. replacement; substitution.

reexpedir to forward.

Tenga la bondad de reexpedir mi correspondencia a esta dirección. Please forward my mail to this address.

referencia f. reference; account, report.

¿Quién puede dar referencia de Ud.? Who can you give as reference?

El asunto de referencia. The matter in question.

referente adj. referring, relating.

REFERIR to refer; to relate; to report.

referirse to refer to.

¿A qué se refiere Ud.? What are you referring to?

refinado adj. refined; polished.

refinería f. refinery.

reflector adj. reflecting; m. searchlight.

reflejar to reflect.

Eso refleja su carácter. That reflects his character.

reflejo m. reflex; glare.

Es un fiel reflejo de la verdad. This is the plain truth.

reflexión f. reflection; thinking something over carefully.

reflexionar to think over, to think carefully, to meditate; to reflect.

Reflexiónelo bien. Think it over carefully.

Tengo que reflexionar sobre eso. I have to think about that. I have to think that over.

reflexivo adj. reflexive.

reforma f. reform; reformation; alteration.

Cerrado por reformas. Closed for alterations (repairs).

reformar to reform; to correct; to renovate.

reformatorio adj. reforming; m. reformatory.

reforzar to reinforce; to strengthen.

refrán m. proverb, saying.

refrenar to curb, to restrain, to refrain.

refrendar to legalize; to countersign, to authenticate.

refrescar to refresh; to cool; to brush up.

refresco m. refreshment; cold drink.

refriega f. fray, skirmish, strife.

refrigerador adj. refrigerating; m. refrigerator.

refrigerar to refrigerate, to cool.

refuerzo m. reinforcement.

refugiado adj. and n. refugee.

refugiar to shelter.

refugiarse to take shelter (refuge).

refugio m. refuge, shelter, haven.

refunfuñar to growl, to grumble.

No refunfuñe tanto. Don't grumble so much.

regadera f. sprinkler; watering pot.

regalado adj. free, given away for nothing; cheap; easy.

Hace una vida muy regalada. He leads an easy life.

regalar to make a gift; to entertain; to treat; to caress.

Le regalaré este libro. I'll give him this book as a gift.

Es muy amigo de regalarse. He's very fond of indulging himself.

REGALO m. gift, present; comfort, good living.

Recibió un bonito regalo. He received a nice gift.

Vivía con mucho regalo. He lived in luxury.

regañar to scold; to quarrel; to growl.

La regañaron por llegar tarde. They scolded her for being late.

Ese hombre se pasa la vida regañando. That man is always quarreling.

regaño m. reprimand, scolding.

regañón adj. and n. growling; growler; a scolding person.

regar to water, to irrigate.

regata f. boat race, regatta.

regatear to bargain, to haggle; to stint; to dodge, to evade.

regateo m. haggling.

regazo m. lap.

regeneración f. regeneration.

regenerar to regenerate.

régimen m. regime; diet.

El médico me ha puesto a régimen. The doctor has put me on a diet.

El país cambió de régimen. The country changed its government.

regimiento m. regiment.

regio adj. royal, regal; splendid, magnificent.

región f. region.

regional adj. regional, local.

REGIR to rule, to govern; to go by; to prevail; to be in force (law, etc.).

Regía los destinos del pueblo. He governed the people.

Aún rige ese decreto. That decree is still in effect.

Los precios que rigen. The prevailing prices.

registrar to inspect, to examine; to search; to register, to put on record.

Es preciso registrarse en el Consulado. You have to register at the Consulate.

En este libro se registran las compras y ventas. *Purchases and sales are entered in this book.*

La policía registró su casa. *The police searched his house.*

¿Dónde registrarán el equipaje? *Where will they examine the baggage?*

registro *m. inspection; search; record, register.*

Firme en el libro de registro. *Sign the register.*

REGLA *f. ruler; rule; principle.*

¿Puede dejarme la regla? *Can you let me have the ruler?*

¿Tiene Ud. el pasaporte en regla? *Is your passport in order?*

Todo está en regla. *Everything is in order.*

Estas son las reglas del juego. *These are the rules of the game.*

Por regla general. *As a general rule.*

reglamentario *adj. according to regulations; usual, customary.*

reglamento *m. rules and regulations, by-laws.*

regocijar *to make glad (happy).*

regocijarse *to rejoice, to be glad.*

Se regocijó mucho por la noticia. *The news made him very glad.*

regocijo *m. rejoicing, pleasure.*

REGRESAR *to return, to go or come back.*

Regresará por Navidad. *He'll come back for Christmas.*

Regresaré a España en junio. *I'll go back to Spain in June.*

regreso *m. return, coming back.*

En nuestro viaje de regreso. *On our return trip.*

A mi regreso. *On my return.*

REGULAR *to regulate; to adjust; adj. regular, ordinary; fair, moderate; medium in size, quality, grade, etc.*

Regular el tráfico. *To regulate traffic.*

Estoy regular. *I'm so, so. Can't complain!*

Disfrutaba de un salario regular. *He received a moderate salary.*

De tamaño regular. *Of medium size.*

Por lo regular le veía todos los días. *Ordinarily I used to see him every day.*

regularmente *regularly.*

rehabilitación *f. rehabilitation.*

rehabilitar *to rehabilitate; to restore.*

rehacer *to make over; to refit.*

rehacerse *to recover, to regain strength; to rally (military).*

rehuir *to withdraw; to shun, to avoid; to refuse.*

Siempre rehuye verme. *He always avoids me.*

rehusar *to refuse; to reject.*

Rehusó la invitación. *He refused the invitation.*

reimprimir *to reprint.*

reina *f. queen.*

reinado *m. reign.*

reinar *to reign; to predominate, to prevail, to exist.*

La reina Victoria reinó durante sesenta años. *Queen Victoria reigned sixty years.*

Reina un malestar general. *There's a general unrest.*

reincidir *to relapse, to fall back into a former state or way of acting, to backslide.*

reino *m. kingdom, reign.*

reintegrar *to restore; to refund.*

Hay que reintegrar la suma. *We have to make good (replace) the sum.*

Le reintegrarán el importe. *They'll refund your money.*

reintegrarse *to recuperate; to return.*

Reintegrarse al trabajo. *To return to work.*

reintegro *m. restitution; refund.*

REÍR *to laugh.*

Se echó a reír. *He burst out laughing.*

Reír a carcajadas. *To laugh uproariously. To laugh out loud.*

reírse *to scoff, to make fun, to laugh.*

¿Por qué se ríe de él? *Why are you laughing at him?*

Se ríe por nada. *The least little thing makes him laugh.*

reiterar *to reiterate.*

reja *f. grate; railing, iron fence; iron bars; plowshare.*

rejuvenecer *to rejuvenate.*

RELACIÓN *f. relation, connection; report, account; pl. connections; relations.*

No hay relación entre estas dos cosas. *There's no relation (connection) between these two things.*

Hizo una relación del suceso. *He gave an account of what happened.*

Tiene muy buenas relaciones. *He has very good connections.*

Relaciones diplomáticas. *Diplomatic relations.*

relacionado *adj. acquainted, related, well-connected.*

Está muy bien relacionado. *He has very good connections.*

relacionar *to relate; to connect; to be acquainted.*

Estamos relacionados con la firma. *We do business with the firm.*

relacionarse *to associate oneself with, to get acquainted, to make connections.*

Se relaciona mucho con artistas y escritores. *He associates a lot with artists and writers.*

Entiende todo cuanto se relaciona con la mecánica. *He understands everything that has to do with mechanics.*

relajarse *to relax.*

relámpago *m. lightning.*

relampaguear *to be lightning.*

Relampaguea (Está relampagueando). *It's lightning.*

relapso *m. relapse; backslider.*

relatar *to relate, tell.*

relativo *adj. relative.*

Relativo a. *With regard to. With reference to.*

relato *m. account, statement; story.*

Hizo un relato de lo que ocurrió. *He gave an account of what had happened.*

releer *to read over again.*

relevo *m. relay (race); release (legal).*

relieve *m. relief.*

religión *f. religion.*

religioso *adj. religious.*

RELOJ *m. clock, watch.*

Reloj de bolsillo. *Pocket watch.*

Reloj de pulsera. *Wristwatch.*

Reloj de pared. *Clock.*

relojero *m. watchmaker.*

relucir *to shine, to glitter; to excel; to bring to light.*

Sacó a relucir aquella vieja cuestión. *He brought up that old question (problem) again.*

relumbrar *to shine, to dazzle.*

rellenar *to refill; to stuff; to pad.*

relleno *adj. stuffed; filled; m. stuffing.*

Pimientos rellenos. *Stuffed peppers.*

remar *to row, to paddle.*

Máquina de remar. *Rowing machine.*

rematar *to complete, to put the finishing touches on; to sell at auction.*

remate *m. end, conclusion; auction.*

De remate. *Utterly. Irremediably.*

Por remate. *Finally.*

remedar *to imitate; to mimic.*

remediar *to remedy; to make good; to help; to avoid.*

No lo puedo remediar. *I can't help it. I can't do anything about it.*

Eso se puede remediar. *That can be remedied.*

Lo que no se puede remediar, se ha de aguantar. *What cannot be cured must be endured.*

REMEDIO *m. remedy; medicine; redress; resource, resort.*

¿Sabe Ud. de algún remedio contra el mareo? *Do you know of any medicine for seasickness?*

Esto no tiene remedio. *This can't be helped.*

No tuvo más remedio que aceptarlo. *He had no alternative but to accept it.*

¡No hay más remedio! *There's nothing else to do.*

Es un caso sin remedio. *It's a hopeless case.*

remendar *to mend, to patch; to darn.*

remesa *f. remittance; shipment.*

remiendo *m. patch; repair.*

remitente *m. and f. sender, shipper. dispatcher.*

REMITIR *to remit, to send, to forward, to ship.*

Me hace el favor de remitir mis cartas a estas señas. *Please forward my mail to this address.*

Le remitimos los géneros. *We sent you the goods.*

remo *m. oar; rowing.*

Bote de remo. *Rowboat.*

remojar *to soak, to steep, to dip.*

remojo *m. soaking, steeping.*

Ponga los frijoles en remojo. *Let the beans soak.*

remolcador *m. tugboat.*

remolcar *to tow; to haul.*

remolino *m. whirlpool; whirlwind; cowlick.*

remolque *m. towing; towline.*

Llevar a remolque. *To tow.*

remontar *to remount; to repair saddles.*

remontarse *to soar, to fly at a great height.*

Remontarse a. *To date back to.*

remorder *to feel remorse.*

Le remuerde la conciencia. *He has a guilty conscience.*

remordimiento *m. remorse.*

remover *to remove; to stir; to dismiss.*

remuneración *f. remuneration; reward.*

remunerar *to remunerate, to reward.*

renacer *to be reborn; to grow again.*

rencor *m. rancor, grudge.*

No le guardo ningún rencor. *I don't bear him any grudge.*

rencoroso *adj. resentful, spiteful.*

rendición *f. rendering; surrendering.*

rendido *adj. tired, worn-out, exhausted, overcome.*

Estoy rendido, no puedo andar más. *I'm exhausted. I can't walk any further.*

rendija *f. slit, crevice, crack.*

rendir *to subdue; to surrender; to produce, to yield; to tire out.*

Este negocio rinde poco. *This business is not very profitable.*

rendirse *to give up, to surrender; to be tired.*

Está por rendirse. *He's about to give up.*

Rendirse incondicionalmente. *To surrender unconditionally.*

renegado *m. renegade.*

renglón *m. line (written or printed).*

Fíjese en el tercer renglón. *Look at the third line.*

Leer entre renglones. *To read between the lines.*

renombre *m. renown, fame.*

renovación *f. renovation; renewal.*

renovar *to renovate; to renew; to reform, to transform.*

renta *f. rent, income; profit; rental; revenue, annuity.*

Vive de sus rentas. *He lives on his income.*

renuncia *f. resignation; renunciation, giving up; waiving.*

Presentó su renuncia. *He turned in his resignation.*

renunciar *to renounce, to resign; to waive; to drop (a claim); to refuse.*

Renunciaré a mi empleo. *I'll resign my position.*

Renunciar un derecho. *To give up a right.*

Renunció el ofrecimiento. *He refused (declined) that offer.*

reñir *to quarrel, to fight; to scold.*

Ha reñido con sus suegros. *She quarreled with her in-laws.*

No le riñas al niño. *Don't scold the child.*

reo *m. criminal; defendant.*

reojo *m. (look) askance.*

Mirar de reojo. *To look askance. To look out of the corner of one's eye.*

reorganización *f. reorganization.*

reorganizar *to reorganize.*

reparable *adj. reparable, remediable.*

reparación *f. reparation, repair; amends; satisfaction.*

REPARAR *to repair; to notice; to make up for.*

Hay que reparar la radio. *Our radio needs to be fixed.*

¿Dónde me podrán reparar esto? *Where can I get this repaired (fixed)?*

¿Reparó Ud. en su acento argentino? *Did you notice his Argentine accent?*

reparo *m. remark, hint; consideration; objection (fencing).*

Poner reparo. *To object. To raise an objection.*

Sin ningún reparo. *Without any consideration.*

repartición *f. distribution; sharing.*

Repartición de premios. *Distribution of prizes.*

repartidor *m. distributor, deliveryman.*

repartir *to distribute; to divide; to deliver (the mail).*

Se repartieron las ganancias. *They divided the profits between (among) themselves.*

Reparten el correo a eso de las ocho. *The mail is delivered at about eight o'clock.*

reparto *m. distribution; delivery; cast (in a play).*

¿A qué hora se hace el reparto? *At what time is the mail delivered?*

repasar *to check, to look over; to go over; to mend (clothes).*

Repase Ud. esa cuenta detenidamente. *Check that account carefully.*

Repasar la lección. *To go over one's lessons.*

Está repasando la ropa. *She's mending the clothes.*

repaso *m. review (of a lesson); revision.*

repatriar *to repatriate.*

REPENTE *m. sudden movement.*

Tuvo un repente de ira. *She had a fit of temper.*

De repente. *Suddenly. All of a sudden.*

De repente se apagaron todas las luces. *All of a sudden the lights went out.*

repentino *adj. sudden.*

Murió de muerte repentina. *He died suddenly.*

repercusión *f. repercussion; reaction.*

repercutir *to have a repercussion; to echo, to reverberate.*

Eso repercutirá en la situación. *That will have an effect on the situation.*

repetición *f. repetition, encore.*

El informe estaba lleno de repeticiones. *The report was full of repetitions.*

El público entusiasmando pidió la repetición. *The enthusiastic audience called for an encore.*

REPETIR *to repeat; to have a second helping.*

Haga el favor de repetir lo que dijo. *Please repeat what you said.*

¿Puedo repetir de este plato? *May I have a second helping?*

repisa *f. bracket; shelf.*

REPLETO *adj. full, replete.*

Tiene la cartera repleta de billetes. *His wallet is full of bills.*

La tienda está repleta de mercadería. *The store is well stocked.*

réplica *f. reply, answer; replica.*

Su réplica fue acertadísima. *His reply was very much to the point.*

replicar *to reply; to retort, to talk back.*

¡No me repliques! *Don't answer back! Don't talk back to me!*

repollo *m. cabbage.*

reponer *to replace; to restore.*

Repuso los fondos. *He replaced the funds.*

reponerse *to recover; to retrieve.*

No podrá reponerse. *She can't possibly recover.*

Ya me he repuesto de mis pérdidas. *I have already retrieved my losses.*

repórter, reportero *m. reporter.*

reposar *to rest; to lie down.*

reposo *m. rest.*

Después de un reposo se sentirá mejor. *You'll feel better after a short rest.*

repostería *f. confectioner's, pastry shop.*

reprender *to reprimand, to reprehend.*

reprensión *f. reproof, reproach, reprimand.*

representación *f. representation; play, performance.*

¿A qué hora empieza la representación? *When does the performance (play) begin?*

representante *adj. representing; m. and f. representative, agent.*

representar *to represent; to stage, to play on the stage.*

¿Qué casa representa Ud.? *Which firm do you represent?*

No representa su edad. *She doesn't look her age.*

reprimir *to repress, to check, to hold in check.*

No me pude reprimir por más tiempo. *I couldn't contain myself any longer.*

reprobación *f. reprobation.*

reprobar *to reprove, to condemn, to find fault with.*

reprochar *to reproach; to upbraid.*

reproducción *f. reproduction.*

reproducir *to reproduce.*

reproducirse *to recur.*

reptil *m. reptile.*

república *f. republic.*

republicano *adj. and n. republican.*

repudiar *to repudiate; to disown.*

repuesto *adj. recovered; m. pl. spare parts.*

De repuesto. *Spare. Extra.*

Envíeme Ud. algunas piezas de repuesto. *Send me some spare parts.*

repugnante *adj. repugnant, distasteful.*

repugnar *to detest; to act with reluctance.*

Me repugna. *I detest it. It's repugnant to me.*

repulsión *f. repulsion; aversion.*

repulsivo *adj. repulsive, repelling.*

reputación *f. reputation, name.*

Gozar de buena reputación. *To have a good name.*

requerimiento *m. request; summons.*

requerir *to summon; to notify; to require.*

Eso requiere mucha atención. *That requires a lot of attention.*

requesón *m. cottage cheese, pot cheese.*

requisito *m. requisite, requirement.*

Llenar los requisitos. *To meet the requirements.*

res *f. steer, cow, bull (Amer.).*

Carne de res. *Beef.*

resaltar *to rebound; to stand out; to be conspicuous.*

Hacer resaltar. *To emphasize. To call attention to.*

Resaltar a la vista. *To be self-evident. To be very obvious. To stare one in the face.*

resbaladizo *adj. slippery.*

resbalar *to slip, to slide.*

resbalón *m. slip, slipping.*

rescatar *to ransom; to redeem.*

rescate *m. ransom.*

resentirse *to feel the effects of; to resent, to be offended, to feel hurt, to show displeasure; to hurt.*

Está resentida. *She's resentful. She feels hurt.*

Resentirse por nada. *To take offense at unimportant things.*

Tengo el cuerpo resentido. *My body aches all over.*

reseña *f. review (book, film, etc.); brief account.*

reseñar *to outline; to review (book, etc.), to give a brief account.*

reserva *f. reserve; reservation; caution; secret.*

Se lo digo a Ud. en reserva. *I'm telling you this in confidence.*

Con la mayor reserva. *In strict(est) confidence.*

Está en la reserva. *He is in the reserve (Army or Navy).*

Reserva mental. *Mental reservation.*

Sin reserva. *Without reservation. Openly.*

De reserva. *Extra. In reserve.*

Tengo una reserva en el banco. *I have some money put away in the bank.*

reservadamente *secretly, confidentially.*

reservado *adj. reserved; cautious; confidential.*

Es muy reservado. *He's very reserved.*

reservar *to reserve; to save; to keep; to conceal.*

Queremos que nos reserve un asiento de primera clase. *We want a first-class seat reservation.*

Le reservó su habitación hasta su regreso. *He reserved the room for him until his return.*

El Club se reserve el derecho de admisión.

The Club reserves the right of admission.

reservarse *to preserve oneself; to bide one's time; to be cautious.*

resfriado *m. a cold.*
He cogido un resfriado. *I've caught a cold.*

resfriar *to cool; to cool off.*

resfriarse *to catch a cold.*
Se resfrió anoche. *He caught a cold last night.*

resguardar *to reserve; to keep safe, to protect.*

resguardarse *to take care of oneself; to be on one's guard; to take shelter.*

resguardo *m. voucher; security; safekeeping; guard; customs official.*
Poner a resguardo de. *To keep safe. To preserve from.*

residencia *f. residence.*

residente *adj. residing; resident; m. resident, inhabitant.*

residir *to reside, to live.*

residuo *m. residue, remainder.*

resignación *f. resignation, patience.*

resignarse *to be resigned, to resign oneself to.*

resistencia *f. resistance.*

resistente *adj. resistant, strong.*

resistir *to resist, to hold out, to withstand, to endure.*
Resistir la tentación. *To resist temptation.*
Resistir un ataque. *To resist (withstand) an attack.*
Ha resistido la prueba. *It stood the test.*
Esto ya no se puede resistir. *This can't be tolerated any longer.*

resistirse *to offer resistance; to refuse.*
Se resistió a hacerlo. *He refused to do it.*

resma *f. ream (paper).*

resolución *f. resolution, determination, decision; solution.*
Tenemos que tomar una resolución. *We must come to some decision.*

resoluto *adj. resolute.*

resolver *to resolve, to determine, to decide; to solve; to dissolve; to settle.*
Estoy resuelto a hacerlo yo mismo. *I'm determined to do it myself.*
Este problema es difícil de resolver. *This problem is hard to solve.*
Es necesario resolver este asunto con toda urgencia. *It's necessary to settle this affair immediately.*

resolverse *to resolve, to make up one's mind, to reach a decision.*
No se resuelve a tomar una decisión. *He couldn't make up his mind.*

resonancia *f. resonance.*

resonante *adj. resonant, resounding.*

resonar *to resound.*

resorte *m. spring (metal).*

respaldo *m. back (of a seat); back, reverse (of a sheet of paper); endorsement.*
Al respaldo. *On the back of.*

respectivamente *respectively.*

respectivo *adj. respective.*

RESPECTO *m. relation, respect, reference.*
Con respecto a. *With regards to.*
A este respecto. *In regard to this.*
Por todos respectos. *By all means.*

respetable *adj. respectable, honorable.*

respetar *to respect, to honor.*

RESPETO *m. respect, regard, consideration.*
Mis respetos a su señor padre. *My best regards to your father.*
Perder el respeto. *To lose respect for.*
Faltar al respeto. *To be disrespectful.*
Por respeto a. *Out of consideration for.*

respetuoso *adj. respectful, polite.*

respiración *f. respiration; breathing.*
Le faltó la respiración. *He was out of breath.*

respirar *to breathe.*
Respire Ud. fuerte. *Breathe deeply.*
Déjeme Ud. respirar. *Give me a chance to get my breath.*
Con aquel dinero pudo respirar un mes más. *With that money he could get by for another month.*

respiro *m. respite, time of relief.*

resplandor *m. splendor; glare.*

RESPONDER *to answer; to respond; to talk back; to correspond; to be responsible for.*
Ni siquiera me respondió. *He didn't even answer me.*
Ese niño siempre responde a sus padres. *That child always talks back to his parents.*
¿Y qué responde Ud. a esto? *And what do you say to this?*
Ha respondido muy bien al tratamiento. *He responded to the treatment very well.*
Respondo de las consecuencias. *I'll answer for the consequences.*
¿Hay alguien que responda por él? *Is there anyone who will stand up for him?*

respondón *adj. saucy, fresh; m. a person who is always answering back.*

responsabilidad *f. responsibility.*

responsable *adj. responsible, liable.*

RESPUESTA *f. answer, reply; retort; response.*

resta *f. subtraction; remainder.*

restablecer *to re-establish; to restore.*

restablecerse *to recover.*
Restablecerse de una enfermedad. *To recover from an illness.*

restante *adj. remaining; m. remainder.*
Hay muchas cosas restantes. *There are many things left over (remaining).*
restar *to subtract; to deduct; to remain; to be left.*
Reste dos de cinco. *Subtract two from five.*
No nos resta más que marcharnos. *There's nothing left for us to do but leave.*
restauración *f. restoration.*
RESTAURANTE *m. restaurant.*
restaurar *to restore; to recover.*
restitución *f. restitution.*
restituir *to restore.*
Le restituyeron sus propiedades. *His property was restored to him.*
RESTO *m. rest, remainder, residue; pl. remains, leftovers.*
Esa cocinera sabe aprovechar los restos. *This cook knows how to make good use of leftovers.*
Echar el resto. *To bet everything one has.*
restorán *m. restaurant.*
restricción *f. restriction, curtailment.*
restringir *to restrain; to curtail; to restrict, to limit.*
resucitar *to resurrect; to revive; to come or bring back.*
Resucitar una moda. *To revive a style.*
resuelto *adj. resolute, daring; determined; prompt; settled, resolved.*
Es un hombre muy resuelto. *He's a very determined person.*
Es cosa resuelta. *It's (a) settled (matter).*
resulta *f. result, effect, consequence.*
De resultas. *As a consequence. Consequently.*
RESULTADO *m. result, outcome; score.*
¿Cuál fue el resultado del partido? *What was the final score of the game?*
RESULTAR *to result, to turn out to be.*
No resultó muy bien la combinación. *The combination didn't turn out to be a good one.*
Si tomamos un cuarto juntos nos resultará más barato. *If we take a room together, it will be cheaper for us.*
Nos resultó muy caro. *It was very expensive for us.*
¿Qué traje le ha resultado mejor? *Which suit wore better?*
La película resultó muy aburrida. *The picture was boring.*
Resultó herido. *He was wounded.*
Esto no me resulta. *This doesn't suit me.*
resumen *m. summary, summing up; résumé.*
resumido *adj. abridged.*
En resumidas cuentas. *In short. To make a long story short.*

resumir *to abridge, to cut short; to summarize, to sum up.*
Resumir un discurso. *To cut a speech short.*
resurgimiento *m. revival.*
resurgir *to reappear.*
retaguardia *f. rear guard.*
retar *to challenge; to reprimand.*
retardar *to retard; to delay.*
¿Qué le ha retardado a Ud.? *What made you so late?*
retardo *m. delay.*
Eso fue la causa del retardo. *That caused the delay.*
Temo que el retardo sea fatal. *I'm afraid that the delay may be fatal.*
retazo *m. remnant, piece (material, cloth).*
retener *to retain; to withhold; to hold, to keep; to remember.*
Le retuvieron el sueldo aquel mes. *They withheld his salary that month.*
No puede retener las fechas en la cabeza. *He can't remember dates.*
retina *f. retina.*
retirada *f. retreat, withdrawal.*
El enemigo se bate en retirada. *The enemy is retreating.*
retirar *to withdraw; to retire; to take away; to back up (printing).*
Quiero retirar cien dólares. *I'd like to withdraw a hundred dollars.*
Retire un poco la silla para que se pueda pasar. *Pull the chair aside a little so there will be room to pass.*
Retire esta silla. *Take this chair away.*
retirarse *to go away; to retire; to retreat.*
Se ha retirado de los negocios. *He has retired from business.*
Nuestras fuerzas se retiraron. *Our forces withdrew.*
Se retiró a su cuarto. *He went to his room.*
Retírese del fuego. *Get away from the fire.*
Puede Ud. retirarse. *You may go now.*
retocar *to retouch, to improve.*
retoño *m. shoot, sprout.*
retoque *m. touch-up; finishing touch.*
retorcer *to twist; to contort; to distort; to retort.*
retornar *to return, to shuttle; to give back; to repay; to reciprocate.*
retorno *m. return; repayment; exchange.*
retractar *to retract, to withdraw.*
retractarse *to retract, to go back on one's word.*
retraer *to dissuade; to draw back.*
retraerse *to keep aloof; to shy away; to retire, to withdraw from; to live a retired life.*

retraído *aloof, solitary, not communicative, secretive.*

Es un hombre retraído. *He's not communicative.*

retraimiento *m. shyness; reserve; retreat, seclusion.*

retrasar *to retard, to delay, to be slow; to put off; to set back.*

Mi reloj retrasa. *My watch is slow.*

El tren viene retrasado. *The train's late.*

retrasarse *to be late; to fall behind (in payment); to be backward.*

Siento haberme retrasado tanto. *I'm sorry to be so late.*

Nos hemos retrasado en los pagos. *We've fallen behind in our payments.*

retraso *m. delay.*

Con retraso. *Late.*

El tren ha tenido retraso. *The train's late.*

retratar *to portray; to draw a portrait; to photograph, to take a picture.*

retrato *m. portrait; photograph, picture; image.*

Este retrato no se parece en nada a ella. *This portrait doesn't resemble her at all.*

Es el vivo retrato de su padre. *He's the living image of his father.*

retrete *m. toilet.*

retribución *f. retribution; reward.*

retribuir *to pay back; to remunerate.*

retroactivo *adj. retroactive.*

retroceder *to back up, to move backward; to draw back, to fall back; to recoil; to grow worse.*

El auto retrocedió hasta quedar enfrente de la puerta. *The car backed up until it was in front of the door.*

Retrocedió unos pasos para reunirse con nosotros. *He came back a few steps to join us.*

No podía retroceder en su decisión. *He couldn't reverse his decision.*

retroceso *m. recoil, drawing back.*

retrógrado *adj. reactionary.*

retrospectivo *adj. retrospective.*

reubicar *to relocate.*

reuma *m. rheumatism.*

reumatismo *m. rheumatism.*

reunión *f. reunion; meeting, assembly.*

Habrá una reunión a las cinco. *There will be a meeting at five o'clock.*

reunir *to gather; to collect, to get (money), to bring together.*

Es preciso que Ud. reuna el dinero hoy mismo. *You must get the money today.*

Reunió a sus amigos en una fiesta. *He brought all his friends together at a party.*

Se han reunido todos contra él. *They've all united against him.*

reunirse *to get together; to meet; to unite; to join.*

¿A qué hora prodríamos reunirnos? *At what time could we get together?*

Se reunen en su casa todos los sábados. *They meet at his home every Saturday.*

revelación *f. revelation.*

revelar *to reveal, to show, to disclose; to develop (photography).*

Revelar un secreto. *To reveal a secret.*

El autor revela gran talento en este libro. *The author shows great talent in this book.*

¿Reveló Ud. ya las fotografías? *Have you developed the pictures yet?*

revendedor *m. retailer.*

revender *to retail; to resell.*

reventar *to burst, to blow up; to blow out; to break; to sprout, to blossom; to tire, to exhaust, to vex.*

Reventar de risa. *To burst into laughter.*

Reventó el neumático. *The tire blew out.*

Estoy reventado de tanto caminar. *I'm exhausted from walking so much.*

Ese tipo me revienta. *I can't stand that fellow.*

reventarse *to burst.*

Se reventó un neumático en el camino. *We had a blowout on the road.*

reventón *m. bursting; blowout; explosion; steep slope; hard work.*

Tuvo que darse un reventón para terminar el trabajo. *He almost worked himself to death to finish the work.*

reverencia *f. reverence.*

reverso *m. reverse.*

REVÉS *m. reverse; wrong side; backhand slap; misfortune.*

Este es el revés. *This is the wrong side.*

La chaqueta está del revés. *The jacket is wrong side out.*

No es así, precisamente es al revés. *It's not like that, it's just the opposite.*

Todo le salía al revés. *Everything he did went wrong.*

revisar *to look over, to go over; to check; to overhaul; to examine, to audit (accounts).*

Revisar las cuentas. *To audit accounts.*

Hágame el favor de revisar el motor. *Please check the engine.*

revisión *f. checking; verification; overhauling. Revisión de cuentas. Audit.*

revisor *m. inspector; auditor.*

revista *f. review, parade; magazine.*

El general pasó revista a los soldados. *The general reviewed the soldiers.*

Tomaré un ejemplar de esta revista. *I'll take a copy of this magazine.*

revivir *to revive.*

revocación *f. revocation, repeal.*

revocar *to revoke, to repeal, to cancel; to plaster.*

revolcar *to knock down, to floor (an opponent).*

revolcarse *to be stubborn.*

revoltoso *adj. rebellious, hard to manage; boisterous; naughty, full of pranks.*

revolución *f. revolution.*

revolucionario *adj. revolutionary.*

revolver *to revolve; to turn upside down; to stir up.*

El niño lo revolvía todo en la casa, *The child turned the house upside down.*

Revuélvalo Ud. con una cuchara. *Stir it with a spoon.*

revólver *m. revolver.*

revuelo *m. commotion, sensation.*

revuelta *f. revolt.*

revuelto *adj. turned upside down; scrambled; boisterous, restless.*

Huevos revueltos. *Scrambled eggs.*

rey *m. king.*

rezagar *to leave behind; to defer.*

rezagarse *to remain behind; to lag.*

rezar *to pray.*

Rezaba todos los días sus oraciones. *He said his prayers every day.*

Eso no reza conmigo. *That's none of my business. That has nothing to do with me.*

ría *f. mouth of a river, estuary.*

riachuelo *m. brook, stream, rivulet.*

ribera *f. shore, bank.*

ribete *m. border, trimming; binding (on seams).*

ricacho, ricachón *m. very rich.*

ricino *m. castor-oil plant.*

Aceite de ricino. *Castor oil.*

RICO *adj. rich, wealthy, delicious.*

Si yo fuera rico no trabajaría tanto. *I wouldn't work so much if I were rich.*

¡Qué sabor más rico el de esta carne! *What a delicious flavor this meat has!*

ridiculizar *to ridicule.*

RIDÍCULO *adj. ridiculous; odd, queer; m. ridicule.*

Es una moda ridícula. *It's a ridiculous fashion.*

Poner en ridículo. *To ridicule.*

Ponerse en ridículo. *To make oneself ridiculous.*

riego *m. irrigation, watering.*

riel *m. rail, track.*

rienda *f. rein; restraint.*

Sujete Ud. bien las riendas. *Hold on to the reins.*

Dar rienda suelta. *To give free rein. To give vent to.*

riesgo *m. risk, danger, hazard.*

Corrió mucho riesgo. *He took a big risk.*

Sin riesgo. *Without risk. Safely.*

rifa *f. raffle.*

rifar *to raffle.*

rifle *m. rifle.*

rigidez *f. rigidity, sternness.*

rígido *adj. rigid; severe, hard, stern.*

rigor *m. rigor.*

riguroso *adj. rigorous, severe, strict.*

rima *f. rhyme.*

rincón *m. corner (of a room, etc.); nook; hidden spot, secluded place.*

Ponga Ud. la silla en el rincón. *Put the chair in the corner.*

rinoceronte *m. rhinoceros.*

riña *f. quarrel, fight.*

riñón *m. kidney.*

río *m. river.*

El Río Grande. *Rio Grande.*

riqueza *f. riches; wealth; fertility.*

RISA *f. laugh, laughter.*

Todo aquello le producía risa. *That made him laugh.*

No es cosa de risa. *It's no laughing matter.*

¡Ay qué risa! *My, how funny! That's very funny!*

Morir de risa. *To die laughing.*

risco *m. steep rock; cliff.*

risible *adj. laughable.*

risueño *adj. smiling; pleasant.*

Es un niño muy risueño. *The child is very goodnatured.*

ritmo *m. rhythm.*

rito *m. rite, ceremony.*

rival *m. rival.*

rivalidad *f. rivalry.*

rivalizar *to vie, compete.*

rizado *adj. curly.*

rizo *m. curl, frizzle; loop (aviation).*

robar *to rob, to steal; to draw (a card).*

Me han robado la cartera. *My wallet's been stolen.*

roble *m. oak.*

robo *m. robbery, theft.*

robusto *adj. robust, strong.*

Es de constitución robusta. *He has a strong constitution.*

roca *f. rock.*

roce *m. friction; close contact.*

Tiene mucho roce con ellos. *He associates a lot with them.*

rociar *to spray, to sprinkle.*

rocío *m. dew.*

rock *m. rock (music).*

rocnrol *m. rock 'n' roll.*

rodar *to roll; to roam around; to shoot (a film).*

Rodó la escalera. *He went rolling down the stairs.*

Desde muy joven empezó a rodar por el mundo. *He began to roam around the world when he was very young.*

Se empezó a rodar la película. *They started shooting the picture.*

rodear *to surround, to encircle; to go around.*

rodeo *m. turn; roundabout way; roundup, rodeo.*

Ese camino da un rodeo muy grande. *That road makes a wide turn.*

Hubo un rodeo la semana pasada. *There was a rodeo last week.*

Déjese de rodeos y conteste claramente. *Stop beating around the bush and give me a straight answer.*

RODILLA *f. knee.*

De rodillas. *On one's knee.*

Ponerse de rodillas. *To kneel.*

rodillo *m. roller; rolling pin; platen.*

roer *to gnaw, to nibble; to pick (a bone); to annoy.*

rogar *to pray, to beg, to entreat, to request.*

Le ruego que . . . *I beg you to . . .*
    Please . . .

ROJO *adj. red.*

La Cruz Roja. *The Red Cross.*

rol *m. roll, list, crew list; role.*

rollizo *adj. plump; m. log.*

rollo *m. roll, bolt (material); roller.*

Roma *f. Rome.*

romance *m. romance; ballad.*

romanticismo *m. romanticism.*

romántico *adj. romantic.*

romería *f. pilgrimage; gathering; tour.*

romero *m. rosemary; pilgrim.*

rompecabezas *m. riddle; puzzle.*

rompenueces *m. nutcracker.*

ROMPER *to break; to smash; to tear; to rip; to fracture.*

¿Ha roto Ud. la botella? *Have you broken the bottle?*

Se cayó del caballo y se rompió una pierna. *He fell from his horse and broke a leg.*

Rompió el documento. *He tore up the document.*

Se me ha roto la media. *I've ripped my stocking.*

Romper relaciones. *To break relations.*

Romper con alguno. *To break with someone.*

Al romper el día. *At daybreak.*

ron *m. rum.*

roncar *to snore; to roar; to brag.*

ronco *adj. hoarse.*

roncha *f. swelling caused by a bite or by a blow; welt.*

ronda *f. night patrol; making the rounds; a round (of drinks, etc.).*

rondar *to patrol.*

ronquido *m. snore; roaring.*

roña *f. scab; filth.*

ROPA *f. wearing apparel, clothing; clothes.*

Tengo que mudarme de ropa. *I have to change my clothes.*

Ropa interior. *Underwear.*

Ropa sucia. *Dirty clothes. Laundry (to be washed).*

ropero *m. wardrobe; closet.*

roquero *m. rock music singer.*

rosa *f. rose.*

rosado *adj. pink, rosy.*

rosal *m. rosebush.*

rosario *m. rosary.*

rosbif *m. roast beef.*

rosca *f. ring (bread or cake); thread (of a screw).*

Deme Ud. una rosca de esas. *Give me one of those rings (bread or cake).*

La rosca de un tornillo. *The thread of a screw.*

rostro *m. face.*

roto *adj. torn; broken; ragged.*

rotular *to label.*

rótulo *m. label; poster, placard.*

rotura *f. breaking, rupture; crack.*

rozar *to grub, to clear (the ground); to nibble (grass); to graze.*

El avión rozó ligeramente el suelo. *The plane grazed the ground.*

rubí *m. ruby.*

rubio *adj. blond; f. blonde.*

rubor *m. blush; bashfulness.*

ruborizarse *to blush.*

rudeza *f. coarseness, roughness.*

rudimento *m. rudiment.*

rudo *adj. rude, rough; severe.*

rueda *f. wheel.*

ruedo *m. hem; round mat.*

ruego *m. request, petition.*

Dirigió un ruego a la Cámara. *He submitted a petition to the legislature.*

A ruego de. *At the request of.*

rugido *m. roar; rumbling.*

rugir *to roar; to bellow.*

RUIDO *m. noise.*

El ruido me impidió dormir. *The noise kept me awake.*

Meter (hacer) ruido. *To make noise. To create a sensation. To attract attention.*

ruin *adj. mean, vile, low.*

ruina f. ruin; downfall; bankruptcy; pl. ruins.

ruinoso adj. ruinous; in ruins.

ruiseñor m. nightingale.

ruleta f. roulette.

rumba f. rumba (Cuban dance).

rumbo m. course; road, route; pomp, showy display.

Tomaremos otro rumbo. We'll take another course (road).

Con rumbo a. Bound for.

rumiar to ruminate; to ponder.

rumor m. rumor.

ruptura f. rupture; breaking off.

rural adj. rural, rustic.

ruso adj. and m. Russian.

rústico adj. rustic.

Un libro en rústica. A paperbound book.

ruta f. route, course.

rutina f. routine, habit; rut.

rutinario adj. according to routine; mechanical.

S

SÁBADO m. Saturday.

sábana f. bedsheet.

sabana f. savanna; grassy plain (Cuba).

saber m. learning, knowledge.

SABER to know; to know how; to be able to; to taste; to hear, to find out. (To know a person or a place = **conocer**.)

¿Sabe Ud. dónde vive? Do you know where he lives?

¿A ver qué sabe Ud.? Let's see what (how much) you know.

Sabe tanto como su professor. He knows as much as his teacher (professor).

¿Sabe Ud. lo que pasó? Do you know what happened?

¿Sabe Ud. escribir? Can you write?

¿Sabe Ud. nadar? Can you swim?

Sabe nadar muy bien. She swims very well.

¿Sabe Ud. algo de nuevo? Have you heard anything new?

Celebro saberlo. I'm glad (delighted) to hear it.

¿Le sabe mal? Does it taste okay to you? Don't you like it?

¿Sabe la noticia? Have you heard the news?

¿Cómo ha sabido Ud. eso? How did you find that out (learn that)?

¿Qué sé yo? How do I know? How should I know?

¡Ya lo sé! I know it!

Yo no sé. I don't know.

¡Quién sabe! Who knows!

No se sabe nunca. One never knows.

¡Sabe Dios! God knows!

Esto sabe mal. This tastes bad.

Esta comida sabe a gloria. This food's delicious.

Le remitimos los géneros siguientes, a saber: We are sending you the following goods:

Hacer saber. To make known.

Como es sabido. As is known.

Que yo sepa. To my knowledge. As far as I know.

No que yo sepa. Not that I'm aware of.

Saber de sobra. To know well enough.

¿Sabe Ud. una cosa? Do you know what? (Do) You know something?

sabiduría f. learning, knowledge, wisdom.

sabio adj. wise, learned; m. scholar.

sable m. saber; cutlass.

sabor m. savor, taste, flavor.

saborear to flavor; to savor, to relish.

saborearse to relish, to enjoy (eating or drinking); to be delighted.

sabotaje m. sabotage.

sabroso adj. delicious, tasty.

La comida es muy sabrosa. The food is very tasty.

sacacorchos m. corkscrew.

sacamanchas m. cleaning fluid; stain remover.

sacapuntas m. pencil sharpener.

SACAR to take out, to put out, to bring out, to get out; to draw; to remove, to pull out; to infer; to publish; to win (a prize); to take (a picture); to buy, to get.

Sacar una copia. To make a copy.

¿Cuánto saca por día? How much does he make a day?

Saque Ud. la cuenta. Figure out the bill.

Esta mañana saqué un poco de dinero del banco. I drew some money from the bank this morning.

Saqué un premio en el sorteo. I won a prize in the drawing.

¿Dónde puedo sacar mis billetes? Where can I buy my tickets?

Sacaré tres butacas. I'll buy three orchestra seats.

Saque las manos de los bolsillos. Take your hands out of your pockets.

¿De dónde ha sacado Ud. esa idea? Where did you get that idea?

Nos sacó de apuro. He got us out of trouble (out of a difficulty).

Saca los niños a pasear. Take the children out for a walk.

Ese hombre saca partido de todo. That man turns everything to profit.

Sacarán la casa a subasta pública. They're

going to sell the house at public
auction.

Sacar una foto. *To take a picture.*

Sacar una muela. *To pull out a tooth.*

Sacar a luz. *To print. To publish. To make
public.*

Sacar en limpio. *To infer.*

No sacar nada en limpio. *Not to be able to
make anything out of.*

saco m. *sack, bag; coat* (Amer.).

¿Qué hay en este saco? *What's in this
bag?*

El viajero llevaba un saco a cuestas. *The
traveler carried a bag on his
shoulders.*

Quítese el saco. *Take your coat off.*

Caer en saco roto. *To come to nothing.*

sacramento m. *sacrament.*

sacrificar *to sacrifice.*

sacrificio m. *sacrifice.*

sacrilegio m. *sacrilege.*

sacristía f. *sacristy, vestry.*

sacudida f. *shock, shake; beating.*

Le dio una buena sacudida. *He gave him a
good beating.*

sacudir *to shake; to jerk; to beat; to dust; to
shake off.*

sacudirse *to get rid of, to object.*

saeta f. *arrow; shaft.*

sagacidad f. *sagacity, shrewdness.*

sagaz adj. *sagacious, shrewd.*

sagrado adj. *sacred.*

sainete m. *farce, burlesque act.*

SAL f. *salt; wit, humor; charm.*

Haga el favor de pasarme la sal. *Please
pass me the salt.*

Tiene mucha sal esta niña. *This girl is very
witty.*

SALA f. *living room, parlor; large room;
room.*

Vamos a la sala a escuchar un poco de
música. *Let's go to the living room
and listen to some music.*

¿Dónde está la sala de espera? *Where is
the waiting room?*

Sala de pruebas. *Fitting room.*

Sala de fiestas. *Nightclub.*

salado adj. *salty; witty.*

Esta carne está muy salada. *This meat is
very salty.*

Es muy salada. *She's very witty.*

salario m. *salary, wages.*

salchicha f. *sausage.*

salchichón m. *large sausage.*

SALDO m. *balance, remainder; sale,
bargain.*

La tienda anuncia un saldo. *The store is
advertising a sale.*

Queda todavía a mi favor un pequeño

saldo. *A small sum still remains to my
credit.*

salero m. *saltshaker; gracefulness, charm.*

Tenga la bondad de alcanzarme el salero.
Please pass me the saltshaker.

Es hermosa y además tiene mucho salero.
*She's pretty and she's also very
charming.*

SALIDA f. *departure; exit; outlet; output;
witty remark; loophole, subterfuge.*

Salida y llegada de trenes. *Departure and
arrival of trains.*

¿Dónde está la salida? *Where is the
electrical outlet?*

Le veré a la salida. *I'll see you on my way
out.*

Tener salida. *To sell well.*

Dar salida. *To dispose of. To sell.*

Salida del sol. *Sunrise.*

Callejón sin salida. *Dead-end street.*

SALIR *to go out; to leave; to depart; to
appear; to come out; to get out; to
come off; to turn out; to rise (the
sun); to cost; to take after.*

¿A qué hora sale el tren? *What times does
the train leave?*

El tren está por salir. *The train is about to
leave.*

¿Piensa Ud. salir esta noche? *Are you
going out tonight?*

Voy a salir a tomar un poco el aire. *I'm
going out for some air.*

Salió hace un rato. *He left a while ago.*

He salido sin dinero. *I left the house
without any money.*

Me sale a mil pesetas la yarda. *It costs me
a thousand peseta a yard.*

Ella sale a su madre. *She takes after her
mother.*

¡Salga de aquí! *Get out!*

Muy en breve saldrá el libro. *The book will
be out (appear) very soon.*

El periódico sale todos los días. *The
paper comes out (appears) every
day.*

Estas manchas no salen. *These spots don't
come off.*

Se le sale mucho el pañuelo del bolsillo.
*His handkerchief sticks way out of his
pocket.*

Salió bien en los exámenes. *He passed his
examination with good marks.*

¿Quién salió ganando? *Who was the
winner?*

Todo le salía al revés. *Everything he did
went wrong.*

Al salir el sol. *At sunrise.*

El sol sale para todos. *The sun shines on
the just and on the unjust.*

El anillo se me ha salido del dedo. *The ring slipped off my finger.*

salirse *to leak; to overflow.*

Esta jarra se sale. *This jar is leaking.*

¡Cuidado que se sale la leche! *Look out, the milk is going to overflow!*

Salirse con la suya. *To get one's way. To accomplish one's end.*

saliva *f. saliva.*

salmón *m. salmon.*

salón *m. hall; salon; parlor.*

¿Hay algún salón de belleza por aquí? *Is there a beauty parlor near here?*

En este salón caben más de cien personas. *This hall can accommodate over a hundred people.*

Salón de baile. *Dance hall.*

salpicar *to splash, to spatter.*

salsa *f. sauce, gravy, dressing; popular Latin music.*

salsera *f. gravy dish.*

salsero *m. popular Latin music singer.*

SALTAR *to jump, to leap, to hop; to skip, to omit; to bounce; to fly off.*

¿Puede Ud. saltar por encima de esa cerca? *Can you jump over that fence?*

Al pasar lista saltó mi nombre. *When he called the roll he skipped my name.*

Esta pelota no salta. *This ball doesn't bounce.*

Saltó en su defensa. *He sprang to his (her) defense.*

Hacer saltar. *To blow up.*

Saltar a la vista. *To be obvious. To stare one in the face.*

salteado *adj. sautéed.*

SALTO *m. jump, leap; sudden promotion; waterfall, cascade.*

Salto de agua. *Waterfall.*

A saltos. *By fits and starts.*

Dar saltos. *To jump.*

De un salto. *At one jump.*

Salto mortal. *A somersault.*

SALUD *f. health.*

Disfruta de muy buena salud. *He's enjoying good health.*

Bueno para la salud. *Good for the health. Healthful.*

Estar bien de salud. *To be in good health.*

Estar mal de salud. *To be in poor health.*

Bebamos a la salud de nuestro anfitrión. *Let's drink to our host.*

¡Salud! *Hello! Good luck! To your health!*

¡Salud y pesetas! *Here's to health and wealth!*

saludable *adj. healthful, good for the health; salutary, beneficial.*

saludar *to salute, to greet.*

Le saludó muy afectuosamente. *He greeted him (her) affectionately.*

Y a mí, ¿no me saluda Ud.? (*Well,*) *Aren't you going to say hello to me?*

Cuando lo vea, salúdele en mi nombre. *Remember me to him when you see him.*

Salude a Juan de mi parte. *Give John my regards.*

saludo *m. salute, greeting.*

Saludos a. *Greetings to.*

salva *f. salvo, volley.*

Una salva de aplausos. *Thunderous applause.*

salvación *f. salvation.*

salvado *m. bran.*

salvaje *adj. savage; wild.*

salvamento *m. salvage, rescue.*

salvar *to salvage; to save; to clear (an obstacle); to avoid (a danger); to jump over (a ditch, etc.), to cover (a distance).*

El médico ha perdido la esperanza de salvarlo. *The doctor has given up hope of saving him.*

Salvando pequeños detalles. *Apart from minor details.*

salvarse *to escape from danger; to be saved.*

Se salvó por un pelo. *He had a narrow escape.*

salvavidas *m. lifeguard; life preserver; lifeboat, lifebelt, life buoy.*

salvedad *f. reserve, exception, qualification.*

SALVO *adj. saved, safe; excepted; save, exempting; but, unless.*

Todos vinieron salvo él. *Everyone came except him.*

Salvo los casos imprevistos. *Except for unforeseen cases.*

Salvo que. *Unless.*

Poner a salvo. *To safeguard. To keep safe.*

En salvo. *Safe. With safety.*

Sano y salvo. *Safe and sound.*

Ponerse a salvo. *To escape.*

A su salvo. *To one's satisfaction.*

salvoconducto *m. pass, safe-conduct.*

sanar *to cure, to heal; to recover.*

La herida sanó pronto. *The wound healed quickly.*

sanatorio *m. sanatorium.*

sanción *f. sanction.*

sancionar *to sanction; to ratify, to confirm.*

sandalia *f. sandal.*

sandía *f. watermelon.*

saneamiento *m. sanitation; drainage.*

sanear *to drain, to improve (lands); to take sanitary meaures, to make sanitary; to make good, to indemnify; to guarantee.*

sangrar to bleed.

SANGRE f. blood.

  A sangre fría. In cold blood.

  A sangre y fuego. Without mercy. With fire and sword.

sangriento adj. bloody; cruel.

sanidad f. health; health department.

  Sanidad pública. Public health.

sanitario adj. sanitary; hygienic.

  Toallas sanitarias. Sanitary napkins.

SANO adj. sound, healthy; sane; safe.

  Regresó sano y salvo. He returned safe and sound.

santiamén m. instant, twinkling of an eye, jiffy.

  Lo haré en un santiamén. I'll do it in a jiffy.

sanitguarse to cross oneself, to make the sign of the cross (on oneself).

santo adj. very good, saintly; saint, holy, sacred; m. saint.

  Semana Santa. Holy Week (Easter).

  Se ha quedado para vestir santos. She's going to be (is) an old maid.

saña f. rage, fury, anger, passion.

sapo m. toad.

saquear to sack, to loot, to pillage.

sarampión m. measles.

sarcasmo m. sarcasm.

sardina f. sardine.

sargento m. sergeant.

sarpullido m. rash, skin eruption.

sartén f. frying pan.

sastre m. tailor.

  Lleve este traje al sastre. Take this suit to the tailor.

sastrería f. tailor shop, tailoring.

Satán, Satanás m. Satan.

satélite m. satellite.

sátira f. satire, sarcasm, irony.

satírico adj. satirical.

SATISFACCIÓN f. satisfaction; pleasure; apology.

  Tuve la satisfacción de conocerla. I had the pleasure of meeting her.

  Eso fue una gran satisfacción para mí. That was a great satisfaction for me.

  El dio un suspiro de satisfacción. He gave a sigh of relief.

  Dar satisfacciones. To apologize.

SATISFACER to satisfy; to please; to pay (debt); to gratify.

  No me satisface su trabajo. His work doesn't satisfy me.

  Eso no me satisface. I'm not satisfied with that.

  Satisfacer una deuda. To pay a debt.

satisfactorio adj. satisfactory.

SATISFECHO adj. satisfied, content.

Deseamos que todos estén satisfechos. We want everyone to be satisfied.

Hágalo Ud. de modo que él quede satisfecho. Do it in a way that will please him.

No deseo comer más, estoy satisfecho. I don't want to eat any more, I've had enough.

sauce m. willow.

sazón f. maturity; seasoning, taste, flavor; opportunity.

  A la sazón estaba yo en Inglaterra. At that time I was in England.

  En sazón. In season. Ripe. Seasonably.

sazonado adj. seasoned; ripe; expressive.

  Un plato bien sazonado. A well-seasoned dish.

sazonar to season; to mature, to ripen.

SE (third person object and reflexive pronoun) to him, to her, to it, to you, etc.; self, oneself, himself, herself, itself, etc. (Se is often used as a reciprocal pronoun and also to introduce the passive form.)

  Se lo diré. I'll tell it to him.

  Se dice. It's said.

  ¡Figúrese Ud.! Just imagine!

  Se me figura. I can imagine.

  Déselo. Give it to him.

  Lávese. Wash yourself.

  Se engañan. They're fooling themselves.

  Se conocen. They know each other (one another).

  Se aman. They love each other.

  ¿Cómo se llama Ud.? What's your name?

  Se sabe. It's known.

  No se sabe. No one knows.

  Se habla español. Spanish spoken here.

  Se alquila. For rent.

  Se prohíbe fumar. No smoking allowed.

SÉ (imperative of ser and first person indicative of saber) be; I know.

  Sé bueno. Be good.

  No lo sé. I don't know.

seca f. drought, dry season.

  Lo dijo a secas. He told it in a matter-of-fact way.

SECAR to dry, to desiccate; to wipe.

  Hay que secar los platos. We have to dry the dishes.

  Séquese bien. Dry yourself well (thoroughly).

sección f. section; division; department; cutting.

  ¿En qué sección trabaja Ud.? In what section (division) do you work?

SECO adj. dry; withered; lean; curt; rude.

  Tengo la garganta seca. My throat is dry.

Quiero que me limpie en seco este traje. *I'd like this suit dry-cleaned.*

Era un hombre muy seco. *He was a very curt person.*

Consérvese en un lugar seco. *Keep in a dry place.*

Clima seco. *Dry climate.*

Vino seco. *Dry wine.*

Lavar en seco. *To dry-clean.*

secretamente *secretly.*

secretaria *f. secretary.*

secretaría *f. secretaryship; secretary's office.*

secretario *m. secretary.*

secreto *adj. secret; private; m. secret; secrecy; mystery.*

Lo he guardado en secreto. *I've kept it a secret.*

Temo que Ud. no guarde el secreto. *I'm afraid you won't keep the secret.*

Era un secreto a voces. *It was an open secret.*

secuestro *m. kidnapping, hijacking.*

secundar *to second, to back up, to aid.*

Lo secunda en todo y por todo. *He supports him in everything.*

secundario *adj. secondary, subsidiary.*

SED *f. thirst; desire, craving.*

Tengo sed. *I'm thirsty.*

seda *f. silk.*

Tiene la piel como seda. *Her skin is soft as silk.*

Papel de seda. *Tissue paper.*

Seda vegetal. *Dental floss.*

sedería *f. silks; silk trade; silk shop.*

sedición *f. sedition, mutiny.*

sediento *adj. thirsty.*

sedimento *m. sediment.*

seducir *to seduce; to tempt, to fascinate; to bribe.*

segadora *f. reaper, harvester (machine).*

segar *to harvest; to mow.*

segregar *to segregate, to separate; to secrete.*

SEGUIDA *f. succession, continuation.*

En seguida. *Right away. Immediately.*

¡Venga en seguida! *Come right away!*

De seguida. *Successively. In succession.*

seguidamente *successively; immediately after, right after.*

seguidilla *f. seguidilla (a lively Spanish dance); the song and music that go with it.*

seguido *adj. continued; straight (ahead).*

Vaya todo seguido y luego tome la primera a la derecha. *Go straight ahead and then take the first street to your right.*

SEGUIR *to follow; to pursue; to continue, to go on, to keep on.*

Sígame. *Follow me.*

Le sigo a Ud. *I'll follow you.*

Seguiré sus consejos. *I'll follow your advice.*

¡Siga adelante! 1. *Go straight ahead!* 2. *Go ahead! Continue!*

Siga derecho. *Keep straight ahead.*

¿Qué sigue después? *What comes afterward?*

Como sigue: *As follows:*

Siga tal como empezó. *Go on just as you started.*

Siguió hablando. *He went on talking. He kept (on) talking.*

La situación sigue de mal en peor. *The situation is going from bad to worse.*

El herido sigue mejor. *The wounded man is improving.*

Seguía diluviando. *It was still pouring.*

Sigo sin comprender. *I still don't understand.*

SEGÚN *according to; in the same way as, just as; it depends.*

Según el informe que me dio. *According to the report he gave me.*

Claro que esto es según se mire. *Of course, this depends on how you look at it.*

Según vayan llegando hágalos Ud. entrar. *Have them enter in their order of arrival.*

Según y conforme. *That depends.*

¿Irá Ud.?—Según y cómo. *Will you go?—That all depends.*

SEGUNDO *adj. and n. second; mate (of a ship).*

Espéreme un segundo, ahora vuelvo. *Wait a second, I'll be right back.*

Ella vive en el segundo piso. *She lives on the second floor.*

¿Qué tomo desea Ud., el primero o el segundo? *Which volume do you want, the first or second?*

Segunda velocidad. *Second gear.*

En segundo lugar. *In the second place. Secondly. On second thought.*

Un billete de segunda. *A coach ticket.*

De segunda mano. *Secondhand.*

seguramente *certainly, surely.*

Seguramente que sí. *Yes, certainly.*

seguridad *f. security; certainty; safety.*

Puede Ud. tener la seguridad de que lo haré. *You may be sure that I'll do it.*

Con toda seguridad. *With absolute certainty.*

Para mayor seguridad. *For safety's sake. For greater safety.*

SEGURO *adj. secure, sure, safe, certain; m. insurance; safety; stop, safety catch.*

¿No está Ud. seguro? *Aren't you sure?*

Tener por seguro. *To be sure. To consider certain.*

Ir sobre seguro. *To be on safe ground.*

A buen seguro. *Certainly.*

Compañía de seguros. *Insurance company.*

Póliza de seguro. *Insurance policy.*

Prima de seguro. *Insurance premium.*

Seguro de vida. *Life insurance.*

Seguro contra incendios. *Fire insurance.*

Tomar un seguro. *To take out an insurance policy.*

SEIS *adj. and n.* six.

seiscientos *adj. and n.* six hundred.

selección *f.* selection, choice, digest.

selecto *adj.* select; distinguished.

Había un público muy selecto. *There was a very distinguished audience.*

selva *f.* forest, woods, jungle.

sellar *to seal; to stamp.*

¿Es necesario sellar esta carta con lacre? *Is it necessary to use sealing wax on this letter?*

Selle Ud esas localidades. *Stamp those tickets.*

SELLO *m.* seal; stamp; postage stamp.

El sello se despegó. *The stamp came off.*

semáforo *m.* traffic signal.

SEMANA *f.* week; week's pay.

Voy al cine cada semana. *I go to the movies every week.*

Lo veremos la semana que viene. *We'll see him next week.*

Al parecer vendrá la semana próxima. *Apparently he's coming next week.*

La semana pasada. *Last week.*

En una semana más o menos. *In a week or so.*

Semana inglesa. *Five-day week.*

Semana Santa. *Holy Week (Easter).*

Un día entre semana. *A weekday.*

A la semana. *Per week.*

Hace una semana. *A week ago.*

semanal *adj.* weekly.

Una revista semanal. *A weekly magazine.*

semanalmente *weekly, by the week, every week.*

Esta revista sale semanalmente. *This magazine appears every week.*

semanario *adj.* weekly; *m.* weekly publication.

semblante *m.* countenance, look; aspect.

Hoy tiene Ud. muy buen semblante. *You look very well today.*

sembrar *to sow; to scatter, to spread.*

semejante *adj.* similar; such; *m.* fellow man.

¿Tiene Ud. algo semejante? *Do you have something (anything) similar?*

Los dos relatos son muy semejantes. *The two stories are very similar.*

No creo en semejante cosa. *I don't believe such a thing.*

Piense que son sus semejantes. *Remember that they are your fellow men.*

semejanza *f.* similarity, resemblance, likeness.

semejar *to resemble, to be like.*

semen *m.* semen, sperm, seed.

semestral *adj.* semi-annually.

semestre *m.* space of six months, half-year, semester; half-year's income or pension.

semi (*prefix*) semi, half, partially.

Semicircular. *Semicircular.*

Semibreve. *Semibreve.*

semilla *f.* seed.

seminario *m.* seminary.

seminarista *m.* seminarist.

sempiterno *adj.* everlasting.

senado *m.* senate.

senador *m.* senator

sencillez *f.* simplicity, lack of affection, plainness, candor.

Atraía por la sencillez de su carácter. *She attracted people by her lack of affection.*

Vestía con mucha sencillez. *She dressed very simply.*

SENCILLO *adj.* simple; plain; single.

Era un problema muy sencillo. *It was a very simple problem.*

Un vestido sencillo. *A plain dress.*

senda *f.* path, footpath.

sendero *m.* path, footpath.

senil *adj.* senile.

seno *m.* breast, bosom; lap; sinus; womb.

sensación *f.* sensation.

sensacional *adj.* sensational.

sensatez *f.* good sense, discretion.

sensato *adj.* sensible, discreet.

sensibilidad *f.* sensibility; sensitivity.

SENSIBLE *adj.* sensitive; regrettable; *f.* sensible.

Los ojos son sensibles a la luz. *The eyes are sensitive to light.*

Es una chica muy sensible. *She's a very sensitive girl.*

Un corazón sensible. *A tender heart.*

Una pérdida sensible. *A regrettable loss.*

sensual *adj.* sensual, voluptuous.

sensualidad *f.* sensuality, lust.

sentado *adj.* seated; judicious; sensible.

Estaba sentado a mi izquierda. *He was sitting on my left.*

Dar por sentado. *To take for granted.*

Puede esperar sentado. *You'll have to wait for it till doomsday.*

SENTAR *to fit, to be becoming; to agree with one (food, etc.); to seat.*

Este sombrero le sienta divinamente. *This hat fits you perfectly.*

¿No le ha sentado bien el desayuno? Didn't your breakfast agree with you?

Le sentará muy bien un descanso. A rest will do him good.

Sentar plaza. To enlist (as a soldier).

SENTARSE *to sit down, to take a seat.*

Sentémonos aquí. Let's sit down here.

¿Dónde me siento? Where shall I sit?

Siéntese Ud. en esta butaca. Sit down in this armchair.

Los invitados se sentaron a la mesa. The guests sat at the table.

sentencia *f. sentence, verdict; maxim.*

sentenciar *to sentence.*

sentencioso *adj. sententious.*

SENTIDO *adj. felt; experienced; offended; disgusted; touchy; m. sense; meaning; understanding; direction.*

Es muy sentida. She's very touchy.

Está sentida con ellos. She's disgusted with them.

Su muerte fue muy sentida. His death affected everyone deeply.

En el sentido de. In the sense of.

Sin sentido. Senseless. Meaningless.

Carece de lógica y de sentido común. It lacks logic and common sense.

No lo tome Ud. en ese sentido. Don't take it that way.

Caminaba en sentido contrario. He was walking in the opposite direction.

Pondré mis cinco sentidos al hacerlo. I'll put everything I've got into it.

Perder el sentido. To become unconscious.

sentimental *adj. sentimental, showing a great deal of feeling.*

Es muy sentimental. She's very sentimental.

sentimentalismo *m. sentimentalism.*

sentimiento *m. sentiment, feeling; grief; resentment.*

Era persona de malos sentimientos. He was a malicious person.

Le acompaño a Ud. en el sentimiento. I'm very sorry to hear about your loss.

SENTIR *to feel; to be sorry; to grieve; to hear; to sense; to be (happy, cold, warm, etc.); m. feeling; opinion.*

Lo siento muchísimo. I'm very sorry.

Siento no poder ir. I'm sorry I can't go.

Siento haberme retrasado tanto. I'm sorry to be so late.

Sentí en el alma la pérdida de tan fiel amigo. I felt very deeply the loss of such a faithful friend.

Ahora siento frío. I'm cold now.

Siento mucha alegría. I'm very happy (glad).

Pasaron las horas sin sentir. The hours passed without our knowing it.

Siento que viene alguien. I hear someone coming.

Díganos cuál es su sentir. Tell us how you feel (about it).

Es de sentir. It's to be regretted. It's regrettable.

Dar que sentir. To hurt one's feelings.

SENTIRSE *to resent; to feel (well, sick, sad, etc.); to ache; to crack (a wall, etc.).*

¿Se siente Ud. mejor? Do you feel better?

Me siento mal. I don't feel well.

¿Siente Ud. dolor en la espalda? Do you have a backache?

Se siente del pecho. His chest aches.

No tenía porque sentirse molesto. He has no reason to feel annoyed.

SEÑA *f. signal; sign, mark, password; pl. address.*

Escriba Ud. a estas señas. Write to this address.

No dejaron ni señas del pastel. They ate up every bit of the cake.

Hacer señas. To motion. To signal.

La policía me pidió sus señas personales. The police asked me for a description of him.

SEÑAL *f. sign, mark; signal; trace; scar; deposit (paid as a pledge); token.*

Esta es la mejor señal de mejoría. That's the best sign of improvement.

Ponga una señal en esa página. Mark that page.

La señal de alarma. The alarm signal.

Se daba a entender por señales. He made himself understood by signs.

¿Quiere Ud. que deje algún dinero en señal? Do you want me to leave you some money as a deposit?

Tiene una señal en la cara. He has a scar on his face.

En señal de. As a token of. In proof of.

Código de señales. Signal code.

señalado *adj. distinguished, noted; marked; appointed (time).*

Al (en el) tiempo señalado. At the appointed time.

señalar *to mark; to signal; to point out; to set (the date).*

Hay que señalar el día de la reunión. The date of the meeting must be set.

Señale Ud. los errores que encuentre. Point out the errors you find.

Señalar con el dedo. To point one's finger at.

SEÑOR *m. mister, sir; gentleman; master; lord.*

Señor Navarro. Mr. Navarro (used when addressing the person directly).

Buenos días, señor Navarro. *Good morning, Mr. Navarro.*

El señor Navarro no podrá venir. *Mr Navarro will not come (use the article el when speaking of the person).*

Muy señor mío. *Dear sir.*

El gusto es mío, señor. *The pleasure is mine, sir.*

Hay un señor esperándole. *There's a gentleman waiting for him.*

Los señores Sucre. *Mr. and Mrs. Sucre.*

SEÑORA f. *Mrs., madam, lady; wife.*

Señora de García. *Mrs. García (direct address).*

La señora de García. *Mrs. Garcia (use the article la when speaking of the person).*

La señora no está en casa. *The lady of the house is not at home.*

Sí, señora. *Yes, madam.*

Mucho gusto en conocer a Ud., señora. *I'm very happy (pleased) to know you, madam.*

Dele un silla a esta señora. *Give this lady a chair.*

¿Cómo está su señora? *How is your wife?*

SEÑORITA f. *miss; young lady.*

Mucho gusto en conocerla, señorita Navarro. *I'm very glad to meet you, Miss Navarro.*

Que pase la señorita Navarro. *Ask Miss Navarro to come in.*

Esta señorita es nórteamericana. *This young lady is an American.*

separación f. *separation.*

separar to *separate.*

Separe Ud. los grandes de los pequeños. *Separate the large ones from the small.*

Una cortina separa las dos habitaciones. *A curtain divides the two rooms.*

Separe Ud. un poco la mesa de la pared. *Move the table from the wall a bit.*

separarse to *part company; to get out of the way; to retire (from business, etc.).*

Decidieron separarse legalmente. *They decided to separate legally.*

SEPTIEMBRE m. *September.*

séptimo adj. *seventh.*

septuagenario adj. and n. *septuagenarian.*

sepulcro m. *grave, tomb, sepulcher.*

sepultar to *bury, to inter; to hide.*

sepultura f. *burial; grave; tomb.*

sequedad f. *dryness.*

sequía f. *drought, lack of rain.*

séquito m. *entourage.*

ser m. *being, creature.*

Ser viviente. *Living being. Living creature.*

Seres humanos. *Human beings.*

SER to *be.*

¿Quién es? *Who is it?*

Soy yo. *It's me (I).*

¿Quién será? *Who can it be?*

¿Es Ud. el Sr. Smith? *Are you Mr. Smith?*

¿De dónde es Ud.? *Where are you from?*

Soy de Boston. *I'm from Boston.*

Somos norteamericanos. *We're Americans.*

Somos viejos amigos. *We are old friends.*

¿Qué será de él? *What will become of him?*

¿En qué puedo serle útil? *What can I do for you? Can I help you?*

¿De quién es este lápiz? *Whose pencil is this?*

Es mío. *It's mine.*

Es de Juan. *It belongs to John.*

¿De quién será esta casa? *Whose house can (could) this be?*

Es la casa de Juan. *It's John's house.*

¿De qué es esta maleta? *What is this suitcase made of?*

Es una maleta de cuero. *It's a leather suitcase. It's made of leather.*

¿Cómo es? *How is it?*

Es algo sordo. *He's rather hard of hearing.*

¿Es guapa la hija? *Is the daughter pretty?*

Es guapísima. *She's very pretty.*

¿Qué es Ud.? *What are you?*

Yo soy escritor. *I'm a writer.*

¿Qué es su hermano? *What does your brother do?*

Es médico. *He is a doctor.*

¿Qué es eso? *What is that?*

¿Cuánto es? *How much is it?*

¿Qué tal ha sido el viaje? *How was the trip?*

¿Qué hora es? *What time is it?*

Es la una. *It's one o'clock.*

Son las dos. *It's two o'clock.*

¿Qué hora será? *I wonder what time it is.*

Son más de las diez. *It's after ten o'clock.*

Es temprano todavía. *It's still early.*

¿Cuándo será la boda? *When will the wedding take place?*

¿Qué fecha es hoy? *What's the date today?*

¿Qué día es hoy? *What day is today?*

Hoy es lunes. *Today is Monday.*

Mañana será otro día. *Tomorrow is another day.*

Es fácil. *It's easy.*

Es difícil. *It's difficult.*

¿Es verdad? *Is it true?*

No es verdad. *It's not true.*

No creo que sea cierto. *I don't believe it's (that's) true.*

¿Será posible? *Would that be possible?*

Puede ser. *That may be. Maybe. Perhaps.*

Eso no puede ser. *That can't be.*

Después llegaron a ser buenos amigos. *Afterward they became good friends.*

Eso no era con Ud. *It wasn't meant for you.*

Haré por Ud. cuanto me sea posible. *I'll do as much as I can for you.*

¿Qué ha sido de su amigo? *What became of your friend?*

Sea Ud. puntual. *Be on time.*

No seas tonto. *Don't be foolish.*

No sea Ud. inoportuno. *Don't come at the wrong time (do things at the wrong time, say the wrong things).*

¡Sé bueno, hijo mío! *Be good, my child!*

Ha llegado a ser gerente. *He became manager.*

Sea quien fuera. *Whoever he might be.*

Son tal para cual. *They're two of a kind.*

serenamente *coolly, calmly.*

serenar *to clear up; to calm down; to pacify.*

serenata *f. serenade.*

serenidad *f. serenity, coolness.*

sereno *adj. serene, calm; clear (sky); m. dew; night watchman.*

Era un hombre sereno. *He was a calm man. He was very calm.*

El cielo está muy sereno. *The sky is very clear.*

Hay mucho sereno en las flores. *There's a lot of dew on the flowers.*

serie *f. series.*

Pertenece a la serie A. *It belongs to series A.*

seriedad *f. seriousness, reliability; earnestness.*

SERIO *adj. serious; earnest; businesslike.*

Es un hombre serio. *He's businesslike.*

La situación se pone seria. *The situation is becoming serious.*

Lo dijo en serio. *He said it in earnest.*

Hablando en serio, eso no está bien. *Joking apart, that's wrong.*

Tomar en serio. *To take seriously.*

sermón *m. sermon; lecture, reproof.*

serpiente *f. serpent.*

serrano *m. mountaineer.*

serrar *to saw.*

serrucho *m. saw.*

servicial *adj. serviceable; obliging, accommodating.*

SERVICIO *m. service, favor, good turn; set, service.*

Servicio de mesa. *Table service.*

Me ha prestado Ud. un gran servicio. *You've done me a great favor.*

Ud. podría hacerme un gran servicio. *You could do me a great favor.*

Se quejó del servicio en el hotel. *He complained about the service in the hotel.*

El servicio de trenes es muy malo aquí. *The train service is very bad here.*

Es muy difícil conseguir servicio doméstico. *It's very difficult to get any domestic help.*

Tenemos que tomar en cuenta sus buenos servicios. *We must take into consideration the work he did.*

De servicio. *On duty.*

Estar a servicio de. *To be working for.*

servidor *m. servant, waiter.*

¡Servidor de Ud.! *At your service.*

"Quedo de Ud. atento y seguro servidor." *"Sincerely yours."*

servidumbre *f. servants, help; slavery.*

servil *adj. servile, low, mean.*

servilleta *f. napkin.*

SERVIR *to serve; to do a favor; to do for, to be useful, to answer the purpose; to be for; to wait on (the table).*

Para servir a Ud. *At your service.*

¿En qué puedo servirle? *What can I do for you? Can I help you?*

¿Le sirvo a Ud. un poco de vino? *Shall I give (serve) you a little wine?*

Permítame servirle otra taza de café. *Let me give you another cup of coffee.*

La comida está servida. *Dinner is served.*

El camarero sirvió a la mesa. *The waiter waited on the table.*

¿Para qué sirve esta máquina? *What's this machine for?*

Sirvió cuatro años en las fuerzas aéreas. *He was in the Air Corps for four years.*

No lo tire, que puede servir para algo. *Don't throw it away! It may be good for something.*

No sirve. *It's no good.*

Él puede servir de intérprete. *He can act as interpreter.*

De nada le servirá escribirles. *Writing to them won't do you any good.*

servirse *to deign, to please; to help oneself (food); to make use of.*

Sírvase venir conmigo. *Please come with me.*

Tenga la bondad de servirse. *Please help yourself.*

Me sirvo del diccionario para traducir. *I use the dictionary for translating.*

SESENTA *adj. and n. sixty.*

sesentón *m. sexagenarian.*

sesgo *adj. sloped, oblique; m. slope; slant, bias.*

Tomar mal sesgo. *To take a bad turn. To take a turn for the worse.*

sesión *f. session, meeting, showing.*

En sesión. *In session.*

SESO *m. brain; brains.*

Devanarse los sesos. *To rack one's brains.*

Perder el seso. *To lose one's head.*

No tiene seso. *He has no brains (coll.).*

setecientos *adj. and n. seven hundred.*

SETENTA *adj. and n. seventy.*

setentón *m. septuagenarian.*

seudónimo *adj. relating to a pseudonym; m. pseudonym; pen name.*

severidad *f. severity, strictness.*

severo *adj. severe, strict.*

sexo *m. sex.*

sexual *adj. sexual.*

sexteto *m. sextet, sextette.*

sexto *adj. sixth.*

short *m. Bermuda shorts.*

show *m. show (variety, musical).*

SI *conj. if; whether.*

Si Ud. quiere. *If you like.*

Si Ud. gusta. *If you please.*

Si tuviese dinero, lo compraría. *I'd buy it if I had money.*

Si le parece nos citamos para las cuatro. *Let's meet at four o'clock if that's convenient for you.*

Si bien. *Although.*

Si por acaso. *If by any chance. In case.*

¡Si lo acabo de ver! *But I just saw it!*

Si no. *If not. Otherwise.*

SÍ *adv. yes; indeed; refl. pron. himself, herself, itself, oneself, themselves; m. consent, assent.*

Sí señor. *Yes, sir.*

Pues sí. *Yes, indeed.*

¿Sí o no? *Yes or no?*

Le dije que sí. *I told him yes.*

Eso sí que no. *I should say not.*

Creo que sí. *I think so.*

Espero que sí. *I hope so.*

Habla demasiado de sí misma. *She talks too much about herself.*

Lo quiere para sí. *He wants it for himself.*

Todavía no ha vuelto en sí. *He hasn't recovered consciousness yet.*

Estaban fuera de sí. *They were beside themselves (with anger, etc.).*

Reírse entre sí. *To laugh up one's sleeve.*

¿A que sí? *I'll bet I do.*

De sí. *Spontaneously. Of itself (himself, etc.).*

Lo dijo de sí. *He said it spontaneously (of his own accord).*

Dar el sí. *To say yes. To give one's consent. To accept a marriage proposal.*

SIDA *m. AIDS*

siderurgia *f. iron and steel industry.*

sidra *f. alcoholic cider.*

siega *f. harvest.*

siembra *f. sowing; seedtime; sown ground.*

SIEMPRE *always; ever.*

Siempre llega tarde. *He's always late.*

Es lo de siempre. *It's the same old story.*

Siempre que pueda le escribiré. *I'll write you provided I'm able.*

Para siempre. *For good. Forever.*

Para siempre jamás. *Forever (and ever).*

siempreviva *f. everlasting, immortelle (plant).*

sien *f. temple.*

sierra *f. saw; sierra, mountain range.*

No corta bien la sierra. *The saw doesn't cut well.*

La Sierra Madre está en México. *Sierra Madre is in Mexico.*

siesta *f. siesta, nap.*

¿Va Ud. a dormir la siesta? *Are you going to take your nap?*

SIETE *adj. and n. seven.*

sigilo *m. seal, secrecy; discretion; caution.*

Obra con sigilo. *He acts cautiously.*

sigiloso *adj. secretive; reserved.*

SIGLO *m. century, age; a long time.*

Vivió en el siglo décimo. *He lived in the tenth century.*

Hace un siglo que no le veo. *I haven't seen him for ages.*

El Siglo de Oro. *The Golden Age.*

significación *f. signification; significance, meaning.*

significado *m. significance; meaning.*

¿Cuál es el significado de esta palabra en inglés? *What does that word mean in English?*

SIGNIFICAR *to mean, to signify.*

¿Qué significa eso? *What's the meaning of that? What does that mean?*

No sé qué significa esa palabra. *I don't know the meaning of that word.*

significativo *adj. significant.*

signo *m. sign, mark.*

El signo de la cruz. *The sign of the cross.*

SIGUIENTE *adj. following, next.*

Al día siguiente. *On the following day. On the next day.*

La página siguiente. *The next page.*

La aduana está en la siguiente cuadra. *The customshouse is on the next block.*

Lo siguiente. *The following.*

sílaba *f. syllable.*

silbar *to whistle; to hiss, to boo.*

El público silbó la comedia. *The audience booed the comedy. (Whistling indicates disapproval in Spanish-speaking countries.)*

silbido *m. whistling, whistle; hiss.*

silencio *m. silence; quiet.*

¡Silencio! *Silence!*

Todo estaba en silencio. *Everything was quiet.*

Su silencio me inquieta. *I'm worried because I haven't had any word from her.*

Eso lo pasó Ud. en silencio. *You avoided mentioning that.*

Sufrir en silencio. *To suffer in silence.*

silencioso *adj. silent, noiseless.*

silueta *f. silhouette.*

silvestre *adj. wild, rustic, uncultivated.*

Flores silvestres. *Wild flowers.*

SILLA *f. chair; saddle.*

Ponga la silla aquí. *Put the chair here.*

Silla de ruedas. *Wheelchair.*

sillón *m. armchair.*

simbólico *adj. symbolic.*

simbolizar *to symbolize.*

símbolo *m. symbol.*

simetría *f. symmetry.*

simétrico *adj. symmetrical.*

SIMILAR *adj. similar, resembling. (See parecido.)*

Es un producto similar. *This is a similar product.*

similitud *f. resemblance, similarity, similitude.*

simpatía *f. sympathy, liking.*

Le inspiró mucha simpatía. *He found him (her) very congenial.*

simpático *adj. nice, pleasant, congenial, nice.*

Es muy simpático. *He's very nice.*

simpatizar *to sympathize; to like.*

SIMPLE *adj. simple; plain; silly, foolish; m. fool.*

Por la simple razón. *For the simple reason.*

A simple vista. *At first sight.*

El procedimiento es muy simple. *The system is very simple.*

Es una mujer muy simple. *She's a very simple woman.*

A un simple cualquiera le engaña. *Anyone can cheat a fool.*

simplemente *simply, merely.*

Eso es simplemente un detalle. *That's simply a detail.*

simpleza *f. naiveté, foolishness.*

simplicidad *f. simplicity.*

simplificar *to simplify.*

simulación *f. simulation; fake.*

simulacro *m. sham, feign.*

simulado *adj. simulated, sham.*

simular *to simulate, to feign, to sham.*

simultáneo *adj. simultaneous.*

SIN *without, besides.*

Iremos sin él. *We'll go without him.*

No puedo leer sin mis anteojos. *I can't read without my glasses.*

Lo hice sin pensar. *I did it without thinking.*

Lo hice sin querer. *I didn't mean to do it.*

Estaba sin dinero. *He was penniless.*

Es un hombre sin educación. *He's ill-bred.*

Es una mujer sin par. *She's in a class by herself. There's no one like her.*

Me he quedado sin gasolina. *I've run out of gas.*

Sin falta. *Without fail.*

Sin duda. *Without a doubt. Undoubtedly.*

Sin novedad. *Nothing new. The same as usual.*

Sin embargo. *Nevertheless. Notwithstanding.*

sinceridad *f. sincerity.*

sincero *adj. sincere.*

Es un amigo sincero. *He's a true friend.*

síncope *f. faint, fainting spell.*

Síncope cardíaco. *Heart attack.*

sincronizar *to synchronize.*

sindical *adj. pertaining to a trade union.*

sindicato *m. trade union; syndicate.*

síndrome *m. syndrome.*

Síndrome de inmunodeficiencia adquirida. *AIDS.*

sinfín *m. an endless number.*

Tengo un sinfín de cosas para hacer. *I have a million and one things to do.*

sinfonía *f. symphony.*

sinfónico *adj. symphonic.*

SINGULAR *adj. singular; unusual; exceptional; strange, odd.*

"Niño" es singular, y "niños" es plural. *"Boy" is singular, "boys" plural.*

¡Qué caso tan singular! *What a strange case!*

Es un hombre singular. *He's an exceptional man.*

Es un caso singularísimo. *It's a very singular (unusual) case.*

singularidad *f. singularity; peculiarity.*

siniestro *adj. sinister; unfortunate; m. disaster, damage.*

Lado siniestro. *Left side.*

Tiene un aspecto siniestro. *It has a sinister look.*

¿Dónde ocurrió el siniestro? *Where did the disaster occur?*

sinnúmero *m. a great many, too many, numberless, no end.*

SINO *(used after a negative) but, except; only; instead; m. fate, luck.*

No es rojo sino rosado. *It's not red, but pink.*

No iré hoy, sino mañana. *I'll go tomorrow instead of today.*

Nadie puede hacerlo sino tú. *No one but you can do it.*

No sólo nos llamó, sino también nos visitó.

She not only called us, but she also
visited us.

Es su triste sino. *It's his hard luck.*

sinónimo *adj. synonymous; m. synonym.*

sintaxis *f. syntax.*

síntesis *f. synthesis.*

sintético *adj. synthetic.*

sintetizador *m. synthesizer.*

sintetizar *to synthesize.*

síntoma *f. symptom.*

sintonizador *m. tuner.*

sintonizar *to tune in* (radio).

sinvergüenza *m. and f. shameless person.*

SIQUIERA *at least; even; although.*

Ni siquiera eso. *Not even that.*

Una vez siquiera. *Once at least.*

Deme siquiera agua fría. *At least give me
some cold water.*

Ni me dio las gracias siquiera. *He didn't
even thank me.*

sirena *f. siren; whistle; foghorn; mermaid.*

sirviente *m. servant.*

sisear *to boo.*

sismo *m. earthquake.*

sistema *m. system.*

Sistema métrico. *Metric system.*

Sistema operativo. *Operating system.*

sistemático *adj. systematic.*

sitiar *to besiege.*

SITIO *m. place; space; room; m. siege.*

Ponlo otra vez en su sitio. *Put it back in
the same place.*

No hay bastante sitio para todos. *There
isn't enough room for everybody.*

Ocupe Ud. su sitio. *Take your seat.*

Me ofreció un sitio en su coche. *He offered
me a lift in his car.*

Está en algún sitio en la casa. *It's
somewhere around the house.*

¿En qué sitio le duele? *Where does it hurt
you?*

Hacer sitio. *To make room.*

Poner sitio. *To besiege.*

SITUACIÓN *f. situation; position;
circumstances; site, location.*

Está en mala situación. *He's in a bad
situation.*

situado *adj. situated, located; m. allowance,
annuity.*

situar *to place, to locate; to situate; to allot
funds.*

situarse *to place oneself, to settle in a place.*

smoking *m. tuxedo.*

so *under, below.*

So (capa) pretexto de. *Under the pretext
of.*

So pena de. *Under penalty of.*

sobar *to knead; to soften; to pummel; to pet;
to beat, to whip.*

soberanía *f. sovereignty.*

soberano *adj. and n. sovereign.*

soberbia *f. pride, haughtiness.*

soberbio *adj. proud, haughty; ill-tempered;
superb; magnificent.*

Un edificio soberbio. *A magnificent
building.*

Es muy soberbio. *He's very proud.*

sobornar *to suborn, to bribe.*

soborno *m. bribe.*

SOBRA *f. too much, too many, more than is
needed; leftover.*

Tengo tiempo de sobra. *I've plenty of time.*

Tengo de sobra con lo que Ud. me dio.
*I've more than enough with what you
gave me.*

Estar de sobra. *To be superfluous.*

Tiene Ud. razón de sobra. *You're quite
right.*

Hay de sobra. *There's more than enough.*

Aproveche las sobras. *Use up the leftovers.*

sobradamente *abundantly.*

Saber sobradamente. *To know only too
well.*

sobrante *adj. remaining; m. remainder,
surplus; leftover.*

SOBRAR *to be more than enough; to have
more than is needed; to remain; to be
left.*

Sobró mucha comida. *A great deal of food
was left over.*

Nos sobran poquísimas provisiones. *We've
got very few supplies* (provisions) *left.*

Me parece que aquí sobro. *It seems to me
that I'm intruding here.*

Sobran cinco. *There are five too many.*

SOBRE *on; over; above; about; m. envelope.*

Ponga el vaso sobre la mesa. *Put the glass
on the table.*

Desgracia sobre desgracia. *Misfortune on
misfortune. Trouble after trouble. Just
one thing after another.*

¿Qué opina Ud. sobre esto? *What do you
think about this?*

Ha escrito un libro sobre los Estados
Unidos. *He has written a book about
the United States.*

Discurramos un poco más sobre esto. *Let's
consider that a little longer.*

Tenía un gran dominio sobre sí. *He had
great self-control.*

Sobre las tres. *At about three o'clock.*

Tengo sobre cincuenta dólares. *I have
about fifty dollars.*

Estar sobre aviso. *To be on guard.*

Sobre todo. *Above all.*

Sobre que. *Besides.*

Deme un sobre. *Give me an envelope.*

sobrealimentar *to overfeed.*

sobrecarga *f. overload; overcharge.*

sobrecargar *to overload; to overcharge.*

sobrecargo *m. purser; supercargo (on a ship).*

sobreceño *m. frown.*

sobrecoger *to surprise, to take by surprise.*

sobreentenderse *to be understood, to go without saying.*

Eso se sobreentiende. *That's understood. That goes without saying.*

sobrehumano *adj. superhuman.*

sobrellenar *to overfill.*

sobrellevar *to shoulder, to ease (another's burden); to bear; to endure.*

Él es el que sobrelleva toda la carga. *He's the one who shoulders the whole burden.*

Sobrelleva sus penas con paciencia. *He endures his difficulties (troubles) patiently.*

sobremanera *excessively, exceedingly.*

sobremesa *f. table cover; dessert; after dinner; after-dinner talk (around the table).*

Después de comer, fuma su cigarro de sobremesa. *After eating he smokes his after-dinner cigar.*

Estuvimos cerca de una hora de sobremesa. *After dinner we sat around the table and talked for about an hour.*

sobrenatural *adj. and m. supernatural.*

sobrepasar *to exceed, to surpass.*

sobreponer *to place over; to overlay; to overlap.*

sobreponerse *to master, to overcome; to prevail on another; to show (prove) oneself superior to.*

sobresaliente *adj. outstanding; excelling.*

sobresalir *to stand out, to excel.*

sobresaltar *to frighten, to startle; to assail, to fall upon.*

sobresaltarse *to be frightened, to be startled.*

Se sobresalta por la menor cosa. *She gets frightened at the least (little) thing.*

sobresalto *m. start, shock.*

sobrestimar *to overestimate.*

sobresueldo *m. extra pay; bonus.*

sobrevenir *to happen, to take place unexpectedly.*

Sobrevino algo inesperado. *Something unexpected happened.*

sobrevivir *to survive.*

sobriedad *f. sobriety, temperance, moderation.*

sobrina *f. niece.*

sobrino *m. nephew.*

sobrio *adj. sober, temperate.*

sociable *adj. sociable.*

social *adj. social.*

Tenía muy buen trato social. *He was very agreeable socially.*

Movimiento social. *Social movement.*

¿Quién representa a esta razón social? *Who's the representative of this firm?*

socialismo *m. socialism.*

socialista *adj. socialistic; m. socialist.*

socializar *to socialize.*

sociedad *f. society; social life; company, corporation; partnership.*

Le gustaba frecuentar la buena sociedad. *He liked to move in society.*

Formaron una sociedad. *They formed a partnership.*

Sociedad anónima. *Corporation.*

socio *m. partner, associate; fellow member.*

Le presento a mi socio, Sr. Gilsanz, *Meet my partner, Mr. Gilsanz.*

¿Es Ud. socio de ese club? *Are you a member of that club?*

sociología *f. sociology.*

sociólogo *m. sociologist.*

socorrer *to aid, to help, to assist; to rescue.*

Hay que socorrerlo. *We have to help him.*

socorro *m. succor, aid, help.*

Primeros socorros. *First aid.*

soda *f. soda.*

soez *adj. indecent, obscene; vulgar, rude.*

sofá *m. sofa.*

sofocante *adj. suffocating.*

sofocar *to suffocate, to stifle, to choke; to vex; to make a person blush; to put out (fire).*

El calor le ha sofocado. *He was suffocated by the heat.*

No se sofoque Ud. *Don't get excited.*

Sofocar el fuego. *To put out a fire.*

Sofocar una rebelión. *To crush (subdue) a rebellion.*

software *m. software (computer).*

soga *f. rope; halter, cord.*

SOL *m. sun, sunshine; Peruvian currency unit.*

Hace sol. *The sun's shining. The sun's out.*

Vamos a tomar sol. *Let's go get some sun.*

Antes de bañarse estuvieron tomando sol mucho rato. *They took a long sunbath before bathing.*

Salida del sol. *Sunrise.*

Puesta del sol. *Sunset.*

De sol a sol. *From sunrise to sunset.*

SOLAMENTE *solely, only.*

Aprendí solamente un poco de español. *I learned only a little Spanish.*

Deme Ud. solamente la mitad. *Give me just half.*

solapa *f. lapel; flap.*

solar *m. lot, plot (land); real estate; mansion.*

solas (a) *all alone, by oneself.*
A mis solas. *By myself. All alone.*
A sus solas. *By himself (herself). All alone.*
SOLDADO *m. soldier, private.*
Soldado raso. *Buck private.*
soldar *to solder; to weld.*
Todavía no han soldado la cañería. *They haven't soldered the pipe yet.*
soledad *f. solitude, loneliness.*
solemne *adj. solemn; serious, grave.*
solemnidad *f. solemnity.*
Pobre de solemnidad. *Very poor.*
SOLER *to be unusual, to be accustomed to, to be in the habit of.*
Suele comer despacio. *He usually eats slowly.*
Suele venir los domingos. *He usually comes on Sundays.*
Como suele acontecer. *As often happens. As is apt to be the case.*
solfear *to sing the scale (music).*
SOLICITAR *to solicit; to ask; to apply for.*
Solicita un empleo. *She's applying for a position.*
Hay que solicitar un permiso para visitar ese edificio. *You'll have to ask for a pass to visit that building.*
Solicitó su mano. *He proposed to her.*
solicitud *f. application; request.*
Llene Ud. el pliego de la solicitud. *Fill out the application.*
solidaridad *f. solidarity.*
solidario *adj. jointly responsible.*
solidez *f. solidity, firmness, soundness.*
SÓLIDO *adj. solid, sound, strong, firm; m. solid.*
Tiene una base muy sólida. *It has a very solid base.*
Cuerpo sólido. *Solid substance.*
Tiene una educación sólida. *He has a sound education.*
solitario *adj. solitary, lonely; m. solitary; hermit; solitaire (game).*
SOLO *adj. alone; single; m. solo (music).*
¿Está Ud. solo? *Are you alone?*
Ni una sola palabra. *Not a single word.*
Vive solo. *He lives alone.*
Estoy muy solo. *I'm very lonely.*
No lo puedo hacer yo solo. *I can't do this all alone (by myself).*
SÓLO *adv. only, solely.*
Sólo tengo dos pesos. *I have only two dollars.*
Sólo para adultos. *Adults only.*
Hace sólo un rato que almorcé. *I had breakfast only a little while ago.*
Sólo Dios sabe lo que pasará. *(Only) God knows what will happen.*

SOLTAR *to loosen; to set free; to let out; to let go.*
Soltaron al preso. *They set the prisoner free.*
¡No lo suelte Ud.! *Hold it! Don't let go!*
Soltaron las amarras. *They loosened the cables.*
De repente soltó una carcajada. *Suddenly he burst into laughter (burst out laughing).*
soltarse *to get loose; to become wild; to lose restraint, to become more dexterous; to start.*
Se soltó a correr. *He started to run.*
Soltarse el pelo. *To let one's hair down.*
soltero *adj. single, unmarried; m. bachelor.*
¿Es Ud. casado o soltero? *Are you single or married?*
Todavía soy soltero. *I'm still a bachelor.*
solterón *m. old bachelor.*
solterona *f. old maid.*
soltura *f. ease; ability; agility; release; looseness.*
Bailaba con mucha soltura. *She danced with great ease (gracefully).*
Hablar con soltura. *To speak freely.*
soluble *adj. soluble; solvable.*
SOLUCIÓN *f. solution, answer, way out; denouement, outcome (of a plot in a play, story, etc.).*
Esto no tiene solución. *There's no solution to this.*
¿Dónde encontraré la solución? *Where can I find the answer?*
Ésa es la mejor solución. *That's the best way out. That's the best solution.*
solvencia *f. solvency.*
solvente *adj. solvent.*
sollozar *to sob.*
sollozo *m. sob.*
SOMBRA *f. shade; shadow; darkness.*
El termómetro marca treinta grados a la sombra. *The thermometer registers thirty degrees in the shade.*
Se sentó a descansar a la sombra de un árbol. *He sat down to rest in the shade of the tree.*
Le pusieron a la sombra. *They imprisoned him.*
sombrerería *f. hat shop; millinery.*
SOMBRERO *m. hat.*
Se puso el sombrero y salió. *He put on his hat and left.*
Quítese Ud. el sombrero al entrar. *Take off your hat on entering (when you enter).*
sombrilla *f. parasol.*
sombrío *adj. shady; gloomy.*

Tenía un aspecto muy sombrío. *He had a very gloomy appearance.*

someter *to suspect; to subdue; to put (to a test); to submit.*

Fue difícil someter a los rebeldes. *It was difficult to subdue the rebels.*

Someta Ud. esto a nuevo estudio. *Give it further study.*

SON *m. sound, tune; guise; a Cuban musical rhythm.*

¿A son de qué? *Why? For what reason?*

En son de. *In the guise of. As.*

En son de broma. *In the guise of. As.*

En son de broma. *As a joke.*

Sin son ni ton. *Without rhyme or reason.*

Bailar uno al son que le tocan. *To adapt oneself to the circumstances.*

sonajero *m. rattle.*

sonámbulo *m. sleepwalker.*

SONAR *to sound; to ring; to be mentioned, to sound familiar.*

Esa nota no me suena bien. *That note doesn't sound right.*

Suena el timbre. *The bell's ringing.*

Ese nombre no me suena. *That name doesn't sound familiar to me.*

Suena mucho su nombre para candidato. *His name is often mentioned as a candidate.*

Sonó un disparo. *There was the sound of a shot.*

sonarse *to blow one's nose.*

sonata *f. sonata.*

sondar (*See* **sondear**).

sondear *to sound, to fathom; to find out, to learn about, to explore.*

Estuvieron sondeando la bahía. *They were sounding the bay.*

Sondee Ud. sus intenciones. *Find out his intentions. Sound him out.*

soneto *m. sonnet.*

sonido *m. sound.*

sonoridad *f. sonority.*

sonoro *adj. sonorous; sounding.*

Tiene una voz muy sonora. *He has a sonorous voice.*

Una película sonora (*hablada*). *A talking picture.*

sonreír *to smile.*

Todos sonrieron satisfechos. *Everyone smiled with satisfaction.*

sonrisa *f. smile.*

Una amable sonrisa. *A pleasant smile.*

sonrojar *to make one blush.*

sonrojarse *to blush.*

Se sonroja por nada. *She blushes at the least little thing.*

soñador *m. dreamer.*

SOÑAR *to dream.*

No debería Ud. soñar con tales cosas. *You shouldn't even dream of such things.*

Vive soñando. *His head's in the clouds.*

soñoliento *adj. sleepy, drowsy.*

SOPA *f. soup.*

¿Le sirvo un poco de sopa? *Shall I serve you some soup?*

Estoy hecho una sopa. *I'm soaked to the skin.*

sopapo *m. a blow under the chin, uppercut; slap.*

sopera *f. soup tureen.*

sopetón *m. blow; toasted bread dipped in oil.*

Se presentó de sopetón. *Suddenly he appeared.*

soplar *to blow; to inflate; to steal, to rob.*

Soplaba un viento suave. *A very gentle wind was blowing.*

Le soplaron el reloj. *They stole his watch.*

soplo *m. blowing; puff (of wind); hint; denunciation*

soplón *m. stoolpigeon.*

sopor *m. stupor; drowsiness.*

soportar *to stand, to endure, to bear.*

Ha soportado muchas penas. *He endured many hardships.*

No puedo soportarlo por más tiempo. *I can't stand it any longer.*

soprano *m. soprano.*

sorber *to sip; to suck; to absorb; to swallow.*

sorbete *m. sherbet.*

sorbo *m. sip, draught, gulp.*

Tómeselo a sorbos. *Sip it.*

sordera *f. deafness.*

SORDO *adj. deaf; not able to hear; not willing to hear; muffled; silent; m. a deaf person.*

Sordo como una tapia. *As deaf as a post.*

Ser sordo a. *To be deaf to.*

sordomudo *adj. and n. deaf and dumb; deaf-mute.*

SORPRENDER *to surprise; to take by surprise.*

No se sorprenda Ud. por eso. *Don't be surprised at that.*

Su llegada nos sorprendió a todos. *His arrival surprised everybody.*

SORPRESA *f. surprise.*

Es una verdadera sorpresa. *This is a real surprise.*

Me ha cogido de sorpresa. *It has taken (it took) me by surprise.*

sortear *to draw lots; to raffle; to avoid, to evade, to dodge.*

sorteo *m. lottery, raffle.*

sortija *f. ring; lock of hair.*

sosa *f. soda (chemical).*

Sosa cáustica. *Caustic soda.*

sosegado *adj. calm, quiet.*

sosegar *to appease, to calm; to rest.*

sosegarse *to calm down; to be quiet.*

Cuando Ud. se sosiegue, hablaremos. *We'll talk it over when you calm down.*

sosiego *m. peace, calmness, quiet.*

No tenía un minuto de sosiego. *He didn't have a moment's peace.*

soslayo *m. slant, askance.*

Mirar de soslayo. *To look askance. To look out of the corner of one's eye.*

soso *adj. insipid, tasteless; uninteresting; simple, homely.*

La comida está sosa. *The food is tasteless.*

Es una chica sosa. *She's an uninteresting girl.*

sospecha *f. suspicion.*

Eso da motivos de sospecha. *That gives ground for suspicion.*

sospechar *to suspect, to have a suspicion.*

Sospecho de él. *I'm suspicious of him. I suspect him.*

sospechoso *adj. suspicious; suspecting.*

Es un individuo sospechoso. *He's a suspicious character.*

sostén *m. support, prop.*

SOSTENER *to support, to sustain; to maintain; to hold; to carry (a conversation).*

Sostenía a su familia. *He supported his family.*

Ahora podemos sostener una conversación en español. *We can now carry on a conversation in Spanish.*

Lo digo y lo sostengo. *I'll stand by what I'm saying.*

sostenerse *to support oneself, to keep up, to hold out.*

Estaba tan borracho que no podía sostenerse. *He was so drunk, he couldn't stand up.*

sostenido *adj. sustained; m. sharp (music).*

sostenimiento *m. support, maintenance; upkeep.*

sotana *f. cassock.*

sótano *m. cellar.*

soya or **soja** *f. soy; soy bean. (Also* **soja**.)

SU *pron. his, her, its, their, your; pl.* **sus**.

Su libro. *His book.*

Sus libros. *His books.*

Su hermana. *His sister.*

Sus hermanas. *His sisters.*

Su novio. *Her fiancé.*

¿Dónde están sus hijos?—Están con sus abuelos. *Where are your children?—They're with their grandparents.*

Este procedimiento tiene sus ventajas y desventajas. *This procedure has its advantages and disadvantages.*

SUAVE *adj. soft, smooth, mild, gentle, mellow.*

Esta tela es muy suave. *This cloth is very soft.*

Es un vino suave. *This wine is very mellow.*

Tabaco suave. *Mild tobacco.*

suavemente *smoothly, softly, mildly; gently, sweetly.*

suavidad *f. softness; suavity.*

suavizar *to soften; to make smooth.*

subalterno *adj. and n. subaltern, subordinate.*

subarrendar *to sublet.*

subasta *f. auction.*

subconsciencia *f. subconscious, subconsciousness.*

subconsciente *adj and n. subconscious.*

subdesarrollado *adj. underdeveloped.*

País subdesarrollado. *Underdeveloped country.*

subdirector *m. assistant director.*

súbdito *m. subject (of a king, etc.); citizen.*

subdivisión *f. subdivision.*

subido *adj. bright, loud, deep (color); high (price).*

Es de un color muy subido. *It's a loud color.*

Es algo subido el precio. *The price is a little high.*

SUBIR *to go up, to walk up; to ascend, to rise; to climb; to mount; to come up; to take up; to bring up; to get on; to raise.*

Suba Ud. a mi cuarto. *Go up to my room.*

Subamos. 1. *Let's go up.* 2. *Let's get on (train, bus, etc.).*

Suban Uds. un piso más. *Walk up another flight.*

Oigo subir a alguien. *I hear someone coming upstairs.*

Me tienes que ayudar a subir el baúl. *You must help me bring the trunk up.*

El mozo le subirá la maleta al tren. *The porter will put your suitcase on the train.*

Subió a lo alto del árbol. *He climbed to the top of the tree.*

El globo subió hasta diez mil pies. *The balloon rose to ten thousand feet.*

Le subió la temperatura. *His temperature rose.*

Los precios suben cada vez más. *Prices are constantly going up (rising).*

Tendrá Ud. que subir un poco la voz, es muy sordo. *You'll have to raise your voice a little; he's very deaf.*

Ha subido muy de prisa ese muchacho. *That boy has made rapid progress.*

¿A cuánto sube la cuenta? *How much is the bill?*

Subir a caballo. *To mount a horse.*

Se le subieron los tragos a la cabeza. *The drinks went to his head.*

SÚBITAMENTE *suddenly.*

SÚBITO *adj. sudden.*

De súbito. *Suddenly. All of a sudden.*

subjefe *m. second in command; chief assistant.*

subjetividad *f. subjectivity.*

subjetivo *adj. subjective.*

subjuntivo *m. subjunctive.*

sublevación *f. insurrection, uprising.*

sublevar *to stir up, to excite to rebellion.*

sublevarse *to revolt.*

sublime *adj. sublime.*

submarino *adj. and n. submarine.*

subordinado *adj. subordinate.*

subordinar *to subordinate.*

subrayar *to underline, to emphasize.*

subsanar *to rectify, to make right, to repair, to make up; to excuse.*

Subsanar un error. *To rectify an error.*

subscribir *to subscribe.*

subscribirse *to subscribe to.*

¿Quiere Ud. subscribirse a esta revista? *Would you like to subscribe to this magazine?*

subscripción *f. subscription.*

subscriptor *m. subscriber.*

subsecretario *m. under secretary; assistant secretary.*

subsecuente *adj. subsequent.*

subsidio *m. subsidy, aid.*

subsistencia *f. subsistence.*

subsistir *to subsist; to exist; to last.*

substancia *f. substance; essence.*

En substancia. 1. *In substance.* 2. *In short. In brief.*

substancial *adj. substantial.*

substanciar *to substantiate.*

substancioso *adj. juicy; nourishing; substantial.*

substantivo *adj. substantive; m. substantive.*

substitución *f. substitution.*

substituir *to substitute.*

substituto *m. substitute.*

substracción *f. subtraction.*

substraer *to subtract.*

subte *m. subway (Arg.).*

subterráneo *adj. subterranean, underground; m. subway (Amer.).*

subtítulo *m. subtitle.*

suburbio *m. suburb.*

subvención *f. subsidy.*

subvencionar *to subsidize.*

subyugar *to subdue, to subjugate.*

SUCEDER *to happen; to succeed; to inherit.*

¿Qué sucedió después? *What happened then (next)?*

¿Qué le ha sucedido? *What happened to you?*

Suceda lo que suceda, yo estaré aquí. *No matter what happens, I'll be here.*

Se cree que su hijo le sucederá. *It's thought that his son will succeed him.*

sucesión *f. succession; estate, inheritance; offspring.*

sucesivamente *successively.*

sucesivo *adj. successive.*

En lo sucesivo. *In the future. Hereafter.*

suceso *m. event; incident.*

Sucesos de actualidad. *Current events. News of the day.*

sucesor *m. successor.*

suciedad. *f. dirt, filth.*

sucio *adj. dirty, filthy, nasty.*

Una jugada sucia. *A dirty trick.*

Palabras sucias. *Nasty (dirty) words.*

sucre *m. Ecuadoran monetary unit.*

sucumbir *to die; to succumb; to give way, to yield.*

sucursal *adj. subsidiary; m. branch, annex.*

sud *m. south. (See sur.)*

sudar *to sweat, to perspire; to toil.*

sudeste *m. southeast.*

sudoeste *m. southwest.*

sudor *m. sweat, perspiration, toil, hard work.*

suegra *f. mother-in-law.*

suegro *m. father-in-law.*

suela *f. sole (of shoe); sole leather.*

sueldo *f. salary.*

SUELO *m. soil; ground; floor.*

Levanta ese papel del suelo. *Pick up that paper from the floor.*

El suelo está resbaladizo (resbaloso). *The pavement is slippery.*

Este suelo produce mucho. *This land is very fertile.*

Estar por los suelos. *To be very cheap (price).*

Suelo natal. *Native land.*

SUELTO *adj. loose; swift; free; fluent (style), single, odd (copy); m. change (money); newspaper item, short editorial.*

Sus cordones están sueltos. *Your shoelaces are untied (loose).*

Tenemos unos números sueltos de esa revista. *I have some odd copies of that magazine.*

Ese muchacho anda suelto. *That boy's running wild.*

Suelto de lengua. *Outspoken.*

Corrió a rienda suelta. *He ran fast.*

¿Tiene Ud. suelto? *Have you any change?*

No tengo suelto. *I haven't any change.*

SUEÑO *m. sleep; dream.*
  ¿Tiene Ud. sueño? *Are you sleepy?*
  Tengo mucho sueño. *I'm very sleepy.*
  Sueño con mucha frecuencia. *I dream very often.*
  Todo me parece un sueño. *Everything seems like a dream.*
suero *m. serum.*
SUERTE *f. chance, lot, fortune, luck; manner, way, kind.*
  ¡Buena suerte! *Good luck!*
  Mala suerte. *Bad luck.*
  Envidio tu suerte. *I envy your luck.*
  Tiene mucha suerte. *He's very lucky.*
  Echemos suertes. *Let's draw lots.*
  ¿A quién le tocó la suerte? *Who won the lottery?*
  De la misma suerte. *The same way.*
  De suerte que. *So that. So. Thus.*
suficiencia *f. sufficiency, capacity.*
SUFICIENTE *adj. enough; sufficient.*
  Eso no es suficiente. *That's not enough.*
  Por más que trabaja, nunca gana lo suficiente. *He never earns enough no matter how hard he works.*
sufijo *adj. suffixed; m. suffix.*
sufragar *to pay, to defray; to aid.*
  Sufragará todos los gastos del viaje. *He'll pay all the expenses of the trip.*
sufragio *m. suffrage, vote; aid.*
sufrido *adj. patient, enduring.*
  Es una mujer sufrida. *She's a very patient woman.*
sufrimiento *m. suffering.*
sufrir *to suffer, to stand.*
  ¿De qué dolencia sufre Ud.? *What (illness) are you suffering from? What do you have?*
  No puedo sufrirlo por más tiempo. *I can't stand it anymore.*
sugerencia *f. suggestion.*
SUGERIR *to suggest, to hint.*
  ¿Qué me sugiere Ud.? *What do you suggest (to me)?*
SUGESTIÓN *f. suggestion, hint.*
  Ésa fue una buena sugestión. *That was a good suggestion.*
sugestionar *to suggest through hypnotism; to influence.*
sugestivo *adj. suggestive.*
suicida *m. and f. suicide (person).*
suicidarse *to commit suicide.*
suicidio *m. (the act of) suicide.*
sujetapapeles *m. paper clip, paper holder.*
SUJETAR *to fasten; to hold; to subdue, to subject.*
  Sujete Ud. bien las riendas. *Hold on to the reins.*
  No está bien sujeto el cinturón. *The belt isn't fastened well.*
  Sujete al perro con una cadena. *Put a leash on the dog.*
sujetarse *to submit to, to keep to, to abide by.*
  Había que sujetarse a la nueva disposición. *We had to submit to the new regulations.*
SUJETO *adj. subject, liable, likely; m. subject; (coll.) fellow, guy.*
  Estar sujeto a. *To be subject to.*
  ¿Quién es ese sujeto? *Who's that fellow (coll.)?*
  Es un buen sujeto. *He's a nice guy (coll.).*
sulfuro *m. sulphide.*
SUMA *f. sum, amount; addition.*
  ¿Cuánto es la suma total? *What's the total amount?*
  Una suma crecida. *A large sum of money.*
  Es hombre de suma cortesía. *He's very (extremely) polite.*
  En suma. *In short.*
sumamente *extremely, exceedingly.*
  Es Ud. sumamente amable. *You're extremely kind.*
sumar *to add; to sum up.*
  Suma muy bien. *He adds accurately.*
  Sumarse a. *To join.*
  Se sumó al movimiento. *He joined the movement.*
sumario *adj. summary; m. summary; indictment, table of contents.*
sumergir *to submerge.*
sumidero *m. sewer, drain, sink.*
suministrar *to supply, to furnish.*
suministro *m. supply.*
sumisión *f. submission, resignation, obedience.*
sumiso *adj. submissive, obedient, docile.*
SUMO *adj. high, great, supreme.*
  Con sumo gusto. *With great pleasure.*
  En sumo grado. *In the highest degree.*
  A lo sumo. *At the most.*
suntuosidad *f. sumptuousness.*
suntuoso *adj. sumptuous, magnificent.*
superabundante *adj. superabundant, very abundant.*
superar *to exceed, to excel, to surpass; to overcome.*
superávit *m. surplus.*
superchería *f. deceit, fraud.*
superficial *adj. superficial.*
superficialidad *f. superficiality.*
superficie *f. surface; area.*
superfluo *adj. superfluous.*
superintendente *m. superintendent; supervisor; quartermaster.*
SUPERIOR *adj. superior; higher, better; above; m. superior.*

Es superior a todo elogio. *It's above all praise.*

Labio superior. *Upper lip.*

Es un hombre superior. *He's a great man.*

Este es un vino superior. *This is an excellent wine.*

superioridad *f. superiority; higher authority.*

superlativo *adj. superlative.*

superproducción *f. overproduction.*

superstición *f. superstition.*

supersticioso *adj. superstitious.*

superviviente *adj. and n. survivor; surviving.*

suplantar *to supplant, to displace.*

suplementario *adj. supplementary.*

suplemento *m. supplementing; supplement, extra charge.*

suplente *adj. and n. substituting, replacing, alternate, substitute, understudy.*

súplica *f. request, entreaty, petition.*

No cedió a sus súplicas. *He didn't give in to her pleas.*

suplicación *f. request; petition.*

suplicar *to beg, to implore, to beseech, to entreat; to petition.*

Suplico a Ud. que le perdone. *I beg of you (entreat you) to forgive him.*

Le suplicó que le ayudara. *She implored him to help her.*

suplicio *m. ordeal, torment, torture; execution (death penalty).*

Pasó por el suplicio de ... *He went through the ordeal of ...*

suplir *to supply; to make up; to substitute.*

SUPONER *to imagine, to suppose, to surmise; to amount to; to expect.*

Ud. podrá suponer lo que ocurrió. *You can imagine what happened.*

¿Cuánto supone todo esto? *What does all this amount to? How important is all this?*

Es de suponer que ... *It's to be expected that ...*

suposición *f. supposition, conjecture, assumption; falsehood.*

supremacía *f. supremacy.*

supremo *adj. supreme; highest.*

supresión *f. suppression.*

ṢUPRIMIR *to suppress; to abolish; to eliminate; to omit, to leave out; to do away with.*

Suprima Ud. los huevos de su régimen. *Eliminate eggs from your diet.*

Suprimieron los impuestos sobre las diversiones. *The amusement taxes were abolished.*

SUPUESTO *adj. supposed, assumed; m. supposition, assumption.*

Usaba un nombre supuesto. *He used an alias.*

Ud. parte de un supuesto equivocado, *You're starting with a false assumption (from a wrong premise).*

Por supuesto, tendrá Ud. que tener el pasaporte en regla. *Of course, you have to have your passport in order.*

En el supuesto de que. *On the assumption that.*

SUR *m. south. (See* **sud.***)*

surco *m. furrow; wrinkle.*

surgir *to spurt; to arise; to appear.*

Han surgido algunas dificultades. *Some (several) difficulties have arisen.*

surtido *adj. assorted; m. assortment, stock, supply.*

Quiero una caja de galletas surtidas. *I want a box of assorted cookies.*

Hemos recibido un surtido de medias de varios tamaños. *We've received an assortment of stockings of various sizes.*

surtidor *m. jet, spout; supplier.*

Surtidor de gasolina. *Filling station (gasoline).*

surtir *to supply, to furnish.*

¿Se ha surtido de todo lo necesario? *Have you supplied yourself with everything necessary?*

SUS *(pl. of* **su***). (See* **su.***)*

susceptibilidad *f. susceptibility.*

susceptible *adj. susceptible, sensitive to.*

suscitar *to stir up, to excite.*

susodicho *adj. above-mentioned; aforesaid.*

SUSPENDER *to suspend; to lay off; to postpone; to put off; to discontinue; to stop (payment); to adjourn.*

La lámpara estaba suspendida del techo. *The lamp was suspended from the ceiling.*

Se ha suspendido la publicación de la revista. *The publication of the magazine was suspended.*

Lo han suspendido de su cargo. *He was laid off from his job.*

Suspendieron el partido por la lluvia. *The game was postponed on account of rain.*

Suspender los pagos. *To stop payment.*

suspensión *f. suspension, cessation, stop.*

suspensivo *adj. suspensive.*

Puntos suspensivos. *Suspension points.*

suspenso *adj. suspended; hung; m. suspense; abeyance.*

El libro lo tiene a uno en suspenso. *The book keeps one in suspense.*

En suspenso. *In suspense. Pending.*

Dejar en suspenso. *To hold over (for future action or consideration). To hold in abeyance.*

suspicacia f. suspicion; distrust.

suspicaz adj. suspicious, distrustful.

suspirar to sigh.

　Suspirar por. To crave. To long for.

suspiro m. sigh, breath.

sustancia f. (See substancia.)

sustantivo m. (See substantivo.)

sustentar to support, to feed, to sustain, to assert.

sustento m. maintenance, support.

sustituto m. (See substituto.)

sustituir (See substituir.)

sustituto adj. (See substituto.)

susto m. fright.

　Dar un susto. To scare.

　Recuperarse de un susto. To recover from a shock.

sustraer (See substraer.)

sutil adj. subtle.

sutileza f. subtleness.

SUYA (f. of suyo) yours; his; hers; theirs; your own; his own; her own; their own; f. view, way. (See suyo.)

　Mi corbata es igual que la suya. My tie is like yours.

　Una amiga suya. A friend of hers.

　Esta pluma es suya. This pen is yours.

　Ha tomado mi pluma y me ha dado la suya. He took my pen and gave me his own.

　Ver la suya. To see one's chance.

　Salirse con la suya. To have one's way.

　Es una de las suyas. It's one of his tricks (pranks).

SUYAS (pl. of suya). (See suya.)

　Son vecinas suyas. They're neighbors of yours.

　Han hecho de las suyas. They are up to their old tricks again.

SUYO yours; his; hers; theirs; one's; your own; his own; her own; their own; its own; sometimes used with the article el, la, lo, los, las. (El suyo, la suya, lo suyo, los suyos, and las suyas are equivalent to el de Ud., el de él, el de ella, el de ellos, el de ellas, los de Ud., los de él, los de ella, los de ellos, las de Ud., las de él, las de ellas, las de ellos.)

　¿Es Ud. primo suyo? Are you his cousin?

　¿Es suyo este lápiz? Is this pencil yours?

　Me gustaría tener un anillo como el suyo. I'd like to have a ring like yours.

　Un conocido suyo. An acquaintance of theirs.

　De suyo. Of one's own accord. Spontaneously. In itself. Of itself.

SUYOS (pl. of suyo). (See suyo).

　Estos libros son los suyos. These are your books.

　Unos amigos suyos. Some friends of yours.

　¿Cómo están Ud. y los suyos? How are you and your family ("yours")?

T

tabaco m. tobacco.

　Tabaco suave (flojo). Mild tobacco.

　Tabaco en rama. Leaf tobacco.

tabaquería f. cigar store.

tabaquero m. tobacconist.

taberna f. tavern, inn, bar.

tabernero m. bartender.

tabique m. partition wall, partition.

tabla f. table (of information); board, plank (of wood); pl. stage.

　Con esta tabla haré un banco. I'll make a bench with this board.

　Tabla de multiplicar. Multiplication table.

tablado m. platform; stage; scaffold.

tablero m. panel, board, keyboard.

　Tablero de damas. Checkerboard.

　Tablero de ajedrez. Chessboard.

　Tablero de instrumentos. Dashboard.

tableta f. tablet.

tablilla f. slab, small board; bulletin board.

taburete m. stool.

tacañería f. stinginess.

tacaño adj. stingy, miserly.

tácito adj. tacit.

taciturno adj. taciturn.

taco m. plug, stopper; pad, wad; billiard cue.

tacón m. heel; heelpiece of a shoe.

　Tacones de goma. Rubber heels.

taconear to tap with the heels.

taconeo m. the act of tapping with the heels.

táctica f. tactics.

tacto m. touch; tact; skill; feel.

　Es un hombre de mucho tacto. He's a very tactful man.

　Es suave al tacto. It feels soft.

tacha f. fault, blemish.

　Poner tacha (a). To find fault. To make objections.

　Sin tacha. Without fault (blemish).

tachar to find fault with; to erase, to cross out; to censure.

tachuela f. tack, small nail.

tafetán m. taffeta.

tahur m. gambler; cardsharp.

tajada f. slice, cut.

tajo m. cut, incision.

TAL adj. such, so, as.

　¿Qué tal? How are you? How are things? What do you say?

¿Qué tal está su familia? *How is your family?*

¿Qué tal se porta? *How is she behaving?*

No permitiré tal cosa. *I won't allow such a thing.*

En mi vida ni he visto ni oído tal cosa. *I haven't seen or heard of such a thing in my life.*

Encontramos el país tal como nos lo habíamos imaginado. *We found the country just as we had imagined it to be.*

Tal era el frío que tuvimos que encender la lumbre. *It was so cold that we had to light a fire.*

Como si tal cosa. *As if nothing had happened.*

Lo dejaron todo tal como estaba. *They left everything just as it was.*

Me lo dijo un tal González. *A certain Gonzalez told me so.*

Tal vez. *Maybe.*

Con tal que. *Provided that.*

No hay tal. *No such thing.*

Tal para cual. *Two of a kind.*

tala *f. felling of trees; havoc.*

taladrar *to drill, to bore.*

taladro *m. auger, bit, drill; drill hole, bore.*

talar *to fell trees; to destroy.*

talco *m. talcum, talc; tinsel.*

talento *m. talent; cleverness.*

Es un escritor de gran talento. *He's a very talented writer.*

talón *m. heel; check, stub, receipt.*

Presente este talón al reclamar su equipaje. *Present this check when you claim your baggage.*

talonario *m. stub; stub book, checkbook.*

talla *f. size, stature; wood carving.*

Es un hombre de talla de media. *He's of medium height.*

tallador *m. engraver.*

tallar *to carve; to engrave.*

tallarín *m. noodle.*

talle *m. waist; size; shape; figure.*

Tiene un talle muy pequeño. *She has a very small waist.*

taller *m. workshop, factory; laboratory.*

Taller de sastre. *Tailor shop.*

Taller de reparaciones. *Repair shop.*

tallo *m. stem; stalk; sprout.*

tamal *m. tamale.*

¿Le gustan los tamales? *Do you like tamales?*

TAMAÑO *adj. of such and such a size; such, so great, so large, so small, etc.; m. size, dimensions.*

Nunca había visto tamaño descaro. *I'd never seen such impudence.*

¿De qué tamaño es? *What size is it?*

¿Tiene Ud. tornillos de este tamaño? *Have you screws of this size?*

Hemos recibido un surtido de medias de varios tamaños. *We've received an assortment of stockings of various sizes.*

De gran tamaño. *Very large.*

De poco tamaño. *Small.*

TAMBIÉN *also, too; as well; likewise.*

Yo también. *I also.*

¿Va Ud. también? *Are you going too?*

También Ud. puede venir. *You may also come. You can come too.*

tambor *m. drum; drummer.*

tamiz *m. fine sieve, sifter.*

tamizar *to sift.*

TAMPOCO *neither (used after a negative).*

A decir verdad, no quiero verlo.—Ni yo tampoco. *To tell the truth I don't want to see him.—Neither do I.*

Su mujer tampoco dijo nada. *His wife didn't say anything either.*

tampón *m. ink pad; pl. tampons.*

TAN *so, as, so much, as well, as much.*

¿Qué le ha hecho volver tan pronto? *What made you return so soon?*

Siendo tan tarde no iré. *Since it's so late, I won't go.*

Tan pronto como sea posible. *As soon as possible.*

Tan largo tiempo. *Such a long time.*

No tan de prisa. *Not so fast.*

Ya es tan alto como su padre. *He's now as tall as his father.*

Habla español tan bien como ella. *He speaks Spanish as well as she.*

Tan bien. *So well. As well.*

Tan mal. *So bad. As bad.*

Además de ser tan encantadora, es inteligente. *She's intelligent as well as charming.*

No le creí tan niño. *I didn't think he was so childish.*

¿Tan aficionado es su hermano al esquí? *Is your brother that enthusiastic about skiing?*

tanda *f. rotation, turn; (work) shift; batch; team.*

tangible *adj. tangible.*

tango *m. tango.*

tanque *m. tank.*

tantear *to measure; to try, to sound somebody out; to keep the score in a game; to estimate.*

tanteo *m. estimate; sounding (somebody out); score (games).*

TANTO *adj. so much, as much; adv. so, in*

such a manner; such a long (time);
m. point (in games), pl. score.

Tanto gusto, señora. I'm very glad
(pleased) to know you, madam.

¡Lo siento tanto! I'm so sorry!

No beba Ud. tanto. Don't drink so much.

¡Tanto bueno por aquí! Look who's here!
I'm glad to see you.

¿Por qué tanta prisa? Why the hurry?

Tanta gente. So many people.

Ciento y tantas libras. A hundred and some
pounds.

Tener tantos años de edad. To be so many
years old.

A tantos de mayo. On such and such a
date in May.

¿Tanto le costó? Did it cost you as much
as that?

A tanto la yarda. At so much a yard.

Algún tanto. A little. Somewhat.

Otro tanto. Just as much. As much more.

Otros tantos. Just as many.

Ni tanto, ni tan poco. Neither too much nor
too little.

Tanto por tanto. For the same price.

Tantos a tantos. Equal numbers.

Tanto uno como otro. The one as well as
the other. Both of them.

Cuanto más le doy, tanto más me pide. The
more I give him, the more he asks for.

Tanto más cuanto (que). All the more
(because).

Tanto como. (Tanto cuanto.) As much as.

En tanto (Entretanto.) In the meanwhile.

Hay tanta gente aquí. There are so many
people here.

Por lo tanto. Therefore. For the reasons
mentioned.

Estar al tanto de. To be informed of. To be
aware of.

Tanto mejor. So much the better.

Tanto peor. So much the worse.

tapa f. cover, lid, cap.

tapas f. pl. snacks.

tapadera f. cover, lid.

tapar to cover, to cover up; to coneal, to
hide.

tapia f. mud wall; fence.

¿Puede Ud. saltar por encima de esta tapia?
Can you jump over that fence?

Es sordo como una tapia. He's deaf as a
post.

tapicería f. tapestry; upholstery.

tapioca f. tapioca.

tapiz m. tapestry.

tapizar tapestry; to upholster.

tapón m. cork; plug.

taponar to plug.

taquígrafo m. stenographer.

taquilla f. box office or ticket window.

¿Dónde está la taquilla? Where's the box
office?

tardanza f. slowness, delay.

Perdone mi tardanza. Pardon my lateness.

TARDAR to delay; to be late; to be slow.

No tarde Ud. Don't take too long. Don't be
late.

No tardaré en volver. I'll be back before
long.

No creo que tarde mucho. I don't think
he'll be long.

Tardó una hora en ir allí. It took him an
hour to go (get) there.

¿Cuánto tiempo se tarda en avión? How
long does it take by airplane?

Tarda mucho en decidirse. He's slow in
making up his mind.

A más tardar. At the latest.

TARDE f. afternoon; adv. late.

¡Buenas tardes! Good afternoon!

¡Qué hermosa tarde! What a lovely
afternoon!

¿De modo que pasaron Uds. allí la tarde?
So you spent the afternoon there?

Esta tarde a las cuatro. This afternoon at
four o'clock.

En la tarde. In the afternoon.

Mañana por la tarde. Tomorrow afternoon.

Ya es tarde. It's late.

Más vale tarde que nunca. Better late than
never.

No quiero llegar tarde. I don't want to be
late.

Puede ser que venga más tarde. Maybe
he'll come later.

Más tarde o más temprano. Sooner or
later.

Hacerse tarde. To grow late.

tardío adj. tardy, slow; late.

tarea f. job, task, work.

La tarea está concluida. The job is finished.

Tarea escolar. Homework.

tarifa f. tariff; fare, rate.

tarima f. movable platform; stand.

tarjeta f. card.

Aquí tiene Ud. mi tarjeta. Here's my card.

Tarjeta de crédito. Credit card.

Tarjeta postal. Postcard.

tarro m. jar; can, pot.

tartamudear to stammer, to stutter.

tartamudo adj. stammering; stuttering; m.
stammerer, stutterer.

tasa f. assessment, rate; valuation.

tasar to appraise, to assess; to value.

tatarabuela f. great-great-grandmother.

tatarabuelo m. great-great-grandfather.

tataranieta f. great-great-granddaughter.

tataranieto m. great-great-grandson.

tatuaje *m. tattoo; tattooing.*

tatuar *to tattoo.*

tauromaquia *f. bullfighting.*

TAXI *m. taxi, taxicab.*
> ¿Iremos a pie o en taxi? *Shall we walk or take a taxi?*

taxímetro *m. meter (of a cab).*

TAZA *f. cup; bowl.*
> Haga el favor de darme otra taza de café. *Please give me another cup of coffee.*

tazón *m. large bowl.*

TE *pron. (direct, indirect, and reflexive form of tú) you, to you.*
> ¿Te duele la cabeza? *Do you have a headache?*
>
> ¿Qué te parece? *What do you think of it?*
>
> Te lo dio a ti. *He gave it to you.*
>
> Si me escribes te contestaré. *I'll answer you if you write to me.*
>
> Ponte el abrigo. *Put on your coat.*

te *f. name of the letter* **t.**

té *m. tea.*
> Ya está el té. *Tea is ready.*

teatral *adj. theatrical.*

TEATRO *m. theater; playhouse.*

tecla *f. key (of a piano, typewriter, computer).*

teclado *m. keyboard (of a piano, typewriter, computer).*
> Teclado numérico. *Keypad (computer).*

técnica *f. technique.*

técnico *adj. technical; m. technician, expert.*

techo *m. roof; ceiling.*

tedio *m. boredom, tediousness.*

tedioso *adj. tiresome, tedious.*

teja *f. tile, slate.*

tejado *m. roof, tiled roof.*

tejer *to weave, to knit.*

tejido *m. texture, fabric, web; tissue.*

tela *f. cloth, material; web, fabric.*
> Esta tela tiene un metro de ancho. *This material (cloth) is one meter wide.*
>
> ¿Se encoge esta tela? *Does this material shrink?*
>
> Ese es el revés de la tela. *That's the wrong side of the material.*

telaraña *f. cobweb.*

TELE *f. coll. for* **televisión.**

TELECOMUNICACIONES *f. pl. telecommunications.*

TELEFONEAR *to phone.*
> Telefonéeme. *Phone me. Give me a ring.*
>
> ¿Se puede telefonear desde aquí? *Can we phone from here?*
>
> Telefoneo de parte del Sr. López. *I'm calling for Mr. Lopez.*

telefonema *m. telephone message, call.*

telefónico *adj. relating to a telephone.*

> ¿Dónde está la central telefónica? *Where's the telephone exchange station?*
>
> Guía telefónica. *Telephone directory (book).*
>
> Cabina telefónica. *Telephone booth.*

telefonista *m. and f. telephone operator.*

TELÉFONO *m. telephone.*
> Llámeme por teléfono. *Phone me. Give me a ring.*
>
> Teléfono celular. *Cellular telephone.*
>
> ¿Qué número tiene su teléfono? *What's your phone number?*
>
> Un momento, que suena el teléfono. *Just a minute, the phone is ringing.*

telégrafo *m. telegraph.*

telegrama *m. telegram.*
> Le pondré un telegrama en cuanto llegue. *I'll send you a telegram as soon as I arrive.*

telescopio *m. telescope.*

televisión *f. television (programming).*

televisor *m. television (set).*

télex *m. telex.*

telón *m. curtain (theater).*

tema *m. theme; subject.*
> Cambiemos de tema. *Let's change the subject. Let's talk about something else.*

temblar *to tremble, to shake, to shiver.*

temblor *m. trembling, tremor; earthquake.*

TEMER *to fear, to dread, to be afraid.*
> No tiene Ud. nada que temer. *There's nothing to be afraid of.*
>
> Temo que esté enfermo. *I'm afraid he's sick.*
>
> No tema, que no le hará daño. *Don't be afraid, it won't hurt you.*
>
> Temo que sea demasiado tarde. *I'm afraid that it's too late.*

temerario *adj. reckless, rash.*

temeridad *f. temerity, rashness, recklessness; folly.*

temeroso *adj. timid; afraid, fearful.*

temible *adj. dreadful, terrible.*

temor *m. fear, dread.*

temperamento *m. temperament, temper, nature.*

temperatura *f. temperature.*

tempestad *f. tempest, storm.*

templado *adj. moderate, temperate, tempered; lukewarm.*

templo *m. temple; church.*

temporada *f. season; period.*
> Este espectáculo es el mejor de la temporada. *This is the best show of the season.*

temporal *adj. temporary; m. storm.*

TEMPRANO *early.*

Salimos por la mañana temprano. *We left early in the morning.*

Me gusta acostarme temprano. *I like to go to bed early.*

Es demasiado temprano aún. *It's too early yet.*

Se sabrá más tarde o más temprano. *It'll become known sooner or later.*

tenacidad *f.* tenacity.

tenaz *adj.* tenacious; stubborn.

tenazas *f. pl.* pincers, tongs, pliers; forceps.

tendencia *f.* tendency, leaning; trend.

tender *to hang* (clothes); *to stretch out, to spread out, to tend.*

Los pescadores tendieron la red. *The fisherman spread out the net.*

tendero *m.* storekeeper.

tendón *m.* tendon.

tenebroso *adj.* dark; gloomy.

TENEDOR *m.* fork; holder.

Deme un tenedor. *Let me have a fork.*

Tenedor de libros. *Bookkeeper.*

Tenedor de póliza. *Policyholder.*

teneduría *f.* keeping (*of books*).

Teneduría de libros. *Bookkeeping.*

TENER *to have, to possess; to keep; to hold, to contain; to take; to be* (hungry, thirsty, cold, warm, *etc.*).

¿Qué tiene Ud. en ese paquete? *What do you have in that package?*

Tendrá que facturar el baúl. *You'll have to check the trunk.*

Tengo que irme ahora. *I have to go now.*

No tengo mucho tiempo. *I haven't much time.*

Tengo mucho que hacer hoy. *I've a lot to do today.*

No tengo suelto. *I haven't any change.*

No tengo más. *I haven't (got) any more. I don't have any more.*

¿Qué tiene Ud. que ver con eso? *What do you have to do with it?*

Aquí tenemos que cambiar de tren. *We have to change trains here.*

¿Qué edad tiene Ud.? *How old are you?*

Tengo treinta años. *I'm thirty years old.*

Aquí tiene Ud. un libro interesante. *Here's an interesting book.*

¿Qué tiene Ud? *What's the matter with you?*

No tengo nada. *There's nothing the matter with me.*

No tenga Ud. miedo. *Don't be afraid.*

Tengo hambre. *I'm hungry.*

No tengo ganas de comer ahora. *I don't feel like eating now.*

Tengo sed. *I'm thirsty.*

Tengo mucho frío. *I'm very cold.*

Tengo dolor de cabeza. *I have a headache.*

Tengo dolor de garganta. *I have a sore throat.*

Tengo escalofríos. *I have the chills.*

Tengo un fuerte resfriado. *I have a bad cold.*

¿Tiene Ud. sueño? *Are you sleepy?*

Tenga paciencia. *Be patient. Have patience.*

¡Tenga cuidado! *Be careful! Watch out!*

Tiene buena cara. *It looks very nice. It looks good.*

Tener razón. *To be right.*

¿Quién tiene razón? *Who's right?*

No tener razón. *To be wrong.*

Tiene los brazos muy largos. *He has very long arms.*

Tiene mucha suerte. *He's very lucky.*

Tener prisa. *To be in a hurry.*

Tener lugar. *To take place.*

Tener malas pulgas. *To be hot-tempered. To be hot-headed (hot-blooded).*

Tener buen diente. *To have a hearty appetite.*

Lo tendré en cuenta. *I'll bear it in mind.*

Lo tiene en poco. *He attaches little value to it.*

Tuve un buen día. *I spent a pleasant day.*

¿Con qué ésas tenemos? *So that's the story!*

Tiene mucho pico. *He's a chatterbox.*

No tengo arte ni parte en el asunto. *I've nothing to do with the matter.*

tenis *m.* tennis.

tenis de mesa *m.* Ping-Pong.

tenor *m.* tenor.

tensión *f.* tension; voltage.

Tensión emocional. *Stress.*

tentación *f.* temptation.

tentar *to touch, to feel; to grope; to tempt; to try, to attempt.*

tentativa *f.* attempt, try.

tenue *adj.* tenuous, thin, delicate.

teñir *to dye, to tinge.*

teoría *f.* theory.

teórico *adj.* theoretical.

terapéutica *f.* therapeutics.

terapia *f.* therapy.

TERCER (*shortening of* **tercero**) third.

Vive en el tercer piso. *He lives on the third floor.*

El tercer día. *The third day.*

Tercer mundo. *Third World.*

TERCERO *adj.* third; *m.* third person; mediator, intermediary.

La tercera parte. *The third part. A third.*

La tercera lección. *The third lesson.*

El sirvió de tercero en la negociación. *He was an intermediary in the negotiations.*

Ya está en tercera (velocidad). *It's in third (gear)*.

tercio *adj. third; m. a third*.

terciopelo *m. velvet*.

terco *adj. stubborn, headstrong*.

tergiversar *to distort, to misrepresent*.

terminación *f. termination; ending*.

terminal *adj. terminal, final; m. terminal*.

TERMINAR *to end, to terminate; to finish*.

Casi he terminado. *I've almost finished*.

La reunión terminó cerca de las diez. *The meeting ended about ten o'clock*.

término *m. term; manner; end; word; boundary*.

¿En qué términos? *On what terms?*

En estos términos. *On these terms. In these words*.

Poner término a. *To put an end to*.

En un término medio. *On an average*.

Me ha hablado en términos lisonjeros de su obra. *She spoke to me in a very flattering way about your work*.

terminología *f. terminology*.

termómetro *m. thermometer*.

termos *m. Thermos bottle*.

termostato *m. thermostat*.

ternera *f. veal; heifer*.

Chuletas de ternera. *Veal cutlets*.

ternero *m. calf*.

ternura *f. tenderness, fondness*.

terraplén *m. embankment*.

terrateniente *m. landowner*.

terraza *f. terrace*.

terremoto *m. earthquake*.

terreno *m. land, soil, field, piece of ground*.

Partieron el terreno en varios lotes. *They divided the land into several lots*.

Sobre el terreno. *On the spot*.

terrestre *adj. ground, terrestrial*.

Fuerzas terrestres. *Ground forces*.

TERRIBLE *adj. terrible, dreadful*.

territorial *adj. territorial*.

Contribución territorial. *Property tax*.

territorio *m. territory*.

terrón *m. clod; lump*.

Un terrón de azúcar. *A lump of sugar*.

terror *m. terror*.

terruño *m. piece of land, native country*.

tertulia *f. evening party, social gathering, friendly conversation*.

tesis *f. thesis*.

tesorería *f. treasury, treasurer's office*.

tesorero *m. treasurer*.

tesoro *m. treasure; treasury*.

testamento *m. testament, will*.

testar *to make a will; to bequeath*.

testarudo *adj. headstrong, stubborn, obstinate*.

No seas tan testarudo y haz lo que te piden. *Don't be so stubborn and do as you are told*.

testigo *m. and f. witness*.

testimonio *m. testimony; attestation; affidavit; evidence; deposition*.

tetera *f. teapot*.

textil *adj. and n. textile*.

texto *m. text*.

Libro de texto. *Textbook*.

textual *adj. textual*.

textualmente *textually, word for word*.

tez *f. complexion, skin*.

Tiene una tez muy suave. *She has a very delicate complexion*.

TI *you (prepositional form of* **tú**).

Para ti. *For you*.

A ti te hablan. *They're talking to you*.

Te estás engañando a ti mismo. *You're fooling yourself*.

tía *f. aunt*.

tibia *f. tibia, shinbone*.

tibio *adj. lukewarm; indifferent*.

Agua tibia. *Lukewarm water*.

tiburón *m. shark*.

tictac *m. ticking*.

TIEMPO *m. time; tense; weather; tempo*.

¿Qué tiempo hace? *How's the weather? What's the weather like?*

Hace muy buen tiempo. Hace un tiempo muy bueno. *The weather's fine. The weather's very nice*.

Hace mal tiempo. *The weather's bad*.

El tiempo se pone bueno. *The weather's getting very nice*.

El tiempo está muy variable. *The weather's very changeable*.

El tiempo se está despejando. *The weather's clearing up*.

Durante algún tiempo. *For some time*.

Por mucho tiempo. *For a long time*.

Hace mucho tiempo. *It's been a long time*.

¿Cuánto tiempo se tarda en avión? *How long does it take by airplane?*

¿Cuánto tiempo hace que vive Ud. aquí? *How long have you been living here?*

Tengo tiempo de sobra. *I have plenty of time*.

No tengo tiempo. *I have no time*.

No hay tiempo que perder. *There's no time to waste*.

Es tiempo de que Ud. hable. *It's time for you to speak*.

Aprovechar el tiempo. *To make good use of one's time*.

Andar con el tiempo. *To keep up with the times*.

Obedecer al tiempo. *To act as circumstances require. To go with the times*.

Matar el tiempo. *To kill time.*

A tiempo. *In time.*

Fuera de tiempo. *Out of season.*

A un tiempo. *At the same time.*

Con tiempo. *Timely.*

Con el tiempo. *In time. In the course of time.*

El tiempo es oro. *Time is money.*

TIENDA *f. store, shop; awning; tent.*

¿A qué hora abren las tiendas? *What time do the stores open?*

¿Hasta qué hora está la tienda abierta? *How late does the store stay open?*

Poner (abrir) tienda. *To open up a store.*

Acamparon en tiendas (de campaña). *They camped in tents.*

tientas (a) *in the dark.*

Andar a tientas. *To feel one's way in the dark. To grope in the dark.*

Encienda la luz, No busque a tientas. *Turn the light on. Don't look for it in the dark.*

tierno *adj. tender; soft; affectionate; young.*

TIERRA *f. earth; soil; land; ground; native country.*

Su fortuna consiste en tierras y valores. *His fortune consists of land and securities.*

Iremos por tierra. *We'll go by land (overland).*

Iremos a tierra en cuanto atraque el barco. *We'll go ashore as soon as the ship docks.*

Ver tierras. *To see the world. To travel.*

Echar a tierra. *To bring down.*

Tomar tierra. *To anchor. To land.*

En tierra. *On land. Ashore.*

Tierra adentro. *Inland.*

Echar por tierra. *To overthrow. To ruin. To destroy.*

¡Tierra a la vista! *Land in sight!*

tieso *adj. stiff, hard; firm, strong; solemn; stubborn.*

Tenérselas tiesas. *To hold to one's opinion. To be stubborn (opinionated).*

tiesto *m. flowerpot.*

tifus *m. typhus.*

tigre *m. tiger.*

tijeras *f. pl. scissors; shears.*

tildar *to put a tilde over.*

tilde *f. tilde, a mark (˜) used over n; trifle, bit.*

timador *m. swindler.*

timar *to swindle, to cheat.*

TIMBRE *m. stamp, seal; bell, buzzer, tone.*

El certificado lleva un timbre. *The certificate has an official stamp.*

Tocar el timbre. *To ring the bell.*

Abrí la puerta luego que sonó el timbre. *I*

opened the door as soon as the bell rang.

timidez *f. timidity, shyness.*

tímido *adj. timid, shy.*

tímpano *m. kettledrum; tympanum, eardrum.*

tina *f. large earthen jar; tub; bathrub; vat.*

tinaja *f. large earthen jar for water.*

tino *m. skill, knack; judgment, tact; a good hit.*

Sacar de tino. *To exasperate. To confound.*

tinta *f. ink; dye.*

La tinta es demasiado espesa, no corre bien. *The ink is too thick; it doesn't flow well.*

Lo sé de buena tinta. *I have that on good authority. I learned that from a reliable source.*

tinte *m. dye; tint, hue; cleaner's.*

Lleve esto al tinte. *Take this to the cleaner's.*

tintero *m. inkstand, inkwell.*

tintorería *f. dry cleaner's.*

tintorero *m. dyer; dry cleaner.*

tintura *f. dyeing; m. tincture; tint; dye; rouge.*

Tintura para el pelo. *Hair-dye.*

Tintura de yodo. *Iodine.*

TÍO *m. uncle; (coll.) fellow.*

Mis tíos. *My uncle and aunt.*

¿Quién es ese tío? *Who's that fellow?*

típico *adj. typical, characteristic.*

tiple *m. and f. treble, soprano.*

tipo *m. type; rate; standard; class; (coll.) fellow.*

¿Cuál es el tipo de cambio hoy? *What is the rate of exchange today?*

Ese tipo me revienta. *I can't stand that fellow.*

Ese es un tipo muy malo. *He's a bad character.*

tipografía *f. printing; printing shop; typography.*

tipógrafo *m. printer, typographer, typesetter.*

tira *f. strip; stripe.*

Tiras cómicas. *Comic strips.*

tirabuzón *m. corkscrew; curl of hair.*

tirada *f. edition, issue; printing; cast, throw; distance; stretch.*

De una tirada. *At a stretch.*

tirador *m. marksman, sharpshooter.*

tiranía *f. tyranny.*

tirano *m. tyrant.*

tirante *adj. strained, taut, tight; m. brace, trace; pl. suspenders.*

TIRAR *to throw, to toss, to cast; to shoot; to pull; to squander; to draw; to print.*

No lo tire. *Don't throw it away.*

Tíremelo. *Toss it over to me. Throw it to me.*

El niño la tiraba de la falda. *The child tugged at her skirt.*

Tire una línea recta. *Draw a straight line.*

Ha tirado su fortuna. *He's squandered his fortune.*

Han tirado una nueva edición. *They've printed a new edition.*

Veamos cuál de nosotros puede tirar mejor. *Let's see which one of us is the better shot.*

Tirar a los dados. *To shoot dice.*

Tirar al blanco. *To shoot at a target.*

Tira de la cuerda. *Pull the cord.*

¡Voy tirando! *I manage to get along.*

Se tiró por la ventana. *He threw himself out the window.*

Vimos como se tiraban los paracaidistas. *We saw the parachutists jump.*

tiritar *to shiver.*

tiro *m. shot; report (of a gun); throw; fling; range; reach, mark made by a throw; team (of horses).*

Tiro al blanco. *Target practice.*

Errar el tiro. *To miss the mark.*

Matar a tiros a. *To shoot to death.*

¿Cuántos tiros ha disparado Ud.? *How many shots did you fire?*

tirón *m. tug, pull.*

De un tirón. *All at once. At one stroke.*

Dormí toda la noche de un tirón. *I slept all night through.*

tiroteo *m. shooting.*

tísico *adj. and n. consumptive; person who has tuberculosis.*

tisis *f. tuberculosis, consumption.*

títere *m. puppet.*

titiritar *to shiver.*

titubear *to hesitate, to doubt.*

El testigo contestaba sin titubear. *The witness answered without hesitation.*

titular *to title; to entitle; adj. and n. titular; head, holder; headline.*

título *m. title, diploma, degree; heading, headline; inscription; pl. shares, securities.*

Recibió el título de abogado. *He became a lawyer.*

A título de. *On the pretense of. Under the pretext of.*

Títulos al portador. *Shares payable to the bearer.*

Título de crédito. *Credit instrument.*

tiza *f. chalk.*

tiznar *to smut, to smudge.*

toalla *f. towel.*

Toallas sanitarias. *Sanitary napkins.*

tobillo *m. ankle.*

tocado *adj. touched; tainted; m. headdress, coiffure.*

tocador *m. vanity, dressing table; boudoir, dressing room.*

tocante *adj. touching, respecting, concerning.*

Tocante a. *Concerning. As regards.*

En lo tocante a. *In regard to. Regarding.*

TOCAR *to touch; to play (an instrument); to ring; to toll; to concern, to interest; to be one's turn; to fall to one's share; to call (at a port).*

¡No tocar! *Don't touch! Hands off!*

Toque el timbre. *Ring the bell.*

¿Qué instrumento toca Ud.? *What instrument do you play?*

La orquesta está tocando un tango. *The band is playing a tango.*

¿A quién le toca ahora? *Whose turn is it now?*

Ahora me toca a mí. *It's my turn now.*

¿A quién le tocó la suerte? *Who won the lottery?*

Nos tocarán partes iguales. *We'll get equal shares.*

Por lo que toca a mí. *As far as I'm concerned. As regards myself.*

El barco no tocará en Cádiz. *The ship won't call (stop) at Cadiz.*

Tocar a la puerta. *To knock at the door.*

tocayo *m. namesake.*

Es mi tocayo. *He's my namesake. He has the same name I have.*

tocino *m. bacon; salt pork.*

Huevos y tocino. *Bacon and eggs.*

TODAVÍA *yet; still.*

Todavía es temprano. *It's still early.*

Todavía no han dado las diez. *It's not ten o'clock yet.*

¿Terminó la carta?—Todavía no. *Have you finished the letter?—Not yet.*

¿Todavía anda Ud. por aquí? *Are you still around?*

TODO *adj. all, each, every; m. the whole, everything, everyone.*

Todo o nada. *All or nothing.*

Eso es todo. *That's all.*

Estoy todo rendido. *I'm all tired out.*

No estoy del todo satisfecho. *I'm not quite (altogether) satisfied.*

¡Ya estamos todos! *We're all here!*

Nos han convidado a todos. *They've invited all of us.*

Esta es la opinión de todos. *This is everyone's opinion.*

Todos son uno. *They're all the same.*

Todos los días. *Every day.*

La veo todos los días. *I see her every day.*

Todo el día. *All day long.*

He esperado todo el día. *I've been waiting all day.*

¿Sale Ud. todas las noches? *Do you go out every night?*

Según parece lloverá toda la tarde. *It looks as if it will rain all afternoon.*

Todo el año. *All year round.*

Espero quedarme todo el otoño. *I hope to stay through the autumn.*

Toda la familia. *The whole family.*

Todo el que. *Whoever. All that. All who.*

Todo el mundo. *Everybody.*

Todo el mundo lo sabe. *Everybody knows it.*

Sabe un poco de todo. *He knows a little about everything.*

Le daré todo lo que necesita. *I'll give him everything he needs.*

Todo tiene sus límites. *There's a limit to everything.*

¿Está todo en buenas condiciones? *Is everything in good order?*

Estamos dispuestos a todo. *We're prepared for anything.*

Ella siempre está en todo. *She doesn't miss a thing.*

Fuimos allí a todo correr. *We rushed there.*

Ante todo. *First of all.*

Después de todo. *After all.*

De todos modos. *At any rate. Anyway.*

A toda costa. *By all means. At any price.*

Una vez por todas. *Once (and) for all.*

Del todo. *Wholly. Completely. Entirely.*

No del todo. *Not completely. Not quite.*

A toda velocidad. *At full speed.*

Así y todo. *In spite of all.*

Con todo, prefiero no ir. *Still, I prefer not to go. I still would rather not go.*

Jugar el todo por el todo. *To stake or risk all.*

Todo cabe en él. *He's capable of anything.*

toldo m. *awning.*

tolerable adj. *tolerable.*

tolerancia f. *tolerance.*

tolerante adj. *tolerant.*

tolerar *to tolerate.*

No podemos tolerar tal atropello. *We can't tolerate such an outrage.*

toma f. *seizure, capture; dose (of medicine); tap (of a water main or electric wire); intake (water, gas, etc.).*

Toma de corriente. *Outlet.*

TOMAR *to take; to get; to seize; to have (drink or food).*

¿Qué quiere tomar? *What will you have to drink?*

Tomaremos café en lugar de té. *We'll take coffee instead of tea.*

¿Qué toma Ud.? *What will you have (to drink)?*

Tomo vino de vez en cuando. *I drink wine occasionally. I have some (take a little) wine every once in a while.*

Tomemos un bocadillo. *Let's have a bite.*

¿Qué toma Ud. para desayunarse? *What do you eat for breakfast?*

Tome la medicina un día sí y otro no. *Take the medicine every other day.*

Le aconsejo que tome el tren de las ocho. *I advise you to take the eight o'clock train.*

Tomaré un ejemplar de esta revista. *I'll take a copy of this magazine.*

¿Quiere Ud. tomar asiento? *Would you like to sit down? Won't you sit down?*

Tome dos de ocho. *Take (subtract) two from eight.*

Tomar nota de. *To take note of.*

Lo toman por tonto. *They take him for a fool.*

No lo tome Ud. en ese sentido. *Don't take it that way.*

Tomar a bien. *To take (it) the right way. To take (it) well.*

Tomar a mal. *To take (it) in the wrong way.*

Tomar a broma. *To take as a joke.*

Esto debe tomarse en consideración. *This should be taken into consideration.*

Tómelo con calma. *Take it easy.*

No lo tome Ud. a pecho. *Don't take it to heart.*

El médico le tomó el pulso. *The doctor took (felt) his pulse.*

Se tomaron las medidas necesarias en contra de la epidemia. *They took the necessary measures against the epidemic.*

No tomaron más tiempo que el necesario para comer. *They only took the time necessary to eat.*

Tomaron la ciudad de noche. *They took (captured) the city during the night.*

Tomar el pelo. *To make fun of. To tease.*

Voy a salir a tomar un poco el aire. *I'm going out for some air.*

Está tomando alas (coll.). *He's putting on airs. He's getting too big for his breeches.*

Tomó razón de todo lo que se dijo. *He made a record of all that was said.*

Tomar cariño. *To become fond of. To take a liking to.*

Tomar las once. *To have a light lunch or some appetizers about noon.*

Tomar la responsabilidad. *To assume (the) responsibility.*

Tomar una resolución. *To make a decision. To decide. To resolve.*

La ha tomado conmigo. *He picked a quarrel with me.*

Ya le estoy tomando el gusto a este juego. *I'm beginning to enjoy this game.*

tomate *m. tomato.*

tomo *m. volume (book).*

Es una obra en tres tomos. *The work's in three volumes.*

tomógrafo *m. tomographer.*

ton *m. tone.*

Sin ton ni son. *Without rhyme or reason.*

tonel *m. barrel, cask.*

tonelada *f. ton.*

tónico *adj. and n. tonic.*

tono *m. tone; tune; key tone; accent; manner; conceit; shade (color).*

Darse tono. *To show off.*

Gente de buen tono. *Fashionable people.*

tontear *to act foolishly; to talk nonsense.*

tontería *f. foolishness, nonsense.*

No digas tonterías. *Don't talk nonsense. Don't say foolish things.*

TONTO *adj. silly, stupid; m. fool.*

No sea Ud. tonto. *Don't be foolish.*

Hablar a tontas y a locas. *To tell idle stories (tales).*

topacio *m. topaz.*

topar *to collide; to run into.*

tope *m. stop (device); buffer (railway); collision, bump.*

topografía *f. topography.*

topógrafo *m. topographer.*

toque *m. touch; ringing, peal; call (bugle).*

tórax *m. thorax.*

torbellino *m. whirlwind; rush, hurly-burly, hurry-scurry.*

torcedura *f. twisting; sprain.*

torcer *to twist; to turn; to sprain; to distort.*

Se me ha torcido el pie. *I've sprained my ankle.*

Tuerza a la derecha. *Turn right.*

torcido *adj. twisted; crooked.*

toreo *m. bullfighting.*

torear *to be a bullfighter; to banter.*

torero *m. bullfighter.*

tormenta *f. storm, tempest.*

tormentoso *adj. stormy.*

tornar *to return; to repeat, to do again; to change.*

tornasol *m. sunflower; litmus.*

torneo *m. tournament.*

tornillo *m. screw.*

La rosca de un tornillo. *The thread of a screw.*

torniquete *m. turnstile; tourniquet.*

torno *m. lathe; winch, windlass; spindle.*

toro *m. bull.*

Vamos a los toros. *Let's go to the bullfight.*

toronja *f. grapefruit.*

torpe *adj. dull, clumsy, slow; awkward.*

torpedero *m. torpedo boat.*

torpedo *m. torpedo.*

torpeza *f. dullness, slowness; awkwardness.*

torre *f. tower; turret; castle (in chess).*

torrente *m. torrent.*

tórrido *adj. torrid.*

torta *f. cake, tart; font (printing).*

tortilla *f. omelet; a kind of pancake (Mex.).*

Tráigame Ud. una tortilla de cebolla. *Bring me an onion omelet.*

tórtola *f. turtledove.*

tortuga *f. turtle; tortoise.*

tortura *f. torture.*

torturar *to torture.*

tos *f. cough.*

Pastillas para la tos. *Cough drops.*

tosco *adj. rough, coarse, clumsy.*

toser *to cough.*

tostada *f. toast.*

Tráigame una taza de café, tostadas y mantequilla. *Bring me a cup of coffee and some toast and butter.*

tostado *adj. toasted; tanned.*

Pan tostado. *Toast (bread).*

tostar *to toast; to roast; to tan (by exposure to sun).*

TOTAL *adj. and n. total, whole, in all.*

¿Cuál es el importe total? *What's the total amount?*

¿Cuántos hay ahí en total? *How many are there in all?*

totalitario *adj. totalitarian.*

tóxico *adj. toxic, poisonous; m. poison.*

traba *f. obstacle, hindrance; trammel, hobble, fetter.*

trabajador *adj. hardworking, industrious; m. worker, laborer.*

TRABAJAR *to work; to labor.*

¿En qué trabaja Ud.? *What work do you do?*

Se gana la vida trabajando. *He works for a living.*

TRABAJO *m. work, labor; workmanship; toil, trouble, hardship.*

Se garantiza el trabajo. *The work is guaranteed.*

Este trabajo está hecho a medias. *This work is only halfway done.*

Todo esto es trabajo perdido. *All this work is wasted. This is all wasted effort.*

¡Qué trabajo más bien hecho! *What an excellent piece of work!*

Sin trabajo. *Unemployed. Out of work.*

Costar trabajo. *To be difficult. To require a lot of work (effort).*

Cuesta trabajo creerlo. *It's hard to believe it.*

Día de trabajo. *Working day.*

Tomarse el trabajo de. *To take the trouble to.*

Trabajo nocturno. *Night work.*

Trabajos forzados. *Hard labor.*

trabar *to join, to unite, to bind; to shackle; to file (legal).*

Trabar conversación. *To open a conversation.*

Trabar amistad. *To make friends.*

Trabar conocimiento. *To make someone's acquaintance.*

tractor *m. tractor.*

tradición *f. tradition.*

tradicional *adj. traditional.*

traducción *f. translation.*

TRADUCIR *to translate.*

Traduzca esta carta al inglés. *Translate this letter into English.*

No hay manera de traducirloa. *There's no way to translate it.*

traductor *m. translator.*

TRAER *to bring, to carry; to wear.*

¡Mozo! Tráigame una cerveza. *Waiter, bring me a glass of beer.*

¿Lo trajo consigo? *Did you bring it with you?*

¿Qué le trae a Ud. acá? *What brings you here?*

¿Qué trae el diario? *What's new in the paper today?*

Todos los días trae un vestido nuevo. *Every day she wears a new dress.*

Traer a cuento. *To bring into the conversation.*

traficante *adj. trading; m. trader, trafficker (drugs).*

traficar *to traffic, to trade, to do business.*

tráfico *m. traffic; trading; trade.*

tragaluz *f. skylight.*

tragar *to swallow; to devour, to glut.*

tragedia *f. tragedy.*

trágico *adj. tragic.*

trago *m. drink, draught.*

Vamos a echarnos un trago. *Let's have a drink.*

Beber a tragos. *To gulp (down).*

tragón *adj. gluttonous; m. glutton.*

traición *f. treason; treachery.*

Hizo traición a su patria. *He betrayed his country.*

traicionar *to betray, to act treacherously.*

traidor *adj. treacherous; m. traitor.*

tráiler *m. trailer.*

traje *m. suit; dress; gown.*

Traje de sastre. *Tailored suit.*

Traje hecho. *Ready-made suit.*

Traje de etiqueta. *Formal dress.*

Traje de baño. *Bathing suit.*

trajinar *to carry, to convey; to travel about.*

trama *f. weft (in weaving), web; plot; conspiracy.*

tramar *to weave; to plot, to scheme.*

Se trama algo. *Something's brewing. Something's in the air.*

tramitar *to conduct, to transact.*

trámite *m. procedure; transaction; pl. formalities.*

trampa *f. trap; fraud; bad debt.*

Trampa para ratones. *Mousetrap.*

tramposo *adj. and n. deceitful; trickster, cheater, deceiver.*

tranca *f. crossbar.*

trance *m. danger; critical moment.*

A todo trance. *By all means. At all costs. To the bitter end.*

tranco *m. a long stride; threshold.*

tranquilidad *f. tranquillity, peace, quietness.*

tranquilizar *to calm, to reassure.*

tranquilo *adj. tranquil, quiet, calm.*

Este es un lugar muy tranquilo. *This is a very quiet place.*

transacción *f. compromise; transaction.*

transatlántico *adj. transatlantic; m. (transatlantic) liner.*

transbordar *to transfer, to change (trains, buses, etc.); to transship.*

transbordo *m. transfer; transshipment.*

transcurso *m. course, lapse (of time).*

transcurrir *to pass, to elapse (time).*

transeúnte *m. and f. passerby.*

transferencia *f. transference; transfer.*

Deme una transferencia. *Give me a transfer.*

Transferencia de fondos. *Funds transfer.*

transformación *f. transformation.*

transformador *adj. transforming; m. transformer.*

transformar *to transform.*

transfusión *f. transfusion.*

transigir *to compromise; to give in.*

transitar *to pass by, to walk along; to travel.*

tránsito *m. passage, transit, transition.*

De tránsito. *In transit.*

transitorio *adj. transitory.*

transmisor *adj. transmitting; m. transmitter.*

transmitir *to transmit, to send, to convey.*

transparencia *f. slide.*

transparente *adj. transparent; m. window shade.*

transpiración *f. perspiration.*

transportar *to transport, to convey; to transpose (music).*

transporte *m. transport; transportation.*

tranvía *m. tram, streetcar.*

trapecio *m. trapeze.*

trapero *m. junkman, ragman.*

trapo *m. rag; pl. old clothes; rags.*

Poner como un trapo. *To reprimand*

severely. To give someone a dressing down.

Trapo de limpiar. *Cleaning rag.*

TRAS *after, behind, besides.*

Uno tras el otro. *One after the other.*

Ponlo tras ese biombo. *Put it behind that screen.*

Buscamos en una tienda tras otra. *We tried store after store.*

trascendencia *f. transcendency, importance.*

trascendental *adj. transcendental; very important, far-reaching.*

trascender *to spread, to pervade; to leak out, to become known; to smell.*

trasero *adj. back, rear.*

La puerta trasera da al jardín. *The back door opens out into the garden.*

Asiento trasero. *Backseat.*

trasladar *to move; to transport; to transfer; to postpone; to transcribe, to translate.*

Se trasladaron de casa. *They moved to another house.*

Acaban de trasladarlo a otra sucursal. *He's just been transferred to another branch.*

traslado *m. transfer; notification (law); transcript, copy.*

trasmitir *(See transmitir.)*

trasnochador *adj. and n. night owl; one who stays up late.*

trasnochar *to keep late hours, to stay up late, to sit up all night.*

traspasar *to cross; to transfer, to trespass.*

Traspasar de un lado a otro. *To cross from one side to the other.*

Traspasar un negocio. *To transfer a business.*

traspaso *m. transfer; assignment; trespass.*

Acta de traspaso. *Deed of assignment.*

traspié *m. slip; trip.*

trasplantar *to transplant.*

trasquilar *to clip, to shear.*

traste *m. fret (on a guitar, etc.).*

Dar al traste con. *To ruin. To spoil. To destroy.*

trastienda *f. back room (in a store).*

trasto *m. an old piece of furniture; trash.*

Trastos de cocina. *Kitchen utensils.*

trastornar *to upset; to turn upside down; to disturb, to disarrange.*

trastorno *m. upsetting; disturbance.*

trata *f. slave trade.*

tratable *adj. sociable, easy to deal with; amenable.*

tratado *m. treaty; treatise.*

tratamiento *m. treatment; form of address.*

Ha respondido muy bien al tratamiento. *He responded to the treatment very well.*

Tratamiento de textos. *Word processing.*

tratante *m. dealer, trader, merchant.*

TRATAR *to treat; to deal; to try; to discuss.*

¿De qué se trata? *What's it all about? What's it a question of?*

Se trata de un asunto importante. *The matter in question is important.*

De eso se trata. *That's the point. That's what it's about.*

De nada de eso se trató. *That wasn't discussed.*

¿De qué trata este artículo de fondo? *What does this editorial deal with?*

Este libro trata de la vida de Washington. *This book deals with (is about) the life of Washington.*

Prefiero tratar con personas serias. *I prefer to deal with reliable (serious) people.*

Todos los que la tratan la quieren. *She's liked by everyone who meets her.*

La trataron como a una hermana. *They treated her like a sister.*

Trató de hacerlo pero no pudo. *He tried to do it but couldn't.*

Trate de ser más puntual en lo futuro. *Try to be more punctual in the future.*

Trataron de un asunto importantísimo. *They discussed a very important matter.*

Le trataron de tonto. *They called him a fool.*

Eso es lo que trataba de decir. *That's what I was trying to say.*

Tratarse con. *To be on friendly terms with. To deal personally with (someone).*

No se tratan desde hace mucho tiempo. *They haven't been on friendly terms for a long time.*

Tratándose de Ud. *In your case.*

Por tratarse de Ud. *In so far as concerns you. In what concerns you.*

trato *m. treatment; form of address; agreement, deal.*

He tenido poco trato con ellos. *I haven't had much to do with them.*

Cerrar el trato. *To close a (the) deal.*

Entrar en tratos. *To start a deal. To enter into (start) negotiations.*

Hagamos un trato. *Let's make a deal.*

Tener buen trato. *To be pleasant. To be nice.*

Tener mal trato. *To be rude. To be impolite.*

TRAVÉS *m. bias; misfortune; crossbeam; traverse.*

A través de. *Through. Across.*

Mirar de través. *To look sideways. To look out of the corner of one's eyes.*

travesía *f. ocean crossing, sea voyage; crossing.*

Es una larga travesía. *It's a long voyage.*

travesura *f. mischief, prank, trick.*

travieso *adj. mischievous, naughty.*

trayecto *m. distance; stretch; route.*

Final del trayecto. *Last stop.*

trayectoria *f. trajectory.*

traza *f. sketch, outline; appearance.*

Llevar trazas de. *To look like.*

Según todas las trazas. *According to all appearances.*

trazar *to draw, to plan, to outline.*

Trace una línea recta. *Draw a straight line.*

Los ingenieros trazaron los planos para un nuevo muelle. *The engineers drew up plans for a new dock.*

trébol *m. clover, trefoil; club (cards).*

trece *adj. and n. thirteen.*

Estarse (mantenerse) en sus treces. *To stick to one's opinion.*

trecho *m. distance, stretch.*

A trechos. *At intervals.*

tregua *f. truce; respite.*

TREINTA *adj. and n. thirty.*

tremendo *adj. tremendous, dreadful, awful.*

TREN *m. train; equipment; retinue; ostentation.*

¿A qué hora sale el próximo tren? *(At) What time does the next train leave?*

El tren va a salir. *The train's about to leave.*

¿Adónde va este tren? *Where does this train go?*

¿Para este tren en todas las estaciones? *Does this train stop at all stations?*

trenza *f. braid, tress.*

trenzar *to braid.*

trepar *to climb; to creep (a plant).*

TRES *adj. and n. three.*

TRESCIENTOS *adj. and n. three hundred.*

treta *f. trick, wile.*

triángulo *m. triangle.*

tribu *f. tribe.*

tribuna *f. tribune; platform.*

tribunal *m. court (of justice).*

tributar *to pay taxes; to pay tribute, to render homage.*

tributo *m. tribute; tax.*

trigo *m. wheat.*

trigonometría *f. trigonometry.*

trigueña *f. brunette, olive skinned.*

trigueño *m. dark blond (hair); olive skinned.*

trilla *f. threshing.*

trilladora *f. thresher, threshing machine.*

trillar *to thresh.*

trimestral *adj. quarterly.*

trimestre *m. quarter (of a year).*

trinchar *to carve (meat).*

trinchera *f. trench.*

trineo *m. sleigh, sled.*

trío *m. trio.*

tripa *f. tripe; intestines; belly (coll.).*

triple *adj. triple, treble.*

triplicar *to triple, to treble.*

tripulación *f. crew.*

tripulante *m. and f. crew member.*

tripular *to man (a ship); to equip.*

TRISTE *adj. sad; gloomy.*

Esto es muy triste. *That's very sad.*

Parecía triste y cansado. *He looked tired and depressed.*

Al oír la noticia se puso muy triste. *She became very sad when she heard the news.*

tristeza *f. sadness, grief, gloom.*

Se muere de tristeza. *She's heartbroken. She's brokenhearted.*

triturar *to grind, to pound.*

triunfal *adj. triumphal.*

triunfante *adj. triumphant.*

triunfar *to triumph, to succeed.*

Triunfó porque era muy determinado. *He succeeded because he was very determined.*

triunfo *m. triumph; trump card.*

trivial *adj. trivial.*

Es algo trivial. *It's a trifling matter. It's a trifle.*

trocar *to change; to barter.*

trofeo *m. trophy; prize.*

trombón *m. trombone.*

trompa *f. trumpet; trunk (of an elephant).*

trompada *f. punch, blow with the fist; bump.*

trompeta *f. trumpet; m. trumpeter.*

trompo *m. top, spinning-top.*

tronar *to thunder.*

tronco *m. trunk (of wood); log; stem.*

trono *m. throne.*

tropa *f. troop.*

tropezar *to stumble, to trip; to come across, to meet accidentally, to run into; to meet with difficulties.*

Por poco me caigo al tropezar con esa piedra. *I almost tripped over that stone.*

¿Ha tropezado Ud. por casualidad con mi libro? *Have you by any chance come across my book?*

Acabo de tropezar con Juan en la calle. *I just ran across John in the street.*

tropezón *m. stumbling; tripping.*

Dar un tropezón. *To stumble.*

A tropezones. *By fits and starts. Painfully. Stumbling along.*

tropical *adj. tropical.*

trópico *m. tropic.*

tropiezo *m. stumble, trip; slip, fault; difficulty.*

Sin tropiezo. *Without any difficulty.*
Without a hitch.
trotar *to trot.*
trote *m. trot.*
trozo *m. bit, piece, morsel; passage of a*
literary work.
truco *m. trick.*
trucha *f. trout.*
trueno *m. thunder.*
trueque *m. barter, exchange.*
A trueque de. *In exchange for.*
TÚ *(familiar form).*
Hablarse de tú. *To address each other in*
the familiar form.
Tú eres un buen muchacho. *You're a good*
boy.
TU *(possessive singular of* **tú**) *your; pl.* **tus.**
Tu libro. *Your book.*
Tus libros. *Your books.*
tuberculosis *f. tuberculosis.*
tuberculoso *adj. and n. tubercular.*
tubería *f. pipeline; tubing.*
tubo *m. tube; pipe.*
Tubo de imagen. *Picture tube.*
tuerca *f. nut (of a screw).*
tuétano *m. marrow.*
Helarse hasta los tuétanos. *To be frozen to*
the marrow.
tufo *m. unpleasant odor, fumes.*
tul *m. tulle, thin fine silk net.*
tulipán *m. tulip.*
tullido *adj. and n. crippled, partially*
paralyzed.
tumba *f. tomb, grave.*
tumbar *to knock down; to tumble.*
tumor *m. tumor.*
tumulto *m. tumult, commotion; mob.*
tunante *adj. leading a wild life; m. rascal,*
rogue.
El muy tunante se ha burlado de nosotros.
The rascal has fooled us.
túnel *m. tunnel.*
tupido *adj. dense, thick, close-woven.*
turba *f. mob, rabble, crowd.*
turbación *f. perturbation; embarrassment.*
turbante *m. turban.*
turbar *to disturb, to upset; to embarrass.*
turbina *f. turbine.*
turbio *adj. turbid, muddy; troubled.*
turbulencia *f. turbulence, disturbance.*
turbulento *adj. turbid; turbulent.*
turismo *m. touring.*
Barco de turismo. *Boat for tourists.*
Coche de turismo. *Touring car.*
Agencia de turismo. *Travel agency.*
Guía de turismo. *Travel guide.*
turista *m. and f. tourist.*
turístico *adj. touristic.*
turnarse *to alternate; to take turns.*

turno *m. turn.*
Espere su turno. *Wait for your turn.*
Es mi turno. *It's my turn now.*
turquesa *f. turquoise.*
turrón *m. nougat, almond and honey paste.*
tutear *to address each other in the familiar*
form. To use **tú.**
tutela *f. guardianship, tutelage.*
tutor *m. tutor, guardian.*
TUYA *(f. of* **tuyo**) *yours, of yours; pl.* **tuyas.**
Una hermana tuya. *One of your sisters.*
Unas amigas tuyas. *Some (girl) friends of*
yours.
Esa camisa es tuya. *This shirt is yours.*
Prefiero la tuya a la mía. *I prefer yours to*
mine.
Las tuyas. *Yours (pl.).*
TUYO *yours, of yours (familiar form); pl.*
tuyos.
Un amigo tuyo. *A friend of yours.*
Unos amigos tuyos. *Some friends of yours.*
Prefiere el tuyo al mío. *I prefer yours to*
mine.
Los tuyos. *Yours (pl.).*
Lo mío y lo tuyo. *Mine and yours.*
Lo mío es tuyo. *What's mine is yours.*

U

u *used instead of* **o** *when the following word*
begins with an **o,** *f. name of the*
letter **u.**
Siete u ocho. *Seven or eight.*
Uno u otro. *One or the other. Either one.*
ufano *adj. proud, haughty; satisfied,*
contented, happy.
Vive muy ufano en Nueva York. *He lives*
very happily in New York.
Ud. *(abbreviation of* **usted**) *you (polite*
form).
úlcera *f. ulcer.*
ulterior *adj. ulterior.*
ÚLTIMAMENTE *lately.*
Ha estado malo últimamente. *He's been*
sick lately.
ultimátum *m. ultimatum.*
ÚLTIMO *adj. last, latest; late, latter; final;*
lowest (price).
Fue el último en llegar. *He was the last*
one to arrive.
A última hora. *At the last moment.*
¿Es ésta la última edición? *Is this the latest*
(last) edition?
Última moda. *Latest style.*
Está en las últimas. *He's at the end of his*
rope.
Por último. *Finally. At last.*

ultrajar *to outrage; to offend, to abuse, to insult, to humiliate.*

ultraje *m. outrage, great offense, insult.*

ultramarino *adj. overseas.*

ultramarinos *m. pl. grocery; fancy groceries.*

ultravioleta *adj. ultraviolet.*

umbral *m. threshold, doorway.*

UN (*indefinite article*) *a, an; adj.* (*shortening of* **uno**) *one.*

Un hombre. *A man.*

Tráigame un vaso de cerveza. *Bring me a glass of beer.*

Un poco. *A little.*

Sabe un poco de todo. *He knows a little about everything.*

Hace un tiempo magnífico. *The weather is fine* (*lovely, wonderful*).

Compraré solamente un libro. *I'll buy only one book.*

UNA (*f. of* **un**) *a, an, one;* (*f. of* **uno**) *one; someone; pl. a few, some.*

Una mujer. *A woman.*

Unas señoras preguntan por Ud. *Some ladies are asking for you.*

Quiero decirle unas palabras. *I'd like to say a few words to you.*

Es una bailarina. *She's a dancer.*

Es una chica encantadora. *She's a charming girl.*

Tengo una sola maleta. *I have only one suitcase.*

Salimos a la una. *We'll leave at one.*

Una vez. *Once.*

Unas veces. *Sometimes.*

Ló intentó una y otra vez. *He tried it time and time again.*

unánime *adj. unanimous.*

unanimidad *f. unanimity.*

Por unanimidad. *Unanimously.*

undécimo *adj. and n. eleventh.*

ungüento *m. unguent, ointment, liniment.*

Este ungüento le quitará el dolor. *This ointment will ease the pain.*

únicamente *only, simply, merely.*

ÚNICO *adj. only, only one, singular, unique, alone.*

Era su hijo único. *It was her only son.*

Es algo único en su género. *It's something unique.*

unidad *f. unity; conformity; unit.*

Unidad central de proceso. *CPU.*

La unidad de discos. *Disk drive.*

unido *adj. united, joined.*

unificar *to unify.*

uniforme *adj. uniform, always the same; m. uniform.*

Uniforme militar. *Military uniform.*

uniformidad *f. uniformity.*

UNIÓN *f. union; unity; coupling; joint.*

La unión hace la fuerza. *In union there is strength.*

En unión de. *Together with. In company with.*

unir *to unite, to join together, to put together.*

Hay que unir esos dos alambres. *Those two wires have to be joined.*

unirse *to become united; to merge.*

Se han unido las dos firmas. *The two firms have merged.*

universal *adj. universal.*

universidad *f. university.*

universitario *adj. collegiate; pertaining to a university.*

universo *m. universe.*

UNO *adj. and n. one; indefinite pronoun, one; someone; pl. some, a few.*

El número uno. *The number one.*

Deme uno nada más. *Give me just one.*

Uno más. *One more.*

Unos señores quieren verlo. *Some gentlemen would like to see you.*

Tenía unos cigarros y los he regalado. *I had a few cigars and gave them away.*

Unos cuantos. *Some. A few.*

¿Qué puede uno hacer? *What can one do?*

Uno pregunta por Ud. *Someone is asking for you.*

Nos parecemos el uno al otro. *We resemble one another.*

Se aman uno a otro. *They love each other.*

No se pueden ver unos a otros. *They can't stand each other.*

Uno y otro *Both.*

Cada uno. *Each one.*

Uno u otro. *Either of the two. Either one.*

Ni uno ni otro. *Neither one.*

Uno a uno. *One by one.*

Uno por uno. *One at a time.*

Uno tras otro. *One after the other.*

Todo es uno. *It's all the same.*

untar *to grease; to rub; to bribe; to anoint.*

Úntelo de aceite. *Rub some oil on it.*

unto *m. grease, fat* (*of animals*).

untura *f. rubbing with salve, unguent, etc.; unguent, salve, ointment.*

uña *f. nail* (*of finger or toe*); *claw; hoof.*

Cortarse las uñas. *To cut one's nails.*

Ser carne y uña. *To be very close friends.*

urbanidad *f. urbanitiy, good manners, politeness.*

urbanización *f. housing development.*

urbano *adj. urban, living in a city; urbane, refined, polite.*

urbe *f. large city.*

urdir *to warp; to scheme, to plot.*

urgencia *f. urgency, pressure.*

La urgencia de los negocios. *The pressure of business.*

Con urgencia. *Urgently.*

De urgencia. *Urgent. Pressing.*

urgente *adj. urgent.*

Es urgente que sepan la noticia. *It's urgent for them to know the news.*

urgir *to urge, to be pressing.*

Nos urgen mucho estos géneros. *We're greatly in need of these goods.*

usado *adj. used, secondhand; worn-out.*

Ropa usada. *Secondhand clothing. Used clothes.*

usanza *f. usage, custom.*

USAR *to use; to be accustomed to; to wear.*

¿Me permite Ud. usar su teléfono? *May I use your phone?*

Uso anteojos porque no veo bien. *I wear (use) eyeglasses because I can't see well.*

Usar de su derecho. *To exercise one's right.*

USO *m. use; usage, customary; wearing, wear.*

Estos artículos son de mi uso personal. *These articles are for my personal use.*

Para uso interno. *For internal use.*

En buen uso. *In good condition.*

Se viste al uso del día. *She keeps up with the style.*

USTED *you (polite form). Usually abbreviated to Ud. (or Vd.).*

Ud. y yo. *You and I.*

¿Cómo está Ud.? *How are you?*

¿Y Ud.? *And you? And how are you?*

¿Es Ud. francés? *Are you French?*

¿Qué toma Ud.? *What will you have (to drink)?*

Después de Ud. *After you.*

¡Cuídese Ud.! *Take good care of yourself!*

USTEDES *(pl. of usted) you. Usually abbreviated to Uds. (or Vds.).*

Todos Uds. son muy amables. *You are all very kind.*

Uds. llegaron antes que nosotros. *You (pl.) arrived before we did.*

USUAL *adj. usual, customary.*

Lo usual. *What's customary (usual). That which is customary.*

Eso es muy usual. *That's very common (usual).*

Son cosas usuales. *They're common (everyday) things.*

usuario *m. user.*

usura *f. usury.*

usurero *m. usurer; moneylender.*

usurpación *f. usurpation.*

usurpar *to usurp.*

utensilio *m. utensil.*

Utensilios de cocina. *Kitchen utensils.*

ÚTIL *adj. useful, profitable; m. pl. implements, tools, equipment.*

¿En qué puedo serle útil? *What can I do for you?*

Lo encontrará muy útil. *You'll find it very useful.*

Útiles para la escuela. *School supplies.*

Útiles de carpintería. *Carpenter's tools.*

utilidad *f. utility, usefulness; profit.*

Esto les será de mucha utilidad. *You'll find this very useful.*

utilizar *to utilize.*

uvas *f. pl. grapes.*

V

VACA *f. cow; beef.*

Carne de vaca. *Beef.*

vacaciones *f. vacation; holidays.*

vacante *adj. vacant; f. vacancy.*

vaciar *to empty; to pour out; to cast, to mold; to make hollow.*

vaciarse *to give vent to one's feelings; to talk too much.*

vacilación *f. vacillation, hesitation.*

vacilante *adj. vacillating, wavering, uncertain, hesitating.*

vacilar *to vacillate, to waver, to hesitate.*

No vaciló en hacerlo. *He didn't hesitate to do it.*

vacío *adj. empty; vacant; m. cold; vacuum.*

vacuna *f. vaccination; vaccine.*

vacunar *to vaccinate.*

vadear *to ford; to surmount.*

vado *m. ford (of a river).*

vagabundo *adj. vagabond, tramp.*

vagancia *f. vagrancy.*

vagar *to rove, to roam, to wander about; to be idle.*

vago *adj. vague; vagrant; m. vagabond.*

vagón *m. coach, car; wagon, freight car.*

vaivén *m. sway; fluctuation.*

vajilla *f. table service, dinner set.*

vale *m. promissory note, voucher; I.O.U.; okay (Spain).*

Firmó el vale. *He signed the I.O.U.*

valentía *f. valor, courage, bravery; boast.*

VALER *to be worth, to amount to; to be valid, to hold good.*

¿Cuánto vale? *How much is it worth?*

¿Cuánto puede valer ese automóvil? *I wonder how much that car would cost.*

Vale lo que pesa. *He's (it's) worth his (its) weight in gold.*

Hacer valer. *To assert (one's rights). To make good (a claim).*

Más vale. *It's better.*

Más vale tarde que nunca. *Better late than never.*

Vale la pena. *It's worthwhile.*

No vale la pena. *It's not worthwhile.*

valerse *to avail oneself of, to make use of.*

Se valió de mi influencia. *He made use of my influence.*

valeroso *adj. courageous, brave, valiant.*

validar *to make valid.*

validez *f. validity.*

válido *adj. valid, binding.*

El pasaporte es válido por diez años. *The passport is valid for ten years.*

valiente *adj. brave, courageous, valiant.*

valija *f. valise, grip; sack, mail bag.*

valioso *adj. valuable; of great influence.*

VALOR *m. value; price; courage, valor; pl. securities, bonds, shares.*

No tuvo valor de decirlo. *He hadn't the courage to say it.*

No tengo objetos de valor que declarar. *I have nothing (of value) to declare (customs).*

Aumentar el valor. *To increase the value.*

De poco valor. *Of little value.*

Sin valor. *Of no value. Worthless.*

Valor nominal. *Face value.*

Valor real. *Actual value.*

Estimar en su justo valor. *To attach the proper value to something.*

valorar *to value, to appraise.*

vals *m. waltz.*

valuación *f. valuation, appraisal, appraisement.*

valuar (en) *to rate, to price, to appraise, to value.*

válvula *f. valve.*

Válvula de seguridad. *Safety valve.*

Válvula de escape. *Exhaust valve.*

valla *f. fence, stockade; obstacle.*

vástago *m. enclosure; stockade.*

valle *m. valley.*

¡vamos! *Well! Come now! Go on! Let's go! (See* **ir.**)

vanagloria *f. vanity, extreme self-pride.*

vanagloriarse *to boast.*

vanamente *vainly, in vain.*

vanguardia *f. vanguard.*

vanidad *f. vanity.*

Lo hace por vanidad. *He does it out of vanity.*

vanidoso *adj. vain, conceited.*

VANO *adj. vain; of no use.*

Esperé en vano toda la tarde. *I waited all afternoon in vain.*

Tratamos en vano de hacerlo. *We tried in vain to do it.*

Toda tentativa fue en vano. *Every attempt was in vain.*

vapor *m. vapor, steam; steamboat, steamer.*

Compañía de vapores. *Steamship company.*

A todo vapor. *At full steam.*

vaquero *m. herdsman; cowherd; cowboy.*

vara *f. measure of about 33 inches; yardstick; rod, pole.*

No se meta Ud. en camisa de once varas. *Don't be so inquisitive.*

varar *to run aground; to be stranded; to launch (a ship).*

variable *adj. variable, changeable.*

variación *f. variation, change.*

Sin variación. *Unchanged.*

Las variaciones del tiempo. *Changes in the weather.*

variado *adj. varied; of different kinds.*

variante *adj. varying; deviating; f. textual variation; variant reading.*

variar *to vary, to change.*

No varía. *It doesn't change.*

variedad *f. variety.*

VARIO *adj. changeable; various; pl. several, some, a few.*

Un carácter muy vario. *A very changeable character.*

Varios hombres descargaban el camión. *Several men were unloading the truck.*

He comprado varios libros. *I bought a few books.*

Llevo ya escritas varias cartas. *I have already written several letters.*

varón *m. man, male.*

varonil *adj. manly, manful.*

vaselina *f. vaseline.*

vasija *f. vessel (pitcher, jar, container, etc.).*

VASO *m. glass (for drinking); vessel (anatomy).*

Deme otro vaso de cerveza. *Give me another glass of beer.*

vástago *m. stem; shoot; offspring.*

vasto *adj. vast, immense.*

vaticinar *to forecast, to predict, to foretell.*

vaticinio *m. forecast, prediction.*

¡vaya! *Go on! Come on! Indeed! Certainly! Go! (See* **ir.**)

¡Vaya historia! *Some story! What a story!*

ve *f. name of the letter* v.

vecindad *f. vicinity, neighborhood.*

vecindario *m. neighborhood; people of a neighborhood.*

VECINO *adj. neighboring, next; m. neighbor; resident.*

El vecino de al lado. *Next-door neighbor.*

veda *f. prohibition, interdiction by law; season when hunting is forbidden.*

vegetación *f. vegetation.*

vegetal *m. vegetal, vegetable.*

vegetariano *adj. and n. vegetarian.*

vehemencia *f. vehemence.*

vehemente *adj. vehement, violent.*

VEINTE *adj. and n. twenty.*

vehículo *m. vehicle.*

vejación *f. annoyance, vexation.*

vejar *to vex, to annoy.*

vejez *f. old age.*

vejiga *f. bladder; blister.*

vela *f. candle; vigil; watch, wake; sail; sailboat; night shift.*

Apague las velas por favor. *Please blow out the candles.*

Pasé la noche en vela. *I didn't sleep all night.*

Darse (hacerse) a la vela. *To set sail.*

velada *f. evening entertainment, soiree, party.*

velador *m. watchman; lamp table, lamp stand.*

velar *to watch; to keep vigil; to work at night; to veil.*

Velar a un paciente. *To keep vigil over a patient.*

Velar por. *To watch over. To take care of.*

velero *adj. fast sailer (ship); m. sailboat.*

velo *m. veil.*

VELOCIDAD *f. velocity, speed; gear.*

Pasaron a toda velocidad. *They tore past at full speed.*

Modere la velocidad. *Slow up.*

Cambio de velocidad. *Gearshift.*

Primera velocidad. *First gear.*

Segunda velocidad. *Second gear.*

Ya está en tercera velocidad. *It's in third gear.*

velocímetro *m. speedometer.*

veloz *adj. swift, fast.*

vello *m. fuzz, down, nap; gossamer.*

vellón *m. fleece; lock of wool.*

velludo *adj. hairy, shaggy.*

vena *f. vein.*

venado *m. deer, vension.*

vencedor *adj. and n. victorious; winner, victor.*

vencer *to conquer, to vanquish.*

vencerse *to control oneself.*

vencido *adj. defeated; due (to be paid).*

¡Me doy por vencido! *I give up!*

Letra vencida. *Overdue draft.*

vencimiento *m. maturity, falling due, expiration (of term); victory.*

Al vencimiento. *When due.*

Mañana es el vencimiento de la letra. *The draft becomes due tomorrow.*

venda *f. bandage.*

vendaje *m. bandage, dressing (of wounds).*

vendar *to bandage, to dress a wound; to blindfold.*

vendaval *m. gale, strong wind.*

vendedor *m. seller, trader, dealer, salesman, vendor.*

Vendedor ambulante. *Street vendor.*

VENDER *to sell.*

¿A cómo se venden estos libros? *What's the price of these books?*

Quiero vender mi automóvil. *I want to sell my car.*

Vender a crédito. *To sell on credit.*

Vender al contado. *To sell for cash.*

Vender a plazos. *To sell on installments.*

vender al por mayor. *To sell wholesale.*

Vender al por menor. *To sell retail.*

vendimia *f. vintage.*

veneno *m. venom, poison.*

venenoso *adj. poisonous.*

venerable *adj. venerable.*

veneración *f. veneration.*

venerar *to venerate.*

vengador *m. avenger.*

venganza *f. vengeance.*

vengar *to avenge, to take revenge.*

vengativo *adj. vindictive, revengeful.*

VENIR *to come; to fit, to suit.*

¡Ven acá! *Come here!*

¡Venga pronto! *Come quickly!*

¿A qué hora vendrá Ud.? *(At) What time will you come?*

¿De manera que no viene Ud.? *So you're not coming?*

¡Venga en seguida! *Come at once!*

Los veo venir. *I see them coming.*

El mes que viene. *Next month.*

Estos zapatos me vienen anchos. *These shoes are too wide for me.*

Le viene como un guante. *It fits you like a glove.*

¿A qué viene eso? *What's that got to do with it?*

Venirse al suelo. *To fall to the ground.*

Venga lo que venga. *Come what may.*

El pobre ha venido muy a menos. *The poor fellow has come down in the world.*

Lo que Ud. dice no viene al caso. *What you're saying is beside the point.*

Esto no viene a cuento. *That's beside the point.*

Eso ni me va ni me viene. *That doesn't concern me.*

VENTA *f. sale, selling; roadside inn.*

Estos días han disminuído las ventas. *Sales have decreased (fallen off) recently (these days).*

Poner a la venta. *To put on sale.*

Está a la venta. *It's for sale.*

Ventas al por mayor. *Wholesale.*

Ventas al por menor. *Retail.*

ventaja f. advantage; profit; odds (games); handicap (sports).

Este procedimiento tiene sus ventajas y desventajas. This procedure has its advantages and disadvantages.

Llevar ventaja. To have an (the) advantage over.

Llevar la ventaja. To get the upper hand.

ventajoso adj. advantageous, profitable.

VENTANA f. window; window shutter; nostril.

Las ventanas dan a la calle. The windows face the street.

Asómese Ud. a la ventana. Lean out of the window.

Tirar por la ventana. To squander. To waste.

ventanilla f. small window.

ventilación f. ventilation.

Este cuarto necesita ventilación. The (this) room needs to be aired.

ventilador m. ventilator; electric fan.

Correa del ventilador. Fan belt.

ventilar to ventilate, to air; to winnow; to discuss.

Favor de ventilar el cuarto. Please air the room.

Abra las ventanas para que se ventile la habitación. Open the windows to air out the room.

Ventilar una cuestión. To discuss a question.

ventisca f. blizzard.

ventura f. happiness; fortune, chance, venture.

venturoso adj. lucky, fortunate.

VER to see; to look at; to look into; to visit; to meet; m. sense of sight; seeing; look; opinion.

Déjeme verlo. Let me see it.

¿Se le puede ver? May I see him?

Me alegro mucho de verla aquí. I'm very glad to see you here.

Hasta más ver. So long. See you later. Good-bye.

A más ver. So long. See you later. Good-bye.

¿Dónde nos vemos antes de la comida? Where shall we meet before dinner?

Nos veremos esta noche. We'll meet tonight.

¿Qué cuadros desea Ud. ver? Which paintings do you wish to see?

Vamos a ver. Let's see.

¿A ver si le gusta esto? See whether you like it.

Veamos el menú. Let's have a look at the menu.

A ver, otro chiste. Come on, tell another joke.

Ya veremos más adelante. We'll see about that later.

¡Allá veremos! (¡Ya veremos!) We'll see. Time will tell.

Ya se ve. It's evident. It's obvious. It's plain.

A lo que se ve. Apparently. As it seems.

¡Para que veas! There you are! I told you so.

Ver y creer. Seeing is believing.

No lo puedo ver ni pintado. I can't bear the sight of him.

Eso queda por ver. That remains to be seen.

Aquello era de ver. It was worthwhile seeing.

No tener nada que ver con. To have nothing to do with.

A mi ver. In my opinion. As it seems to me.

Hacer ver. To show.

Hacer ver que . . . To make it clear that . . .

VERANO m. summer.

VERAS f. pl. truth, reality; earnestness.

¿De veras? Really? No fooling? Do you really mean it?

¡De veras! You don't say so! You don't mean it! Really! Indeed!

De veras. In earnest. Absolutely so. Really.

veraz adj. veracious, truthful.

verbal adj. verbal, oral.

verbalmente verbally, orally.

verbigracia for example, for instance, e.g.

verbo m. verb.

VERDAD f. truth.

Todo lo cual no es verdad. All of which isn't true.

Diga Ud. la verdad. Tell the truth.

Quiero averiguar si es verdad. I want to find out if it's true.

Falta Ud. a la verdad. You're lying. You're not telling the truth.

Hace frío, ¿no es verdad? It's cold, isn't it?

¿Verdad? Is that so? Is it? Isn't it? Doesn't it?

¿De verdad? Really?

De verdad. In earnest.

La pura verdad. The plain truth.

En verdad. Truly.

A la verdad. Truly. In fact.

A decir verdad. As a matter of fact. To tell the truth.

Bien es verdad que . . . It's true that . . .

Decir cuatro verdades. To give someone a piece of one's mind.

verdaderamente truly, really; in fact, indeed.

Es verdaderamente bonito. It's really very pretty.

verdadero adj. true, real, veritable; sincere.

Es una verdadera sorpresa. *This is a real surprise.*

Es un amigo verdadero. *He's a true friend.*

verde *adj. green; immature, unripe; m. green color.*

El verde le cae muy bien. *Green is very becoming on you.*

Legumbres verdes. *Greens. Green vegetables.*

Uvas verdes. *Sour grapes.*

Estas judías verdes son excelentes. *These string beans are excellent.*

Fruta verde. *Green (unripe) fruit.*

verdugo *m. hangman; very cruel person; young shoot of a tree.*

verdulero *m. vegetable man.*

verdura *f. vegetable greens.*

vereda *f. path, footpath, trail; sidewalk (Amer.).*

veredicto *m. verdict.*

vergonzoso *adj. bashful, shy; shameful, disgraceful.*

Este niño es muy vergonzoso. *This child is very bashful.*

vergüenza *f. shame; disgrace.*

¿No le da vergüenza? *Aren't you ashamed of yourself?*

¡Qué vergüenza! *What a shame!*

Perder la vergüenza. *To lost all sense of shame.*

Tener vergüenza. *To be ashamed.*

Sin vergüenza. *Shameless.*

verídico *adj. truthful, veracious.*

verificación *f. verification.*

verificar *to check up, to verify; to take place.*

Verifique la cuenta. *Check the account.*

La reunión se verificará mañana. *The meeting will take place tomorrow.*

verja *f. grate, grating; iron gate; iron railing.*

vermut *m. vermouth.*

verosímil *adj. likely, probable, credible.*

versar *to go about; to deal with; to be about.*

versátil *adj. versatile.*

versatilidad *f. versatility.*

VERSE *to see each other; to be seen; to find oneself; to be (in).*

Nos vemos con frecuencia. *We see each other quite often.*

Se veía pobre y sin amigos. *He found himself poor and friendless.*

Verse obligado a. *To find it necessary to. To be compelled to.*

Verse con alguien. *To see someone. To have a talk with someone.*

Verse en apuro. *To be in trouble.*

Verse negro. *To be in a fix.*

Véase la página . . . *See page . . .*

versión *f. version.*

Cada uno de ellos dio una versión distinta del suceso. *Each one of them gave a different version of the incident.*

Esta es la mejor versión del Quijote en inglés. *This is the best version of "Don Quixote" in English.*

verso *m. verse; pl. verses, poetry; poem.*

vértebra *f. vertebra.*

vertedero *m. sewer, drain; garbage dump.*

verter *to pour; to spill; to empty; to translate.*

vertical *adj. vertical.*

vértice *m. vertex, apex, top.*

vertiente *f. flowing; stream; watershed; slope.*

vértigo *m. dizziness; giddiness, vertigo.*

vesícula *vesicle.*

Vesícula biliar. *Gall bladder.*

vestíbulo *m. hall, lobby.*

Hay un teléfono en el vestíbulo. *There's a phone in the lobby.*

VESTIDO *adj. dressed; m. dress; garment; clothing.*

Siempre va bien vestida. *She's always well dressed.*

¿Cómo estaba vestida? *What was she wearing? How was she dressed?*

Iba vestido de paisano. *He was dressed in civilian clothes.*

Vestido de etiqueta. *Evening dress.*

Vestido de verano. *Summer dress.*

Vestido de casa. *Housedress.*

vestigio *m. vestige.*

VESTIR *to dress; to put on; to cover.*

Tengo que vestir a los niños. *I have to dress the children.*

Eso viste mucho. *That's very stylish.*

Se ha quedado para vestir santos. *She's an old maid.*

VESTIRSE *to dress oneself, to get dressed; to wear.*

Date prisa y vístete que se nos hace tarde. *Hurry up and get dressed—we're late.*

Iba vestida de punta en blanco. *She was all dressed up.*

Se viste muy bien. *She dresses well.*

Estoy a medio vestir. *I'm (only) half dressed.*

vestuario *m. clothes, wardrobe, wearing apparel; dressing room (in a theater), locker room.*

veterano *m. veteran.*

veterinario *m. veterinarian.*

veto *m. veto.*

VEZ *f. time; turn.*

Una vez. *Once.*

Dos veces. *Twice.*

Otra vez. *Again.*

Repetidas veces. *Again and again.*

De una vez. *At once.*

De una vez para siempre. *Once (and) for all.*

Rara vez. *Seldom.*

Muchas veces. *Often.*

Tal vez. *Perhaps.*

Cada vez. *Each time. Every time.*

Cada vez más. *More and more.*

Todas las veces que. *Whenever. As often as. Every time that.*

De vez en cuando. *Now and then.*

Alguna (una) que otra vez. *Sometimes. Once in a while.*

Una vez que otra. *Sometimes. Once in a while.*

A la vez que. *While.*

Esta vez. *This time.*

VÍA *f. road, way; via; track, line (railroad).*

Por vía de. *By way of.*

Vía ancha. *Broad gauge (railroad).*

Vía angosta. *Narrow gauge (railroad).*

Doble vía. *Double track.*

Vía férrea. *Railroad. Railway.*

Vía aérea. *Airway; airmail.*

Por la vía marítima. *By sea. By boat.*

Vía terrestre. *Land route.*

En vía de fabricación. *In process of manufacture.*

En vías de. *Under way.*

Vía pública. *Public road. Thoroughfare. Street.*

viable *adj. viable, capable of maintaining life; feasible.*

VIAJAR *to travel.*

¿Ha viajado Ud. alguna vez por avión? *Have you ever traveled by plane?*

Ha viajado mucho por Europa. *He's traveled a lot in Europe.*

VIAJE *m. trip, voyage, journey, travel.*

¡Buen viaje! *Bon voyage! Pleasant journey!*

¡Feliz viaje! *A pleasant journey!*

Tuvimos una tormenta durante el viaje de ida. *We ran into a storm on our way over.*

En viaje para. *En route for.*

Estar de viaje. *To be on a trip. To be away traveling.*

Viaje redondo. *A round trip.*

Viaje de novios. *Honeymoon.*

Viaje de recreo. *Pleasure trip.*

Viaje de ida. *A one-way trip. Trip to a place.*

Viaje de vuelta (regreso). *A return trip. A trip back.*

Viaje de ida y vuelta. *A round trip.*

VIAJERO *m. traveler; passenger.*

¡Señores viajeros, al tren! *(Passengers.) All aboard!*

vianda *f. food, viands; pl. vegetables for a dish called* **ajiaco.**

víbora *f. viper.*

vibración *f. vibration.*

vibrar *to vibrate, to throb.*

vicepresidente *m. vice-president.*

viciar *to mar; to spoil; to corrupt; to tamper with, to forge; to make void.*

El aire aquí está viciado. *The air here is impure.*

Este manuscrito está viciado. *The manuscript has been tampered with.*

viciarse *to give oneself up to vice; to acquire vices.*

vicio *m. vice; habit; bad habit; defect; exuberance; growth of plants.*

Ese niño llora de vicio. *That child is always crying.*

Dinero para los vicios. *Pocket money.*

Tener el vicio de. *To be in the habit of.*

Vivir en el vicio. *To lead a dissolute life.*

vicioso *adj. vicious; having bad habits, given to vice.*

Es muy vicioso. *He has many bad habits.*

Círculo vicioso. *Vicious circle.*

vicisitud *f. vicissitude.*

víctima *f. victim.*

victoria *f. victory.*

victorioso *adj. victorious.*

VIDA *f. life; living.*

En mi vida he visto ni oído tal cosa. *I've never seen or heard of such a thing in my life.*

Me gano la vida escribiendo. *I write for a living.*

Mi vida. *My dearest. My darling.*

Vida mía. *My dearest. My darling.*

Buscar la vida. *To try to make a living.*

Ganarse la vida. *To earn (make) a living.*

Darse buena vida. *To live comfortably.*

Dar mala vida. *To mistreat. To abuse.*

Vida alegre (airada). *A merry life.*

Pasar la vida. *To live frugally. To eke out an existence.*

El coste de la vida. *The cost of living.*

Entre la vida y la muerte. *Between life and death.*

En su vida. *Never.*

¡Por mi vida! *My word!*

Escapar con vida. *To have a narrow escape.*

video *m. video.*

videocasete *m. videocassette.*

videocinta *f. videotape.*

videograbadora *m. VCR.*

vidrio *m. glass.*

Vidrio de aumento. *Magnifying glass.*

Vidrio tallado. *Cut glass.*

Pagar los vidrios rotos. *To be made the scapegoat.*

viejecito m. *a little old man.*

VIEJO adj. *old; worn-out; ancient; m. an old man.*

Somos viejos amigos. *We're old friends.*

Le creí más viejo. *I thought you were older.*

Su madre es muy vieja. *His mother is very old.*

Ese viejo tiene muy mal genio. *That old man has a bad (vile) temper.*

VIENTO m. *wind; scent (hunting); airs.*

Hace mucho viento. *It's very windy.*

Corre un viento glacial. *There's an icy wind.*

Sus negocios van de viento en popa. *His business is very successful.*

vientre m. *belly, stomach.*

VIERNES m. *Friday.*

viga f. *beam, rafter, girder.*

vigésimo adj. and n. *twentieth.*

vigilancia f. *vigilance.*

vigilante adj. *vigilant; watchful; m. watchman.*

vigilar *to watch over, to look after.*

vigilia f. *vigil; fast; eve; burning the midnight oil.*

Esta novela es el producto de sus vigilias. *He spent his nights working on this novel.*

vigor m. *vigor, strength.*

vigoroso adj. *vigorous, strong.*

vil adj. *mean, low, vile, despicable.*

vileza f. *meanness, infamous deed.*

villa f. *village; villa.*

vinagre m. *vinegar.*

vinicultura f. *viniculture, wine growing.*

vinicultor m. *wine grower.*

VINO m. *wine.*

¿Le sirvo a Ud. un poco de vino? *Shall I pour (serve) you a little wine?*

Jerez es famoso por sus vinos. *Jerez is famous for its wines.*

Vino tinto. *Red wine.*

Vino blanco. *White wine.*

Vino espumoso. *Sparkling wine.*

Vino de Jerez. *Sherry.*

Vino de Oporto. *Port Wine.*

viña f. *vineyard.*

viñedo m. *vineyard.*

violación f. *violation, breach, rape.*

violar *to violate, to infringe, to offend, to rape.*

violencia f. *violence.*

violento adj. *violent.*

violeta f. *violet (plant).*

violín m. *violin.*

violinista m. and f. *violinist.*

violoncelo m. *violoncello.*

virar *to tack, to veer, to change direction, to turn.*

Vire a la derecha (izquierda). *Turn right (left).*

virgen f. *virgin.*

viril adj. *virile, manly.*

virilidad f. *virility.*

virtud f. *virtue, a good quality.*

En virtud de. *By virtue of.*

Por virtud de. *Because of. On account of.*

En tal virtud. *In view of which. On account of which.*

virtuoso adj. and n. *virtuoso.*

viruela f. *smallpox.*

Viruelas locas. *Chicken pox.*

virulencia f. *virulence.*

virulento adj. *virulent; malignant.*

virus m. *virus.*

viscosidad f. *viscosity.*

viscoso adj. *viscous, clammy.*

visibilidad f. *visibility.*

visible adj. *visible.*

visión f. *vision, sight; revelation.*

VISITA f. *visit, call.*

Está esperando la visita en la sala. *The guest is waiting in the living room.*

Tenemos visitas. *We have company.*

Hacer una visita. *To pay a call.*

Visita de inspección. *Inspection tour.*

Pagar una visita. *To return a call.*

VISITAR *to visit; to call on.*

¿Por qué ha dejado Ud. de visitarnos? *Why have you stopped visiting us?*

Los visito de vez en cuando. *I call on them now and then.*

visitarse *to call on one another, to be on visiting terms.*

víspera f. *eve.*

Estar en vísperas de. *To be on the eve of.*

VISTA f. *sight; view; glance; looks; trial (law); m. a customs official.*

¡Hasta la vista! *I'll be seeing you! See you soon!*

Solamente le conozco de vista. *I know him only by sight.*

No lo pierdas de vista. *Don't lose sight of him.*

Bajar la vista. *To look down.*

Alzar la vista. *To look up.*

A la vista. *On sight.*

A primera vista. *At first sight.*

Corto de vista. *Nearsighted.*

Cansar la vista. *To strain one's eyes.*

En vista de. *In view of. Considering.*

Hacer la vista gorda. *To turn a blind eye.*

Echar una vista a. *To glance at.*

Vista de pájaro. *A bird's-eye view.*

Hay una hermosa vista desde aquí. *There's a nice view from here.*

¡Que vista! *What a view!*

vistazo *m. glance.*

Echar un vistazo. *To glance.*

visto *adj. seen; obvious, clear.*

Está visto. *It's obvious. It's evident.*

Nunca visto. *Unheard of.*

Por lo visto. *Evidently. Apparently.*

Visto Bueno. (V°.B°.) *O.K. All right. Approved.*

Visto que. *Considering that.*

Bien visto. *Respected. Highly regarded. Proper.*

Mal visto. *Not respected. Looked down on.*

vistoso *adj. beautiful, showy; dressy.*

visual *adj. visual.*

visualizar *to display.*

vital *adj. vital.*

vitalicio *adj. for life; during life.*

Renta vitalicia. *Life pension.*

vitalidad *f. vitality.*

vitamina *f. vitamin.*

vitorear *to acclaim, to cheer.*

vituperio *m. bitter abuse; infamy, shame.*

viuda *f. widow; mourning bride (plant).*

viudez *f. widowhood.*

viudo *f. widower.*

¡viva! *Long live! Hail! Hurrah!*

¡Viva España! *Long live Spain!*

vivamente *vividly, deeply, very much.*

vivaracho *adj. lively, sprightly, frisky.*

vivaz *adj. lively; vivid; ingenious, bright, witty.*

vivero *m. warren; hatchery; nursery (plants).*

viveza *f. liveliness; vividness; perspicacity, keenness; sparkling (eyes).*

VIVIR *to live; to last; m. life, living.*

Vive solo. *He lives alone.*

¿Dónde vive? *Where do you live?*

¿Cuánto tiempo hace que vive Ud. aquí? *How long have you been living here?*

Se viene a vivir con nosotros. *He's coming to live with us.*

Ella vive en el segundo piso. *She lives on the second floor.*

Se vive bien aquí. *One can live well (nicely, comfortably) here.*

Vive de su pluma. *He makes his living as a writer.*

Tiene para vivir. *He has enough to live on.*

Vive soñando. *His head's in the clouds.*

Vivir para ver. *Live and learn.*

VIVO *adj. living, alive; lively; smart.*

Está vivo. *He's alive.*

Es un hombre muy vivo. *He's a very clever man.*

Color vivo. *Bright color.*

En vivo. *Alive.*

De viva voz. *By word of mouth.*

Tocar en lo vivo. *To cut to the quick.*

Los vivos y los muertos. *The quick and the dead.*

vizconde *m. viscount.*

vizcondesa *f. viscountess.*

vocablo *m. word, term.*

vocabulario *m. vocabulary.*

vocación *m. vocation.*

vocal *adj. vocal, oral; f. vowel, m. voter (in an assembly); member of a board of directors.*

vocear *to cry out.*

vocero *m. spokesman; advocate.*

vociferar *to vociferate, to shout, to cry out loudly.*

volante *adj. flying; m. steering wheel; balance wheel (watch).*

VOLAR *to fly; to blow up, to blast; to spread, to disseminate (news, a rumor).*

Volamos desde Madrid a Barcelona. *We flew from Madrid to Barcelona.*

Las horas vuelan. *The hours flew by.*

La noticia voló de boca en boca. *The news spread from mouth to mouth.*

Echar a volar la imaginación. *To let one's imagination run away with one.*

Sacar (echar) a volar. *To spread. To publish.*

volátil *adj. volatile, changeable.*

volcán *m. volcano.*

volcar *to overturn; to turn upside down; to turn over; to tilt.*

vólibol *m. volleyball.*

voltear *to turn over (position); to tumble, to roll over (an acrobat).*

voltereta *f. somersault.*

volubilidad *f. volubility.*

voluble *adj. voluble; fickle, changeable.*

volumen *m. volume; size; bulk. (For "volume" in the sense of "volume two of a set," see* tomo.)

voluminoso *adj. voluminous, bulky.*

VOLUNTAD *f. will, desire; disposition, consent; intention.*

Lo puede hacer pero le falta voluntad. *He can do it but he's unwilling to.*

Lo hice contra mi voluntad. *I did it against my own will.*

Mala voluntad. *Bad disposition.*

De buena voluntad. *With pleasure. Willingly.*

De mala voluntad. *Unwillingly.*

A voluntad. *At will.*

Ultima voluntad. *Last will and testament.*

voluntariamente *voluntarily, of one's own free will.*

voluntario *adj. voluntary, willing; m. volunteer.*

voluptuoso *adj. voluptuous, sensual.*

VOLVER *to come back, to return; to turn; to turn back; to put back.*

Vuelva mañana. *Come back tomorrow.*

No ha vuelto todavía. *He hasn't returned yet.*

Volverá pronto. *He'll come back soon.*

Se ha marchado para no volver. *He's gone for good.*

Vuelva la página. *Turn the page.*

El camino vuelve hacia la izquierda. *The road turns to the left.*

Vuelve el libro a su sitio. *Put the book back in its place.*

Volvió a salir. *He went out again.*

Vuelva a hacerlo. *Do it again.*

Volver la cabeza. *To turn one's head.*

Volver a trabajar. *To resume work.*

Volver atrás. *To come or go back.*

Volver en sí. *To recover one's senses.*

Volver a uno loco. *To drive someone crazy.*

Volver a poner. *To play back.*

VOLVERSE *to turn, to become.*

Este papel se ha vuelto amarillo. *This paper has turned yellow.*

Se ha vuelto loco. *He's become insane.*

Volverse atrás. *To retract.*

Volverse contra. *To turn on (someone, something).*

vomitar *to vomit, to throw out.*

vomitivo *adj. and n. emetic.*

vómito *m. vomiting.*

voracidad *f. voracity, greediness.*

vorágine *f. vortex, whirlpool.*

voraz *adj. voracious, greedy.*

vos *(personal pronoun) you (singular and familiar; used in Arg., Costa Rica, and Uruguay).*

Vos y yo. *You and I.*

Es como vos. *He's like you.*

Vos tenés que venir mañana. *(Arg.) You have to come tomorrow.*

VOSOTRAS *(f. pl. of* **tú***) you (familiar).*

Vosotras sois sus hermanas. *You're his sisters.*

Esto es para vosotras. *This is for you (pl. f.).*

VOSOTROS *(m. pl. of* **tú***) you (familiar).*

Vosotros sois mis amigos. *You (pl.) are my friends.*

Vosotros tenéis la culpa. *You're (pl.) to blame.*

Vosotros os engañáis. *You're (pl.) fooling yourselves.*

Os aguardábamos a vosotros. *We were waiting for you (pl.).*

votación *f. voting.*

Votación secreta. *Ballot. Secret vote.*

Poner a votación. *To put to a vote.*

votante *m. and f. voter, elector.*

votar *to vote; to vow.*

No votaré ni por el uno ni por el otro. *I won't vote for either one.*

voto *m. vote; ballot; vow; wish.*

Fue elegido por una gran mayoría de votos. *He was elected by a large majority (of votes).*

Hacemos votos por que obtenga lo que desea. *We hope you'll get your wish.*

Hacemos votos por su felicidad. *We wish you a lot of happiness.*

Hago votos por su prosperidad. *I wish you success.*

VOZ *f. voice; outcry; word; rumor.*

Tiene muy buena voz. *He has a very good voice.*

Él es quien lleva la voz cantante. *He's the spokesman.*

Alza la voz. *To raise one's voice.*

Tener voz y voto. *To have a voice in a (the) matter.*

Voz de mando. *Word of command.*

La voz pasiva. *The passive voice (grammar).*

A media voz. *In an undertone. In a whisper.*

Dar voces. *To cry. To shout.*

Corre la voz. *It's rumored. It's said.*

De viva voz. *By word of mouth.*

En voz alta. *Aloud.*

En voz baja. *In a low tone.*

Estar en voz. *To be in voice.*

A una voz. *Unanimously.*

vuelco *m. overturning, upset.*

vuelo *m. flight; distance flown; frill, ruffle; width, flare (dress, skirt, etc.).*

Esta falda tiene mucho vuelo. *There's plenty of flare in that skirt.*

Acaban de hacer un vuelo alrededor del mundo. *They have just made a flight around the world.*

Tomar vuelo. *To grow. To progress.*

Alzar (levantar) vuelo. *To fly off.*

De alto vuelo. *Of great importance. Of high standing.*

VUELTA *f. turn, turning; return; reverse; back (of a page); a walk; change (money).*

Estar de vuelta. *To be back. To know beforehand.*

Me dijo que estaría de vuelta pronto. *She told me she would be back soon.*

Dar una vuelta. *To take a walk.*

¿Le gustaría dar una vuelta después de comer? *Would you like to take a walk after dinner?*

Dar vueltas. *To turn. To walk back and forth. To keep thinking about the same thing. To hammer on a point.*

Por más que doy vueltas, no acierto a comprenderlo. *No matter how hard I think about it, I can't understand it.*

Deme la vuelta. *Give me the change.*

Quédese con la vuelta. *Keep the change.*

Eso no tiene vuelta de hoja. *There are no two ways about it.*

Lo puso de vuelta y media. *She gave him a good dressing-down.*

Billete de ida y vuelta. *Round-trip ticket.*

Viaje de vuelta. *Return trip.*

A la vuelta de la esquina. *Around the corner.*

Dé la vuelta. *Turn around.*

Otra vuelta. *Again. Once more.*

¡Otra vuelta! *Another round (of drinks)!*

A vuelta(s) de. *Around. Approximately.*

A la vuelta. *On the next page. Turn over. Carried over (bookkeeping).*

De la vuelta. *Continued. Brought forward (bookkeeping).*

¡Media vuelta! *Right about-face!*

vuelto *m. change, money returned (Amer.).*

Guarde el vuelto. *Keep the change.*

VUESTRA *(f. of* **vuestro**) *your, yours; pl.* **vuestras.**

Vuestra madre. *Your mother.*

Vuestras hijas. *Your daughters.*

VUESTRO *(pers. pron.) your, yours; pl.* **vuestros.**

Vuestro amigo. *Your friend.*

Es un amigo vuestro. *He's a friend of yours.*

Vuestros amigos. *Your friends.*

vulgar *adj. vulgar; common; ordinary.*

vulgaridad *f. vulgarity.*

vulgarmente *vulgarly; commonly.*

vulgo *m. the common people; populace; mob.*

vulnerable *adj. vulnerable.*

whisky *m. whiskey.*

x *the letter equis.*

Rayos X. *X rays.*

xenofobia *f. hatred of foreigners.*

Y *and*

Tú y yo. *You and I.*

Hoy y mañana. *Today and tomorrow.*

Pan y queso. *Bread and cheese.*

¿Y después? *What next? What then?*

¿Pero y ella? *But what about her?*

YA *already; now; finally.*

Tengo que irme ya. *I have to go now.*

Ya es tarde. *It's late. It's late now.*

Ya son las doce pasadas. *It's after twelve now.*

Es ya hora de leventarse. *It's time to get up.*

¡Ya voy! *I'm coming.*

Ya está el té. *Tea is ready.*

Ya no lo necesito. *I no longer need it. I don't need it anymore.*

El niño ya puede andar. *The child can walk now.*

Pasa ya de los cincuenta. *He's over fifty.*

¡Ya está! *It's all done!*

Ya no puedo más. *I'm worn out. I can't stand it any longer.*

Ya caigo en la cuenta. *Now I see the point.*

¡Ya me las pagará! *I'll get even with him.*

¡Ya lo haré! *I'll do it in time. Certainly I'll do it.*

¡Ya lo creo! *I should think so! Of course! Certainly!*

¡Ya lo decía yo! *Didn't I say so! I had a feeling that it might happen. I was sure of it.*

¡Ya lo ves! *See there! There you are! Now you see it!*

¡Ya veremos! *We'll see.*

yacer *to lie; to be lying (ill in bed); to be lying (in the grave).*

yacimiento *m. bed, layer, deposit (of ore); field (oil).*

Yacimiento petrolífero. *Oil field.*

yanqui *adj. and n. a native of the United States; Yankee.*

yapa *(also* ñapa) *f. bonus, something extra given to a customer with a purchase.*

yarda *f. yard (a measure).*

yate *m. yacht.*

yedra *f. ivy.*

yegua *f. mare.*

yema *f. bud, shoot; yolk (of an egg); fingertip.*

Me he lastimado la yema del dedo. *I hurt the tip of my finger.*

Este huevo tiene dos yemas. *This egg has two yolks.*

Hay muchas yemas en ese rosal. *There are a lot of buds on that rosebush.*

yerba *f. herb; weed; grass; mate. (See* **hierba**).

Yerba mate. *Mate.*

Yerba buena. *Mint.*

yermo *adj. waste, bare; m. desert, wilderness.*

Tierra yerma. *Wasteland.*

yerno *m. son-in-law.*

yerro *m. error, mistake, fault.*

yerto *adj. stiff; motionless.*

yeso *m. gypsum; plaster; cast (of plaster).*

YO *I.*

Soy yo. *It's me (I).*

¡Soy yo mismo! *Yes, it's me. It's me in the flesh.*

Fui yo el que telefoneó. *I was the one who phoned.*

Yo mismo se lo dí. *I gave it to him myself.*

Yo no hablo español. *I don't speak Spanish.*

yodo *m. iodine.*

yoga *m. yoga.*

yogur(t) *m. yogurt.*

yuca *f. yucca (a plant).*

yudo *m. judo.*

yugo *m. yoke; bondage, slavery; marriage ties.*

Sacudir el yugo. *To throw off the yoke. To free oneself. To become free.*

yunque *m. anvil.*

yunta *f. yoke (of oxen, horses, etc.); couple, pair.*

Una yunta de bueyes. *A yoke of oxen.*

yute *m. jute.*

yuxtaponer *to juxtapose, to place side by side.*

yuxtapuesto *adj. juxtaposed, side by side.*

Z

zacate *m. grass; hay (Mex, Central America, the Philippines).*

zafar *to untie; to lighten (a ship).*

zafarse *to get rid of; to escape, to get out of; to slip off, to come off; to break loose.*

zafiro *m. sapphire.*

zafra *f. sugar crop; crop of sugar cane.*

zaga *f. rear, back; load in the rear of a carriage. m. last player (at cards).*

Ir a la zaga. *To lag behind.*

Dejar en zaga. *To leave behind. To outstrip. To do better than.*

Quedarse en zaga. *To be left behind. To be outstripped.*

No ir en zaga. *To be as good as the next one.*

zagal *m. lad, young man; young shepherd.*

zaguán *m. hall, foyer.*

zaguero *adj. laggard; m. defense (soccer); backstop (in Basque ballgame).*

zaherir *to blame, to reproach.*

zalamería *f. flattery.*

zalamero *adj. flatterer.*

Es una niña muy zalamera. *She's a flatterer.*

zambo *adj. bowlegged; m. mulatto.*

zambullida *f. dive, plunge.*

zambullir *to duck, to plunge.*

zambullirse *to dive, to plunge (into the water).*

Se zambulló en el río. *He dived into the river.*

zampar *to gulp, to swallow down; to conceal.*

zamparse *to rush in, to barge in.*

zanahoria *f. carrot.*

zanca *f. shank; long leg.*

zancada *f. stride; long step.*

De dos zancadas. *In a jiffy. In no time.*

zanco *m. stilt.*

zancudo *adj. long-legged; wading (bird); m. mosquito; waders, wading birds.*

zángano *m. drone; idler, lazy person.*

zanja *f. ditch.*

zanjar *to ditch, to dig a ditch; to settle in a friendly manner.*

Hay que zanjar ese asunto. *We must settle that matter in a friendly way. That matter has to be settled amicably.*

zapa *f. spade (tool).*

Trabajo de zapa. *Underhanded work.*

zapatazo *m. a blow with a shoe; stamping (with the feet).*

Mandar a zapatazos. *To mistreat. To treat badly.*

zapateado *m. Spanish tap dance.*

zapatear *to tap (with the feet).*

Baile zapateado. *Tap dance.*

zapateo *m. tapping; keeping time with the feet.*

zapatería *f. shoestore; shoemaker's; shoemaking.*

zapatero *adj. poorly cooked (vegetables); m. shoemaker, shoe dealer.*

zapatilla *f. slipper; pump (shoe); washer (ring of leather).*

ZAPATO *m. shoe.*

Un par de zapatos. *A pair of shoes.*

¿Le lastiman los zapatos? *Do your shoes hurt (you)?*

Átese bien los zapatos. *Tie your shoelaces.*

Estos zapatos me vienen anchos. *These shoes are too wide for me.*

Estos zapatos me aprietan mucho. *These shoes are too tight.*

Zapatos de lona. *Sneakers.*

Encontrarse uno con la horma de su zapato. *To find one's match.*

¡zape! *Scat!*

zarco *adj. of a light blue color.*

Ojos zarcos. *Light blue eyes.*

zarpar *to weigh anchor, to sail.*

Acaban de dar el último aviso, va a zarpar
  el barco. *They have just given the last
  signal. The boat is about to sail.*
zarza *f. bramble; brier.*
zarzamora *f. blackberry (fruit).*
zarzaparrilla *f. sarsparilla.*
zarzuela *f. a Spanish operetta.*
¡zas! *Smack! Slap! Bang!*
zeda *or* **zeta** *f. name of letter z.*
zenit *m. zenith.*
zigzag *m. zigzag.*
zinc *m. zinc.*
zócalo *m. pedestal stand; public square
  (Mexico).*
zodíaco *m. zodiac.*
zonzo *adj. boring; stupid; m. a bore; stupid
  person.*
zoología *f. zoology.*
zopenco *adj. dumbbell, blockhead.*
zoquete *m. block (of wood); morsel (of
  bread); boor; worm; little, ugly
  person.*
zorra *f. fox; vixen; streetwalker (coll.);
  drunkenness.*
zorro *m. fox (male); foxy (cunning; sly,
  crafty) person.*

zozobra *f. foundering, sinking; anguish.*
zozobrar *to capsize, to sink.*
zueco *m. wooden shoe, clog.*
zumbar *to buzz; to ring (one's ears); to
  joke; to hit, to slap.*
  El abejarrón zumba. *The bumblebee buzzes.*
  Me zumban los oídos. *My ears are ringing.*
zumbido *m. buzzing; ringing (in one's ear).*
zumo *m. juice; profit.*
  Zumo de limón. *Lemon juice.*
  Zumo de naranja. *Orange juice.*
zurcido *adj. darning; m. a place that has
  been darned.*
zurdo *adj. left-handed.*
zurra *f. tanning (hide, skin); a beating, a
  whipping, a flogging.*
zurrar *to tan (hide, skin); to whip, to beat,
  to spank.*
  Al llegar a casa su padre le zurró la
  badana. *When he came home his
  father gave him a (good) spanking.*
zutano *m. so-and-so; such a one. (See
  fulano.)*
  ¿Cómo se llama ese zutano? *What's that
  fellow's name?*

GLOSSARY OF PROPER NAMES

Alberto	Albert.
Alejandro	Alexander.
Alfonso	Alphonse.
Alfredo	Alfred.
Alicia	Alice.
Ana	Ann, Anne, Anna Hannah.
Andrés	Andrew.
Antonio	Anthony.
Arturo	Arthur.
Beatriz	Beatrice.
Bernardo	Bernard.
Carlos	Charles.
Carlota	Charlotte.
Consuelo	Constance.
Diego	James.
Dorotea	Dorothy.
Eduardo	Edward.
Elena	Ellen, Helen.
Emilia	Emily.
Enrique	Henry.
Ernesto	Ernest.
Ester	Esther, Hester.
Eugenio	Eugene.
Eva	Eve.
Federico	Frederic.
Felipe	Philip.
Fernando	Ferdinand.
Francisco	Francis.
Gertrudis	Gertrude.
Gustavo	Gustavus, Gustave.
Ignacio	Ignatius.
Inés	Agnes, Inez.
Isabel	Elizabeth.
Javier	Xavier.
Jesús	Jesus.
Joaquín	Joachim.
Jorge	George.
José	Joseph.
Josefa	Josephine.
Josefina	Josephine.
Juan	John.
Juana	Jane, Jennie, Jean, Joan, Joanna.
Julián	Julian.
Julio	Julius.
León	Leo, Leon.
Leonor	Eleanor.
Luis	Louis.
Luisa	Louise.
Manuel	Emmanuel.
Margarita	Margaret.
María	Mary, Maria, Miriam.
Marta	Martha.
Miguel	Michael.
Pablo	Paul.
Pedro	Peter.
Rafael	Raphael.
Raimundo	Raymond.
Ramón	Raymond.
Ricardo	Richard.
Roberto	Robert.
Rosa	Rose.
Rosalía	Rosalie.
Rosario	Rosario.
Santiago	James.
Susana	Susan.
Teresa	Theresa.
Vicente	Vincent.

GLOSSARY OF GEOGRAPHICAL NAMES

Africa	Africa.
Africa del Sur	South Africa.
Alemania	Germany.
Alpes	Alps.
Amazonas	Amazon.
Amberes	Antwerp.
América Central	Central America.
América del Norte	North America.
América del Sur	South America.
América Latina	Latin America.
Andes	Andes.
Angola	Angola.
Antillas	Antilles. West Indies.
Arabia Saudita	Saudia Arabia.
Argelia	Algeria.
Argentina	Argentina.
Asia	Asia.
Atenas	Athens.
Atlántico	Atlantic (Ocean).
Australia	Australia.
Bélgica	Belgium.
Bolivia	Bolivia.
Brasil	Brazil.
Bretaña	Brittany.
Bretaña, Gran	Great Britain.
Bruselas	Brussels.
Camboya	Cambodia.
Canadá	Canada.
Canal de la Mancha	English Channel.
Caribe	Caribbean.
Castilla	Castile.
Cataluña	Catalonia.
Centroamérica	Central America.

Colombia	Colombia.
Costa Rica	Costa Rica.
Cuba	Cuba.
Checoslovaquia	Czechoslovakia.
Chile	Chile.
China	China.
Chipre	Cyprus.
Comunidad	Commonwealth
Estados	of Independent
Ecuadientes	States.
Egipto	Denmark.
El Salvador	Ecuador.
Emiratos Arabes	Egypt.
Unidos	Unated.
	Emirats
Escandinavia	Scandinavia
Escocia	Scotland.
España	Spain.
Estados Unidos	United States
de América	of America.
Europa	Europe.
Filipinas	Philippines.
Finlandia	Finland.
Flandes	Flanders.
Francia	France.
Gales	Wales.
Galicia	Galicia.
Génova	Genoa.
Ginebra	Geneva.
Golfo Pérsico	Persian Gulf.
Gran Bretaña	Great Britain.
Grecia	Greece.
Guatemala	Guatemala.
Habana	Havana.
Hispanoamérica	Spanish America.
Holanda	Holland
Honduras.	Honduras.
Hungría	Hungary.
Indonesia	Indonesia.
Inglaterra	England.
Irán	Iran.
Iraq	Iraq.
Irlanda	Ireland.
Irlanda del Norte	Northern Ireland.
Israel	Israel.
Italia	Italy.
Jamaica	Jamaica.
Japón	Japan.
Jordania	Jordan.
Kenia	Kenya.
Laos	Laos.
Latvia	Latvia.
Líbano	Lebanon.
Libia	Libya.
Lisboa	Lisbon.
Lituania	Lithuania
Londres	London.
Madrid	Madrid.
Malasia	Malaysia.
Mallorca	Majorca.
Marruecos	Morroco.
Marsella	Marseilles.
Mediterráneo	Mediterranean.
México	Mexico.
Moscú	Moscow.
Mozambique	Mozambique.
Nicaragua	Nicaragua.
Nigeria	Nigeria.
Normandía	Normandy.
Norteamérica	North America.
Noruega	Norway.
Nueva York	New York.
Nueva Zelandia	New Zealand.
Oceanía	Oceania.
Pacífico	Pacific (Ocean).
Países Bajos	Low Countries.
	Netherlands.
Paquistán	Pakistan.
Palestina	Palestine.
Panamá	Panama.
Paraguay	Paraguay.
París	Paris.
Perú	Peru.
Pirineos	Pyrenees.
Polonia	Poland.
Portugal	Portugal.
Prusia	Prussia.
Puerto Rico	Puerto Rico.
Reino Unido	United Kingdom.
República	
Dominicana	Dominican Republic.
Roma	Rome.
Rumania	Romania.
Rusia	Russia.
Sevilla	Seville.
Sicilia	Sicily.
Siria	Syria.
Sudamérica	South America.
Suecia	Sweden.
Suiza	Switzerland.
Suramérica	South America.
Tailandia	Thailand.
Taiwán	Taiwan.
Tejas	Texas.
Tokio	Tokyo.
Turquía	Turkey.
Uruguay	Uruguay.
Venezuela	Venezuela.
Viena	Vienna.
Viet Nam	Vietnam.
Zaire	Zaire.
Zimbabwe	Zimbabwe.

English-Spanish

A

a (an) un, uno, una.
able *adj.* capaz.
able (to be) poder.
abolish abolir.
abortion aborto.
about cerca de; sobre; acerca; con respecto a.
above sobre, encima de.
abroad fuera del país, extranjero.
absent ausente.
absolute absoluto.
absorb (to) absorber.
absurd absurdo.
abundant abundante.
abuse abuso.
abuse (to) abusar, maltratar.
academy academia.
accent acento.
accent (to) acentuar.
accept aceptar.
acceptance aceptación.
access acceso.
accident accidente.
accommodate acomodar, ajustar.
accomodations acomodo, alojamiento.
accomplish (to) efectuar, llevar a cabo.
according (to) según, conforme.
account cuenta; relación, narración.
accuracy exactitud.
accuse (to) acusar.
acid ácido (*noun and adj.*)
acquaintance conocido (person).
acre acre.
across a través de, al otro lado.
act acto, hecho, acción.
act (to) actuar; conducirse (to behave);
     representar (theater).
active activo.
activity actividad.
actor actor.
actual real, verdadero.
add añadir.
addict adicto.
address dirección, señas.
address (to) dirigir (a letter).
adequate adecuado.
adjective adjetivo.
adjoining contiguo, inmediato.
administrative administrativo.
admiral almirante.
admiration admiración.
admire admirar.
admirer admirador.
admission admisión; entrada.
    Free admission. Entrada gratis.
admit admitir, confesar, reconocer.
admittance entrada.

No admittance.   Se prohibe la entrada.
admonish amonestar, advertir.
adopt (to) adoptar.
adoption adopción.
adult adulto.
advance *n.* anticipo; adelanto; avance.
advance (to) avanzar, adelantar.
advantage beneficio, provecho.
advantageous ventajoso.
adventure aventura.
adverb adverbio.
adversity adversidad.
advertise (to) anunciar.
advertisement anuncio, publicidad.
    classified ad clasificados.
advice consejo.
advise (to) aconsejar.
aerobics aeróbica.
affected afectado.
affection afecto, cariño.
affectionate cariñoso, afectuoso.
    Affectionately yours.   Afectuosamente.
affirm (to) afirmar.
affirmative afirmativo.
afternoon tarde.
    Good afternoon! ¡Buenas tardes!
afterward después.
again otra vez; de nuevo.
against contra.
age edad.
age (epoch) época.
age (to) envejecer.
agency agencia.
agent agente.
aggravate (to) agravar.
aggressive agresivo, dinámico.
ago
    a long time ago   hace mucho tiempo.
    How long ago? ¿Cuánto tiempo hace?
agony angustia, agonía.
agree (to) acordar, convenir en.
agreeable agradable.
agreed convenido.
agreement convenio, acuerdo.
agricultural agrícola.
agriculture agricultura.
AIDS SIDA.
air aire.
airmail correo aéreo.
airplane avión.
aisle pasillo.
alarm (to) alarmar.
alarm clock despertador.
album álbum.
alcohol alcohol.
alight (to) apearse.
alike igual; semejante.
alive vivo.
all todo.

all day   todo el día.
all right   está bien, bueno.
all the same   igual, lo mismo.
allergy alergia.
allied aliado.
allow (to)   permitir.
   Allow me.   Permítame.
allowable permisible.
ally aliado.
almond almendra.
almost casi.
alone solo.
along a lo largo de.
   along with   junto con, con.
   along the side   al costado.
   all along   siempre, constantemente.
   to get along with   llevarse bien con.
   to go along with   acompañar, aceptar.
also también; además.
alternate (to)   alternar.
alternately alternativamente.
although aunque, no obstante.
always siempre.
ambassador embajador.
amber ámbar.
ambition ambición.
ambitious ambicioso.
ambulance ambulancia.
amend enmendar; corregir.
amends compensación, satisfacción.
America América.
   North America   América del Norte.
   Central America   Centroamérica.
   South America   Sudamérica.
American americano, norteamericano.
among entre.
amount importe, cantidad, suma.
amount (to)   ascender, sumar.
ample amplio.
amuse (to)   divertir.
amusement diversión, entretenimiento.
analyze (to)   analizar.
anchor ancla.
anchorman (news) locutor, presentador.
ancient antiguo.
and y, e.
anecdote anécdota.
angel ángel.
anger cólera, ira.
anger (to)   enfadar.
angry enfadado, enojado.
   to get angry   enfadarse.
animal animal.
animate (to)   animar.
ankle tobillo.
annex anexo.
annex (to)   anexar, anexionar.
anniversary aniversario.
announcement anuncio.

annual anual.
anonymous anónimo.
another otro.
answer repuesta, contestación.
answer (to)   responder, contestar.
anxious ansioso.
any cualquier, cualquiera, alguno, alguna.
anybody alguno, alguien, quienquiera.
anyhow de cualquier modo, de todos modos.
anyone cualquiera.
anything cualquier cosa, algo.
anyway comoquiera, de cualquier modo.
anywhere en cualquier lugar, dondequiera.
apart aparte, separado.
apartment departamento, apartamento, piso.
apiece cada uno; por cabeza, por persona.
apologize (to)   disculpar; excusarse.
apology excusa, disculpa.
apparatus aparato.
appeal apelación (law); súplica (request);
          atracción, simpatía (attraction).
appeal (to)   apelar, recurrir; atraer, llamar la
          atención (to attract).
appear (to)   aparecer.
appetite apetito.
applaud (to)   aplaudir.
applause aplauso.
apple manzana.
applicant aspirante, candidato.
application aplicación; solicitud (job).
apply (to)   aplicar (put on).
   to apply for solicitar.
appreciate apreciar; subir de valor.
appreciation aprecio, reconocimiento.
approach acceso (access), táctica, manera de
          plantear un asunto o de acercarse a
          una persona.
approach (to)   acercarse a (come near);
          aproximar; abordar (a subject).
approval aprobación.
approve (to)   aprobar.
April abril.
apron delantal.
arbitrary arbitrario.
arcade arcada, galería.
architect arquitecto.
architecture arquitectura.
Argentina La Argentina.
Argentinian argentino.
argument argumento; debate (to convince or
          persuade); disputa (dispute).
arid árido.
arm brazo (part of body).
arm (to)   armar.
armpit axila.
army ejército.
around alrededor.
   around here   cerca de aquí.
arrangement disposición, arreglo.

arrival llegada.
arrive (to) llegar.
art arte; destreza, técnica.
article artículo.
artificial artificial.
artist artista.
artistic artístico.
as como
    as ... as ...   tan ... como ...
    as it were   por decirlo así.
    as little as   tan poco como.
    as long as   mientras.
    as much as   tanto como.
ascertain (to) asegurar; determinar.
ashes ceniza.
aside aparte; al lado.
ask (to) preguntar (a question); pedir
    (request).
asleep dormido.
    to fall asleep   dormirse, quedarse dormido.
aspire (to) aspirar.
assassinate (to) asesinar.
assemble (to) reunir (to gather); montar,
       armar (a machine); juntar (collect).
assembly asamblea.
assets activo; capital; bienes.
assign (to) asignar.
assimilate (to) asimilar.
assist (to) ayudar, asistir.
assistance asistencia, ayuda.
associate asociado.
associate (to) asociar, asociarse.
assume (to) asumir.
assumption suposición.
assurance seguridad, certeza.
assure (to) asegurar.
astonish (to) asombrar.
astounded atónito.
astounding asombroso, sorprendente.
astronaut astronauta.
at a, en.
    at first   al principio.
    at last   al fin, por fin.
    at once   inmediatamente, al instante, de
       una vez.
    at the same time   a la vez, a un tiempo.
    at two o'clock   a las dos.
    at that time   en aquel tiempo, entonces.
    We were at John's.   Estábamos en la casa
       de Juan.
    at home   en casa.
athlete atleta.
athletic atlético.
athletics atletismo.
atmosphere atmósfera, ambiente.
atom átomo.
attach (to) prender, unir, adjuntar.
attack ataque.
attack (to) atacar.

attempt intento, tentativa.
attempt (to) intentar; tratar de; probar.
attend (to) acudir, asistir, prestar atención.
attention atención.
attentive atento.
attic buhardilla, desván.
attitude actitud.
attorney abogado.
attract (to) atraer.
attraction atracción.
attractive atractivo.
audience auditorio, público.
August agosto.
aunt tía.
authentic auténtico.
author autor.
authority autoridad.
authorize (to) autorizar.
automobile automóvil.
autumn otoño
avenue avenida.
average promedio.
    on the average   por término medio.
avoid (to) evitar.
awake *adj.* despierto.
awake (to) despertar.
aware enterado, consciente.
away ausente, fuera, lejos.
    to go away   marcharse.
awful tremendo; horrible.
awkward torpe; embarazoso, difícil
       (embarrassing, difficult).
ax, axe hacha.

B

babble parlotear.
baby nene, criatura, bebé.
bachelor soltero.
back espalda (of the body); posterior; atrás,
       detrás (behind); respaldo (of a chair).
    behind one's back   a espaldas de uno.
    back door   la puerta de atrás, puerta
       trasera.
    to go back   volver.
    to be back   estar de vuelta (regreso).
background fondo (scenery, painting, etc.);
       educación (education); antecedentes
       (of a person).
backward atrasado; tardo; retrógrado.
    to go backward   andar de espaldas.
bacon tocino.
bad mal, malo.
badge insignia; placa (of metal).
bag saco; bolsa.
bait cebo.
baker panadero.
bakery panadería.

balance balanza (for weighing); equilibrio (equilibrium); balance (bookkeeping).
bald calvo.
ball bola, pelota.
balloon globo.
banana plátano, banana.
band banda.
bandage venda.
banister baranda, barandilla.
bank banco; orilla, ribera (of river).
bank book libreta de banco.
bankruptcy quiebra, bancarrota.
baptize bautizar.
bar bar (where liquor is served); barra (of metal, etc.); tableta (of chocolate).
barbecue barbacoa, parrillada.
barber barbero, peluquero.
barbershop barbería, peluquería.
bare desnudo.
barefoot descalzo.
bargain trato, negociación; ganga (at a low price).
barge barcaza.
bark corteza (of a tree); ladrido (of a dog).
bark (to) ladrar.
barley cebada.
barn granero, establo.
barrel barril.
barren estéril.
base base.
basin palangana (bowl).
basis base, fundamento.
basket cesta, canasto.
bath baño.
bathe (to) bañar, bañarse.
battle batalla.
bay bahía.
be (to) ser; estar.
   to be hungry   tener hambre.
   to be right   tener razón.
   to be sleepy   tener sueño.
   to be slow   ser lento; atrasar, estar atrasado (of a watch).
   to be sorry   sentir.
   to be thirsty   tener sed.
   to be used to   estar acostumbrado.
   to be wrong   no tener razón.
beach playa.
beam *n.* viga, madero (of timber, etc.); rayo, destello (of light, etc.).
beaming radiante.
bean habichuela, judía, frijol, haba.
bear oso.
bear (to) aguantar, sobrellevar, sufrir (to endure, to suffer); soportar (to support); portar (to carry); tener (in mind); parir (children, etc.); producir (fruit, etc.).
   to bear a grudge   guardar rencor.

   to bear in mind   tener presente.
bearer portador.
beat (to) latir, palpitar (heart); golpear, pegar (strike); tocar (a drum); batir (eggs, etc.); ganar (in a game).
beating paliza, zurra (whipping); latido, pulsación (heart).
beautiful hermoso; bello.
beauty hermosura, belleza.
because porque.
   because of   debido a; a causa de.
become llegar a ser, convertirse (to come to be); sentar, quedar bien (to be becoming); volverse, ponerse (*sudden change*).
becoming conveniente (appropriate); gracioso, mono, que sienta bien (speaking of a dress, hat, etc.).
bed cama.
bedclothes ropa de cama.
bedroom alcoba, dormitorio.
bee abeja.
beech haya.
beef carne de vaca (meat).
beehive colmena.
beer cerveza.
beet remolacha.
before antes, antes que; ante, delante de, enfrente de.
beforehand de antemano, previamente.
beg (to) rogar.
beggar mendigo.
begin (to) empezar; comenzar.
beginning principio, comienzo.
behind atrás; detrás.
Belgian belga, bélgico.
Belgium Bélgica.
belief creencia; opinión.
believe (to) creer.
bell campana.
belong (to) pertenecer.
below abajo, debajo; más abajo.
belt cinturón.
bench banco; tribunal (court).
bend doblar; inclinarse.
beneath debajo.
benefit beneficio.
benefit (to) beneficiar.
beside al lado de, contiguo.
besides además de, por otra parte.
best mejor.
bet apuesta.
bet (to) apostar.
better mejor; más preferible.
between entre; en medio de.
beverage bebida.
beyond más allá.
bicycle bicicleta.
big grande.

bill cuenta (check, account); factura (invoice).
  bill of fare menú, lista de platos.
billion mil millones, billón.
bind (to) atar, unir; encuadernar (a book).
binding encuadernación (book); obligatorio.
birch abedul.
bird pájaro, ave.
birth nacimiento.
  to give birth dar a luz.
birthday cumpleaños.
biscuit bizcocho.
bishop obispo.
bit (a) pedacito (small amount); bit, bitio
  (computer).
bite mordedura.
bite (to) morder.
bitter amargo.
bitterness amargura.
black negro.
blackbird mirlo.
blacken (to) ennegrecer.
blame culpa.
blame (to) culpar.
blank en blanco.
blanket manta, frazada; cobija.
bleed (to) sangrar.
bless (to) bendecir.
blessing bendición.
blind *adj.* ciego.
blind (to) cegar.
blindness ceguera.
blister ampolla.
block up bloquear, obstruir.
blond rubio.
blouse blusa.
blow golpe.
blow (to) soplar.
blue azul.
blush rubor.
blush (to) ruborizarse.
board tabla (wood); pensión (food); cartón
  (pasteboard); junta, consejo (of
  directors, etc.); tablero (for chess, etc.).
  on board a bordo.
boarder pensionista.
boast jactancia.
boast (to) jactarse, hacer alarde.
boat bote, barca; barco, buque.
body cuerpo.
boil grano (on the body).
boil (to) hervir.
boiler caldera.
boiling *adj.* hirviendo.
bold audaz, termerario.
Bolivia Bolivia.
Bolivian boliviano.
bomb bomba.
bond bono (stocks).
bone hueso.

book libro.
bookseller librero.
bookshop librería.
boot bota.
border frontera; linde, límite (boundary);
  borde, ribete (edge).
bore (to) aburrir; taladrar, hacer aguejeros
  (to make holes).
boring aburrido (dull).
born nacido.
born (to be) nacer.
borrow (to) tomar prestado.
both ambos.
bother molestia (trouble).
bother (to) molestar.
bottle botella.
bottom fondo.
bound atado, amarrado (tied).
bound for destinado; con rumbo a, con
  destino a.
boundless ilimitado.
bow saludo, reverencia (greeting); arco
  (weapon, bow of a violin); proa
  (ship).
bow (to) saludar, hacer reverencia (to bend
  in reverence); doblegarse, ceder,
  someterse (to submit or yield).
bowl tazón, bol; bolos (bowling).
box caja.
boy muchacho, niño; hijo varón (male child).
boyfriend novio.
bracelet pulsera, brazalete.
braid trenza.
brain cerebro.
brake freno.
bran salvado, afrecho.
branch rama (of tree); ramal (railroad, etc.);
  sucursal (local office, etc.).
brand marca (of goods).
Brazil Brasil.
Brazilian brasileño, brasilero.
bread pan.
break ruptura.
break (to) romper.
breakdown avería; colapso (medical);
  descomposición (chemical).
breakfast desayuno.
breakfast (to) desayunarse.
breath aliento, respiración.
breathe respirar.
breathing respiración.
breeze brisa.
bribe soborno.
bribe (to) sobornar.
bride novia.
bridegroom novio.
bridge puente.
brief breve, corto.
briefly brevemente.

bright claro (opposite of dark); radiante (radiant); inteligente (clever); vivo (lively).

brighten aclarar (to make clearer); alegrar, dar vida, avivarse (to make or become cheerful).

brilliant brillante, luminoso.

brim borde, ala (hat).

bring traer.

    to bring together   juntar, reunir.

    to bring toward   acercar.

    to bring up   educar, criar (to rear); traer a discusión (a matter, etc.); subir (upstairs).

bringing up educación.

Britain La Gran Bretaña.

British británico.

broad ancho.

broadcaster locutor.

broil (to)   asar (meat).

brook arroyo.

broom escoba.

brother hermano.

brother-in-law cuñado.

brotherly fraternal.

brown café; moreno; marrón.

bruise contusión.

bruise (to)   magullar.

brush brocha, cepillo.

    clothesbrush   cepillo para la ropa.

    toothbrush   cepillo para los dientes.

brush (to)   cepillar.

brute bruto.

bubble *n.* burbuja; pompa (soap).

    bubble gum   chicle de globo.

buckle *n.* hebilla.

bud *n.* yema, brote.

buffet aparador (sideboard); buffet (restaurant).

build (to) construir.

building *n.* edificio.

bulb (electric) bombilla (eléctrica).

bull toro.

bullfighter torero.

bulletin boletín.

bundle atado; bulto.

burden carga; agobio.

bureau tocador (in a bedroom); oficina (an office).

bureaucracy burocracia.

burial entierro.

burn quemadura.

burn (to)   quemar.

    to burn up   quemarse, consumirse por completo.

burst reventón, estallido.

burst (to)   reventar, estallar.

    to burst out laughing   soltar una carcajada.

bury enterrar.

bus autobús; camión (Mexico); guagua. (P. R.)

bush arbusto.

business ocupación; negocio, firma.

businessman comerciante, hombre de negocios.

businesswoman comerciante, mujer de negocios.

busy ocupado.

but pero.

butcher carnicero.

butcher's (shop) carnicería.

butter mantequilla.

button botón.

buy (to) comprar.

buyer comprador.

by por, a, en, de, para; junto a, cerca de (near).

    by and by   poco a poco.

    by and large   por lo general, de una manera general.

    by hand   a mano.

    by reason of   por razón de.

    by that time   para entonces.

    by the way   de paso.

    by then   para entonces.

    by virtue of   en virtud de.

    Finish it by Sunday.   Termínelo para el domingo.

    Send it by airmail.   Envíelo por correo aéreo.

byte byte.

C

cab taxi, coche de alquiler.

cabbage col, repollo.

cabinet gabinete.

cable *n.* cable, cabo.

café café.

cage jaula.

cake pastel, bizcocho, torta; pastilla (soap).

calendar calendario.

calf ternera.

call llamada (act of calling, a phone call, etc.); visita (visit).

call (to)   llamar (in a loud voice); convocar (a meeting); citar (to summon); visitar (to call upon).

    to call back   llamar, hacer volver.

    to call forth   llamar a.

    to call out   gritar.

calm *adj.* quieto, tranquilo.

calm *n.* calma, silencio.

camp campamento.

camp (to) acampar.

can *n.* lata, bote, tarro.

can poder (to be able); saber (to know how); envasar en lata (to put in a can).

canal canal.

candidate candidato, aspirante.

candle vela, candela.

candy dulce, bombón, caramelo.

cap gorra, gorro.

capital capital (city, *f.*); (assets, *m.*).

captain capitán.

capture (to) capturar.

car carro automóvil, coche (passenger car).

card tarjeta; naipe, carta (playing card).

cardboard cartón.

care cuidado.

   to take care of   tener cuidado.

   to take care of   cuidar de, ocuparse de.

   in care of (c/o)   al cuidado de (a/c).

care (to) importar, interesarse, tener cuidado.

   I don't care to go.   No me interesa ir.

   He doesn't care a hang.   No le importa nada.

   I don't care.   No me importa.

   What do I care?   ¿Qué me importa?

care about (to) interersarse por, estimar.

   I don't care about him/it.   Me tiene sin cuidado. No me importa.

   He cares about his appearance.   Se cuida de su aspecto.

career carrera.

care for interesarse por, estimar, querer, gustar, desear.

   I don't care for it.   No me interesa. No me importa nada.

   I don't care for wine.   No quiero vino. No me gusta el vino.

   Would you care for some dessert?   ¿Le gustaría tomar algo de postre?

careful cuidadoso, prudente.

   Be careful!   ¡Cuidado!

careless descuidado.

carpenter carpintero.

carpet alfombra.

carry llevar, conducir, portar.

   to carry away   llevarse.

   to carry out   llevar a cabo.

   to carry on   continuar (continue), conducir (manage).

cart *n.* carro, carreta.

carve tajar, trinchar (meat); esculpir, tallar (marble, wood, etc.).

case caso (a particular instance; grammar, etc.); estuche (box for small articles); caja (case of wine, etc.).

   in case of   en caso de.

cash dinero en efectivo, caja.

   cash on hand   efectivo en caja.

   cash payment   pago al contado.

cash (to) cobrar o hacer efectivo un cheque, etc.

cashier cajero.

cask tonel.

castle castillo.

casual casual.

casually casualmente.

cat gato.

catch (to) coger, agarrar.

   to catch cold   resfriarse.

   to catch on   caer en la cuenta, comprender.

   to catch (on) fire   encenderse, prender.

   to catch up   alcanzar (overtake).

catholic católico.

cattle ganado.

cause causa; razón; motivo.

cause (to) causar, provocar.

cavalry caballería.

ceiling techo, cielo raso.

celebrate (to) celebrar.

celebration celebración, conmemoración.

celery apio.

cellar sótano.

cement cemento.

cemetery cementerio.

censorship censura.

cent céntimo.

center centro.

century siglo.

ceremony ceremonia.

certain seguro; cierto, claro, evidente.

certainly ciertamente, sin duda, a buen seguro.

certificate certificado.

chain cadena.

chain (to) encadenar.

chair silla.

chairman presidente (of a meeting).

chalk tiza.

champion campeón.

chance azar, acaso, casualidad (happening by chance); oportunidad (opportunity); probabilidad (probability); riesgo (risk).

   by chance   por casualidad.

   to take a chance   correr un riesgo, aventurarse.

chance (to) aventurar, arriesgar.

chances probabilidades, oportunidades.

change cambio (money).

change (to) cambiar.

chapel capilla.

character carácter.

characteristic *adj.* característico. típico.

charge carga (load; quantity of powder, electricity, fuel, etc.); orden, mandato (order); costo (price); cargo, acusación (accusation); carga, ataque (attack); partida cargada en cuenta (bookkeeping).

   in charge   encargado; intenno.

charge (to) cargar (a battery, etc.; to debit an account; to load; to attack); llevar, costar, cobrar (a price); acusar (to accuse).

How much do you charge for this? ¿Cuánto cobra Ud. por esto?

charges gastos (expenses); partes (cost of carriage, freight, etc.); instrucciones (to a jury, etc.).

charitable caritativo.

charity caridad.

charm encanto.

charm (to) encantar.

charming encantador.

chart carta (for the use of navigators); mapa (outline, map); cuadro, gráfico (graph).

chase (to) perseguir.

chat (to) charlar, platicar.

cheap barato.

check cheque (banking); talón de reclamo, contraseña (slip of paper); cuenta (in a restaurant); jaque (chess); control, inspección (control); restricción (restraint); obstáculo, impedimento (hindrance); verificación, comprobación (verification).

check (to) examinar (to investigate); verificar (to verify); refrenar, reprimir (to curb, to restrain); facturar (baggage); dar a guardar, dejar (to leave for safekeeping); dar jaque (chess).

checkup chequeo.

cheek mejilla (part of face).

cheer n. alegría, buen humor (gaiety); vivas, aplausos (applause).

cheerful alegre, animado.

cheer up animar; animarse, cobrar ánimo.

cheese queso.

chemical químico.

chemistry química.

cherish querer, estimar (to hold dear); acariciar, abrigar (a thought, etc.).

cherry cereza.

chest pecho (body); arca, cajón (box).

chestnut castaña.

chew (to) mascar.

chicken pollo.

chief adj. principal.

chief jefe (m.); jefa (f.).

child niño (m.); niña (f.).

childhood infancia, niñez.

Chile Chile.

Chilean chileno.

chili chile.

chimney chimenea.

chin barbilla, mentón.

china porcelana, loza.

chocolate chocolate.

choice adj. selecto, escogido.

choice n. opción, elección.

choir coro.

choke (to) sofocar, ahogar.

cholesterol colesterol.

choose (to) escoger; elegir.

chop chuleta (cut of meat).

chop (to) cortar (wood, etc.); picar carne (meat).

Christian cristiano.

Christmas Navidad.

church iglesia.

cider sidra.

cigar cigarro, puro.

cigarette cigarrillo.

cigarette lighter encendedor, mechero.

cinema cine.

cinnamon canela.

circle círculo.

circulation circulación.

cite (to) citar, mencionar.

citizen ciudadano.

city ciudad.

city hall ayuntamiento.

civil civil.

civilize (to) civilizar.

claim demanda, petición (demand); pretensión (pretension); título, derecho (title, right).

claim (to) demandar (to demand); reclamar (to seek, to obtain); sostener, pretender (to assert as a fact).

clam almeja.

clamor clamor.

clap (to) aplaudir.

class clase.

class (to) clasificar.

clause cláusula.

claw garra.

clay arcilla.

clean adj. limpio.

clean (to) limpiar.

cleanliness aseo, limpieza.

clear claro; neto (net).

clear (to) aclarar, despejar (to make clear); aclararse (to clear up); absolver (of blame, guilt); liquidar (to settle a debt, account, etc.); quitar la mesa (a table).

clearly claramente.

clerk dependiente; oficinista.

clever diestro, hábil; inteligente.

climate clima.

climb (to) trepar, subir.

cloak capa, manto.

clock reloj.

close (near) cerca; junto a.

    close by muy cerca.

close (to) cerrar (to shut, to shut down);
terminar (a meeting, etc.); finiquitar,
saldar (an account); cerrar (a deal).

closed cerrado.

closet ropero (clothes)· armario.

cloth tela, paño.

clothe (to) vestir.

clothes ropa.

cloud nube.

cloudy nublado.

clover trébol.

club club, círculo (association); porra, garrote
(stick).

clue pista.

coach coche.

coal carbón.

coast costa.

coat saco; abrigo; capa (paint).

cocaine cocaína.

cockroach cucaracha.

cocktail cóctel.

cocoa cacao.

coconut coco.

code código.

zip code código de área.

coffee café.

coffin ataúd.

coin moneda.

coincidence coincidencia.

by coincidence   por casualidad.

cold frío.

coldness frialdad.

collaborate (to) colaborar.

collar cuello.

collect (to) coleccionar; cobrar (money
due).

collection colección.

collective colectivo.

college escuela de estudios universitarios
(university); colegio (of cardinals,
etc.).

Colombia Colombia.

Colombian colombiano.

colonial colonial.

colony colonia.

color color.

color (to) colorear.

colored de color.

colt potro.

column columna.

comb peine.

comb (to) peinar.

combat combate.

combination combinación.

combine (to) combinar.

come (to) venir.

to come back   volver.

to come forward   adelantar.

to come across   encontrarse con.

to come for   venir por.

to come in   entrar en.

to come down (stairs)   bajar.

to come up (stairs)   subir.

Come on!   ¡Vamos! ¡Déjate de tonterías!

comedy comedia.

comet cometa.

comfort confort, comodidad; consuelo
(consolation).

comfort (to) confortar, consolar.

comfortable cómodo.

to be comfortable   estar a gusto, estar
bien.

comma coma.

command orden (order); mando (computer);
mando, comando (authority to
command).

command (to) mandar, ordenar.

commerce comercio.

commercial comercial, anuncio, publicidad.

commission comisión.

commit (to) cometer.

common común.

communicate (to) comunicar.

community comunidad.

companion compañero.

company compañía, sociedad anónima
(business); huéspedes, visitas
(guests).

compare (to) comparar.

comparison comparación.

by comparison   en comparación.

compassion compasión.

compatible compatible.

compete with competir con.

competent competente.

competition concurso (contest); competencia
(business).

complain (to) quejarse.

complaint queja.

complete completo.

complete (to) completar, acabar.

complex complejo.

complexion cutis, tez (skin); aspecto
(appearance).

complicate (to) complicar.

complicated complicado.

complication complicación.

compliment elogio, galantería.

compliment (to) elogiar.

compose (to) componer.

composition composición.

comprise (to) comprender, abarcar.

compromise compromiso.

compromise (to) transigir (to settle by
mutual concessions); arreglar, zanjar
(a difference between parties);
comprometer (to endanger life or
reputation).

computer computador, computadora, ordenador.

computer science   informática.

computerize computarizar.

comrade camarada.

conceit presunción.

conceive (to) concebir.

concentrate (to) concentrar.

concentration concentración.

concept concepto.

concern asunto, negocio (business, affair); interés, incumbencia (interest); empresa, casa de comercio (a business organization); ansiedad, inquietud (worry).

concern (to) importar, concernir; interesarse, preocuparse (to be concerned).

concert concierto.

concrete *adj.* concreto.

concrete *n.* hormigón.

reinforced concrete   cemento armado.

condemn (to) condenar.

condense condensar.

condom condón, goma, preservativo.

conduct conducta (behavior); manejo, dirección (direction).

conduct (to) conducir, manejar, guiar (to lead, to manage); portarse (to conduct oneself).

conductor conductor.

cone cono; barquillo (ice cream).

confer (to) conferir (to grant); conferenciar (to hold a conference); tratar, consultar (to compare views).

confidence confianza (trust); confidencia (secret).

confident *adj.* seguro, cierto, confiado.

confidential confidencial, en confianza.

confirm (to) confirmar, asegurar.

confirmation confirmación.

conflict conflicto.

confront (to) enfrentar.

confused contundido; confuso.

congeal helar.

congratulate felicitar.

congratulation enhorabuena, felicitación.

Congratulations! ¡Felicitaciones! ¡Enhorabuena!

congress congreso.

conjunction conjunción.

connect (to) conectar.

connection conexión; relación.

conquer (to) conquistar, vencer.

conquest conquista.

conscience conciencia.

conscientious concienzudo, escrupuloso.

conscious consciente.

consent consentimiento.

consent (to) consentir.

consequence consecuencia.

consequently por consiguiente, en consecuencia, por lo tanto.

conservative conservador.

consider (to) considerar.

considerable considerable.

consideration consideración.

consist of (to) consistir en, constar de, componerse de.

consistent coherente (in ideas, etc.); consistente (solid).

console (to) consolar.

consonant consonante.

constable alguacil, policía.

constant constante.

constitution constitución.

consultant consultor.

consume (to) consumir.

consumer consumidor.

consumption consumo (use of goods); consunción, tisis (med.).

contagion contagio.

contagious contagioso.

contain (to) contener.

container envase; recipiente; buque de carga.

contaminate (to) contaminar.

contemplation contemplación.

contemporary contemporáneo.

contend (to) sostener, afirmar (to assert, to maintain); contender, disputar, competir (to strive, to compete).

contents contenido.

contest concurso, competencia.

continent continente.

continuation continuación.

continue (to) continuar.

contraception contracepción.

contract contrato.

contract (to) contraer; contratar.

contractor contratista.

contradict (to) contradecir.

contradiction contradicción.

contradictory contradictorio.

contrary contrario.

on the contrary   al contrario, por el contrario.

contrast contraste.

contrast (to) contrastar.

contribute (to) contribuir.

contribution contribución.

control control, mando, dirección.

remote control   control remoto.

control (to) controlar, dominar, dirigir, verificar.

convenience conveniencia.

at your convenience   cuando le sea cómodo, cuando le venga bien.

convenient conveniente.

if it's convenient to you si le viene bien.
convent convento.
convention convención, asamblea, junta,
    congreso.
conversation conversación.
converse (to) conversar.
convert (to) convertir.
conviction convicción.
convince (to) convencer.
cook cocinero.
cook (to) cocinar.
cool fresco.
cool (to) enfriar.
cooperation cooperación.
cooperative cooperativa.
copy copia; ejemplar (of a book).
copy (to) copiar.
cordial cordial.
cork corcho; tapón (stopper).
corn maíz.
corner esquina (street); rincón (nook, corner
    of a room).
corporation corporación, sociedad anónima.
correct correcto.
correct (to) corregir.
correction corrección.
correspond (to) corresponder.
correspondence correspondencia.
correspondent corresponsal.
corresponding correspondiente.
corrupt corrompido.
corrupt (to) corromper.
cosmetics cosméticos, maquillaje.
cost costo; precio.
cost (to) costar.
Costa Rica Costa Rica.
Costa Rican costarricense, costarriqueño.
costume traje, vestido, indumentaria.
cottage casa de campo, chalet.
cotton algodón.
couch sofá.
cough tos.
cough (to) toser.
council consejo, junta, concillo (religious).
count conde (title).
count (to) contar.
counter mostrador (in a store).
countess condesa.
countless innumerable.
county país (nation); campo (opposed to
    city); patria (fatherland).
country house casa de campo.
countryman compatriota.
coup d'état golpe de estado.
courage valor, coraje.
course curso; marcha (of events); estadio
    (grounds); plato (of a meal); rumbo
    (route).
court tribunal (law); corte.

courteous cortés.
courtesy cortesía.
courtyard corral, patio.
cousin primo.
cover cubierta, tapa, tapadera.
cover (to) cubrir; tapar (to place a lid over,
    to conceal); recorrer (a distance);
    abarcar (to include).
cow vaca.
crab cangrejo.
crack hendidura, raja (split); chasquido (of a
    whip); chascarrillo (joke).
cradle cuna.
cramp n. calambre.
crash estrépito, estruendo (noise); quiebra,
    bancarrota (business); choque
    (collision).
crash (to) romperse con estrépito (to
    break); estrellarse (a plane, etc.).
cream nata, crema.
create (to) crear; ocasionar (to cause).
creation creación.
credit n. crédito.
creditor acreedor.
cricket grillo (insect).
crime crimen, delito.
crisis crisis.
critic crítico.
critical crítico.
criticism crítica.
criticize (to) criticar.
crooked torcido (bent).
crop cosecha (harvest).
cross cruz (symbol).
cross (to) cruzar, atravesar (a street);
    tachar, borrar (to cross out).
  to cross one's mind ocurrírsele a uno,
    pasarle a uno por la imaginación.
  to cross over cruzar, pasar al otro lado.
cross-examination interrogación.
cross-eyed bizco.
crossing cruce; travesía (sea); paso, vado
    (river).
crossroads encrucijada.
crouch (to) agacharse.
crow cuervo.
crowd gentío, muchedumbre.
crowded apiñado, lleno.
crown corona.
crown (to) coronar.
cruel cruel.
cruelty crueldad.
crumb migaja (a small piece).
crumbling derrumbe.
crush (to) aplastar.
cry grito; lloro (weeping).
cry (to) gritar (shout); llorar (weep).
crystal cristal.
Cuba Cuba.

Cuban cubano.
cube cubo.
cucumber pepino.
cuff puño.
culture cultura.
cup taza.
cure cura.
cure (to) curar.
curiosity curiosidad.
curious curioso.
curl rizo.
curl (to) rizar.
current *adj.* corriente.
current *n.* corriente.
curtain cortina.
curve curva.
cushion cojín.
custard flan, natilla.
custom costumbre.
customer cliente.
customshouse aduana.
customs (duties) derechos de aduana.
cut corte.
cut (to) cortar.
cycle ciclo.
cynic cínico.

D

dad papá, papacito, papáto.
dagger puñal.
daily *adj.* diario, cotidiano.
　daily newspaper diario, periódico.
dainty delicado.
dairy lechería.
dam dique, presa, embalse.
damage daño, perjuicio.
damage (to) dañar, perjudicar.
damp húmedo.
dance baile.
dance (to) bailar.
dancer bailarín *m.;* bailarina *f.*
danger peligro.
dangerous peligroso.
dare atreverse (venture); desafiar
　　(challenge).
dark o(b)scuro.
darkness o(b)scuridad.
darling amado, querido.
darn (to) zurcir, ¡maldición!
data datos
　data processing procesamiento de datos.
date fecha (time); cita (rendezvous); dátil
　　(fruit).
date (to) datar, poner la fecha.
daughter hija.
dawn madrugada, alba, aurora.
　at dawn de madrugada, al amanecer.

day día.
　day after tomorrow pasado mañana.
　day before yesterday anteayer.
　every day todos los días.
　day care cuidado diurno.
daze atontamiento, aturdimiento.
dead muerto.
deadly mortal.
deaf sordo.
dealer vendedor comerciante, traficante
　　(drugs).
dear querido, estimado, caro (expensive).
death muerte.
debatable discutible.
debate debate, discusión.
debate (to) discutir.
debt deuda.
debtor deudor.
decade década.
decay decadencia (decadence); mengua
　　(decrease); podredumbre (rot).
decay (to) decaer, declinar (decline);
　　deteriorarse (deteriorate); pudrirse,
　　dañarse (fruit, etc.); picarse, cariarse
　　(teeth).
deceit engaño.
deceive (to) engañar.
December diciembre.
decency decencia.
decent decente.
decide (to) decidir; resolver, terminar (a
　　dispute, etc.); optar por.
decision decisión.
　to make a decision tomar una decisión.
decisive decisivo.
declaration declaración.
declare (to) declarar, manifestar.
decrease mengua, diminución.
decrease (to) disminuir, reducir.
decree *n.* decreto.
dedicate dedicar.
deduct deducir, descontar, restar, subtraer.
deduction deducción, descuento, rebaja.
deep hondo, profundo.
deeply profundamente.
default incumplimiento.
defeat derrota.
defeat (to) derrotar, vencer.
defect defecto.
defective defectuoso.
defend (to) defender.
defender defensor.
defense defensa.
defer (to) diferir (to put off).
defiance desafío.
definite definido, preciso.
definition definición.
defy (to) desafiar, resistir.
degenerate (to) degenerar.

degree grado.

delay tardanza, demora, retardo.

delay (to) tardar, demorarse (to linger); retardar, diferir (to defer).

delegate delegado.

delegate (to) delegar.

delegation delegación.

deliberate adj. circunspecto, cauto (careful); pensado, premeditado (carefully thought out).

deliberate (to) deliberar.

delicacy delicadeza (finesse); golosina, bocado exquisito (food).

delicate delicado.

delicious delicioso.

delight deleite, encanto, gusto, placer.

delight (to) encantar, deleitar.

deliver (to) entregar (hand over); librar de (delivery from); pronunciar (a speech).

delivery entrega (of goods); distribución, reparto (mail).

demand demanda; reclamo.

demand (to) demandar, exigir, reclamar.

democracy democracia.

demonstrate (to) demostrar.

demonstration demostración, manifestación.

denial negativa, denegación.

denounce (to) denunciar.

dense denso.

density densidad.

dental floss hilo dental.

dentist dentista.

deny (to) negar; rehusar (to refuse to grant).

department store tienda de departamentos; almacén.

depend (to) depender.

dependence dependencia.

dependent adj. dependiente, sujeto, pendiente.

deplore (to) deplorar, lamentar.

deposit depósito.

deposit (to) depositar.

depreciate (to) despreciarse.

depreciation depreciación; desprecio (dislike).

depth profundidad.

descend (to) descender, bajar.

descendant descendiente.

descent descenso.

describe (to) describir.

description descripción.

desert desierto.

desert (to) desertar, abandonar.

deserve (to) merecer.

desirable deseable.

desire deseo.

desire (to) desear.

desirous deseoso.

desk escritorio.

desolation desolación.

despair desesperación.

despair (to) desesperar.

desperate desesperado.

despite a pesar de, a despecho de.

dessert postre.

destroy (to) destruir.

destruction destrucción.

detach (to) separar, despegar, desprender (to separate or disunite); destacar (soldiers).

detain (to) detener.

determination determinación.

determine (to) determinar.

detour desvío.

develop desarrollar; revelar (photography).

development desarrollo; revelado (photography).

devil demonio, diablo.

devilish diabólico, endiablado, satánico.

devote (to) dedicar.

devotion devoción.

devour (to) devorar, engullir.

dew sereno, rocío.

dial (clock) esfera.

dial(to) marcar un número (telephone).

dialogue diálogo.

diameter diámetro.

diamond diamante.

dictionary diccionario.

die (to) morir.

diet dieta, régimen.

differ (from) diferenciarse (to stand apart); no estar de acuerdo (to disagree).

difference diferencia; distinción (of persons, etc.).

different diferente, distinto.

difficult difícil.

difficulty dificultad.

diffuse (to) difundir.

dig (to) cavar.

digest (to) digerir.

digestion digestión.

digital digital.

dignify dignidad.

dim o(b)scuro, vago.

dimple hoyuelo.

dinner comida principal.

diplomacy diplomacia.

diplomat diplomático.

diplomatic diplomático.

direct directo (without deviation); en línea recta (straight line); derecho (straight forward).

direct (to) dirigir.

direction dirección, instrucción; modo de empleo (use).

directly directamente.
director director.
dirt mugre, suciedad.
dirty sucio.
disadvantage desventaja.
disappear (to) desaparecer.
disappearance desaparición.
disappoint (to) desengañar, desilusionar.
disappointment decepción, desengaño.
disapprove (to) desaprobar.
disarm (to) desarmar.
disaster desastre.
disastrous desastroso, funesto.
discipline disciplina, castigo.
discontent descontento.
discord discordia.
discourage (to) desanimar, desalentar.
discouragement desaliento, desánimo.
discover (to) descubrir.
discovery descubrimiento.
discreet discreto.
discretion discreción.
discuss (to) discutir (to argue); tratar (to talk over).
discussion discusión.
disease enfermedad.
disgrace deshonra.
disgrace (to) deshonrar.
disgust disgusto, asco.
disgust (to) ` disgustar, repugnar.
disgusting repugnante, odioso.
dish plato.
dishonest deshonesto.
dishwasher lavaplatos.
disillusion desilusión.
disk, diskette (floppy) disco.
dismal lúgubre, tétrico.
dismiss (to) despedir.
disobey (to) desobedecer.
disorder desorden.
dispatch despacho.
dispatch (to) despachar.
display despliegue (of troops); exhibición (show); ostentación; representación (computer).
display (to) desplegar; exhibir, mostrar (to show); representar (computer).
displease (to) desagradar.
dispute disputa.
dispute (to) disputar, discutir.
dissolve (to) disolver.
distance distancia.
distinct distinto, claro.
distinction distinción.
distinguish (to) distinguir.
distinguished distinguido.
distort (to) falsear, tergiversar.
distract (to) distraer (divert).
distraction distracción.

distribute (to) distribuir, repartir.
distribution reparto, distribución.
district distrito.
distrust desconfianza.
distrust (to) desconfiar.
disturb estorbar (to interfere with); turbar, inquieta (to disquiet); molestar (to put to inconvenience).
disturbance disturbio.
dive zambullida (into water); picado (a plane).
dive (to) zambullirse, sumergirse (into water), picar (aviation).
divide (to) dividir.
dividend dividendo.
divine divino.
diving board trampolín.
division división.
divorce divorcio.
divorce (to) divorciar.
divorced (to be) divorciarse.
dizzy mareado, aturdido.
do (to) hacer.
   How do you do? ¿Cómo le va? ¿Cómo está Ud.? ¿Qué tal?
   to do one's best hacer lo posible.
   to do without pasarse sin, prescindir de.
   to have to do with tener que ver con.
   That will do. Eso basta. Eso sirve.
   Do you believe it? ¿Lo cree Ud.?
   Do come. Venga sin falta.
dock (pier) muelle.
doctor doctor; médico.
doctrine doctrina.
document documento.
dog perro.
dogma dogma.
dome cúpula.
domestic *adj.* doméstico (pertaining to the household); casero (homemade); del país, nacional (domestic trade, etc.).
Dominican Republic República Dominicana.
Dominican dominicano.
door puerta.
double doble.
doubt duda.
doubt (to) dudar.
doubtful dudoso.
doubtless sin duda.
dough masa, pasta.
down abajo; hacia abajo.
   to go down bajar.
   to come down bajar.
   Come down! ¡Baje!
downstairs abajo, en el piso de abajo.
downward descendente, hacia abajo.
dozen docena.
draft corriente de aire (air); letra de cambio, giro (bank); quinta, conscripción

(military); borrador, anteproyecto (sketch or outline).

draft (to) redactar, escribir (a document, etc.); hacer un borrador (a tentative outline).

drag arrastrar.

drama dama.

draw (to) dibujar (with a pencil); sacar (money, liquids, etc.); correr, descorrer (curtains); librar, girar (a bank draft); cobrar (a salary); tirar (to putt); redactar, escribir (to draw up); robar, tomar (a card); sortear (lottery, etc.).

to draw back ·reintegrarse de (to get something back); retroceder (to go back).

drawer gaveta, cajón (of a desk, etc.).

drawing dibujo.

dread (to) temer.

dreaded temido.

dreadful horrible.

dream sueño.

dream (to) soñar.

dreamer soñador.

dress vestido, traje.

dress (to) vestirse (to get dressed); vendar (a wound).

dressmaker modista, costurera.

drink bebida (a beverage); trago, copa.

drink (to) beber; tomar.

drip (to) gotear.

drive paseo en coche (a ride in a car, etc.); paseo, calzada (a road); campaña (to raise money, etc.).

drive (to) conducir, guiar (a car, etc.); ir en coche (to take a ride); clavar (a nail); ahuyentar (to drive away).

driver chófer, conductor (of a car).

drop gota (of water, etc.); caída, baja (fall). cough drops pastillas para la tos.

drop (to) soltar, dejar caer (to release, to let fall); verter a gotas (fall in drops); abandonar, desistir de, dejar (to let go).

to drop in on visitar.

to drop a subject cambiar de tema.

drown ahogar.

drug droga.

drug (to) drogar.

drug addict narcómano, drogadicto.

drug trafficker traficante de drogas.

drug pusher púcher (de drogas).

druggist farmacéutico, boticario.

drugstore botica, farmacia.

drum tambor.

drunk borracho, ebrio.

drunkard borracho.

drunkenness embriaguez, borrachera.

dry seco.

dry (to) secar.

dryness sequedad.

duchess duquesa.

due debido; pagadero (payable); vencido (at a given time).

duke duque.

dull opaco, muerto (color); pesado, aburrido, sin gracia (slow, boring); estúpido (stupid).

dumb mudo (deaf and dumb); estúpido (stupid).

durable duradero.

during durante, mientras.

dusk crepúsculo.

dust polvo.

dust (to) quitar el polvo.

dusty polvoriento.

duty deber; derechos de aduana (customs).

duty free libre de derechos.

dwelling morada, residencia.

dye tinte, tintura.

dye (to) teñir.

dynasty dinastía.

E

each cada.

each one cada uno.

each other mutuamente, el uno al otro, unos a otros.

eager ansioso, deseoso.

eagle águila.

ear oído (the organ of hearing or the internal ear); oreja (the external ear); mazorca (of corn); espiga (of wheat, rye, etc.).

early temprano.

earn (to) ganar.

earnest serio (serious); ansioso (eager). in earnest de buena fe, en serio.

earth tierra.

earthquake temblor de tierra, terremoto.

ease tranquilidad, alivio; facilidad (with ease); con desahogo, cómodamente (at ease).

ease (to) aliviar, mitigar.

easily fácilmente.

east este, oriente.

Easter Pascua florida.

eastern oriental.

easy fácil.

eat (to) comer.

ecology ecología.

economic económico.

economy economía.

economy class clase turista.

Ecuador Ecuador.

Ecuadoran ecuatoriano.

edge orilla, borde (of a stream, etc.); canto (of a table, a book); filo (of a blade).

edit (to) redactar (to write); corregir, editar; montar (film).

editing redacción.

edition edición.

editor redactor, editor.

education educacion.

eel anguila.

effect efecto.

effect (to) efectuar, realizar.

efficiency eficacia.

effort esfuerzo.

egg huevo.

eggplant berenjena.

eggshell cascarón.

egoist egoista.

eight ocho.

eighteen dieciocho.

eighth octavo.

eighty ochenta.

either o, u (*conj.*); uno u otro, el uno o el otro, cualquiera de los dos.

  either one el uno o el otro, cualquiera de los dos.

elastic elástico.

elbow codo.

elder *adj.* mayor, de más edad.

elderly mayor, de edad.

elect (to) elegir.

elected electo, elegido.

election elección.

electric eléctrico.

electricity electricidad.

elegance elegancia.

elegant elegante.

element elemento.

elementary elemental.

elephant elefante.

elevation elevación; altitud.

elevator ascensor, elevador.

eleven once.

eleventh undécimo.

eliminate (to) eliminar.

eloquence elocuencia.

eloquent elocuente.

else otro, más, además.

  nothing else nada más.

  something else algo más.

  or else o bien, o en su lugar, si no.

  nobody else ningún otro.

elsewhere en alguna otra parte, en otro lugar.

elude (to) eludir, evitar.

embark (to) embarcar.

embarrass (to) desconcertar, poner en aprieto.

embarrassing desconcertante.

  in an embarrassing situation en una situación difícil, en un apuro, en un compromiso.

embassy embajada.

embody (to) encarnar.

embrace abrazo.

embrace (to) abrazar.

embroidery bordado.

emerge (to) surgir.

emergency emergencia, aprieto, apuro, necesidad urgente.

emigrant emigrante.

emigrate (to) emigrar.

emigration emigración.

eminent eminente.

emit (to) emitir.

emotion emoción.

emphasis énfasis.

emphasize (to) hacer hincapié; enfatizar.

emphatic enfático, categórico.

empire imperio.

employ (to) emplear, usar.

employee empleado.

employer patrono, patrón.

employment empleo.

empty vacío.

empty (to) vaciar.

enable (to) posibilitar; autorizar.

enclose (to) cercar (ground, etc.); incluir (in a letter, etc.).

enclosed adjunto.

encourage (to) animar.

encouragement estímulo, aliento.

end fin; final (of a street); extremidad (tip).

end (to) acabar, terminar.

endeavor esfuerzo.

endeavor (to) esforzarse.

endorse (to) endosar.

endorsement endoso.

endow (to) dotar.

endure (to) soportar, resistir, aguantar.

enemy enemigo.

energetic enérgico

energy energía.

energy crisis crisis de energía.

solar energy energía solar.

enforce hacer cumplir, poner en vigor (a law); forzar, compeler (to compel).

engage ajustar (a servant); emplear (a clerk, etc.); alquilar (a room, etc.); trabar (in a conversation, etc.).

engagement compromiso, cita (date); promesa de matrimonio, compromiso (promise of marriage); contrato (employment for a stated time).

engineer ingeniero.

English inglés.

engrave (to) grabar.

enjoy (to) gozar, disfrutar.

  to enjoy oneself divertirse.

enjoyment goce.
enlarge (to) aumentar, agrandar, ampliar.
enlargement ampliación.
enlist (to) alistarse.
enlistment alistamiento.
enough bastante, suficiente.
enrich (to) enriquecer.
entangle (to) enredar, embrollar.
enter (to) entrar (a house, etc.); anotar,
    registrar (in a register, etc.); entablar
    (into a conversation); ingresar,
    matricularse (a school); afiliarse (a
    society, etc.).
entertain (to) tener invitados, agasajar
    (guests); conversar, entretener (to talk
    to); acariciar, abrigar (ideas); divertir
    (to amuse).
entertainment entretenimiento, diversión
    (amusement); show, espectáculo
    (show).
enthusiasm entusiasmo.
enthusiastic entusiasta.
entire entero.
entitle (to) titular, poner un título (title);
    autorizar, dar derecho a (right).
entrance entrada.
entrust (to) confiar a.
entry entrada (entrance); asiento, íngreso
    (records, bookkeeping).
enumerate (to) enumerar.
envelope *n.* sobre.
enviable envidiable.
envious envidioso.
envy envidia.
envy (to) envidiar.
epidemic *adj.* epidémico; *n.* epidemia.
episode episodio.
epoch época, era.
equal igual.
equal (to) igualar.
equality igualdad.
equador ecuador.
equilibrium equilibrio.
equip (to) equipar, dotar de.
equipment equipo.
equity equidad; valor líquido.
era era, época.
erase (to) borrar, raspar.
eraser goma de borrar, borrador.
err (to) errar, equivocarse.
errand recado, mandado.
error error.
escape fuga.
escape (to) escapar, escaparse de.
escort escolta (a body of soldiers, etc.);
    acompañante (an individual).
escort (to) escoltar, acompañar.
especially especialmente, particularmente.
essay ensayo; composición (school).

essence esencia.
essential esencial, indispensable.
establish (to) establecer.
establishment establecimiento.
estate bienes, propiedades (properties,
    possessions); finca, hacienda (a
    country estate).
esteem estimación, aprecio.
esteem (to) estimar.
estimate presupuesto, cálculo, estimación
    (value).
estimate (to) tasar, calcular, estimar (judge
    value).
eternal eterno.
eternity eternidad.
ether éter.
evacuate (to) , evacuar.
even *adj.* par (not odd); parejo, llano, plano.
    to be even with   estar en paz con, estar
        mano a mano.
even *adv.* aun, hasta, no obstante.
    even as   así como
    even if   aun cuando
    even so   aun así.
    even that   hasta eso.
    not even that   ni siquiera eso.
evening tarde.
    Good evening!   ¡Buenas tardes!
    yesterday evening   ayer por la tarde.
    tomorrow evening   mañana por la tarde.
event suceso.
    in the event that   en el caso de.
ever siempre (always); nunca (never).
    as ever   como siempre.
    ever so much   muy, mucho, muchísimo.
    ever since   desde entonces.
    not . . . ever   nunca.
    nor . . . ever   ni nunca.
every cada
    every bit   enteramente.
    every day   todos los días.
    every other day   un día sí y otro no.
    every one   cada uno, cada cual.
    every once in a while   de cuando en
        cuando.
    every time   cada vez.
everybody todos, todo el mundo.
everyone todos, todo el mundo.
everything todo.
everywhere en (por) todas partes.
evidence evidencia, prueba, testimonio.
    to give evidence   dar testimonio, deponer.
evident evidente.
evil *adj.* malo.
evil *n.* mal.
evoke (to) evocar.
exact preciso, exacto.
exaggerate (to) exagerar.
exaggeration exageración.

exalt (to) exaltar.
examination examen.
examine examinar.
example ejemplo.
exasperate (to) exasperar, irritar.
excavate (to) excavar, cavar.
exceed (to) exceder.
excel (to) sobresalir, superar.
excellence excelencia.
excellent excelente.
except excepto, menos; sino, a menos que.
except (to) exceptuar, excluir.
exception excepción.
   to make an exception   hacer una excepción.
exceptional excepcional.
exceptionally excepcionalmente.
excess exceso.
excessive excesivo.
exchange cambio.
   in exchange for   a cambio de.
   rate of exchange   tipo de cambio.
exchange (to) cambiar.
excite (to) excitar.
excitement excitación, conmoción.
exclaim (to) exclamar.
exclamation exclamación.
exclude (to) excluir.
exclusive exclusivo.
excursion excursión.
excuse excusa.
excuse (to) excusar, dispensar, disculpar.
   Excuse me.   Dispense Ud.
execute (to) ejecutar.
executive ejecutivo.
exempt (to) exentar, eximir.
exercise (to) ejercer; hacer ejercicios
      (physical exercise); ejercitar (drill).
exhaust (to) agotar.
exhausted agotado, exhausto.
exhausting agotador.
exile *adj.* exilado, desterrado.
exile *n.* destierro, exilio.
exile (to)   desterrar.
exist (to) existir.
existence existencia.
exit salida.
expand (to) extender(se), ensanchar(se);
      dilatar(se), desarrollar(se).
expansion expansión.
expansive expansivo.
expect (to) esperar, aguardar.
expectation expectativa, esperanza.
expel (to) expulsar.
expense gasto, coste.
   at one's expense   a costa de uno.
expensive caro, costoso.
experience experiencia, práctica.
experience (to) experimentar; pasar por
     (undergo).

experiment experimento.
experiment (to) experimentar.
experimental experimental.
expert experto.
expire (to) expirar.
explain (to) explicar.
explanation explicación.
explanatory explicativo.
explode (to) estallar.
exploit hazaña, proeza.
exploit (to) explotar, sacar partido.
exploration exploración.
explore (to) explorar.
explorer explorador.
explosion explosión.
export exportación.
export (to) exportar.
expose (to) exponer.
express *adj.* expreso.
express (to) expresar.
expression expresión.
expulsion expulsión.
exquisite exquisito.
extend (to) extender.
extensive extensivo.
extent extensión.
   to a certain extent   hasta cierto punto.
exterior exterior.
exterminate (to) exterminar.
external externo.
extinguish (to) extinguir.
extra extra, extraordinario.
extract extracto.
extract (to) extraer.
extravagance extravagancia.
extravagant extravagante.
extreme extremo.
extremity extremidad.
eye ojo.
eyebrow ceja.
eyeglasses anteojos, espejuelos, lentes, gafas.
eyelash pestaña.
eyelid párpado.
eyewitness testigo ocular.

F

fable fábula.
fabric tela.
fabulous fabuloso.
face cara.
   face value   valor nominal.
fact hecho.
   in fact   en realidad.
factory fábrica; factoría (U.S. Span.).
faculty facultad (school); profesorado
     (teachers).

fade palidecer, marchitarse; desteñirse (color).

fail omisión, falta.

   without fail   sin falta.

fail (to) fracasar, no tener suerte (in an undertaking); salir mal (in an exam); decaer, ir a menos (health); faltar, dejar de (to do something).

   not to fail   no dejar de.

failure fracaso; falta (fault, defect); quiebra (bankruptcy).

faint (to) desmayarse.

fair adj. rubio (hair); blanco (complexion); claro (clear); justo, recto (just); regular, mediano (moderate); despejado, buen (weather).

   fair play   juego limpio.

   fair weather   buen tiempo.

fair n. feria (exhibition, place for trade).

fairness justicia, equidad.

fairy tale cuento de hadas.

faith fe, confianza.

faithful fiel.

fall caída; otoño (autumn).

fall (to) caer; caerse (fall down).

false falso.

fame fama, renombre.

familiar familiar.

familiarity familiaridad, confianza.

family familia.

famine hambre.

famous famoso.

fan abanico; ventilador (electric fan).

fancy fantasía; capricho (whim).

fantastic fantástico.

far lejos.

   How far?   ¿A qué distancia?

   far away   muy lejos.

   so far   hasta aquí, hasta ahora.

   As far as I'm concerned.   En cuanto a mí toca.

   by far   con mucho.

fare tarifa, pasaje.

farmer agricultor, labrador, campesino.

farming agricultura, cultivo de la tierra.

farther más lejos, más allá; además de.

fashion moda.

fashionable a la moda, de moda, elegante, de buen tono.

fast pronto, de prisa (quickly).

fasten fijar, sujetar.

fat adj. gordo.

fat n. manteca, grasa.

fate destino, fatalidad.

father padre.

fatherhood paternidad.

father-in-law suegro.

fatten engordar.

faucet grifo, llave, canilla.

fault falta, culpa.

favor favor, servico.

favor (to) hacer un favor, favorecer.

favorite favorito, preferido.

fear miedo, temor.

fearless intrépido.

feast fiesta, banqueta.

feather pluma.

feature rasgo, característica.

February febrero.

federal federal.

fee honorarios; cuota.

feeble débil, enfermizo.

feed alimentar, dar de comer.

feeding alimentación.

feel (to) sentir; tocar (touch).

feeling tacto (tact); sentimiento (sentiment); sensibilidad (sensitiveness).

fellow sujeto, individuo.

   fellow student   condiscípulo.

   fellow traveler   compañero de viaje.

   fellow worker   compañero de trabajo.

female hembra, femenino.

feminine femenino.

fence valla, cerca.

ferment (to) fermentar.

fermentation fermentación.

ferry ferry, barca de transbordo.

fertile fecundo, fértil.

fertilize (to) fertilizar, fecundar.

fertilizer abono.

fervent ferviente.

fervor fervor.

festival fiesta, festival.

fever fiebre.

feverish febril.

few pocos.

   a few   unos cuantos, unos pocos.

   a few days   unos pocos días.

fewer menos.

fiber fibra.

fickle variable, caprichoso.

fiction ficción; novela (novel).

field campo; campaña (military); ramo, especialidad (specialty).

fierce feroz.

fiery vehemente, furibundo.

fifteenth decimoquinto.

fifth quinto.

fifty cincuenta.

fig higo.

   fig tree   higuera.

fight riña, pelea, lucha, conflicto.

fight (to) pelear, luchar, combatir.

figure figura, silueta (body).

file lima (for nails, etc.); archivo, fichero (for papers, cards, etc.).

file (to) limar (with an instrument); archivar (papers etc.).

fill (to) llenar.
film película.
filthy sucio, inmundo.
final final.
finally finalmente, por último.
finance n. hacienda, finanzas.
finance (to) financiar.
financial financiero.
financing financiamiento, financiación.
find (to) hallar, encontrar.
fine adj. fino, buen, magnífico, excelente.
    Fine! ¡Muy bien!
fine n. multa.
finger dedo.
finish (to) terminar; acabar.
fire fuego, incendio.
fire (to) incendiar (burn); disparar (a gun);
    despedir, dejar cesante (an employee).
fireman bombero.
firm adj. seguro, firme.
firm n. firma (business).
firmness firmeza.
first primero.
    at first al principio.
    at first glance a primera vista.
firstly primeramente.
fish pez (in water); pescado (when caught).
fish (to) pescar.
fisherman pescador.
fishing pesca.
fist puño.
fit adj. apto, idóneo, adecuado, conveniente, a
    propósito.
    to see fit juzgar conveniente.
    If you think fit. Si a Ud. le parece.
fit (to) ajustar, adaptar; entallar (to fit a
    dress, etc.); caer bien, sentar bien (to
    have the right size or shape).
    to fit into encajar en.
    That would fit the case. Eso sería lo
    propio.
    The dress fits you well. El vestido le
    sienta bien.
    It fits badly. Me sienta mal.
fitness aptitud; estado físico.
fitting (to be) sentar bien, venir bien.
five cinco.
fix (to) arreglar, componer, reparar (to
    repair).
flag bandera.
flagrant flagrante, descarado.
flame llama.
flannel franela.
flash n. destello (light); relámpago
    (lightning).
flashlight linterna.
flat plano, chato; insípido, soso (taste).
flatten (to) aplastar, aplanar.
flatter adular.

flattery adulación, lisonja.
flavor sabor, gusto.
flavor (to) sazonar, condimentar.
flax lino.
flea pulga.
    flea market mercado de artículos usados.
fleet flota, armada.
flesh carne; pulpa (fruit).
flexibility flexibilidad, docilidad.
flexible flexible.
flight vuelo (in the air); fuga (from jail,
    etc.).
float flotar; fluctuar (currency).
flood inundación.
flood (to) inundar.
floor piso.
floss, dental seda vegetal, hilo dental.
flour harina.
flow (to) fluir, manar, correr.
flower flor.
flowery florido.
fluency dominio; fluidez.
fluid fluido, líquido.
fly mosca.
fly (to) volar.
foam espuma.
foam (to) hacer espuma.
focus foco.
fog niebla, neblina.
fold pliegue, doblez.
fold (to) doblar, plegar.
foliage follaje.
follow (to) seguir.
following siguiente.
food comida.
fool tonto, bobo, necio.
foolish tonto, disparatado.
foolishness tontería.
foot pie.
    on foot a pie.
football fútbol (soccer).
footnote anotación.
for para, por.
    This is for her. Esto es para ella.
    for example por ejemplo.
    for the first time por la primera vez.
    for the present por ahora.
    for the time being por de pronto.
forbid (to) prohibir.
forbidden prohibido.
force fuerza.
force (to) forzar, obligar.
forced obligado.
forecast pronóstico.
forecast (to) pronosticar, vaticinar.
forehead frente.
foreign extranjero, exterior, ajeno.
foreigner extranjero.
foresee (to) prever.

forest selva, bosque.
forget (to) olvidar.
forgive (to) perdonar.
forgiveness perdón.
fork tenedor.
form forma.
form (to) formar.
formal ceremonioso (ceremonial);
    convencional (official).
formality formalidad, ceremonia.
formation formación.
former previo, anterior.
former (the) aquél, aquélla, aquéllos,
    aquéllas, aquello.
formerly antiguamente, en otros tiempos.
formula fórmula.
forsake desamparar, abandonar.
fortunate afortunado.
fortunately afortunadamente.
fortune suerte, fortuna.
fortune-teller adivino.
fortune-telling adivinación.
forty cuarenta.
forward *adv.* adelante, en adelante.
forward (to) remitir, reexpedir.
found encontrado.
found (to) fundar
foundation fundación.
founder fundador.
fountain fuente.
fountain pen estilográfica, pluma fuente.
four cuatro.
four-letter word palabrota (palabra) taca.
fourteen catorce.
fourth cuarto.
fowl aves.
fragment fragmento.
fragrance fragrancia, aroma.
fragrant oloroso, fragante.
frail débil, frágil.
frame marco (of a picture, door, etc.);
    armazón, entramado, estructura
    (structure).
  frame of mind estado de ánimo.
frame (to) encuadrar, poner en un marco (a
    picture, etc.).
France Francia.
frank franco, sincero.
frankness franqueza.
free *adj.* libre; gratis.
  free of charge gratis.
free (to) libertar, librar.
freeze (to) helar, congelar.
freight carga; flete.
French francés.
frequent frecuente.
frequent (to) frecuentar.
frequently frecuentemente.
fresh fresco.

Friday viernes.
friend amigo.
friendly amistoso.
friendship amistad
frighten (to) asustar.
frightening espantoso.
frivolity frivolidad, trivialidad.
frivolous frívolo.
frog rana.
from de, desde.
  from a distance desde lejos.
  from memory de memoria.
front *adj.* anterior, delantero, de frente.
  front door puerta de entrada.
  front view vista de frente.
front frente.
  in front of frente a.
frown ceño, entrecejo.
frown (to) fruncir el ceño.
fruit fruta.
fry (to) freír.
frying pan sartén.
fuel combustible.
fugitive fugitivo.
fulfill (to) cumplir.
full lleno.
fully plenamente, enteramente.
fun broma; diversión.
  to have fun divertirse, pasar un buen rato.
  to make fun of burlarse de.
function función.
function (to) funcionar.
fundamental fundamental.
funds fondos.
funeral funeral, entierro.
funny divertido, cómico.
fur piel(es).
furious furioso.
furnace horno.
furnish amueblar (a room, house, etc.);
    suplir (supply); proveer (provide).
furniture muebles.
furrow surco.
further *adv.* más lejos, más allá; además,
    aún.
  further on más adelante; y además de eso
    (in speech).
fury furor.
fusion fusión.
future futuro.
  in the future en lo sucesivo, en adelante,
    en lo futuro.

G

gaiety alegría, alborozo.
gain ganancia.
gain (to) ganar.

gallon galón.

gamble (to) jugar por dinero.

game juego; partida, partido; caza (hunting).

    a game of chess   una partida de ajedrez.

garage garage.

garden jardín, huerta.

gardener jardinero, hortelano.

gargle (to) hacer gárgaras.

garlic ajo.

garment prenda de vestir, vestido.

garter liga.

gas gas; gasolina (gasoline).

    gas station   gasolinera.

gasoline gasolina.

    gasoline station   gasolinera.

gate puerta.

gather (to) reunir, juntar.

gay adj. alegre; homosexual.

gearbox caja de cambios.

gem piedra preciosa.

gender género; sexo.

general adj. general.

    in general   en general, por lo general.

general n. general.

generality generalidad.

generalize (to) generalizar.

generally generalmente, por lo general.

generation generación.

generosity generosidad.

generous generoso.

genius genio.

gentle suave; amable, delicado (of a person).

gentleman caballero.

    gentlemen   señores; muy señores
        míos/nuestros (in a letter).

gentleness amabilidad, delicadeza.

gently suavemente; amablemente.

genuine genuino, auténtico.

geographical geográfico.

geography geografía.

geometric geométrico.

geometry geometría.

germ germen; microbio.

German alemán.

Germany Alemania

gesture n. gesto, ademán.

get (to) adquirir, obtener, conseguir, recibir.

    to get ahead   adelantarse.

    to get away   partir, marcharse; huir.

    to get back   recuperar.

    to get home   llegar a casa.

    to get in   entrar.

    to get married   casarse.

    to get off   apearse, bajar.

    to get on   montar, subir.

    to get out   salir.

    to get up   levantarse; subir.

ghost fantasma.

giant gigante.

gift regalo, obsequio.

gifted agraciado; talentoso, inteligente.

ginger jengibre.

girl chica, niña, muchacha.

give (to) dar.

    to give in   ceder, acceder.

    to give up   desistir, darse por vencido.

    to give a gift   regalar, hacer un regalo.

glad contento, feliz.

    to be glad   alegrarse de, tener gusto en.

glance ojeada, vistazo.

glance (to) echar un vistazo, dar una ojeada.

    to glance at a book   hojear un libro.

glass vidrio; vaso (for drinking).

    looking glass   espejo.

    drinking glass   vaso.

glimpse n. ojeada, vistazo.

glitter (to) brillar, resplandecer.

globe globo.

gloomy triste, sombrío.

glorious glorioso.

glory n. gloria.

glove guante.

glue n. cola, goma de pegar.

go (to) ir.

    to go away   irse, marcharse.

    to go back   volverse atrás, retroceder;
        regresar, volver.

    to go down   bajar.

    to go forward   ir adelante, adelantarse.

    to go out   salir; apagarse (a light, fire,
        etc.).

    to go up   subir.

    to go with   acompañar.

    to go without   pasarse sin.

goal meta, objetivo, fin.

    to reach one's goal   alcanzar el objetivo,
        llegar a la meta, obtener lo que uno se
        había propuesto.

goalpost poste.

God Dios.

godfather padrino.

godmother madrina.

gold oro.

golden de oro, dorado.

good buen(o).

    good morning   buenos días.

    good evening   buenas tardes.

    good night   buenas noches.

good-bye adiós, hasta luego.

goodness bondad

    Goodness! (Goodness gracious!) ¡Válgame
        Dios! ¡María santísima!

    Goodness knows! ¡Quién sabe!

goods mercancías, géneros, efectos.

goodwill buena voluntad; nombre, reputación.

goose ganso.

gossip chisme, chismografía, murmuración.

gossip (to) chismear, murmurar.

gourmet *n.* gastrónomo.
govern (to) gobernar.
government gobierno.
governor gobernador.
grab (to) agarrar, arrebatar
grace *n.* gracia.
graceful gracioso.
gracious bondadoso, afable, cortés.
grade grado, calidad.
gradual gradual.
gradually gradualmente.
graduate (a) graduado, recibido de (doctor, etc.).
graduate (to) graduarse, recibir un título.
graduated (be) graduarse, recibirse.
grain grano.
grammar gramática.
grammatical gramatical.
grand grand, grandioso, magnífico, espléndido.
   Grand! ¡Estupendo! ¡Magnífico!
grandchild nieto.
granddaughter nieta.
grandfather abuelo.
grandmother abuela.
grandparents abuelos.
grandson nieto.
grant concesión; donación.
grant (to) conceder, otorgar.
   to take for granted   dar por sentado, presuponer.
   granting (granted) that   supuesto que, concedido que.
grape uva.
grapefruit toronja, pomelo.
grasp (to) empuñar, agarrar; comprender, percibir.
grass hierba, pasto, césped; yerba (marijuana).
grasshopper saltamontes.
grateful agradecido.
gratefully agradecidamente, gratamente.
gratis gratis, de balde.
gratitude agradecimiento.
grave *adj.* grave, serio.
grave *n.* sepultura, tumba.
gravel grava.
gravity gravedad, seriedad.
gravy salsa.
gray gris (color), cano (hair).
   gray-haired   canoso.
grease grasa.
grease (to) engrasar.
great gran, grande.
   a great man   un gran hombre.
   a great many   muchos.
   a great deal   mucho.
   Great!   ¡Estupendo! ¡Magnífico!
Great Britain Gran Bretaña.
greatness grandeza, grandiosidad.

green verde.
greet (to) saludar.
greeting saludo.
grief pesar, dolor, pena.
grieve (to) penar, afligirse.
grill (to) asar a la parrilla.
grind (to) moler.
groan gemido.
groan (to) gemir.
grocer tendero; bodeguero; abarrotero (Mex.).
groceries comestibles, abarrotes (Amer.).
grocery (store) tienda de comestibles, abarrotes (Amer.), bodega.
groove ranura.
grope (to) andar a tientas.
ground *n.* tierra, suelo, terreno.
group grupo.
group (to) agrupar.
grow (to) crecer.
   to grow old   envejecer.
   to grow late   hacerse tarde.
   to grow better   ponerse mejor, mejorar.
   to grow worse   ponerse peor, empeorar.
growth crecimiento.
grudge rencor.
gruff áspero, brusco.
grumble (to) refunfuñar, grunir.
guarantee garantía
guarantee (to) garantir.
guard guardia; guarda; guardián.
guard (to) guardar, vigilar.
   to guard against   guardarse de.
Guatemala Guatemala.
Guatemalan guatemalteco.
guess conjetura, suposición.
guess (to) adivinar, conjeturar.
   to guess right   acertar.
guest huésped, invitado.
   guest house   pensión, casa de huéspedes.
guide guía.
guide (to) guiar.
guidebook guía (de viajeros).
guilt culpa.
guilty culpable.
guitar guitarra.
gulf golfo.
gum encía (teeth).
   chewing gum   chicle.
gun arma de fuego, pistola, fusil, revólver.
gymnasium gimnasio.
gypsy gitano.

H

habit costumbre, hábito.
   to be in the habit of   estar acostumbrado
habitual acustombrado.

hail granizo (during thunderstorm); viva
    (cheering, greeting).
hail (to) granizar (in a thunderstorm);
    aclamar (to cheer).
hair pelo, cabello.
    hairbrush   cepillo para el pelo.
    haircut   corte de pelo.
    hairdye   tintura para el pelo.
    hairpin   horquilla.
    hairdo   peinado
half medio; mitad.
    half and half   mitad y mitad.
    half past two   las dos y media.
    half hour   media hora.
    half year   semestre.
half brother hermanastro.
half sister hermanastra.
halfway a medio camino, a medias.
hall vestíbulo (entrance, foyer); salón
    (assembly room).
halt alto, parada.
halt (to) parar, detener.
    Halt   ¡Alto!
ham jamón.
hamburger hamburguesa.
hammer martillo.
hammer (to) martillar.
    to hammer on a subject   machacar.
hand mano; manecilla (of a watch).
    by hand   a mano.
    in hand   entre manos; (dinero) en mano.
    offhand   improvisadamente, de repente;
        sin preparación.
    on hand   disponible, a la mano.
    on the other hand   por otra parte.
hand over (to) entregar.
handbag bolso cartera,
handbook manual
handful puñado.
handkercheif pañuelo.
handle mango, asa.
handle (to) manejar, manipular.
handmade hecho a mano.
handshake apretón de manos.
handsome guapo.
hang (to) colgar.
hanger (clothes) colgadero, percha.
happen (to) suceder, acontecer.
happening suceso, acontecimiento.
happiness dicha, felicidad.
happy feliz, contento.
harbor puerto.
hard duro; difícil.
    hard luck   mala suerte.
    hard work   trabajo difícil.
    to rain hard   llover a cántaros.
    to work hard   trabajar duro.
harden (to) endurecer.
hardly apenas, difícilmente, escasamente.

hardness dureza.
hardware ferretería, quincalla, hardware
    (computer).
hardware store ferretería.
hardy fuerte, robusto.
hare liebre.
harm n. mal, prejuicio, daño.
harmful nocivo, dañoso, dañino.
harmless inofensivo, inocuo.
harmonious armonioso.
harmonize (to) armonizar.
harmony armonía.
harness n. aparejo, arnés.
harsh áspero, tosco; desagradable.
harvest n. cosecha.
haste prisa.
    in haste   de prisa.
hasten (to) darse prisa, apresurarse.
hasty apresurado.
hat sombrero.
hatch (to) empollar.
hatchet hachuela.
hate odio.
hate (to) odiar, detestar.
hateful odioso.
hatred odio, aborrecimiento.
haughty soberbio, altivo.
have (to) tener (to possess); haber
    (auxiliary).
    to have in mind   tener en cuenta.
    to have to   tener que.
    to have a mind to   querer, tener ganas de.
hay heno.
he él.
head cabeza, jefe (chief).
head (to) encabezar.
headache dolor de cabeza.
heading encabezamiento, título.
headline n. encabezamiento, titular.
headphones auriculares.
headquarters cuartel general (Army); oficina
    principal (main office).
heal (to) curar; recobrar la salud; cicatrizarse
    (a wound).
health salud.
    to be in good heatlh   estar bien de salud.
healthful saludable, sano.
healthy sano.
heap n. montón.
    in heaps   a montones.
heap (to) acumular, apilar.
hear (to) oír.
    to hear from   saber de, tener noticias de.
heart corazón.
    heart and soul   en cuerpo y alma.
    by heart   de memoria.
    to have no heart   no tener corazón.
    to take to heart   tomar a pecho.
hearth hogar.

hearty cordial (warm); voraz (appetite).
heat calor.
heat (to) calentar.
heater calentador.
heating calefacción.
heaven cielo.
   Heavens! ¡Cielos!
heavy pesado.
   heavy rain lluvia fuerte, aguacero.
hedge seto.
heel talón (of foot); tacón (shoe).
height altura.
heir heredero.
hell infierno.
Hello! ¡Hola!
help ayuda, auxilio.
help (to) ayudar.
   to help oneself to servirse (comida).
helper asistente, ayudante.
helpful útil, provechoso.
hemisphere hemisferio.
hemorrhage hemorragia.
hen gallina.
henceforth de aquí en adelante, en lo futuro.
her la, le (a ella), ella (de ella), su
herb hierba
here aquí; acá.
   Here it is. Aquí está.
   Come here. Ven acá.
   around here cerca de aquí, por aquí.
   near here cerca de aquí.
hereabout por aquí, por aquí cerca.
hereafter en adelante.
herein aquí dentro, adjunto.
herewith con esto.
heritage herencia.
hero héroe.
heroic heroico.
heroin heroína.
heroine heroína.
heroism heroísmo.
herring arenque.
hers suyo, suya, de ella; el suyo, la suya, los
      suyos, las suyas.
herself ella misma; sí misma; se, sí.
   by herself sola; por sí, por su cuenta.
   she herself ella misma, en persona.
hesitant indeciso, vacilante.
hesitate (to) vacilar.
hesitation vacilación, titubeo.
hiccup hipo.
hidden escondido.
hide (to) esconder, esconderse.
hideous horrible, espantoso.
high alto, elevado, caro (price).
   It is five inches high. Tiene cinco
      pulgadas de alto.
higher más alto; superior.
highway carretera, autopista

hill colina, cerro.
him él, le (a él).
himself el mismo; sí mismo, se, sí.
   by himself solo; por sí, por su cuenta.
   he himself él mismo, en persona.
hinder (to) impedir, estorbar.
hindrance impedimento, estorbo, obstáculo.
hinge gozne, bisagra.
hint insinuación, idea, indirecta, alusión.
hint (to) insinuar.
   to hint at aludir a.
hip cadera.
hire (to) alquilar, emplear.
his su, sus, suyo, suya, el suyo, la suya, los
      suyos, las suyas, de él.
hiss (to) silbar.
historian historiador.
historic historico.
history historia.
hit golpe.
hit (to) golpear.
   to hit the mark dar en el blanco.
hive colmena.
hoarse ronco.
hobby pasatiempo.
hoe azada.
hog cerdo, puerco.
hold (to) tener (in one's hands, arms, etc.);
      coger, agarrar, asir (to grasp); caber,
      contener (to contain, to have capacity
      for); tener, desempeñar (a job, etc.).
   to hold good valer, ser válido.
   to hold a meeting celebrar una reunión.
   to hold one's own mantenerse firme,
      defenderse bien.
   to hold a conversation sostener una
      conversación.
hole agujero; hueco.
holiday día festivo, día feriado.
holidays vacaciones.
holy santo.
homage homenaje.
home hogar, casa, domicilio.
   at home en casa.
   hometown pueblo natal.
homely sencillo.
homemade casero, hecho en casa.
homework deber, tarea.
homosexual homosexual.
Honduras Honduras.
Honduran hondureño.
honest honrado.
honesty honradez.
honey miel.
honor honor, honra.
honor (to) honrar.
honorable honroso; honorable.
hoof casco, pezuña.
hook n. gancho; anzuelo (for fishing).

hope esperanza.
hope (to) esperar.
hopeful lleno de esperanzas, optimista.
hopeless desesperado, sin remedio.
horizon horizonte.
horizontal horizontal.
horn cuerno (of animals); bocina (of car).
horrible horrible, terrible.
horror horror.
horse caballo.
   on horseback   a caballo
hosiery medias, calcetines.
hospitable hospitalario.
hospital hospital.
hospitality hospitalidad.
host anfitrión.
hostess anfitriona.
hot caliente.
hotel hotel.
hour hora.
house casa.
housewife ama de casa, madre de familia.
how cómo; qué, cuánto.
   How do you do?   ¿Cómo le va? ¿Cómo
     está Ud.? ¿Qué tal?
   How many?   ¿Cuántos?
   How much?   ¿Cuánto?
   How far?   ¿A qué distancia?
   How early?   ¿Cuándo? ¿A qué hora?
   How late?   ¿Hasta qué hora? ¿Cuándo?
   How long?   ¿Cuánto tiempo?
   How soon?   ¿Cuándo a más tardar?
however sin embargo.
huge inmenso, enorme.
human humano.
   human race   género humano.
humane humanitario, bienhechor.
humanity humanidad.
humble humilde.
humid húmedo.
humiliate (to) humillar.
humiliation humillación.
humility humildad.
humor humor.
humorous humorista, chistoso, jocoso.
hundred cien, ciento.
hundredth centésimo.
hunger hambre.
hungry (to be) tener hambre.
hunt caza.
hunt (to) cazar.
hunter cazador.
hunting caza.
hurry prisa.
   to be in a hurry   tener prisa, estar de prisa.
hurry (to) apresurar.
   to hurry up   darse prisa.
   Hurry up!   ¡Date prisa! (familiar). ¡Dése
     prisa!

hurt (to) lastimar, herir; ofender (one's
     feelings).
husband esposo.
hydrant boca de agua.
hygiene higiene.
hyphen guión.
hypnotism hipnotismo.
hypnotize (to) hipnotizar.
hypocrisy hipocresía.
hypocrite hipócrita.
hysteria histeria.
hysterical histérico.

I

I yo.
ice hielo.
ice cream helado.
idea idea.
ideal ideal.
idealism idealismo.
idealist idealista.
identical idéntico.
identification identificación.
identify (to) identificar.
identity identidad.
   ID card   tarjeta de identificación.
idiom modismo.
idiot idiota, imbécil.
idle ocioso.
idleness ocio.
idol ídolo.
if si
   if not   si no.
   even if   aun cuando.
   If I may.   Con su permiso. Si me permite.
ignorance ignorancia.
ignorant ignorante, inculto.
ignore (to) ignorar, pasar por alto, no hacer
     caso.
ill enfermo (sick) mal, malo (wrong, bad).
   ill breeding   malos modales.
   ill will   mala voluntad.
illegal ilegal.
illegible ilegible.
illiteracy analfabetismo.
illiterate analfabeto.
illness enfermedad.
illogical ilógico.
illuminate (to) iluminar, alumbrar.
illumination iluminación, alumbrado.
illusion ilusión.
illustrate ilustrar.
illustrated ilustrado.
illustration ilustración (picture, etc.); ejemplo
     (example).
image imagen.
imaginary imaginario.

imagination imaginación.
imaginative imaginativo.
imagine (to) figurar, imaginar.
 Just imagine! ¡Imagínese!
imitate (to) imitar.
imitation imitación.
immediate inmediato.
immediately inmediatamente, en seguida, en
 el acto.
immense inmenso.
immigrant inmigrante.
immigrate (to) inmigrar.
immigration inmigración.
imminent inminente.
immoderate inmoderado, excesivo.
immoral inmoral.
immorality inmoralidad.
immortal inmortal.
immorality inmortalidad.
impartial imparcial.
impatience impaciencia.
impatient impaciente.
imperative imperativo.
imperceptible imperceptible.
imperfect imperfecto, defectuoso.
impersonal impersonal
impertinence impertinencia.
impertinent impertinente.
impetuous impetuoso, arrebatado.
implement herramienta, utensilio.
implied implícito.
imply (to) implicar; querer decir, significar.
impolite descortés.
import (to) importar
importance importancia.
important importante.
importation importación.
importer importador.
impose (to) imponer; abusar de (impose
 upon).
imposing imponente; abusivo.
impossibility imposibilidad.
impossible imposible.
impress (to) impresionar.
impression impresión.
 to have the impression tener la impresión.
impressive impresionante, grandioso.
imprison encarcelar, aprisionar.
improbable improbable.
improper improprio.
improve (to) mejorar, perfeccionar;
 adelantar, progresar; aliviarse;
 mejorarse (health).
improved mejorado, perfeccionado.
improvement mejora, adelanto, progreso,
 perfeccionamiento; alivio, mejoría
 (health).
improvise (to) improvisar.
imprudence imprudencia.

imprudent imprudente.
impure impuro.
in en.
 in fact en efecto.
 in the morning por la mañana.
 in a week de aquí a una semana, dentro
  de una semana.
 to be in estar en (casa, en la oficina,
  etc.).
 in front enfrente, delante.
 in general en general, por lo general.
 in part en parte.
 in reality en realidad.
 in spite of a pesar de.
 in turn por turno.
 in vain en vano.
 in writing por escrito.
inability ineptitud, inhabilidad, incapacidad.
inaccessible inaccesible.
inaccuracy inexactitud.
inaccurate inexacto.
inactive inactivo.
inadequate inadecuado.
inaugurate inaugurar.
incapability incapacidad.
incapable incapaz.
incapacity incapacidad.
inch pulgada.
incident incidente.
inclination inclinación, propensión.
include incluir, comprender.
included inclusive, incluso, comprendido.
inclusive inclusivo.
incoherent incoherente.
income renta, ingreso.
incomparable incomparable.
incompatible incompatible.
incomprehensible incomprensible.
inconsistent inconsistente.
inconvenience inconveniencia; molestia.
inconvenience (to) incomodar, molestar.
inconvenient inconveniente; incómodo,
  molesto.
incorrect incorrecto.
increase aumento.
increase (to) aumentar.
incredible increíble.
incurable incurable
indebted endeudado, lleno de deudas.
indecent indecente.
indeed verdaderamente, realmente, de veras,
  a la verdad, sí, claro está.
 Indeed? ¿De veras?
 Yes indeed! ¡Claro que sí! ¡Claro está!
 No indeed! ¡Quiá! ¡De ninguna manera!
indefinite indefinido.
independence independencia.
independent independiente; acomodado.
indescribable indescriptible.

index índice.
index finger índice.
indicate indicar.
indifference indiferencia.
indifferent indiferente.
indigestion indigestión.
indignant indignado.
indignation indignación.
indirect indirecto.
indiscreet indiscreto.
indispensable indispensable.
indisputable indisputable.
indistinct indistinto.
individual *adj.* individual, particular.
individual *n.* individuo.
individuality individualidad, personalidad.
individually individualmente.
indivisible indivisible.
indolence indolencia.
indolent indolente.
indoors dentro, en casa.
indulge dar rienda suelta a, darse gusto;
    entregarse a (to indulge in).
indulgence indulgencia; complacencia
    (self-indulgence).
indulgent indulgente.
industrial industrial.
industrious diligente, trabajador.
industry industria.
inefficient ineficaz.
inequality desigualdad.
inevitable inevitable.
inexcusable inexcusable, imperdonable.
inexhaustible inagotable.
inexpensive barato.
inexperience inexperiencia.
infallible infalible.
infant infante, niño.
infantry infantería.
infection infección.
infectious infeccioso, contagioso.
infer (to) inferir; colegir.
inference inferencia.
inferior inferior.
inferiority inferioridad.
infest (to) infestar, plagar.
infinite infinito.
infinitive infinitivo.
infinity infinidad.
inflate (to) inflar.
inflation inflación.
influence influencia.
influence (to) influir.
    to influence by suggestion   sugestionar.
influential influyente.
influenza influenza.
inform (to) informar, hacer saber, poner al
    corriente.
information información.

information bureau   oficina de
    información.
infrequent raro, infrecuente.
infrequently raramente.
ingenious ingenioso.
ingenuity ingenio, talento.
ingratitude ingratitud.
inhabit (to) habitar.
inhabitant habitante.
inherit (to) heredar.
inheritance herencia.
initial inicial.
initiative iniciativa.
injection inyección.
injure (to) injuriar, agraviar (the feelings,
    reputation, etc.); dañar, hacer daño,
    lastimar (to damage).
injurious nocivo, dañino, perjudicial.
injury daño, avería; perjuicio; herida.
injustice injusticia.
ink tinta.
inkwell tintero.
inland interior, tierra adentro.
    inland navigation   navegación fluvial
inn posada, mesón.
innate innato.
inner interior.
innocence inocencia.
innocent inocente.
input entrada (computer, etc.).
insane loco, demente.
insanity locura.
inscribe (to) inscribir.
inscription inscripción.
insect insecto.
insecticide insecticida.
insecure inseguro.
insecurity inseguridad.
insensible insensible.
inseparable inseparable.
insert (to) insertar, introducir.
insertion inserción.
inside dentro; interior.
    on the inside   por dentro.
    toward the inside   hacia dentro.
    inside out   al revés.
insignificance insignificancia.
insignificant insignificante.
insincere falto de sinceridad, poco sincero.
insincerity falta de sinceridad.
insist (to) insistir.
insistence insistencia.
insolence insolencia.
insolent insolente.
insolvency insolvencia.
inspect (to) inspeccionar, examinar.
inspection inspección.
inspector inspector.
inspiration inspiración.

install (to) instalar, colocar.
installation instalación.
installment plazo
    installment payment pago a plazos.
instance ejemplo; caso.
    for instance por ejemplo.
    in this instance en este caso.
instead of en lugar de, en vez de.
instinct instinto.
institute instituto.
institute (to) instituir.
institution institución.
instruct (to) instruir, enseñar; dar
    instrucciones.
instruction instrucción, enseñanza.
instructive instructivo.
instructor instructor.
instrument instrumento.
insufficiency insuficiencia.
insufficient insuficiente.
insult insulto.
insult (to) insultar.
insulting insultante.
insuperable insuperable.
insurance seguro.
insure a segurar.
insurgence insurgencia.
intact intacto.
integral íntegro.
intellectual intelectual.
intelligence inteligencia.
intelligent inteligente.
intend (to) intentar; tener intención de,
    proponerse (to have in mind).
    to be intended for tener por objeto.
intense intenso.
intensity intensidad.
intention intención.
intentional intencional.
intentionally intencionalmente.
intercom sistema de intercomunicación.
interest interés.
interest (to) interesar.
interested interesado.
interesting interesante.
interior interior, interno.
intermission intermisión, entreacto (theater).
internal interno.
international internacional.
interplay interacción.
interpret interpretar.
interpretation interpretación.
interpreter intérprete.
interrupt interrumpir.
interruption interrupción
interval intervalo.
intervention intervención.
interview entrevista.
intestines intestinos.

intimacy intimidad.
intimate íntimo.
intimidate intimidar.
into en, dentro.
intonation entonación.
intoxicate embriagar; intoxicar (to poison).
intoxicated borracho.
intoxicating embriagante.
intoxication embriaguez; intoxicación
    (poison)
intricate intrincado, enredado, complicado.
intrigue intriga, trama.
intrinsic(al) intrínseco.
introduce (to) introducir; presentar (a
    person).
    to introduce a person presentar a una
    persona.
introduction introducción (book);
    presentación (person).
introductory preliminar.
intruder intruso.
intuition intuición.
invade (to) invadir.
invalid *adj.* inválido (person), nulo (void).
invalid *n.* inválido.
invasion invasión.
invent (to) inventar.
invention invención.
inventor inventor.
invert (to) invertir, volver al revés.
invest (to) invertir, colocar (money).
investigate (to) investigar, inquirir.
investigation investigación.
investment inversión.
investor inversionista.
invisible invisible.
invitation invitación.
invite (to) invitar, convidar.
invoice factura.
involuntary involuntario.
involve (to) comprometer, implicar; enredar.
involved complicado.
iodine yodo.
IOU pagaré, nota promisoria.
iris iris.
iron hierro; plancha (for ironing).
iron (to) planchar (clothes).
ironical irónico.
ironing planchado.
irony ironía.
irregular irregular.
irrelevant inaplicable.
irresponsible irresponsable.
irrigate (to) regar, irrigar.
irrigation riego.
irritable irritable.
irritate (to) irritar, exasperar.
irritation irritación.
island isla.

isolation aislamiento.

issue edición, tirada (books, etc.); punto, cuestión.

issue (to) publicar, dar a luz (books, magazines, etc.); emitir (money, stocks).

it ello, él, ella; lo, la, le; esto, este, esta. ("It" is not translated in phrases like "it's raining" [llueve], "it's late" [es tarde], "it's two o'clock" [son las dos], etc.).

     I have it.   Lo *m.* tengo.

     I have it.   La *f.* tengo.

     I said it.   Yo lo dije.

     Isn't it?   ¿No es verdad?

     That's it.   Eso es.

Italian italiano.

Italy Italia.

itch picazón.

itinerary itinerario.

its su, sus (de él, de ella, de ello, de ellos, de ellas).

itself sí, sí mismo, se.

     by itself   por sí.

ivory marfil.

ivy hiedra.

J

jack gato (tool).

jacket chaqueta (a short coat); cubierta (covering, casing).

jail cárcel.

jam mermelada; apuro, aprieto (a fix).

janitor portero, conserje.

January enero.

jar *n.* tarro, pote, jarra.

jaw quijada.

jazz jazz.

jealous celoso.

jealousy celos, envidia.

jelly jalea.

jeopardy peligro.

jerk (to) sacudir.

jest broma.

jest (to) bromear.

Jesuit jesuita.

jewel joya, alhaja.

jewelry shop joyería.

job empleo; tarea.

join unir, juntar (to put together); unirse, asociarse (to unite); afiliarse, adherirse a, ingresar en (an organization).

joint coyuntura, articulación (anatomical); juntura, ensambladura (the place or part where two things are joined).

joke broma.

joke (to) bromear, embromar.

jolly *adj.* alegre, divertido, jovial.

journal diario.

journalist periodista.

journalistic periodístico.

journey viaje.

journey (to) viajar.

jovial jovial.

joy alegría, júbilo.

joyful alegre, gozoso.

judge juez.

judge (to) juzgar.

judgment juicio.

judicial judicial.

juice zumo, jugo.

juicy jugoso.

July julio.

jump salto.

jump (to) saltar.

June junio.

junior *adj.* más joven (younger); hijo (Jr. after a name).

     junior partner   socio menos antiguo.

junk chatarra, cachivache.

junkie drogadicto.

jurisprudence jurisprudencia.

juror jurado (individual).

jury jurado.

just *adj.* justo.

     It's not just.   No es justo.

just *adv.* justamente, exactamente; solamente, simplemente, no más que.

     just as   al momento que, en el mismo instante en que; no bien.

     just as I came in   en el mismo instante en que entraba.

     just a moment   un momentito.

     just now   ahora mismo.

     I just wanted to   yo solamente quería.

     to have just   acabar de.

     I have just come.   Acabo de llegar.

     It is just two o'clock.   Son las dos en punto.

     Just as you please.   Como Ud. guste.

justice justicia.

justifiable justificable.

justification justificación.

justify (to) justificar.

K

keen agudo.

keep (to) guardar.

     to keep away   mantener alejado; no dejar entrar.

     to keep back (retain)   detener, retener.

     to keep from   impedir (hinder); abstenerse (refrain).

     to keep quiet   callar.

to keep house   tener casa puesta.

to keep in mind   recordar, tener presente.

to keep late hours   acostarse tarde.

to keep one's hands off   no tocar, no meterse en.

to keep one's word   tener palabra, cumplir su palabra.

to keep track of   no perder de vista; tener en cuenta.

kerosene querosén, queroseno.

kettle marmita, caldera.

key llave; principal (main); tecla (machine).

keyboard teclado.

kick puntapié; patada, coz.

kick (to) patear; cocear.

kidney riñón.

kill (to) matar.

kind *adj.* bueno, amable, bondadoso.

kind *n.* clase, calidad.

     a kind of   una especie de.

     of the kind   semejante.

     nothing of the kind   no hay tal, nada de eso.

     of a kind   de una misma clase.

kindergarten jardín de niños.

kindhearted bondadoso.

kindly bondadosamente; tenga la bondad, haga el favor, sírvase.

     Kindly do it.   Tenga la bondad de hacerlo.

kindness bondad.

king rey.

kingdom reino.

kiss beso.

kiss (to) besar.

kitchen cocina.

kite cometa.

kitten gatito.

knee rodilla.

kneecap rótula.

kneel (to) arrodillarse.

knife cuchillo.

knit tejer.

knock golpe (blow); llamada (on the door).

knock (to) golpear; tocar, llamar (on the door).

knot nudo.

know (to) saber; conocer (be acquainted with).

knowledge conocimiento.

     to the best of my knowledge   según mi leal saber y entender.

known conocido.

knuckle covuntura, nudillo.

L

label etiqueta.

labor trabajo, labor

laboratory laboratorio

laborer jornalero, trabajador.

lace *n.* encaje.

lack falta, escasez, carencia, necesidad.

lack (to) career, faltar algo, necesitar.

lacking (to be) hacer falta.

ladder escalera de mano.

lady señora.

     Ladies.   Señoras.

     Ladies and gentlemen.   Señoras y caballeros.

lake lago.

lamb cordero.

     lamb chops   chuletas de cordero.

lame cojo (limping); lisiado (crippled); defectuoso, inaceptable (unsatisfactory).

lame (to be) cojear (to limp).

lament (to) lamentar.

lamentation lamento.

lamp lámpara.

land tierra (ground); terreno (terrain), país (country).

land (to) desembarcar (ship); aterrizar (plane).

landing *n.* desembarco (from a ship); aterrizaje (of an airplane); meseta, descanso (a staircase).

landlady propietaria, dueña, patrona.

landlord propietario, dueño, casero, patrón.

landmark patrimonio nacional, monumento histórico.

landscape paisaje, vista.

language lengua, idioma; lenguaje.

languid lánguido.

languish languidecer.

languor languidez.

lantern farol, linterna.

lap falda.

lard manteca, lardo.

large grande.

     at large   en libertad, suelto (free, loose); extensamente, sin limitación (widespread); en general, en conjunto (in general).

large-scale en gran escala.

lark alondra.

larynx laringe.

laser rayo laser.

last último; pasado.

     lastly   al fin, finalmente, por último.

     at last   al fin, al cabo, por fin.

     last night   anoche.

     last week   la semana pasada.

     last year   el año pasado.

last (to) durar.

lasting duradero, durable.

latch aldaba, picaporte.

late *adj.* tarde.

to be late   llegar tarde.
late in the year   a fines de año.
How late?   ¿Hasta qué hora?
lately recientemente, últimamente.
lateness tardanza, demora, retraso.
later más tarde.
latest último.
latest style   última moda.
at the latest   a más tardar.
lather espuma de jabón.
Latin latino *adj.*; latín *n.*
latter (the) éste, último.
laudable laudable, loable.
laugh risa.
to make someone laugh   hacer reír.
laugh (to) reír.
laughable risible, que causa risa, divertido.
laughter risa.
launder lavar y planchar la ropa.
laundress lavandera.
laundry lavandería; ropa sucia (clothes to be
     washed); ropa lavada (washed
     clothes).
lavish pródigo, generoso.
lavish (to) prodigar.
law ley; jurisprudencia (legal science);
     derecho (body of laws); código
     (code).
law school   escuela de derecho.
international law   derecho internacional.
lawful legal, conforme a la ley.
lawless ilegal.
lawn césped.
lawyer abogado.
laxative laxante.
lay (to) poner.
to lay away (aside, by)   poner a un lado,
     guardar, ahorrar.
to lay hands on   sentar la mano a.
to lay hold of   asir, coger.
to lay off   quitarse de encima; despedir
     (to fire).
to lay the blame on   echar la culpa a.
laziness pereza.
lazy perezoso.
lead (metal) plomo.
lead (to) conducir, guiar.
to lead the way   mostrar el camino, ir
     delante.
to lead up to   conducir a.
leader líder, caudillo, conductor, jefe; guía
     (guide); director (band leader).
leadership dirección, mando.
leading principal, capital.
leading article   editorial.
leading man   protagonista.
leading edge   puesto de avanzada.
leaf hoja.
lean (to) inclinar; apoyarse.

to lean back   recostarse.
to lean over   reclinarse.
leaning inclinación, propensión, tendencia.
leap salto, brinco.
leap (to) saltar, brincar.
learn (to) aprender (to acquire knowledge,
     skill); enterarse de, tener noticia de,
     saber (to find out about).
learned sabio, docto, erudito.
learning saber, ciencia, erudición.
lease arriendo, contrato de arrendamiento.
lease (to) arrendar, dar en arriendo.
least mínimo, el mínimo, menos.
at least   a lo menos, por lo menos.
not in the least   de ninguna manera, bajo
     ningún concepto.
the least possible   lo menos posible.
least of all   lo de menos.
leather cuero, piel.
leave (to) dejar (quit); abandonar (desert);
     salir (go out); irse (go away).
to leave behind   dejar atrás.
to leave out   omitir, excluir.
lecture *n.* conferencia; disertación (a
     discourse), regaño (a reprimand).
lecturer conferenciante, conferencista.
left izquierdo
left hand   mano izquierda.
to the left   a la izquierda.
left-handed   zurdo.
left (to be) quedarse.
leg pierna; pata (of a chicken, etc.); pata, pie
     (of a table, etc.).
legal legal.
legend leyenda.
legible legible.
legislation legislación.
legislator legislador.
legislature legislatura.
leisure ocio, holganza, comodidad.
lemon limón.
lemonade limonada.
lend (to) prestar, dar prestado.
to lend an ear   dar oídos, prestar atención.
to lend a hand   arrimar el hombro, dar una
     mano.
length largo, longitud.
at length   al fin, finalmente;
     detalladamente (with all the details).
at full legnth   a lo largo, a todo lo largo.
lenient indulgente.
lens lente.
less menos.
more or less   más o menos.
less and less   cada vez menos.
lessen reducir, disminuir, disminuirse.
lesson lección.
let (to) dejar, permitir; arrendar, alquilar (to
     rent).

Let's go. Vamos.

Let's see. Veamos.

to let alone dejar en paz, no molestar.

to let be no meterse con.

to let go soltar.

to let it go at that dejar pasar, no hacer o decir más.

to let in dejar entrar, hacer pasar.

to let know hacer saber, avisar.

letter carta; letra (of the alphabet).

lettuce lechuga.

leukemia leucemia.

level *adj.* plano, llano, igual.

level crossing paso a nivel.

level nivel.

to be on the level jugar limpio, ser honrado.

level off (to) nivelar; planear (a plane).

liable sujeto, expuesto a (exposed to); propenso a, capaz de (liable to think, say, do).

liar embustero.

liberal liberal.

liberty libertad.

library biblioteca.

license licencia, permiso.

lick (to) lamer,

lid tapa, tapadera.

eyelid pestañas.

lie mentira (falsehood).

lie (to) mentir (tell a falsehood); reposar, acostarse, echarse (lie down).

lieutenant teniente.

life vida.

lifeguard salvavidas.

lifeboat bote salvavidas.

life insurance seguro sobre la vida.

lifetime toda la vida.

lift alzar, levantar.

light luz; claridad.

in the light of según, a la luz de.

in this light desde este punto de vista.

light *adj.* liviano, ligero (in weight), claro (color).

light complexion tez blanca.

light reading lectura amena.

light-headed mareado.

light (to) encender (a match, etc.); alumbrar, iluminar (to illuminate).

lighten aligerar, quitar peso.

lighthouse faro.

lighting alumbrado, iluminación

lightness ligereza.

lightning relámpago.

like parecido, semejante (similar).

in like manner del mismo modo, análogamente.

be like ser semejante, parecido.

like (to) querer, gustar, agradar.

to like someone tener simpatía por.

I like her very much. La quiero mucho.

She doesn't like me. Ella no me quiere.

As you like. Como Ud. quiera (guste).

Do you like it? ¿Le gusta? ¿Le agrada?

I like it. Me gusta.

I don't like it. No me gusta.

likely probable; probablemente.

likeness semejanza.

likewise igualmente, asimismo.

liking afición; simpatía; gusto.

limb miembro.

lime cal.

limit límite.

limit (to) limitar

limp (to) cojear.

line línea.

line (to) rayar, trazar líneas.

to line up alinear, alinearse.

linen lino, hilo (goods, material); ropa de cama.

lingerie lencería.

linguist lingüista; poliglota.

lining forro.

link eslabón; enlace.

link (to) unir, enlazar, eslabonar, encadenar.

lip labio.

lipstick lápiz para los labios, lápiz labial.

liquid líquido.

liquor licor.

lisp (to) cecear

list lista.

list (to) anotar, registrar, poner en lista.

listen (to) escuchar.

literal literal, al pie de la letra.

literally literalmente.

literary literario.

literature literatura.

little pequeño.

a little un poco, un poquito

very little muy poco.

little boy chico, chiquillo.

little girl chica, chiquilla.

a little child un muchachito.

a little dog un perrito.

little by little poco a poco.

live *adj.* vivo.

live (to) vivir.

liver hígado.

living *adj.* viviente

living *n.* vida; mantenimiento.

to make a living ganarse la vida.

living room sala, sala de estar.

load carga.

load (to) cargar.

loaf pan, panecillo, hogaza (bread).

loan préstamo.

lobby vestíbulo, sala de espera.

lobster langosta.

local local.
locate (to) situar.
located situado.
location sitio, localidad (place, locality);
    ubicación, situación, posición (site).
lock cerradura.
lock (to) cerrar con llave.
locomotive locomotora.
locust cicada.
log leño, tronco (wood).
    log book   diario de navegación.
logic lógica.
logical lógico.
lonely solitario, solo.
long *adj.* largo; de largo.
    It's five inches long.   Tiene cinco
      pulgadas de largo.
    A long time ago.   Hace mucho tiempo.
      Mucho tiempo atrás.
    long distance   a larga distancia (phone
      call).
long *adj.* a gran distancia; mucho, mucho
    tiempo.
    long ago   hace mucho tiempo.
    all day long   todo el santo día.
    not long ago   no hace mucho.
    How long ago?   ¿Cuánto tiempo hace?
    How long?   ¿Cuánto tiempo?
    as long as   mientras.
longer *adj.* más largo.
longer *adv.* más tiempo.
    How much longer?   ¿Cuánto tiempo más?
    no longer   ya no.
    to long for   anhelar.
longing anhelo.
look cara, aspecto (appearance); mirada;
    ojeada (glance).
look (to) ver, mirar.
    Look!   ¡Mire!
    Look in the mirror!   ¡Mírate al espejo!
    to look for   buscar; esperar.
    to look after   cuidar.
    to look alike   parecerse.
    to look forward to   esperar.
    to look into   examinar, estudiar.
    to look like snow   parece que va a nevar.
    to look out   tener cuidado (be careful).
    Look out!   ¡Cuidado!
    to look over   repasar, revisar.
loose suelto.
loosen (to) desatar, soltar.
Lord Señor.
lose (to) perder.
loss pérdida.
    at a loss   perdiendo, con pérdida, perplejo
      (puzzled).
    to be at a loss   estar sin saber que hacer.
lot (a) mucho.
    a lot of money   mucho dinero.

loud ruidoso, fuerte.
    a loud laugh   risotada.
love amor, cariño.
    to be in love   estar enamorado.
love (to) amar, querer.
lovely encantador, precioso, bonito, hermoso.
low bajo
lower más bajo, inferior.
    lower case   letras minúsculas.
lower (to) bajar; rebajar (price); arriar, abatir
    (a flag, etc.).
lox salmón ahumado.
loyal leal.
loyalty fidelidad, lealtad.
luck suerte, fortuna.
    good luck   buena suerte.
    to have luck   tener suerte.
luckily por fortuna, afortunadamente.
lucky afortunado.
    to be lucky   tener suerte.
ludicrous ridículo, absurdo.
luggage equipaje.
lukewarm tibio, templado.
lumber madera.
luminous luminoso.
lunch merienda, almuerzo.
lunch (to) almorzar, merendar.
    to have lunch   almorzar, merendar.
lung pulmón.
luxury lujo.
luxurious lujoso.
lying mentiroso.
lyric lírico.

M

macaroni macarrones.
machine máquina.
machinery maquinaria.
macrobiotic macrobiótico.
mad loco.
    to go mad   volverse loco.
made hecho, fabricado.
madness locura, furia.
magazine revista.
magic *adj.* mágico.
magic *n.* magia.
magistrate magistrado.
magnanimous magnánimo.
magnet imán.
magnetic imagnético.
magnificent magnífico.
magnify (to) aumentar.
magnifying glass lente (cristal) de aumento,
    lupa.
mail correo.
mailbox buzón.
mailman cartero.

main principal, esencial.
  the main issue la cuestión principal.
  main office casa matriz.
  the main point el punto esencial.
mainly principalmente, sobre todo.
maintain mantener, sostener, conservar.
maintenance matenimiento; conservación,
  reparación (property, equipment).
majestic majestuoso.
majesty majestad.
major *adj.* mayor, más importante.
major *n.* mayor, comandante.
majority mayoría.
make (to) hacer; fabricar, producir.
  to make sad poner triste, entristecer.
  to make happy poner alegre, alegrar.
  to make a good salary ganar un buen
    sueldo.
  to make a living ganarse la vida.
  to make possible hacer posible.
  to make ready preparar.
  to make room hacer lugar.
  to make known dar a conocer.
  to make a hit dar golpe, producir
    sensación.
  to make a mistake equivocarse.
  to make a stop detenerse.
  to make friends granjearse amigos.
  to make fun of burlarse de.
  to make haste apurarse.
  to make headway progresar, adelantar.
  to make into convertir.
  to make for a place dirigirse a un lugar,
    encaminarse hacia.
  to make no difference ser indiferente, no
    importar.
  to make out comprender, descifrar, sacar
    en limpio; salir bien o mal.
  to make sick causar repugnancia, fastidiar
    (to annoy).
  to make the best of sacar el mayor
    provecho de, sacar el mejor partido
    de.
  to make tired cansar.
  to make one's mind up decidirse,
    determinarse.
maker fabricante.
malady enfermedad.
male varón, macho.
malice malicia.
malicious malicioso
malignant maligno, pernicioso.
mammal mamífero.
man hombre, señor.
  young man joven.
manage (to) administrar; gestionar;
  arreglárselas.
management administración, dirección,
  gerencia.

manager administrador, director, gerente.
maneuver maniobra.
manifest (to) manifestar.
manipulate (to) manipular.
mankind humanidad.
manly viril, varonil.
manner manera, modo.
manners modales.
mansion mansión, casa grande.
manual manual.
manufacture (to) manufacturar, fabricar.
manufacturer fabricante.
manuscript manuscrito.
many muchos.
  many times muchas veces.
  as many as tantos como.
  How many? ¿Cuántos?
map mapa.
maple arce.
marble mármol; canica, bolita (for children).
March marzo.
march marcha.
march (to) marchar.
margin margen.
marina marina.
mark marca; seña, señal.
mark (to) señalar, marcar.
market mercado.
marketing mercadeo.
marriage matrimonio, boda.
married casado.
  to get married casarse.
marrow meollo, médula.
marry casar; casarse.
marvel *n.* maravilla, prodigio.
marvel at (to) admirarse.
marvelous maravilloso.
marvelously maravillosamente.
mask máscara.
mason albañil.
mass masa; misa (religious).
  mass media medios de comunicación.
massage masaje.
massage (to) dar masaje.
massive macizo, sólido.
mast mástil.
master amo, dueño.
masterpiece obra maestra.
mat estera (straw).
match fósforo, cerilla (to light with); partida,
  partido (sport); compañero, pareja (a
  pair); noviazgo, casamiento
  (marriage).
match (to) hacer juego (a vase, a picture,
  etc.); casar (colors).
material material.
maternal materno.
mathematical matemático.
mathematics matemáticas.

matinee matinée, función de tarde.
matriculate (to) matricularse.
matrimony matrimonio.
matter materia; cosa (thing); asunto, cuestión (question).
   an important matter   un asunto importante.
   What's the matter?   ¿Qué pasa? ¿Qué ocurre?
   Nothing's the matter.   No es nada.
matter (to) importar
   it doesn't matter.   No importa.
mattress colchón.
mature *adj.* maduro.
mature (to) madurar.
   to become mature   madurar; alcanzar la edad madura.
maturity madurez.
maximum máximo.
   at the maximum   a lo sumo.
May mayo.
may poder, ser posible.
   It may be.   Puede ser.
   It may be true.   Podrá ser verdad,
   May I?   ¿Me permite Ud.? Si Ud. me permite. Con su permiso.
   May I come in?   ¿Puedo entrar?
maybe acaso, quizás, tal vez.
mayonnaise mayonesa.
mayor alcalde.
maze laberinto.
   to be in a maze   estar perplejo.
meadow prado.
meal comida.
mean bajo, vil, despreciable; medio (average).
mean (to) significar, querer decir, dar a entender.
   What do you mean?   ¿Qué quiere Ud. decir?
meaning designio, intención (intent); sentido, significado (of a word, etc.).
means medio; medios, recursos.
   by all means   sin falta.
   by no means   de ningún modo.
   by some means   de alguna manera.
   by this means   por este medio.
meantime entretanto.
   in the meantime   mientras tanto.
meanwhile mientras tanto, entretanto.
   in the meanwhile   mientras tanto.
meanwhile *n.* ínterin.
measles sarampión.
measure medida.
   in a great measure   en gran manera.
   in some measure   en cierto modo, hasta cierto punto.
measure (to) medir.
   to measure up to   ponerse a la altura de, ser igual.

measurement medición; medida.
meat carne.
mechanic mecánico.
mechanical mecánico.
mechanism mecanismo.
medal medalla.
meddle (to) intervenir, entremeterse.
media medios publicitarios.
mediate (to) mediar
medical médico.
   medical school   escuela de medicina.
medicine medicina.
medieval medieval.
meditate (to) meditar.
meditation meditación.
Mediterranean Mediterráneo.
medium *adj.* mediano.
meet (to) encontrar, econtrarse (to come across); conocer (to know); pagar, honrar (a bill, etc.); hacer frente a (expenses, etc.); reunirse (to get together, assemble).
   to go to meet   salir al encuentro, ir a recibir.
   Glad to meet you.   Me alegro de conocerlo.
   I hope to meet you again.   Espero tener el gusto de verle otra vez.
meeting *n.* mitin, reunión.
melancholy *adj.* melancólico.
melody melodía.
melon melón.
melt (to) derretir, disolver; fundir (metals).
member miembro.
memorable memorable.
memorandum memorándum apunte.
memory memoria.
mend remendar, componer; enmendarse, corregirse (mend one's ways, etc.).
mental mental.
mention mención.
mention (to) mencionar.
menu menú, lista de platos.
merchandise mercancía.
merchant comerciante, negociante.
merciful misericordioso.
merciless desapiadado, sin piedad.
mercury mercurio.
mercy misericordia.
mere mero, puro.
   by mere chance   de pura casualidad.
merely meramente, simplemente, puramente.
merit mérito.
merit (to) merecer.
merry alegre.
message mensaje, recado.
messenger mensajero.
metal *adj.* metálico.
metal *n.* metal.

meter metro (measurement); medidor,
  contador (for gas, electricity, etc.).
method método.
methodic(al) metódico.
metric métrico.
 metric system sistema métrico.
metropolis metrópolis.
metropolitan metropolitano.
Mexican mexicano.
Mexico Mexico.
microchip microplaqueta.
microcomputer microcomputadora.
microscope microscopio.
microwave microondas.
midday mediodía.
middle *adj.* medio.
 Middle Ages Edad media.
 middle-aged entrado en años.
 middle-class clase media.
middle medio, centro.
 in the middle en el centro.
 about the middle of March a mediados de
  marzo.
midnight medianoche.
might poder, fuerza.
mighty fuerte, potente.
migraine migraña, jaqueca.
mild suave (tobacco, etc.); moderado
  (moderate); leve, ligero (light);
  apacible, manso (character).
mile milla.
military militar.
milk leche.
milkman lechero.
milkshake batido.
mill molino; fábrica (factory).
miller molinero.
million millón.
millionaire millonario.
mind mente.
 to have in mind pensar en, tener presente.
 to have on one's mind tener en la mente,
  preocuparse por.
mine mío, el mío, lo mío.
 a friend of mine un amigo mío.
 your friends and mine sus amigos y los
  míos.
mine *n.* mina.
miner minero.
mineral mineral.
miniature miniatura.
minimum mínimo.
 at the minimum lo menos, el mínimum.
minister ministro.
minor *adj.* menor; secundario.
minor *n.* menor (age).
minority minoría.
mint menta (plant); casa de la moneda
  (money).

minus menos.
minute minuto (time); diminuto (size).
 minute hand minutero.
 just a minute, please. Un minuto, por
  favor.
 any minute de un momento a otro.
 Wait a minute! ¡Aguarde un momento!
miracle milagro.
miraculous milagroso.
mirror espejo.
mirth júbilo, alegría.
misbehave (to) portarse mal.
misbehavior mal comportamiento.
mischief travesura.
mischievous travieso.
miser avaro.
miserable miserable.
misery miseria.
misfortune desgracia, mala suerte.
Miss señorita (title).
miss (to) echar de menos (someone or
  something); perder (train, etc); errar
  (mark, etc.).
 to miss the point no comprender el
  verdadero sentido.
mission misión.
missionary misionero.
mistake equivocación, error.
mistake (to) equivocar.
 to be mistaken equivocarse, estar
  equivocado.
mistrust desconfianza.
mistrust (to) desconfiar de.
misunderstand entender mal una cosa, tomar
  algo en sentido erróneo.
misunderstanding malentendido, concepto
  falso, error.
mix (to) mezclar.
mixture mezcla.
moan gemido.
moan (to) gemir.
mobilization movilización.
mobilize (to) movilizar.
mock (to) burlar.
mockery burla.
mode modo; moda (fashion).
model modelo.
moderate *adj.* moderado.
moderate (to) moderar.
moderately moderadamente; módicamente.
moderation moderación.
modern moderno.
modest modesto.
modesty modestia.
modify (to) modificar.
moist húmedo, mojado.
moisten (to) humedecer.
moisture humedad.
moisturizer loción humectante.

moment momento.
  Just a moment! ¡Un momento!
momentary momentáneo.
momentous trascendental, importante.
monarch monarca.
monarchy monarquía.
Monday lunes.
money dinero.
monk fraile, monje.
monkey mono.
monologue monólogo.
monopoly monopolio.
monorail monorriel.
monosyllable monosílabo.
monotonous monótono.
monotony monotonía.
monster monstruo.
monstrous monstruoso, grotesco.
month mes.
monthly mensual.
monument monumento.
monumental monumental.
mood humor, disposición.
moon luna.
moonlight luz de la luna.
moral adj. ético, moral.
morale moral, estado de ánimo.
morals conducta, moralidad, ética.
morbid morboso.
more más.
  more or less   más o menos.
  once more   una vez más.
  no more   no más.
  the more ... the better   cuanto más ...
    tanto mejor.
moreover además.
morning mañana.
  Good morning! ¡Buenos días!
morsel bocado.
mortal mortal.
mortgage n. hipoteca.
mosquito mosquito.
moss musgo.
most lo más, los más, el mayor número, la
  mayor parte.
  at most   a los más, a lo sumo.
  for the most part   generalmente, en su
    mayor parte.
  most of us   casi todos nosotros, la mayor
    parte de nosotros.
moth polilla.
mother madre.
mother-in-law suegra.
motion movimiento; moción.
motive motivo.
motorcycle motocicleta.
motor n. motor.
mount n. monte (hill); montaje (artillery);
  soporte, tripode (for instruments).

mount (to) montar, subir.
mountain montaña.
mountainous montañoso.
mourn (to) lamentar.
mournful triste, fúnebre
mourning lamento.
  in mourning   de luto.
mouse ratón.
mouth boca.
mouthful bócado.
mouthwash enjuague bucal.
movable móvil, movible.
move (to) mover, moverse (to set in
    motion), mudar de casa, mudarse (to
    another house), mudar, trasladar;
    poner en otro sitio (to change place,
    position).
movement movimiento.
movie cine, cinema; película (film).
moving adj. conmovedor (emotionally).
Mr. don, señor (abbre. Sr.).
Mrs. doña, señora de (abbre. Sra.).
much mucho.
  as much   tanto.
  as much as   tanto ... como.
  How much? ¿Cuánto?
  too much   demasiado.
  much the same   casi lo mismo, más o
    menos lo mismo.
  this much more   esto más, tanto así más.
  much money   mucho dinero.
.nud barro, fango, lodo.
muddy turbio.
mug (to) asaltar.
mugger asaltante.
mugging asalto.
mule mula.
multiple múltiple.
multiplication multiplicación.
multiply multiplicar, multiplicarse.
murder asesinato, homicidio.
murder (to) asesinar.
murderer asesino.
murmur n. mumuracíon.
muscle músculo.
museum museo.
music música.
musical musical.
musician músico.
must tener que, haber que, deber.
  I must go.   Tengo que irme.
  It must be.   Debe ser.
  It must be late.   Debe de ser tarde.
  I must confess.   Debo confesar. Debo
    reconocer.
mustache bigotes.
mustard mostaza.
mutton carnero.
mutual mutuo, recíproco.

my mi, mis.
myself yo mismo; me, a mí, mí mismo.
mysterious misterioso.
mystery misterio.
myth mito.
mythology mitología.

N

nail uña (fingernail); clavo (metal).
　　nail polish　esmalte de uñas.
nail (to) clavar.
naive cándido, ingenuo.
naked desnudo.
name nombre.
　　Christian name　nombre de pila.
　　surname　apellido.
name (to) nombrar, designar.
namely es decir, a saber.
nap *n.* siesta.
napkin servilleta.
narcotics narcóticos.
narration narración.
narrative relato.
narrow estrecho, angosto.
nation nación.
national nacional.
nationality nacionalidad; ciudadanía.
nationalize (to) nacionalizar.
native *adj.* nativo, oriundo.
　　native country　país natal.
natural natural.
naturalist naturalista.
naturally naturalmente.
naturalness naturalidad.
nature naturaleza; carácter, índole.
　　good nature　buen humor.
　　good-natured man　bonachón.
naughty malo, travieso.
naval naval.
navigable navegable.
navigator navegante.
navy armada, marina de guerra.
near cerca de; cerca.
nearby cerca, a la mano.
nearer más cerca.
nearest lo (el, la) más cerca.
nearly casi, cerca de.
nearsighted miope.
neat esmerado, pulcro (tidy); bonito, lindo
　　(nice).
neatness esmero, pulcritud.
necessary necesario.
　　to be necessary　hacer falta, ser necesario.
necessitate (to) necesitar.
necessity necesidad.
　　of necessity　por necesidad.
neck cuello, garganta, pescuezo.

　　neck and neck　parejos (in a race).
necklace collar, gargantilla.
necktie corbata.
need necesidad.
need (to) hacer falta, necesitar.
　　to be in need of　tener necesidad de.
　　to be in need　estar necesitado.
needle aguja.
negative *adj.* negativo.
　　a negative answer　una respuesta negativa.
negative *n.* negativa; negativo (photography).
neglect descuido, negligencia.
neglect (to) descuidar.
neighbor vecino.
neighborhood vecindad, barrio.
neither *conj.* ni; *adj.* ningún, ninguno de los
　　dos; *pron.* ninguno.
　　neither . . . nor　ni . . . ni.
　　neither this one nor that one　ni uno ni
　　　otro, ni éste ni aquél.
　　neither one　ni el uno ni el otro.
nephew sobrino.
nerve nervio.
nervous nervioso.
nest nido.
net *n.* red.
network red.
neuter neutro.
neutral neutral.
never jamás, nunca.
nevertheless no obstante, sin embargo, con
　　todo.
new nuevo.
　　new moon　luna nueva.
　　New Year　año nuevo.
　　What's new?　¿Qué hay de nuevo?
news noticia, noticias.
newsboy vendedor de periódicos.
newspaper diario, periódico.
newsstand puesto de periódicos quiosco.
next siguiente, próximo.
　　the next day　al día siguiente, al otro día.
　　(the) next week　la semana entrante.
　　(the) next time　la próxima vez, otra vez.
　　next to　al lado de, junto a.
　　to be next　seguir en turno.
　　Who's next?　¿Quién sigue?
nice bonito, lindo; gentil, amable; simpático.
nickname apodo.
niece sobrina.
night noche.
　　by night　de noche.
　　good night　buenas noches.
　　last night　anoche.
nightmare pesadilla.
nighttime *adj.* nocturno; *n.* noche.
nine nueve.
nineteen diez y nueve (diecinueve).
ninety noventa.

ninth noveno.

no no; ningún, ninguno, ninguna.

  no other   ningún otro.

  no one   nadie.

  no longer   ya no.

  no more   no más.

  no matter   no importa.

  no matter how much   por mucho que.

  by no means   de ningún modo.

  No admittance.   No se permite la entrada.

  No smoking.   No se permite fumar.

nobility nobleza.

noble noble.

nobody nadie, ninguno.

  nobody else   nadie más, ningún otro.

nod (to) mover, inclinar la cabeza en sentido
      afirmativo; cabecear (become sleepy).

noise ruido.

  to make noise   hacer ruido

noisy ruidoso, bullicioso.

none nadie, ninguno; nada

  none of us   ninguno de nosotros.

nonsense tontería, disparate.

noon mediodía.

nor ni.

  neither ... nor ...   ni ... ni ...

normal normal.

north norte.

  North America.   América del Norte.

northern del norte.

nose nariz.

nostril fosa nasal, ventana de la nariz.

not no; ni, ni siquiera.

  if not   si no.

  not any   ningún, ninguno.

  not one   ni uno solo.

  not a word   ni una palabra.

  not at all   de ninguna manera.

  not even   ni siquiera, ni aun.

notable notable.

note nota.

  bank note   billete de banco.

note (to) notar.

notebook cuaderno.

nothing nada, ninguna cosa.

  nothing doing   nada de eso.

  It's nothing.   No es nada.

  nothing much   poca cosa.

  for nothing   de balde, gratis.

  That's nothing to me.   Eso no me importa.

notice aviso

  Notice to the public.   Aviso al público.

notice (to) advertir, notar.

notwithstanding no obstante, a pesar de, aun
      cuando, aunque, si bien, sin embargo.

noun nombre, substantivo.

nourish (to) alimentar.

nourishment alimento; nutrición.

novel novela.

novelist novelista.

novelty novedad.

November noviembre.

now ahora; ahora bien, ya.

  until now   hasta ahora, hasta aquí.

  now and then   de vez en cuando.

  Is it ready now?   ¿Ya está hecho?

nowadays hoy día.

nowhere en ninguna parte.

nuclear nuclear

  nuclear reaction   reacción nuclear.

  nuclear energy   energía nuclear.

  nuclear wastes   desechos nucleares.

null nulo,

  null and void   nulo y sin valor.

number número.

number (to) numerar.

numerous numeroso.

nun monja.

nurse *n.* enfermero.

nursery cuarto de los niños (room).

nut nuez (for eating); tuerca (for a screw).

nutrition nutrición.

nylon nilón.

oak roble.

oar remo.

oat avena.

oath juramento.

obedience obediencia.

obedient obediente.

obey (to) obedecer.

object objeto; complemento (grammar).

object (to) oponer, desaprobar.

objection objeción, reparo.

objective objetivo; acusativo (grammar).

obligation obligación.

oblige (to) obligar.

oblique oblicuo.

obscure o(b)scuro.

obscure (to) o(b)scurecer, ocultar.

observation observación.

observatory observatorio.

observe (to) observar; notar.

observer observador.

observing observador, atento.

obstacle obstáculo.

obstinacy porfía, obstinación.

obstinate terco, porfiado.

obstruct (to) obstruir, dificultar.

obstruction obstrucción.

obtain (to) obtener.

obvious obvio, evidente.

occasion ocasión, oportunidad.

occasional ocasional, accidental, casual

(casual); poco frecuente (not frequent).

occasionally a veces, de vez en cuando.

occidental occidental.

occupation ocupación, empleo.

occupy (to) ocupar; emplear (the time).

occur (to) ocurrir, suceder.

occurrence suceso, acaecimiento.

ocean océano.

o'clock

at nine o'clock   a las nueve.

It's ten o'clock.   Son las diez.

October octubre.

oculist oculista.

odd impar (number); raro (strange); suelto, que no hace juego (an odd shoe, etc.).

odor olor.

of de, del.

to taste of   saber a.

to think of   pensar en.

of course   naturalmente, por supuesto.

of himself   por sí mismo.

It's ten of one.   Faltan diez para la una.

That's very kind of you.   Ud. es muy amable.

off lejos, a distancia, fuera; cerca; quitado, sin; suspendido.

off and on   de vez en cuando.

The meeting is off.   Se ha suspendido la reunión.

The cover is off.   Está destapado.

off the coast   cerca de la costa.

ten miles off   a diez millas de aquí.

off the track   despistado.

a day off   un día libre.

to be well off   disfrutar de una posición desahogada.

to take off   quitar de; quitarse.

Take it off the table.   Quítelo de la mesa.

Take your hat off.   Descúbrase. Quítese el sombrero.

offend ofender.

offended (to be) resentirse, enfadarse.

offense ofensa, agravio; delito.

offensive adj. ofensivo; desagradable (smell, etc.).

offensive n. ofensiva.

offer oferta, ofrecimiento, propuesta.

offer (to) ofrecer.

offering n. ofrenda (gift).

office oficina, despacho (a building, a room, etc.); puesto, cargo (position).

officer oficial, funcionario.

official adj. oficial.

official n. funcionario.

often muchas veces, frecuentemente, a menudo, con frecuencia.

oil aceite.

olive oil   aceite de oliva.

oil painting   pintura al óleo.

ointment ungüento, pomada.

old viejo, antiguo.

to be twenty years old   tener veinte años.

old man   viejo.

old age   vejez.

olive oliva.

olive oil   aceite de oliva.

olive tree   olivo.

omelette tortilla.

omission omisión.

omit (to) omitir.

omnibus ómnibus.

on sobre, encima de, en; a, al; con, bajo; por.

on the table   sobre la mesa.

on the train   en el tren.

on that occasion   en aquella ocasión.

on the left   a la izquierda.

on my arrival   a mi llegada.

on foot   a pie.

on credit   al fiado, a crédito.

on time   a tiempo, a la hora indicada.

on my word   bajo mi palabra.

on my part   por mi parte.

on the (an) average   por término medio.

on the contrary   por el contrario.

on the whole   en conjunto, en general, por lo general.

on Saturday   el sábado.

on adv. puesto; comenzado.

with his hat on   con el sombrero puesto.

The show is on.   Ya ha empezado la función.

and so on   y así sucesivamente, etcétera.

once una vez.

once (and) for all   una vez por todas.

at once   cuanto antes, en seguida.

all at once   de una vez, de seguida.

once more   otra vez más.

one (numeral) un, uno, una.

one (impersonal "you") se, uno.

onion cebolla.

only adj. sólo, único.

only adv. solamente, únicamente.

not only . . . but also   no sólo . . . sino también

onward hacia adelante.

opaque opaco.

open abierto.

open (to) abrir.

opening abertura.

opera ópera.

operate (to) operar; hacer funcionar (a machine, etc.).

be operated on   operarse.

operation operación.

to have (undergo) an operation   operarse.

operator telefonista; operario, maquinista (*factory worker*).

opinion opinión.
　in my opinion　a mi ver.
opponent antagonista, adversario.
opportune oportuno.
opportunity oportunidad.
oppose (to) oponer, resistir.
opposite opuesto.
opposition oposición.
oppress (to) oprimir.
oppression opresión.
optic óptico.
optician óptico.
optimism optimismo.
optimistic optimista.
or o, u.
oracle oráculo
oral oral, verbal.
orange naranja.
oratory oratoria.
orbit órbita.
orchard huerto.
orchestra orquesta.
order orden; pedido (of goods).
　in order that　a fin de, para que.
order (to) ordenar (command); hacer un
　　pedido (goods).
ordinary ordinario, vulgar.
organ órgano.
organic orgánico.
organism organismo.
organization organización.
organize (to) organizar.
organizer organizador.
orgasm orgasmo.
orient oriente.
oriental oriental.
origin origen, principio.
original original.
originality originalidad.
originate (to) originarse.
ornament ornamento.
orphan huérfano.
orthodox ortodoxo.
ostentation ostentación.
other otro, otra, otros, otras.
　the other day　el otro día, hace poco.
　the others　los otros.
　Give me the other one.　Deme el otro.
ought to (to) deber.
　I ought to　Debo.
　you ought not to　Ud. no debe.
ounce onza.
our(s) nuestro, nuestra, nuestros, nuestras,
out fuera, afuera.
　out of breath　sin aliento.
　out of date　anticuado.
　out of doors　fuera de casa.
　out of order　descompuesto.
　out of place　fuera de lugar.

　out of print　agotada (una edición).
　out of respect for　por respeto a.
　out of style　fuera de moda.
　out of the way　donde no estorbe;
　　apartado.
　out of work　sin trabajo.
outcome resultado.
outdoor(s) fuera de casa; al aire libre, a la
　　intemperie.
outgoing desalida; sociable.
outline perfil, contorno; bosquejo, croquis.
outline (to) bosquejar, esbozar, delinear.
output producción, rendimiento, salida
　　(computer).
outrage *n.* atropello, ultraje.
outrageous atroz.
outside externo, exterior; fuera, afuera; fuera
　　de ajeno.
outstanding sobresaliente, notable,
　　extraordinario.
outward externo; aparente.
　outward bound　de ida.
oven horno.
over sobre, encima; al otro lado de; más de;
　　mientras, durante; por; en.
　overnight　durante la noche.
　to stay over the weekend　pasar el fin de
　　semana.
　to be over　haber pasado; acabarse,
　　terminarse.
　all over　por todas partes.
　all the world over (over the whole world)
　　por todo el mundo.
　over again　otra vez.
　over and over　repetidas veces.
overcast nublado.
overcoat sobretodo, abrigo.
overcome (to) vencer; superar.
overflow (to) rebosar.
overseas de ultramar, exterior.
oversight inadvertencia, descuido.
overtake alcanzar.
overthrow derrocar.
overtime horas extra.
overwhelm (to) abrumar.
overwhelming abrumador, irresistible.
overwork trabajo excesivo.
overwork (to) trabajar demasiado.
owe (to) deber, adeudar.
　owing to　debido a.
owl buho, lechuza.
own propio, mismo.
　to write with one's own hand　escribir con
　　su propio puño.
　my own self　yo mismo.
　This is your own.　Esto es lo suyo.
own (to) poseer, ser dueño de, tener.
owner amo, dueño, propietario.
ox buey.

oxygen oxígeno.
ozone ozono.
  ozone layer   ozonosfera, capa de ozono.
oyster ostra

P

pace paso; ritmo.
pack (to) empacar, empaquetar, hacer el baúl
  (la maleta), arreglar el equipaje.
package bulto, paquete.
packing n. embalaje.
paddle pagaya; paleta.
page página.
pail balde, cubo.
pain n. dolor, dolencia.
painful doloroso.
painkiller calmante.
paint pintura.
paint (to) pintar.
painter pintor.
painting pintura, retrato, cuadro.
pair n. par; pareja.
pajamas pijamas, piyama.
palace palacio.
palate paladar.
pale adj. pálido.
  to turn pale   palidecer.
paleness palidez.
palm palma (of the hand).
palm tree palmera.
pamphlet folleto.
pancake panqueque, panquec, tortilla hecha
  con harina y azúcar.
pane vidrio, cristal de la ventana (glass).
panel panel; painel.
panic pánico.
pant (to) jadear.
pantry despensa.
pants pantalones.
panty hose pantimedias.
papa papá.
paper papel.
  writing paper   papel de escribir.
  newspaper   diario, periódico.
parade parada, desfile.
paradise paraíso.
paragraph párrafo.
parallel adj. paralelo.
paralysis parálisis.
paralyze (to) paralizar.
parcel paquete.
  Send it parcel post.   Mándelo como
    paquete postal. Envíelo por
    encomienda (Amer.).
pardon perdón.
  I beg your pardon.   Perdone Ud.
    ¡Dispense! ¡Perdón!

pardon (to) perdonar, dispensar.
  Pardon me.   Perdone Ud. Perdóneme.
    Dispénseme.
parenthesis (parentheses) paréntesis.
parents padres.
parish parroquia.
park parque.
park (to) estacionar, parquear (cars).
parking estacionamiento, parqueadero (cars).
parliament parlamento.
parliamentary parlamentario.
parlor sala.
parrot loro, papagayo.
parsley perejil.
part parte.
  a great (large) part of   la mayor parte de.
  part of speech   parte de la oración.
  for one's part   por lo que a uno toca.
  to do one's part   cumplir uno con su
    obligación, hacer uno su parte, hacer
    lo que pueda.
partial parcial.
participant participante, partícipe.
participle participio.
particular adj. particular.
particularly particularmente.
partly en parte, en cierto modo.
partner socio.
party partido; velada, fiesta (entertainment).
pass paso; pase (permit).
pass (to) pasar; ser aprobado (a student, a
  bill, etc.).
boarding pass pase de embarque.
passage pasaje.
passenger pasajero, viajero.
passerby transeúnte.
passion pasión.
passionate apasionado.
passive pasivo.
past prep. más allá de.
  past ten o'clock   las diez dadas, más de la
    diez.
  half-past seven   las siete y media.
past adj.pasado.
  the past year   el año pasado.
past n. pasado.
  in the past   en otros tiempos,
    anteriormente.
paste pasta (dough).
pastime distracción, diversión, pasatiempo.
pastry pasteles.
past tense pretérito.
patent patente.
paternal paternal, paterno.
path senda, sendero, camino.
patience paciencia.
patient adj. paciente.
patient n. enfermo, paciente.
patriot patriota.

patriotic patriótico.
patriotism patriotismo.
pause pausa.
pave (to) pavimentar.
  to pave the way   preparar (allanar) el camino.
pavement pavimento.
pavilion pabellón.
paw pata.
pawn (to) empeñar.
pawnshop casa de préstamos (empeños).
pay pago, sueldo, salario.
pay (to) pagar; prestar (attention); hacer (a visit).
  to pay attention   prestar atención.
  to pay a call   hacer una visita.
  to pay one's respects   presentar (ofrecer) sus respetos.
  to pay on account   pagar a cuenta.
  to pay cash (down)   pagar al contado.
  to pay dearly   costarle a uno caro.
payment pago, paga.
payoff soborno.
payroll nómina de pagos.
pea guisante; chícaro (Mex.); arveja (Arg., etc.).
peace paz.
peach melocotón, durazno (Amer.).
peak punta; pico (mountain).
peanut cacahuete, maní.
pear pera.
pearl perla.
peasant campesino.
peculiar peculiar.
peddler vendedor ambulante.
pedestal pedestal.
pedestrian transeúnte, caminante, peatón.
peel cáscara, corteza.
peel (to) pelar, mondar.
peg clavija, estaca.
pen pluma.
penalty pena; multa (fine); penalty (sports).
pencil lápiz.
penetrate (to) penetrar.
penetration penetración.
peninsula península.
pension pensión.
pensive pensativo.
people gente; pueblo.
  many people   mucha gente.
  the Spanish people   el pueblo español.
pepper pimienta.
perceive (to) percibir.
percent por ciento.
percentage porcentaje.
perfect *adj.* perfecto.
  Perfect!   ¡Muy bien!
perfection perfección.

perform (to) ejecutar, llevar a cabo, desempeñar.
performance ejecución, actuación, funcionamiento, rendimiento (of a machine); representación, función (theater).
perfume perfume.
perfume (to) perfumar.
perhaps quizá, tal vez, acaso.
period período; punto final (punctuation).
periodical periódico.
perish (to) perecer.
permanent permanente.
permanently permanentemente.
permission permiso.
permit (to) permitir.
perpendicular perpendicular.
perplex (to) confundir, dejar perplejo.
perplexed perplejo.
persecute (to) perseguir.
persecution persecución.
persist (to) persistir, empeñarse, obstinarse.
persistent persistente.
person persona.
personal personal.
personality personalidad.
personally personalmente.
personnel personal, empleados; tripulantes (crew).
persuade (to) persuadir, inducir.
persuasion persuasión.
persuasive persuasivo.
pertaining perteneciente, concerniente, tocanto, relativo.
pessimist pesimista.
pessimistic pesimista.
petal pétalo.
petition petición.
petroleum petróleo.
petty insignificante, trivial, sin importancia (trifling).
  petty cash   caja chica
pharmacist farmacéutico.
pharmacy farmacia.
phase fase.
phenomenon fenómeno.
philosopher filósofo.
philosophical filosófico.
philosophy filosofía.
phone *n.* teléfono.
phone (to) telefonear.
phonograph fonógrafo.
photograph foto, fotografía.
photograph (to) fotografiar, retratar.
  to be photographed   retratarse.
physical físico.
physician médico.
physics física.
piano piano.

pick (to) escoger (choose).
  to pick up alzar, levantar (with the
    fingers), acelerar (speed); tomar
    incremento (business); restablecerse
    (to recover).
  to pick a quarrel buscar bronca.
  to have a bone to pick with habérselas
    con uno.
pickle encurtido, pepinillo.
picnic picnic.
picture retrato, foto, cuadro, pintura, grabado.
  to be out of the picture quedar fuera del
    juego.
picturesque pintoresco.
piece pedazo, trozo.
pier muelle.
pig puerco, cerdo.
pigeon paloma.
pill píldora.
pillow almohada, almohadón, cojín.
pilot piloto.
pimple grano.
pin *n.* alfiler.
pinch (to) pellizcar.
pink rosado.
pipe pipa (smoking); tubo, caño, tubería,
    cañería (for water, etc.).
pistol pistola.
pitch pez, brea, alquitrán (tar); tono (music).
pitcher jarro, cántaro (for water, etc.);
    pitcher, lanzador (in baseball).
pitiful lastimoso.
pity lástima, piedad, compasión.
  It's a pity. Es lástima.
  What a pity! ¡Qué lástima!
  Out of pity. Por compasión.
  to have pity tener piedad.
pity (to) compadecer.
place lugar, sitio, parte, local.
  in the first place en primer lugar.
  in the next place luego, en segundo lugar.
  in place en su lugar.
  in place of en lugar de.
  out of place fuera de lugar (propósito).
  to take place tener lugar.
place (to) colocar, poner.
plain llano, simple, sencillo; franco.
  plain speaking hablando con franqueza.
  plain truth la pura verdad.
  plain food alimentos sencillos.
plaintiff demandante.
plan plan; plano (of a city, etc.).
plan (to) proyectar, hacer planes, pensar.
planet planeta.
plant planta.
plant (to) plantar, sembrar.
plantation plantación.
planter sembrador; colono, hacendado
    (owner of a plantation).

plaster yeso.
plastic plástico.
plate plato (food); plancha, lámina (metal in
    sheets); estereotipo, clisé (printing);
    placa (photography).
  a plate of soup un plato de sopa.
plateau meseta.
platform plataforma; andén (railroad station);
    programa político (politics).
play juego (game); drama, representación,
    función (theater).
play (to) jugar; tocar (to play an instrument);
    dar, representar, poner en escena (in a
    theater).
  to play a part representar un papel.
  to play a game jugar una partida (un
    partido).
  to play a joke hacer una broma.
  to play a trick on someone hacer una
    mala jugada.
player jugador.
playful juguetón.
playground patio de recreo, campo de
    deportes.
plea ruego, súplica; alegato (law).
plead (to) rogar, suplicar; alegar, defender
    una causa (law).
pleasant agradable; grato; simpático (of a
    person).
please (to) gustar, agradar; complacer, dar
    gusto.
  I'm pleased. Estoy satisfecho. Estoy
    contento.
  It pleases me. Me place. Me agrada.
  It doesn't please me. No me agrada.
  He was quite pleased. Quedó bastante
    complacido.
  please hágame el favor, por favor.
  Please tell me. Hágame el favor de
    decirme. Sírvase decirme.
  Pleased to meet you. Mucho gusto en
    conocerle.
pleasing agradable.
pleasure placer, gusto.
plenty abundancia.
plot *n.* complot, intriga (scheme); solar (of
    land); trama (of a novel, play, etc.).
plow arado.
plow (to) arar.
plug enchufe (electric plug); bujía (spark
    plug).
plum ciruela.
plumber plomero, fontanero.
plumbing plomería, cañería.
plump gordo, rollizo.
plural plural.
plus más.
pneumonia pulmonía.
pocket bolsillo.

pocketbook   libro de bolso.
poem poema
poetic poético.
poetry poesía.
point punto; punta (of a pin, etc.).
 point of view   punto de vista.
 to come to the point   ir al grano.
point (to) señalar.
 to point out   indicar, señalar.
pointed puntiagudo; agudo.
poise porte; aplomo.
poison veneno.
poison (to) envenenar.
poisoning envenenamiento.
poisonous venenoso.
polar polar.
pole polo (north pole, etc.); poste, palo (of
 wood).
polemic polémica.
police policía.
policeman policía, agente de policía.
police station comisaría.
policy política (of government, etc.); norma,
 sistema, costumbre (a settled course);
 póliza (insurance).
 insurance policy   póliza de seguro.
polish pulimento, lustre, pasta o líquido para
 sacar brillo.
 shoe polish   betún.
polish (to) pulir, lustrar; esmaltar (nails).
polished pulido.
polite cortés.
political político.
politician político.
politics política.
pollute (to) contaminar.
pollution contaminación, polución (del medio
 ambiente).
pond charca, estanque.
pool piscina (swimming pool).
poor pobre.
popcorn rosetas de maíz.
pope papa
poppy amapola.
popular popular.
popularity popularidad.
populate (to) poblar.
population población.
porch vestíbulo, portal, porche.
pore poro.
pork puerco, cerdo; carne de puerco (meat).
 pork chops   chuletas de puerco.
port puerto
portable portátil.
porter mozo; portero (building).
portion porción, parte.
portrait retrato.
 portrait painter   retratista.
position posición.

positive positivo.
positively positivamente, ciertamente.
possess (to) poseer.
possession posesión.
 to take possession of   apoderarse de.
possessive posesivo.
possessor poseedor.
possibility posibilidad.
possible posible.
 as soon as possible   cuanto antes.
possibly quizá, quizás, posiblemente.
post n. poste, pilar (pillar, etc.); correo (post
  office); puesto, guarnición (soldiers).
 post card   tarjeta postal.
 post office   correo oficina (casa) de
  correos.
 post office box   apartado de correos.
postage franqueo.
postage stamp sello (de correo), estampilla.
postal postal.
posterity posteridad.
postman cartero.
postscript posdata.
pot cazuela (cooking); maceta (flowers).
potato patata, papa (Amer.).
 fried potatoes   patatas fritas.
 mashed potatoes   puré de patatas (papas).
pound libra.
pour verter, vaciar; llover a cántaros (rain).
poverty pobreza.
powder polvo (for the face, teeth, etc.);
  pólvora (gunpowder).
 tooth powder   polvo dentífrico.
 face powder   polvos para la cara.
power poder, fuerza, potencia, energía.
 electric power   energía eléctrica.
 horsepower   caballo de fuerza.
 the great powers   las grandes potencias.
 power of attorney   poder.
 to grant power of attorney   dar poder.
 civil power   autoridad civil.
powerful poderoso.
practical práctico.
practice práctica; regla, uso (usage);
  costumbre (habit); ejercicio (of a
  profession).
practice (to) practicar; ejercer (a profession).
praise alabanza, elogio.
praise (to) elogiar, alabar, encomiar.
prank travesura, broma.
pray (to) rezar, orar (to God).
prayer rezo, oración, plegaria.
precede (to) anteceder, preceder.
preceding precedente, anterior.
 preceding year   el año anterior.
precept precepto.
precious precioso.
precipice precipicio.

precise preciso, exacto.
precisely precisamente, exactamente.
precision precisión.
precocious precoz.
precursor precursor.
predecessor predecesor.
predicament situación difícil, dificultad,
    apuro.
predict (to) predecir.
prediction predicción.
predominant predominante.
preface preámbulo, prólogo.
prefer (to) preferir.
preferable preferente, preferible.
preferably preferiblemente, preferentemente.
preference preferencia.
preferred preferente, preferido, predilecto.
pregnant embarazada, en cinta, en estado.
prejudice *n.* prejuicio.
preliminary preliminar.
premature prematuro.
preparation preparación.
prepare (to) preparar.
preposition preposición.
prescribe (to) prescribir; recetar ('medicine).
prescription prescripción, receta.
presence presencia.
present presente; regalo, obsequio (gift).
    at present   al presente, ahora.
    for the present   por ahora.
    in the present   al presente, actualmente.
    present participle   participio presente,
        gerundio.
    present-day   actual.
    the present month   el actual, el corriente.
    to give a present   hacer un regalo,
        regalar.
    to be present   asistir, estar presente.
present (to) presentar, dar a conocer; dar un
    regalo, regalar (to make a gift).
presentation presentación.
presentiment presentimiento.
preservation preservación.
preserve (to) preservar, conservar.
preside (to) presidir.
president presidente.
press prensa (machine, daily press); imprenta
    (printing plant).
    the press   la prensa.
press (to) apretar, prensar; planchar
    (clothes); apremiar, instar (to urge).
pressing urgente, apremiante.
pressure presión.
prestige prestigio.
presumable presumible.
presume (to) presumir.
pretend (to) pretender.
pretense pretensión, apariencia, disimulo.
    under pretense of   con el pretexto de.

    under false pretenses   bajo falsas
        apariencias.
preterite pretérito.
pretext pretexto.
pretty *adj.* bello, bonito, lindo.
pretty *adv.* algo, un poco, algún tanto;
    bastante.
    pretty tired   algo cansado.
    pretty good   bastante bueno.
    pretty near   bastante cerca.
    pretty well   medianamente, así así.
    pretty much   casi (almost).
    pretty much the same   parecido, casi lo
        mismo.
prevail (to) reinar, prevalecer, predominar.
    to prevail over   vencer, triunfar.
    to prevail upon   persuadir, convencer.
prevent (to) prevenir, impedir.
prevention prevención.
previous previo.
    previous to   antes de.
    previous question   cuestión previa.
previously previamente, de antemano.
price precio.
    unit price   precio por unidad.
    price war   guerra de precios.
    price freeze   congelación de precios.
    price fixing   fijación de precios.
pride orgullo.
    to take pride in   estar orgulloso de.
priest sacerdote, cura.
primarily principalmente; en primer lugar.
primary primario, primero, principal (first,
    principal); elemental (elementary).
    primary color   color elemental.
    primary school   escuela primaria.
prince príncipe.
principal principal.
principally principalmente.
principle principio.
    in principle   en principio.
    as a matter of principle   como cuestión de
        princípios, por principio.
    on general principles   por regla general.
print (to) imprimir.
printed impreso.
    printed matter   impresos.
printer impresor.
printing tipografía, imprenta; impresión.
prior *adj.* anterior, precedente, previo.
    prior to   antes de.
prison cárcel, prisión.
prisoner preso; prisionero (of war).
private privado, particular, personal,
        confidencial, reservado, secreto.
    private affair   asunto de carácter privado.
    private hearing   audiencia secreta.
    private office   despacho particular.
    private secretary   secretario particular.

in private en secreto, confidencialmente.
privately en secreto, reservadamente.
privilege privilegio.
prize premio.
pro pro.
    the pros and the cons el pro y el contra.
probability probabilidad.
probable probable.
probably probablemente.
problem problema.
procedure procedimiento, proceder.
proceed (to) seguir, proseguir, proceder.
process procedimiento, método (method);
    proceso (of growth, etc.); curso (of
    time); causa, procedimiento (law).
    in the process of en vía de.
    in the process of time con el tiempo
    data processing procesamiento de datos.
    word processing procesamiento de
        palabras.
process (to) tramitar, transformar, procesar
procession cortejo; procesión.
proclaim (to) proclamar.
proclamation proclama, proclamación.
produce (to) producir, rendir.
product producto.
production producción.
productive productivo.
profession profesión.
professional profesional.
professor profesor.
proficient competente, capaz.
profile perfil.
profit beneficio, ganancia.
profit (to) sacar provecho, ganar.
    to profit by sacar partido de, sacar
        provecho de, beneficiarse con.
profitable provechoso, lucrativo.
program programa.
program (to) programar.
programmer programador.
programming programación.
progress progreso, adelanto.
progress (to) progresar, adelantar, hacer
    progresos.
progressive progresivo.
prohibit (to) prohibir.
prohibited prohibido.
    prohibited by law prohibido por la ley.
prohibition prohibición.
project proyecto, plan.
project (to) proyectar.
prolong (to) prolongar.
prominent prominente.
    to be prominent sobresalir, ser
        prominente.
promise promesa.
promise (to) prometer.
promote (to) promover, ascender (in grade);

    fomentar (industry, etc.).
promotion promoción, ascenso (in grade);
    fomento (of industry).
prompt pronto, puntual.
promptly pronto, puntualmente.
promptness prontitud.
pronoun pronombre.
pronounce (to) pronunciar.
pronunciation pronunciación.
proof prueba.
propaganda propaganda.
propeller hélice (of a ship, plane, etc.).
proper propio, conveniente, adecuado (right,
    fit); correcto, decoroso (correct).
properly propiamente, apropiadamente;
    correctamente.
property propiedad.
prophecy profecía.
prophesy (to) predecir, profetizar.
prophet profeta.
proportion proporción.
    in proportion en proporción.
    out of proportion desproporcionado.
proposal propuesta, proposición.
propose (to) proponer.
proprietor dueño, propietario.
prose prosa.
prosper (to) prosperar.
prosperity prosperidad.
prosperous próspero.
protagonist protagonista.
protect (to) proteger.
protection protección.
protector protector.
protein proteína.
protest protesta.
protest (to) protestar.
Protestant protestante.
proud orgulloso.
prove (to) establecer, probar; resultar (to
    turn out).
proverb refrán, proverbio.
provide (to) proveer.
    to provide oneself with proveerse de.
    provided that con tal que, a condición de
        que.
providence providencia.
province provincia.
provincial provinciano.
provisions provisiones, víveres, comestibles.
prudence prudencia.
prudent prudente.
prune ciruela pasa.
psychiatrist psiquiatra.
psychiatry psiquiatría.
psychological psicológico.
psychology psicología.
public público.
publication publicación.

publicity publicidad.
publish (to) publicar.
publisher editor.
publishing house casa editorial.
pudding pudín, budín.
pull (to) tirar de, tirar hacia, arrastrar.
  to pull in   tirar hacia uno.
  to pull out (off)   arrancar.
  to pull up   desarraigar.
  to pull apart   despedazar, hacer pedazos.
  to pull through   salir de un apuro.
pullover suéter, jersey.
pulpit púlpito.
pulse pulso.
pump bomba.
punctual puntual.
punctuate puntuar.
punctuation puntuación.
puncture *n.* pinchazo (tire).
punish (to) castigar.
punishment castigo.
pupil alumno (school); pupila (eye).
purchase compra.
purchase (to) comprar.
purchaser comprador.
pure puro.
purely puramente, meramente, simplemente.
purple púrpura, cárdeno.
purpose propósito, fin, objeto, intención.
  on purpose   intencionadamente, de
    propósito.
  to no purpose   inútilmente.
  for the purpose   a propósito, al caso.
  With what purpose?   ¿Con qué fin?
purse portamonedas (change purse).
pursue (to) perseguir.
pursuit persecución.
push (to) empujar.
pusher (drugs) púcher.
put (to) poner, colocar.
  to put away   poner aparte, apartar.
  to put in order   arreglar, ordenar.
  to put off   diferir, aplazar.
  to put up for sale   poner en venta.
  to put up with   tolerar, aguantar.
  to put on   vestir, ponerse (clothes);
    ponerse gordo (weight).
  to put on the spot   poner en aprieto.
  to put out   apagar (a light, etc.); publicar
    (a book, etc.).
  to put out of the way   quitar, apartar,
    poner algo donde no estorbe.
  to put to bed   acostar.
  to put to sleep   hacer dormir.
  to put together   juntar; armar (a machine,
    etc.).
  to put to a vote   poner a votación.
puzzle *n.* enigma; crucigrama (crossword);
  rompecabezas (jigsaw, etc.).

puzzled (be) (estar) perplejo.
pyramid pirámide.

quadrangle cuadrángulo; patio.
quaint curioso, raro.
qualify (to) calificar.
quality calidad; cualidad (of character).
quantity cantidad.
quark quark.
quart cuarto de galón.
quarter cuarto (fourth).
  a quarter hour   un cuarto de hora.
quarters alojamiento; cuartel (for soldiers).
queen reina.
queer extraño, raro.
  a queer person   un tipo raro.
quell (to) reprimir, sofocar.
quench (to) apagar.
question pregunta.
  to ask a question   hacer una pregunta.
  to be a question of   tratarse de.
  question mark   signo de interrogación.
  What's the question?   ¿De qué se trata?
  without any question   sin duda.
  to be out of the question   ser imposible.
questioning *n.* interrogatorio.
quick pronto, rápido, presto.
quickly prontamente, rápidamente, con
  presteza.
  Come quickly.   Venga pronto.
quiet quieto, tranquilo.
quiet (to) calmar, tranquilizar.
quietly silenciosamente, tranquilamente.
quietness silencio, tranquilidad.
quilt edredón, cobertor, colcha.
quinine quinina.
quit (to) dejar, parar, cesar de, desistir de.
  to quit work   dejar de trabajar.
quite bastante, más bien; muy.
  quite good   bastante bueno.
  quite soon   bastante de prisa.
  quite difficult   bien difícil.
  quite well done   muy bien hecho.
  She seems quite different!   ¡Parece otra!
quotation citación, cita, texto citado.
  quotation marks   comillas.
quota cuota.
quote (to) citar.

R

rabbi rabino.
rabbit conejo.
race *n.* carrera; raza (ethnic).

racism racismo.
racket raqueta (sports).
radiance brillo, esplendor.
radiant radiante, brillante.
radiator radiador
radio radio.
radio station radioemisora, emisora.
radish rábano.
raft balsa.
rag trapo.
rage rabia, ira, cólera.
rage (to) rabiar, enfurecerse.
ragged andrajoso, harrapiento.
rail riel, carril.
railroad ferrocarril.
   by railroad   por ferrocarril.
railway ferrocarril.
rain lluvia.
rain (to) llover.
rainbow arco iris.
raincoat impermeable.
rainfall precipitación.
rainy lluvioso
raise aumento (salary).
raise (to) levantar, alzar, elevar; aumentar,
       subir (prices, salary); criar (children,
       animals); cultivar (a crop.)
   to raise an objection   objetar, poner una
     objeción.
   to raise a question   suscitar una cuestión.
   to raise a row   armar un alboroto, armar
     un lío.
   to raise money   reunir dinero.
raisin pasa.
rake rastrillo.
rake (to) rastrillar.
   to rake in   ganar mucho.
ranch rancho, hacienda.
range alcance (of a gun, of the voice, etc.);
       radio de acción (of a plane, etc.);
       cadena (of mountains).
   range of mountains   sierra, cordillera,
     cadena de montañas.
rank grado (army, etc.); rango (status);
       posición (social rank).
   rank and file   los miembros, la tropa
     (military).
ransom rescate
rape violación.
rapid rápido.
rapidity rapidez.
rare raro
rarity rareza.
rascal tunante, pícaro, bribón.
rash *adj.* precipitado, temerario (reckless).
rash *n.* sarpullido.
rat rata; traidor.
rate tarifa, precio; interés.
   at the rate of   a razón de.

interest rate   tipo de interés.
   rate of exchange   tipo de cambio.
   at any rate   de todos modos, sea como
     fuere.
rather más bien, un poco, algo.
   rather expensive   algo caro.
   rather than   más bien que, antes que.
ratio proporción, razón.
ration ración.
rational racional, razonable.
rationing racionamiento.
rave (to) delirar; estar loco por.
raw crudo.
   in a raw state   en bruto.
   raw materials   materias primas.
ray rayo.
rayon rayón.
razor navaja.
   razor blade   hoja de afeitar.
   safety razor   maquinilla de afeitar.
reach alcance (range).
   beyond one's reach   fuera del alcance de
     uno.
   within one's reach   al alcance de uno,
     dentro del poder de uno.
reach (to) alcanzar, llegar a, llegar hasta
       (arrive at).
   to reach the end   terminar, llegar al fin,
     lograr su objeto.
   to reach out one's hand   extender la mano.
react (to) reaccionar.
reaction reacción.
reactionary reaccionario.
read (to) leer.
readable legible.
reader lector.
reading lectura.
reading room sala de lectura.
ready listo.
ready-made confeccionado, ya hecho.
ready-made clothes ropa hecha.
real real, verdadero.
   real estate   bienes raíces.
reality realidad.
realization realización; comprensión,
       conciencia, cierta (understanding,
       awareness).
realize (to) darse cuenta, hacerse cargo;
       llevar a cabo, realizar, obtener.
   to realize a danger   darse cuenta del
     peligro.
   to realize a project   llevar a cabo un
     proyecto.
   to realize a profit   obtener un beneficio,
     lograr un provecho.
really en verdad, realmente, verdaderamente.
   Really!   ¡De veras!
reap (to) segar.
rear *adj.* de atrás, trasero, posterior.

rear *n.* parte posterior.
reason razón, juicio, causa.
  by reason of   con motivo de, a causa de.
  for this reason   por esto.
  without reason   sin razón.
reason (to) razonar, raciocinar.
reasonable razonable; módico.
reasoning razonamiento.
rebel rebelde.
rebel (to) rebelarse.
rebellion rebelión.
rebellious rebelde, refractario.
recall (to) recordar (remember).
receipt recibo.
  to acknowledge receipt   acusar recibo.
receipts ingresos.
receive (to) recibir.
receiver receptor.
recent reciente.
reception recepción, acogida.
recipe receta de cocina.
recite (to) recitar.
reckless imprudente, temerario.
recline (to) reclinar.
recognition reconocimiento.
recognize (to) reconocer
recoil (to) retroceder.
recollect (to) recordar (to remember).
recollection recuerdo, reminiscencia.
recommend (to) recomendar.
recommendation recomendación.
reconcile (to) conciliar, reconciliar.
reconciliation reconciliación.
record *n.* registro; acta; disco (phonograph); record (sports); constancia, comprobante (voucher, etc.).
  on record   registrado, que consta, que hay o queda constancia.
records datos, memorias, archivo, anales.
recover (to) cobrar (damages); recuperar (health).
  to recover one's health   reponerse, recobrar la salud.
recovery recuperación (of money, etc.).
recreation recreación, recreo.
recuperate (to) restablecerse, recuperarse.
recycle reciclar.
red rojo, colorado.
redeem redimir.
redhead pelirrojo.
reduce (to) reducir, rebajar.
reduction reducción, rebaja.
  arms reduction   desarme
refer (to) referir;
  to refer to   recurrir a, acudir.
reference referencia.
  reference book   libro de consulta, fuente de referencia.

  with reference to   en cuanto a, con referencia a.
refine (to) refinar.
refinement cortesía, cultura, esmero.
reflect (to) reflejar (light); reflexionar (think).
reflection reflejo (light); reflexión (thought).
reform reforma.
reform (to) reformar; reformarse.
refrain from (to) refrenarse, abstenerse de.
refresh (to) refrescar.
  to refresh one's memory   recordar, refrescar la memoria.
  a refreshing drink   refresco.
refreshment refresco.
refrigerator refrigeradora, nevera; frigorífico.
refuge refugio, asilo.
refugee refugiado, asilado.
refusal negativa.
refuse (to) rehusar.
refute (to) refutar, rebatir.
regard consideración, respeto.
  in regard to   en cuanto a, respecto a, con respecto a.
  in this regard   en este respecto.
  with regard to   con respecto a, a propósito de.
  without any regard to   sin tomar en cuenta.
regard (to) estimar, considerar, mirar.
regarding relativo a, respecto de.
regardless of a pesar de.
regards recuerdos, memorias, afectos.
  to give (send) one's regards   dar memorias, dar recuerdos.
regime régimen.
regiment regimiento.
region región.
register registro.
register (to) inscribir, registrar.
  registered letter   carta certificada.
regret pesar, pena, remordimiento.
regret (to) sentir, deplorar, lamentar.
  I regret it.   Lo siento.
  I regret that.   Siento que.
regular regular.
regularity regularidad.
regulation reglamento, regla, regulación, reglamentación.
rehearsal ensayo.
rehearse (to) ensayar (theater).
reign reinado.
reign (to) reinar.
reject (to) rechazar, negar, desechar.
rejection rechazo, repudiación.
rejoice (to) alegrar, regocijarse.
rejoicing regocijo.
relapse recaída.
relate (to) relatar, contar (tell).

to be related estar emparentado (kinship);
  relacionarse (be connected with).
everything relating to cuanto se relaciona
  con.
relation relación; pariente (a relative).
relationship relación; parentesco (family).
relative *adj.* relativo.
relative pariente (family).
release (to) soltar; dar al público (release
  news); exonerar, descargar (from a
  debt, penalty, etc.).
reliability confianza.
reliable digno de confianza.
relief alivio (from pain); socorro (aid);
  relevo (of a sentry, etc.).
relieve aliviar (from pain); socorrer, auxiliar
  (to aid); relevar (a sentry, etc.).
religion religión.
religious religioso.
relish (to) saborear; gustar de.
reluctance mala gana, disgusto.
  with reluctance de mala gana.
reluctant mal dispuesto, reacio.
rely on (to) confiar en, contar con.
remain (to) quedar; quedarse, permanecer.
  to remain silent callar, guardar silencio.
  to remain undone quedar sin hacer.
  remains restos, sobras.
remark observación, nota.
  to make a remark hacer una observación.
remark (to) observar, advertir, comentar,
  notar.
remarkable notable, interesante,
  extraordinario.
remedy remedio.
remedy (to) remediar.
remember (to) recordar, acordarse.
  I don't remember. No me acuerdo.
  Remember me to him. Dele expresiones
    mías.
remembrance memoria, recuerdo.
remind (to) recordar.
reminder recordatorio, recuerdo; advertencia.
remit (to) remitir.
remorse remordimiento.
removal remoción, acción de quitar; cesantía,
  deposición (from a position).
remove (to) mudar, trasladar, cambiar (to
  take to another place); quitar (a stain,
  etc.); deponer, destituir, dejar cesante
  (from a job).
renew (to) renovar; extender, prorrogar (to
  obtain an extension).
renewal renovación, prórroga (extension).
rent alquiler renta (Amer.), arriendo.
  for rent se alquila.
rent (to) alquilar, arrendar.
repair reparación, compostura, remiendo.
repair (to) reparar, componer.

repeal (to) derogar, revocar.
repeat (to) repetir.
repeated repetido, reiterado.
repeatedly repetidamente, repetidas veces.
repetition repetición.
reply respuesta, contestación.
reply (to) contestar, responder.
report relación, informe, parte.
  to give a report dar un informe.
report (to) informar, dar parte; denunciar (to
  the police).
  to report on the progress of dar cuenta de
    la marcha de.
  it is reported se dice, corre la voz.
represent (to) representar.
representation representación.
representative representante, agente;
  diputado (to Congress, etc.).
reproach censura, reproche.
reproach (to) reprochar, censurar.
reproduce reproducir.
reproduction reproducción.
reptile reptil, lagarto.
republic república.
reputation reputación.
request ruego, petición.
request (to) pedir, rogar.
require (to) requerir, necesitar.
rescue rescate; salvamento.
rescue (to) rescatar; salvar, librar
research investigación.
researcher investigador.
resemblance semejanza, parecido.
resemble (to) parecerse a.
  She resembles her mother. Se parece a su
    madre.
resent (to) resentirse de, ofenderse por.
reservation reservación (hotel); reserva
  (land).
  to make a reservation mandar a reservar.
reserve reserva.
  without reserve sin reserva; con toda
    franqueza.
  Speak without reserve. Hable con
    franqueza.
reserve (to) reservar.
reservoir embalse.
reside (to) residir, morar.
residence residencia.
resident residente.
resign (to) resignar, renunciar; resignarse (to
  resign oneself).
resignation resignación; renuncia (of a
  position, etc.).
resist (to) resistir; rechazar, oponerse,
  negarse a (to repel, to refuse).
resistance resistencia.
resolute resuelto.
resolution resolución.

resolve resolver; resolverse.

resource recurso.

respect respecto; respeto (esteem, regard).
  in this respect   a este respeto.
  in some respect   en cierto sentido.
  in (with) respect to   tocante a, con respecto a
  with due respect   con todo respeto.
  in all respects   en todo sentido, en todos sus aspectos.
  in every respect   en todo sentido.

respect (to) respetar.

respectable respetable.

respected considerado.

respectful respetuoso.

respective respectivo.

response respuesta.

responsibility responsabilidad.
  on your (own) responsibility   bajo su responsabilidad.

responsible responsable.

rest resto (what is left over), descanso, reposo (when tired).

rest (to) reposar, descansar.

restaurant restaurante, restorán.

restful sosegado, tranquilo.

restless inquieto.

restore (to) restaurar, reponer.

result resultado, consecuencia.

result (to) resultar.
  to result in   venir a parar, acabar en, conducir a, causar.

retail venta al por menor.

retail (to) vender al por menor.

return vuelta.
  in return   a cambio.
  by return mail   a vuelta de correo.
  return trip   viaje de vuelta.
  Many happy returns!   ¡Feliz cumpleaños!

return (to) volver, regresar (to go or come back); devolver (to give back).
  to return a book   devolver un libro.
  to return a favor   corresponder a un favor.
  to return home   regresar a casa.

reverse adj. opuesto, contrario; n. lo opuesto, revés.

review revista; examen, análisis (examination), revisión (law).

review (to) revisar; pasar revista, revistar (military).

revise (to) revisar, modificar.

revision revisión.

revive (to) hacer revivir, resucitar.

revolt rebelión.

revolt (to) rebelarse.

revolution revolución.

revolver revólver.

reward recompensa, premio.

reward (to) recompensar, premiar.

rheumatism reuma, reumatismo.

rhyme rima.

rhythm ritmo.

rib costilla (anatomy).

ribbon cinta.

rice arroz.
  Chicken and rice.   Arroz con pollo.

rich rico; muy fuerte (food).

riches riqueza, riquezas.

riddle acertijo, adivinanza, enigma.

ride paseo en coche (in a car); paseo a caballo (on horseback).

ride (to) cabalgar, montar a caballo (on horseback); ir en coche, pasear en automóvil (in a car).

ridiculous ridículo.

rifle fusil, rifle.

right adj. derecho; recto, justo (just); correcto (correct); adecuado (fit).
  right hand   mano derecha.
  the right time   la hora exacta, la hora justa.
  at the right time   a buen tiempo, a su debido tiempo.
  right or wrong   bueno o malo, con razón o sin ella.
  right side   lado derecho.
  Is this right?   ¿Está bien esto?
  It's right.   Está bien. Es justo.
  It's not right.   No es justo. No está bien.
  to be right   tener razón.

right n. derecho.
  to be in the right   tener razón.
  to the right   a la derecha.
  to keep to the right   seguir por la derecha.
  to have a right   tener derecho.
  by rights   de (por) derecho, con razón.

right adv. bien; rectamente, justamente, correctamente, perfectamente, propiamente; mismo.
  right here   aquí mismo.
  right away   inmediatamente, en seguida.
  right now   ahora mismo, al instante.
  all right   bien, está bien.
  Everything is all right.   Todo va bien.
  Go right ahead.   Siga todo derecho. Vaya todo seguido.
  right along   sin cesar.
  right in the middle   en medio de.
  to know right well   saber perfectamente bien.

ring anillo.

ring (to) tocar, sonar.

riot motín, tumulto.

riot (to) amotinarse, armar motines.

ripe maduro.

ripen (to) madurar.

rise n. subida; alza (prices).
  sunrise   salida del sol.

rise (to) subir, ascender (to move upward);
    levantarse (to stand up, to get up);
    salir (the sun); sublevarse (to rebel);
    alzar (prices); aumentar (salary).
risk riesgo.
    to run the risk arriesgar, correr el riesgo.
risk (to) arriesgar.
river río.
road camino, carretera.
    main road camino principal.
roar rugido.
roar (to) rugir, bramar.
roast asado.
    roast chicken pollo asado.
roast (to) asar.
    roast beef rosbif, carne de vaca asada.
rob (to) robar; asaltar.
robber ladrón.
robbery robo.
rock roca, peña, peñasco; rocnrol (music).
rock (to) mecer.
rocking chair mecedora.
rocky rocoso, peñascoso.
roll rollo; panecillo (bread).
roll (to) rodar; arrollar, enrollar (to roll up).
romance romance; novela (novel).
romantic romántico.
roof techo.
room cuarto, pieza, habitación; lugar, sitio,
    espacio (space).
    inside room cuarto interior.
    to make room hacer lugar.
    There's not enough room. No hay
        suficiente sitio.
    There's no room for doubt. No cabe
        duda.
rooster gallo.
root raíz.
rooted arraigado.
rope cuerda, cordel.
    to be at the end of one's rope estar sin
        recursos.
rose rosa.
rosebush rosal.
rotten estropeado, podrido.
rouge colorete.
rough áspero, rudo, tosco.
    rough draft borrador.
    rough sea mar alborotado (agitado).
    a rough guess a ojo, aproximadamente.
    rough diamond diamante en bruto.
round *adj.* redondo.
    a round table una mesa redonda.
    round number número redondo.
    round sum suma redonda.
    round trip viaje de ida y vuelta; viaje
        redondo (Mex.).
    all year round todo el año, el año entero.
round tanda, vuelta (of drinks, etc.).

route ruta, via, camino, curso, itinerario.
routine rutina.
row fila, hilera (rank, file); riña (brawl).
row (to) remar.
rub (to) frotar.
rubber goma, caucho.
    rubber band goma, elástico.
    rubbers chanclos, zapatos de goma.
rude rudo, descortés, tosco, chabacano.
rug alfombra, tapete.
rugged escabroso (land); robusto (health).
ruin ruina.
rule regla, norma; reinado, dominio (reign).
    as a rule por lo general, por regla general.
    to be the rule ser la regla, ser de
        reglamento.
rule (to) gobernar, mandar (to govern); rayar
        (to draw lines); disponer, determinar
        (court); establecer una regla (to
        establish a rule).
    to rule out descartar, excluir, no admitir.
    to rule over mandar, dominar.
ruler gobernante; regla (for drawing lines).
rumor rumor.
run correr; andar, funcionar (a watch, a
        machine, etc.).
    to run across tropezar con.
    to run into chocar con, topar con.
    to run away escapar, huir.
    to run the risk of correr el riesgo de,
        arriesgar.
    to run over derramarse, salirse (a liquid);
        atropellar (a car, etc.).
    to run up and down correr de una parte a
        otra.
    to run wild desenfrenarse.
rural rural.
rush prisa (haste).
    in a rush de prisa.
rush (to) ir de prisa, apresurarse.
    to rush in entrar precipitadamente.
    to rush through ejecutar de prisa, hacer
        algo de prisa.
    rush hour hora de punte.
rust moho, herrumbre.
rust (to) enmohecer, oxidarse.
rusty mohoso, oxidado.
rye centeno

Sabbath sábado, día de descanso.
sabotage sabotaje.
sack saco.
sacred sagrado.
sacrifice sacrificio.
sacrifice (to) sacrificar.
sad triste.

saddle silla de montar.
saddle (to) ensillar.
sadness tristeza.
safe *n.* caja fuerte, caja de caudales.
safe *adj.* seguro; slavo, ileso (unhurt); sin
    peligro (safe from danger); sin riesgo
    (safe from risk).
  safe and sound sano y salvo.'
  Safe trip. Feliz viaje.
safely a salvo.
safety seguridad.
  safety razor maquinilla de afeitar.
  safety zone zona de seguridad.
  safety bolt cerrojo de seguridad.
sail vela; buque de vela, velero (boat).
sail (to) darse a la vela, zarpar; navegar.
sailor marinero.
saint santo.
  Saint Valentine's Day día de San
    Valentín.
sake causa, motivo, amor, bien,
    consideración.
  for your sake por Ud., por su bien.
  for the sake of por causa de, por amor de.
  for the sake of brevity por brevedad.
  for mercy's sake por misericordia.
  for God's sake por Dios, por amor de
    Dios.
salad ensalada.
salary sueldo, salario.
sale venta.
  for sale de (en) venta.
salesclerk vendedor, dependiente.
salesgirl vendedora, dependienta.
salesman vendedor.
saleswoman vendedora.
salmon salmón.
salt sal.
salt (to) salar.
salted salado.
same mismo, propio, igual.
  the same lo mismo, el mismo, los
    mismos; otro tanto.
  all the same todo es uno.
  It's all the same to me. Me da lo mismo,
    me es igual.
  if it's the same to you si le es a Ud.
    igual.
  much the same casi lo mismo.
  the same as lo mismo que, el mismo que,
    los mismos que.
sample muestra.
sand arena.
sandpaper papel de lija.
sandwich sandwich, emparedado, bocadillo.
sandy arenoso.
sane sano, cuerdo.
sanitarium sanatorio.
sanitary sanitario.

sanitation saneamiento.
sanity cordura, juicio sano.
sap savia; vitalidad.
sarcasm sarcasmo.
sarcastic sarcástico.
sardine sardina.
Satan Satanás, Satán.
satellite satélite.
satin raso.
satire sátira.
satisfaction satisfacción.
satisfactory satisfactorio.
satisfied satisfecho.
satisfy (to) satisfacer.
Saturday sábado.
sauce salsa.
saucer platillo.
sausage salchicha, chorizo.
sauté (to) saltear.
savage salvaje; silvestre (growing wild).
save *prep.* salvo, excepto; *conj.* sino, a menos
    que, a no ser que.
save (to) salvar, librar (a person);
    economizar, ahorrar (money).
savings ahorros, economías.
savings account cuenta de ahorros.
savings bank caja de ahorros.
saw sierra; serrucho (handsaw).
say (to) decir.
  that is to say es decir, esto es.
  it is said se dice.
saying dicho, proverbio, adagio, refrán.
  as the saying goes como dice el refrán.
scale *n.* escala; balanza, báscula (for
    weights); escama (of fishes, etc.).
scales peso, báscula.
scalp cuero cabelludo.
scandal escándalo.
scanty escaso.
scar *n.* cicatriz.
scarce raro, escaso.
scarcely apenas, escasamente, con dificultad.
scarcity escasez.
scare (to) asustar.
scarf bufanda.
scarlet escarlata.
scene escena.
scenery vista, paisaje; decoración (theater).
scent aroma, olor.
schedule *n.* programa, cuadro, lista; horario
    de trenes (train schedule).
scheme plan, proyecto, designio; ardid, treta.
school escuela.
  schoolteacher maestro de escuela.
  schoolbook texto de escuela.
  schoolmate condiscípulo.
  schoolroom aula.
science ciencia.
  science fiction ciencia ficción.

scientific científico.

scientist científico.

scissors tijeras.

scold (to) reñir, regañar.

scorn desdén, desprecio.

scorn (to) despreciar.

scornful despreciativo, desdeñoso.

score tantos, puntaje, puntuaje (in games), partitura (music).

score (to) marcar los tantos, llevar la cuenta (to keep a record in a game, etc.); apuntarse uno un tanto, ganar un tanto (to gain points, etc.).

to score a point   ganar un tanto.

scout explorador.

scrape (to) raspar (on a surface).

scratch rasguño, arañazo (on the hand, etc.); raspadura, raya (on a table, etc.).

scratch (to) rascar (from itching), rasguñar, arañar (to cause injury with the claws or nails); rayar (a glass, a table, etc.).

scream (to) chillar, gritar.

screen *n.* biombo, tela metálica, rejilla (for windows, etc.); pantana, cine (movies); cortina (of smoke); barrera (of fire).

screw tornillo; rosca (screw thread).

screw (to) atornillar.

scruple escrúpulo.

scuba diving buceo.

sculpture escultura.

sea mar, océano.

seal sello; foca (animal).

seal (to) sellar; lacrar (with wax).

seam costura.

search busca, búsqueda (act of looking for); pesquisa, investigación (scrutiny, investigation); registro (for concealed weapons, etc.).

in search of   en busca de.

search (to) buscar (to search for); registrar (a house, etc.); explorar (to explore); indagar, inquirir, investigar (to inquire, to investigate).

to search after   indagar, preguntar por.

to search for   buscar, procurar.

seasick mareado.

season estación (of the year).

in season   en sazón.

out of season   fuera de sazón.

to be in season   ser de la estación, ser del tiempo.

season (to) sazonar, condimentar (food).

seat *n.* asiento.

to take a seat   tomar asiento, sentarse.

front seat   asiento delantero.

backseat   asiento trasero.

secede (to) separarse.

second segundo.

second class   de segunda clase.

second year   el segundo año.

Wait a second!   ¡Espere un instante!

on second thought   después de pensarlo bien.

secondary secundario.

secondhand de segunda mano, usado.

secondly en segundo lugar.

secrecy secreto, reserva.

secret secreto.

in secret   en secreto.

secretary secretario.

private secretary   secretario particular.

section sección.

secure seguro, firme

secure (to) asegurar; conseguir (obtain).

securely seguramente, firmemente.

see (to) ver.

See?   ¿Sabe? ¿Comprende?

Let's see.   A ver. Vamos a ver. Veamos.

to see about   averiguar.

to see someone off   ir a despedir a alguien.

to see someone home   acompañar a alguien a casa.

to see the point   caer en la cuenta, comprender.

to see through   llevar a cabo.

to see fit   creer conveniente.

to see one's way clear   ver el modo de hacer algo.

to see to   atender a, cuidarse de.

seeing that   visto que, puesto que.

seed semilla, simiente.

seek (to) buscar.

to seek after   tratar de obtener, buscar.

seem (to) parecer, figurarse.

it seems to me   me parece.

it seems   parece, a lo que parece.

see-through transparente.

segregate (to) segregarse.

seize agarrar (to grasp); coger, prender (to apprehend); apoderarse de (to take possession of); darse cuenta de, comprender (to comprehend).

seldom rara vez, raramente.

select *adj.* selecto, escogido.

select (to) elegir, escoger.

selection selección.

self mismo, por sí mismo; sí, se.

myself   yo mismo, me.

yourself   tu mismo, te.

himself   él mismo, se.

herself   ella misma, se.

itself   ello mismo, se.

ourselves   nosotros mismos, nosotras mismas, nos.

yourselves   vosotros mismos, vosotras mismas, os.

themselves　ellos mismos, ellas mismas, se.

oneself　uno mismo, una misma, se.

you yourself　tú mismo, tú misma.

Wash yourself.　Lávate.

by himself　por sí mismo.

by herself　por sí misma.

I shave myself.　Yo mismo me afeito.

self-conceited presumido, presuntuoso.

self-confidence confianza en sí mismo.

self-defense defensa propia.

self-determination autonomía, independencia.

self-evident patente, evidente.

selfish egoísta.

selfishness egoísmo.

self-help esfuerzo propio.

self-interest interés propio.

self-service autoservicio.

self-sufficient que se basta a sí mismo.

sell (to) vender.

senate senado.

senator senador

send (to) enviar, despachar, mandar, expedir.

to send away　despedir, echar a la calle.

to send word　mandar recado, avisar, enviar a decir.

to send back　devolver, enviar de vuelta.

to send in　hacer entrar.

to send for　envira por, mandar a buscar.

sending despacho.

senior mayor, de mayor edad, más antiguo.

Mr. Suarez, Sr.　Suárez padre.

sense n. sentido.

common sense　sentido común.

to be out of one's senses　haber perdido e juicio.

sensible sensato, razonable.

sentence oración (grammar); sentencia (court)

sentence (to) sentenciar, condenar.

sentiment sentimiento.

sentimental sentimental.

separate adj. separado, aparte.

under separate cover　por separado.

separate (to) apartar, separar.

separation separación.

September septiembre.

serene sereno.

sergeant sargento.

serial adj. de serie, de orden (a number, etc.); por partes, por entregas (publications); en episodios, en serie (a picture).

series serie.

in series　en serie.

serious serio; grave (grave).

seriousness seriedad, gravedad.

sermon sermón.

servant criado, sirviente; criada, sirvienta (maid).

serve (to) servir.

to serve the purpose　venir al caso.

to serve notice　notificar, hacer saber, dar aviso.

It serves you right.　Bien se lo merece.

to serve as　servir de.

service servicio.

at your service　servidor, a sus órdenes.

to be of service　ser útil, servir.

session sesión.

set adj. fijo, establecido.

set price　precio fijo.

set n. juego.

tea set　juego de té.

set of dishes　vajilla.

set (to) poner.

to set aside　poner a un lado, apartar; ahorrar (money).

to set back　atrasar.

to set free　poner en libertad.

to set in order　arreglar, poner en orden.

to set on fire　pegar fuego a.

to set to work　poner manos a la obra, poner(se) a trabajar.

settle (to) arreglar, ajustar, saldar (an account, a matter, etc.); instalarse, fijar su residencia, establecerse (to be established); posarse, asentarse (liquids).

to settle an account　saldar una cuenta.

settlement acuerdo, arreglo (adjustment of an account, etc.); colonia, caserío (a small village); colonización (colonization).

seven siete.

seventeen diecisiete.

seventh séptimo.

seventy setenta.

several varios.

several times　varias veces.

severe severo.

severity severidad.

sew (to) coser.

sewing costura.

sewing machine máquina de coser.

sex sexo.

shade sombra.

shade (to) sombrear, dar sombra.

shadow sombra.

shady sombreado, umbroso.

shake sacudida, temblor; apretón de manos (handshake).

shake (to) sacudir; temblar (to tremble); estrechar, darse (shake hands); cabecear, mover (one's head).

to shake one's head　mover la cabeza.

to shake hands　darse la mano.

to shake in one's shoes   temblar de miedo.

shall, will (*auxiliary*) the future tense of the
  indicative is formed by adding -é, -ás,
  -á, -emos, éis, and -án to most
  infinitives.

I shall go   iré.
you will go   irás.
he will go   irá.
we shall go   iremos.
you will go   iréis.
they will go   irán.

shame vergüenza.
shame (to) avergonzar.
shameful vergonzoso.
shameless desvergonzado, sin vergüenza.
shampoo champú.
shampoo (to) dar champú, lavar la cabeza.
shape forma, figura.
shape (to) formar, dar forma.
share porción, parte; acción (stock).
share (to) partir, repartir (to apportion);
  participar, tomar parte en (to share
  in).
  to share alike   tener una parte igual.
shareholder accionista.
sharp agudo; puntiagudo (sharp-pointed);
  afilado, cortante (sharp-edged).
  a sharp pain   un dolor punzante (agudo).
  a sharp answer   una respuesta tajante
    (áspera).
  a sharp curve   una curva muy
    pronunciada.
  sharp-witted   perspicaz, de ingenio agudo.
  at two o'clock sharp   a las dos en punto.
sharpen (to) afilar, aguzar; sacar punta a (a
  pencil).
shatter (to) destrozar, hacer pedazos, hacer
  añicos; romperse.
shave afeitado.
shave (to) afeitar, rasurar (someone);
  afeitarse, rasurarse (oneself).
shaving afeitado
  shaving cream   crema de afeitar.
  shaving brush   brocha de afeitar.
shawl chal, mantón.
she ella; hembra.
shears tijeras grandes, cizalla.
shed cobertizo; cabaña, barraca (a hut).
shed (to) verter, derramar (tears, etc.).
sheep oveja(s).
sheet sábana (bed); hoja, pliego (paper).
shelf estante.
shell concha (of mollusks); cáscara (of nuts,
  eggs, etc.); granada (artillery).
shelter refugio, abrigo.
  to take shelter   refugiarse.
  to give shelter   albergar, dar albergue.
shelter (to) proteger, albergar, refugiar,
  poner al abrigo, poner a cubierto.

shepherd pastor.
sheriff sheriff.
sherry jerez.
shield escudo, resguardo, defensa.
shield (to) defender, amparar, resguardar.
shift cambio; tanda, turno (work).
shift (to) cambiar (gears, etc.).
shine (to) brillar; limpiar, lustrar, dar lustre
  (to shine shoes).
shining brillante, radiante, reluciente.
shiny lustroso, brillante.
ship buque, barco, vapor.
  merchant ship   buque mercante.
ship (to) embarcar; enviar, despachar
  (goods).
shipment embarque (act of shipping); envío,
  despacho (dispatch of goods);
  cargamento (goods shipped).
shipwreck naufragio.
shipyard astillero.
shirt camisa.
  shirt store   camisería.
  sport shirt   camisa de deporte.
shiver escalofrío, temblor.
shiver (to) tiritar.
shock choque; sacudida (shake); sobresalto,
  emoción (emotion).
shock (to) sacudir, dar una sacudida (to
  cause to shake); chocar, ofender (to
  offend); conmover (to move);
  escandalizar (to scandalize).
shoe zapato.
  shoe store   zapatería.
  shoelaces   cordones para los zapatos.
  shoe polish   betún, crema para los
    zapatos.
shoehorn calzador.
shoemaker zapatero.
shoot (to) tirar, disparar.
shooting tiro, tiroteo.
shop tienda.
shop (to) hacer compras, ir de tiendas
  to go shopping   ir de compras.
shoplifter ratero de tiendas.
shore costa, orilla.
short corto (not long); bajo, de escasa
  estatura (not tall); breve, conciso
  (brief); falto, escaso (of goods).
  short cut   atajo.
  short circuit   corto circuito.
  short story   cuento corto.
  for short   para abreviar, para mayor
    brevedad.
  in short   en suma, en resumen.
  to be short   estar escaso, quedarse corto,
    andar escaso (of money, etc.).
  in a short while   dentro de poco.
  a short time ago   hace poco.
shortage falta.

shorten (to) acortar, abreviar (to make short).

shorts calzoncillos (underwear); short (bermuda).

shortsighted corto de vista.

short term a corto plazo.

shot tiro, disparo, balazo (of a gun).

should, would debe, deberá, debiera, debería.
   I should go.   Yo debería ir.
   I would go.   Yo iría.
   if I should go   si yo fuese.
   The window should be left open.   Debe dejarse abierta la ventana.
   Things are not as they should be.   No están las cosas como debieran estar.

shoulder hombro.
   shoulder to shoulder   hombro a hombro.
   shoulder blade   omoplato.

shout grito.

shout (to) gritar, vocear.

shovel pala.

show exposición (exhibition); espectáculo, show. (spectacle); función (theater); apariencia (appearance); ostentación, boato (ostentation).
   show window   escaparate, vidriera (Amer.).
   showcase   vitrina.

show (to) mostrar, enseñar; demostrar, probar.
   to show someone in   hacer entrar.
   to show to the door   acompañar a la puerta.
   to show off   hacer alarde.
   to show up   presentarse, parecer.

shower lluvia, chaparrón, chubasco; ducha (bath).
   to take a shower   darse una ducha.

shrewd astuto, sagaz.

shrimp camarón.

shrink encogerse; contraer.
   to shrink from   huir de, apartarse de.

shrub arbusto.

shut (to) cerrar.
   to shut in   encerrar.
   to shut out   cerrar la puerta a uno; excluir.
   to shut up   hacer callar, callarse (to be quiet).

shutdown cierre.

shutter persiana (window); obturador (photography).

shuttle lanzadera (space).
   space shuttle   transbordador espacial.

shy tímido, corto.

sick malo, enfermo.
   to feel sick   sentirse enfermo.

sickness enfermedad.
   seasickness   mareo.

side lado, costado.

side by side   lado a lado, hombro a hombro, juntos.
   on this side   de (a, en, por) este lado.
   on that side   de (a, en, por) ese lado.
   on the other side   al otro lado, a la otra parte.
   (the) wrong side out   al revés, del revés.

sidewalk acera, vereda (Arg.).

sieve tamiz.

sigh suspiro.

sigh (to) suspirar.

sight vista, aspecto.
   at first sight   a primera vista.
   What a sight!   ¡Qué espectáculo!

sight-seeing (to go) ver las cosas de interés, visitar los lugares notables.

sign seña, señal (mark); letrero, rótulo (over a shop); aviso (notice).
   sign language   lenguaje por señas.

sign (to) firmar.
   to sign a check   firmar un cheque.

signal señal, seña.

signal (to) hacer señas.

signature firma.

significance significación, importancia.

significant significativo, expresivo.

silence silencio.

silence (to) hacer callar.

silent silencioso, callado.

silk seda.

silly tonto, bobo.

silver plata; monedas de plata (silver money).

silverware vajilla de plata.

similar similar, semejante.

similarity semejanza, similitud.

simple simple, sencillo.

simplicity sencillez.

simplification simplificación.

simplify (to) simplificar.

simply sencillamente, puramente, simplemente.

simultaneous simultáneo.

sin pecado.

sin (to) pecar.

since *adv.* desde entonces, hace.
   ever since   desde entonces.
   not long since   hace poco.

since *conj.* ya que, puesto que, pues que.

since *prep.* desde, después.
   since then   desde entonces.

sincere sincero.

sincerely sinceramente.
   sincerely yours   su seguro servidor (s.s.s.).

sincerity sinceridad.

sing (to) cantar.

singer cantante, cantor, cantora.

single solo, sin compañero; soltero (unmarried).

not a single word   ni una sola palabra.
  single room   habitación individual,
    habitación para uno.
singly individualmente, separadamente, de
  uno en uno.
singular singular.
sink lavabo (for washing); fregadero (kitchen
  sink).
sink (to) hundir, echar a pique, hundirse.
sinner pecador.
sip sorbo.
sip (to) tomar a sorbos, sorber.
sir señor, caballero.
  Dear Sir (My dear Sir):   Muy señor mío:
siren sirena.
sister hermana.
sister-in-law cuñada.
sit (to) sentar, sentarse.
  to sit down   sentarse.
sitting room sala, sala de estar.
situated situado, ubicado.
situation situación.
six seis.
sixteen dieciséis.
sixteenth décimo sexto.
sixth sexto.
sixty sesenta.
size tamaño, medida.
skate patín
  ice skate   patín de hielo.
  roller skate   patín de ruedas.
skate (to) patinar.
skeleton esqueleto.
sketch bosquejo, dibujo.
sketch (to) bosquejar, esbozar.
skill destreza, habilidad.
skillful diestro, experto, hábil.
skim (to) hojear (book); desnatar (milk).
skin piel.
skindive (to) bucear.
skinny flaco.
skirt falda.
skull cráneo.
sky cielo, firmamento.
  sky blue   azul celeste.
skyjack secuesta en vuelo.
skyjack (to) secuestrar en vuelo.
skylight claraboya, tragaluz.
skyline horizonte; la línea del cielo.
slander calumnia, tragaluz.
slang caló, jerga.
slap bofetada.
slap (to) dar una bofetada.
slate pizarra; lista de candidatos.
slaughter *n.* matanza.
slave esclavo.
slavery esclavitud.
slay (to) matar.
sleep sueño.

sleep (to) dormir.
  to go to sleep   irse a dormir, acostarse.
sleepy soñoliento.
  to be sleepy   tener sueño.
sleeve manga.
slender delgado, esbelto.
slice tajada, rebanada.
slice (to) rebanar, cortar en rebanadas.
slide (to) resbalar, deslizarse.
slight *adj.* ligero, leve.
slight (to) despreciar.
slim delgado.
sling honda (weapon); cabestrillo (medical).
slip resbalón.
slip (to) resbalar, resbalarse.
  to slip one's mind   irse de la memoria.
  to slip away   escabullirse, deslizarse.
slippers zapatillas, babuchas.
slippery resbaladizo, resbaloso.
slope pendiente, declive.
slow lento, despacio.
  to be slow   atrasar; ser lento.
slow down (to) reducir la marcha.
slowly lentamente, despacio.
  Drive slowly.   Conduzca despacio.
  Go slowly.   Vaya despacio.
slowness lentitud, tardanza.
slumber sueño ligero.
slumber (to) dormitar.
slums barrios bajos, barriadas, limonadas.
sly astuto.
small pequeño.
  small change   suelto.
smallness pequeñez.
smallpox viruela.
smart inteligente (clever).
smash (to) romper, quebrantar.
smell olor.
smell (to) oler.
smile sonrisa.
smile (to) sonreír.
smoke humo; cigarrillo (a cigarette).
smoke (to) humear; fumar (tobacco).
  No smoking.   Se prohibe fumar.
smoker fumador.
smooth liso, llano, suave.
  smooth wine   vino suave.
  smooth surface   superficie lisa.
snack merienda, bocadito.
snail caracol.
snake serpiente, culebra.
snatch (to) arrancar, arrebatar.
sneeze estornudo.
sneeze (to) estornudar.
snob snob.
snore (to) roncar.
snoring ronquido.
snow nieve.
snow (to) nevar.

snowflake copo de nieve.

snowy nevado.

so *adv.* así, tal; de modo que.

  That is so. Así es. Eso es.

  and so forth y así sucesivamente, etcétera.

  so and so fulano de tal.

  so much (many) tanto.

  at so much a yard a tanto la yarda.

  so that para que, de suerte que, de modo que.

  so then conque.

  so, so así, así; regular.

  if so si así es.

  Is that so? ¿De veras?

  I think so. Lo creo. Así lo creo.

  I hope so. Así lo espero.

  not so good as no tan bueno como.

  ten dollars or so cosa de diez dólares.

soak (to) empapar.

soap jabón.

  cake of soap pastilla de jabón.

sob sollozo.

sob (to) sollozar.

sober sobrio.

sociable sociable.

social social.

socialism socialismo.

society sociedad.

socket casquillo (for an electric bulb).

  eye socket órbita.

socks calcetines.

soda soda.

  soda water gaseosa; agua de Seltz (seltzer, carbonated water).

sofa sofá.

soft blando, suave.

  soft-boiled eggs huevos pasados por agua.

soften (to) ablandar.

softness suavidad.

soil tierra (ground).

soil (to) ensuciar.

soiled sucio.

solar solar.

sold vendido.

  sold out agotado.

soldier soldado.

sole *adj.* único, solo.

sole *n.* suela (shoe); planta (foot).

solemn solemne.

solemnity solemnidad.

solid sólido.

  solid color color entero.

solidarity solidaridad.

solidity solidez.

solitary solitario.

solitude soledad.

soluble soluble.

solution solución.

solve (to) resolver (a problem, etc.).

some algo de; un poco; alguno; unos; unos cuantos.

  Some (people) think so. Hay quienes piensan así.

  at some time or other un día u otro.

  Bring me some cigars. Tráigame unos puros.

  I have some left. Me sobra algo.

  some of his books algunos de sus libros.

  some two hundred unos doscientos.

somebody alguien, alguno.

  somebody else algún otro.

somehow de algún modo.

something alguna cosa, algo.

  something else otra cosa, alguna otra cosa.

sometime algún día, en algún tiempo.

sometimes algunas veces, a veces.

somewhat algún tanto un poco.

  somewhat busy algo ocupado.

somewhere en alguna parte.

  somewhere else en alguna otra parte.

son hijo.

  son-in-law yerno.

song canto, canción.

soon presto, pronto, prontamente, a poco.

  as soon as tan pronto como, luego que, en cuanto.

  as soon as possible lo más pronto posible.

  sooner or later (más) tarde o (más) temprano.

  the sooner the better mientras más pronto mejor.

  How soon will you finish? ¿Cuánto tiempo tardará Ud. en terminar?

soothe (to) aliviar, calmar, tranquilizar.

sophisticated sofisticado.

soprano soprano.

sore *adj.* dolorido; resentido (offended).

  sore throat dolor de garganta.

sore *n.* llaga (on the body).

sorrow pesar, tristeza.

sorry triste, afligido.

  to be sorry sentir.

  I'm very sorry. Lo siento muchísimo.

sort especie, clase, manera, suerte.

  all sorts of people toda clase de gente.

  a sort of una especie de.

  nothing of the sort nada de eso.

  What sort of person is he? ¿Qué tal persona es?

soul alma.

sound *adj.* sano, robusto.

  sound judgment juicio cabal.

  safe and sound sano y salvo.

  sound sleep sueño profundo.

sound *n.* sonido.

soup sopa.

  soup plate sopero, plato hondo.

vegetable soup   sopa de legumbres.
sour agrio.
source fuente.
south sur, sud.
　South America   América del Sur.
　　Sudamérica.
　South American   sudamericano.
　The South Pole   El polo sur.
southern meridional, del sur.
sow (to) sembrar.
space espacio.
spaceflight vuelo espacial.
spaceship nave espacial, aeronave.
spacious espacioso, amplio, vasto.
spade pala; espada (cards).
Spain España.
Spaniard español.
Spanish español.
　Spanish America   Hispanoamérica.
　Spanish American   Hispanoamericano.
　Spanish language   castellano.
Spanish-speaking hispanoparlante.
spare *adj.* disponible, sobrante; de repuesto.
　spare time   horas de ocio, ratos perdidos.
　spare money   dinero de reserva, ahorros.
　spare room   cuarto para huéspedes, cuarto
　　de sobra.
　spare parts   repuestos, piezas de repuesto.
　spare tire   neumático de repuesto.
spare (to) ahorrar, economizar (to save);
　　escatimar, ser frugal (to be sparing);
　　perdonar (to forgive); ahorrarse
　　trabajo, molestias (to spare oneself
　　trouble, etc.).
　They spared his life.   Le perdonaron la
　　vida.
　to have (money, time, etc.) to spare   tener
　　(dinero, tiempo, etc.) de sobra.
　I was spared the trouble of   Me ahorré la
　　molestia de.
sparingly escasamente, parcamente,
　　frugalmente; rara vez.
spark chispa.
spark (to) echar chispas, chispear.
sparrow gorrión.
speak (to) hablar.
　to speak for   hablar en favor de, hablar en
　　nombre de.
　to speak for itself   ser evidente, hablar por
　　sí mismo.
　to speak one's mind   decir uno lo que
　　piensa.
　to speak out   decir, hablar claro.
　to speak to   hablar a.
　to speak up   hablar, decir.
speaker orador; presidente de (las cortes), la
　　cámara de diputados (congress);
　　portavoz (spokesperson).
spear lanza.

spearmint hierbabuena, menta.
special especial, particular.
　special delivery   entrega inmediata.
specialist especialista.
specialize (to) especializar, especializarse;
　　tener por especialidad, estar
　　especializado (to be specialized).
specially especialmente, particularmente,
　　sobre todo.
specialty especialidad.
specific específico.
specify (to) especificar.
specimen espécimen, muestra.
spectacle espectáculo.
spectacles anteojos, espejuelos, gafas.
spectator espectador.
speculation especulación.
speech habla, palabra; discurso, disertación
　　(address, discourse).
　to make a speech   pronunciar un discurso.
speechless mudo, sin habla.
speed velocidad, rapidez.
　at full speed   a toda velocidad, a todo
　　correr.
　speed limit   velocidad máxima, velocidad
　　permitida.
speed (to) acelerar, apresurar, dar prisa (to
　　speed up); apresurarse, darse prisa (to
　　hasten).
spell (to) deletrear.
spellbound hechizado.
spend (to) gastar.
　to spend time   emplear el tiempo, pasar un
　　tiempo.
　to spend the night   pasar la noche,
　　trasnochar.
　I'll spend the winter in Florida.   Pasaré el
　　invierno en Florida.
sphere esfera.
spice *n.* especia.
spicy picante.
spider araña.
spin giro, vuelta (motion); barrena (aviation).
spin (to) hilar (thread, cotton, wool, etc.);
　　girar, dar vueltas (to turn, to revolve);
　　tornear (on a lathe, etc.).
spinach, espinaca.
spine espina dorsal (backbone).
spiral espiral.
spirit espíritu.
spiritual espiritual.
spit asador, espeto, espetón (for roasting);
　　saliva.
spit (to) escupir.
spite *n.* rencor, despecho, malevolencia
　　in spite of   a pesar de, a despecho de.
spiteful rencoroso, vengativo.
splash salpicadura, chapoteo.
splash (to) salpicar, chapotear.

splendid espléndido, magnífico.

Splendid! ¡Espléndido!

splendor esplendor.

split *adj.* hendido, partido; dividido (divided).

split (to) hender, partir, rajar; dividir (to divide).

to split the difference   partir la diferencia.

to split up   repartir, dividir.

to split hairs   pararse en pelillos.

to split one's sides with laughter   partirse de risa.

spoil (to) echar a perder, dañar, estropear (to damage); estropearse, dañarse, echarse a perder (to get spoiled); pudrirse (to rot).

to spoil a child   mimar demasiado a un niño.

spoiled estropeado, dañado, echado a perder.

a spoiled child   un niño mimado.

spoke *n.* rayo de la rueda (of a wheel); travesaño (rung, crossbar).

sponge esponja.

sponsor patrocinador; anunciante (radio sponsor).

sponsor (to) patrocinar, fomentar, apadrinar; costear un programa.

spontaneity espontaneidad.

spontaneous espontáneo.

spool carrete, carretel.

spool of thread   carrete (carretel) de hilo.

spoon cuchara.

teaspoon   cucharilla, cucharita.

tablespoon   cuchara.

soupspoon   cucharón (ladle).

spoonful cucharada.

sport *adj.* deportivo, de deporte.

sport shirt   camisa de deporte.

sports deportes.

spot mancha (stain); borrón (of ink); sitio, lugar, paraje (place); apuro, aprieto (fix, difficulty).

on the spot   allí mismo, en el mismo lugar; al punto, inmediatamente (at once).

sprain torcedura, distensión.

sprain (to) torcerse, distenderse.

spray (to) rociar.

sprayer vaporizador.

spread difusión.

spread (to) difundir, divulgar (news, etc.); esparcir, desparramar (to scatter); tender, extender, desplegar, abrir (to stretch out, to unfold, etc.), untar (butter).

speakers (radio) altoparlantes, altavoces.

spring primavera (season); manantial, fuente (water); salto (jump); resorte, muelle (of wire, steel, etc.).

bedspring   colchón de muelles.

spring (to) saltar, brincar.

to spring at   lanzarse sobre, saltar.

sprinkle (to) rociar (liquid); polvorear (powder).

sprout (to) brotar.

spry activo.

spy espía.

spy (to) espiar.

squad escuadra; pelotón (military).

squadron escuadrón; escuadra, flotilla (Navy).

square cuadrado; plaza (town).

squash *n.* calabaza.

squeeze (to) exprimir (crush); apretar (compress).

squirrel ardilla.

stab puñalada.

stab (to) apuñalar, dar de puñaladas.

staff palo, asta (pole); báculo, bastón (rod, stick); bastón de mando (baton); jalón de mira (for surveying); personal (personnel); plana mayor, estado mayor (body of officers).

office staff   personal de oficina.

editorial staff   cuerpo de redacción.

staff officer   oficial de estado mayor.

stage etapa; escenario, tablas (theater).

by stages   por etapas.

stage (to) representar, poner en escena (theater).

stagnant estancado, inactivo.

stagnate (to) estancarse.

stain mancha.

stain (to) manchar.

stair escalón, peldaño.

staircase escalera.

stake estaca, piquete (for driving into the ground).

at stake   comprometido, envuelto, en peligro.

His life is at stake.   En eso le va la vida. Su vida está en peligro.

stake (to) estacar, poner estacas; jugar, aventurar, arriesgar (to risk, to put at hazard).

to stake all   jugarse el todo por el todo, echar el resto.

stammer tartamudear.

stamp sello, estampilla (for letters); timbre (for documents).

postage stamp   sello de correo.

stamp (to) estampar, sellar; poner un sello, poner los sellos (a letter).

stand *n.* puesto (stall); tribuna (platform); mesita, velador, estante, pedestal, soporte (a piece of furniture).

newsstand   puesto (quiosco) de periódicos.

stand (to) poner derecho, colocar *or* poner
    de pie (to set something on end);
    ponerse *or* estar de pie (to take or
    keep an upright position); resistir,
    hacer frente (to resist); aguantar,
    sufrir (pain, etc.); pararse (to stop
    moving).

Stand back! ¡Atrás!

Stand up! ¡Levántese! ¡Póngase de pie!
    ¡Párese! (Amer.)

I am standing. Estoy de pie.

I can't stand him. No lo puedo aguantar.

to stand a chance tener probabilidades.

to stand by estar listo (ready); estar cerca
    (near); estar de mirón (to be looking
    at); atenerse a, sujetarse a (to abide
    by).

to stand for estar por, ser partidario de,
    defender, mantener, aprobar,
    favorecer; querer decir, significar
    (to mean); tolerar, aguantar (to
    tolerate).

to stand in line hacer cola.

to stand in the way cerrar el paso,
    estorbar, ser un estorbo.

to stand off mantenerse a distancia.

to stand on one's feet valerse de sí
    mismo.

to stand one's ground resistir mantenerse
    firme.

to stand out resaltar, sobresalir, destacarse
    (to be prominent, conspicuous).

to stand out of the way hacerse a un
    lado.

to stand still no moverse, estarse
    quieto.

to stand the test pasar, resistir la
    prueba.

to stand together mantenerse unidos,
    solidarizarse.

to stand up levantarse, ponerse de pie,
    pararse (Amer.).

to stand up for sacar la cara por.

standard norma, tipo, pauta, patrón, standard;
    estandarte (flag).

standard of living nivel de vida.

gold standard patrón de oro.

standard price precio corriente.

standpoint punto de vista.

star estrella, astro.

starch almidón.

starch (to) almidonar.

stare (to) mirar fijamente.

start principio, comienzo (beginning);
    partida, salida (departure); arranque
    (of a car, an engine).

to get a start tomar la delantera.

start (to) comenzar, principiar (to begin);
    partir, salir, ponerse en marcha (to

    start out); poner en marcha, arrancar
    (an engine, etc.).

starvation hambre.

starve (to) morir de hambre; matar de
    hambre (to cause to starve).

state *n.* estado, condición, situación.

state (to) decir, expresar, declarar, exponer,
    manifestar, afirmar.

statement declaración, manifestación,
    exposición, relación; informe,
    memoria (report); cuenta, estado de
    cuenta (of an account).

stateroom camarote.

statesman estadista, hombre de estado.

station estación.

railroad station estación de ferrocarril.

stationmaster jefe de estación.

stationery papel para cartas, efectos de
    escritorio.

stationery store papelería.

statistical estadístico.

statistics estadística.

statue estatua.

statute estatuto.

stay estancia, permanencia, residencia (visit);
    suspensión temporal de un proceso
    (court).

stay (to) quedar, quedarse, parar, detenerse,
    hospedarse; aplazar, suspender (to put
    off).

to stay in quedarse en casa, no salir.

to stay in bed guardar cama.

to stay away estar ausente, no volver.

He's staying at the Waldorf Astoria. Para
    en el Waldorf Astoria.

steadily constantemente, invariablemente.

steady firme, fijo, estable, constante.

steak bistec, biftec.

steal (to) robar.

They've stolen my watch. Me han robado
    el reloj.

steam vapor.

steam engine máquina de vapor.

steamship buque, vapor

steamship line compañía de vapores,
    compañía de navegación.

steel acero.

steep empinado, escarpado.

steer (to) guiar, conducir, gobernar.

steering wheel volante.

stem tallo; raíz (grammar).

step paso; escalón, peldaño (stair).

step by step paso a paso.

to be in step llevar el paso.

to be out of step no llevar el paso.

flight of steps tramo.

step (to) dar un paso, pisar, andar,
    caminar.

to step aside hacerse a un lado.

to step back   retroceder.

to step down   bajar, descender; disminuir (decrease).

to step in   entrar, visitar; meterse, intervenir (take part).

to step on   pisar, poner el pie sobre.

to step out   salir.

stepbrother hermanastro, medio hermano.

stepchild hijastro.

stepdaughter hijastra.

stepfather pedrastro.

stepmother madrastra.

stepsister hermanastra.

stepson hijastro.

stern *adj.* austero, severo.

stew guisado, estofado.

veal stew   guisado de ternera.

steward camarero, azafato.

stewardess camarera, azafato.

stick palo, garrote; bastón (cane).

stick (to) apuñalar (to stab); clavar, hincar (to thrust); pegar (to glue); fijar, prender (to fasten); perseverar (to keep on).

to stick by   solidarzarse con, apoyar; mantenerse en.

to stick out   sacar; asomar (one's head); perseverar hasta el fin (to put up with until the end).

to stick up   atracar.

to stick up for   defender, sacar la cara por.

to stick to   atenerse a, perseverar, mantenerse en.

stiff tieso, duro, rígido; estirado, afectado (not natural in manners); ceremonioso (formal); fuerte (strong); caro (of prices).

stiff collar   cuello duro, cuello planchado.

stiff neck   torticolis.

stiff resistance   resistencia obstinada.

stiffen endurecer(se), obstinarse.

stiffness rigidez, dureza.

still *adj.* quieto, inmóvil, tranquilo.

still water   agua estancada.

to stand still   estarse quieto.

still life   naturaleza muerta.

Be still!   ¡Cállate!

still *adv.* aún, todavía, hasta ahora, no obstante.

She's still sleeping.   Está durmiendo todavía,

stillness calma, quietud.

stimulate (to) estimular.

sting aguijón; picadura (wound).

sting (to) picar; pinchar (to prick).

stir (to) agitar; revolver.

to stir the fire   atizar el fuego.

to stir up   conmover, excitar, alborotar, despertar.

stirrup estribo.

stock surtido, existencias, mercancías (supply of goods); acción (share); valores, acciones (stocks); caja (of a rifle); raza (race).

stock market/exchange   bolsa.

stock company   sociedad anónima.

in stock   en existencia.

out of stock   agotado.

stockbroker corredor de bolsa

stockholder accionista.

stockings medias.

stomach estómago.

stone piedra.

stool taburete, banqueta (seat).

stool pigeon   soplón.

stop parada (of bus, etc.).

stop (to) parar, pararse, detener, detenerse, hacer alto; quedarse (to stay).

to stop raining   dejar (cesar) de llover.

Stop!   ¡Alto!

Stop that now!   ¡Basta!

Stop a minute.   Deténgase un instante.

to stop talking   dejar de hablar.

to stop working   dejar de trabajar.

to stop payment   suspender el pago.

to stop payments   suspender pagos.

to stop at   detenerse en, poner reparo.

to stop short   parar en seco.

to stop over   detenerse durante el viaje; quedarse.

stoplight semáforo.

storage almacenamiento.

store tienda (shop).

department store   almacenes, tienda de variedades.

store (to) almacenar (computer, etc.).

stork cigüeña.

storm tempestad, tormenta.

stormy tempestuoso, turbulento.

story historia, cuento, historieta (tale); piso (building); mentira, embuste (falsehood).

short story   cuento (corto).

as the story goes   según se dice, según cuenta la historia.

stout corpulento, gordo.

stove estufa.

straight derecho, recto.

straight line   línea recta.

Go straight ahead.   Vaya todo seguido.

straighten (to) enderezar, poner en orden.

straightforward *adj.* derecho; recto; franco (frank); íntegro, honrado (honest).

strain tensión (tension); esfuerzo (effort).

strain (to) colar (through a strainer); cansar

(the eyes, etc.); esforzarse (to make an effort).

Don't strain yourself.   No se canse Ud.

to strain the voice   forzar la voz.

strange extraño, raro (unusual); desconocido (not known).

strange face   cara desconocida.

stranger extraño, desconocido, extranjero (foreigner).

strap correa, tira.

strategic estratégico.

strategy estrategia.

straw paja.

straw hat   sombrero de paja.

the last straw   el colmo.

strawberry fresa.

stream *n.* corriente de agua, río, arroyo.

street calle.

street crossing   cruce de calle.

street intersection   bocacalle.

streetcar tranvía.

streetcar conductor   cobrador.

strength fuerza, vigor.

to gain strength   cobrar fuerzas.

on the strength of   fundándose en.

strengthen (to) fortalecer(se), reforzar.

stress fuerza (force); esfuerzo (effort); estrés, tensión (strain); presión (pressure); acento (accent); énfasis, importancia (importance).

stress (to) acentuar, dar énfasis.

stretch (to) estirar, extender, ensanchar; dar de sí (to become longer or wider).

to stretch oneself   desperezarse.

to stretch out   estirar, alargar.

stretcher camilla.

strict estricto, riguroso, severo.

strike huelga (of workers).

strike (to) golpear, pegar, chocar.

to strike at   atacar, acometer.

to strike a match   encender un fósforo.

to strike against   chocar con.

to strike back   dar golpe por golpe.

to strike home   dar en el vivo.

to strike out   borrar, tachar (to cross out).

to strike one as funny   hacer gracia.

striking notable; llamativo (attracting attention).

stripe lista.

stroll paseo, vuelta.

to go for a stroll   dar una vuelta.

stroll (to) pasear(se).

strong fuerte, poderoso.

stronghold fortaleza, fuerte.

structure estructura.

struggle lucha.

struggle (to) luchar.

stubborn obstinado, terco.

student estudiante.

studious estudioso.

study estudio.

study (to) estudiar.

stuff *n.* tela, paño, género (cloth, material); cosa (thing), cachivaches, chismes, muebles (belongings, furniture).

stuffy sofocante.

stumble (to) tropezar.

stump tocón, cepa (of tree).

stupid estúpido.

to be stupid   ser estúpido.

stupidity estupidez.

stupor estupefacción, estupor.

style estilo, modo; moda (fashion).

suave afable, amable.

subdue (to) amansar, sojuzgar.

subject sujeto; materia, asunto, tema (subject matter).

subject (to) sujetar, someter.

submarine submarino.

submission sumisión.

submit (to) someter; someterse.

subordinate subordinado.

subscribe (to) subscribir(se).

subscriber abonado, subscriptor.

subscription subscripción; abono.

subsequent subsiguiente, ulterior.

substance substancia.

substantial substancial.

substitute substituto.

substitute (to) substituir.

substitution substitución.

subtract (to) quitar, restar, sustraer.

suburb suburbio, arrabal.

subway subterráneo, metro, subte (Arg.).

succeed (to) salir bien, tener buen éxito (turn out well); suceder (come next after another).

success (buen) éxito, buen resultado.

successful próspero, afortunado.

successive sucesivo.

successor sucesor.

such tal, semejante.

such as   tal como.

in such a way   de tal modo.

no such (a) thing   no hay tal.

sudden *adj.* repentino, súbito, imprevisto.

all of a sudden   de repente.

suddenly repentinamente, de pronto, súbitamente.

suffer (to) sufrir.

suffering *n.* sufrimiento, padecimiento.

sugar azúcar.

sugar bowl   azucarero.

sugar cane   caña de azúcar.

sugar mill   ingenio de azúcar.

suggest (to) sugerir, proponer.

suggestion sugestión, sugerencia.

suicide suicidio.

to commit suicide   suicidarse.

suit traje (clothes); causa, pleito (court); palo (in cards).

ready-made suit   traje hecho.

suit made to order   traje a la medida.

to bring suit   entablar juicio.

suit (to) cuadrar, convenir, acomodar (to be suitable); venir *or* ir bien, sentar (to be becoming); satisfacer, agradar (to please, to satisfy).

suitable adecuado, apropiado, conveniente.

sulfur azufre.

sum suma.

in sum   en suma.

sum total   suma total.

summary sumario.

summer verano.

summer resort   lugar de veraneo.

summit cima, cumbre.

summon (to) citar, emplazar, requerir, convocar.

summons citación.

sum up (to) resumir, recapitular.

sun sol.

sunbath   baño de sol.

to take a sunbath   tomar un baño de sol.

sunbeam rayo de sol.

sunburn quemadura de sol.

sunburned tostado por el sol.

to get sunburned   tostarse por el sol.

Sunday domingo.

sunlight luz del sol.

sunny de sol, asoleado; alegre, risueño (sunny disposition).

sunrise salida de sol, amanecer.

sunset puesta del sol.

sunshine luz solar.

in the sunshine   al sol.

sunstroke insolación.

superb soberbio, grandioso.

superfluous superfluo.

superintendent superintendente, conserje.

superior superior.

superiority superioridad.

supersonic supersónico.

superstition superstición.

superstitious supersticioso.

supper cena.

to have supper   cenar.

supplement suplemento.

supply abastecimiento; surtido (stock); oferta (business).

supply and demand   oferta y demanda.

supply (to) abastecer, proveer, surtir.

support apoyo, sostén; sustento, manutención (act of providing for).

support (to) sostener, apoyar; mantener (to provide for).

suppose (to) suponer.

supposition suposición, supuesto.

suppress (to) suprimir.

suppression supresión.

supreme supremo, sumo.

Supreme Court   Corte Suprema, Tribunal Supremo.

sure cierto, seguro.

to be sure   estar seguro, sin duda.

be sure to   no deje de, sin falta.

surf (to) hacer surfing.

surface superficie.

surgeon cirujano.

surgery cirugía; sala de operaciones (room).

surname apellido.

surprise sorpresa, extrañeza.

surprise (to) sorprender.

surprising sorprendente.

surrealistic surrealista.

surrender rendición, entrega.

surrender (to) rendir(se), entregar(se), ceder.

surround (to) cercar, rodear.

surrounding circunvecino.

surroundings inmediaciones, alrededores; medio, ambiente (atmosphere).

survey examen, estudio; inspección (inspection); levantamiento de planos (surveying).

survey (to) examinar, estudiar; reconocer, inspeccionar (to inspect); levantar un plano (in surveying).

survival supervivencia.

survive (to) sobrevivir.

survivor sobreviviente.

susceptible susceptible.

suspect *n.* persona sospechosa.

suspect (to) sospechar.

suspend (to) suspender.

suspenders tirantes.

suspicion sospecha.

suspicious sospechoso, desconfiado, suspicaz.

sustain (to) sostener.

swallow golondrina (bird).

swallow (to) tragar.

swamp pantano, ciénaga.

swan cisne.

swarm enjambre.

swarm (to) pulular, hormiguear.

swear jurar, tomar *or* prestar juramento.

to swear by   jurar por, poner confianza implícita en.

sweat sudor.

sweat (to) sudar.

sweater suéter.

sweep (to) barrer.

sweet dulce.

sweet potato   batata, patata dulce, boniato (Cuba); camote (Amer.).

to have a sweet tooth   ser goloso.

She's very sweet. Ella es muy dulce.

sweetheart novio, novia.

sweetness dulzura.

swell *adj.* excelente, magnífico, estupendo.

swell (to) hinchar(se), subir, crecer (to rise above the level).

swelling hinchazón.

swift rápido, veloz.

swim (to) nadar.

My head's swimming. Se me va la cabeza.

swimmer nadador.

swimming pool piscina.

swing columpio (a seat hung from ropes), balanceo, oscilación (movement).

in full swing en pleno apogeo.

swing (to) columpiar, mecer; girar.

switch la llave de la luz, el botón de la luz, interruptor, conmutador (electric switch); cambiavía, aguja de cambio (railroad); cambio (change, shift).

switch (to) dar vuelta la llave de la luz (to turn the switch); desviar, apartar (rails); cambiar (to change, to shift); azotar (to whip).

sword espada.

syllable sílaba.

symbol símbolo.

sympathetic compasivo.

sympathize (to) simpatizar.

sympathy simpatía.

symphony sinfonía.

symphony orchestra orquesta sinfónica.

symptom síntoma.

synonym sinónimo.

synthetic sintético.

synthesizer sintetizador.

syringe jeringa.

syrup almíbar.

system sistema.

systematic metódico, sistemático.

T

table mesa; tabla (of measures, etc.).

to set the table poner la mesa.

tablecloth mantel.

tablespoon cuchara.

tablet tableta, pastilla (of aspirin, etc.); bloc de papel (for writing); tabla, lápida (with an inscription).

tableware servicio de mesa.

tacit tácito, implícito.

tact tacto.

tactical táctico.

tactics táctica.

tactful cauto, discreto.

tactless falta de tacto.

tag etiqueta.

tail cola.

tailor sastre.

take (to) tomar; coger (to grasp).

to take a bite comer algo.

to take a bath bañarse.

to take a picture sacar un retrato.

to take a walk dar un paseo.

to take a stroll dar una vuelta.

to take a nap tomar la siesta.

to take a look at echar un vistazo a, mirar.

to take a trip hacer un viaje.

to take an oath prestar juramento.

to take apart desarmar (a machine).

to take a step dar un paso.

to take away quitar, llevarse.

to take back retractarse, desdecirse de; devolver.

to take account of tomar en cuenta.

to take advantage of aprovecharse de, abusar de.

to take a liking to coger (tomar) cariño a.

to take advice hacer caso, tomar consejo.

to take care tener cuidado.

to take care of cuidar de.

to take chances correr el riesgo, arriesgar.

to take down bajar, poner más bajo (to lower); tomar nota (to take note).

to take for granted tomar por sentado.

to take charge of encargarse de.

to take effect surtir efecto.

to take into consideration tener en cuenta.

to take to heart tomar pecho.

to take it easy no apurarse.

Take it or leave it. ¿Sí o no? Tómelo o déjelo.

to take from quitar de; restar de (to subtract).

to take leave despedirse.

to take notes tomar apuntes

to take notice advertir, observar, notar percatarse de.

to take out sacar, quitar.

to take after salir a, parecerse, ser como.

to take it out on desquitarse con otro, desahogarse con.

to take off despegar (a plane).

to take one's clothes off quitarse la ropa, desnudarse.

to take one's shoes off descalzarse.

Take your hat off. Quítese el sombrero.

Take my word for it. Créame Ud. Bajo mi palabra.

to take pains cuidar.

to take part tomar parte.

to take place suceder, ocurrir.

to take possession of apoderarse.

to take refuge refugiarse.

to take time   tomar tiempo.

to take one's time   tomarse tiempo, no darse prisa.

to take up a subject   abordar un tema.

to take up room   ocupar espacio.

to take upon oneself   encargarse de, asumir la responsabilidad, hacerse cargo de.

talcum talco.

talcum powder polvo de talco.

tale cuento; chisme (gossip).

talent talento, aptitud.

talented talentoso.

talk conversación (conversation); charla (chat); discurso (speech); comidilla (gossip); rumor (rumor).

talk (to) hablar, conversar, charlar.

to talk back   replicar, responder irrespetuosamente.

to talk over   discutir, tratar acerca de.

to talk to   hablar a.

talkative locuaz, hablador.

tall alto.

tallness altura, estatura.

tame adj. domesticado, amansado, dócil.

tame (to) domar, domesticar.

tan n. color de canela, color café claro (color).

tan adj. atezado, tostado (skin); de color café claro, de color de canela.

tan (to) curtir; atezarse, tostarse (to become tan).

tangent tangente.

tank tanque, cisterna; tanque (military); depósito, tanque (for gasoline).

tantalize (to) tentar.

tape cinta, tira de tela, de papel o de metal.

tape measure   cinta para medir.

adhesive tape   esparadrapo.

tape cinta; cinta adhesiva (Scotch Tape); grabación (recording) videocinta videotape.

tape (to) grabar.

tape recorder grabadora.

tapestry tapiz, tapicería.

tar brea, alquitrán.

target blanco, objetivo.

to hit the target   dar en el blanco.

task tarea, faena, labor.

taste gusto.

in bad taste   del mal gusto.

in good taste   de buen gusto.

to have a taste for   tener gusto por.

taste (to) gustar, saborear, probar; saber a, tener gusto a (to have a flavor of).

Taste it.   Pruébelo.

The soup tastes of onion.   La sopa sabe a cebolla.

tasteful de buen gusto; sabroso.

tavern taberna.

tax impuesto, contribución.

income tax   impuesto sobre la renta.

tax collector   recaudador de impuestos.

tax rate   tarifa de impuestos.

tax (to) cobrar impuestos, imponer contribuciones.

taxi taxi, coche de alquiler.

tea té.

teach (to) enseñar.

teacher maestro, profesor.

teacup taza para té.

teakettle olla para calentar agua.

team pareja, tronco (horses); equipo (sports).

team work   trabajo de equipo.

teapot tetera.

tear lágrima.

in tears   llorando.

tear (to) desgarrar, rasgar, romper.

to tear down   demoler.

to tear to pieces   despedazar.

to tear one's hair out   arrancarse los cabellos.

tease (to) tomar el pelo.

technical técnico.

technique técnica.

technology tecnología.

tedious aburrido, cansado.

teenager adolescente.

teeth dientes.

false teeth   dientes postizos.

set of teeth   dentadura.

telegraph telégrafo.

telegraph (to) telegrafiar.

telephone teléfono.

telephone booth   cabina telefónica.

telephone call   llamada telefónica.

telephone operator   telefonista.

telephone directory   guía telefónica, directorio telefónico.

telephone (to) telefonear.

telescope telescopio.

telex (to) enviar un télex.

tell (to) decir; contar, relatar, referir.

to tell a story   contar un cuento.

Who told you so?   ¿Quién se lo dijo?

Tell it to him.   Cuénteselo a él.

Do what you are told.   Haz lo que se la mande.

temper genio, carácter.

bad temper   mal genio.

to lose one's temper   enfadarse, perder la paciencia.

temperament temperamento.

tempest tempestad.

temple templo (for worship); sien (anatomy).

temporarily provisionalmente, temporalmente, transitoriamente.

temporary provisorio, temporal, interino.

tempt (to) tentar.

temptation tentación.

tempting tentador.

ten diez

tenacious tenaz, porfiado.

tenant inquilino.

tendency tendencia.

tender *adj.* tierno, frágil.

　tenderhearted　compasivo.

tennis tenis.

　tennis court　cancha de tenis.

tense tenso.

tension tensión.

tent tienda de campaña.

tentative tentativa.

tenth décimo.

term término; plazo (period of time);
　especificaciones, condiciones (terms).

　in terms of　en concepto de; un función de
　　(mathematics).

　on no terms　por ningún concepto.

　to be on good terms with　estar en buenas
　　relaciones con.

　to come to terms　llegar a un acuerdo,
　　convenir.

　to bring to terms　imponer condiciones a,
　　hacer arreglos con.

　On what terms?　¿En que términos?

terminal *adj.* terminal, final, último.

terminal término; estación terminal, final de
　trayecto (station, end of a line);
　terminal (elec.).

terrace terraza, balcón.

terrible terrible, espantoso.

　How terrible!　¡Qué espantoso!

terrify (to) aterrorizar.

territory territorio, región.

terror terror, espanto.

terrorist terrorista.

terse terso, sucinto, conciso.

terseness concisión.

test prueba, ensayo, examen, análisis.

test (to) ensayar, probar, analisar.

testify (to) atestiguar, testificar, declarar.

testimony evidencia, prueba, testimonio.

text texto.

textbook libro de texto.

textile téxtil.

texture textura.

than que.

　more than that　más que eso.

　fewer than ten　menos de diez.

　She's older than I.　Ella es mayor que yo.

thank (to) agradecer, dar las gracias.

　Thank you.　Gracias.

thankful agradecido.

thanks gracias.

　thanks to　gracias a.

that ese, esa, eso, aquel, aquella, aquello

　(*dem. adj.*); ése, ésa, eso, aquél,
　aquélla, aquello (*dem. pron.*); que,
　quien, el cual, la cual, lo que, lo cual
　(*rel. pron.*).

　that man　ese hombre.

　that woman　esa mujer.

　That's the one.　Ese es.

　That's it.　Eso es.

　That's to say.　Es decir.

　That may be.　Es posible. Eso puede ser.

　That's all.　Eso es todo.

　and all that　y cosas por el estilo.

　That way.　Por allí. Por aquel camino.

　that's how　así es como es, así es como se
　　hace.

　That's that.　Eso es lo que hay. No hay
　　más que decir.

　to let it go at that　conformarse con eso,
　　dejar correr.

that *adv.* tan, así de.

　not that far　no tan lejos.

　that many　tantos.

　that much　tanto.

　that big　así de grande.

that *conj.* que, para que.

　so that　de modo que, de suerte que, para
　　que.

　in order that　para que, de modo que.

　except that　salvo que.

　in that　por cuanto, en que.

the el, la, lo; los, las.

　the man　el hombre.

　the men　los hombres.

　the woman　la mujer.

　the women　las mujeres.

　the sooner the better　cuanto más pronto,
　　tanto mejor.

　the most interesting part　lo más
　　interesante.

theater teatro, auditorio.

theatrical teatral.

their su, suyo, suya, de él, de ella; sus,
　suyos, suyas, de ellos, de ellas.

theirs el suyo, la suya, los suyos, las suyas,
　de ellos, de ellas.

them los, las, les; ellos, ellas.

theme tema, asunto.

themselves ellos mismos, ellas mismas; sí
　mismos.

then entonces, en aquel tiempo, a la sazón.

　now and then　de cuando en cuando, de
　　vez en cuando.

　but then　si bien es cierto que, sin
　　embargo.

　and then　y entonces.

　just then　entonces mismo, en aquel
　　mismo momento.

　by then　para entonces.

　And what then?　¡Y entonces! ¿Pues y

qué? ¿Y que pasó después?
(What happened then?) ¿Y que
pasará después? (What will happen
then?)

theoretical teórico.

theorize (to) teorizar.

theory teoría.

there allí, allá, ahí (near the person
addressed).
Put it there. Ponlo ahí.
There she goes. Ahí va.
I was there. Yo estuve allí.
She lives there. Ella vive allí.
Go there. Vaya allá.
Over there. Por allí. Allá.
There in Spain. Allá en España.
There you are. Ahí tiene Ud. Para que
vea. Eso es todo.
There! ¡Toma! ¡Vaya! ¡Mira!

thereabouts por ahí, por allí, cerca de allí.

thereafter después de eso; conforme.
There are many things. Hay muchas
cosas.

thereby por medio de eso; con eso, con lo
cual; de tal modo, así.

therefore por lo tanto, por esto, por esa
razón; a consecuencia de eso, por
consiguiente.

there is (there are) hay.
There's plenty (enough). Hay bastante.

thereupon en eso, sobre eso; por lo tanto;
inmediatamente después, en seguida,
luego.

thermometer termómetro.

these estos, estas; éstos, éstas.

thesis tesis.

they ellos, ellas.

thick espeso (like glue); tupido, denso
(dense); grosor, grueso (not thin).
three inches thick tres pulgadas de
espesor.
thick-headed torpe.

thickness grueso, espesor, grosor.

thief ladrón.

thigh muslo.

thimble dedal.

thin flaco (lean); delgado (not thick);
delgado, esbelto (slender).

thing cosa, objeto.
something algo, alguna cosa.
anything cualquier cosa.

think (to) pensar; creer, opinar (believe).
to think of pensar en, reflexionar acerca
de.
to think well of pensar bien de, tener
buen concepto de.
As you think fit. Como Ud. quiera, como
a Ud. le parezca mejor.
to think it over pensarlo, meditarlo.

to think nothing of no dar importancia a;
tener en poco.
to think twice andar con tiento, pensarlo
bien, relexionar mucho.
I don't think so. Creo que no.
I think so. Creo que sí.

thinness delgadez, flacura.

third tercero.
a third person un tercero.
thirdly en tercer lugar.
Third World tercer mundo.

thirst sed.
to be thirsty tener sed.

thirteen trece.

thirty treinta.

this este, esta; esto; éste; ésta.
this man este hombre.
this woman esta mujer.
this morning esta mañana.
this one and that one éste y aquél.
this and that esto y aquello.

thorn espina.

thorough *adj.* entero, cabal minucioso,
perfecto.

thoroughfare vía pública, calle, carretera.
No thoroughfare. Se prohíbe el paso.

thoroughgoing cabal, completo, entero, hasta
el final.

thoroughly enteramente, cabalmente.

those esos, esas; aquellos, aquellas.

though aunque, sin embargo, no obstante, si
bien, bien que, aun cuando.
as though como si.

thought pensamiento.
to give thought to pensar en.

thoughtful pensativo, meditabundo;
precavido (careful); atento,
considerado (considerate).
It's very thoughtful of you. Ud. es muy
atento.

thoughtfulness reflexión, meditación,
atención, consideración, previsión.

thoughtless inconsiderado, descuidado,
insensato.

thousand mil, millar.

thread hilo.

thread (to) enhilar, enhebrar.

threat amenaza.

threaten (to) amenazar.

three tres.

threefold triple.

threshold umbral.

thrift economía, frugalidad.

thrifty frugal, económico.

thrill emoción, estremecimiento.

thrill (to) emocionarse, estremecerse,
temblar; causar una viva emoción.

throat garganta.
sore throat dolor (mal) de garganta.

I have a sore throat.   Me duele la
  garganta.
throne trono.
through *adj.* continuo, directo.
  a through train from Barcelona to
    Valencia   un tren directo de
    Barcelona a Valencia.
through *adv.* a través, de parte en parte, de
    un lado a otro; enteramente,
    completamente.
  through and through   enteramente, hasta
    los tuétanos.
  I'm wet through and through.   Estoy
    mojado hasta los huesos. Estoy heco
    una sopa.
  to be through   haber terminado.
  to be through with   no tener más que ver
    con, haber terminado, no ocuparse ya
    en.
through *prep.* por, por entre, a través, por
    medio de, por conducto de; mediante.
  through the door   por la puerta.
  through the strainer   a través del colador.
  through the trees   por entre los árboles.
  through his influence   mediante su
    influencia.
throughout *prep.* durante todo, en todo, a lo
    largo de, por todos lados; *adv.* de
    parte a parte, desde el principio hasta
    el fin, en todas partes.
throw (to) echar; tirar (a ball, stone, etc.).
  to throw out   echar fuera, arrojar.
  to throw away   tirar, arrojar, botar
    (Amer.).
  to throw light on   esclarecer, aclarar.
thumb pulgar.
thumbtack chinche, tachuela.
thunder trueno.
thunder (to) tronar.
  It's thundering.   Truena.
thunderbolt rayo, centella.
thundershower chubasco con truenos y
    relámpagos.
thunderstorm tronada, tormenta.
Thursday jueves.
thus así, de este modo, en estos términos,
    como sigue.
  thus far   hasta aquí, hasta ahora.
  thus much   no más, basta, baste esto.
ticket billete, boleto (Amer.).
  round-trip ticket   billete de ida y vuelta.
  season ticket   abono, billete de temporada.
  ticket window   taquilla.
tickle (to) hacer cosquillas.
ticklish cosquilloso; quisquilloso.
tide marea.
  high tide   pleamar, plenamar.
  low tide   bajamar.
tie *n.* corbata (to wear); lazo (bond); atadura,

  nudo (a knot); traviesa, durmiente
    (railroad tie).
  family ties   lazos de familia.
tie (to) atar, amarrar.
tiger tigre.
tight apretado, muy ajustado, bien cerrado.
tighten (to) apretar.
tile azulejo, losa, baldosa; teja (for roof).
tiling azulejos, tejas (tiles); tejado (roof
    covered with tiles).
till hasta; hasta que.
  till now   hasta ahora.
  till further notice   hasta nueva orden.
till (to) cultivar, labrar.
timber madera.
time tiempo; hora; vez; época; plazo.
  What time is it?   ¿Qué hora es?
  the first time   a la primera vez.
  on time   a tiempo.
  a long time ago   hace mucho tiempo.
  at the proper time   a su debido tiempo, en
    el momento oportuno.
  at the same time   al mismo tiempo.
  any time   a cualquier hora; cuandoquiera.
  at no time   jamás.
  one at a time   uno a la vez.
  at this time   ahora, al presente.
  at this time (of the day)   a estas horas.
  at times   a veces.
  for the time being   por ahora, de
    momento.
  time and again   una y otra vez.
  from time to time   de vez en cuando.
  in no time   en un instante, en un abrir y
    cerrar de ojos.
  in an hour's time   en una hora.
  Be on time.   Sea puntual.
  Have a good time!   ¡Que se divierta!
  We had a good time.   Pasamos un buen
    rato.
  to take time   tomarse tiempo.
  spare time   tiempo desocupado, ratos de
    ocio.
timely oportunamente, a propósito (*adv.*);
    oportuno, a buen tiempo (*adj.*).
timid tímido.
timidity timidez.
tin lata.
  tin can   lata.
  tin foil   hoja de estaño.
  tin plate   hoja de lata.
tincture tintura.
  tincture of iodine   tintura de yodo.
tint tinte.
tip punta, extremidad, cabo (point, end);
    propina (gratuity); soplo, delación
    (secret information); advertencia
    (warning).
tip (to) ladear, inclinar (to slant); dar una

propina (to give a tip); prevenir,
precaver (to warn); delatar, soplar (to
tip off).

tire neumático, llanta.
flat tire   pinchazo, neumático desinflado.
tire (to) cansar; aburrir (to bore).
to tire out   reventar de cansancio.
tired cansado.
tired out   rendido de cansancio, agotado.
to become tired   cansarse.
tiredness cansancio, fatiga.
tireless incansable, infatigable.
tissue tejido (a mass of cells, skin tissue,
etc.); gasa, tisú (cloth).
tissue paper   papel de seda.
title título.
title page   portada.
to a, para, de, por, hasta, que.
to give to   dar a.
to go to   ir a.
to speak to   hablar a.
ready to go   listo para marcharse.
It's time to leave.   Es hora de partir.
the road to Madrid   la carretera de
Madrid.
from house to house   de casa en casa.
to be done   por hacerse.
letters to be written   cartas por escribir.
to this day   hasta ahora.
in order to   a fin de, para.
to and fro   de un lado a otro, de acá para
allá.
I have to go.   Tengo que irme.
I have something to do.   Tengo algo que
hacer.
It's five (minutes) to three.   Son las tres
menos cinco.
toad sapo.
toast tostada.
toast (to) tostar.
toasted. tostado.
toaster tostadora.
tobacco tabaco.
tobacco shop   estanco (Spain) cigarrería,
tabaquería (Amer.).
today hoy
a week from today   de hoy en ocho días.
toe dedo del pie.
together juntos; juntamente; a un tiempo,
simultaneamente.
Let's go together.   Vamos juntos.
together with   junto con, en compañía de.
to call together   reunir, congregar.
toil trabajo, angustia, fatiga.
toilet retrete, inodoro; tocado (combing the
hair, bathing, etc.).
toilet water   colonia, agua de colonia.
toilet paper   papel higiénico.
tolerance tolerancia.

tolerant tolerante.
tolerate (to) tolerar, aguantar, sufrir.
tomato tomate.
tomato juice   jugo de tomate.
tomb tumba, sepulcro.
tomcat gato.
tomorrow mañana.
day after tomorrow   pasado mañana.
tomorrow morning   mañana por la
mañana.
tomorrow noon   mañana al mediodía.
tomorrow afternoon   mañana por la
tarde.
tomorrow night   mañana por la noche.
ton tonelada.
tone tono.
tongs tenazas, alicates.
tongue lengua; espíga.
to hold one's tongue   callarse.
tonic tónico.
tonight esta noche, a la noche.
tonsil amígdala.
tonsilitis amigdalitis.
too demasiado (too much), tambien (also).
too much   demasiado, excesivo.
too many   demasiados, muchos.
It's too bad.   Es lástima.
It's too early.   Es demasiado temprano.
It's a little too early.   Es un poco
temprano.
That's too much.   Eso ya es demasiado.
Es el colmo.
You have gone a little too far.   Ud. se ha
excedido un poco.
He's too good.   Es, muy bueno. Se pasa de
bueno.
me (I) too   yo también.
I am only too glad to do it.   Lo haré con
muchísimo gusto.
one dollar too much   un dolar de más.
That's too little.   Eso es muy poco.
tool herramienta, utensilio.
tooth diente.
tooth powder   polvo dentífrico.
toothache   dolor de muelas.
toothbrush   cepillo de dientes.
toothpaste   pasta dentífrica.
toothpick   mondadientes, palillo.
top cima, cumbre (of a mountain); copa (of a
tree); la parte superior, la parte de
arriba, superficie (upper side); cabeza
(head), pináculo (pinnacle); trompo
(toy).
the top of the mountain   la cumbre de la
montaña.
top hat   sombrero de copa.
at top speed   a todo correr.
at the top   a la cabeza, en la cumbre.
from top to bottom   de arriba abajo.

from top to toe   de píes a cabeza.

on top of   encima de, sobre.

top (to) aventajar, exceeder, llegar a la cima.

to top off   coronar, rematar, dar cima.

topcoat abrigo, sobretodo.

topic tema, tópico.

torch antorcha.

torment tormento.

torrent torrente.

torrid tórrido.

torrid zone   zona tórrida.

tortoise tortuga.

tortoise shell   carey.

torture tortura, tormento.

torture (to) torturar, atormentar.

toss (to) tirar, lanzar.

to toss aside   echar a un lado.

to toss up   jugar a cara o cruz.

total total.

sum total   suma total.

touch contacto.

to be in touch with   estar en comunicación con, en relación con.

touch (to) tocar.

touching *adj.* patético, conmovedor.

touchy quisquilloso.

tough duro, fuerte; difícil, penoso (hard to bear).

toughen (to) endurecer (se).

toughness endurecimiento, rigidez.

tour viaje, gira.

tour (to) recorrer, viajar por.

touring turismo.

touring agency   agencia de turismo.

touring car   coche de turismo.

touring guide   guía de turismo.

tourist turista.

tourist class   clase económica.

tournament torneo.

tow (to) remolcar (a ship, etc.).

toward hacia, para con, tocante a.

to go toward (a place)   ir hacia (un lugar).

His attitude toward me.   Su actitud para conmigo.

towel toalla.

face towel   toalla para la cara.

hand towel   toalla para las manos.

bath towel   toalla de baño.

tower torre.

town ciudad, pueblo.

hometown   cuidad natal.

town hall   ayuntamiento.

toxic tóxico.

toy juguete.

trace indicio, huella, pista.

trace (to) trazar (to mark out); seguir la pista (to follow).

track huella; vía, rieles (metal rails); andén (in a railroad station).

trade comercio.

trademark   marca de fábrica, marca registrada.

trade name   razón social; nombre de fábrica (for products).

trade union   sindicato.

trading comercio.

tradition tradición.

traditional tradicional

traffic circulación, tráfico.

tragedy tragedia.

tragic trágico.

train tren.

train (to) entrenar, adiestrar, instruir.

trainer entrenador.

training preparación, entrenamiento.

traitor traidor.

tramp vago, vagabundo.

tranquil tranquilo.

transatlantic transatlántico.

transfer transferencia; traspaso (a store, a farm, etc.); transbordo (from one train, bus, etc., to another).

transfer (to) transferir (to change hands); transbordar (trains, busses, etc.); trasladar (from one place to another).

translate (to) traducir.

translation traducción.

translator traductor.

transmission transmisión.

automatic transmission   cambio automático.

transparent transparente.

transport transporte.

transport (to) transportar.

transportation transporte.

trap trampa.

trap (to) atrapar.

travel (to) viajar.

traveler viajero, viajante (salesman).

tray bandeja.

treacherous traidor.

treachery traición.

tread pisada.

tread (to) pisar, pisotear.

treason traición.

treasure tesoro.

treasure (to) atesorar, guardar.

treasurer tesorero.

treasury tesorería.

treat (to) tratar; convidar, invitar (with food, drinks, etc.).

to treat a patient   tratar a un enfermo.

to treat well (badly)   dar buen (mal) trato.

treatment trato, tratamiento (med.).

treaty tratado.

tree árbol.

tremble (to) temblar.

trembling *adj.* trémulo, tembloroso.

trembling *n.* temblor.

tremendous tremendo, inmenso.

trench zanja; trinchera (fortification).

trend tendencia, giro, rumbo.

trial prueba, ensayo (test); juicio, vista de una causa (law).

triangle triángulo.

tribe tribu.

tribunal tribunal.

tribute tributo.

trick artificio, jugada, artimaña; truco; juego de manos (with cards, etc.); maña, destreza (skill).

    to do the trick   resolver el problema.

    He played a trick on me.   Me hizo una jugarreta.

trifle friolera, bagatela.

trim (to) adornar (a dress, etc.); podar (a tree); cortar ligeramente (the hair).

trimming adorno, decoración.

trinket dije, chuchería.

trip *n.* viaje (voyage); traspié, tropezón (stumble); zancadilla (act of catching a person's foot).

    one-way trip   viaje de ida.

    round trip   viaje de ida y vuelta.

trip (to) tropezar (to stumble); hacer una zancadilla (to cause to stumble).

triple triple.

triumph triunfo.

triumph (to) triunfar.

triumphant triunfante.

trivial trivial.

trolley car tranvía.

troops tropas.

trophy trofeo.

tropic trópico.

tropic(al) *adj.* tropical.

trot (to) trotar.

trouble preocupación, pena (worry); dificultad (difficulty); molestia (bother); apuro, aprieto (distress); disgusto, desavenencia (disagreement) mal, enfermedad (sickness).

    to cause trouble   causar molestia, dar que hacer.

    to be in trouble   estar en apuro.

    not to be worth the trouble   no valer la pena.

    It's no trouble at all.   No es ninguna molestia.

    stomach trouble   mal de estómago.

    I have stomach trouble.   Padezco del estómago.

trouble (to) molestar, importunar.

    Don't trouble yourself.   No se moleste Ud.

troubled preocupado, afligido.

    to be troubled with   padecer, sufrir de.

troublesome molesto, embarazoso; importuno, alborotador (person).

trousers pantalones.

trout trucha.

truck camión.

true cierto, exacto, verdadero, fiel.

    It's true.   Es verdad.

trunk tronco (of a tree); cofre, baúl (for packing).

trust confianza.

    on trust   al fiado.

    in trust   en depósito.

trust (to) tener confianza, confiar, fiar.

    I trust him.   Le tengo confianza.

    I don't trust him.   No me fío de él.

trustworthy digno de confianza.

truth verdad.

truthful verídico, veraz.

truthfulness veracidad.

try (to) probar, tratar de, esforzarse.

    to try on clothes   probarse ropa.

    Try to do it.   Trate de hacerlo.

    to try hard   hacer lo posible por.

tub cuba, tonel.

    bathtub   baño, bañera.

tube tubo.

tuberculosis tuberculosis, tisis.

Tuesday martes.

tuition matrícula.

tumor tumor.

tumult tumulto, motín.

tuna atún.

tune tonada, tono, melodía.

    to be out of tune   desafinar.

tune (to) afinar, entonar; sintonizar (radio).

    to tune in   sintonizar.

tunnel túnel.

turkey pavo.

turn turno (time, order); vuelta, giro (motion); favor (favor).

    by turns   por turnos.

    in turn   a su turno, a su vez.

    to take turns   turnarse.

    It's my turn now.   Ahora me toca a mí.

turn (to) dar vuelta; dar vueltas, girar (to revolve); volver, doblar, torcer (to change direction); ponerse, volverse (to become pale, etc.).

    to turn against   predisponer en contra, volverse en contra.

    to turn around   dar vuelta a.

    to turn down   rehusar, rechazar (to refuse).

    to turn into   convertir en, cambiar en.

    to turn off   cerrar la llave del (gas, steam, etc.).

to turn off the light   apagar la luz.

to turn off the water   cortar el agua; cerrar el grifo.

to turn off the gas   apagar el gas.

to turn on the light   encender la luz.

to turn on the water   dejar correr el agua, abrir el grifo.

to turn back   dar la vuelta, volverse, retroceder.

to turn one's back on   voltear la espalda a.

to turn out to be   resultar, venir a ser.

to turn over   transferir (to transfer), entregar, dar (to hand over); volcar, tumbarse (to tumble); dar vuelta, volver (to change in position).

to turn sour   agriarse (milk, etc.).

to turn to   recurrir a, acudir a; convertir en, convertirse en.

to turn up   aparecer (to appear), poner más alto, levantar (to give upward turn to), volver (a card, etc.); resultar, acontecer, venir a ser (to occur).

to turn a cold shoulder to   desairar.

to turn upside down   poner patas arriba.

turnip nabo

turtle tortuga.

tweezers pinzas.

twelfth duodécimo, décimo segundo.

twelve doce.

twentieth vigésimo.

twenty veinte.

twice dos veces.

twilight crepúsculo.

twin mellizo, gemelo.

twin brother   hermano gemelo.

twin brothers   mellizos.

twist (to) torcer, retorcer.

two dos.

type tipo.

typewrite (to) escribir a máquina.

typewriter máquina de escribir.

portable typewriter   máquina de escribir portátil.

typewriter ribbon   cinta para la máquina de escribir.

typical típico.

typist mecanógrafo.

tyrannical tiránico.

tyranny tiranía.

tyrant tirano.

U

UFO OVNI.

ugliness fealdad.

ugly feo.

ulcer úlcera.

ultimate último.

ultrasound ultrasonido.

umbrella paraguas.

umbrella stand   paragüero.

umpire árbitro.

unable incapaz.

I was unable to.   No pude. Me fue imposible.

unanimous unánime.

unaware ignorante; desprevenido, de sopresa; inadvertidamente, sin pensar.

to take someone unawares   coger a uno de sorpresa.

unbearable insoportable.

unbutton (to) desabrochar.

uncertain incierto.

uncertainty incertidumbre.

unchangeable inmutable, inalterable.

uncle tío.

uncomfortable. incómodo, molesto; indispuesto.

to feel uncomfortable   estar incómodo.

unconquered invicto.

undecided indeciso no resuelto.

under bajo, debajo de.

under the table   debajo de la mesa.

under consideration   en consideración.

underage   menor de edad.

under contract   bajo contrato; conforme al contrato.

undercover   al abrigo, a cubierto; dentro de un sobre (in an envelope).

underarms   bajo las armas.

under way   en camino, andando, en marcha.

under the circumstances   en las circunstancias.

under an obligation   deber favores.

under one's nose   en las barbas de uno.

underclothes ropa interior.

underdeveloped subdesarrollado.

underdeveloped countries   países en vía de desarrollo

undergo (to) someterse a, pasar por, sufrir.

to undergo an operation   operarse.

underground subterráneo.

underline (to) subrayar.

underneath bajo, debajo de.

understand (to) comprender, entender; estar de acuerdo.

Do you understand Spanish? ¿Entinede Ud. español?

That's easy to understand.   Eso se comprende.

understanding entendimiento, modo de ver; acuerdo, inteligencia (agreement).

to come to an understanding   llegar a una inteligencia.

understood entendido, sobreentendido, convenido.

to be understood   sobreentenderse.

be it understood   entiéndase bien.

That's understood.   Está entendido. Por supuesto. Estamos de acuerdo.

undertake (to) emprender; comprometerse a.

undertaking empresa; compromiso, promesa (promise).

undo (to) deshacer, desatar; anular.

undress (to) desnudar (se).

uneasiness malestar, inquietud, desasosiego.

uneasy inquieto, molesto, incómodo, desasosegado.

unequal desigual.

uneven desigual, irregular; impar (numbers).

unexpected inesperado.

unfair injusto.

unfaithful infiel.

unfavorable desfavorable.

unfinished incompleto.

unfit inadecuado, impropio; inepto, incapaz de (unable).

unfold (to) desenvolver, desplegar; descubrir, revelar, mostrar (to reveal, to show).

unforeseen imprevisto, inesperado.

unforgettable inolvidable.

unfortunate desgraciado, desdichado.

unfortunately por desgracia, desgraciadamente.

unfurnished sin muebles, desamueblado, no amueblado.

     unfurnished apartment   piso sin muebles.

ungrateful ingrato, desagradecido.

unhappy infeliz, desdichado.

unhealthy enfermizo, achacoso; malsano.

unheard of inaudito.

unhurt ileso, intacto.

uniform uniforme.

union unión.

     labor union   sindicato.

unique único.

unit unidad.

     intensive care unit   unidad de cuidado intensivo.

unite (to) unir (se).

united unido.

     United States   Estados Unidos.

unity unidad.

universal universal.

universe universo.

university universidad.

unjust injusto.

unkind poco amable; despiadado (cruel); tosco, duro (harsh).

unknown desconocido.

unlawful ilegal, ilícito, ilegítimo.

unless a no ser que, a menos que, si no.

unlike diferente.

unlikely improbable, inverosímil.

unload (to) descargar.

unlucky desgraciado, desafortunado, de mala suerte.

unmarried soltero.

     unmarried man   soltero.

     unmarried woman   soltera.

unmoved impasible, inmutable, frío.

unnecessary innecesario.

unpaid sin pagar, no pagado.

unpleasant desagradable

unquestionable indiscutible, indisputable.

unreasonable irrazonable, desatinado.

unruly ingobernable.

unsatisfactory inaceptable, poco satisfactorio.

unseen invisible; inadvertido.

unselfish desinteresado.

unsettled revuelto, turbio (liquid); variable, inestable (not stable); sin pagar, pendiente (a bill, etc.).

unsteady inestable, inconstante, inseguro.

unsuccessful infructuoso, sin éxito; desafortunado.

unsuitable impropio, inadecuado.

until hasta.

untiring incansable, infatigable.

unusual extraordinario, poco común.

unwelcome mal acogido, importuna.

unwilling maldispuesto.

     to be unwilling   no estar dispuesto.

unwillingly de mala gana.

unwritten no escrito, en blanco.

unworthy indigno.

up arriba, en lo alto, hacia arriba; en pie, de pie.

     up and down   arriba y abajo; de un lado a otro.

     to go up   subir.

     to go upstairs   subir.

     to walk up and down   ir de un sitio para otra, dar vueltas.

     up the river   río arriba.

     one flight up   en el piso de arriba.

     Up there!   ¡Alto ahí!

     to be up to one   ser asunto de uno, ser cosa de uno.

     What's up?   ¿Qué pasa? ¿De qué se trata?

     The time is up.   Ya ha vencido el plazo. Ya es tiempo.

     She's not up yet.   Todavía no se ha levantado.

     this side up   arriba (on cases).

     up to   hasta; capaz de (capable of doing).

     up to anything   dispuesto a todo.

     up-to-date   al día.

     up to now   hasta la fecha.

upon sobre, encima.

     upon my word.   bajo mi palabra.

     upon which   sobre lo cual.

upper superior, alto.

     the upper floor   el piso de arriba.

upper lip   labio superior.

upright vertical; derecho, recto, justo (character).

upset (to) trastornar, perturbar, desarreglar.

upside

upside down   al revés, patas arriba; desconcierto.

upstairs arriba; en el piso de arriba.

to go upstairs   subir.

upstart *n.* advenedizo.

upwards hacia arriba.

urgency urgencia.

urgent urgente, apremiante.

use uso.

to make use of   utilizar.

in use   en uso.

of no use   inútil.

to be of no use   no servir.

to have no use for   no servirle a uno; no tener buena opinión de, tener en poco.

It's no use.   Es inútil.

What's the use?   ¿Para qué? Es inútil. ¿De qué sirve?

use (to) usar, servirse de, hacer uso de; soler, acostumbrar.

to use one's own judgment   obrar uno conforme le parezca.

to use up   gastar; agotar.

I'm used to it.   Estoy acostumbrado a ello.

I used to see her every day.   Solía verla todos los días.

used usado.

used clothes   ropa usada.

useful útil.

useless inútil, inservible.

usher acomodador.

usual usual; común, general, ordinario.

as usual   como de costumbre.

usually usualmente, ordinariamente, de costumbre, por lo común, por lo general, comunmente.

I usually get up early.   Por regla general me levanto temprano.

utensil utensilio.

kitchen utensils   batería de cocina.

utility utilidad.

utilize (to) utilizar, emplear.

utmost extremo, sumo.

to the utmost   hasta no más.

to do one's utmost   hacer cuanto esté de la parte de uno, hacer uno cuanto pueda.

utterly enteramente, del todo.

V

vacancy vacante (unoccupied position); cuarto para alquilar (room); piso para alquilar (apartment).

vacant vacío, desocupado.

vacation vacaciones.

vaccinate (to) vacunar.

vaccine vacuna (med.).

vacuum vacío.

vague vago.

vain vano.

in vain   en vano.

valid válido.

validate (to) validar.

valise maleta, valija.

valley valle.

valuable valioso.

value valor; valuación (estimated value); aprecio, estimación (regard).

value (to) valuar, tasar (to estimate the value); preciar, apreciar, tener en mucho (to think highly of).

valve válvula.

vanguard vanguardia.

vanilla vainilla.

vanish (to) desvanecerse, desaparecerse.

vanity vanidad.

vantage ventaja.

vantage point   posición de ventaja.

variable variable.

variety variedad.

various varios; diversos.

varnish (to) barnizar.

vary (to) variar.

vase florero.

Vaseline vaselina.

vast vasto, inmenso.

VCR videograbador(a).

veal ternera.

veal cutlet   chuleta de ternera.

vegetable vegetal, planta.

vegetable man   verdulero.

vegetable soup   menestra, sopa de legumbres.

vegetable oil   aceite vegetal.

vegetables legumbres, verduras, hortalizas.

vegetation vegetación.

vehement vehemente.

vehicle vehículo.

veil velo, mantilla.

vein vena.

velvet terciopelo.

vengeance venganza.

ventilate (to) ventilar.

ventilation ventilación.

venture aventura; riesgo.

verb verbo.

verdict veredicto, sentencia.

verse verso.

vertical vertical.

very muy, mucho, mucha.

very much   mucho, muchísimo.

very many   muchísimos, muchísimas.

very much money   mucho dinero.
(Very) Much obliged.   Muy agradecido.
Very well, thank you.   Muy bien, gracias.
the very man   el mismo hombre.
at the very latest   a más tardar
vessel vasija, vaso (container); buque (ship).
vest chaleco.
veteran veterano.
veterinary veterinario.
vex (to) molestar, enfadar.
vexation molestia, enfado.
vexing molesto, importuno.
vibration vibración.
vice vicio.
vice president vicepresidente.
vice versa viceversa, al contrario.
vicinity vecindad, cercanía.
vicious malvado, depravado.
   vicious circle   círculo vicioso.
victim víctima.
victor vencedor.
victorious victorioso.
victory victoria.
video *m.* vídeo
   video recorder   videograbador(a).
   video game   video juego.
   videotape   cinta de video.
   videorecording   videograbación.
view vista, perspectiva, panorama.
   bird's-eye view   vista de pájaro.
   in view of   en vista de.
   point of view   punto de vista.
   What a view!   ¡Que vista!
view (to) mirar, ver, contemplar.
vigil vigilia.
vigilant vigilante.
vigor brío, vigor.
vigorous vigoroso.
vile vil, bajo.
villa casa de campo.
village aldea, pueblo, pueblecito.
villager aldeano.
villain villano.
vine parra.
vinegar vinagre.
vineyard viña.
vinyl vinilo.
violate (to) violar.
violation violación.
violence violencia.
violent furioso, violento.
violet violeta.
violin violín.
violinist violinista.
violoncello violoncelo.
viper víbora.
virgin virgen.
virtue virtud.
virtuous virtuoso.

visa visto bueno, visado.
visible visible
vision vista, visión.
visit visita.
   to pay a visit   hacer una visita.
visit (to) visitar.
visitor visitante.
visual visual.
vital vital.
vitamin vitamina.
vivid vivo, vívido, gráfico.
vocal vocal.
   vocal cords   cuerdas vocales
vogue moda.
   in vogue   de moda
voice voz.
void *adj.* vacío; nulo, inválido, sin valor ni
      fuerza (null).
void *n.* vacío.
volcano volcán.
volt voltio.
volume volumen; tomo (book).
voluntary voluntario.
volunteer voluntario.
vomit vómito.
vomit (to) vomitar.
vote voto, sufragio.
vote (to) votar.
voter votante.
vow voto.
vow (to) hacer promesa, hacer voto.
vowel vocal.
voyage viaje.
vulgar vulgar.
vulture buitre.

W

wade vadear; caminar en.
   to wade through the mud   andar por el barro.
wage(s) sueldo, paga, jornal.
   monthly wages   sueldo mensual, salario.
   daily wages   jornal.
   wage earner   jornalero, trabajador, obrero.
wage (to) emprender.
   to wage war   hacer guerra.
wager apuesta.
wager (to) apostar.
wagon carro; furgón (freight car); vagón
      (railroad car).
waist cintura.
wait (to) esperar, aguardar.
   Wait for me.   Espéreme.
   to keep waiting   hacer esperar.
   to wait on   atender a, despachar (in a
      store, etc.); servir a (to serve).
waiter mozo, camarero, mesero.
waiting espera.

waiting room   sala de espera.
waitress camarera, mesera.
wake (to) despertar(se).
　to wake up   despertar, llamar; despertarse.
　Wake me at seven.   Despiérteme a las
　　siete.
　I woke up at seven.   Me desperté a las
　　siete.
waken (to) despertar.
walk paseo.
　to take a walk   dar un paseo.
walk (to) andar, caminar.
　to walk away   marcharse.
　to walk down   bajar.
　to walk up   subir.
　to walk out   salir; declararse en huelga (to
　　go on strike).
　to walk arm in arm   ir del brazo.
　to walk up and down   pasearse, ir y venir.
walking paseo, acción de pasear.
　to go walking   ir de paseo; ir a pie.
　walking cane   bastón.
wall muro, pared, muralla.
　wallpaper   papel de empapelar.
walnut nuez (nut); nogal (tree).
waltz vals.
waltz (to) valsar.
wand vara, varita.
wander (to) vagar; perderse, extraviarse (to
　　go astray); divagar, delirar (of the mind)
want necesidad, falta, carencia.
　to be in want   estar necesitado.
　for want of   por falta de.
want (to) necesitar, tener necesidad de (to
　　need); querer, desear (to desire).
　What do you want?   ¿Qué quiere Ud.?
　Don't you want to come?   ¿No quiere Ud.
　　venir?
　Cook wanted.   Se busca cocinera.
wanting defectuoso, deficiente; necesitado,
　　escaso (lacking).
　to be wanting   faltar.
war guerra.
　War Department   Ministerio de la guerra.
　to wage war   hacer la guerra.
ward sala, pabellón (in a hospital); barrio,
　　distrito (of a city); pupilo, menor en
　　tutela (person under the care of a
　　guardian, etc.).
warden guardián, celador; carcelero (of a
　　prison); director (of school, etc.).
ward off (to) detener, desviar.
wardrobe guardarropa, armario, ropero.
　wardrobe trunk   baúl ropero.
warehouse almacén, depósito.
wares mercancías, mercadería, géneros or
　　artículos de comercio.
warfare guerra.
warlike belicoso.

warm caliente, cálido, caluroso.
　It's warm.   Hace calor.
　I am warm.   Tengo calor.
　warm water   agua caliente.
warn (to) calentar.
　to warm up   calentarse; acalorarse, tomar
　　bríos.
warn (to) advertir, prevenir, avisar.
warning advertencia, prevención, aviso;
　　lección, escarmiento.
　to give warning   prevenir, advertir.
warrant autorización; mandamiento, auto (a
　　written order).
warrior guerrero.
wash lavado; ropa sucia (clothes to be
　　washed); ropa lavada (clothes that
　　have been washed).
　washing machine   máquina de lavar.
　washbasin   lavabo.
wash (to) lavar.
　to wash one's hands   lavarse las manos.
waste despilfarro, derroche; desperdicio.
　nuclear wastes   desechos nucleares.
waste (to) malgastar, desperdiciar; perder,
　　gastar.
　to waste time   perder tiempo.
wastebasket cesto de papeles.
watch reloj; guardia (guard).
　wristwatch   reloj de pulsera.
　to be on the watch   estar alerta, estar
　　sobre sí.
　to wind up a watch   dar cuerda a un reloj.
watch (to) vigilar.
　to watch out   tener cuidado con.
　to watch over   guardar, vigilar.
　to watch one's step   tener cuidado;
　　andarse con tiento.
watchful alerta, vigilante, despierto.
watchmaker relojero.
watchman vigilante, sereno, guardián.
watchword contraseña; consigna, lema.
water agua.
　fresh water   agua fresca.
　hot water   agua caliente.
　mineral water   agua mineral.
　running water   agua corriente.
　seawater   agua de mar.
　soda water   agua de seltz, soda.
　toilet water   colonia, agua de colonia.
　water faucet   grifo.
　waterpower   fuerza hidráulica.
　to make one's mouth water   hacer la boca
　　agua.
　water bag   bolsa para agua, calientapiés.
water (to) regar (to sprinkle); mojar,
　　humedecer (to wet).
waterfall cascada, catarata.
waterfront muelles.
watermelon sandía.

waterproof impermeable.
waterski esquí acuático.
wave ola; onda (radio, etc.), ondulación (hair).

  short wave onda corta.
  sound wave onda sonora.
  wavelength longitud de onda.
  to be on the same wavelength estar en la misma onda.

wave (to) ondular; flotar (in the air); hacer señas (to signal by waving); agitar (a handkerchief, etc.).

  to wave one's hand hacer señas con la mano.

waver (to) vacilar, titubear; cejar, ceder (to give way).
wavering irresoluto, vacilante.
waving *n.* ondulación.
wavy ondulado.
wax cera.

  wax candle vela de cera.
  wax paper papel encerado.

wax (to) encerar.
way camino, vía, ruta; modo, manera (manner).

  way in entrada.
  way off muy lejos.
  way out salida.
  by way of por la vía de; pasando por.
  by the way a propósito, dicho sea de paso.
  in such a way de tal manera.
  in this way de este modo.
  any way de cualquier modo.
  in no way de ningún modo.
  this way así.
  Go this way. Vaya por aquí.
  on the way en ruta; de camino.
  out of the way fuera de camino; donde no estorbe.
  across the way al otro lado, en frente.
  Which way? ¿Por dónde?
  Get out of the way! ¡Fuera!; quitarse de en medio.
  Step this way. Venga Ud. acá.
  in some way or other de un modo o de otro.
  under way en camino, en marcha.
  to have (get) one's way salirse con la suya.
  the other way around al contrario, al revés.
  all the way en todo el camino, durante el trayecto; del todo; hasta el fin.
  to give way ceder.
  ways and means medios y arbitrios.

we nosotros, nosotras.

  we Americans nosotros los norteamericanos.

weak débil, frágil.
weaken debilitar.
weakness debilidad, flaqueza.
wealth riqueza, bienes.
wealthy rico, adinerado.
weapon arma.
wear uso, desgaste.
wear (to) llevar, usar, llevar puesto, poner.

  to wear down cansar, fastidiar (to tire, annoy); vencer (to overcome).
  to wear off gastarse; borrarse (color).
  to wear out gastarse.
  to wear well durar (to last).
  Which dress will you wear tonight? ¿Qué vestido te vas a poner esta noche?
  I like the blouse she's wearing. Me gusta la blusa que lleva puesta.

weariness cansancio, hastío, aburrimiento.
wearing apparel ropa, prenda de vestir.
weary *adj.* cansado, hastiado, fastidiado.
weary (to) cansar, hastiar, molestar.
weather tiempo.

  bad weather mal tiempo.
  nice weather buen tiempo.
  The weather is fine. Hace buen tiempo. Hace un tiempo muy bueno.
  weather conditions condiciones meteorológicas.
  weather report boletín meteorológico.

weave (to) tejer.
web tela, tejido.

  spider web tela de araña.

wedding boda, nupcias.

  wedding dress traje de boda.
  wedding present regalo de boda.

wedge cuña.
Wednesday miércoles.
weed maleza, mala hierba.
week semana.

  weekday día de trabajo.
  last week la semana pasada.
  next week la semana que viene.
  a week from tomorrow de mañana en ocho días.

weekend fin de semana.
weekly *adj.* semanario.

  weekly publication semanario.

weekly *adv.* semalmente, por semana.
weep (to) llorar.

  to weep for llorar por, llorar de.

weigh (to) pesar; levar (anchor).
weight peso.

  gross weight peso bruto.
  net weight peso neto.
  weights and measures pesos y medidas.
  weight lifting levantamiento de pesas.

weighty de peso, ponderoso, serio, importante.
welcome *adj.* bienvenido.

Welcome! ¡Bienvenido!

You're welcome (answer to "Thank you."). De nada. No hay de qué.

welcome *n.* bienvenida.

welcome (to) dar la bienvenida.

welfare bienestar.

welfare work   obra de beneficiencia, labor social.

well pozo.

well *adj.* bueno, bien; *adv.* bien.

to be well   estar bien.

very well   muy bien.

I am quite well.   Estoy muy bien.

I don't feel well.   No me siento bien.

to look well   tenor buena cara.

well and good   la enhorabuena, bien está.

well-being   bienestar.

well-bred   bien educado.

well done   bien hecho.

well-to-do   acomodado, rico.

well-known   bien conocido.

well-timed   oportuno.

as well as   así como, lo mismo que.

well then   con que.

Well!   ¡Cómo!

Well, well!   ¡Vaya! ¡Qué cosa!

Very well!   ¡Está bien!

west oeste, occidente.

western Occidental.

wet *adj.* mojado; húmedo.

to get wet   mojarse.

wet (to) mojar.

whale ballena.

wharf muelle.

what qué.

What's that?   ¿Qué es eso?

What's the matter?   ¿Qué pasa?

What else?   ¿Qué más?

What for?   ¿Para qué?

What about?   ¿Qué le parece? ¿Que hay en cuanto a eso? ¿Qué diremos?

What of (about) it?   ¿Y eso qué importa?

what if   y si, qué será si, qué sucederá si, y qué importa que, aunque.

whatever cualquier cosa que, sea lo que fuere, lo que.

whatever you like   lo que Ud. quiera.

whatever reasons he may have   sean cuales fueren las razones que tenga.

wheat trigo.

wheel rueda.

steering wheel   volante.

wheelchair   silla de reudas.

wheelbarrow carretilla.

when cuando.

Since when?   ¿Desde cuándo? ¿De cuándo acá?

whenever cuandoquiera, siempre que, en cualquier tiempo que sea.

whenever you like   cuando Ud. quiera.

where donde, dónde, adonde, en donde, por donde, de donde.

Where are you from?   ¿De dónde es Ud.?

Where are you going?   ¿Adónde va?

whereby por lo cual, por el que, por medio del cual, con lo cual.

wherever dondequiera que.

whether si, sea que, que.

I doubt whether   dudo que.

whether he likes it or not   que quiera, que no quiera.

which cual, que, el cual, la cual, lo cual.

Which book?   ¿Qué libro?

Which way?   ¿Por dónde? ¿Por qué camino?

Which of these?   ¿Cuál de éstos?

all of which   todo lo cual.

both of which   ambos.

whichever cualquiera.

while instante, momento, rato.

a little while   un ratito.

a little while ago   hace poco rato, no hace mucho.

for a while   por algún tiempo.

once in a while   de vez en cuando.

to be worthwhile   valer la pena.

while *conj.* mientras, mientras que, a la vez que.

whip látigo, azote.

whip (to) azotar, dar latigazos; batir (cream, eggs, etc.).

whipped cream   nata batida.

whirl giro, rotación.

whirl (to) dar vueltas, girar.

whirlpool remolino, vorágine.

whirlwind torbellino.

whisper cuchicheo, susurro.

whisper (to) cuchichear, decir al oído.

to whisper in someone's ear   decir al oído.

whistle silbido.

whistle (to) silbar.

white blanco.

white of an egg   clara de huevo.

white lie   mentirilla.

White House   Casa Blanca.

whiten (to) blanquear.

who quien, quinese, que, el que, la que, los que, las que; quien.

Who is he?   ¿Quién es?

whoever quienquiera, cualquiera.

whoever it may be   quienquiera que sea.

whole todo, entero, integral.

the whole   todo el.

whole wheat bread   pan integral.

on the whole   en conjunto, en general.

whole number   número entero.

wholehearted sincero, de todo corazón; enérgico, activo.

wholesale (al) por mayor.

wholesome sano.

  wholesome food   alimento sano, alimento nutritivo.

wholly totalmente, enteramente.

whom a quien, a quienes.

whose cuyo, de quien.

why *adv.* por qué; *n.* porqué.

  Why not? ¿Por qué no? ¿Pues y qué?

  the why and the wherefore el porqué y la razón.

wicked mala, malvado, perverso.

wickedness maldad, iniquidad.

wide ancho, vasto, extenso.

  two inches wide dos pulgadas de ancho.

  wide open abierto de par en par.

wide-awake muy despierto, alerta, vivo.

widely muy, mucho.

  widely different diametralmente opuesto, completamente diferente.

  widely used se usa mucho.

  widely known muy conocido.

widen (to) ensanchar, extender, ampliar.

widespread divulgado, esparcido.

widow viuda.

widower viudo.

width ancho, anchura.

wife esposa, señora, mujer.

wig peluca.

wild salvaje (savage); silvestre (plants, flowers, etc.); atolondrado, descabellado, desenfrenado (of a person).

wilderness desierto.

will voluntad; testamento.

  at will a voluntad, a discreción.

  against one's will contra la voluntad de uno.

will (to) querer, desear; testar, hacer testamento (to make a will). (*See also* **shall**.)

  Will you tell me the time? ¿Me hace Ud. el favor de decirme la hora?

  Will you do me a favor? ¿Me quiere Ud. hacer un favor?

  I won't do it, but she will. Yo no lo haré, pero ella sí.

  Will you go? ¿Irá Ud.?

  I will not go. No iré. No quiero ir.

willing dispuesto, gustoso, pronto, inclinado.

  to be willing estar dispuesto, querer.

  God willing Dios mediante.

willingly de buena gana, gustosamente.

willingness buena voluntad, buena gana.

win (to) ganar, vencer, prevalecer, lograr.

  to win out salir bien, triunfar.

wind viento

  wind instrument instrumento de viento.

wind (to) enrollar; dar cuerda (a watch).

windmill molino (de viento).

window ventana.

  windowpane vidrio (cristal) de la ventana.

  window shade transparente, visillo.

windshield parabrisas.

windy ventoso.

  to be windy hacer viento.

wine vino.

  red wine vino tinto.

  white wine vino blanco.

wing ala.

wink guiñada.

  not to sleep a wink no pegar los ojos.

wink (to) guiñar.

winner ganador.

winter invierno.

wintry invernal.

wipe (to) limpiar con un trapo, etc. (the floor, etc.); secar, enjugar (to dry).

  to wipe out arrasar, extirpar, destruir.

wire *n.* alambre (metal); telegrama (telegram).

  barbed wire alambre de púa.

wire (to) telegrafiar; alambrar.

wisdom sabiduría, juicioso; sentido común.

  wisdom tooth muela del juicio.

wise sabio; juicioso, prudente.

wish deseo.

wish (to) desear, querer.

  to make a wish concebir un deseo, pensar en algo que se quiere.

wit ingenio, agudeza, sal.

witch bruja.

with con, en compañía de; a, contra, de, en, entre.

  coffee with milk café con leche.

  to speak with caution hablar con prudencia.

  to touch with the hand tocar con la mano.

  She came with a friend. Vino con un amigo.

  identical with idéntico a.

  to struggle with luchar contra.

  to fill with llenar de.

  with the exception of a excepción de.

  with regard to en cuanto a, con respecto a.

  with the exception a excepción de.

  the girl with the red dress la chica del vestido rojo.

  That always happens with friends. Eso ocurre siempre entre amigos.

withdraw (to) retirar, retirarse; retractarse de (to retract).

withdrawal retiro, retirada.

within dentro de; a poco de, cerca de.

  within a short distance a poca distancia.

  within a week dentro de una semana.

within one's reach   al alcance de uno.

from within   de adentro.

without sin; *adv.* fuera, afuera, por fuera, de la parte de afuera.

tea without sugar   té sin azúcar.

without fail   sin falta.

within and without   dentro y fuera.

without doubt   sin duda.

without noticing it   sin advertirlo.

witness testigo.

witness (to) presenciar, ver; declarar, atestiguar, dar testimonio, servir de testigo (to act as a witness).

witty ingenioso, ocurrente, gracioso, salado.

a witty remark   una gracia, una agudeza.

She's very witty.   Es muy salada.

wolf lobo.

woman mujer.

young woman   joven.

wonder maravilla.

No wonder.   No es extraño. No es para menos.

wonder (to) admirarse, maravillarse de, preguntarse.

I wonder whether it's true.   Yo me pregunto si será verdad. ¿Será verdad?

I wonder what she wants.   ¿Qué querrá?

to wonder at   maravillarse de.

to wonder about   extrañarse, tener sus dudas acerca de; tener curiosidad por.

I wonder why?   ¿Por qué será?

I wonder!   ¡Si será cierto!

wonderful estupendo, admirable, maravilloso.

wood madera (matinal); monte, bosque (woods).

firewood   leña.

woodwork maderaje.

wool lana.

woolen de lana.

word palabra.

too funny for words   lo más gracioso del mundo.

in so many words   en esas mismas palabras, exactamente así, claramente.

word for word   palabra por palabra.

in other words   en otros términos.

by word of mouth   de palabra, verbalmente.

on my word   bajo mi palabra.

to leave word   dejar dicho, dejar recado.

to send word   mandar a decir.

work trabajo, labor.

to be at work   estar en el trabajo; estar ocupado, estar trabajando.

out of work   sin trabajo.

work of art   objeto de arte, obra de arte.

work (to) trabajar; funcionar (machine); explotar (a mine); tallar (a stone); elaborar, fabricar.

to work out   resolver (a problem); llevar a cabo (to carry out); salir bien, tener éxito (to come out all right).

The machine doesn't work.   La máquina no funciona.

worker obrero, trabajador.

working trabajo, funcionamiento.

working day   día de trabajo.

workman obrero, trabajador.

workshop taller.

world mundo.

all over the world   por todo el mundo.

worldwide   mundial.

world war   guerra mundial.

Third World   tercer mundo.

worm gusano.

worn out rendido, gastado.

worn-out clothes   ropa usada.

I'm worn out.   Estoy rendido.

worry preocupación, cuidado, ansiedad.

worry (to) preocupar(se), inquietar(se).

Don't worry.   No se preocupe. No se apure.

to be worried   estar preocupado.

worse peor.

to get worse   empeorarse.

so much the worse   tanto peor.

worse and worse   de mal en peor.

worse than ever   peor que nunca.

to take a turn for the worse   empeorar.

worship culto, adoración.

worship (to) adorar, venerar.

worst pésimo, malísimo.

the worst   lo peor, lo más malo.

at the worst   en el peor de los casos.

if worse comes to the worst   si sucediera lo peor.

to have the worst of it   salir perdiendo, llevar la peor parte.

worth valor, mérito.

What's it worth?   ¿Cuánto vale?

It's worth the money.   Eso vale su precio. Es una buena compra.

He's worth a lot of money.   Tiene mucho dinero.

It's worthwhile trying.   Vale la pena intentarlo.

worthless inútil, sin valor.

to be worthless   ser inútil.

worthwhile (to be) valer la pena.

worthy digno, meritorio.

would The conditional is generally expressed by adding -ía, -ías, -ía, -íamos, -ías, -ían to the infinitive of the verb.

I would go.   Iría.

I would like to go.   Quisiera ir.

I wouldn't go if I could.   No iría si pudiera.

She wouldn't come.   No quiso venir.

I wish she would come.   Querría que
   viniese. Ojalá que venga.

I would like to ask you a favor.   Quisiera
   pedirle un favor.

Would you do me a favor?   ¿Me haría
   Ud. un favor?

wound herida.

wound (to) herir.

wounded herido.

wrap (to) envolver (to wrap up).

wrapper empaquetador (person).

wrapping *n.* envoltura.

   wrapping paper   papel de envolver.

wreath corona (of flowers, etc.), guirnalda.

wreck naufragio (shipwreck); ruina (ruin).

wreck (to) arruinar; hacer naufragar.

   to be shipwrecked   irse a pique,
      naufragar.

wrench torcedura (wrenching), llave de
      tuercas, llave inglesa (tool).

wrench (to) torcer, dislocar.

   to wrench one's foot   torcerse el pie.

wrestle luchar.

wrestler luchador.

wring torcer, retorcer; escurrir (wet
      clothes, etc.).

   to wring out   exprimir, escurrir.

wrinkle arruga.

wrinkle (to) arrugar.

wrist muñeca.

   wristwatch   reloj de pulsera.

write (to) escribir.

   to write down   poner por escrito, anotar.

writer escritor, autor.

writing escritura, escrito.

   in writing   por escrito.

   to put in writing   poner por escrito.

   writing desk   escritorio.

   writing paper   papel de escribir.

written escrito.

wrong *n.* mal; daño (harm); injuria, injusticia
      (injustice); agravio; *adj.* mal(o),
      incorrecto, falso, erróneo, injusto; *adv.*
      mal.

   the knowledge of right and wrong   el
      conocimiento del bien y el mal.

   to do wrong   hacer daño, obrar mal.

   You are wrong.   Ud. no tiene razón. Ud.
      está equivocado.

   to be wrong   no tener razón; estar mal
      hecho.

   wrong side out   al revés.

   That's wrong.   Eso está mal. Está mal
      dicho (said). Está mal escrito
      (written). Está mal hecho (done).

   Something is wrong with the engine.   El
      motor no funciona bien.

   Something is wrong with him.   Le pasa
      algo. Tiene algo raro.

I took the wrong road.   Erré el camino.
   Me equivoqué de camino.

X rays rayos X (equis).

yard yarda, vara (measure); patio (court);
      corral (around a barn).

yawn bostezo.

yawn (to) bostezar.

year año.

   last year   el año pasado.

   all year round   todo el año.

   many years ago   hace muchos años.

yearbook anuario, anales.

yearly *adj.* anual.

yearly *adv.* anualmente, todos los años.

yeast levadura.

yell grito.

yell (to) gritar, chillar.

yellow amarillo.

yes sí.

yesterday ayer.

   day before yesterday   anteayer.

yet *adv.* todavía, aún; *conj.* sin embargo, con
      todo.

   not yet   aún no, todavía no.

   as yet   hasta ahora, hasta aquí.

   I don't know yet.   Todavía no lo sé.

yield rendimiento, provecho.

yield (to) rendir, producir; ceder (to give in).

yoga yoga.

yogurt yogur.

yoke yugo.

yolk yema.

you tú (fam.); usted (polite).

young joven, mozo.

   young man   joven.

   young lady   señorita, joven.

   young people   jóvenes.

   to look young   verse joven, tener la traza
      de joven, aparentar poca edad.

your tú, tus, su, sus, vuestro(s), de usted(es).

yours suyo(s), suya(s), tuyo(s), tuya(s),
      vuestro(s), vuestra(s), el suyo, la
      suya, el tuyo, la tuya, la vuestra, los
      (tuyos, suyos, vuestros), las (tuyas,
      suyas, vuestras), de (usted, ustedes).

   This book is yours.   Este libro es tuyo
      (suyo, de usted, vuestro, de ustedes).

   a friend of yours   un amigo tuyo (suyo,
      vuestro, de usted, de ustedes).

   Yours sincerely   Su seguro servidor

(S.S.S.), Su afectísimo y seguro
servidor (Su afmo, y s.s.).
yourself usted mismo, tú mismo, te, se.
Wash yourself.   Lávate. Lávese.
yourselves ustedes mismos, vosotros mismos,
os, se.
youth juventud.
youthful juvenil.

Z

zeal celo, fervor.
zealous celoso.

zenith cenit.
zero cero.
zest entusiasmo, brío.
zigzag zigzag.
zinc cinc.
zipper cremallera, cíper.
zodiac zodíaco.
zone zona.
zoo jardín zoológico.
zoological zoológico.
zoology zoología.

GLOSSARY OF PROPER NAMES

Rose	Rosa.
Susan	Susana.
Theresa	Teresa.
Thomas	Tomás.
Vincent	Vicente.
William	Guillermo.

Albert	Alberto.
Alexander	Alejandro.
Alfred	Alfredo.
Alice	Alicia.
Andrew	Andrés.
Ann, Anna	Ana.
Anthony	Antonio.
Arthur	Arturo.
Beatrice	Beatriz.
Bernard	Bernardo.
Catharine,	
Catherine	Catalina.
Charles	Carlos.
Charlotte	Carlota.
Dorothy	Dorotea.
Edward	Eduardo.
Elizabeth	Isabel.
Ellen	Elena.
Emily	Emilia.
Ernest	Ernesto.
Esther	Ester.
Eugene	Eugenio.
Frances	Francisca.
Francis	Francisco.
Frederic(k)	Federico.
George	Jorge.
Gertrude	Gertrudis.
Helen	Elena.
Henry	Enrique.
Isabella	Isabel.
James	Jaime, Diego.
Joan,	
Joana,	
Joann	Juana.
John	Juan.
Joseph	José.
Josephine	Josefina.
Juliet	Julia.
Julius	Julio.
Leo	León.
Louis	Luis.
Louise	Luisa.
Margaret	Margarita.
Martha	Marta.
Mary	María.
Michael	Miguel.
Paul	Pablo.
Peter	Pedro.
Philip	Felipe.
Raymond	Raimundo, Ramón.
Richard	Ricardo.
Robert	Roberto.

GLOSSARY OF GEOGRAPHICAL NAMES

Africa	Africa.
Algeria	Argelia.
Alps	Alpes.
Amazon	Amazonas.
Andes	Andes.
Angola	Angola.
Antilles	Antillas.
Antwerp	Amberes.
Argentina	Argentina.
Asia	Asia.
Athens	Atenas.
Atlantic Ocean	Océano Atlántico.
Australia	Australia.
Barcelona	Barcelona.
Basque Provinces	Provincias Vasconga-
	das.
Belgium	Bélgica
Bilboa	Bilboa.
Biscay	Vizcaya.
Bolivia	Bolivia.
Brazil	Brasil.
Brittany	Bretaña.
Brussels	Bruselas.
Buenos Aires	Buenos Aires.
Cambodia	Camboya.
Canada	Canadá.
Castile	Castilla.
Catalonia	Cataluña.
Central America	Centroamérica.
Chile	Chile.
China	China.
CIS	Communidad de Esta-
	dos Independientes.
Colombia	Colombia.
Costa Rica	Costa Rica.
Cuba	Cuba.
Cyprus	Chipre.
Czechoslovakia	Checoslovaquia.
Denmark	Dinamarca.
Dominican Republic	República Dominicana.
Ecuador	Ecuador.
Egypt	Egipto.
El Salvador	El Salvador.
England	Inglaterra.

English Channel	Canal de la Mancha.	**Norway**	Noruega.
Europe	Europa.	**Pacific Ocean**	Océano Pacífico.
Finland	Finlandia.	**Pakistan**	Paquistán.
Flanders	Flandes.	**Palestine**	Palestina.
France	Francia.	**Panama**	Panamá.
Galicia	Galicia.	**Paraguay**	Paraguay.
Geneva	Genebra.	**Paris**	París.
Georgia	Georgia.	**Persian Gulf**	Golfo Pérsico.
Germany	Alemania.	**Peru**	Perú.
Great Britain	Gran Bretaña.	**Philippines**	Filipinas.
Greece	Grecia.	**Pyrenees**	Pirineos.
Guatemala	Guatemala.	**Poland**	Polonia
Havana	Habana.	**Portugal**	Portugal.
Holland	Holanda.	**Prague**	Praga.
Honduras	Honduras.	**Prussia**	Prusia.
Hungary	Hungría.	**Puerto Rico**	Puerto Rico.
Iceland	Islandia.	**Rome**	Roma.
Indonesia	Indonesia.	**Romania**	Rumania.
Iran	Irán.	**Russia**	Rusia.
Iraq	Irak.	**Saudi Arabia**	Arabia Saudita.
Ireland	Irlanda.	**Scandinavia**	Escandinavia.
Israel	Israel.	**Scotland**	Escocia.
Italy	Italia.	**Seville**	Sevilla.
Jamaica	Jamaica.	**Sicily**	Sicilia.
Japan	Japón.	**South Africa**	Africa del Sur.
Jordan	Jordania.	**South America**	Suramérica.
Kenya	Kenia.	**Spain**	España.
Laos	Laos.	**Spanish America**	Hispanoamérica.
Latin America	América Latina.	**Sweden**	Suecia.
Latvia	Latvia.	**Switzerland**	Suiza.
Lebanon	Líbano.	**Syria**	Siria.
Libya	Libia.	**Taiwan**	Taiwán.
Lisbon	Lisboa.	**Texas**	Tejas.
Lithuania	Lituania.	**Thailand**	Tailandia.
London	Londres.	**Tokyo**	Tokio.
Madrid	Madrid.	**Turkey**	Turquía.
Majorca	Mallorca.	**United Arab**	Emiratos Arabes
Malaysia	Malasia.	**Emirates**	Unidos.
Morocco	Marruecos.	**United Kingdom**	Reino Unido.
Marseilles	Marsella.	**United States**	Estados Unidos de
Mediterranean Sea	Mar Mediterráneo.	**of America**	América.
Mexico	México.	**Uruguay**	Uruguay.
Moscow	Moscú.	**Valencia**	Valencia.
Mozambique	Mozambique.	**Venezuela**	Venezuela.
Naples	Nápoles.	**Venice**	Venecia.
Netherlands	Países Bajos, Holanda.	**Vienna**	Viena.
New York	Nueva York.	**Vietnam**	Viet Nam.
New Zealand	Nueva Zelandia.	**Wales**	Gales.
Nicaragua	Nicaragua.	**Warsaw**	Varsovia.
Nigeria	Nigeria.	**Yugoslavia**	Yugoslavia.
North America	Norteamérica.	**Zaire**	Zaire.
Northern Ireland	Irlanda del Norte.	**Zimbabwe**	Zimbabwe.